*"The Encyclopedia of Weight Training is a must resource book for body builders, athletes and general fitness participants. The "Encyclopedia" is a synthesis of theoretical, scientific and practical principles of weight training that should form the foundation for any successful weight training, sport training or body building program. The information contained in the "Encyclopedia" is appropriate for males and females of all ages and levels of interest. **"DON'T GO TO THE GYM WITHOUT IT!"***

Jim Wright, PhD
Exercise Scientist

*"The Encyclopedia of Weight Training is one of the most comprehensive books on weight training I have read. It is a valuable addition to my reference library - one I will **NOT** loan out."*

Bill Pearl
Former Mr. America & Mr. USA
Five Times Mr. Universe

"A terrific book, I highly recommend it."

Joe Weider
Trainer of Champions since 1936 and
Publisher: *Muscle & Fitness, Flex and Shape Magazines*

THE ENCYCLOPEDIA OF WEIGHT TRAINING:

WEIGHT TRAINING FOR GENERAL CONDITIONING, SPORT AND BODY BUILDING

BY

PAUL E. WARD, PED

ROBERT D. WARD, PED

SECOND EDITION

QPT PUBLICATIONS
LAGUNA HILLS, CALIFORNIA

1997

Published by:

QPT PUBLICATIONS
27068 LA PAZ, # 401
LAGUNA HILLS, CA 92656

First Printing   February, 1992

Second Printing   April, 1997 (Revised Edition)

ISBN No. 0-9632019-1-3

First edition 1992 - Printed in the United States of America
Second edition 1997 - Printed in the United States of America

Additional copies of this book may be purchased for $ 49.95 (California residents add 7.75% of price for sales tax) plus $ 6.00 for shipping and handling. **Foreign countries:** shipping and handling is $ 15.00.

ORDER FROM:

QPT PUBLICATIONS
27068 LA PAZ, # 401
LAGUNA HILLS, CA 92656

PREFACE

This book is not meant to be read from page one to the last page; it is a reference book - encyclopedic in form. Therefore, select the topic of interest from the Table of Contents for each section:

1. The Scientific, Theoretical and Practical Basis For Weight Training.
2. General Fitness Programs.
3. Weight Training For Sport.
4. Body Building.
5. Nutritional Support Of Weight Training Programs For General Fitness, Sport and Body Building.

The information contained in this book is by no means all inclusive: however, it includes most of the important topics relevant to weight training for General Fitness, Sport and Body Building. Moreover, the last section is devoted to Nutritional Support For Weight Training Programs.

The encyclopedia should be a part of the library of every person involved in the application of functional weight training as a means of conditioning. Educators, coaches, athletes, body builders, fitness participants and the general public will find it an invaluable reference.

The information contained in this encyclopedia presents the principles and practices that will enable anyone at any level of training to design a sensible weight training program. The particulars of how to perform specific exercises have purposely not been addressed in this volume because there are many other books that have amply addressed the exercise techniques. The focus of the encyclopedia is the synthesis of the theory of weight training integrated with practical observations derived from years of training and teaching all levels and motivations of people participating in weight training programs. In addition, Part V discusses the basics of nutrition in an effort to maximize the results of a scientific approach to weight training.

The authors are indebted to thousands of male and female students, junior high school, high school athletes, collegiate athletes, professional athletes and average people who have helped them develop the body of knowledge contained in this encyclopedia. The combined experience of the two authors extends over ninety six (96) years of practical application, scientific research, personal training, coaching and teaching all aspects of training with weights. This truly represents a storehouse of information pertaining to weight training in all its dimensions which will be very useful for all levels of weight training participants.

Along with the vast amount of practical information, the authors have spent a lifetime studying exercise science and application of exercise science for improving human performance. Both authors have been driving forces in the training of Olympic athletes in Track and Field and in professional football, basketball and baseball. Moreover, the authors have researched and are responsible for the world wide application of circuit weight training, super circuit weight training, cross training and the 30 minute workout for athletes and general fitness participants. They have been the driving force in the upgrading and sophistication of the commercial fitness center's multi-dimensional facilities and equipment; advanced and effective physical training regimens; and, sensible, scientific and advanced nutritional programs for the general public.

The authors have, also, strongly impacted the design, development and sophistication of high-tech exercise equipment including conventional machines, free weight equipment, home exercise equipment, and, more recently, the design, development and introduction of the Life Circuit computerized exercise machines.

The authors realize that they "stand upon the shoulders of giants that have preceded them." A great debt is owed to Dr. John Cooper, Dr. James Counsilman, Dr. James Lounsberry, Geoffrey Dyson, Tom Landry, George Allen, Leo Stern, Bill Pearl and Ralph Davis for their significant impact on the experiences and intellectual refinement of the authors.

RESEARCH YOUR EXPERIENCE, ABSORB WHAT IS USEFUL, REJECT WHAT IS USELESS, SYNTHESIZE AND ADD YOUR OWN WRINKLE FOR SUCCESS IN LIFE AND WEIGHT TRAINING!

Dr. Paul E. Ward   Dr. Robert D. Ward

THE ENCYCLOPEDIA OF WEIGHT TRAINING: WEIGHT TRAINING FOR GENERAL CONDITIONING, SPORT AND BODY BUILDING

By
Dr. Paul E. Ward and Dr. Robert D. Ward

GENERAL TABLE OF CONTENTS

PART I

THE ENCYCLOPEDIA OF WEIGHT TRAINING:

The Scientific, Theoretical And Practical Basis For Weight Training

PART I

THEORY & PRACTICE

PART I

THEORY & PRACTICE

THE ENCYCLOPEDIA OF WEIGHT TRAINING: WEIGHT TRAINING FOR GENERAL CONDITIONING, SPORT AND BODY BUILDING

PART I: THE SCIENTIFIC, THEORETICAL AND PRACTICAL BASIS FOR WEIGHT TRAINING

TABLE OF CONTENTS — PART I

PART I

THEORY & PRACTICE

TABLE OF CONTENTS — PART I (CONTINUED)

TABLE OF CONTENTS — PART I (CONTINUED)

PART I

THEORY & PRACTICE

TABLE OF CONTENTS — PART I (CONTINUED)

PART I

THEORY & PRACTICE

TABLE OF CONTENTS — PART I (CONTINUED)

PART I

THEORY & PRACTICE

THE ENCYCLOPEDIA OF WEIGHT TRAINING: PART I

LIST OF FIGURES

PART I

THEORY & PRACTICE

THE ENCYCLOPEDIA OF WEIGHT TRAINING: PART I

LIST OF TABLES

PART I

THEORY & PRACTICE

LIST OF TABLES — PART I (CONTINUED)

PART I

THEORY & PRACTICE

PART I

THE SCIENTIFIC, THEORETICAL AND PRACTICAL BASIS OF WEIGHT TRAINING

GENERAL CONCEPTS AND INTRODUCTION TO WEIGHT TRAINING

Weight training has become one of the most widespread methods of conditioning utilized today for sport and for general physical fitness. It can be observed in action in any up-to-date physical education program in schools, in commercial health clubs and in other community resources across America. Major sports at all levels of performance utilize some form of weight training as an adjunct to the sport specific training program. A predominant reason that weight training has become so popular may be because it has been able to produce positive changes in the **structure** and **function** of the bodies of those individuals who train with weights. In addition, there seems to be a positive change in the personality of those who weight train reflected by increased self esteem and self worth. This phenomenon is observed at all age levels and at all levels of performance.

A second reason for the widespread utilization of weight training is the systematic way a weight training program can be developed, thereby, providing a very convenient and efficient means of conditioning the basic components of physical fitness (strength, local muscle endurance, aerobic endurance and optimization of body composition). In other words, participation in a weight training program enables one to <u>Look Better Physically and Perform More Effectively</u> in their daily tasks and in recreational or sporting interests. These benefits are worthy goals to seek, and therefore, should be considered when individual, school or community health and fitness programs are being developed and implemented.

A CHANGING VIEW OF WEIGHT TRAINING

The present view of weight training has taken many years to develop. It has been an uncertain path to its present position of widespread acceptance as a scientifically established method of conditioning the body for sport and general fitness. During the 1940's and 1950's a great many teachers of physical education, as well as athletic team coaches, did not approve of using weight training in their programs. It was not uncommon during this era for teachers and coaches to discourage their students from using weight training as a means of conditioning for their sports.

The reasons these educators gave for their opposition to weight training were usually related to the **assumed** negative influences that weight training had on skilled performance. Surprisingly, some of these unfounded beliefs still exist today even with the overwhelming accumulation of scientific and empirical evidence to the contrary. Since many of the negatives were based solely on unreliable opinion, not on scientific investigations, a period of time followed in which studies were designed and conducted to investigate some of the important questions involved in this issue.

The positive results of these scientific investigations on the influence of weight training on human anatomy, physiology, appearance and physical performance plus the overwhelming mass of very positive empirical observations concerning weight training in humans are reflected in the increasing number of physical education programs that have included some form of weight training as a course offering in their school curriculum today. Furthermore, almost all athletic programs today, at all levels of competition, integrate weight training programs into their training protocols pre-season, in-season and off-season for injury rehabilitation and to improve the conditioning and physical performance levels of their athletes. The community at large has a variety of other opportunities that range from commercial health clubs and private clubs to sports medicine centers that have included weight training for their members or clients.

It is interesting to note that average women as well as women in sport have, in very recent times, enthusiastically endorsed all forms of resistive training. Women by the droves are rapidly becoming involved in weight training programs. Women's body building has become very popular in the late 1970's and early 1980's. Also, American women in many sports have truly become international in caliber, primarily as a result of their participation in scientific functional strength training programs.

Another health reason for women to become involved in weight training is in the prevention of osteoporosis. Current research reports have indicated that weight training may be a defense against osteoporosis in aging women. Also, a large number of younger as well as older women are using weight training to more effectively contour their bodies, to reduce body fat and to improve physical performance.

Women are slowly but surely turning away from the ineffective physical exercise programs that have been jammed down their throats in the past. They are realizing that weight training in any one of its forms is a superior body contouring and fat reducing program. Females are finally discovering that muscle developed by weight training normalizes the body curves and does not negatively affect their femininity.

THE TOTAL CONDITIONING PROCESS AND WEIGHT TRAINING

Excellence in any sport, as well as in general physical fitness training, involves many factors, but basically it represents a fulfillment of one's potential. It is obvious that humans perform at various levels for a variety of psychological and physiological reasons. However, no matter what these reasons may be, or what the performance levels are, one should never leave readiness to chance. Therefore, an intelligent resistive training program will prepare one for the task selected, and should be one of the basic conditioning methods employed in the overall training plan.

If optimum readiness is to be attained prior to performing, it will be necessary that all elements required to meet the goal be included in the training plans. Another important fact to know about conditioning is that it takes time to become as good as one can possibly be in any activity. The body requires time to grow or adjust to the stresses placed on it in the conditioning program. Therefore, one should not become discouraged if they are not instantly successful. It may take months, or years, to achieve the goals selected. Remember, also, that performance at any time will be determined by the potential that one possesses physically and mentally, minus any losses because of improper application of the skill enhancement program and the weight training and conditioning program.

The most efficient approach to take in the search for a scientific basis for sports conditioning is to study the actual skill in question. Then add, subsequent to this analysis, an exercise program that will train all systems of the body as specifically as possible. Stress studies conducted by many scientists over the years have shown what adaptation can be expected as a result of normal and abnormal stress on the body. It depends on the quantity and quality of the specific stressor used and the proper balance of work, rest and nutrition. Bruce Lee, the late martial art sensation, also focused on the issue at its essence. In a "Fortune Cookie" he states, "If one desires to become proficient at fighting, one fights". Any practice not emphasizing this principle is operating on questionable grounds. **SPECIFICITY RULES!**

While "specificity rules", the average person as well as the athlete is obliged to add a resistive training (weight training) component to their exercise regimen. This has to be done to provide the stimulus for improvement of athletic or recreational skills by increasing the force that a muscle can produce; to protect from injury in pursuing aerobic activities, athletic and recreational skills; and optimizing body composition by increasing lean body mass and reducing body fat. Research and practical experience have demonstrated that weight training is the most effective means to accomplish these goals.

A graphic representation of all the elements of human movement will serve to demonstrate the interrelationships between all these elements. The conditioning model and its graphical presentation are discussed below.

THE CONDITIONING MODEL

Down through the years, physical educators have attempted to develop a model that would best describe the elements of human movement. Clarke (1967) graphically illustrated these relationships in his writings in measurement and evaluation. However, the authors have taken the liberty of adding elements to illustrate the holistic nature of human movement. Figure 1-1 shows the elements of this conditioning model.

The health of humans and their performance capacities are based on organic soundness and adequate nutrition. Physical fitness includes strength, local muscle endurance and cardio-vascular-respiratory endurance and is supported by organic soundness and adequate nutrition. Motor fitness is based on all the factors of organic soundness, adequate nutrition and the components of physical fitness with the addition of muscular power, agility, speed and body balance. General athletic ability includes all the elements of organic soundness, adequate nutrition, physical fitness and motor fitness with the addition of hand/eye coordination and foot/eye coordination. Specific athletic ability is based on all the ingredients of organic soundness, adequate nutrition, physical fitness, motor fitness and general athletic ability augmented with those unique attributes that are needed for performance of a specific skill. These specific attributes are denoted by "X" and "Y" in Figure 1-1, The Conditioning Model and are special to each skill trained.

Clarke, H. Harrison; Application of Measurement to Health & Physical Education; Prentice-Hall Inc., Englewood Cliffs, N.J.; 4th Ed., © 1967, p. 202.

THEORY & PRACTICE   PART I

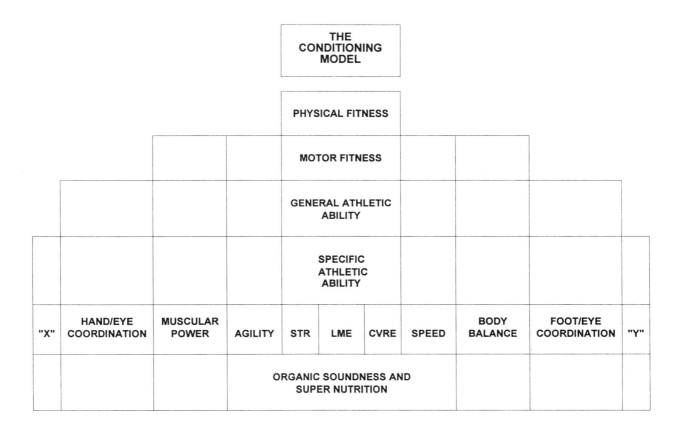

Figure 1-1. The Conditioning Model

THE USE OF WEIGHT TRAINING IN THE CONDITIONING PROCESS

It is important to understand the objectives of a conditioning program before one can intelligently develop a systematic program that will ensure success. Therefore, it is very critical to understand where weight training can be more effectively used as a conditioning tool. By changing the mode, i.e., the sets, repetitions and intensity, weight training can be adapted so that many aspects of physical fitness can be conditioned with various weight training methods.

To have a **Total Conditioning Program**, the following elements should be studied to see how they satisfy the conditioning objectives. It should be recognized that each one of the conditioning qualities should be planned for in a **Total Conditioning Program**. However, the main topic of this book is Weight Training; therefore, the qualities that are influenced to a greater extent by weight training will be listed first.

PHYSICAL QUALITIES HIGHLY DEVELOPED THROUGH WEIGHT TRAINING

MUSCULAR POWER: Muscular Power is the ability to do heavy workloads in very short periods of time. The power clean and power snatch are commonly used measures of this quality.

MUSCULAR STRENGTH: Muscular Strength is the ability to develop maximum force, or tension in an exercise. This quality is usually measured by doing a one repetition maximum (1RM) for an exercise. The dead lift would be an excellent example of total body muscular strength.

LOCAL MUSCLE ENDURANCE: Local Muscle Endurance is the ability to do an exercise, series of exercises or circuit weight training with below maximum weight for a prolonged period of time. Various exercises can be done for repetitions with a percentage of the 1RM or a percentage of body weight.

SPEED OF MOVEMENT: Speed of movement generally relates to the movement of the total body. However, the speed of movement of each segment (arms, legs and trunk) is also important. Improvement in muscular strength directly influences in a very positive manner the speed of movement of the overall body as well as each of the limbs.

OPTIMIZATION OF BODY COMPOSITION: Weight training is the single most effective system of training to optimize body composition that exists. Other systems of training, i.e., aerobic programs, stretching regimens and skill development programs usually have a very large but specific impact on the physiological component for which those systems are designed. There is generally only a small modification of lean body mass when training with systems other than some form of weight training except where those other systems mimic resistive training programs which significantly increase lean body mass; such as, gymnastics, wrestling and, possibly, swimming. Of course, sensible application of nutritional principles potentiates the effects of a good weight training program. Research has shown the weight training is most effective for increasing lean (muscle) body mass and reducing body fat, concurrently.

Gettman, Ward and Hagan (1981) have published an article which includes Table 1-1 that demonstrates the overall effectiveness of various forms of weight training compared to traditional aerobic training systems with regard to the exercise program's impact on body composition.

Notice that some form of weight training (circuit training, super circuit weight training or traditional sets and repetitions) has been shown to be more effective in **reducing body fat** and **increasing lean body mass** than traditional aerobic programs. This finding is in direct conflict with what is erroneously taught in most fitness programs which push aerobic exercise as the best method of controlling body composition. However, a honest and objective evaluation of the effectiveness of basic physical training methods would favor the use of some form of weight training when body fat reduction and increases in lean body mass are the primary goals. An additional benefit gained by employing weight training programs for reducing body fat is the substantial increase in muscular strength produced by all forms of weight training compared to the rather ineffective impact of traditional aerobic training programs on strength improvement.

Table 1-1. Changes In Strength, Aerobic Capacity, And Body Composition With Various Types Of Training.

TYPE OF TRAINING	STRENGTH %	VO2 MAX %	BODY WEIGHT %	LBW %	BODY FAT %
Weight Training (Traditional)	+30	0	0 to +1	+2	-2
Aerobic Programs	0 to +12	+15 to 25	0 to -1	0 to +2	-2
Circuit Weight Training	+18	+5 to 12	0 to -1	+2	-2
Super Circuit	+23	+17	-1	+3	-3

Gettmann, L., Ward, P., and Hagan, D.; Strength and endurance changes through circuit weight training; National Strength & Conditioning Association Journal; Aug.-Sept., 1981.

CONDITIONING FOR SPORTS

Sports offer a tremendous challenge to the coaches who attempt to train beginners or champions. Today, more than any other time in history, there are numerous available facts and principles regarding training for sports, discovered, and elaborated upon, by past and present researchers, coaches, athletes and practitioners. **The coach still operating only at the intuitive level is doing his athletes a disservice by not utilizing this wealth of knowledge.** Many times the study of these facts and principles will produce a sound basis for changing or improving technique, changing or improving the physical preparation process or possibly serve only to explain the reasons for present skill performance. No matter what the reasons, coaching of motor skills can only improve if these facts are applied properly.

Many technical questions arise in the teaching and training of skills, and these questions must be answered if ultimates in performance are to be reached. The coach who is unwilling to make an assessment of the situation and produce sound solutions to the problems is just as guilty of an error of omission as he would be for one of commission. One thing must be thoroughly recognized by both the coach and the athlete, and this is that progress may not be rapid. For instance, in the case of altering some element of an already grooved skill, the progress in most cases is negative; therefore, the coach and athlete pursuing this type of solution must be prepared for a comprehensive struggle to get top results. Needless to say, the situation can produce maximum stress factors that will take a mature individual to comprehend.

Many times, it has been observed that athletes were not able to cope with such stress factors...**when success didn't come easily**...and completely gave up. Therefore, coaching involves much more than just dispensing data; it is concerned with the individual as a unit. To put it another way, there must be a holistic approach to physical preparation, mental preparation and skill performance. To disregard this fact is to spell almost certain failure for the coach and athlete.

THEORY & PRACTICE   PART I

If the modern era in sports has contributed anything as a result of specialization, it has been in the area of **pre-season preparation**. Athletes are better today primarily because they are better prepared both physically and mentally to participate in sports. Still there is a tremendous gap between what some athletes are and what they potentially would be. **The major weakness that can be seen in most aspiring athletes is in the area of strength <u>development.</u>** This is a sad situation because with little internal impetus, and some external guiding, it is a relatively easy matter to increase muscle mass, and concurrently, the individual's strength which may have the most weighted impact on performance when compared to all possible factors that influence performance, besides genetics.

The concept of improving strength has found fruition in many amateur and professional athletes. One of the greatest thrills in coaching is to be able to observe the great improvement in strength and consequently, performance in athletes. No matter the level at which this growth is observed, it should always be an inspirational experience. Many examples can be thought of that vividly reinforce the need for a comprehensive year-round weight training and conditioning program.

FACTORS AFFECTING PERFORMANCE

The difference between winning and losing many times is minute. One of the reasons for this is that ability levels of each athlete is becoming very comparable. Due to this fact, preparation has become an even more important factor for successful performance. A major consideration in the preparation process is **CONDITIONING**. It should be pointed out also that proper conditioning is invariably the result of sound planning. In the final analysis, however, success is related directly to how the plan is applied.

An interesting question to ponder at this time is, **"Do we fail to attain our goals because of inadequate physical endowment or because of insufficient training?"** The program for training for sport should be developed primarily so that insufficient training **WILL NOT** be a major reason for unacceptable levels of performance. To evaluate productivity, one should take the relationship expressed by the following equation and apply it to their own situation.

PRODUCTIVITY = POTENTIAL - LOSSES DUE TO FAULTY PROCESS

Figure 1-2 contains a few of the general factors that affect human performance. There are many factors that have a strong influence on physical performance. Among them are: coach-athlete interaction, sleep, heredity, injury, work, school, social life, nutrition, training and environmental factors. While it is important to control as many of these general factors as possible when training (for general fitness or sport) the single most important factor is physical training. This is the one factor that can be best controlled and, therefore, most strongly influences physical performance.

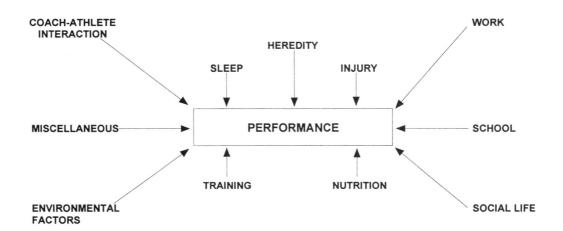

Figure 1-2. Factors Affecting Performance

While there is strong interaction between all factors, the inherent dimensions of physical training will dictate to the greatest degree, the level of physical performance one can attain. The application of the physical training program determines to a large degree whether one will be successful in their efforts. Of course, all other factors must be optimally controlled, however, one does not exert the control of these other factors as they can with their own efforts in the physical training program. Therefore, training must be grounded on scientific principles and a significant amount of time is needed to apply the general training program in order to maximize performance.

Changes do not take place all at once or in a short period of time. Rather, it is the accumulation of many months and years of hard training that produces uncommon levels of performance. The training process is an ever-ascending spiral to maximum achievement. In the yearly training plan, one should expect to participate four to five months (16 to 20 weeks) in general and specific training prior to the beginning of training for a specific sport or activity.

For any skill performance, outside of practicing the exact skill, the single most important training factor is the absence or presence of a weight training program. For endurance oriented sports the weight training program is necessary for injury prevention as well as performance enhancement.

Studies that have been conducted over the years have confirmed some very important training concepts. Among these concepts can be found some guiding rules to action that have helped to improve a conditioning program. A general rule that weaves through all human behavior states that, **"Exercise prepares you to do additional exercise."** The body will adapt to the loads placed on it. Therefore, when the sport season ends, the tendency is to adapt to the loads encountered "at that time." If they are lower than previous levels, negative changes occur. Briefly, some of these changes that are observed immediately post season when training is abruptly interrupted are:

1. Decreases in Performance (speed, strength, endurance, flexibility, and skills).
2. Decrease in Lean Body Weight (muscle and bone).
3. Increase in Body Fat.

It is essential that these changes be held to a minimum if performance is to be improved or maintained at previous levels. Year-round weight training and skill training for athletes based on the principles of periodization will help to minimize fitness and performance entropy.

It is helpful to restate some key concepts with regard to factors affecting human performance:

1. Winning or losing is many times determined by slight margins in athletic potential.
2. Conditioning can make the difference.
3. Productivity = Potential - Losses due to the faulty training and conditioning process.
4. The training process is an ever ascending spiral to maximum achievement that requires many years of work.
5. Plan on taking 4 to 5 months of general and specific training prior to the beginning of the sport season.
6. Remember, the human body adapts to the loads placed on it. If these loads are lower than previous levels, negative changes occur.
7. Success is based on a logical systematic plan.
8. The reason for playing the sport will determine the level of achievement one can attain.
9. The body is like a computer - "quality in, quality out." Remember, the body only adapts to the specific types of activities that are included in the training program.

PSYCHOLOGICAL FACTORS

The mind and body are one unit, and therefore, they should not be thought of and physically trained as separate parts. However, it may be interesting to discuss some of the qualities that behavioral scientists have considered as extremely important personality traits. This should give us a better understanding of how one can perform at higher personal levels.

Although it may be difficult to predict physical performance by personality evaluation, there are some commonly accepted factors and traits that may provide a better understanding of the interaction that exists between the mental and physical aspects of performance. Six of these personality traits are discussed briefly below to allow the reader to mentally evaluate their own traits.

1. **INTELLIGENCE.** The ability to acquire and retain knowledge, mentally and physically. Does one learn the techniques and strategy of the sport easily? Can they absorb it in a short time? Can they carry out the assignments or techniques in competition?

2. **CHARACTER.** An individual's pattern of behavior or personality or moral constitution. Are they disloyal? Selfish? Uncooperative? Break Rules?

3. **PRIDE.** This is the ability to continue striving until the goal is reached. To be unwilling to settle for anything less. A job well done.

4. **INTENSITY.** Enthusiasm and high levels of energy are evident in the individuals that possess exceptional levels of intensity. Do you approach the objectives of the day with a positive attitude and eagerness?

5. **AGGRESSIVENESS.** Boldness and an energetic pursuit of goals are qualities of positive aggressive behavior associated with individuals who are high achievers.

6. **LEADERSHIP.** Do you have the combination of mental and physical qualities that inspire and lead others to perform more effectively? Good leaders many times exhibit the following qualities: fairness, aggressiveness, enthusiasm, resourcefulness, desire to excel, cooperativeness, conscientiousness, and therefore are usually popular individuals.

D.A. Kelly has developed an excellent measurement device that can be used as a self-test or to evaluate the sport demand by the coach, athlete or any person wanting to become involved in a sport or physical activity. There are eight factors that cover the psycho/social domain. The following test should allow one to evaluate their possible involvement in a sport or physical activity. To use this device one should first rate themselves and then rate the sport. A comparison of the individual rating and the sport/activity of interest rating will help one determine if one has some affinity for that sport or activity. Score each item from 1-10. Ten is the greater amount of a trait. Subtotal each trait and then total all the subtotals for an overall score. **SEE THE PSYCH/SOCIAL EVALUATION SELF-TEST ON THE FOLLOWING PAGES.**

If one scored a ten on each item on this test they would accumulate 460 points. **There are no standards regarding the results of this assessment**. It is merely a private and personal evaluation of one's feelings about their participation in a selected activity. It may assist in directing one into a physical activity or sport that would specifically appeal to their emotional assessment of themselves. It is important to understand that the results of this assessment will vary at different phases in one's lifetime. Table 1-2 contains an arbitrary guide to rating the score of this test for physical activity affinity or sport affinity.

Table 1-2. Arbitrary Guide For The Rating Of Physical Activity Affinity Or Sport Affinity.

RATING	SCORE TOTAL
High Affinity	376-460
Moderately High Affinity	329-375
Good Affinity	235-328
Moderately Low Affinity	141-234
Low Affinity	000-140

PSYCHO/SOCIAL EVALUATION

TRAITS	INDIVIDUAL VALUE	SPORT/ACTIVITY VALUE
1. PHYSICAL EXERTION		
A. Gross motor (large muscle) activity	_____	_____
B. Physical Strength	_____	_____
C. Overall good physical condition	_____	_____
D. Endurance and stamina	_____	_____
E. Tolerating pain or discomfort	_____	_____
F. The expenditure of energy	_____	_____
Subtotal for Physical Exertion	_____	_____
2. INDIVIDUAL CONTROL		
A. Much practice and preparation	_____	_____
B. Precision of movement	_____	_____
C. Patience	_____	_____
D. Intense concentration	_____	_____
E. Self-Control	_____	_____
F. The ability to ignore irrelevant or distracting stimuli	_____	_____
G. The progressive learning of specific skills	_____	_____
H. Focused attention on things happening inside your body	_____	_____
I. The ability to bounce back after making mistakes	_____	_____
Subtotal for Individual Control	_____	_____
3. COORDINATED SPEED		
A. Fine motor (small muscle) activity	_____	_____
B. Agility	_____	_____
C. Overall speed of movement	_____	_____
D. Precision of movement	_____	_____
E. Quick reactions	_____	_____
F. The progressive learning of specific skills	_____	_____
G. The coordination of many different abilities	_____	_____
Subtotal for Coordinated Speed	_____	_____
4. INTERPERSONAL SUPPORT		
A. Interaction with coaches	_____	_____
B. Teamwork and cooperation	_____	_____
C. Team cohesiveness and team spirit	_____	_____
Subtotal for Interpersonal Support	_____	_____
5. EMOTIONAL AROUSAL		
A. Emotional arousal	_____	_____
B. Feeling psyched-up	_____	_____
C. Feelings of anger or hostility	_____	_____
D. Relaxed and calm feelings	_____	_____
Subtotal for Emotional Arousal	_____	_____

THEORY & PRACTICE

PART I

PSYCHO/SOCIAL EVALUATION (CONTINUED)

TRAITS	INDIVIDUAL VALUE	SPORT/ACTIVITY VALUE
6. COGNITIVE EFFICIENCY		
A. Understanding complicated rules	_____	_____
B. A good memory	_____	_____
C. Thinking and analysis of complex situations	_____	_____
D. Recognizing & responding to many things simultaneously	_____	_____
E. Strategy and planning	_____	_____
F. Taking risks and changes	_____	_____
G. Focused attention on things happening outside your body	_____	_____
H. Intelligence	_____	_____
Subtotal for Cognitive Efficiency	_____	_____
7. EXTERNAL ATTENTION		
A. Self-pacing (i.e., going at your own speed)	_____	_____
B. Reacting to somebody or something else	_____	_____
C. Competing against a standard	_____	_____
D. Quick reactions	_____	_____
E. Focused attention on things happening outside your body	_____	_____
F. Focused attention on things happening inside your body	_____	_____
Subtotal for External Attention	_____	_____
8. DISINHIBITION		
A. Aggressive physical contact with other people	_____	_____
B. Disregard for personal injury	_____	_____
C. Feelings of anger or hostility	_____	_____
Subtotal for Disinhibition	_____	_____

PSYCHO/SOCIAL EVALUATION - COMPOSITE SCORE

TRAITS	INDIVIDUAL VALUE	SPORT/ACTIVITY VALUE
1. Physical Exertion	_____	_____
2. Individual Control	_____	_____
3. Coordinated Speed	_____	_____
4. Interpersonal Support	_____	_____
5. Emotional Arousal	_____	_____
6. Cognitive Efficiency	_____	_____
7. External Attention	_____	_____
8. Disinhibition	_____	_____
Total Psycho/Social Evaluation	_____	_____

Adapted from Psycho/Social Evaluation developed by D. A. Kelly, PHD, LCDR, MSC USN; Psychiatry Department; Naval Hospital; Groton, Connecticut 06349-5600.

BODY STRUCTURE FACTORS

The elements of body structure help describe the human body, first. Secondarily, a relationship can be identified between these elements and physical performance. Essentially, the following factors play an important role in success in physical activity:

1. Size - height, weight, bone lengths and circumferences of major body parts.
2. Optimum Weight - The total body weight that is best suited for each individual. It is influenced by age, size, sex, and skill or sport.
3. Lean Body Weight - Bone, muscle, organ and related tissue.
4. Total weight, fat weight and lean body weight ratios.
5. Percent Fat - The total amount of fat that the body contains can also be expressed as a percent of the total body weight. The levels of body fat vary with age, sex, size, nutrition, and exercise.

In Table 1-3 is found the percent fat values for selected age groups of males and females. It is important to remember that these values may vary greatly when humans are very active or are quite inactive. In general lean athletes perform better than fatter athletes. This, of course, may vary greatly among sports and also among various positions or disciplines within a specific sport. It is important to remember there is a wide range of percent body fat among elite performers in all sports. Arbitrary percent fat levels are not good guidelines; the level of performance of the individual should be the criterion for determining if they are too fat.

Table 1-3. Percent Fat Values For Selected Ages In Humans

AGE	MALE %	FEMALE %
15 Years Old	12	20
20 Years Old	15	25
30 Years Old	19	28
40 Years Old	22	30
50 Years Old	26	35
Athletes	6-20	6-20

The primary concern is how much fat and lean body weight one has. In general, the higher the percent fat, the poorer the performance; the lower the percent fat, the better the performance. There are some exceptions: for instance, one of the United State's best discus throwers and a former world record holder was found to be 20% fat in a scientifically controlled body composition study. Other American discus throwers in the same study who were at world class performance levels and former World Record holders were only 6 % body fat. It is important to note that the discus thrower who had 20% body fat did not experience diminished performance levels because of his relatively high percent of body fat. **As stated before, the performance level should dictate what percent fat that an athlete should be, not some arbitrary standard imposed by the coach or exercise scientist.** Conditioning will greatly influence body composition by reducing fat weight and increasing lean body weight.

FUNCTIONAL STRENGTH FACTORS

There are many ways of organizing the functional strength factors. An individual program can be developed by body part, joint action, multi-jointed fast-slow action, light and heavy weight, or any combination. The factors that are presented here have been based on patterns discovered from studying college, olympic and professional athletes.

The factors draw from all of the methods given above.

1. **POWER.** Power is the ability to lift heavy weights quickly. The loads lifted can vary from 80% to 100% of 1 repetition maximum. This is the most important functional strength factor, because it utilizes total body actions, and requires a tremendous amount of energy to be developed in a short time period. Olympic lifting and variations, have been used for training this factor. However, various dumbbell exercises done with one hand can bring in a 3-plane action that helps develop all aspects of the body.

2. **LEG AND BACK STRENGTH.** Leg and back strength are very important in determining the maximum strength of the body. The greater the strength in these areas, the better the foundation will be for developing the power exercises. It is extremely important that the legs and back have much greater strength than the power exercises require, so that proper techniques will be used.

3. **SHOULDER AND ARM STRENGTH.** There are two divisions in shoulder and arm strength. They are based on joint action. The exercises are categorized according to a pushing (away from the body), or pulling (toward body) action. Both pushing and pulling movements are important to many sports activities.

4. **MUSCLE ENDURANCE.** Muscular strength endurance includes exercises, or series of exercises, that develop the ability to work at loads below the maximum levels of muscular strength (lifting level). It is interesting to note that any of the other factors can serve as a muscular strength or muscular endurance exercise simply by varying the amount of weight lifted, and the number of repetitions done. This can be made a part of any single exercise, or can include any number of exercises desired.

5. **TRUNK AND ABDOMEN STRENGTH AND ENDURANCE.** The trunk and abdomen need to be trained in all possible directions of movement. The energy required for sports skill must be transmitted properly through the trunk. Therefore, a well conditioned trunk and abdomen are essential.

6. **NECK STRENGTH AND ENDURANCE.** The neck and head play a major role in all kinds of contact and non-contact sports. The benefits of proper conditioning of the neck may be of value in performance, injury prevention, or both.

7. **SPECIAL AND REHABILITATION EXERCISES.** There may be weaknesses, muscle imbalances, injuries, or just areas of special concern that can be taken care of in this category. Dumbbell exercises allow unlimited movements of the joints and, consequently, are an excellent means of working in this area.

ENERGY ORIENTED FACTORS

The superior performer in any sport position/skill must be able to transmit or receive a large amount of energy in a short period of time. Therefore, the athlete must develop a degree of physical toughness to withstand the rigors of a game under full speed conditions. A careful study of those factors important in energy absorption and transmission will help in handling situations that arise during the game, by seeking ways to train them prior to the contest. The previous factor areas have included most of the elements of this section. However, the following discussion may serve as a summary of the physical factors that need to be considered when planning a conditioning program.

1. **KIND OF SPORT OR ACTIVITY.** Does the sport involve contact, quick starting and stopping, or continuous sub-maximal effort, etc.?
2. **RANGE OF MOTION OF JOINTS.** Total body flexibility.
3. **MUSCLE QUALITIES.** The rate at which the muscles can contract and relax, the length of the muscles, and the tension in the muscles, are qualities that influence the ability to perform.
4. **PERCEPTION.**
   A. Reaction Time = (Sense Organ + Brain + Nerve) + Muscle.
   B. Reflex Time = (Sense Organ + Nerve) + Muscle.

C. Movement Time = Time that it takes from first visible movement to completion of the task.
D. Total Movement Time = Reacting time or reflex time + Movement Time.
E. Response to Pressure = Reaction Time (Touch - Pressure).

5. **STRENGTH OF MUSCLES.** The absolute maximum amount of tension that can be developed.
6. **ENDURANCE OF MUSCLES.** The ability to continue to exercise at levels below absolute strength.

The tissues of the body will hold up in direct proportion to their ability to withstand the tensile (pulling), compression (pressing), shear (side), and torsion (twisting) forces they are called upon to withstand. These forces can be either internally developed by the muscles and levers, or developed externally by gravity and impacts with players, or other hard surfaces.

A thoroughly planned conditioning program will be built on the idea of improved performance and injury prevention. Consequently, the conditioning program either has to develop the ability of the tissues of the body to resist large amounts of force, or to develop neuromuscular skills that will allow the player to control, or redirect the forces to his advantage. Controlling or redirecting the forces that are present in the playing environment is by far the best approach because the forces present can easily exceed those levels that cause injury to body tissues. Injury prevention is a major concern; however, a player can improve his performance by becoming aware of what is taking place on the field and by using the forces available to his advantage, and at the same time, reduce the possibility of injury.

TRAINING INTENSITY LEVELS

The intensity levels are based on a percentage of a standard. Usually, this can be determined by testing, or by previous performances. One repetition maximums are commonly used standards. However, this does not mean that other standards may not be appropriate. In Table 1-4 is a guide that will help in establishing a system of intensity prescription.

Table 1-4. Rating Of Intensity Of 1RM For Exercise Prescription.

% 1RM	RATING
90% +	Very Heavy
80% - 90%	Heavy
70% - 80%	Medium
60% - 70%	Medium Light
50% - 60%	Light
40% - 50%	Easy - Threshold of Training Effect

SUMMARY STATEMENT ON FACTORS

Factors that impact human performance at any level are: physiological factors, body structural factors, functional strength factors, energy oriented factors and training intensity levels. It would be very difficult to pick out any one of the above factors and develop a program based on it alone with the omission of all the other factors. Remember that conditioning for sport includes many factors that work together to produce improved performance. However, the art and science of putting a conditioning program together should account for the varying amounts of each factor that are included in the program. The concepts and methods presented in this book relating to individual program prescriptions will help one to organize the conditioning program for the activity of choice.

PART I

THEORY & PRACTICE

REASONS FOR A LACK OF TRAINING PROGRESS

People who train with weights often experience times when improvements are not forthcoming. This is a very confusing and frustrating time in one's training career. This confusion and frustration can be greatly reduced by carefully designing the weight training program with consideration given to all the factors affecting performance. The following is a list of reasons for a lack of training progress which will help coaches and athletes understand appropriate program structure and design for functional strength programs:

1. Poor program structure.

    (a) Poor choice of exercises or using too many or too few exercises.
    (b) Improper execution of exercises.
    (c) Continuous alterations in the program from week to week.
    (d) Exercises used do not relate to the training goals.
    (e) Absence of variation in training intensity and duration from day to day, week to week, etc.

2. Missing workouts.
3. Excessive overload — program too advanced.
4. Insufficient overload — program too easy.
5. Poor Diet.
6. Insufficient rest.
7. Excess "outside" stressors — work, study, social relationships.

It is essential to develop a well planned and scientifically grounded weight training program for successful attainment of individual goals; whether they be focused on general fitness, body building or training for sport. First the objectives of the program must be clearly defined followed by the application of scientific principles of training. The principles of periodization must be applied to be successful in any weight training program at any level of participation.

PHYSICAL FITNESS AND STRENGTH TRAINING IN PUBESCENCE AND DURING AGING

Discussions of physical fitness, strength training in prepubescent males and females, and strength and aging are presented in this section. It is important to note that strength is an important component of fitness and that strength training at all ages of life is effective and desirable. Unfortunately, strength fitness has not been encouraged at all ages which has resulted in a population of people that are sub-par in strength and muscular development. This lack of strength training programs impacts the functional capacity for daily living, recreational pursuits, predisposes people to injuries and distorts the normal curves of the body. While strength training is important for all ages in males and females, it is only one of four components of physical fitness. All factors of physical fitness must be addressed in designing and participating in general fitness programs as well as training for sport and body building.

THE CONCEPT OF PHYSICAL FITNESS

Physical education literature and popular writings contain many varied yet similar descriptions of physical fitness. Perception of physical fitness is highly related to how people anticipate using their bodies. For example, the degree of physical fitness needed by an athlete is considerably higher than that needed for a sedentary office worker. Moreover, each sport has its own specific conditioning requirement. Likewise every individual has specific needs that will dictate modifications of a physical fitness program and, therefore, impact their definition of physical fitness.

There must be specificity of fitness training to meet the needs of a specific activity interest, but at the same time, there exists a need for the general development of fitness components in preparation for these specific activities and general health. Therefore, it is necessary to define the **basic components of fitness** and adapt programs that develop them in concert with one's individual needs and goals.

Only those factors that relate to the development of health and increase the functional capacity of the body should be cataloged as physical fitness components. Those abilities that are necessary for motor skill proficiency (basic movement factors) should be classified as motor components and are not normally included in the general definitions of physical fitness. These motor ability factors are: agility, balance, coordination, speed, power, flexibility and reaction time. These characteristics are often erroneously included in the definition of physical fitness; however, they must be properly considered as unique and specific motor components.

Clarke (1967) defined physical fitness as "...the ability to carry out daily tasks with vigor and alertness, without undue fatigue, and with ample energy to enjoy leisure time pursuits, and to meet unforeseen emergencies."

COMPONENTS OF PHYSICAL FITNESS

Most authorities in the field of physical fitness agree that the components of physical fitness are as follows:

(1) **STRENGTH:** Strength is defined as the ability of a muscle or muscle group to execute one maximum contraction against a maximum resistance.

(2) **LOCAL MUSCLE ENDURANCE (LME):** LME is the ability of a muscle or muscle group to make repeated submaximal contractions.

(3) **CARDIOVASCULAR-RESPIRATORY ENDURANCE (CVRE):** CVRE is the ability to execute submaximal (moderate intensity) general exercise over extended periods of time.

(4) **BODY COMPOSITION:** Body Composition is defined as the proportions of bone, muscle, fat and organ weight in the body. The average male from 18 to 26 years of age is between 12% and 15% body fat. The average woman in the same age range varies between 26% and 30% body fat. Male and female athletes range between 6% and 20% body fat. Men and women who are older than 26 years tend to become fatter as they age. This creeping obesity occurs mainly because of gross inactivity, however, a small portion may be due to decreases in hormonal output.

In Table 1-5 is shown the relationship between physical fitness components and muscularity components. More information concerning this relationship is presented in subsequent sections.

With regard to weight training programs, it can be observed in the table that as intensity increases and the number of repetitions decreases in a given training strategy there is a greater impact on the muscularity components (strength and size). Using lower weights and a greater number of repetitions (up to, but no more than 15 repetitions for multiple sets) focuses more on the energy producing (metabolic) elements of the muscle and, therefore, impacts the muscular endurance dimension of performance, i.e., the ability to execute more work (repetitions) at a low to moderate workload (weight).

Extending the repetitions beyond 15 becomes more a matter of metabolic endurance rather than producing structural changes in the contractile proteins of the muscle. Performing repetitions beyond 15 dictates that the training intensity (% 1RM) be significantly lowered. Extremely high repetition exercises may have some value, but research needs to be performed to precisely define its impact on the contractile proteins, metabolic apparatus and connective tissue in the muscle.

Generally, when using various weight training formats, **CVRE** is produced by using **Circuit Weight Training (CWT)** and **Super Circuit Weight Training (SCWT)**. A good number of research projects have shown that CVRE can be significantly enhanced when using these formats. When using CWT or SCWT it has been found that generally the repetitions should range from 12 to 15 at an intensity of 40-60 % 1RM while performing

Table 1-5.   The Relationship Between Physical Fitness Components And Muscularity Components.

PHYSICAL FITNESS COMPONENTS	CVRE* ———————————————— LME ————————————————— STRENGTH (NOTE: CAN BIAS PROGRAM TOWARD STRENGTH OR CARDIOVASCULAR ENDURANCE)		
	◄——————————————— SLIDING SCALE ———————————————►		
MUSCULARITY COMPONENTS	DIMINUTION IN MUSCLE SIZE AND FURTHER LOSS OF SUBCUTANEOUS FAT	DEFINITION (MUSCULARITY)	SIZE (BULK)
REPETITIONS	CWT/SCWT (10-15 REPS)	9-15 REPS	1-8 REPS
SETS	3-4 LAPS OF CIRCUIT	3-5 SETS	3-5 SETS
TIME OR REST BETWEEN SETS	CONTINUOUS ACTIVITY	CONTINUOUS ACTIVITY OR MINIMAL REST (UP TO 2 MINUTES)	2-5 MINUTES REST BETWEEN EXERCISES
INTENSITY	40%-60% OF 1RM	40%-70% OF 1RM	70%-100% 1RM
TRAINING DAYS PER WEEK	DAILY IF DESIRED OR 3 DAYS PER WEEK	DAILY IF DESIRED OR 2-3 DAYS PER WEEK FOR EACH BODY PART	2-3 DAYS PER WEEK FOR EACH BODY PART

* CVRE = CARDIOVASCULAR ENDURANCE
** LME = LOCAL MUSCLE ENDURANCE

from 20 to 30 stations or three laps of a 10 station circuit. The activity is continuous with little (10-15 seconds) time between exercises in standard CWT while in SCWT the activity is continuous with no time between weight exercises and aerobic exercises, both periods being 30 seconds.

This type of CVRE training can occur daily because the metabolic and muscular intensity is low to moderate. If desired, one could increase the intensity and reduce the repetitions to work for more local muscular endurance and less CVRE. If the intensity of the programs extends above 60% 1RM, then daily training sessions are not recommended and, of course, the training effects becomes more muscular (structural) and less endurance (metabolic).

Local muscle endurance (LME) is improved by performing from 9-15 reps in 3-5 sets with 40-70 % 1RM. Activity can be continuous if more general endurance is desired. Longer rest periods places the focus on muscular endurance. Remember that increased fatigue is not the stimulus to muscle growth. Intensity (% 1RM) and total amount of work are the stimuli to growth. LME training allows more work to be produced and, therefore, more calories are consumed causing a greater reduction of body fat. This principle is practically applied by body builders (male and female) during the cutting phase of their training when they execute from 9-15 repetitions or more in preparation for contests. This practice demonstrates that along with some rigid control of caloric intake, weight training does reduce the percent body fat.

One can bias LME training toward the metabolic (CVRE) or toward local muscular endurance and strength enhancement by simply changing the repetitions, intensity and rest periods.

Strength and size are maximally improved by performing 1-8 repetitions for 3-5 sets with 70 - 100 % of 1RM. The rest periods should be long with complete recovery. **To enhance the increase of contractile proteins**, 5-8 repetitions should be used for 3-5 sets at 75% to 85% 1RM with a long rest between sets. **To enhance the maximal recruitment (CNS control of muscle force)** of muscle one should use from 1-4 repetitions for 3-5 sets (or more) using between 90% and 100% 1RM with complete recovery between sets. Attention needs to be given to the number of times per week that this heavy weight/low reps format is used. The number of heavy training days per week depends upon one's developmental level, genetic potential, age, recovery capacity, hormonal profile, nutritional state and the training objectives of the program.

SUMMARY OF PHYSICAL FITNESS

Physical fitness is a lifetime pursuit. It is impossible to store fitness once it is developed. Inactivity leads to a reversal or deterioration of fitness, so one must continually remain active to retard the degeneration of fitness components. Many myths exist about exercise and physical fitness in the mind of the public. There is no easy road to physical fitness. It requires constant attention and effort. It demands hard work and extended time to effect changes. Nutrition, rest and cycling of training intensities and volumes (known as periodization) all interact to produce effective functional strength and fitness programs for both elite athletes in all sports as well as the common man, woman, boy or girl of all ages.

A balanced approach to fitness training dictates that all components of the physical fitness quadrangle (strength, local muscle endurance, cardiovascular-respiratory endurance and optimal body composition) be actively and consistently developed. The specific objective of the training program will determine the component or components that should be emphasized. **It should be remembered, however, that overemphasis of any one factor may be detrimental to human performance, appearance or general health. A fitness training program should be employed throughout the human life-span.**

Immediately following is a summary of the American College of Sports Medicine (ACSM) Guidelines for Exercise which identifies and quantifies the minimum activity levels for the exercise parameters of cardiovascular training and resistance training.

AMERICAN COLLEGE OF SPORTS MEDICINE GUIDELINES FOR EXERCISE

BACKGROUND

The recommendation for all people (including older people) to engage in weight training exercises is becoming fashionable in the 1990's. **The prestigious American College of Sports Medicine (ACSM) is now vigorously endorsing the use of weight training and includes weight training as a major component of a total fitness program.** The previous position of this organization (prior to the 1990 ACSM Guidelines) was to minimize the importance of weight training in the total fitness program.

The ACSM in 1978 published a position paper entitled *The Recommended Quantity and Quality of Exercise for Developing and Maintaining Fitness in Healthy Adults.* This original paper defined what was considered to be the significant exercise parameters and their magnitudes, primarily for aerobic activities. The paper set the standards for the *frequency, intensity, duration and mode of aerobic exercise*.

Since 1978, 19 scientific studies have been quoted by the ACSM which support the inclusion of weight training recommendations in the exercise program for healthy adults. In addition, the ACSM has cited 6 scientific studies conducted prior to 1978 supporting the inclusion of weight training in an exercise program. Consequently, the *1990 Revised Guidelines* have been given the title of: *The Recommended Quantity and Quality of Exercise for Developing and Maintaining Cardiorespiratory and Muscular Fitness in Health Adults.*

WEIGHT TRAINING IS NOW BEING RECOMMENDED AS A MAJOR COMPONENT IN A TOTAL FITNESS PROGRAM.

SUMMARY OF THE 1990 ACSM GUIDELINES

The 1990 ACSM Guidelines ends with a statement on recommended exercise for healthy adults with the following statement: **"The important factor is to design a program for the individual to provide the proper amount of physical activity to attain maximal benefit at the lowest risk. Emphasis should be placed on factors that result in permanent life-style change and encourage a lifetime of physical activity."** The following is a synopsis of the 1990 guidelines for exercise for healthy adults:

Cardiovascular Training

1. **Frequency of Training:** 1 to 5 days a week.
2. **Intensity of Training:** 60% to 90% of maximum heart rate, or 50% to 85% of VO_2 max or, as an alternative, the **perceived exertion method**, wherein you need not monitor your pulse during exercise. Here you make a subjective evaluation of how hard you are working - somewhere between "moderate" and "very heavy," which should correspond to 60% to 90% of heart rate maximum.
3. **Duration of Training:** 20 to 60 minutes of continuous aerobic activity. Lower intensity activity for a longer period of time is preferred to higher intensity for the nonathletic adult.
4. **Mode of Activity:** Any activity that uses large muscle groups, can be maintained continuously, and is rhythmic and aerobic in nature, such as walking-hiking, running-jogging, cycling-bicycling, cross-country skiing, dancing, rope skipping, rowing, stair-climbing, swimming, skating and various endurance game activities.

Resistance Training

1. **Frequency of Training:** At least 2 days a week.
2. **Number of exercises:** A minimum of 8 to 10 exercises involving the major muscle groups.
3. **Intensity of Training:** A minimum of one set of 8 to 12 repetitions to near fatigue.
4. **Mode of Activity:** Resistance training (weight training) is recommended, but traditional calisthenics exercises "…can still be effective in improving and maintaining strength."

Stretching and Warm-up

"An appropriate warm-up and cool-down, which would include flexibility exercises, is also recommended."

1990 ACSM position paper: The Recommended Quantity and Quality of Exercise for Developing and Maintaining Cardiorespiratory and Muscular Fitness in Healthy Adults. ACSM, P.O. BOX 1440, Indianapolis, IN 46206-1440.

STRENGTH TRAINING IN PREPUBESCENT MALES AND FEMALES

INTRODUCTION

There has been considerable concern and a prodigious invalid pontification concerning the use of strength training in young boys and girls (prepubescent). The invalid criticism of strength training for boys and girls stems from genuine concern for their health and well being, but it is based on little, if any, objective and unbiased data.

Most opposition to the employment of weight training in prepubescent and adolescents children emanates from uninformed medical doctors, educators and physical education leaders that project value judgments based on spurious opinions and philosophical biases, not on objective research or valid empirical observations. This becomes a widespread problem because the general public forms its opinions based on what it perceives are valid sources of information (medical doctors, educators and physical education leaders). These sources have been shown to be unreliable and bogus from a research point of view and, also, from analysis of what is observed in the everyday world. Young boys and girls at all age levels, benefit from weight training programs and exercise programs, in general, that are properly formulated, applied and supervised.

It is generally accepted by most contemporary authorities that research into the effects of strength training on young boys and girls is lacking. A Position Paper on Prepubescent Strength Training disseminated by the National Strength and Conditioning Association states, **"It is clear that the available literature does not provide a definitive position; few studies have specifically addressed the issue of strength training in prepubescent children."** This position paper continues, stating, **"Our analysis of the strength training literature, both pro and con, has established the clear need for ongoing research into the effects of this training on the prepubescent athlete."**

National Strength and Conditioning Association (NCSA, 1985). Position paper on prepubescent strength training. National Strength and Conditioning Association Journal, 7 (6), 70-73.

The opposition to using weight training in preadolescent children has been based on three fundamentally incorrect assumptions:

1. Preadolescent children are incapable of making significant gains in strength because they lack sufficient circulating androgens.
2. Stresses placed on the bones and ligaments could cause serious injuries and hinder the growth process.
3. Strength training and consequent increases in strength will not improve flexibility, motor performance or reduce the risk of injuries.

There are some research studies that have resulted in convincing information upon which valid and reasonable approaches to strength training with prepubescent and pubescent children can be formulated. The studies that have demonstrated this convincing evidence for using weight training in preadolescent children will be reviewed latter in this section.

THE NEED OF YOUTH FITNESS PROGRAMS

In a brochure entitled, **THE UNITED STATES FITNESS ACADEMY - 1988**, the following facts which come from a recent survey conducted by the President's Council on Physical Fitness and Sports are introduced:

Among children under 17 years of age:

1. Forty (40%) percent cannot run a mile within ten (10) minutes.
2. Fifty (50%) percent cannot hold their chin over a bar for more than ten (10) seconds.
3. Fifty-five (55%) percent cannot do more than one pull up.
4. Less than fifty (50%) of all schools in America conduct any kind of a fitness testing program.
5. Two-Thirds of all students in grades 5-12 have no Physical Education classes at all.

In 1985, The President's Council on Physical Fitness and Sports supported and funded a survey called the PCPFS 1985 National School Population Fitness Survey. There were three primary objectives for this survey:

(1) to assess the physical fitness status of American public school children and youth ages 6-17, and establish norms for this age range by sex and age, in five percent increments.

PART I

THEORY & PRACTICE

(2) to compare these data with the results of three similar national studies completed in 1958, 1965 and 1975.

(3) to review and modify, if necessary, the standards for the President's Council on Physical Fitness and Sports Presidential Physical Fitness Award for school children.

1. **PCPFS 1985 National School Population Fitness Survey, S/N 017-001-00463-4; Superintendent of Documents, U.S. Government Printing Office, Washington, D.C. 20402.**

2. **Hunsicker, P. "National Norms For Fitness." Report of The 7th National Conference On Physicians and Schools. Chicago: American Medical Association, 1959.**

3. **Hunsicker, P. and Reiff, G. "Comparison of Youth Fitness,1958-65." Cooperative Research Project No. 2418. (Office of Education: Washington, D.C.).**

4. **Hunsicker, P. and Reiff, G.; "Comparison of Youth Fitness, 1958-65-75." Research Contract #OEC-0-74-9332. (U.S. Office of Education, Washington, D.C.); 1986.**

Some of the important conclusions that were reported in this research report are:

1. "...Extrapolated to the entire population, the study data show there is still a low level of performance in important components of physical fitness by millions of our youth."

2. "Upper arm and shoulder muscle girdle strength and endurance for both boys and girls was poor, although not worse than 1965 or 1975. It remains a significant weakness in our youth, boys as well as girls. Many have insufficient strength to handle their own body weight in case of emergency and were judged as being often unable to carry on daily work or physically demanding recreational activities successfully or safely. Upper arm and shoulder girdle strength and endurance for both men and women have previously been identified as major physical weaknesses for those who served in two world wars; the improvement of this component of fitness still waits to be addressed."

"This study supports a growing volume of both evidence and opinion that increased emphasis is required to improve the levels of youth physical fitness. (Authors' note: This starts at an early age - prepubescence.) Physical fitness has been found to be significantly related to the ability to do physical activities such as household chores, work, sport, dance and a capacity to meet emergency situations and to improved health.

Every youth serving agency, institution and organization at all levels, Federal, State and Regional, in both the private and public sector, should look critically at their responsibilities to improve youth fitness. Families can also provide encouragement and motivation towards good fitness habits. Youth must be self-motivated to develop physically and learn how to maintain at least a minimum level of fitness throughout life.

It is suggested that a great challenge for the 1990's and into the 21st century is the revitalization of school physical education programs which provide opportunities to develop fitness components, learn important concepts in exercise science, and experience fitness tests on a serial basis which provide a profile of the youth's fitness, relationships to peer age and sex group, and changes in fitness achievement."

In addition the United States Office of Disease Prevention and Health Promotion in 1983-84 conducted the National Children and Youth Fitness Study (NCYFS). This study involved school children between the ages of ten and seventeen. This study concluded, among other things, that children were significantly fatter than in the 1960's.

Ross, James G. and Gilbert, Glen G. "The National Children and Youth Fitness Study." Journal of Health; **Physical Education, Recreation and Dance. January, 1985.)**

Updyke (1982) reported a study involving over four million school children, ages 6-17, from over 10,000 public and private schools. He concluded, "that there was large room for improvement in all physical fitness performance tests, and that children are not as fit as they could or should be."

Updyke, Wynn F. "Profile reveals fitness levels lower than desirable"; Stress; July, 1982.

The PCPFS 1985 (National School Population Fitness Survey) reported the following facts: "The United States has more physical educators, more health educators, more gymnasia, more swimming pools, and more recreational opportunities than any country in the world. Buttress this with the best medical science system in the world, not only in quality of care, but in medical research, equipment, facilities, and the like. Yet we lead the world in degenerative diseases."

The former Secretary of Health, Education and Welfare, Joseph Califano made a speech to the Institute of Medicine, National Academy of Science in 1980. In that speech he stated, "...some 29,000,000 adolescents are in poor physical condition...We need better preventive emphasis through exercise to prevent latent disorders."

Reiff, G. "Physical fitness guidelines for school aged youth." Proceeding of the First National Conference on Physical Fitness and Sports for All (U.S. Government Printing Office: Washington, D.C.), 1981.

To add insult to injury, American youth participating in a Soviet youth physical fitness test demonstrated less than desirable results. Two hundred children from Maryland, Virginia and the District of Columbia were administered the Soviet youth physical fitness test. The Soviet youth physical fitness test included the 60 meter sprint, 1,000 meter run, alternate leg jump, long jump, pull-ups, sit-ups, target throw and 25 meter and 50 meter swim. The conclusion of the initial testing project revealed that, "Most American children who took the Soviet youth fitness test scored at the "acceptable" or "outstanding" level in events that required coordination, **but were somewhat weak in upper body strength test and were below expectations in the endurance categories as reflected in the distance runs.**"

Newsletter, Summer 1987, National Association of Governors' Councils on Physical Fitness and Sports.

The foregoing information on the poor physical fitness state and fatness of our prepubescent and pubescent boys and girls coupled with the empirical observations that demonstrate the complete safety, efficacy and desirability of weight training starting early in life, provide a strong indictment of the invalid philosophy and ignorance of those medical doctors, educators, physical educators and, anyone else, who would deny young boys and girls the opportunity to improve their physique and physical fitness with weight training or like activities. If the United States is going to survive as a strong nation, it must inculcate the need and desirability to maintain the highest level of physical fitness in the population, starting with our young boys and girls and ending with our senior men and women.

EMPIRICAL OBSERVATIONS

Young boys and girls regularly engage in a variety of sports activities in today's world, regardless of what country in which they reside. Among these activities are: football, soccer, baseball, volleyball, swimming, wrestling, gymnastics and track and field and many more activities. Performance in all of these sports activities is highly correlated to the strength, local muscular endurance, cardio-vascular-respiratory endurance and body composition of those young children participating in these sports.

Generally, very little time is devoted to developing the physical fitness components on which sports performance depends unless the level of competition is at the very elite tier. Furthermore, many of these sports activities require contact and collisions involving forces five to ten times body weight because of the mass, speed and collision of the bodies and/or solid objects involved (implements, other human bodies and earth). Sport in itself has a degree of risk. However, when sport is conducted under the supervision of qualified coaches, the risks are minimized and the potential benefits are optimized.

Practical experience over many years has demonstrated that when young boys and girls engaged in heavy training schedules under the proper and sometime improper supervision and guidance, have developed good healthy bodies with no impairment of structure or function. One of the authors remembers that he and many of his young male friends would jump out of second story windows into sand piles at building projects at the ages of 10-13 years of age with no injuries or life long structural problems becoming manifested. There is a wide range of activities, duration of participation, intensity levels and individual responses to them in humans, young and old.

Competitive weight lifting amongst school children flourishes in foreign countries: Great Britain, Australia and Eastern European countries. Weight lifting and weight training programs by prepubescent and pubescent children seems to be strongly supported by medical doctors, educational philosophers and leaders in physical education in these foreign countries.

In contrast, the general approach to the inclusion of weight lifting competition and application of weight training programs in prepubescent and pubescent children in the United States is unnaturally over- protective and over-cautious. This misguided philosophy as manifested in the attitudes of some medical doctors, educational philosophers and leaders in physical education is one of the main reasons for the poor physical fitness scores by American children. While there is acceptance by these leaders of the fact that American children are fat and sub-par in strength, local muscular endurance and aerobic endurance, there is reluctance or lack of will to employ effective programs to improve the situation. Indeed, there is a prejudice and bias against the use of weight training by many of these leaders. **"Where the leader's lack vision, the people perish." (The Holy Bible: Proverbs 29:18)**

It was not long ago when young girls would not be allowed to engage in tackle football, little league baseball, or long distance running because medical doctors, educators and physical education leaders led the general public to erroneously think it would harm them. They were wrong again. In the 1980's we observe federal courts ruling that young girls must be given the same athletic opportunities as young boys. Participation in sport by young girls has not lead to stunted growth or damaged physical or mental structures. Furthermore, girls and women are now allowed to run marathon distances and longer today because it has been found that to engage in such activity does not produce irreparable damage to the female (or male) at any age.

What happens when young boys and girls engage in reasonable and well supervised exercise programs like gymnastics, wrestling, weight training, track and field? They become better fit and develop well defined, functional and aesthetically pleasing bodies.

Strength training with weights and other resistive devices executed with the proper technique and under the proper supervision is very safe and effective for developing strength and local muscular endurance while optimizing body composition within genetic limitations of young boys and girls. Weight training under the right conditions has not resulted in stunted growth or damage to the structure of the skeleton in young boys and girls. Compared to other sports activities, weight training has been shown to be relatively absent of injuries.

The prevailing philosophy regarding the restricted use of weight training by prepubescent and pubescent children is very disturbing, since weight training has the greatest potential to improve the physical fitness and reduce the deplorable fatness of the American youth.

Recently, some enlightened medical professionals have recognized that weight training is good for prepubescent and pubescent boys and girls. This vanguard group is the American Orthopaedic Society for Sports Medicine

(AOSSM) which conducted a recent workshop in Indianapolis dealing with strength training in prepubescent youth. The workshop group developed the conclusion that, **"STRENGTH TRAINING FOR PREPUBESCENT BOYS AND GIRLS IS SAFE WITH PROPER PROGRAM DESIGN, INSTRUCTION AND SUPERVISION. THE BENEFITS OUTWEIGH THE RISKS...."**

Duda, M.; Prepubescent strength training gains support; The Physician and Sportsmedicine; Vol 14(2); 1986; pp. 157-161.

Finally there is a reasonable philosophical statement coming from at least one segment of the medical community concerning the application of weight training in prepubescent and pubescent children. The tragedy is that more medical groups, as well as educational philosophers and physical educators, still have difficulty in seeing the light, even when presented with the overwhelming evidence of the safety and efficacy of weight training for children.

The country of Bulgaria has produced the best competitive weight lifters in the world over the last 20 years. They have consistently subdued the Russians and the rest of the World in weight lifting competition. Professor Angell Spassov of the Department of Weightlifting in the Bulgarian Higher Institute for Physical Education and Sport Instruction in Sofia, Bulgaria has recently stated the following: **"Promising boys are selected at age 11 to train and compete in competitive weight lifting. From age 11 through 22 years is the most important time of life in the development of strength; one has the shortest recovery time; and is able to withstand the highest training volumes."**

Seminar at USC, July 22, 1989. "The Bulgarian approach to maximal strength and power development." Angell Spassov.

One of the most famous young Bulgarians is Naim Suleimanov. **(NOTE: NAIM SULEIMANOV HAS RECENTLY DEFECTED TO TURKEY)** Naim started training and competing in Olympic Weight Lifting when he was twelve. At the age of 14 years, he won the Junior World Championships in Sao Paulo, Brazil in 1981, just 5.5 pounds off the world record for the combined total of the snatch and clean and jerk lifts. At age fifteen, Naim became a world record holder while subsequently, at age 16, he lifted three times his body weight in the clean and jerk lift. He is only the second man **(BOY)** in the history of weight lifting to accomplish such a task. This is an amazing feat considering his young age and body stature, height of barely five feet and a body weight of 123 pounds. According to the Sinclair formula, a series of coefficients used by the International Weightlifting Federation to decide who is the Champion of Champions, Suleimanov's total of 656 pounds lifted in the snatch and clean and jerk lifts in the 1984 European Championships made him the greatest lifter in the history of weight lifting. **THIS WAS ACCOMPLISHED AT THE TENDER AGE OF SIXTEEN (16).**

One might say that this was a just a freak happenstance in nature. Not true! In 1960, another Bulgarian boy was allowed to train and compete. His name was Riko Florov. He established a junior world record at the age of 17 years in the 60-kilo (132 pound) class. Many more young boys would be emerging as world class athletes if only the physicians, educators, philosophers, coaches and parents would encourage the participation of young boys and girls in controlled and supervised weight training and lifting programs. Only narrow closed minded thinking has allowed the adoption of a physical education philosophy that has lead to the substandard level of fitness in our youth today.

WEIGHT TRAINING RESEARCH IN PREPUBESCENT AND PUBESCENT CHILDREN

The **"ineffectiveness of strength training in youth because of low levels of circulating androgens myth"** has been discredited by a number of studies. Sewall and Micheli (1986) studied the effects of a progressive resistance program in boys and girls trained for nine weeks. They found that a weight training program performed three times per week for 25-30 minutes produced a 42.9 percent increase in strength in the experimental group while the control group improved only 9.5 percent. Cahill (1985) and Servedio, Bartels and Hamlin (1985) demonstrated corresponding results with preadolescent subjects.

---

1. **Cahill, B. R. (1985). Strength training for the prepubescent. Unpublished study reported in Journal of Physical Education, Recreation and Dance, February, 1988.**

2. **Servedio, F. J., Bartels, R. L., & Hamlin, R. L. (1985). The effects of weight training, using Olympic style lifts, on various physiological variables in prepubescent boys (Abstract). Medicine and Science in Sport and Exercise, 17, 288.**

3. **Sewall, L. and Micheli, L. J.; Strength training for children. Journal of Pediatric Orthopedics; Vol. 6; March 1986; pp. 143-146.**

Mc Govern (1983) studied the effects of circuit weight training on the physical fitness of prepubescent children. He concluded that after 12 weeks of circuit weight training there was a significant impact on the strength of prepubescent males and females, 9 through 11 years of age. Changes in girths, skinfolds, and maximal oxygen uptake were not statistically different in these prepubescent children. It should be noted that a twelve week training period may not be long enough to produce significant changes in girths, skinfolds and maximal oxygen uptake. Furthermore, since valid body composition techniques were not employed in this study, it is impossible to access any changes in lean mass. Also, it may be possible to demonstrate positive changes in lean mass, girths and maximal oxygen uptake if the physical training periods were applied over longer durations.

Mc Govern, Michael, "Effects Of Circuit Weight Training On The Physical Fitness Of Prepubescent Children," Unpublished doctoral dissertation, Northern Illinois University, August, 1983.

While few studies have been conducted on prepubescent children there have been studies that have been conducted using adolescent children.

Kusinitz and Keeney (1958) studied the effect of weight training on the physical fitness of adolescent boys. Their conclusions were that no harmful effects were experienced while hypertrophy, absolute strength and endurance made positive changes.

Ivan Kusinitz and Clifford Keeney, "Effect of Progressive Weight Training on Health and Physical Fitness of Adolescent Boys," The Research Quarterly of the American Association of Health, Physical Eduction and Recreation, 29:294, October, 1958.

Vrijens (1969) studied circuit endurance exercises in adolescents (average age of 16.7 years) as it impacted maximal oxygen uptake, pulse adaptation and chest, thigh and arm girths. After only six weeks of training all these measures showed good changes.

---

1. **Vrijens, J. Muscle strength development in the pre- and post- pubescent age. <u>Medicine and Sports</u>, 1978, Vol. 11; pp. 152-158.**

2. Vrijens, J.The influence of interval circuit exercises on physical fitness of adolescents. <u>Research Quarterly,</u> 1969, Vol. 40(3); pp. 595-599.

Cahill (1985) and Sewall and Micheli (1986) demonstrated in their studies that preadolescent children maintained or improved flexibility when engaging in weight training programs if flexibility exercises were included in the program. Cahill (1985) also reported significant increases in motor performance, specifically the standing long jump and the vertical jump.

1. Cahill, B. R. (1985). Strength training for the prepubescent. Unpublished study reported in Journal of Physical Education, Recreation and Dance, February, 1988.

2. Sewall, L., & Micheli, L. J. (1986, March) Strength training for children. Journal of Pediatric Orthopedics.

<u>SUMMARY STATEMENT ON STRENGTH TRAINING IN PREPUBESCENT MALES AND FEMALES</u>

The results of the small amount of research that has been completed regarding the utilization of weight training in prepubescent and pubescent children have produce evidence that weight training for these ages is strongly indicated. This research evidence combined with empirical evidence plus the findings in a number of national physical fitness surveys that demonstrate the strong need for strength development in our young boys and girls, is compelling confirmation that weight training programs are not only safe and effective for prepubescent and pubescent children but must be vigorously pursued to develop acceptable strength levels in our children.

When weight training programs are properly conceived, organized and implemented and the proper equipment is available there is no reason to believe that injuries will occur or that the children will not benefit. The existing research evidence and empirical observations have shown that weight training is safe and produces good results at any age.

The key to success of any weight training activity is the construction of a scientific program and the monitoring of the program with adequate supervision. Children can begin to use reasonable resistance work at any age, if it is properly supervised and the equipment is adaptable to their physical dimensions.

<u>RELATED LITERATURE:</u>

1. Bjornarra, B.S.; Flexibility and strength considerations for young athletes; NSCA Journal; Vol 4(4); 1982; pp. 62-64.

2. Bloom, T.; At age 11, they build 40% more strength. (Review); American Health; June, 1984; P.20.

3. Caron, A.V. and Bailey, D.A.; Strength development in boys 10 through 16 years; Monogr Soc Res Child Dev 1974:39:1-37.

4. Funato, K.; Fukunaga, T.; Asami, T., et al; Strength training for prepubescent boys and girls; Proceedings of the Department of Sports Science; Vol. 21; University of Tokyo; 1987; pp. 9-19.

5. Hejna, W.F.; Rosenberg, A.; Butukusis, D. and Krieger, A.; Prevention of sports injuries in high school students through strength training; NSCA Journal; Vol. 4(1); 1982; pp.28-31.

6. Munson, Wayne. W. and Pettigrew, Frank F., Cooperative Strength Training: A Method for Preadolescent, JOPERD, February 1988, p 61-66.

7. **National Strength and Conditioning Association (NSCA); Position paper on prepubescent strength training; NSCA Journal; Vol. 7(4); 1985; pp.27-31.**

8. **Pfeiffer, R. and Francis, R.S.; Effects of strength training on muscle development in prepubescent, pubescent and postpubescent males; Physician and Sportsmedicine; Vol.14(9); 1986; pp. 134-143.**

9. **Sailors, M. and Berg, K.; Comparison of responses to weight training in pubescent boys and men; Journal of Sports Medicine and Physical Fitness; Vol. 27; 1987; pp. 30-37.**

10. **Weltman, A., et al; The effects of hydraulic resistance strength training in pre-pubertal males; Medicine and Science in Sports and Exercise; Vol. 18; 1986; pp.629-638.**

STRENGTH TRAINING RECOMMENDATIONS FOR PREPUBESCENT MALES AND FEMALES

In the February 1986 issue of the magazine, ***THE PHYSICIAN AND SPORTS MEDICINE***, there are some guidelines and recommendations for application of strength training programs in prepubescent and pubescent children. They are:

EQUIPMENT
1. Strength-training equipment should be of appropriate design to accommodate the size and degree of maturity of the prepubescent.
2. It should be cost effective.
3. It should be safe, free of defects and inspected frequently.
4. It should be located in an uncrowded area free of obstructions with adequate lighting and ventilation.

PROGRAM CONSIDERATIONS
1. A pre-participation physical exam is mandatory.
2. The child must have the emotional maturity to accept coaching and instruction.
3. There must be adequate supervision by coaches who are knowledgeable about strength training and the special problems of prepubescents.
4. Strength training should be a part of an overall comprehensive program designed to increase motor skills and level of fitness.
5. Strength training should be preceded by a warm-up period and followed by a cool-down.
6. Emphasis should be on dynamic concentric contractions.
7. All exercises should be carried through a full range of motion.
8. Competition is prohibited. **"AUTHOR'S NOTE: WHY?"**
9. No maximum lift should ever be attempted. **"AUTHOR'S NOTE: WHY?"**

PRESCRIBED PROGRAMS
1. Training is recommended two or three times a week for 20-30 minute periods. (**AUTHOR'S NOTE: WHY SO SHORT?**)
2. No resistance should be applied until proper form is demonstrated. Six to fifteen repetitions equal one set; one to three sets per exercise should be done.
3. Weight or resistance is increased in 1 pound to 3 pound increments after the prepubescent does 15 repetitions in good form.

AUTHOR'S NOTE: On items 8 and 9 under Program Considerations and item 1 under Prescribed Programs the authors of this book have concerns about why these restrictions are recommended. Empirical observations contradict every restriction that is listed in these items. Competition is not prohibited in prepubescent children in all kinds of sports where significantly more trauma is endured by those participating in these activities compared to weight training and weight lifting. In all these sports activities there are maximal efforts performed but not under the same safe and controlled situations naturally found in weight lifting. Furthermore, training sessions for many sports activities for prepubescent children extend for 1 1/2 to 2 hours. It is important to protect the health and well-being of our children but to impose irrational and rather naive weight training and weight lifting restrictions will be more detrimental to overall physical fitness of the children.

Strength-Training Recommendations, The Physician and Sportsmedicine, Volume 14, NO. 2, February, 1986; p. 160.

COMMENT

While guidelines and recommendations are good to set boundaries, some of the above recommendations are not reasonable **"where the rubber meets the road," i.e., <u>the real world</u>**. Competition is not contraindicated in most sports in which prepubescent youth participate; eg, wrestling, swimming, gymnastics, football, basketball, baseball, soccer, skiing, volleyball, running, jumping, throwing and more. Physical competition in itself is not deleterious if the athletes are conditioned for the activity in which they will be competing.

Maximal performances are required in all the above listed activities. In these cases the forces developed are infinitely greater than any amount of weight that could be lifted by prepubescents. In addition, the velocity of movement and the impact forces in most athletic activities are considerably above what would be encountered in any weight lifting movement. Properly executed lifts at maximum intensities are considered to be safe under supervised conditions but only after being properly conditioned and only when reasonable mastery of lifting technique has been demonstrated by the youth.

Many of the sports activities per se as well as training for them extend for one to two hours, therefore, to curtail the length of time for strength training may be ridiculous. Furthermore, training for sports activities occurs daily. Again, the real life experiences mitigates against the **<u>strict adherence</u>** to the strength training guidelines and recommendations for prepubescent males and females referenced in the preceding paragraphs.

Abuse, sadism or ignorance should never be accepted in the training of youth or anyone. There is much of that, especially in volunteer coaches who have no professional coaching training or physical education training. Youth need to be intelligently and scientifically programmed to work physically harder to attain their pre-programmed God-given physical potential. This is best accomplished when guided by qualified, competent and formally educated coaches and physical educators.

STRENGTH AND AGING

All people are interested in being physically functional throughout their lifetime. Some people place even greater emphasis on the ability to achieve higher performance levels in physical skills such as, golf, tennis, weightlifting, track and field, swimming and running, etcetera. While decreases in physical performances are inevitable as humans age, decrements in performance can be retarded or minimized by participation in strength training programs. In addition to enhancement of physical performances, weight training improves physical appearance and reduces the potential for injuries associated with a high activity levels.

Aging impacts the strength of humans in three ways: (1) The cross sectional area of muscle (hypertrophy); (2) The expression of maximal strength; (3) The neural system (ability to recruit the muscle fibers).

THE CROSS SECTIONAL AREA (CSA)

It is intuitively obvious that the size of a muscle relates to its strength. Throughout life the strength of males and females parallel the increases and decreases in muscle mass; however, in a more limited way in females. At any age, and, especially in older ages, increases in strength of females is impacted more by increased muscle fiber recruitment patterns instead of muscle hypertrophy. As the human ages and when weight training is not used, there is a loss of muscle fibers, primarily the fast twitch (type II) fibers, although there is some loss of the slow twitch muscle fibers, also.

Regular engagement in weight training exercises can retard the loss of muscle mass and, therefore, higher levels of strength can be maintained as one ages. This enhances physical appearance by helping control the accumulation of body fat and the normalization of muscular curves. A larger muscle mass allows for a higher metabolic rate which helps to control the accumulation of body fat. The maintenance of high strength levels also enhances the performance levels in recreational skills and daily activities.

Endogenous testosterone levels to a large extent, as well as using proper intensities, sets and repetitions in a weight training program, control the amount of muscle hypertrophy (cross sectional area) that can be achieved and retained. Even in prepubescent and older ages, when testosterone levels are normally lower than in the prime of life, a well designed weight training program does improve muscle mass, retards atrophy and loss of strength. Females tend to lose strength faster than males as they age. It is hypothesized that this stems from two factors: (1) lower levels of testosterone; and, (2) lack of engagement in weight lifting programs and other activities that improve cross sectional areas.

STRENGTH EXPRESSION

Most authorities agree that strength increases rapidly as humans grow, reaching a peak somewhere between 30 to 40 years of age. After this age range, strength declines gradually as one ages. However, de Vries (1966) states that at age 60 the loss usually does not exceed more than 10% to 20% of the younger maximum levels for men, while in women the loss of strength with aging is somewhat greater. The rate of strength loss accelerates as one ages if weight training programs are not part of the general exercise plan. It is possible to maintain or achieve relatively high levels of strength through the older ages providing that one engages in regular weight training programs.

Some people may criticize the striving for strength improvement or maintenance at older ages; however, **both strength and endurance fitness are noble and worthy goals because they enhance one's potential for enjoying life.** Authorities also believe that the changes in strength parallel increases or decreases in muscle mass. Exercising at intensities that produce increases in muscle size will also increase the strength in concert with the genetic potential and the increase in muscle mass. When properly applied, weight training is beneficial and safe to employ at any age for both males and females.

In the 1980's and into the 1990's, Master's power lifting and Master's Olympic weight lifting for men and women has become very popular. For example, the World Masters Olympic Lifting Championships conducted in Orlando, Florida in 1988, had the most contestants of any weight lifting contest ever conducted in the history of the World up until 1988, including the various Olympic Games or World Weight Lifting Championships. Two hundred and twenty men participated in this event. The 1990 World Masters Olympic Weight Lifting Championships conducted in Mattersburg, Austria had an even larger participation of 385 men.

Since the advent of masters competition in power lifting and Olympic weight lifting it has been observed that older men and women can manifest impressive amounts of strength. It is believed that because of continued activity in strenuous weight training, application of scientific weight training programs, better nutrition and the use of periodization principles, that these men and women have been able to maintain a larger amount of their maximum lifetime strength. As mentioned above, 220 masters lifters participated in the 1988 World Masters Weight Lifting Championships. The ages of the participants ranged from 40 years up to the oldest of 84 years, Henri Soudieres who won his weight class. Henri is also a US National Powerlifting Champion and has set world records in power lifting for his age and weight classification.

The participation of 385 master lifters in the 1990 World Masters Weight Lifting Championships conducted in Mattersburg, Austria on September 19-23, 1990, demonstrates the escalating interest as well as the potential for older men to exhibit impressive strength. Twenty five countries were represented. In Table 1-6 is listed the number of contestants in the fourth, fifth, sixth, seventh and eighth decade of life who participated in the 1988 and 1990 World Master Weight Lifting Championships. In addition, the tables displays the number of contestants that performed a snatch of 90 kilograms (198 pounds) or more and a clean and jerk of 135 kilograms (297.5 pounds) or more.

Table 1-6.   The Number Of Contestants Who Participated in the 1988 and 1990 World Masters Olympic Lifting Championships And The Number Who Performed A Snatch Of 90 Kilograms And Above And A Clean And Jerk Of 135 Kilograms And Above.

AGE DECADE	NUMBER OF PARTICIPANTS		LIFTING PERFORMANCES (ALL LIFTERS)			
			90 KG SNATCH		135 KG CLEAN & JERK	
	1988	1990	1988	1990	1988	1990
40-49	107	199				
50-59	69	140	N = 79	N = 162	N = 34	N = 52
60-69	38	36	36%	42%	15%	13%
70-79	5	10				
80-89	1	0				
TOTAL LIFTERS	220	385	The numbers above represent the absolute number of total lifters and the % of all lifters.			

1.   **National Masters Weightlifting Newsletter; December 1, 1990; 1990 World Masters Weightlifting Championships; Mattersburg, Austria; September 19-23, 1990.**

2.   **Official results, 1988 World Masters Weightlifting Championships; Orlando, Florida; December 9-11, 1988; Ed Wojchick Meet Director; Florida Weightlifting Federation.**

One can get a good feel for the potential for retaining strength into the older ages by analyzing the results of the 1988 and 1990 World Masters Weight Lifting Championships. For instance, 79 lifters including all the weight and age classifications performed a Snatch of 198 pounds (90 kgs) or more, which represents 36 % of the total number of lifters in the 1988 competition. In the 1990 competition, 162 lifters performed a Snatch of 198 pounds (90 kg) or more, which represented 42.1 % of the total lifters.

Similarly, in the 1988 Championships, 34 lifters including all the weight and age classifications performed a Clean and Jerk of 300 pounds or more, which represents 15% of the total number of lifters. In the 1990 competition, 52 lifters exceeded 297 pounds or more in the Clean and Jerk, which represents 13.5% of the total number of lifters.

These masters competitions include men and women ranging from 40 to over 80 years of age. Empirically, it is observed that participation in weight training through the 4th, 5th, 6th, 7th, 8th decade and beyond allows men and women to reacquire some of their lost strength and/or maintain a higher percent of their lifetime maximum strength. The reason that most older people lose muscle mass with consequent large decreases in strength is because they do not continue to perform resistive exercises that maintain strength and/or produce increases in strength. Most men and women just do not make it a priority to train with weights as they age, to their detriment.

People who do not weight train lose muscle mass, strength and the ability to recruit motor units as they age. Those who continue to train retard the loss of muscle mass, retain high levels of strength, can more effectively activate a good percentage of their muscle, have better physical appearance and perform at higher skill levels.

PART I

THEORY & PRACTICE

Older people who are detrained can make significant improvements in strength as a result of participation in weight training programs at any age. The extent of these gains are about the same as would be expected in younger people. The percentage strength gains for older people who weight train regularly are the same as young people but the absolute magnitude is somewhat lower.

Dr. Brunno Balke, originator of the Balke graded treadmill exercise test and one of the founders of the American College of Sports Medicine reported at the 1987 annual Health and Tennis Corporation of America convention in Orlando, Florida that he improved his strength by an average of 25% in 10 different exercises by weight training over a 12 week period. He was 84 years of age during this experiment. These results are interesting when compared to studies with younger subjects involved in weight training programs which have demonstrated improvements between 20% and 34%. It appears that older people when compared to younger people, can make similar improvements if sufficiently motivated. Of course, the magnitudes of improvements will not be comparable, just the percentage increases.

Many examples of body builders who had the ability to maintain muscle mass at older ages can be given. In 1990, the following male body builders have been recognized as retaining a lot of their muscle mass (note: ages are in parentheses after the name): Clarance Bass (56), Albert Beckles (60), Boyer Coe (44), Chris Dickerson (51), Dave Draper (47), Bill Pearl (60), Larry Scott (52) and Frank Zane (48).

In Track and Field Al Oerter threw the discus a lifetime best throw of 227' 11" at age 50 in 1980 while preparing for the United States Olympic Trials. This throw would have won the gold medal in the 1988 Seoul Olympic Games. Furthermore, Hal Connolly and Ed Burke, both who were former American Record holders in the hammer were able to perform at international competition levels well into their forties. These Track and Field performers were able to perform at international levels well into the 4th decade because they maintained high strength levels combined with a large muscle mass. This was accomplished by participation in regular weight training programs. **Most people don't maintain muscle mass or the ability to manifest high levels of strength because they quit weight training at an early age.**

A research project concerning the improvement of strength in elderly men and women appeared in the September 1990 issue of the Physician and Sport Medicine. Six women and four men whose ages ranged from 86 to 96 years volunteered to participate in an eight week strength training study with a four week post study evaluation. The subjects had sedentary habits, nutritional inadequacies, multiple functional disabilities, arthritis and coronary artery disease. The study was conducted at the Boston Hebrew Rehabilitation Center for the aged. Analysis of the results of the study revealed that strength improved 174%, thigh mass improved 9% and speed of gait improved 48%.

The researchers stated that, **"Our findings indicate that the known hazards of immobility and falls seem to outweigh the potential risks of muscle-strengthening exercise, even for frail, very old men and women with underlying cardiovascular disease. The increased strength may in fact help prevent falls, the most common cause of injury in older persons."** It was also shown in this study that the strength gains were not maintained without continued training which is true for younger people, also.

The authors of the study state further that, **"Our findings suggest that a portion of the muscle weakness attributable to aging may be modifiable through exercise."** The concern for safety of older people participating in weight training programs was shown to be unfounded. The participants in this study actually improved the quality of their life. The authors stated that, **"There used to be a fear that if very old people exercised, they would sustain musculoskeletal injuries, such as strains, or a cardiovascular complication. But this doesn't happen in a monitored situation."**

As mentioned above, it is possible to maintain high strength levels and large muscle masses well into the fourth and fifth decade of life and to a lesser degree in the 6th, 7th, 8th decades and beyond. It is only the lack of desire to do so that keeps people from achieving this goal. Only a few humans, male and female, make it a life priority to maintain strength or muscularity or both in the latter years of life. The main reasons for lack of retention of strength and muscle mass is discontinuance of training at higher intensities and the natural reduction of endogenous testosterone. Some people produce higher levels of testosterone as they age and have a distinct advantage for maintaining strength and muscularity. However, a good amount of strength and muscularity can be maintained by the proper application of periodization principles in the weight training program along with sensible nutritional practices regardless of the levels of testosterone present.

Engagement in a sensible weight training program by itself will enhance muscularity and maintenance of strength. It is extremely important to include short periods of training where higher intensities and lower repetitions are employed in order to maintain muscularity and strength as humans age. **Hakkinen and Hakkinen (1990) recommend that both older men and women should include explosive exercises and weight training at high intensities in their training programs to maintain muscle mass, strength and the ability to produce explosive actions.**

CHANGES IN THE NERVOUS SYSTEM

As humans age there seems to be a decrease in the structure and function of the central nervous system. McArdle, Katch and Katch (1991) state that there is a 37% decline in spinal cord connections and a 10% decline in nerve conduction speed. These authors present data that show older men who maintain and active lifestyles have reaction times that are equal or faster than inactive men in their 20's. Brooks and Fahey (1985) state that there is a selective loss of type II fibers (the fast twitch) accompanying the lack of participation in resistive exercise as one ages. In other words, if the fast twitch fibers are not conditioned by proper intensities and exercises they will disappear as one ages. Hakkinen and Hakkinen (1990) state that the decreases in maximum strength are related to negative changes in the central nervous system and the rate of neural activation. The fast twitch motor neurons atrophy and the nerve conduction magnitude and speed decrease.

Gains in strength in older people are thought to be primarily from improvement of the stimulus of the central nervous system; increases in strength of stimulus, recruitment of more muscle fibers, and frequency of stimulus. Older people have a limited potential for hypertrophy because of lower testosterone levels, however it is possible to improve and maintain muscle mass as well as retard the loss of muscle with good weight training programs throughout life.

SUMMARY STATEMENT ON STRENGTH AND AGING

After about 30 years of age, males and females experience a decrease in lean body mass (muscle cross sectional area) as they age. Concurrent with this loss of muscle mass are negative changes in the nervous system. These negative changes in the nervous system and the loss of muscle mass combine to produce decrements in strength. This impacts the human by reducing physical performances in recreational skills and predisposes them to a higher incidence of muscular-skeletal injuries and detracts from physical appearance.

The impact of aging on the muscular-skeletal system in humans can be minimized by proper application of weight training programs. Throughout life, strength training in general and explosive type exercises should be incorporated as part of a general physical training program for all people, as they age (up until death). This action would minimize the loss of muscle mass and help control the decrease in neural activation of muscle caused by endurance training and/or physical inactivity. In addition, the inclusion of strength training, including reasonable application of explosive type movements, can be useful in the attempt to maintain or improve daily functional capacity throughout one's total lifespan. The application of a weight training program using the principles of periodization will insure that strength and muscle mass can be optimized at any age in a safe manner.

RELATED REFERENCES

1.   Brooks, G.A. and Fahey, T.A.; Exercise Physiology: Human Bioenergetics and Its Application; Macmillan Publishing Co.; New York; 1985; pp 692-693.

2. deVries, H.; Physiology of Exercise for Physical Educations and Athletics; Wm. C. Brown Co. Publishers; Dubuque, Iowa; 1966; p. 337.

3. Hakkinen, K. and Hakkinen, A.; Muscle Cross-Sectional Area, Force Production And Relaxation Characteristics In Females At Different Ages; Paper presented at the First World Congress of Biomechanics, August 30 - September 4, 1990; University of California, San Diego.

4. Lamb, D.R.; Physiology of Exercise: Responses and Adaptations; Macmillan Publishing Co., Inc.; New York; 1978; pp 117-118.

5. McArdle, W.D.; Katch, F.I.; Katch, V.I.; Exercise Physiology: Energy, Nutrition and Human Performance; Lea and Febiger; Philadelphia; 1991: p 702-703.

6. Stovas, Jane; 90 Year Olds Increase Strength Dramatically; In, Wrap-Up; The Physician And Sports Medicine; September, 1990; p 26.

7. Westcott, Wayne; Strength Fitness: Physiological Principles and Training Techniques; Allyn and Bacon Inc.; Boston; 1982; pp 212-215.

8. Wilmore, J.H.; Training For Sport and Activity: The Physiological Basis of The Conditioning Process; Allyn and Bacon Inc.; Boston; 1982; pp 221-222.

SELECTED PHYSIOLOGICAL ASPECTS OF WEIGHT TRAINING

BREATHING TECHNIQUES

Generally, breathing is a response to the body's need for oxygen. Breathing technique during weight training is important for two reasons: (1) The body requires a good oxygen supply for the muscles to do their work, and (2) In some lifts it is necessary to stabilize the shoulders, chest, abdominal, low back and hip regions. This is only accomplished by holding the breath (in order to stabilize the vertebral column) during part of the movement and results in a greater force being exerted on the weight being lifted. There are many different theories of the correct breathing technique for lifting weights or using progressive resistance exercise machines. In the authors' view there is only one correct method for breathing, however, there are some necessary variations when lifting heavier weights, using positive and negative training and when executing some more sophisticated exercise movements.

FOR GENERAL TRAINING

For general training one should inhale on the lowering (eccentric or negative) phase and exhale on the lifting (concentric or positive) phase. In other words, exhale on the working phase and inhale on the return phase. With low to moderate intensities one should never hold their breath but breathe in a natural pattern that fits the rhythm and the intensity of the exercise.

FOR HIGH INTENSITY TRAINING

When training at higher intensities and lower repetitions the breathing technique is slightly modified. The exerciser would take a moderate to deep breath in, hold it and execute the movement. The breath should be exhaled after the exercise sticking point. When more than one repetition is performed at higher intensities there may be multiple breaths between repetitions and then a repeating of the appropriate breathing pattern.

PART I

THEORY & PRACTICE

IN COMPOUND EXERCISES

There are various compound exercises that require a more drastically modified breathing pattern. An example of these compound exercises are: power cleans, power snatches, squat cleans, squat snatches, dead lifts, push jerks, jerks and many like lifts. In these cases the exerciser would take a moderate to deep breath in and would hold it until the exercise sticking point. In the last part of the movement the breath would then be forcefully exhaled. The reason for holding the breath briefly in these movements is to stabilize the shoulders, chest, abdominal, back, low back and hip regions so that the force of the prime movers (muscle causing the action) can be effectively transmitted through the necessary body segments and directly transferred to the bar and, also, to unload and protect the spine.

IN DOUBLE POSITIVE OR POSITIVE/NEGATIVE TRAINING

When a push/pull exercise (double positive) and/or in an exercise where a positive contraction is followed by a negative contraction, the exerciser should execute a **double breathing pattern (exhalation followed by inhalation)** on each stroke of the motion. Exhalation should occur on the exertion phase of the movement. Inhalation would occur at the turn around place or just before the return motion starts. The intensity of the exercise will dictate the precise application of the breathing pattern. The higher the intensity the more strictly one would adhere to the double breathing pattern. At moderate to low intensity, other breathing patterns may be used.

THE VALSALVA PHENOMENON

It is important to discuss the **valsalva phenomenon** during the presentation of breathing techniques. During heavy lifting, usually in overhead pressing movements and heavy dead lifting movements, the breath is held with the glottis closed. The holding of the breath plus the compression of the chest and abdominal area is the most effective way to unload the spine in heavy lifting movements. However, as the movement progresses the chest and the abdominal muscles produce high internal pressures that collapse the thin veins in the chest area reducing blood flow back to the heart. Since the blood return to the heart is diminished there is reduced blood flow to the brain. This can cause dizziness, spots before the eyes or even fainting in sustained effort while holding one's breath. Once the breath is released the chest pressure is reduced and blood flow is returned to normal and there is little chance of experiencing these discomforts.

Maintenance of high intra-abdominal pressure and intra-thoracic pressure is necessary to relieve the spine of great forces experienced in heavy lifting. Fortunately, holding one's breath on a short-term and intermittent basis is acceptable and sensible since it results in effectively unloading of the spinal column. In a sense it is a protective mechanism while insuring application of maximal force.

Providing there is nothing inherently wrong in one's cardiovascular system and one does not drop the weight on their head, experiencing the valsalva phenomenon is of little concern. Such an experience does not inhibit one's ability to continue to train, providing no cardiovascular problem has become manifested by the experience. However if one knows about the potential of the valsalva maneuver and the conditions that produces its onset, one can completely eliminate the potential for experiencing the valsalva phenomenon. The basic precaution is to use one of the appropriate breathing patterns discussed above in the applicable lifting situation.

After performing the correct breathing pattern for the appropriate situation for many repetitions it becomes second nature. Until it becomes a correct habit pattern one should adhere to the rule: exhale during the exertion phase (positive contraction) of an exercise and inhale on the return (negative contraction) phase.

Lander, Jeffrey; Why use a belt?; Strength-Power Update, Volume I, No.3, Summer, 1986.

WEIGHT TRAINING AND BLOOD PRESSURE

High blood pressure (hypertension) is a common health problem in the United States. It represents a serious risk for development of coronary heart disease, stroke, and congestive heart failure. Roughly 50 million adults- 28% of the population-have blood pressure levels that exceed the normal values (130/85). High blood pressure is found in 33% of adults in the black segment of the U.S. population and in 23% of the adults in the white and latino population. Research and clinical observations demonstrate that control of mild to high blood pressure elevation clearly reduces the risk of developing problems related to hypertension.

Blood pressure increases with age and more than half of the American population over 60 years of age have high blood pressure. The number of people with high blood pressure is likely to increase as the American population ages and more people reach older ages. In addition, lifestyle patterns are likely to be a significant cause of high blood pressure in the American society.

Exercise (aerobic exercise and weight training) as well as dietary modification are suggested for initial and long term treatment of high blood pressure. For more serious and intractable high blood pressure, physicians use a variety of drugs. In all cases some sort of exercise is recommended whether drug therapy is used or not used.

High blood pressure has been called "the silent killer" because it can easily go undetected and produces no symptoms until it seriously damages the heart, kidneys, brain or some other vital organ. When high blood pressure is identified it is very effectively controlled in most people through lifestyle modifications and, when necessary, drug treatment. It is important to have your blood pressure checked occasionally (at least once a year) under non-stressful circumstances by a competent healthcare worker to monitor any upward trend that may contribute to future ill health. Your family physician can verify any tendency to develop high blood pressure.

BLOOD PRESSURE: WHAT IS IT?

When the heart beats, a surge of blood is pumped through large blood vessels called arteries. The arteries conduct blood from your heart to other parts of the body. The walls of the arteries are distended when the heart pumps the blood through them. This force against the artery walls is called blood pressure.

Every heart beat produces a flow of blood into the arteries and, thereby, increases the blood pressure in the arteries. This is called the systolic pressure and is represented by the larger number in the blood pressure reading. When the heart relaxes between beats, the pressure in the arteries goes down. This is called the diastolic pressure and is represented by the smaller number in the blood pressure reading.

The systolic pressure shows the maximum amount of pressure pushing out on the arterial wall. And, the diastolic pressure is the minimum amount of pressure pushing out on the arterial wall. The more resistance to blood flow through your blood vessels, the higher the systolic and diastolic pressure will be—and the more strain on your heart.

When your blood pressure is assessed, both levels are measured and recorded as numerical values. For example, if your blood pressure is 119/80 (verbalized as 119 over 80), the systolic reading is 119 and the diastolic reading is 80. These numbers are calculated in millimeters of mercury and are expressed as 119/80 mm Hg.

There is no "ideal" blood pressure reading and it varies throughout the day depending upon your activity level and metabolic needs. Acceptable blood pressure ranges between 110 to 130 systolic and 70 to 85 diastolic. It is not a specific pair of numbers. According to an American Heart Association pamphlet entitled "**ABOUT HIGH BLOOD PRESSURE,**" resting blood pressure readings below 140/90 mm Hg means there is no cause for worry.

WHAT IS HIGH BLOOD PRESSURE?

The smaller branches of the arteries are called arterioles and these arterioles control the blood pressure. If the arterioles are narrowed for some reason, the resistance to blood flow is greater. The narrowing of the arterioles increases your blood pressure making your heart work harder. A practical example demonstrates this principle. A nozzle on the end of a hose regulates the water pressure in the hose. If the nozzle is wide open, there is very low pressure forcing the water out of the hose. As you close the nozzle (or you clamp your thumb over the opening), the water pressure in the hose increases and the water is forced out with greater pressure.

As mentioned above, if the pressure in your arteries reaches 140/90 mm Hg and stays there, you have high blood pressure. But, high blood pressure does not manifest any symptoms. People have high blood pressure over many years without knowing it because there are no specific warning signs. High blood pressure over a long period of time can damage many of the body organs and increase your risk for heart attack and stroke. Remember that high blood pressure can only be confirmed by your physician.

If high blood pressure is not treated, both the large and small blood vessels throughout the body can be damaged. Over time, the tissues and organs supplied by damaged blood vessels may develop perilous complications. The most effective way to prevent or minimize the severity of these complications is to control high blood pressure with lifestyle changes, drug therapy or both.

There are two kinds of high blood pressure (hypertension): (1) primary (essential); and, (2) secondary.

PRIMARY OR ESSENTIAL HYPERTENSION

In 90 to 95% of primary (essential) hypertension cases, no specific reason can be identified as the cause. Since, primary hypertension does not exist in every society, it is a disease of specific cultural patterns suggesting that easily controlled factors such as eating habits, lack of exercise, accumulation of excessive body fat and possibly stress, play a consequential role in the development of hypertension.

Other factors that contribute to the development of primary high blood pressure are genetics, race, sex, age, retention of water and sodium, and nitric oxide abnormalities. The development of high blood pressure may be the result of lifestyle patterns and a combination of these factors, or some unknown element.

SECONDARY HYPERTENSION

A less common type of hypertension is secondary hypertension. This type of hypertension is a symptom of an underlying problem. Secondary hypertension is caused by a number of factors including: kidney disorders, adrenal tumors, other hormonal gland dysfunctioning (thyroid, pituitary and parathyroid), a narrowing of the aorta, and the use of medications (oral contraceptives, corticosteroids, cold remedies, nasal decongestants, appetite suppressants, nonsteroidal anti-inflammatory drugs (NSAIDs), cyclosporine, erythropoietin, MAO inhibitors, tricyclic antidepressants, the antidepressant venlafaxine (Effexor), cocaine, anabolic steroids, and amphetamines). When the source problem is corrected, the secondary hypertension is reduced to normal levels.

ISOLATED SYSTOLIC HYPERTENSION (ISH)

Isolated systolic hypertension is defined as a systolic blood pressure of 160 mm Hg or higher, along with a diastolic pressure less than 90 mm Hg. ISH increases in frequency with increasing age and is the most common form of hypertension in the elderly. It affects about 65% of those people over the age of 65. Drug treatment helps to reduce ISH and, therefore, reduces the incidence of strokes and less fatal and nonfatal heart attacks, and fewer deaths from all causes.

THEORY & PRACTICE   PART I

CLASSIFYING BLOOD PRESSURE

A new system of classifying blood pressure has been recommended by The Fifth Report of the Joint National Committee on Detection, Evaluation, and Treatment of High Blood Pressure (the JNC report), sponsored by the National Heart Lung, and Blood Institute of the National Institutes of Health in January of 1993 (see Table 1.7).

Three main changes have been made.

(1) This committee defined normal blood pressure as levels less than 130 mm Hg systolic and less than 85 mm Hg diastolic.

(2) A new category of high-normal was added (130 to 139 mm Hg systolic and 85-89 mm Hg diastolic) because an estimated 30 million Americans with values in this range are twice as likely to develop hypertension and have a greater risk of cardiovascular problems than people with lower blood pressures.

(3) This new classification replaces the terms "mild" and "moderate" hypertension with stages of hypertension to avoid the possibility that patients may mistakenly believe that "mild" and "moderate" hypertension are medically insignificant.

HYPERTENSION AND WEIGHT TRAINING AND BODY BUILDING

Weight training and body building myths "die hard." One of those myths is that if you engage in weight training, weight lifting or body building, you will increase your resting and exercise blood pressure beyond acceptable levels. Many men and women refrain from weight training because they have apprehensions that this type of exercise will increase their exercise and resting blood pressure beyond safe levels. However, there is accumulating evidence that body building and weight lifting does not adversely affect your resting blood pressure and there is some evidence that it reduces the peak pressures during lifting movements.

Linn Goldberg, M.D., at the Oregon Health Sciences University states the following: **"There is a preponderance of evidence that shows general weight training reduces resting blood pressure. Also, we have found that weight training reduces intra-ocular pressure, which is a risk factor for the development of glaucoma. In drug-free body builders, we have observed that resting blood pressure and cholesterol is similar to aerobically trained endurance athletes."**

In addition, Michael Stone, Ph.D., exercise physiologist and consultant for the United States Weight Lifting Federation makes the following observation regarding the effects of competitive weight lifting and heavy weight training on blood pressure. **"We have routinely measured resting blood pressure in junior and elite weight lifters at the Olympic Training Center in Colorado Springs for over ten years. We have never observed any evidence of the development of high blood pressure even when weight lifters move to higher weight categories (movement upward two to three weight classes with body weight gains of up to 50 pounds)".**

Discussion of the effects of weight training on blood pressure must focus on two separate issues: (1) The effects of this type training on resting blood pressure, and, (2) What happens to blood pressure during the lifting actions (acute response).

THE IMPACT OF WEIGHT TRAINING AND BODY BUILDING ON RESTING BLOOD PRESSURE

Since 1986 there has been a lot of research conducted on the impact of weight training and body building on resting blood pressure, among other cardiovascular parameters. Verill (1992) and his coworkers of the Mecklenburg Cardiovascular Consultants in Charlotte, North Carolina, published a review article concerning resistive exercise training in cardiac patients in **Sports Medicine 13: 1992**. There appeared over 50 studies concerning the effect of resistive exercise training as it impacted cardiovascular factors. Goldberg and Elliot

Table 1-7. Evaluating Blood Pressure Levels

> ### THE NEW BLOOD PRESSURE GUIDELINES
>
> The blood pressure classifications below, developed by the National Blood Pressure Education Program, apply to adults who are not taking antihypertensive drugs and who are not acutely ill. When determining which category an individual falls into, the higher number in the blood pressure reading should prevail. For example, someone with a reading of 140 mm Hg systolic and 100 mm Hg diastolic would fall into the Stage 2 (moderate) category.

CATEGORY	SYSTOLIC (mm Hg)	DIASTOLIC (mm Hg)	RECOMMENDED FOLLOW UP
Optimal	≤110	≤70	Recheck in 2 years
Normal	<130	<85	Recheck in 2 years
High-Normal	130-139	85-89	Recheck in 1 year
HYPERTENSION			
Stage 1 (Mild)	140-159	90-99	Confirm within 2 months
Stage 2 (Moderate)	160-179	100-109	Undergo complete medical evaluation and/or begin treatment within 1 month
Stage 3 (Severe)	180-209	110-119	Undergo complete medical evaluation and/or begin treatment within 1 week
Stage 4 (Very Severe)	≥210	≥120	Undergo complete medical evaluation and/o begin treatment immediately
ISOLATED SYSTOLIC HYPERTENSION	≥140	<90	Confirm within 2 months*

*   Applies only to initial blood-pressure readings. Multiple readings at these levels may require more aggressive treatment.

Margolis, Simeon, M.D. and Klag, Michael, M.D.; Hypertension—The John Hopkins White Papers, 1995; The John Hopkins Medical Institutions, Baltimore, Maryland.

(1994) reported over 80 studies of the effects of exercise on blood pressure. This review of the scientific literature shows that there is overwhelming evidence that resistive training, in all its various forms, does not adversely affect resting blood pressure. In fact, many of the studies report reductions in resting blood pressure in response to weight lifting and body building activities.

Moreover, the observations in these studies that demonstrate no adverse change or the reduction of resting blood pressure in response to weight lifting and body building appears to occur in all age groups, in males and females, and in normal and hypertensive subjects. General body building exercise, circuit weight training, super circuit weight training and competitive weightlifting can produce a decrease in resting blood pressure levels. Furthermore, all types of resistive training, produce many other helpful results; for example, increase in strength, growth of lean body mass, reduction of body fat, improvement of performance levels, enhancement of general physical appearance and elevated self esteem.

It has been noted that even with a large increase in lean body mass (muscle mass), that weight training and body building can produce decreases in resting blood pressure. Some professionals have postulated that as a result of habitual weight training the resting blood pressure is elevated as a result of increased muscle mass. This theory suggests that with increases in muscle mass there is a need for more high resistance small-diameter blood vessels and, therefore, the blood pressure rises. However, the research clearly shows that resting blood pressure exhibits no change or a reduction in those people that habitually engage in weight training and body building. The myth "dies hard."

It is interesting to observe that weight training and body building is being used more and more by the medical community in people who exhibit various kinds and severity of cardiovascular disease (**McKelvie & McCartney, 1990**). Verill and his coworkers (**1992**) state that it is now recommended to incorporate dynamic weight training and nonsustained isometric arm and leg exercise into cardiopulmonary rehabilitation programs to improve muscular strength and endurance. They state further that there appears to be considerable benefit and minimal risk for patients who participate in properly supervised cardiac resistive training programs. In healthy people the benefits of a sensible weight training and body building program override any possible risks.

BLOOD PRESSURE RESPONSE DURING EXERCISE

The human body is more ruggedly constructed than we realize and there seems to be a built-in protective mechanism against blood pressure surges. In addition, weight training is able to induce adaptations within the cardiovascular system which are protective in nature. Paffenbarger and coworkers (1970 & 1975) have shown that longshoremen who worked at a high energy expenditure level demonstrated lower incidence of cardiovascular disease and a lower death rate compared with longshoremen that were less active. The work that these active longshoremen performed is like weight training exercises involving intense bursts of energy creating moderate to large forces and performed for a number of repetitions.

Blood pressure response during exercise is related to the type of exercise (rhythmic, static, dynamic or mixed), the intensity (percent 1 repetition maximum), the number of repetitions (the closer you work to muscle failure), and the muscle groups involved. It is a natural response for blood pressure to increase during all kinds of exercises. For example, in progressive endurance activities, the systolic blood pressure increases while the diastolic blood pressure decreases. Systolic pressure goes up in response to the metabolic demand and is produced by the increased heart beat and increased stroke volume. More blood is ejected from the heart with each heart beat. Diastolic pressure goes down because peripheral resistance is reduced. The smaller arterioles and many of the capillaries are opened causing a reduction of pressure.

In contrast, in isometric and dynamic resistance exercises both the systolic and diastolic blood pressure increase. Even though the smaller arterioles and capillaries are opened, there is tremendous compression of them by the contractions of the muscles involved in the exercise.

There is no evidence that exercise blood pressure increases are dangerous for people with a normal resting blood pressure and no cardiovascular complications. However, if your blood pressure is higher than normal (135/85), check with your physician for guidance before engaging in vigorous exercise programs whether they be resistive or endurance oriented.

Blood pressures (peak systolic and diastolic) reach high values in various lifting movements, especially if breath is held and if you work to failure (work above 60% 1RM) or any combination of the previously mentioned factors. However, exercising blood pressures when working below 60% 1RM are not dissimilar to other high intensity activities (anaerobic and aerobic) such as stationary cycling. In body building and weightlifting activities, the peak blood pressures are intermittent while in cycling the blood pressures are sustained. High peak blood systolic and diastolic pressures in isometric and weight lifting activities, lasting a few seconds appear not to be more detrimental than moderately high levels sustained over long periods of time as achieved in cycling.

People who are sick with cardiovascular disease have been subjected to various weight training regimes under proper supervision using up to 80% 1RM with no reported health problems **(Franklin, 1991)**. Moreover, a significant amount of a body builder's training occurs at 70% to 85% of one repetition maximum with repetitions ranging between 5-8 repetitions and frequently working to failure. With regard to cardiovascular factors, sensible body building and weight training programs are safe methods of exercise for healthy people as well as people who have developed cardiovascular problems but are engaged in medically supervised programs.

Practical observations demonstrate the validity of this author's previous statements that the human body is more ruggedly constructed than we realize and there seems to be a built-in protective mechanism against blood pressure surges. In addition, weight training is able to induce adaptations within the cardiovascular system which are protective in nature. After many years (over 50 years) of weight training by millions of people, these observations have been empirically verified.

The highest blood pressures in weight lifting actions occur in the last few repetitions regardless of the weight intensity (% 1RM). However, the greatest increase in blood pressure is dependent upon the weight intensity (% 1RM) and if lower body exercise is being used and the closer you work to muscle failure. Upper body exercise, generally elicits lower exercise blood pressures. In any case when using upper or lower body exercises, the closer to your maximum that you lift and the closer you work to muscle failure, the higher will be your exercise systolic and diastolic blood pressure.

In weight training exercises, systolic pressure can range between 175-480 mm Hg, while the diastolic pressure can range between 115-350 mm Hg, depending on the percent of 1 repetition maximum that is used, the degree of breath holding (valsalva maneuver), the closeness one works to muscle failure, and whether upper body or lower body exercises are used. These high blood pressures have been observed in studies where blood pressure sensors have been directly implanted in the arteries. The arterial blood pressures where directly monitored during a number of weight training exercises at various percentages of the one repetition maximum (1RM).

MacDougall and his colleagues (1985) reported a study where the average group peak systolic and diastolic blood pressures while performing a double leg press was 320/250 mmHG. Furthermore, one of their subjects recorded peak systolic and diastolic blood pressures of 480/350 mmHG. These high exercise systolic and diastolic pressures seem to be natural physiological responses to very intensive weight lifting activities.

It appears that in healthy people, these high exercise blood pressures are normal and acceptable when the training exercises and intensities elicit them. **You just do not see body builders and weight lifters blowing up their hearts or exploding their brains in the gyms as they engage in intensive weight training. Nor do you observe them in hospitals on the day after training with cardiovascular problems.**

PART I

THEORY & PRACTICE

Lower body exercise, training at higher percents of 1RM, breath holding and working close to muscular failure will elevate systolic and diastolic blood pressure to high values. This appears to be acceptable in healthy and conditioned people.

Regardless of the percent 1RM used in body building exercises, the closer you push towards absolute muscle failure, the higher will be the exercise blood pressure. Working the muscle until the muscle is unable to contract with enough force to produce full exercise range of motion is called "the pump" or "the burn" and will increase both systolic and diastolic exercise blood pressure. In normal healthy people this does not present a health risk.

Research has shown that previous weight training will illicit smaller increases in blood pressure responses to acute resistive exercise. Fleck and others (1987) state that body builders demonstrate lower exercise systolic and diastolic blood pressures than novice weight trainers and controls. There is some conflicting evidence that suggest that exercise blood pressures increase during exercise. The apparent conflict is explained by the weight trainers holding their breath (the valsalva maneuver) during blood pressure measurements. Holding the breath during the performance of any exercise, or course, will increase exercise blood pressure, and is not necessarily dangerous.

The exercising systolic and diastolic blood pressures increase during weight lifting activities. Likewise the systolic blood pressure increases in progressive aerobic exercise. These increases are normal responses to exercise. The healthy human body has the capacity to handle these very high levels of blood pressure during exercise as demonstrated in billions of people in the execution of their daily pursuit of life. Outside of diagnosed severe cardiovascular problems, there is no need to worry about engaging in weight lifting or body building activities.

There is evidence to suggest that strength training may be used as an alternative to endurance training in order to improve overall health. Long-term strength training, as performed by body builders, does not increase the magnitude of risk factors for cardiovascular disease. In fact, resistive training may eventually produce favorable changes in this regard.

Fighting ignorance is a never-ending process. Every day experience strongly demonstrates that the results of body building produces healthy, good-looking bodies at all ages. Joe Weider's statement of truth regarding body building is relevant: **"There are no negative consequences by body building. It is the perfect form of exercise."**

CUFF SIZE

It is important to use the proper cuff size when measuring blood pressure. The rubber bladder itself should encircle at least two thirds of the arm. If the person's arm is large, the normal size cuff will be too small, making the blood pressure reading larger than it actually should be and vice versa. A cuff that is too wide causes less error than one that is too narrow. Thigh cuffs should be used for arms that are above 16" circumference to insure accurate measurements. A cuff error of only a few millimeters of mercury may cause you to be misclassified as normotensive or hypertensive.

WHITE COAT HYPERTENSION

Some people show "white coat hypertension"—consistently high blood pressure readings only when examined by a physician or in a medical environment. In these people the blood pressure measurements are normal when taken at home by the individual, family members, or friends. About 20% of all "white coat hypertension" cases actually have mild hypertension, so it is important to verify this problem with home monitoring of blood pressure or with 24 hour ambulatory blood pressure monitoring.

RELATED REFERENCES

1. Fleck, Steven; Dean, Larry; Resistance training experience and the pressor response during resistance exercise. Journal of Applied Physiology 63(1):116-120, 1987.

2. Franklin, Barry; Bonsheim, Kimberly; Gordon, Seymour; and Timmis, Gerald; Resistance training in cardiac rehabilitation. Journal of Cardiopulmonary Rehabilitation 1991:11:99-107.

3. Goldberg, Linn; Elliot, Diane; Exercise For Prevention And Treatment Of Illness. F. A. Davis Company, Philadelphia, PA. 1994.

4. MacDougall, J.D.;Tuxen, D.; Sale, D.G.; Moroa, J.R. and Sutton, J.R.; Arterial blood pressure response to heavy resistance exercise. Journal of Applied Physiology, 58 (3): 785-790; 1985.

5. McKelvie, Robert and McCartney, Neil; Weightlifting training in cardiac patients: Considerations. Sports Medicine, 10 (6): 355-364, 1990.

6. Paffenbarger, RS; Laughlin, ME; Gima, AS; et al. Work activity of longshoremen as related to death from coronary heart disease and stroke. New England Journal of Medicine 282: 1109-1114; 1970.

7. Paffenbarger, RS; Hale, WE. Work activity and coronary heart mortality. New England Journal of Medicine 292:545-550, 1975.

8. Verrill, David; Shoup, Eric; McElveen, Gregory; Witt, Kenneth; Bergey, Donald. Resistive exercise training in cardiac patients: Recommendations. Sports Medicine 13 (3): 171-193, 1992.

THE EFFECTS OF COMBINED STRENGTH AND AEROBIC ENDURANCE TRAINING ON STRENGTH DEVELOPMENT

Many arm-chair physiologists and ignorant coaches frequently recommend and/or implement cardio-vascular endurance training programs for speed/explosion athletes and body builders. Knowledgeable people do not make this mistake. For the "in the trenches" athletes, coaches and exercise physiologists there has never been a question of the counter-productivity of combining strength and endurance for speed and explosion athletes and body builders. These people intuitively know or have learned that aerobic training combined with speed and explosion training reduces the potential to move fast, to be explosive, to be strong, to produce power and to maximize muscle growth.

Empirical observations demonstrate that endurance runners are not muscular. Low body fat, yes; but not muscular. In contrast, it can be observed also that sprinters and jumpers, in general are quite muscular. To the insightful athletes, coaches and physiologists these are expected consequences for the specificity of training.

Recent research has demonstrated the folly of combining strength and aerobic endurance programs when strength and size are the training objectives. Despite the practical observations and, more recently, the research, many coaches still adhere to the concept of a need for an aerobic base.

It must be remembered that occasional short off-season aerobic endurance training cycles could be used for a training break, a cardio-vascular emphasis (for whatever reason), or as an easy training cycle. However, it must be understood that combining strength and aerobic endurance training programs is basically a bad training concept, if maximum speed/explosion or maximum size/strength is the ultimate goal.

This does not rule out an application of a combined strength/endurance program, it merely emphasizes the need to properly place it in the planning of the total training year (macrocycle). It is best to stay within the resistance training envelope (40% - 100% 1RM) and to minimize aerobic endurance training when training for speed/explosion and/or size/strength.

Aerobic training in combination with weight training is of benefit in the final stages of reducing body fat (cutting) in preparation for a body building contest. Usually at this time all the muscle mass that can be achieved is present and the "cutting" program requires more repetitions executed at lower intensities (% 1RM). Combining both aerobic training and weight training during this phase makes good sense because it allows the body builder to perform large amounts of work in an effort to strip off as much body fat as possible.

Empirical observations have demonstrated that non-impact or very low impact aerobic training minimizes the loss of muscle mass. Examples of low impact exercise that should be employed in the "cutting program" are stationary cycling, stairstepping, rowing, walking and low impact step classes. Furthermore, very rigid and disciplined dieting during this phase potentiates the effects of the combined weight training and aerobic training program in reducing body fat to it lowest level.

RESEARCH

Hickson (1980) studied the compatibility of strength and aerobic endurance training. In this study three groups were defined; strength only group, the aerobic endurance only group and the combined strength and aerobic endurance group.

The strength only group trained five days per week over a 10 week period. Three days per week, parallel squats were performed executing 5 sets of 5 repetitions and leg flexion and leg extension were performed for 3 sets of 5 repetitions using the maximum weight for five repetitions for all exercises. The remaining two alternate days involved performing leg presses 3 sets of 5 repetitions and calf raises 3 sets of 20 repetitions with the maximum resistance possible for the required number of sets and repetitions.

The aerobic endurance only group trained 6 days per week over a 10 week period. Interval training was performed 3 days per week on a cycle ergometer performing six 5 minute work bouts at approximately maximum aerobic capacity. On the alternate days, 3 days of running as fast as possible for 30 minutes the first week, 35 minutes the second week and 40 minutes during weeks 3 through 10 were performed.

The combination group used the exact same programs as the strength only group and the aerobic endurance only group in a mixed regimen, i.e., strength workouts five days and aerobic endurance workouts six day per week. On the days where both regimens were performed, there was at least 2 hours between training sessions.

The results of this study were:

1. Training simultaneously for strength and aerobic endurance increased aerobic power. There was no statistical difference in the aerobic power improvement between the combined group and the group that only trained for aerobic endurance.
2. Training simultaneously for strength and aerobic endurance increased strength 25 % in the squat 1RM.
3. Aerobic endurance training only (alternate days of interval cycling and continuous running) did not increase strength.
4. Aerobic endurance training only increased aerobic power, but no more effectively than the combined strength and aerobic endurance training program.
5. Strength training only increased strength 44% with only a small positive change in aerobic power which was not statistically significant. There was no change in relative aerobic power.
6. The thigh girth increased in the combination group and the strength group but not in the aerobic endurance only training group.

The conclusion of this study was that concurrent training for strength and aerobic endurance compromised improvement in strength. Aerobic endurance training should not be used if maximum size/strength is

the objective of the training program. It can be inferred that strength training may enhance aerobic endurance running training by preventing breakdown of muscle that may occur with the constant pounding of running and, therefore, prevent running associated injuries. Furthermore, to the extent that increased strength may allow for more speed development, distance running performance may be improved by supplementation of strength training for the total body.

Hickson, R.C., Interference of strength development by simultaneously training for strength and endurance; European Journal of Applied Physiology and Occupational Therapy; 45:255-269; 1980.

In 1985, Dudley and Djamil researched the incompatibility of aerobic endurance and strength training modes of exercise. They used a Cybex II to train and test isokinetic strength throughout the range of motion. Three training groups were used: (1) Strength only training group; (2) Aerobic endurance only training group; and, (3) Concurrent training group. Untrained males and females participated for seven weeks.

The **strength only group** trained three times per week for seven weeks. They performed knee extensions on the Cybex II machine executing 2 sets of 30 seconds (26-28 repetitions) at 4.19 rad/second (240 degrees per second).

The **aerobic endurance only group** trained three days per week for seven weeks on a cycle ergometer. Each subject performed five 5 minute bouts of cycling at an intensity designed to elicit peak cycling aerobic power at 4 to 5 minutes of each bout, with rest intervals of five minutes between exercise repetitions.

The **concurrent exercise group** trained six times per week for seven weeks, alternating strength and aerobic endurance training days. This group used the exact training protocols as used for the strength only group and the aerobic endurance only group.

The findings of this study are as follows:

1. The **aerobic endurance trained group** and **concurrent trained group** increased aerobic capacity approximately 18 %. These improvements were not significantly different.
2. The **strength only group** increased strength at all speeds up to 4.19 rad/sec (240 degrees per second).
3. The **concurrent exercise group** increased strength at the lower angular velocities (up to 1.68 rad/sec or 96.23 degrees/sec).

This study found that concurrent training for strength and aerobic endurance does not affect gains in aerobic capacity but does compromise the ability to produce force at the high velocity-low force region of the force-velocity curve. Further analysis of the data by Chromiak and Mulvaney suggest that if the concurrent group was compared to the strength group, the strength trained group had greater absolute and relative improvements in angle specific torque at every angular velocity tested. Therefore, the training effect of concurrent training for strength and aerobic endurance has a negative impact on force development throughout the range of motion when compared to strength training only. Chromiak and Mulvaney suggest that a neural factor is the mechanism limiting strength gains, and that it is likely to be operative at slow and fast speeds.

Dudley, G. and Djamil, R. Incompatibility of endurance and strength training modes of exercise. Journal of Applied Physiology, Volume 59; Number 5; pp. 1446-1451, 1985.

In 1988, Hickson and others reported a study on the potential for strength and endurance training to amplify aerobic endurance performance. This study used well trained cyclists and runners and supplemented their aerobic endurance training programs with heavy resistance weight training.

PART I

THEORY & PRACTICE

The strength training program consisted of 5 sets of 5 repetitions for the squat; 3 sets of 5 repetitions for knee extension and flexion and 3 sets of 25 reps for heel raises. The subjects lifted 3 times per week and used as much weight that would allow for the execution of the precise prescription of sets and repetitions. After 10 weeks of strength training, the 1RM squat was increased by an average of 27 percent. Aerobic capacity remained unchanged consequent to supplementation of the cycling and treadmill running training programs with heavy resistance training.

Short term endurance improved by 11% for cycling and 13% during running. Cycling time to exhaustion at 80% aerobic capacity improved 20%, but the performance times for the 10 km run remained unchanged. This study revealed no concurrent changes in total body mass, thigh girth or muscle fiber size. The gains in strength were probably caused by learning specific activation and motor unit recruitment patterns, rather than intramuscular adaptations. **The conclusion of this study was that certain types of endurance performance could be improved by strength training, especially those that require the recruitment of fast twitch fibers.**

Hickson, R.C.; Dvorak, B.A.; Gorostiaga, E.M.; Kurowski, T.T. and C. Foster; Potential for strength and endurance training to amplify endurance performance; J. Applied Physiology; 65(5):2285-2290; 1988.

In a number of research projects the relationship between aerobic endurance training and vertical jumping (VJ) ability has been investigated. Ono (1981) investigated the inhibitory effect of long distance running training on the VJ and other performances in aged males. Thirty six males, age 30 - 71 ran an average of 4 kilometers daily for 18 weeks.

It was noted that VJ height decreased approximately 8% to 18% in subjects between ages 40 and 60 years. The men in the age groups 30-39 and 60-69 years demonstrated only a slight decline in VJ height. It is important to note that the group that demonstrated the largest increases in aerobic capacity and running time to exhaustion consequent to training had the largest decrement in VJ height. **This report did not treat the data with inferential statistical analysis, however, the trend in the descriptive statistics demonstrates that running 4 km daily for 18 weeks will diminish one's vertical jumping capacity. The VJ is indicative of the explosive power of the muscles moving the legs and hips.**

Ono, M., Miyashita, M. and T. Asami. Inhibitory effect of long distance running training on the vertical jump and other performances among aged males. In: Biomechanics V-B, P. Komi (Ed); Baltimore, Md: University Park Press, 1981, pp.94-100.

Komi and others (1979) studied the effects of subjects training with light weighted fast movements and explosive type jumps. After 8 weeks of this type training, VJ height declines but with continued training over 16 weeks the VJ height returns to pretraining level. It was noted that as training volume increases, vertical jumping ability declines until neuromuscular adaptations occur in response to the training load.

A practical consideration concerning the application of light weight and explosive type jump training is that if it takes 16 weeks for the body to adapt, then this training method is inefficient and must be replaced by more effective training patterns. Coaches and athletes just do not have the time for involvement in ineffective and protracted training theories.

Komi, P.V., Suominen, H., Heikkinen, E., Karlaaon, J. and P. Tesch. Effects of heavy resistance and explosive-type strength training on mechanical, functional and metabolic aspects of performance., In: Exercise and Sport Biology, P.V. Komi (Ed), Champaign, Il: Human Kinetics Publishers., 1979, pp.90-102

Costill and others (1967 and 1985) have observed impaired jumping ability in distance runners and competitive swimmers. This phenomenon can be reversed simply by detraining. This suggests that a high volume of aerobic endurance training, or a neuromuscular factor that is altered as a result of aerobic endurance training, limits ability to develop force during high velocity movements. D. G. Sale and others compared same day strength and aerobic endurance training to determine the impact of such training on aerobic power, voluntary strength, voluntary muscle endurance, muscle cross sectional area, muscle cross- sectional area, muscle enzyme activities, muscle fiber areas, muscle fiber composition and capillarization.

Two groups of young men were subjects for this study. Group A trained twice per week combining strength and endurance training. This group did a combined exercise program on Monday and Thursday or Tuesday and Friday. In the first training session of each week, endurance training preceded strength training. In the second training session, strength training preceded endurance training. Group B used the same strength and endurance program as group A, but performed the strength workout on two days per week and the endurance workout on the other days. In the first week, strength training occurred Monday and Thursday and endurance training happened on Tuesday and Friday. In the second week, endurance training occurred on Monday and Thursday, and strength training occurred on Tuesday and Friday. This pattern was alternated throughout the course of the study.

The strength training program included six to eight sets of 15-20 RM (repetition maximum; for example, the maximum weight that can be used for the designated number (15-20) of repetitions) on a leg press weight machine. There were rest periods of 2 minutes between sets and each strength training session lasted from 30-40 minutes. **It is important to note that this is not a typical weight training technique for gaining strength or muscle size. Nevertheless, it is what was employed as the strength training program.**

Endurance training was performed on a cycle ergometer. Each subject was required to perform a series of 3 minute repetitions ranging from 6 to 8 repetitions over a 20 week training period. The intensity ranged from 60% to 100% of their aerobic capacity. Rest periods between cycling repetitions were three minutes. The endurance training session lasted 35-45 minutes.

Performing strength training and aerobic endurance training on different days proved to be superior to combined strength and aerobic endurance training on the same day, relative to improving strength. Muscle hypertrophy (both fast twitch and slow twitch muscle fibers) increased similarly in both groups in response to the respective training programs. Furthermore, neither training regimen proved to be superior to the other when comparing aerobic capacity and weight lifting endurance.

The results of this study intimate that training for strength and aerobic endurance should be done on alternate days. One must remember that combining strength and aerobic endurance training will impair the development of strength whereas endurance development will not be impaired. **Concurrent strength and aerobic training results in "antagonism" of the training effects. Therefore, if maximum strength, speed and explosion are desired such combining of strength training with aerobic endurance is contraindicated.** However, combining strength and aerobic endurance can be implemented, for whatever reason, at various times in the training year as a mental and physical diversion. One must be careful to place this type of a program at a time in the training cycle when it will not interfere in any manner with the long term training objectives.

---

1. **Sale, D.G.; Jacobs, I.; MacDougall, J.D.; and Garner, S.; Comparison of two regimens of concurrent strength and endurance training. Medicine and Science in Sports and Exercise; Volume 22; No. 3; June, 1990; pp 348-356.**

2. **Stamford, Bryant; Strength vs Endurance; The Physician and Sportsmedicine; November, 1990; pp 105-106.**

PRACTICAL APPLICATION

Now that the evidence, empirical and research has been evaluated, the big question for coaches and athletes is whether or not the speed/explosion/power athlete or the body builder should engage in aerobic training, or if the aerobic endurance athlete should engage in weight training. The authors of this book have for years advocated that aerobic endurance athletes should use weight training for injury prevention, performance enhancement and for prevention of muscle wasting consequent to aerobic endurance training.

In contrast, the authors have insisted that speed/explosion/strength athletes need to minimize aerobic training in order to maximize their performance capabilities (i.e., train specifically). However, this does not mean the exclusion of aerobic training for the speed/explosion/strength athletes. It means that aerobic training programs must be strategically placed in the periodization of training in order to enhance long term cardio-vascular health of the athlete and to make sure that such training does not negatively impact speed/explosion/strength performance.

As mentioned earlier, the body builder may find that aerobic endurance training in addition to their weight training program will help in the fight to reduce body fat. These aerobic programs **should not be** emphasized at times where maximum increases in muscle mass and strength are desired. Aerobic endurance activity combined with conventional body building programs using low to moderate intensities may be beneficial for cutting body fat and defining muscles in preparation for physique contests or in general muscle maintenance programs.

Empirical observations over many years indicate that the loss of muscle mass and decreases in strength that occur when a combined strength training and endurance training program is employed can be minimized when low impact or non-impact endurance activities are used. On the other hand, the participation in running with the attendant constant pounding (high impact) causes a greater reduction of muscle mass and a larger decrease in strength.

For speed/explosion/strength athletes, an aerobic base in not needed and is physiologically imprudent to train. Aerobic conditioning contributes very little to the performance capacity of speed/explosion/strength performance and, furthermore, aerobic capacity is not the limiting factor for performance or training in these activities. **In contrast weight training for aerobic endurance athletes is prudent. It prevents injury, enhances performance and retards muscle breakdown.** Those people training for body building can employ aerobic training in combination weight training as they wish in their overall training program except in cycles where mass and strength are the goals.

Strength training decreases the capillary density (in a practical sense the amount of blood supply in the muscle per cross sectional area) because of hypertrophy, whereas aerobic endurance training increases it. In addition, strength training reduces mitochondrial (this structure produces the aerobic energy for long term endurance activity) volume density which is detrimental to aerobic endurance performance. In short weight training produces major changes in the contractile proteins and in the short term energy system, like glycogen storage, atp-pc storage and the enzymes needed in the anaerobic metabolic processes.

On the other hand, aerobic endurance training produces major changes in the energy making structures in the muscle; mainly the capillary density, mitochondrial volume density and oxidative enzyme activity which enhance aerobic endurance. In addition, it is observed that aerobic endurance training significantly reduces strength and muscle fiber size which impede strength improvement.

The coach and athlete for each sports activity, as well as body builders and people who train for general fitness, need to be aware of the energy systems utilized in their activity or sport and, therefore, train specifically. Weight training in all its forms is a must application for modern day coaches, athletes, body builders and people in general fitness training. It is the basis for performance enhancement, injury prevention, injury rehabilitation and aesthetic presentation of the body.

Chromiak and Mulvaney make the following recommendations regarding the concurrent utilization of strength and aerobic endurance programs in training athletes:

1. The athlete and coach should be aware of the concept of training and performance specificity, i.e., training must emphasize the energy systems used in competition.
2. To increase muscular endurance, high volume weight training should be undertaken instead of moderate or long distance running or cycling.
3. Running should be limited to interval training of short distances and high intensity for athletes in sports that are primarily anaerobic.
4. Aerobic endurance athletes can benefit from strength training for injury prevention, enhanced performance and muscle wasting associated with aerobic endurance training. (This last item has been added by the authors of this book.)

RELATED REFERENCES

1. Costill, D. The relationship between selected physiological variables and distance running performance. Journal of Sports Medicine and Physical Fitness, 7(2):61-66, 1967.

2. Costill, D., King, D.S., Thomas, R. and M Hargreaves. Effects of reduced training on muscular power in swimmers. The Physician and Sports Medicine, 13(2):94-101, 1985.

3. Chromiak, Joseph and Mulvaney, Donald; A Review: The effects of combined strength and endurance training on strength development; Journal of Applied Sport Science Research; A Supplement of The National Strength and Conditioning Association Journal; Volume 4, Number 2; pp. 55-60, 1990.

4. Dudley, Gary and Fleck, Steven; Strength and endurance training: are they mutually exclusive? Sports Medicine; Volume 4, Number 2; pp. 69-85, March/April, 1987.

HYPERTROPHY AND FIBER TYPES

Hypertrophy is an increase in the size of the muscle in general and, specifically, an increase in the size of individual muscle fibers which is usually accompanied by an increase in strength and local muscle endurance. Gross muscle hypertrophy involves an increase in connective tissue as well as increased muscle fiber size. The hypertrophy of individual muscle fibers is accounted for by one or more of the following changes:

1. Increased number and size of myofibrils per muscle fiber.
2. Increased total amount of contractile protein, especially the myosin filament.
3. Increased capillary density per muscle fiber.
4. Increased amounts and strength of connective, tendinous, and ligamentous tissues.

Recently, there has been talk about hyperplasia of muscle tissue. Hyperplasia is defined as the increase in the number of muscle fibers (cells). The research is rather tenuous and only a few animal studies indicate that hyperplasia **might** be occurring. Also, these studies used animals as subjects and it is very difficult to infer from animal studies to humans. At this point in time there is not enough evidence to support the concept that hyperplasia occurs in human muscle tissue. It is the general consensus of researchers in exercise physiology and sport science that hyperplasia does not occur in human muscle.

There are two general classifications of muscle fibers in the human: slow twitch (red endurance fibers) and fast twitch (white speed fibers) which are subcategorized into 3 classes. Table 1-8 displays three classification schemes for the slow and fast twitch muscle fibers. All three classification schemes can be found in the literature regarding the fiber typing of human muscle. Every muscle fiber has a nerve connected to it which activates it. **The nerve, its endings and the muscle fibers to which they connect is called a motor unit.**

THEORY & PRACTICE   PART I

The motor nerves that control slow twitch fibers are different from those that activate the fast twitch fibers. It is believed that muscle fibers do not change from slow twitch to fast twitch as a result of physical training, however, endurance training will force some sub-categories of fast twitch fibers (basically the fast intermediate) to physiologically adapt to endurance work. When this occurs, there is a concurrent loss of ability to contract quickly with large forces. It is not wise for speed and explosion athletes to perform large volumes of endurance work, however, small to moderate amounts performed in the off season or at times when maximum speed or forces are not needed or desired is acceptable. The only rational purposes to include aerobic training in the training program for speed and explosion athletes would be to enhance the circulation of the heart, to reduce blood lipids, increase capillary density in the muscles and for diversity in the training program. However, it is very important to remember that **extensive aerobic training will negatively impact the performance of speed and explosion athletes.**

Table 1-8.   Three Classification Schemes For Slow And Fast Twitch Fibers.

FIBER TYPES	SCHEMES		
	1	2	3
SLOW	I	SLOW	-S-
FAST INTERMEDIATE	IIA	-FO- FAST OXIDATIVE	-FR- FAST, FATIGUE RESISTANT
FAST INTERMEDIATE	IIAB	-FOG- FAST, OXIDATIVE PLUS GLYCOLYTIC	-FI- FAST, INTERMEDIATE FATIGABILITY
FAST	IIB	-FG- FAST, GLYCOLYTIC	-FF- FAST, FATIGABLE (SPRINTS)

The motor unit arrangement allows humans to match force with the task. If a person wants to lift a pencil a small number of motor units are needed. On the other hand, if there is a need to lift a 100 pound dumb bell, the activation of a large number of motor units would be required.

Fast twitch fibers are larger than slow twitch fibers and have a greater capacity for hypertrophy. The nervous system can vary the force (strength) of muscle contraction by changing any one of the following: (1) the number of motor units recruited; (2) by modulating the frequency of the nerve impulses; and maybe, (3) by learning to activate more motor units in a synchronized way. Each motor unit can vary its force output over a 10 fold range by modulating its firing frequency (eg, from 5 to 50 impulses per second).

Progressive resistance exercise is more effective in recruiting the higher threshold motor units than less intense modes of conditioning. Furthermore, just the prolongation of an exercise at low intensity does not stimulate the higher threshold motor units. It is important to use effective intensities to maximize training for size and, also, training for strength. This percent intensity may be different for each individual because of different individual biological profiles. However, one could probably express the minimum effective percent intensity for improving strength as a range of intensity (i.e., 40% to 60% of 1RM). It follows, that the higher the intensity up to 80% to 85% 1RM, the more effective the program to produce hypertrophy because all the slow twitch and many of the fast twitch muscle fibers are recruited and hypertrophied.

Exercising at intensities from 86% to 100% improves strength by specifically training the human to recruit motor units; very little hypertrophy is developed because the amount of work is small and, therefore,

the stimulus is not sufficient to increase the size of the muscles. None-the-less, the central nervous system (CNS) is trained to recruit many of the muscle fibers including the slow twitch and the fast twitch. The person training with this procedure will get strength without a great increase in size.

Motor units are either fast twitch or slow twitch units. Each person is born with a certain percentage of slow twitch and fast twitch fibers which remain unchanged throughout life. Slow twitch muscle fibers are used in low intensity exercise of long duration (exercise that is aerobic in nature). Their contraction time is slow and they are preferentially recruited for endurance activities. They have a low potential for creating force but can contract for long periods of time. Slow twitch fibers are smaller is size than fast twitch and have a limited capacity for hypertrophy.

Research indicates that high intensity training will not improve the slow twitch fiber's capacity to perform as fast twitch fibers. In contrast however, specific endurance training of certain fast twitch fibers may improve their capability to perform endurance activities but only at the expense of their fast twitch capacities. **The explosive athlete should be very careful to not overdo endurance activities that will detract from their ability to perform as an explosive athlete.** There are sub-categories of fast twitch fibers that have been reported to increase their capacity for endurance. Such improvement requires specific endurance exercises for a training stimulus. However, there is a large amount of research evidence and even a large amount of practical observations that indicates that the utilizing low intensity, long duration work significantly detracts from strength and power development.

Strength, speed and explosion athletes should confine any significant aerobic endurance training for the off-season part of their training cycle. Caution should be executed in involving these athletes in extensive aerobic programs. One must train the specific energy system and muscle fibers in the specific way they are used in performance. Otherwise, as research and empirical observations demonstrate, you may be converting a racehorse into a plow horse.

Fast twitch fibers are used in moderate to high intensity exercise of short duration. Their contraction time is fast and they produce large forces. Their endurance potential is very low. Slow twitch motor units are recruited at low forces whereas both fast and slow twitch motor units are recruited at higher tension levels. Research is limited on the exact percentage of the 1RM that should be used where most motor units are activated. It seems rather clear though that motor units are effectively recruited from about 40% 1RM through 100% 1RM. The greater the tension needed the greater the number of motor units recruited and of course the greater the rate of firing of previously recruited motor units.

Motor units are recruited in order of size, from smallest to largest. The recruitment pattern is fixed regardless of rate of force development or speed of contraction. Slow twitch motor units are recruited first regardless of how fast the contraction rate. The fast twitch motor units are recruited after the slow twitch motor units. There does not appear to be a jump-over procedure in motor unit recruitment. This means the nervous system does not jump over slow twitch motor units in fast/strong contractions. It recruits progressively the slow twitch motor units and upward into the fast twitch motor units as the need for more force, speed and explosion increases.

Electromyographic studies do not support the theory of selective recruitment of fast twitch motor units in high velocity contractions. The pattern of recruitment is not changed but the rate of motor unit firing increases dramatically in high velocity movements. The importance of this concept is to correctly understand the physiology of muscle fiber recruitment so that one does not waste their time using ineffective training procedures. In summary, when executing fast contractions the pattern of recruitment is from slow twitch fibers to fast twitch fibers but all fibers are stimulated with a high frequency of stimuli.

In progressive resistance exercise programs both fiber types are utilized. However, fast twitch fibers are involved to a greater degree when intensity is high. As the intensity of contraction increases, the greater the involvement of fast twitch fibers in addition to slow twitch muscle fibers that have previously been recruited. **An important principle to remember is that intensity controls the amount of involvement of the fiber types, not fatigue: both fast and slow twitch muscle fibers are primarily used in exercises**

of high intensity (high muscle force/tension); and slow twitch muscle fibers are selectively utilized in low intensity exercise.

As muscles fatigue, the number of active motor units decrease so the tension a muscle group can develop decreases. Prolongation of exercise produces a further decrease in muscle tension. This type of training produces a maximal stress on the energy system (glycolytic) but in no way does a maximal recruitment of motor units occur.

Maximal recruitment of motor units occurs at maximal intensity (high forces). The production of hypertrophy occurs best at intensities between 75% and 85% 1RM, executing repetitions of from 5 to 8 performed for 3 to 5 sets. Maximal motor unit recruitment occurs at intensities ranging between 90% and 100% 1RM, executing from 1 to 3 repetitions according to the load utilized for 5 to 7 sets. Moreover, training in the 90% to 100% 1RM range will not increase the size of the muscle to a great extent; it is basically used for training the central nervous system.

Strength and size are related, but to maximize strength, programs aimed at hypertrophy must be accompanied by programs that work on the facilitation and recruitment of motor units (training of the central nervous system [CNS]). These two dimensions (hypertrophy and recruitment) are unique and distinct from each other. The training of both dimensions with specific programs is necessary in order to achieve maximum strength. **Programs for hypertrophy involve executing 3 to 5 sets of from 5 to 8 repetitions at intensities of from 75% to 85% 1RM; whereas, motor unit recruitment is trained by executing 5 to 7 sets of 1 to 3 repetitions at intensities from 90% to 100% 1RM.**

The body builder is concerned with maximum size, shape and minimum subcutaneous fat. Their program should involve sets and repetitions and various exercises performed at different intensities to insure the utmost development of all fiber types (Type I, Type IIA, Type IIAB and Type IIB). Each distinct fiber type requires a specific training intensity and volume to maximally develop, however, no research has been done to clearly identify the specific number of sets, repetitions and intensity range that could generate the greatest size of each specific fiber type. The body builder is consigned to determine, by trial and error, what specific programs can be used to maximally develop all the various fibers in their muscles; however, application of basic weight training principles will minimize the search.

Theoretically, the body builder should spend time working all levels of intensities and volumes. Also, it may be possible to train more than one level in the same training session, however, no research is available to point the way. Again the body builder must employ trial and error procedures or seek out body building coaches who have developed an effective system of training to maximize muscular development of all the various muscle fibers.

FLEXIBILITY AND WEIGHT TRAINING

Training with weights and other resistive conditioning programs does not negatively impact the flexibility of individuals using these programs. However, it has been empirically noted that in some individuals the size of certain muscle groups, caused by the individual's genetically controlled hypertrophy combined with a weight training program, may affect the range of motion of the related joints but does not seem to interfere with or inhibit physical performances. The size of the muscle can be controlled by using different exercises and/or modifying the number of sets, repetitions and modulating the intensity of the resistive training.

This section on flexibility is written to give a basic understanding of flexibility and the kinds of stretching programs one might employ. The discussion does not give specific flexibility exercises. The focus is on the variety of stretching methodologies possible. If specific stretching exercises are desired there are a number of excellent stretching and flexibility exercise books where one can select the exercises needed for their program. The goal of this section is to present the theory of stretching and flexibility so that the reader can correctly comprehend flexibility and stretching programs and their potential impact on performance, and to understand how to apply flexibility exercises without undue emphasis so that performance can be enhanced and will not be negatively impacted. This section gives the theory for application of a sound flexibility program.

Before directly dealing with the theory and practice of flexibility and stretching, it is important to point out that adopting conventional wisdom and the consensus of medical and coaching opinion may not be the correct approach to understanding flexibility. Furthermore, this pseudo-knowledge may not provide adequate information upon which to base one's flexibility enhancement or stretching program. The relationship between flexibility, performance and injury is a more complex topic than was once thought. There is no conclusive data to support the contention that lack of flexibility predisposes one to injury and, if so, the minimal amount of flexibility needed to prevent injuries.

Alter, M.J.; Science of Stretching; Human Kinetic Books; Champaign, Illinois; 1988; p. 10.

Empirical observations and research is starting to cause a lot of rethinking about the past and present theories, practices and overemphasis on flexibility programs. For example, an epidemiological study at McMaster University in Hamilton, Ontario, Canada, has shown that stretching before running may not reduce the risk of musculoskeletal injury. It is interesting to note that stretching only some of the time may be worse than not stretching at all.

The stretching practices and training related variables of 1,288 runners were studied with respect to the 1 year incidence of injuries in runners ranging in age from 14 to 76 years (average age was 34 years). It was found that 49% of the runners always stretched before running, while 43% stretched sometimes and 8% never stretched at all. **This study demonstrated that runners who always stretched had about the same injury rate as those who never stretched, but the runners who stretched sometimes had a significantly higher injury rate.** The authors speculated that inappropriate stretching techniques may have contributed to higher injury rate among the runners who only stretched some of the time.

The study identified two important risk factors for increased injury rate in runners: (1) Running more that 40 miles per week; and, (2) A previous history of injury. The age or sex of the runners had no apparent impact on the risk of injury while running. This study should not be considered as evidence that stretching before running is bad. Although one may speculate that a good deal of improper stretching techniques are being applied before running and that there is generally lack of understanding about what flexibility is and the theory and practice of flexibility training. More is not better, harder is not smarter nor does longer time spent doing flexibility programs produce injury prevention or increase performance. Flexibility and stretching programs are very complex issues which need a lot of well designed research to produce definite principles and practices upon which to base effective and safe flexibility and stretching programs.

Physician and Sports Medicine, Vol 18, No. 1, January, 1990: News Briefs: Ontario study raises doubt about stretching. Also to be printed in the following reference: Walter, S.D., Hart, L.E., Sutton, J.R., Et Al: The Ontario cohort study on running-related injuries. Arch Int Med.

People using weight training programs also abuse flexibility and stretching programs. Some never employ a stretching program while others greatly exaggerate these programs. There seems to be a lot of room for error in the application of stretching programs. Most injuries to muscles and tendons do not occur during stretching programs per se. Injuries usually occur in the actual performance of the athlete or exerciser. These injuries cannot be predicted or foreseen. Furthermore, there is no data to demonstrate conclusively that stretching prevents injury. However, one can postulate that improper stretching and overemphasis on stretching may produce micro-traumas to the tissue that accumulate over the years of training and performance. At the least

THEORY & PRACTICE   PART I

expected moment the athlete exhibits a muscle injury resulting from a long time misapplication of stretching programs, excessive stretching or improper application of physical training methods. The injuries are produced over time by too much stretching, improper stretching techniques and poorly designed and implemented training programs and exercises.

The term flexibility is misunderstood and misinterpreted by many coaches, athletes and the general population resulting in misapplication of flexibility and stretching programs. It is important to remember that there is no one measure that indicates a person's total overall flexibility. Flexibility is the ability to move the parts of the body around the joints in a free and easy manner within a prescribed range of motion which is specific to each individual and each specific joint. Every human has a body structure that allows more or less movement at each joint. Humans are unique in the extent of their movement patterns. Furthermore, participation in a specific activity requires a specific flexibility pattern and indeed participation in the specified activity may increase or decrease the extent of movement (flexibility) around various joints. To grossly distort this adapted activity related flexibility pattern may be to predispose the individual to injury, significantly reduce performance levels or waste time in applying flexibility and stretching programs that are ineffective and dangerous. It is, also, interesting to note that flexibility does differ significantly within the various joints of the body.

DEFINITION OF FLEXIBILITY

Flexibility is the ability of a joint to be freely and maximally moved through its range of motion in all directions. This may involve movement in one or more of the following antagonistic movements: flexion/extension, abduction/adduction or clockwise and counter-clockwise rotation or circumduction. Flexibility or range of motion is highly joint specific. That means a person may have great shoulder flexibility and poor hip flexibility, et cetera. Furthermore, one may have good range of motion in one direction and limited range of motion in the opposite direction.

Factors that affect flexibility and range of motion are: bone and joint architecture, joint capsules, ligaments, muscles and tendons. Each of these factors impact flexibility; some can be changed and some cannot. It is important to ascertain what factors are limiting the range of motion in order to properly develop the approach to improving flexibility. If one's skeletal structure predisposes them to limited range of motion then continuous emphasis on flexibility is counterproductive and leads to no improvement, discouragement and possibly injury. Overemphasis in this case may lead to unwanted laxity in the joint ligaments, therefore, predisposing one to injury. In this case it is better to concentrate on other dimensions of physiology to improve performance; for example, a change in performance biomechanics (style or technique) and the improvement in size, strength and speed. On the other hand, if the range of motion is limited by the muscles and their facial sheaths, general flexibility programs or advanced flexibility programs (PNF) will assist in improving range of motion (flexibility).

Stretching programs can be passive or active. When a muscle is stretched passively, it is relaxed with very little tension. The portion of muscle being worked (loaded) is predominately the connective tissue surrounding the muscle and its muscle fibers (the fascia, perimysium, epimysium and endomysium). These tissues are known as the parallel elastic components of the muscle. In passive stretching the muscle is stretched until the person feels a significant pull but no pain. This position is held from 10 to 30 seconds and then the muscle tension is reduced as the stretching action is reduced. The effect of low-load long duration stretching is a more permanent elongation of the connective tissue surrounding the muscles and its fibers.

Active stretching involves the muscle activation during movement which may be a positive (shortening) or negative (lengthening) contraction. When a muscle is actively stretched, the main structures being loaded are the tendons and other muscular elements (the smallest contractile unit of the muscle fibers -sarcomere). All these tissues (the tendons and the sarcomere) are known as the series elastic components of the muscles and are conditioned mainly during active stretching.

Can stretching prevent athletic injuries?, The Journal of Musculoskeletal Medicine; March 1990; pp. 21-31.

The stretching and flexibility program should include both active and passive stretching to condition the parallel elastic fibers and the series elastic fibers of the muscular-tendinous structures.

There are two basic categories of tissue that affect range of motion. Both of these categories can be impacted by scientific stretching programs. These categories are : fibrous connective tissue and muscle tissue.

FIBROUS CONNECTIVE TISSUE

Fibrous connective tissue involves the tissues of the joint capsule, ligaments, tendons and the surrounding sheaths of the muscle fibers, bundles of fibers and finally the entire muscle. All of these fibrous connective tissues are basically composed of the same material with similar basic functions and the same mechanical and biological properties. This fibrous connective tissue contains abundant quantities of collagen and other fibrous material. Collagen is highly inelastic and is responsible for the tremendous tensile strength of tissues such as tendons.

Frost, H.M.; Orthopaedic Biomechanics, Springfield, Illinois, Charles C. Thomas, 1973; p 238.

Ligament strength is dependent upon the total cross-sectional area. It is like skeletal muscle in that sense: i.e., the greater the cross-sectional area the greater the strength. Activity strengthens the ligaments while inactivity weakens ligaments; therefore demonstrating the need for a gradual adaptation program after injuries, illness or long periods of inactivity.

Ligaments connect bone to bone, stabilizes the joint and confines the degree of movement to within proper limits. Loose ligaments produce loose joints and may predispose to injury. In this case stretching may be contraindicated. Ligaments are arranged so that they remain taut while the joint is in the position of greatest stability, usually in the completely extended position or slightly hyper-extended position.

The tendon attaches muscle to bone. As the muscle end is approached there is an increase in the connective tissue framework which extends beyond the muscle fibers as a dense white cord or tendon. These cable-like tendons are very strong and not appreciably extensible, but, at the same time, able to bend in all directions. Their function is to transmit the muscle force directly to the bone. Tendons are stronger than muscle and, therefore, can withstand the tension forces developed by a large muscle contraction. The tendon's maximal strength is about four times greater than the usual tension to which it is likely to be subjected. There seems to be no close relationship between the muscle and the tendon cross-sectional area. Slow twitch fibers have been observed to have thicker tendons than fast twitch fibers which implies a direct relationship between tendon size and work (duration).

Edington, D.W. and Edgerton, V.R.; The Biology Of Physical Activity; Houghton Mifflin Company; Boston; 1976; p. 236.

These fibrous connective tissues respond to tension strain (stretch) first by elongating slightly, then by exhibiting a slow adaptation (overtime) to the force being applied (creep) resulting in a permanent elongation. Care must be taken to make sure over stretching does not render the joint too flaccid (loose).

PART I

THEORY & PRACTICE

Russell, K.W.; A comparison of six methods of stretch on the passive range of hip flexion; Master's Thesis, UBC; 1973, p. 17.

MUSCLE TISSUE

Muscle tissue can be stretched up to about twice its resting length and can contract to about one-half its resting length. This long excursion happens without any apparent damaging effects. Muscle has the ability to permanently increase in length as observed in the normal growth of individuals. As the bones grow in length so do the muscles. This is accomplished by adding length (new sarcomere) serially to the ends of the existing muscle fibers. It has been shown that muscle adapts to being immobilized in an elongated position by growing longer. It has also been observed that there is a reduction of muscle length when muscles have immobilized in a shortened position. Exercises should be performed through the greatest range of motion possible without exaggeration. Partial movements will negatively impact flexibility.

Increase in range of motion can be attributed to fibrous connective tissue elongation (creep) and muscle elongation (serial addition of sarcomeres). These adaptations occur over a long period of time.

1. **Russell, K.W.; A comparison of six methods of stretch on the passive range of hip flexion; Master's Thesis, UBC; 1973, p. 17.**

2. **Tabary, J.C.; Tabary, C; Tardieu, C; Tardieu, G; Goldspink, G.; Physiological and structural changes in the cat's soleus muscle due to immobilization at different lengths by plaster casts. Journal of Physiology; 222:231-244.**

3. **Williams, P.E. and Goldspink, D; Longitudinal growth of striated muscle fibers; Journal of Cell Science; 9:751, 1972.**

TYPES OF STRETCHING PROGRAMS

There are three basic techniques for improving range of motion (flexibility):
1.   Static stretching
2.   Ballistic stretching
3.   Proprioceptive Neuromuscular Facilitation (PNF)

There are many sub-categories and techniques of stretching but all can be generally classified in one of the three basic areas mentioned above. All three techniques have been shown to increase flexibility in scientific studies. They all have a place in the stretching program. Many people only stress static stretching programs but only to the detriment of their followers. It is best to employ a stretching program that combines some static stretching, specific ballistic stretching and PNF.

STATIC STRETCHING: This type of stretching involves assuming and holding a static position or posture for a period of time. These positions often require the joints involved to be locked in complete flexion or extension. This procedure places the muscles and connective tissues at their greatest possible length. Each position is held from 10 to 30 seconds.

Static stretching has been found to produce good improvements in range of motion (flexibility) but not any more effectively than other flexibility techniques. Many authorities recommend this technique over ballistic techniques because they think that it minimizes the danger of injury, soreness and facilitates relaxation. This theory sounds logical but there are no scientific studies that demonstrate that static stretching is less traumatic than other types of stretching. **The key to injury free stretching and performance is proper training, warmup, cool down, rest, nutrition and application of restorative techniques. The basic** reason for using static stretching techniques is to condition the parallel elastic components of the muscle (the fascia, perimysium, epimysium and endomysium).

BALLISTIC STRETCHING: Ballistic stretching involves the movement of a limb against a relatively fixed body or another limb. This procedure employs a controlled and sometimes uncontrolled movement pattern. The limb is put into motion by a prime mover muscle group and the momentum is absorbed by the antagonists as the movement limit is reached. The antagonistic muscles are dynamically stretched by the ballistic movement of the limb put into motion by the prime movers.

Many authorities do not recommend this method of stretching, to their discredit and misunderstanding of performance in all sports. Inherent in all human movements is the ballistic stretching phenomenon and to eliminate it is to limit performance and to make the performer unprepared for the reality of movement. **The key to injury free stretching and performance is proper training, warmup, cool down, rest, nutrition, and application of restorative techniques.** Care and common sense must be used when using specific ballistic stretching programs. Plyometric exercises and skill performance itself are examples of ballistic stretching.

Ballistic stretching has been found to be just as effective as other stretching techniques. However, it has not be demonstrated that it is superior to the other techniques.

---

1. deVries, H.A.; Physiology of Exercise For Physical Education and Athletics; Wm. C. Brown Company, Dubuque, Iowa; 1974; p.437.

2. Wilmore, J.H.; Training For Sport and Activity: The Physiological Basis of the Conditioning Process; Allyn and Bacon Inc.; Boston; 1982; p. 102.

The authors of this *Encyclopedia of Weight Training* suggest that this ballistic stretching does have a place in the flexibility program at all levels of training, however, care and common sense should limit over emphasis on this technique. All sports and physical activities require ballistic stretch because it is inherent in all ballistic movement patterns. The caution is to produce general and specific warm-up involving static and or PNF stretching techniques before moving into ballistic patterns and only after a general warm-up.

PROPRIOCEPTIVE NEUROMUSCULAR FACILITATION (PNF): PNF is a special form of resistive exercise. It is based on the concept that after a maximal or near maximal contractions the muscle spindles are re-set to a different length allowing for greater range of motion. Furthermore the golgi tendon organ is stimulated to relax the prime mover and contract the antagonist when the opposing force cannot be overcome.

There are some specialized immediate neuromuscular organ responses to stretch which have direct application to the need to increase range of motion in a more functional way. Two sensory organs of the muscle/tendon apparatus can dramatically effect the range of motion independent of skeletal and ligamentous limitations. These two sensory organs are the muscle spindles and the golgi tendon organs. The two organs work independently of each other and have different functions. **The muscle spindles** are primarily located in the belly of the muscle and are specialized muscle tissues that are sensitive to muscle length, tension, shortening and lengthening velocity. **They are the muscle length sensors.**

The golgi tendon organs are specialized collagenous tissue located in the tendons close to the musculotendinous junction. They are considered as the muscle **tension sensors**.

The muscle spindles react to the length of the muscles and may be thought of as **length sensors**. Stretching of the muscle causes a reflex contraction to relieve the stretch.

PART I

THEORY & PRACTICE

Gardener, G.W. and O'Connell, A.L.; Understanding The Scientific Basis of Human Movement; The Williams and Wilkins Co.; Baltimore; 1972; p. 200.

This is known as the stretch reflex and can be used to advantage under the proper conditions, i.e., properly warmed up and performance of technically correct movements. Fast (ballistic-spring) stretches produce greater reflexive contraction of the muscle being stretched compared to slow-prolonged stretch. Ballistic stretching is a basic part of all movements and performances. The muscles are quickly stretched followed immediately by a strong contraction. **Ballistic stretching should be executed only after a thorough general warm-up and only after static or PNF stretching programs have been implemented as a protective action.**

The muscle spindles have a mechanism that allows it to be adjusted at various muscle lengths. In a muscle which is not warmed up this adjustment is considerably shorter than the "physiological" stretch limit. This of course limits the range of motion and is often described a tightness. The muscle spindle length can be safely and effectively pre-set prior to performance or exercise most effectively by PNF.

The golgi tendon organ responds to the tension produced by the muscle and its primary function is inhibition of the muscle with which it is associated if the muscle is unable to overcome applied force. This inhibition acts as a protective mechanism for the muscle to prevent it from self-destruction. Many muscles have the ability to produce forces that push the limits of structural strength. Any failure of muscle control would result in a tearing of the muscle or a pulling of the muscle attachment away from the bone. The stimulation of the golgi tendon organs prevents the muscle from going beyond its structural capabilities.

APPLICATION OF PNF: The PNF technique of producing changes in the range of motion involves the interplay of the proprioceptors (muscle spindles, golgi tendon organs and joint capsule sensors), the nervous system and the muscles. There are various methods of applying PNF. Two simple applications are presented below:

STATIC RESISTIVE (PNF) STRETCHING: Only after a general warmup of 5-15 minutes should one execute a specific stretching program. The procedure for applying static resistive (PNF) stretching programs is discussed below.

The exerciser places a limb in a position just short of painful stretch and then performs a 6-10 second near maximal isometric contraction against an immoveable object or a partner. This is followed by a 1 - 2 second relaxation. A new position is assumed just short of painful stretch and then the process is repeated. This procedure can be applied as many times as necessary to produce the desired flexibility, however it has been found that two to three positions is enough. All the major joints can be stretched in this manner.

DYNAMIC RESISTIVE (PNF) STRETCHING: This method incorporates resistive movement throughout the range of motion against a resistance followed by a resistive return movement. It involves a positive (concentric) contraction followed by a negative (eccentric) contraction. This technique like other techniques of stretching should be preceded by a 5-15 minute general warmup. The procedure for applying dynamic resistive (PNF) stretching is discussed below.

Any particular limb and movement pattern can be selected for dynamic resistive (PNF) stretching. A partner must assist in using this technique. The exerciser begins the concentric (muscle shortening) movement against a light to moderate resistance until the one way movement is completed. At the end of the one way completed movement the partner then provides the eccentric (muscle lengthening) movement against a light to moderate resistance provided by the exerciser until the end of the range of motion is achieved. This movement pattern is repeated from 3 to 6 times attempting to increase the range of motion in each direction without pain.

GENERAL GUIDELINES FOR FLEXIBILITY PROGRAMS

Many scientists have studied flexibility and have developed a variety of flexibility programs to improve it. Some of the conclusions these researchers have drawn should help one see why flexibility is important in the training program.

1. Test all of the joints for level of flexibility.
2. Properly conducted stretching exercises done before practice (but not before a general warm-up) can prepare the athlete psychologically for the training session.
3. The distance body parts move will determine the distance through which force can be applied, and thereby influence performance (speed, height, distance, etc.)
4. Flexibility may prevent some injuries, however, flexibility does not ensure that one will be injury free.
5. Special stretching exercises will increase flexibility.
6. Flexibility is different for each individual.
7. Total body nutrition may be shown to be more important to flexibility training in the future.
8. Draw the best from all the different schools of thought on flexibility. Static - no bouncing, ballistic - swing or bounce, partner and PNF.
9. Observe the movements in the sport and identify the many situations requiring different forms of stretching. These may range from passive to extremely forceful ballistic movements.
10. Study those activities that require a great amount of flexibility to be successful (gymnastics, dance).
11. Body temperature is important for ease of stretching. Therefore, include a pre-stretching general warm-up period before engaging in the stretching routine. If practical, include stretching at various points in the practice, and after practice, while the body is warm.
12. An ideal stretch program will take 10-15 minutes.

RELATED REFERENCES

1. **Anderson, Bob; Stretching; Shelter Publications; Bolinas, CA; 1980.**

2. **Beaulieu, John; Stretching For All Sports; The Athletic Press; Pasadena, California; 1980.**

3. **Harper, P.R.; Mobility Exercise; British Amateur Athletic Board; King and Jarett Ltd; London; 1978.**

4. **Hatfield, Frederick; Flexibility Training For Sports: PNF Techniques; Fitness Systems, USA Inc; 1982.**

5. **Michael, J.A.; Science of Stretching; Human Kinetics Books; Champaign, Illinois; 1988.**

RESISTANCE EXERCISE (WEIGHT TRAINING) AND ITS INFLUENCE ON FLEXIBILITY, COORDINATION AND AGILITY

DISCUSSION

The myth about the detrimental effects to human performance caused by weight training, are difficult to extinguish. Research and empirical observations have shown that **Progressive Resistance Weight Programs** contribute in a positive way to improving flexibility, coordination, and agility. The reason is that, to a high degree, strength and local muscle endurance play a major role in agility and coordination. Meanwhile, working through the full range of motion and conditioning antagonistic muscle groups improves flexibility. **Increasing the strength level of a person is the most important factor besides the actual practice of a skill for improving physical performance.** It provides the platform from which the serious athlete, weekend athlete, or anyone, in general, can become more skillful.

PART I

THEORY & PRACTICE

An additional word about flexibility and weight training is necessary since there still prevails the myth about weight training producing a decrease in flexibility. Flexibility is defined as the range of motion around a joint. It can be measured statically by selected tests or dynamically by cinematographical or video tape techniques. The latter technique while being more specific to the real world is generally not used because of the complexity of the measuring technique.

Empirical observations have shown that people can have limited static flexibility but very great dynamic flexibility. There are no controlled research studies that have shown that increases in flexibility can or does reduce injuries or produce improvements in performances. The judgments concerning increasing flexibility and injury prevention or reduction are basically derived by conjecture and emotional prejudicial rationalizations. Research has strongly supported that where weight training programs work both sides of the joints and through the full range of motion there is improvement in static flexibility and no adverse effect on skill performances. In fact, long term studies and empirical evidence have demonstrated generally that weight training enhances range of motion (flexibility).

A study conducted during the 1976 Olympic Games in Montreal demonstrated that olympic weight lifters were second best in flexibility after gymnasts in a composite score of various static flexibility tests.

Jensen, C.R. and Fisher, A.G. <u>Scientific Basis of Athletic Conditioning</u>, Philadelphia, Lea & Febiger, 1979.

<u>RELATED REFERENCES</u>

1. Brodt, A.E.; "Change in physical fitness associated with weight lifting." Urbana, Il.: University of Illinois, Unpublished Master's Thesis, 1950.

2. Capen, E.K.; "The effect of systematic weight training on athletic power, strength and endurance." Research Quarterly. 21:83-93, May, 1950.

3. Chui, E.; "The effect of systematic weight training on athletic power." Research Quarterly. 21:188-94, October, 1950.

4. Counsilman, J.E.; "Does weight training belong in the program?" Journal of Health, Physical Education and Recreation. P. 17, January, 1955.

5. Fox, E.L.; Sports physiology (2nd edition). Philadelphia, W.B. Saunders, 1984.

6. Kusinitz, I. and Keeney, C.E.; "Effects of progressive weight training on health and physical fitness of adolescent boys." Research Quarterly. 29:294, October, 1958.

7. Leighton, J.R.; "Flexibility characteristics of three specialized skill groups of champion athletes," Archives of Physical Medicine and Rehabilitation; 38 (September 1957), p. 580-583.

8. Leighton, J.R.; "A study of the effect of progressive weight training on flexibility," Journal of the Association of Physical and Mental Rehabilitation; 18 (July/August 1964), p. 101.

9. Masely, J.W.; Hairabedian, A. and Donaldson, D.N.; "Weight training in relation to strength, speed and coordination." Research Quarterly. 24:308-15; October, 1953.

10. Massey, B.H. And Chaudet, N.L.; "The effects of systematic, heavy resistive exercise on range of joint movement in young adult male adults;" Research Quarterly, 27 (March 1956), p. 41-51.

11. Murray, J. and Karpovich, P.V.; Weight Training in Athletics. Englewood Cliffs, N.J.: Prentice-Hall, Inc.; 1956.

12. O'Shea, J.P.; **Scientific principles and methods of strength fitness. (2Nd edition). Reading, Massachusetts, Addison-Wesley, 1976.**

13. Rasch, P.J.; **Weight Training. Dubuque, Iowa, Wm. C. Brown, 1979.**

14. Wilkin, B.M.; **"The effect of weight training on speed of movement." Research Quarterly. 23:361-9, October, 1952.**

15. Wilson, A.L.; **"The effect of weight training on the physical fitness of young men." Urbana, Il.: University of Illinois, Unpublished Masters's Thesis, 1947, p. 114.**

16. Zorbas, W.S. and Karpovich, P.V.; **"The effect of weight lifting on the speed of muscle contraction." Research Quarterly. 22:145-8, May, 1951.**

MUSCLE SORENESS

Muscle soreness is divided into two categories: acute and delayed. Muscle soreness occurs during high intensity training (this is called acute soreness) or it may be experienced 12 to 48 hours post exercise (this is called delayed soreness). The acute soreness is a temporary soreness, while the delayed soreness usually appears the next day and may persist 3 to 4 days after the exercise session that caused the delayed soreness, depending upon the state of conditioning of the individual.

ACUTE MUSCLE SORENESS

The immediate soreness associated with intense exercise is short lived. It is thought to be caused by lack of blood flow producing an accumulation of exercise end products such as lactic acid and potassium. It is also thought that internal pressures cause a fluid shift from the blood plasma into the tissues along with engorgement of the muscles with blood. This produces the feeling of being pumped up after executing a large number of repetitions with a moderate to heavy weight in an exercise like arm curls, et cetera. **(Wilmore 1982)**

It has been shown in scientific experiments investigating muscular pain and fatigue that:

1. Muscular pain is produced during contractions in which the tension generated is great enough to block the blood flow to the active muscles.
2. Because of the lack of blood flow, there is a build up of metabolic waste products, such as lactic acid and potassium which cannot be removed until blood flow is restored and thus points to the stimulation of the pain receptors located in the muscles.
3. The acute pain continues until either the intensity of the contraction is reduced or the contraction ceases which allows increased blood flow removing the accumulated waste products. **(FOX & MATHEWS 1981)**

Acute soreness is a natural consequence of vigorous exercise and is eliminated simply by stopping the action causing the immediate exercise pain. When the exercise is stopped the blood flow is restored and the waste products are removed and the pain stops. When one continues a resistance exercise to the point of failure there is of course acute pain (soreness) and a depletion of energy so that none is available to continue the exercise. When the resistance exercise is stopped and recovery is allowed the pain disappears while the energy is quickly restored. Acute soreness may occur at any time when the exercise is of sufficient intensity and duration. Incidentally, **TRAINING TO FAILURE** produces some acute pain and is not necessarily effective for increasing size or strength. Training to failure is foolish training. One should **"TRAIN FOR SUCCESS."**

DELAYED MUSCLE SORENESS

Delayed muscle soreness appears from 12 to 48 hours after moderate to heavy exercise. This type of soreness usually occurs:

(1) After a period of deconditioning;
(2) When moving to higher levels of intensity or volume; and
(3) When introducing new and unaccustomed movements into the training routine.

The exact cause of delayed muscular soreness is not known but the degree of muscular soreness is related to the type of muscle contraction performed. Eccentric (lengthening or negative contractions) contractions have been shown to produce the greatest amount of muscular soreness. Concentric (shortening or positive contractions) contractions and isometric contractions do produce delayed muscular soreness but to a much lesser extent. Little or no muscular soreness has been observed when using isokinetic exercises (those where only concentric (shortening) contractions are involved and the velocity is controlled while the force of contractions are allowed to vary). It has not been demonstrated that isokinetic or isometric exercise is superior to isotonic (eccentric/concentric or vice versa) exercise. Isotonic resistive exercise programs are considered by experts to be superior to isokinetic or isometric programs at this time. In typical weight training programs for body building, sport and general conditioning it is inadvisable to eliminate the eccentric component of the exercise. Therefore one must properly cycle their training volume and intensity to reduce the soreness to a minimum.

There are three theories of delayed muscle soreness at the present time: (1) The Torn Tissue Theory; (2) The Spasm Theory; and (3) The Connective Tissue Disruption Theory.

(1) **THE TORN TISSUE THEORY:** This theory states that muscle soreness is produced by tissue damage, such as the tearing of muscle tissue.

(2) **THE SPASM THEORY:** This theory suggests that blocked blood flow causes pain which causes a reflex contraction of greater tension that causes further blood restriction to the muscle. This continues in a vicious cycle and results in delayed muscle soreness.

(3) **THE CONNECTIVE TISSUE DISRUPTION THEORY:** This theory proposes that the connective tissues, including the tendons, are damaged during contraction producing the muscular pain. Most exercise physiologists believe that this theory has the most evidence supporting it.

While there is no universal agreement on which theory is correct there is good understanding on how to minimize and reduce muscle soreness when it appears. First of all, muscle soreness can be minimized by properly cycling the volume and intensity of the weight training program, working from moderate volumes of moderate intensity to higher volumes of higher intensity. Gradual progression is important as well as proper rest and days of training at lower intensities and volumes intermixed with more intense days. It is believed that nutritional supplementation of vitamin C has a big influence in minimizing muscle soreness, but specific research is lacking.

Once delayed muscular soreness is experienced there are certain steps that one can take to reduce the delayed muscular soreness. The following steps can be taken to reduce delayed muscular soreness:

1. Repeat the exercise at a moderate intensity and volume that produced the soreness in the first place.
2. Massage is very effective in reducing delayed muscular soreness.
3. Heat therapy in the form of whirlpool, sauna and steam baths are effective for relief of delayed muscle soreness.
4. Stretching in its many forms has been shown to reduce delayed muscular soreness. Stretching after each training session may be very effective.

RELATED REFERENCES

1. Fox, Ed and Mathews, Don; The Physiological Basis of PE & Athletics, Saunders College Publishing, 1981, p. 152-155.

2. Lamb, David; Physiology of Exercise; Macmillan Publ. Co, 1978, p. 190-192.

3. McArdle, Katch and Katch; Exercise Physiology: Energy, Nutrition and Human Performance. Lea & Febiger, 1981; p. 486-491.

4. Wilmore, Jack; Training For Sport; Allyn & Bacon, 1982; p. 87-88.

SPECIFICITY OF EXERCISE

EXERCISE SPECIFICITY

Research has repeatedly confirmed that physiological results or benefits of training are specific to the activity. What this means is that endurance training programs result in the preferential recruitment of only the slow twitch fibers and employs only the aerobic energy system utilized in endurance training. On the other hand, training for strength and size develops both the slow twitch and fast twitch fibers while increasing the ability of the muscle to apply strength. Consequently, in general weight training programs there is little or no influence on cardiovascular endurance performance unless circuit weight training, super circuit weight training or local muscle endurance training formats are employed.

In addition, the angle at which the muscle is exercised results only in the recruitment of selected fibers in the muscle or muscle groups that are responsible for that movement. To train all the muscle fibers in a muscle or muscle group would require that many exercises and all the possible angles be trained in a structured and methodical manner. This principle is of prime importance in body building, but to implement it requires a great amount of time for application in the daily training sessions. While this might be ideal for body building, it may be impractical for general conditioning or training for sport. When training for sport (pre-season and in-season) and for general conditioning, one would select exercises that condition the fibers directly involved in the sport, or in the case of general conditioning, the exercises that naturally influence (recruit) the greatest number of muscle fibers. This procedure will reduce the time needed to complete the exercise program.

During post-season training for the athlete, a wide variety of exercises and exercise angles would be of benefit. Likewise, for those people training for general conditioning, there should be training phases where a wide variety of exercises and exercise angles should be employed. This procedure provides a balanced muscle development and conditioning for both athlete and the person training for general fitness.

It is also important to train the muscles in the same metabolic manner in which they will be utilized in the sport performance, and in the case of general conditioning, the metabolic training must meet the objectives of the general condition program. During the off season for sports training a more general program that works the many different angles and muscle fibers can be utilized. For general training programs part of the yearly training cycle should be devoted to training as many different angles and muscle fibers as practicable.

Planning training programs for athletes, body builders or for general conditioning requires that certain clearly defined metabolic and neuromuscular objectives be defined and the specific ranges of motion needed at each joint identified. When this is done, there can be prudent selection of exercises, sets, repetitions, intensities and number of training days per week that will produce results commensurate with the program objectives. While there may be many exercises that will benefit the trainee to varying degrees, there are a few general exercises

THEORY & PRACTICE

PART I

that will produce good results for most activities. The important thing to remember is to maintain muscle symmetry and muscle strength balance in all the major antagonistic muscle groups of the body. In the overall scheme of the training program it may be wise at selected times to include a wide variety of exercises and movements. However, when focusing on a specific championship objective it is necessary to use just those specific exercises that contribute directly to the performance objective.

In summary, specificity involves metabolic and neuromuscular plans of action. The basic energy system used in a sport or physical activity should be trained while the angles of application of force involved in the sport activity should be closely approximated in the resistance exercises included in the training program. **"You get what you train for."** Following the principle of training specificity, if you were to take a thoroughbred race horse and train it by pulling a plow you would get a very strong but slow race horse. Another way of considering training specificity is that one would go to a Spanish teacher to learn Spanish, not to a teacher specializing in the Chinese language. Specificity of training involves two distinct broad areas: (1) metabolic specificity and (2) neuromuscular specificity.

METABOLIC SPECIFICITY

Two major components make up metabolic specificity: (1) the energy systems and (2) the cardiovascular system. The three basic energy systems are: (1) the ATP-PC (adenosinetriphosphate - phosphocreatine); (2) lactic acid system (anaerobic glycolysis); and, (3) the oxygen transport (aerobic) system. In Table 1-9 appears the different phases of energy use, the corresponding performance times, the major energy system used and specific examples.

Table 1-9. Performance Times and Major Energy System Used in Sport Performances.

PHASE	PERFORMANCE TIMES	MAJOR ENERGY SYSTEM USED	EXAMPLES
1	0 - 30 SEC	PHOSPHAGEN (ATP-PC)	SHOTPUT, WT. LIFTING, 100M, 200M SPRINT
2	30 - 90 SEC	ATP-PC + LACTIC ACID	300M - 400M SPRINT, 100M SWIM
3	90 - 180 SEC	LACTIC ACID + AEROBIC SYSTEM	800M RUN, WRESTLING (2'), GYMNASTICS, BOXING, TEAM SPORTS (3')
4	BEYOND 180 SEC	AEROBIC SYSTEM	EXTENDED RUN, SWIM, BIKE
ADAPTED AND MODIFIED FROM FOX; SPORTS PHYSIOLOGY; SAUNDERS COLLEGE PUBLISHING; N.Y.; 1984; P.35.			

For any given exercise or sports activity, the main energy system supplying the energy for the task must be trained. Low intensity and long duration activities require the predominate use of the aerobic energy system. High intensity and very short duration activities involve primarily the anaerobic energy systems. Most weight lifting requires the use of the ATP-PC and lactic acid systems, the exception being circuit weight training and super circuit weight training formats as well as super-setting, tri-setting, quad-setting and giant-setting programs, which involves the aerobic system as well. It is essential that the correct exercise program be utilized to condition the correct energy system that is used in physical performances.

There is metabolic specificity in various patterns of repetitions and sets in weight training, circuit weight training and super circuit weight training patterns which involve both the aerobic and anaerobic energy systems. High resistance and low repetitions involve only the ATP-PC and lactic acid systems. Many of the patterns of exercises used in weight training closely approximates the metabolic requirements of various sports and, therefore, transfers directly to those sports.

For athletes, during selected off-season periods it is wise to devote some time to aerobic conditioning to build-up the cardiovascular system function. This is merely a wise procedure implemented for long term health reasons and really doesn't contribute significantly to high intensity and short duration performance. This is more a preventative health measure rather than an absolute contributor to anaerobic performance.

Cross training is a concept that is frequently touted by exercise enthusiasts. It involves the engagement in various physical training activities and sports that are unrelated such as swimming, running or cycling. It is important to remember that only similar components (metabolic or neuro-muscular) are transferred between activities. While there might be some crossover benefits from swimming to running or vice versa, research has shown that the crossover benefits are minimal.

Similar corresponding observations between cycling and swimming, and, cycling and running have been reported. These observations point to the fact that the for maximal benefits the method of exercise in training **must coincide** with that used when performing. Cross training may be of benefit for a break from what has been the usual training program. Cross training provides diversity in training which facilitates motivation, but one must never forget that **"Specificity Rules."** However, for long term health benefits, cross training may be the best program for the general fitness enthusiast.

For any given performance, it is important to train the correct energy system as well as making sure that the correct neuromuscular pattern is specifically practiced. When it comes to weight training exercises there seems to be a generality of exercises if the above conditions are fully satisfied.

While there are no scientific studies to support the above hypothesis, the generality of weight training exercises, it has been observed in the trenches for many years by the authors. That is to say, that for most sports it is sufficient to utilize only the standard exercises employing the appropriate intensity and the proper number of sets and repetitions for the development of strength and to increase muscle mass. It has been observed that the execution of standard exercises for all the major muscle groups has been efficacious for the improvement of most sports skills. The creation and practice of special specific weight lifting exercises for various sports is not necessary and can sometimes produce unnecessary hazards to muscular and skeletal health. The principle that needs to be applied when training for all sports activities, is to use the standard weight training exercises to increase strength and size as needed using the concepts of periodization. In addition, practice the specific sport skill to refine the athletic performance level desired.

It is easy to stay within the required sports specific energy system when weight training. One can merely change the volume (repetitions) and intensity to match the specific energy requirement. Of course this must be part of a long term periodization plan. There are times in the training year where little consideration is given to metabolic specificity when designing exercises and programs. An example is an aerobic program executed in the off-season of a football player or track and field thrower. These athletes might become involved in an aerobic cycle strictly for health reasons and to strengthen the cardiovascular system.

While it is good to perform aerobic exercise for the health of one's heart and vascular system, the impact on speed and explosion skills is detrimental because one trains the wrong energy system, muscle fibers and neuromuscular patterns. However, application of aerobic exercise can be effectively performed at strategically selected spots and for short phases in the yearly training cycle of the speed/explosion/strength athletes. If properly cycled, aerobic exercise can provide a needed low intensity exercise program that will help restore the metabolic and psychological energy needed to make another long term assault on high intensity training.

PART I

THEORY & PRACTICE

RELATED REFERENCES

1. Edward Fox; Sports Physiology, Saunders College Publishing, N.Y.; 1984; p. 202-5.

2. Edward Fox & Donald Mathews; The Physiological Basis of Physical Education and Athletics; Saunders College Publishing, N.Y., 1981; P. 324-330.

3. William Mc Ardle, Frank Katch and Vic Katch; Exercise Physiology: Energy, Nutrition and Human Performance, Lea & Febiger, Philadelphia, 1981; p. 268-9.

4. M. Stone and H. O'Bryant, Weight Training: A Scientific Approach; Burgess Publishing Company; Minneapolis, Minn., 1984; p. 151-3.

VELOCITY OF MOVEMENT AND FORCE DEVELOPMENT

EXERCISE SPEED

The maximal speed of performing an exercise relates to the complexity of the movement and the weight on the bar. For general conditioning (40%-60% 1RM) the tempo of each exercise movement should be at about 20%-30% of the maximal unloaded velocity. This is relatively slow. The slow movement of the weight minimizes the amount of momentum gained in the movement and, consequently, optimizes the work of the muscle throughout the range of motion. In contrast, during heavier weight training exercises the speed of movement is necessarily reduced because of the heavier work loads (70% -100% 1RM). It follows that the speed of an exercise approaches zero as the resistance on the bar approximates one's maximal strength. The theoretical maximal force a muscle or muscle group can exert is against an immovable object. This is known as an isometric contraction. The relationship between velocity and force of contraction is shown in Figure 1-3. As the speed of movement (muscle contraction) increases the amount of force the muscle can produce is decreased. (A.V. HILL-1922; Fox-1979; McArdle, Katch & Katch-1981; Astrand & Rohdahl- 1977; Fox & Mathews-1981.)

Isometric contractions only strengthen the muscle at the specific length of the muscle during its training contraction. Therefore, for effective isometric training it is necessary to perform a series of isometric contractions at various lengths of the muscle to insure strength development throughout the range of motion. This training procedure takes an inordinate amount of time and thus it is not recommended as a major method of training. Isometric training may have some benefit in injury rehabilitation, for special training problems or as a short training diversion.

The analysis of the force velocity curve of a contracting muscle supports the statements above. The curve displays the fact that as the speed of contraction increases the ability of the muscle to produce force is reduced. Empirical observations show that as loads increase to 70% through 100% of 1RM the velocity of movement is drastically reduced compared to lighter training loads. Furthermore, when exercising at heavier work loads it is impossible to move the weight at high velocities.

When there is an increase in work load the speed of movement is slow but the muscle tension remains high. It is important to remember that it is the appropriate tension in the muscle that produces increases in size and strength, not merely moving the weight for more repetitions or at higher speeds. Also, it is the increasing of the strength of the muscles and the practice of the specific movement pattern that produces increases in speed of movement. One should not move the light weight faster, they should use the appropriate training load and move it with a slow controlled action to optimize strength development. Furthermore, it is wise to employ cycles and exercises using various intensities and volumes to train the full contraction spectrum of force and velocity. However, specific speed and movement patterns must be performed in the specific skill acquisition training program.

Consequent to participation in a scientifically designed strength training program, it is possible to increase the force at a given velocity. **(See A and B in Figure 1-3.)** Because of improvement in the strength potential of the muscles and improved skill performance, the individual is able to apply more force at a given velocity. Velocity of muscle contractions may not change appreciably, however, the ability of the muscular system to apply force can be dramatically improved, thus increasing the amount of force that can be applied at a given velocity. This increasing of muscular force at a given velocity may account for a high percentage of the improvement in a skill performance as the athletes becomes better conditioned.

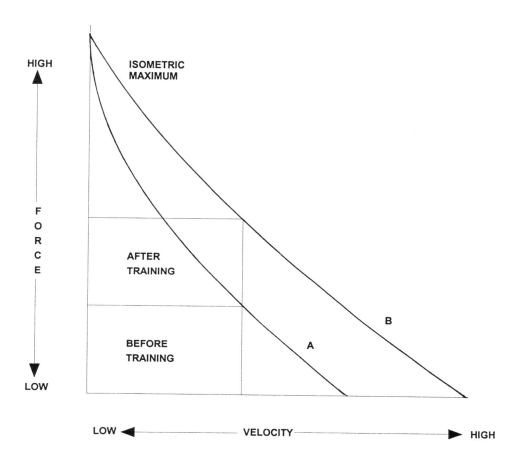

Figure 1-3.   The theoretical force and velocity of contraction relationship. (A) Force/Velocity Curve Before Training. (B) Movement of The Force/Velocity Curve After Training.

Moving light weights at fast velocities recruits a limited number of motor units (muscle fibers and the nerve endings that activate them) while heavier weights necessarily move at slower velocities but will by necessity recruit more motor units. When low intensity and fast movements are used, only a few small slow twitch muscle fibers are recruited.

When high resistance movements are performed with necessarily fewer repetitions, numerous intermediate and fast twitch fibers are recruited, along with the slow twitch muscle fibers to produce greater force and, consequently, greater velocity. Greater muscle mass is involved in the higher intensity exercises that are performed at slower speeds which produces greater hypertrophy and strength development. **The key is to translate the increased strength to improved speed of movement in a selected performance. This is done by practicing the specific speed of movement actions as well as the strength training.**

When weights or constant resistance weight machines are moved the total mass begins to gather momentum. This results in the mass (weights or machines) tending to move on its own, once in motion. Sir Isaac Newton defined this as **INERTIA**; the tendency of a mass to remain at rest or continue in the direction of the force initiating the movement until acted upon by another force. The greater the mass and the greater the speed of movement the greater the tendency of the weight to **"run light."** This means that the muscle force necessary to move the mass is less than when it is moved slower. The tendency of the mass to run light may be thought of as a ballistic movement; a movement that is like a missile that has burned all its rocket fuel and the missile continues to have movement.

How does this apply to weight training? When using free weights or weight machines, the faster one moves the weight or machine the less muscle force is needed to complete the movement. By the very nature of moving fast, the resistance (weight load) has to be reduced to perform the movement at the increased speed. This low intensity fast movement does not recruit many muscle fibers and, thus, limited strengthening occurs. In contrast, when the resistance (intensity [percent of 1RM]) is very high, the movement velocity is naturally very slow, but many muscle fibers are being recruited and conditioned.

For general fitness training, body building and training for sport one should move the heavy resistance with correct form and at a relatively slow speed of movement. Contrary to popular belief, this does not result in loss of speed of movement in sports activities. Some authorities suggest that even though the heavier weights are moving slow that the exerciser should think - FAST. It has yet to be shown experimentally that this concept is valid. However, from an in-the-trenches point of view it may be of some value.

When training high level athletes it is important to shift the force/velocity curve for each muscle group upward. This means that for any given velocity the force is greater. **(SEE FIGURE 1-3)** Moving the force/velocity curve upward will theoretically increase the performance level. This is accomplished by correct application of the periodization concept and using the proper exercises with varying volumes and intensities which are performed at the appropriate velocities to increase the force developing capabilities of the muscles involved in the movement. Moreover, practicing the specific motor pattern where the speed improvement is desired is imperative.

RELATED REFERENCES

1. Astrand, P.O. and Rodahl, K.; Textbook of Work Physiology; McGraw-Hill Book Company; New York; 1977; pp. 101-5.

2. Fox, E.L.; Sports Physiology; W.B. Saunders Company, Philadelphia, 1979; pp. 104-5.

3. Fox, E.L. and Mathews, D.K.; The Physiological Basis of Physical Education and Athletics: Saunders College Publishing; New York; 1981; pp. 101-4.

4. Hill, A.V., 1922; The maximum work and mechanical efficiency of human muscles and their most economical speed. Journal of Physiology; 56:19-41.

5. McArdel, W.D.; Katch, F.I. and Katch V.L.; Exercise Physiology: Energy, Nutrition and Human Performance; Lea & Febiger, Philadelphia, 1981. pp. 294-5.

THE EFFECTS OF WEIGHT TRAINING ON SPEED OF MOVEMENT

DISCUSSION

Many coaches and athletes erroneously believe that weight training will impair athletic ability, speed of movement and flexibility. The myth dies hard. Even in this enlightened age of knowledge in exercise physiology and biomechanics, there are many authorities that believe that weight training is detrimental to speed. The real truth is that a scientifically sound weight training program will improve the speed of movement of any body segment appropriately weight trained.

There are an overwhelming number of research studies and a vast amount of empirical evidence that support the application of weight training programs for improving speed of movement. Merely increasing the strength of a muscle will produce an increase in the speed of muscular contraction. An example from automobile racing will illustrate the principle. If you replace a Volkswagen engine with a V-8 engine, the car will increase its ability to move very fast even though there will be an increase in total vehicular weight. Why? The power (strength) to weight ratio has been dramatically improved.

The speed of movement of any body limb is directly dependent upon the strength of the muscles involved in its movement. A scientifically designed and implemented weight training program will enhance the speed of movement of any body segment. It is useful to elucidate the parameters of weight training programs to ensure productive weight training programs. The following guidelines are recommended for programs utilized to improve speed of movement:

1. The weight training program should include cycles (phases) that focus on increasing the size of the muscles involved in the specific movement and cycles that concentrate on maximal recruiting of the muscle fibers involved in the movement. These are two very distinct phases of resistive muscle training and each needs specific and separate weight training programs to accomplish.

2. The intensity of the cycles (phases) should vary between 75% and 100% 1RM in a planned program.

3. The size (hypertrophy) phase involves exercising at intensities ranging between 75% and 85% 1RM and performing 5 - 8 repetitions for 3 to 5 sets, excluding warmup and cooldown.

4. The CNS (muscle fiber recruitment) phase involves intensities ranging between 90% and 100% 1RM and performing 1 - 4 repetitions for 5 to 7 sets, excluding warmup and cooldown.

5. The muscle groups involved in the program should include the prime movers (the muscles that cause the desired action), the synergistic muscles (the muscles that assist in the action), the stabilizers (the muscles that stabilize various parts of the body related to the action), the antagonistic muscles (the muscles that oppose the prime movers) and the neutralizers (the muscles that may neutralize undesired actions).

6. The specific speed of movement action should be practiced. For example in baseball, football, javelin, shot and discus throwing, any weight loaded movements should be performed within a very narrow range of additional weight or lighter weight. It is understood that there is a very narrow range of weight variance application of overweight and underweight training for speed of movement. This is known as the overload and underload envelope (the training sensitive zone for specific speed training) and is specific for every action.

Type IIb (fast twitch - fast glycolytic) fibers are improved by training between 1 - 6 repetitions with high intensity. To exceed six repetitions the muscle tension is reduced and the type IIb (fast twitch) fibers drop out (Palmierri 1983). Tesch and Larsson (1982) have shown that there is a lack of fast twitch fiber hypertrophy in body builders whose workout consist of 8-20 repetitions maximum. Powerlifters had significantly larger fast twitch fibers because they trained at high intensity and low repetitions.

---

1. Palmierri, G.; The Principles of Muscle Fiber Recruitment Applied to Strength Training: NSCA Journal; Oct/Nov 1983; pp. 22 - 24.

2. Tesch, P. and Larsson; 1982; Muscle hypertrophy in body builders; European Journal of Applied Physiology; 49:301-6.

In the weight training program, there is little advantage in executing rapid repetitions with light weights as a means for increasing the speed of various athletic movements. These rapid light weight exercises employ too much resistance to improve the specific speed (i.e., outside the overload and underload envelope) of movement and too little resistance for increasing strength (i.e., outside the strength training overload envelope) and, therefore, are essentially non-productive for improving athletic speed performance. None-the-less, there are many coaches and athletes that adopt this fallacious and worthless training method to improve speed. By performing many quick repetitions with a light weight, one recruits mainly the slow twitch fibers (intensity [percent of 1RM] determines what fibers are recruited). Fast movements with low resistance do not tax the muscles enough to recruit the fast fibers because the resistance falls outside the training sensitive zone (strength training overload envelope).

Research studies using isokinetic strength measuring devices have been conducted to investigate the relationship of increases in strength and speed of training. Recent investigations have demonstrated that slow (60-90 degree/second) to moderate (180 degrees/second) training velocity are optimal for increasing strength at a variety of speeds. As early as the 1920's and 1930's it was demonstrated that as speed of movement increases, the tension developed within the muscle decreases. (Hill, 1922; Fenn, et al; 1931) In the recent studies it has been demonstrated that nearly twice as much work is performed at an isokinetic velocity of 60 degrees/sec (classified as slow) compared to 300 degrees/sec (classified as fast). The amount of work completed as well as the higher intensity of that work, seems to be the most important factors for improving strength and, therefore, enhancing speed of movement.

The majority of research evidence have found that constant moderate to heavy resistance isotonic exercise is superior to speed loading for gaining strength. Isotonic speed resistance training (many light weight repetitions performed in a fast cadence) may not create sufficient tension in the muscle to elicit a training effect. This recent research has concluded that isokinetic training at a slow (60 degree/sec) to intermediate (96 degree/sec) training velocity can maximize tension in the muscle, increase strength over a wide range of velocities and minimize risk of injuries. (Brooks and Fahey 1996)

Brooks, G.A. and T.D. Fahey; Exercise Physiology: human bioenergetics and its applications; Mayfield Publishing Company, New York; 1996; p 387-89.

Fibers are recruited in harmony with the force requirement and not in accordance with the speed requirement for a specific movement. If one quickly moves their hand in any direction they would not recruit many fast twitch (large) muscle fibers because the resistance to this action is very small. The body recruits the small slow fibers first, followed by the larger fibers as the intensity (% 1RM) increases. In addition to the small (slow) muscle fibers, the large fast twitch fibers are used extensively when training at loads between 75% and 100% 1RM. The closer one trains to their 1RM the more large fast twitch fibers are employed in addition to the smaller slower muscle fibers.

Recruitment is from small (slow) to large (fast) and there is no jumping over smaller fibers. As movements become progressively more intense, other intermediate and fast fibers are recruited in addition to the ones already employed. The slow, intermediate and fast muscle fibers work together to produce the force needed for a particular movement pattern. When intensity (% 1RM) drops lower, which allows for more repetitions to be executed, the intermediate and fast twitch fibers drop out of use and only the slower twitch muscle fibers are preferentially recruited.

Proper weight training uses training loads that recruit both the fast twitch and the slow twitch fibers which allows their appropriate conditioning. The nervous system simply does not jump over the slow fibers to preferentially recruit fast fiber. There is orderly muscle fiber recruitment from slow (small) to fast (large) depending upon the force requirement needed for the specific task.

Contrary to what one has heard or read, slow, controlled weight training will not decrease speed of movement. As mentioned above, speed is enhanced by strength improvement. More muscle fibers (slow, intermediate and fast) are recruited by training with it's heavy weights and by using slow, controlled movements. The heavy weight is moved very slowly because of its mass, but all the needed muscle fibers are being recruited to accomplish the task of lifting the heavy weight.

It is like a train locomotive starting to move a long and heavy series of box cars. All the horsepower in the engine are working to start the very heavy train but it is moving very, very slowly because of it large mass. On the other hand, the best method to condition a specific speed of movement pattern is to practice that activity within a very narrow overload and underload envelope. The training of muscles at higher intensities with slow controlled movements enhances the speed of movement by augmenting the strength level of the muscle utilized in the action. Meanwhile, the practice of the specific movement at fast speeds will produce the best neuromuscular pattern needed for fast movement. **The plan of attack for increasing speed of movement calls for increased strength of muscles involved and the refinement and practice of the specific motor pattern within a narrow overweight/underweight envelope.**

Power is often talked about by exercise scientists, coaches and athletes. Power is the amount of work done in a unit of time **(FORCE X DISTANCE / TIME).** Power is definitionally stated as weight (force) times distance divided by time. Power is increased by:

1. Boosting the movement force (increasing the number of fibers recruited, increasing the force output of fibers or both).
2. Increasing the distance over which the force is applied (increasing work [force X distance]).
3. Decreasing the time needed to perform the movement (speed).
4. Producing a combination of the changes in the conditions stated in 1, 2 and 3 above.

Speed of contraction (number 3 above) and work (number 2 above) have very limited potential for changes, while force (number 1 above) can be dramatically changed. The best method to increase power is to increase the muscular force required for a specific action. The muscular force can be augmented by increasing the strength of the muscles involved by employing a weight training program. The muscle has the ability to make large increases (over time) and, therefore, has the greatest potential to increase power. Increases in strength have been shown to be between 3% and 6% per week and from 30% to 35% over longer periods of time. Most athletes have not begun to realized their potential for strength and, consequently, the potential for increasing their speed of movement by increasing their strength.

Strength training for increased power should not take the form of fast repetitions and light loads. This method of training involves work but does not produce the desired nervous system or muscular adaptations because the resistance is not within the training sensitive zone which is 75% to 100% 1RM. In other words, the weight is too light to produce strength and to heavy to produce specific nervous system changes. This type training preferentially recruits the slow twitch muscle fibers.

The peak power of both slow and fast twitch muscle fibers occurs at approximately one-third of its maximum shortening velocity. The fast twitch fibers produce four times as much power as the slow twitch fibers. (Faulkner, et al 1986) In any one physical activity or performance, no body segment is moving at maximum velocity except possibly the hand at release in throwing activities and foot at contact in kicking activities. There is an optimum speed of movement for each limb involved in a specific movement which must be summed and coordinated by the central nervous system for a high level of performance. Consideration of these factors leads one to adopt the concept that training with heavy weight in slow controlled movements does in fact enhance the speed of movement.

J.A. Faulkner, D.R. Claflin and K.K. McCully; Power output of fast and slow fibers from human skeletal muscles; in Human Muscle Power, N.L. Jones, N. McCartney and A.J. McComas; Human Kinetic Publishers, Inc., Champaign, Illinois, 1986; pp. 81-94.

PART I

THEORY & PRACTICE

SUMMARY STATEMENT ON THE EFFECTS OF WEIGHT TRAINING ON THE SPEED OF MOVEMENT

Improvement in strength enhances speed of movement. Increasing the strength of the muscles responsible for moving any body limb will increase the potential for speed of movement of that limb. Weight training with slow and controlled movements performed at high intensity and few repetitions does not slow the speed of movement in the muscles being trained in this manner. This method of training recruits and strengthens all the muscle fibers (slow, intermediate and fast twitch) that are utilized in the weight training exercises which are the muscle fibers needed to perform at higher speeds of movement. On the other hand, performing rapid repetitions with light weight just does not adequately recruit the larger fast twitch fibers and such training methodology is worthless for improving speed of movement.

It is best to practice the exact action desired for improving speed of movement; for example; football, baseball, javelin, shot and discus throwing. However, it must be remembered that there is a very small envelope of overload and underload training intensities that are effective for improving the speed of specific motor skills or sports activities. The main purpose of weight training is to strengthen the muscles involved in the action where speed of movement is desired. Furthermore, the weight training program should be coupled with the actual practice of the specific sports action under the precise circumstances of the desired performance.

The correct approach to improving speed of movement is to strengthen all the muscles involved in the desired movement and then practice and refine the desired movement patterns at very fast speeds.

RELATED REFERENCES

1. Caiozzo, V.J., J.J. Perine and V.R. Edgerton; 1981; Training induced alterations of the in vivo force velocity relationship of human muscle. Journal of Applied Physiology: Respiratory, Environmental and Exercise Physiology: 51 (3): 750-754.

2. Fenn, W.H., Brady, H and A. Petrilli, 1933; The tension developed by human muscles at different velocities of shortening. American Journal of Physiology, 97 (1);1-4.

3. Hill, A.V., 1922; The maximum work and mechanical efficiency of human muscles and their most economical speed. Journal of Physiology; 56:19-41.

4. Kaneshisa, H. and M. Miyashita. 1983; Specificity of velocity in strength training. European Journal of Applied Physiology and Occupation Physiology; 52:104-6.

5. Reid, C.M.; R.A. Yeater and H. Ulrich, 1987. Weight Training and strength, cardiorespiratory functioning and body composition of men. British Journal of Sports Medicine; 21 (1): 40-44.

WEIGHT TRAINING TECHNOLOGY AND EQUIPMENT

THE USE OF A WEIGHT LIFTING BELT DURING TRAINING

INTRODUCTION

Power lifters, Olympic weight lifters and the general weight trainee use lifting belts during training with weights. The obvious purpose is to support and protect the lower back. There is a current trend to use a weight lifting belt at all times during weight training regardless of the type of exercise, the intensity of the exercise or the number of repetitions that are being performed. The wearing of a weight belt has become a status symbol in the modern day fitness centers and gyms. One can observe males and females wearing lifting belts during exercises where there is no need for low back support. It is the opinion of the authors and many weight training authorities that lifting belts should only be used when attempting heavy lifts or when a strained back must be supported during any lift. Frankly, if the back is strained one should drastically alter their training, seek medical assistance and undergo physical therapy until the back is healed. Continued training with a strained back will retard healing and inhibit physiological progress.

There are fundamentally four types of belts that are commonly used during weight training:

(1) **A WIDE BELT.** The wide belt is made up of a single layer of leather that is narrow (2-3 inches) in the front and very wide (6 inches) in the rear. It may have a single or double row of holes for the respective buckle.

(2) **A REGULAR BELT.** The regular belt is made up of single layer of leather that is narrow (2-3 inches) in the front and only 4 inches wide in the rear. It may have a single or double row of holes for the respective buckle.

(3) **A POWER BELT.** The power belt is 4 inches wide for the entire length of the belt and is usually made up of a double or triple thickness of leather. It may have a single or double row of holes for the respective buckle. A competition (legal) belt is no more than 10 centimeters (4 inches) wide and must only have one row of holes. These belts are much stiffer and provide greater support for the back.

(4) **AN AIR BLADDER SUPPORT BELT.** The air bladder support belt was introduced to weight training around 1990. These devices use air bladders of various sizes and shapes combined with leather or other fabrics. Some of these devices have pumps while others require the occasional inflation by mouth. The effectiveness of these devices vary with the design.

The fundamental reason for using a weight belt is to support the back in heavy lifting. The mechanics of how the belt supports the back are not understood by most users. Simply stated, the belt supports the back by allowing the exerciser to push against the belt with his abdominal muscles which increases the intra-abdominal pressure which unloads the spine. It is the increased intra-abdominal pressure coupled with increased intra-thoracic pressure that supports the spine and not merely the physical constraining of the back.

The ligamentous spine can withstand only 4 to 5 pounds of force before it will crumble. In lifting actions that demand the use of the total body, a stable and firm spine can withstand tons of force. The structures that provide this great support are: (1) The muscles surrounding the vertebral column; (2) The air filled ball of the chest cavity; and, (3) the semi-fluid filled ball of the abdominal cavity. The contraction of the muscles surrounding the vertebral column, the thoracic cavity and the abdominal cavity act together to decompress the vertebral column by increasing the intra-abdominal and intra-thoracic pressures, thus making the trunk a strong rigid lever to apply a great amount of force in lifting activities.

TRUNK PRESSURES

A thin piece of leather pressed against the back will not by itself provide the necessary support to the lower back to allow the lifting of very heavy weights. It makes no difference if the belt is 4 or 6 inches wide or one to three layers thick relative to providing support for the back. The basic function of the belt is allow the abdominal muscles to push against the front of the belt to increase the intra-abdominal pressure (IAP). The increased intra-abdominal pressure essentially unloads and protects the vertebral column.

Another procedure used by lifters is to take a large inhalation, holding it while closing their glottis and attempting to forcefully exhale (Valsalva maneuver). This practice increases the intra-thoracic pressure (ITP) which stabilizes the thoracic vertebra while the large inhalation pushes down on the abdominal cavity which further increases the intra-abdominal pressure. This results in a tremendous increase in the intra-abdominal and intra-thoracic pressure which takes the load off the spine and back muscles to a great degree. The increased intra-abdominal and intra-thoracic pressure is augmented by the constriction action of the muscles of the trunk while the manual support and constriction of the weight belt and further unloads the spine providing great low back support.

INTRA-THORACIC PRESSURE (ITP): Many researcher have investigated the unloading of the thoracic spine by increasing the intra-thoracic pressure. Increasing the ITP will unload the thoracic vertebra during heavy weight lifting. It has been observed that ITP is less than IAP while ITP estimates have been reported to be about 150 mmHG.

INTRA-ABDOMINAL PRESSURE (IAP): There have been numerous investigations of IAP in manual lifting (industrial). Only a few studies have been conducted using common weight-training lifts such as the dead lift and the squat (Eie, 1966; Eie & Wehn, 1962; Hall, 1985; Lander, 1986). IAP estimates during weight lifting movements have been shown to be as high as 375 mmHG. Lander states the IAP clearly has a profound effect in the unloading the lumbar and lower thoracic vertebra.

PRACTICAL APPLICATION

Performance in weight lifting exercises involving overhead lifts, pulling actions from the floor, all variations of leg pressing and squatting can be enhanced by using a lifting belt to assist in increasing intra-abdominal pressure along with the proper application of breath holding and release to increase and to control the ITP. Increasing IAP and ITP must be coordinated to receive greatest benefit and maximal unloading of the vertebral column.

Prior to executing the weight lifting exercise a large inhalation followed by attempted exhalation with a closed glottis greatly increases the ITP. The diaphragm, which is on the top of the abdominal cavity is pushed down and serves as a solid surface. Concurrent forceful pushing of the abdominal muscles against the weight belt and the unyielding thoracic balloon increases the intra-thoracic and the intra-abdominal pressure which dramatically unloads the total spine.

Application of advanced breath holding with the use of low back supports (weight belts) has been found to increase significantly the ability to apply force in a number of exercises. It has been shown that breath holding in heavy lifting activities is safe and desirable to unload the spine so that greater weights can be safely and effectively lifted. Maintaining the increased IAP and ITP during heavy lifting is necessary to relieve the vertebral column of the large forces experienced in these actions. High IAP and ITP can be safely tolerated for short time periods and also on an intermittent basis. Furthermore, if the lifter continues to breathe between the repetitions of a set, the IAP changes can serve as an "abdominal pump" to move blood from the abdomen to the heart.

Lander (1986) makes a few good recommendations regarding the use of weight belts:

1. Use a belt that is 4 inches wide all around. The stiffer the belt, the better it will perform. Depending upon body size a 4 inch belt or a thick powerlifting belt may interfere with lifts that require a deep squat position. This problem can be avoided by using a belt that is narrower in the front. Also, when performing the snatch lift, many weight lifters will not use a belt at all, since the bar can catch on it as it moves past the waist.
2. Just prior to doing a set, tighten the belt as much as possible.
3. Take a trunk stabilizing breath and close the glottis (Valsalva maneuver) to increase ITP.
4. Tighten the abdominal muscles and push or squeeze against the belt to increase IAP as needed. The IAP will vary throughout the lift.
5. Perform the lifting action, making sure to maintain a stable and tight feeling trunk throughout the lift.
6. Perform the lifting action and begin to exhale after the "sticking point."
7. At the completion of the lift one should exhale completely and be ready to perform the next repetition in the same manner as the first.

Lander, Jeffrey E., Why Use A Belt?; Strength-Power Update; Auburn University; Volume 1 Number 3; p. 1-4; Summer, 1986.

THEORY & PRACTICE

A WORD ABOUT AIR BELTS

The air inflatable belt has been recently introduced to the weight training and body building arena (around 1990). It has great potential for improving the ability to train effectively and comfortably. It is a uniquely designed air inflatable nylon covered rubber air bladder combined with a leather backing which provides non-baffled air chambers that conforms to the waist. This advanced design allows complete unrestricted activity while providing support, warmth and passive massage when the belt is used at all levels of activity.

There are many sizes and types of air belts that have been introduced into the fitness market since 1990. The most efficacious belt uses a large (6-8") non-baffled air bladder backed by leather in combination with a secure fastening device (buckle or velcro). The 6-8" back tapers to about three inches as it wraps around the sides of the waist. This design follows the natural curves of the midsection of the body. A three inch fabric strap continues to the front from both sides of the non-baffled air bladder which is fastened with a sliding adjustable velcro/buckle arrangement to allow one belt to fit a variety of sizes.

The more sophisticated large air belt (like the Astro-Back) functions on the principle of distributed air pressure on the muscles and soft tissues. The design allows the belt to exactly contour to the shape of the body while intra-abdominal pressure increases during activity. The benefit of this device is that it prevents muscle and soft tissue distortion while providing increased lumbar support. When movement of the body occurs there is increased intra-abdominal pressure which supports and unloads the spine.

Dr. Paul Ward, former Indiana University/Washington Redskin Stewart O'Dell and EHOB Incorporated were intimately involved in the design and introduction of the first air belt to the marketplace known as the Astro-Back. To improve the unloading of the spine, Dr. Ward introduced the concept of adding a large abdominal pad to the belt. This supplemental four to six inch square abdominal pad provides extra surface area on which the abdominal muscles can push against when the belt is securely fastened around the waist. This increases the intra-abdominal pressure which unloads and supports the spine.

In the past, increasing the abdominal surface area using a leather weight belt has been observed to raise the intra-abdominal pressure which resulted in unloading the spine during performing heavy squats. The additional abdominal surface area was provided by turning a leather weight belt with a 6-8 inch back so that the large part (6-8" back) of the belt was in the front. This allowed a broad comfortable surface area for the abdominal muscles to push against which made it easier to greatly increase IAP and thus many lifting performances.

Dr. Ward and two of his athletes (1972 Olympian Ken Patera and World Class Power Lifter Gary Young [1964-68]) discovered this concept during a weight training session at Portland State University in the early 1965. Subsequent applications and observations of this procedure has proven to substantiate this innovation. Most training concepts and innovations have their origin **"in the gym,"** and are not generated in the scientific laboratory.

THE APPLICATION OF THE "SUPPLEMENTAL ABDOMINAL PAD" WITH THE USE OF A TRADITIONAL LOW BACK SUPPORT DEVICE OR ANY OTHER LOW BACK SUPPORT DEVICE IS DESTINED TO BECOME THE MOST EFFECTIVE LOW BACK SUPPORT APPARATUS FOR PHYSICAL TRAINING, ATHLETIC PARTICIPATION AND INDUSTRIAL LOW BACK SUPPORT.

Traditional leather weight belts and other lower back support devices cause distortion of the back muscles and soft tissue plus they mechanically restrict blood flow within the active muscles. These conventional devices present an undesired pressure gradient which is ineffective in preventing the deformation of body tissues. The entrapment and resulting deformation of muscle and other soft tissue between the skeleton and these traditional lumbar back supports produce the undesirable effects mentioned above.

It is known that support surfaces are necessary to maintain the viability of muscle and soft tissue; however, various types of pressure surfaces can detrimentally affect the muscle and soft tissue integrity between the skeletal structure and the support surface. This is the case with most leather and other none yielding weight belts. **The most effective supportive device will equalize and distribute pressure over the entire contact surface.** Air belts with large non-baffled bladders having broad surface areas, very effectively equalizes and distributes pressure across the entire contact surfaces.

Low back support belts using large non-baffled air bladders which have a large back (6-8") allow the muscles of the low back and midsection to remain in proper alignment, increase muscle temperature and provide a massaging effect during movement with use. These devices deliver equalized pressure against the entire contact surface and prevent muscle and soft tissue distortion.

During increased physical activity muscles require additional oxygen and nutrients, and removal of harmful metabolic by-products such as lactic acid. Therefore, **preventing this internal distortion and facilitating blood flow is the key to maintaining healthy muscle, optimal muscle functioning, while preserving musculo-skeletal alignment which allows one to train more vigorously.**

Air belts with large non-baffled bladders which conform agreeably to the lumbar and waist areas offer at least two notable advantages.

1. Normal breathing and body movement create a light massaging pressure variant to the lower back muscles to further relax the lumbo-sacral region. Massage is a noted benefit in soothing muscles, decreasing spasm and increasing blood flow to the muscles.

2. The lumbar support device responds with higher pressure when more support to the lower back is needed; during aerobic activity, increased bending and lifting, or increased strain on the lower back. This is due to the fact that the volume of the air bladder is decreased secondary to the tightening of the circumferential device around the body because of increased abdominal pressure. This increased air pressure in the non-baffled single chamber which is compliant enough to allow conformation to the low back area produces great support to the lumbar region. This same structure, when backed by a rigid leather surface and placed in a circumferential way around the body provides comfortable, unrestricted support to the lower back during all types of passive and aggressive movement.

These advantages are of great benefit to body builders, athletes and general fitness participant who desire support of the low back during training and performance. Furthermore, the use of the this device is beneficial when performing aerobic exercises, biking and running as well as participation in any sporting or work activity. This device does not restrict movement or range of motion in activity; is comfortable at rest and in physical activity; and provides support to the lower back in vigorous physical activity and sports participation.

Exercise to increase muscular strength and flexibility training of the abdominal and low back area is of utmost importance in lower back care. Any support device used should promote these goals as well as promoting correct, comfortable posture. In conjunction with the intended purpose of a supportive device, it is extremely important that the circulation in the soft tissue and muscle be protected from the adverse effects of constriction and pressure-related distortion. Delivering the low back support by equalized air pressure using these non-baffled air bladder low back support devices, has proven advantages because of the lack of distortion of the muscles and soft tissues as well as the lack of restriction of blood flow to the low back and midsection. The unique design enables fluctuating pressures to create a massaging variant, as well as to act as a self-regulated pressure support of the lumbar area.

The large non-baffled air bladders backed with leather are very effective when used in non-active situations and in vigorous physical training, work and sports participation.

THEORY & PRACTICE

RELATED REFERENCES

1. Barnes, G., Laine, G., Giam, P., Smith, E., & Granger, H. (1985). Cardiovascular responses to elevation of intra-abdominal hydro-static pressure. "Am J Physiol," 248, (2), R208-213.

2. Chaffin, Don & Anderson, Gunar, (1991). "Occupational Biomechanics;" John Wiley & Sons, Inc.; New York, 1991; Chapter 5.

3. Davis, P. (1959). Posture of the trunk during the lifting of weights. "Brit Med J," 1, 87-89.

4. Davis, P., & Troup, J. (1964). Pressure in the trunk cavities when pulling, pushing, and lifting. "Ergonomics," 7, 465-474.

5. Eie, N. (1966). Load capacity of the low back. "J Oslo City Hosp," 16, 73-98.

6. Eie, N. (1973). Recent measurements of the intra-abdominal pressure. In R.M. Kenedi (Ed.), "Perspectives in Biomedical Engineering." Baltimore: University Park Press.

7. Eie, N., & Wehn, P. (1962). Measurements of the intra-abdominal pressure in relation to weight bearing of the lumbosacral spine. "J Oslo City Hosp.," 12, 205-217.

8. Elisberg, E.I. (1963). Heart rate responses to he valsalva maneuver as test of circulatory integrity. "JAMA," 186, 200-205.

9. Fox, I. (1966). Effects of the valsalva maneuver on blood flow in the thoracic aorta in man. "Appl Physiol," 21, 1553-1560.

10. Grew, N., & Deane, G. (1982). The physical effect of lumbar spinal supports. "Pros Orth Int," 6, 79-87.

11. Grieve, D. (1977). The dynamics of lifting. "Exer Sports Sci Rev." 5, 157-179.

12. Grillner, S., Nilsson, J., & Thorstensson, A. (1978). Intra-abdominal pressure changes during natural movements in man. "Acta Phys Scand," 103(3), 275-283.

13. Hall, S. (1985). Effect of attempted lifting speed on forces and torque exerted on-the lumbar spine. "Med Sci Sports Exer," 17(4), 440-444.

14. Harman, E.A., et al. (1988) Intra-abdominal and intra-thoracic pressures during lifting and jumping. "Med Sci Sports Exerc." 20(2):195-201.

15. Harman, E.A., et al., (1987) Generation of IAP and intra-thoracic pressure (ITP) during weight lifting. "J. Appl Sport Sci Res" 1(3):54, abstract.

16. Hemborg, B., Moritz, U., & Lowing, H. (1985). Intra-abdominal pressure and trunk muscle activity during lifting. "Scand J Rehab Med," 17, 25-38.

17. Hemborg, B., Moritz, U., (1985) Intra-abdominal pressure and trunk muscle activity during lifting; II. Chronic low-back patients; "Scan J Rehab Med" 17;5-13.

18. Hemborg, B., Moritz, U., Hamberg, J., Holmstrom, E., Lowing, H., Akesson, I., (1985). Intra-abdominal pressure and trunk muscle activity during lifting; III. Effect of abdominal muscle training in chronic low-back patients; "Scan J. Rehab Med," 17:15-24.

19. Hemborg, B., Noritz, U., Lowing, H, (1985). Intra-abdominal pressure and trunk muscle activity during lifting; IV. The causal factors of the intra-abdominal pressure rise; "Scan J Rehab Med" 17:25-38.

20. Hemborg, B., Moritz, U., Hamberg, J., Lowing, H., Akesson, I., (1983) Intra-abdominal pressure and trunk muscle activity during lifting - effect of abdominal muscle training in healthy subjects; "Scan J Rehab Med" 15:183-196.

21. Jager, M., Luttman, A., (1989) Biomechanical analysis and assessment of lumbar stress during load lifting using a dynamic 19-segment human model. "Ergonomics," 32(1):93-112.

22. Kumar, S., & Davis, P. (1976). Interrelationship of physiological and biomechanical parameters during stoop lifting. In F. Landry & W. Orban (Eds.), "Biomech Sp & Kin" (pp. 181-191). Miami: Symposia Specialists.

23. Kumar, S., & Godfrey, C. (1986). Spinal braces and abdominal support. In W. Karwowski (Ed.), "Trends in Ergonomics/Human Factors III" (pp. 717-726). North-Holland: Elsevier Science.

24. Kumar, S., & Davis, P. (1983). Spinal loading in static and dynamic postures: EMG and intra-abdominal pressure study. "Ergonomics," 26(9), 913-922.

25. Lander, J. (1986). Biomechanics of the squat exercise using a modified center of mass bar. "Med Sci Sports Exerc," 18(4).

26. Lander, J. (1980). Heart rate, valsalva maneuver and maximal isometric contractions. Unpublished research paper.

27. Lander, J.E., Hundley, J.R., Simonton, R.L., (1992). The effectiveness of weight belts during multiple repetitions of the squat exercise. "Med. Sci. Sports Exerc." Accepted for publication 1992.

28. Lander, J., Simonton, L. and J. Giacobbe, (1990). The Effectiveness of weight-belts during the squat exercise. "Medicine and Science in Sports and Exercise," Volume 22, # 1, February, 1990; pp. 117-126.

29. Levine, A. (1984). Spinal orthoses. "Am Fed Pros," 29(3), 277-280.

30. Leskinen T., et al., (1985). Hip torque, L-S compression and IAP in lifting and lowering tasks. In: "Biomechanics IXb," Winter, DA (ed) Human Kinetics Publ. Champaign, IL, pp 5-59.

31. McGill, S.M., Norman, R.W., Sharratt, M.T., (1990). The Effect of an abdominal belt on trunk muscle activity and intra-abdominal pressure during squat lifts. "Ergonomics," 33(2):147-160.

32. Million, R., Nilsen, K., Jayson, M., & Baker, R. (1981). Evaluation of low back pain and assessment of lumbar corsets with and with-out back supports. "Ann Rheu Dis," 40, 449-454.

33. Morris, J., Lucas, D., & Bresler, B. (1961). Role of the trunk in stability of the spine. "J Bone Jt. Surg," 43-A, 327-351.

34. Nordin, M., Eflstrom, G., & Dahlquist, P. (1984). Intra-abdominal pressure measurements using a wireless radio pressure pill and two wire connected pressure transducers: A comparison. "Scand J Rhab Med," 16, 139-146.

35. Primiano, F. (1962). Theoretical analysis of chest wall mechanics. "J Biomechanics," 13912, 919-931.

36. Schultz, A., Warwick, D., Berkson, M., & Nachemson, A. (1979). Mechanical properties of human lumbar spine segments: Part I. "Trans ASME," 101, 46-52.

37. Troup, J.D.G., Leskinen, T.P.J., Stalhammar, H.R., Kuorinka, I.A.A., (1983). A comparison of intra-abdominal pressure increases, hip torque, and lumbar vertebral compression in different lifting techniques. "Human Factors," 25(5):517-525.

38. Wedin, S., Leanderson, R., Knutsson, W. (1988). The effect of voluntary diaphragmatic activation on back lifting; "Scand J Rehab Med" 20:129-132.

USE OF WRIST AND KNEE WRAPS, SUPER SUITS, SUPER SHIRTS AND LIFTING SHOES

INTRODUCTION

In the 1950's, the authors as young boys observed that they were able to squat with heavier weights when training in Levis. The crotch of more Levi jeans were torn than can be remembered. In the 1960's, while teaching at Portland State University, one of the authors observed World Champion power lifters wrapping bed sheets around their waists, wearing women's girdles and placing tennis balls at back of knees wrapped tightly with knee wraps all for the purpose of squatting with greater poundage. Of course the rules and officiating at that time were somewhat lax. **THE AUTHORS OF THIS BOOK DO NOT RECOMMEND THAT THESE BIZARRE TECHNIQUES BE USED. THEY ARE MENTIONED HERE, ONLY FOR HISTORICAL PURPOSES.**

Furthermore, it was empirically observed that the shoes or lifting boots worn during lifting weights can impact the amount of weight lifted in pulling, squatting and overhead pushing exercises. This led to the use of work boots and military style boots being used for training and competitions until specifically designed weight lifting shoes became available.

Over the years of training in many gyms with very strong men and women, it has been observed that wrapping the wrists, knees and elbow joints, as well as, the muscles of the arms and legs and using supportive boots increased the ability to lift more weight in a variety of exercises. These observations have resulted in the commercial development of knee wraps, wrist wraps, super suits, super shirts and lifting boots. The knee and wrist wraps were developed in the 1960's and 1970's; the super suites (by Inzer) were first introduced in the late 1970's; and, the super shirts were introduced in the early 1980's. **(Conversation with Dr. Fred Hatfield, the first man to officially squat over 1000 pounds in competition.)**

Specially designed lifting boots and shoes have been used for a long time in elite Olympic lifting but their commercial development and use in power lifting and general training appeared in the 1970's. Lifting shoes have been more commonly used in training and competition in recent times. Presently, there are rigid regulations controlling the use of wrist and knee wraps, super suits, super shirts, belts and boots when lifting in competition. However, training variants of these supportive devices are employed very frequently in gyms all over the world. More will be said about this latter.

There is very little research and a dearth of written information regarding the use of these training aids. The authors have found only three publications that have presented research reports on lifting aids. Escamilla (1987) reported the results of a study in the use of powerlifting aids in the squat exercise. The aids used in this study were super-suits and knee wraps. In addition to using these aids the powerlifters used belts which were worn all the time during the squatting activities.

Since 1RM's were considered too hazardous for testing, 3RM's were used as an indicator of strength. This procedure was followed because the subjects would not agree to perform maximum lifts without lifting aids. Three males and three females competitive powerlifters were used as subjects. The average difference between the use and non-use of powerlifting aids was 12.94 percent in favor of the lifting aids. Five out of the six lifters

THEORY & PRACTICE   PART I

increased between 10 and 18 percent when using powerlifting aids while one only increased 6 percent. The subjects ranged 20-43 years in age; 116-201 pounds in body weight and 60-72 inches in height. The 3RM squatting poundage ranged between 280 and 550 pounds.

The study concluded that the use of powerlifting aids (super-suits and knee wraps) during the squat caused an increase in the amount of weight that could be lifted.

Escamilla, Rafael, "A cinematographical examination of powerlifting aids while performing the squat," Master's Thesis, Washington State University; May, 1987.

THE RATIONALE FOR USING SUPER-SUITS, SUPER SHIRTS, KNEE WRAPS AND WRIST WRAPS IN TRAINING

While it has been empirically shown that super-suits will increase one's ability to squat heavy poundage, it is the authors' recommendations that suits should not be used routinely in training. Firstly, it takes some time and a lot of effort to get into the suit. Secondly, while the suit allows lifting heavier weight, it is good to train without all this supportive devices to adequately strengthen the muscles, tendons, ligaments and connective tissue. Using this supportive device routinely in training may serve to weaken some tissues that are not adequately stressed when using the suit. Thirdly, super suits can be used occasionally in training when going for a heavy weight to assess the level of one's strength and or to train for maximum force development in some lifting movements, primarily the bench press, squat and dead lift.

The same evaluation as stated for the super suits can be made concerning the super shirts. Generally, it is not wise to use the super-shirt routinely in training for the same reasons stated for the super suit. Occasional use of the super shirt in training is acceptable when assessing one's strength level, however, the super shirt should not be routinely used.

Wrist wraps and knee wraps may be used in daily training with some reservations. These supportive wraps should only be used in lifts that are above 80% 1RM, unless one is injured. On the other hand, if one is injured it would be best to use lighter, non-stressing weights until any knee or wrist injury is healed. Furthermore, there should be times when wraps are not used at all during training to strengthen the supporting structures in the wrists and knees.

Olympic lifters may have to use wrist straps at lower intensities than the suggested 80% 1RM. This is acceptable, although, if injuries persist, the lifter should seek medical advice and reduce the training stress on the wrists until healed. More information about knee wraps is presented in the next few pages. No research was found regarding the use of super shirts or wrist straps in training and competition.

THE USE OF KNEE WRAPS IN TRAINING AND COMPETITION

There are many opinions about the use of knee wraps, but no valid scientific research to support their use in training or competition. However, there is a vast amount of practical experience that can be used to draw satisfactory conclusions about the use of knee wraps. Empirical observations, definitely have demonstrated that the use of knee wraps with various methods of wrapping will increase squatting performance by 10% to 20%.

Some people show concern about those who abuse the use of knee wraps. This is commendable, however, objectivity should be the driving force behind educational efforts. Unfortunately, many self proclaimed authorities have let their opinions and philosophical positions motivate a negative opinion of the use of knee wraps.

It is a flaw in human nature to abuse just about any training tool or technique. When this happens, some people may get injured. This happenstance does not invalidate the proper use of the training tool or technique. Knee wraps have been found to be effective and safe when applied in an intelligent manner. However, research should be performed to investigate the biomechanical implications, the physiological costs and benefits, the methods of wrapping along with the study of prevention of injury when using knee wraps.

It is not useful to condemn the use of knee wraps based on philosophical positions and the lack of valid scientific research. This is especially ignorant in view of the practical experience of literally millions of humans who use knee wraps in training. The approach to educating people about using knee wraps in training and, where appropriate, in competition, should be one of presenting the facts and developing guidelines for their use.

Knee wraps can be used effectively and safely in training and competition, where appropriate.

REASONS FOR USING KNEE WRAPS

Knee wraps are used for the following reasons:

1. Joint warmth.
2. External support to the joint which increases the ability to apply maximum force.
3. Reduction of joint injury.

If joint warmth is desired, a neoprene sleeve is the safest and best method of increasing and sustaining warmth in the knee joint area. Also, external support of the knee joint is enhanced by the reasonable application of knee wraps. For general training, they may be used regularly if not applied with "competition tightness." The application of very tight knee wraps during precompetition training and competition should be limited to very short time periods. The potential for knee wraps to prevent injuries to the knee joint has not been thoroughly substantiated in the scientific literature. Knee joint injury seems to be related more to improper performance technique and to continued training misuse and competition abuse.

FIVE MECHANISMS THAT EXPLAIN THE BENEFIT OF USING KNEE WRAPS

Harman and Frykman (1990) suggest five mechanisms that may explain the known benefits for using knee wraps. These five mechanisms are:

1. The use of knee wraps provide direct mechanical assistance in which the elastic knee wrap material when stretched over the kneecap exerts a force that tends to extend the knee.

2. The use of knee wraps increases the warmth of the knee joints, which enhances blood flow and increases the pliability of the knee tissues, making them less likely to tear when exposed to high forces.

3. The use of knee wraps improves kinesthetic cuing, wherein the physical sensation of the wraps on the knees provides the lifter with better awareness of the knee angle, thereby improving motor control and the ability to make adjustments in technique.

4. The use of knee wraps assists in maintaining the patella in its proper track. If the vastus lateralis and vastus medialis muscles on the thigh do not exert equal force, there is a tendency for the patella (knee cap) to be pulled to either side, out of its normal track. Neuromuscular control could suppress the asymmetrical component of muscle force to avert such de-tracking. The wraps might eliminate the need for such neural inhibition, allowing greater muscle force to be exerted and more weight lifted.

5. The use of knee wraps enhances the psychological state. The wraps might improve the lifter's feeling of security, increasing the likelihood of an maximal effort.

METHODS OF COVERING THE KNEES

There are four basic methods of wrapping the knees.

1. **MULTI-LAYER HORIZONTAL WRAP:** The multi-layer horizontal wrap is effective for providing external support to the knee joint. This technique has been found to be effective for increasing squatting performance. This technique involves starting a short distance below the knee with the wrap coming from behind the knee and up on the inside of the knee with succeeding overlapping ascending horizontal wraps extending from below the knee to just above the knee. The end of the wrap is tucked into the preceding layer to secure.

2. **MULTI-LAYER CROSS PATELLAR WRAP:** The multi-layer cross patella wrap is effective for providing external support to the knee joint. This technique has been found to be effective in increasing squatting performance. This technique involves starting below the knee with one or two ascending overlapping horizontal wraps and then crossing diagonally over the patella to the upper leg, followed by a horizontal wrap and then a crossing of the patella to the lower leg. This procedure is duplicated until the wrap is fully used and then tucked into the preceding layer to secure.

3. **SINGLE-LAYER SLEEVE:** A single layer elastic sleeve can be used for providing warmth. This type of wrap does not give external support and does not produce increases in squatting performance beyond the warmth effect. A neoprene sleeve is a better method of providing warmth for the knee. It does not provide external joint support and therefore will not produce increases in squatting performance beyond the warmth effect.

4. **MULTI-LAYER WRAP OVER THE PATELLAR LIGAMENT ONLY:** This technique involves placing an elastic wrap around the lower leg just below the knee cap for two to three inch multi-layered area. This device is not particularly effective for relieving pain and definitely does not provide external support to the knee joint. This technique is not used very much.

RESEARCH ON USING KNEE WRAPS DURING SQUATTING EXERCISES

A search of the scientific literature has not produced any quality research in the effectiveness of using knee wraps during training with regard to their effectiveness in improving squatting performance or for preventing injury. Harman and Frykman (1990) attempted to investigate the existence and magnitude of a direct mechanical effect of using knee wraps for the squatting exercise. The validity of their method of ascertaining this effect is seriously questioned.

The results of their study showed that the use of knee wraps did in fact increase the vertical force on the feet in a back squatting position. They claimed that in one subject the vertical force of the wraps could be tripled by using two knee wraps on each knee when compared to just one knee wrap on each knee.

These authors claimed that the one diagonal wrapping across the patella created approximately 11 pounds of tension. In most wrapping techniques the wrap crosses the patella from six to nine times which would have accounted for 66 to 99 pounds of tension for each leg. They estimated that a total wrap tension per leg of 75 pounds would be created and that this amount of force would be necessary to produce the increased vertical force they observed in their experiment.

Unfortunately, these authors presented a philosophical discussion about the ethics of using knee wraps in competition. While they have every right to express their opinions, opinions supported only on a philosophical basis have no place in the presentation of a research report.

GENERAL USE OF KNEE WRAPS IN TRAINING AND COMPETITION

Olympic weight lifters are allowed during competition to use knee wraps which cover only 30 centimeters (12") of the leg. There is no limit on the length of the knee wrap. The extensive use of knee wraps during competition is not observed because they impede the free movement into a deep squat in the snatch and clean lifts.

For powerlifting competition the leg can only be covered up to 30 centimeters (12"). The knee wrap must not exceed 2 meters (78.7") in length and must be no wider that 8 centimeters (3.1') in width in the unstretched state. There is extensive use of knee wraps in the squat lift during powerlifting competition.

Knee wraps are primarily used during weight training in the squatting exercise. Powerlifters use knee wraps in training and competition. Many general weight trainers, body builders as well as athletes at all levels, use knee wraps during weight training. Some Olympic lifters use knee wraps when back squatting with very heavy weights during training while most of the other lifts are performed without the use of knee wraps for good reasons.

The logic that governs the limited use of knee wraps during all training exercises except very heavy back squats by Olympic lifters is based on three factors:

1. Large amounts of wrapping may interfere with the bar clearance at the knee level.
2. The added knee wrapping makes it difficult to easily drop into a deep squatting position under the weight.
3. The added wrapping produces forces on the knee joint that pulls the knee joint apart when squatting under the bar which predisposes the knee joint to injury.

In powerlifting competition and in general training, their are two concerns.

1. If the knee wraps are applied very tightly a "scribe effect" occurs on the muscle tissue at the edge of the wrapping resulting in tissue damage.
2. Chondromalacia patellae (wearing down and roughening of the inner surface of the knee cap) has been observed in powerlifting and has been attributed to prolonged use of overly tight knee wraps.

These two concerns can be minimized by using the following guidelines:

1. Use good quality wraps that have maintained their elasticity.
2. Pay attention to how the wrap is applied; i.e., horizontal wrapping or cross the patella wrapping. Both methods are acceptable but each one may result in different problems. Very tight horizontal wrapping may produce the "scribe effect," while the tight cross the knee cap wrapping may contribute to chondromalacia patellae. Reasonable use does not seem to produce either the "scribe effect" or chondromalacia patellae.
3. Very tight competition knee wrapping should be applied in training for short periods during precompetition and competition, but never on a day-to-day basis.
4. During each training session where knee wraps are used, they should be removed immediately after the completion of each set of the exercise.
5. Knee wraps should not be used in ballistic squatting exercises like going under the weight in the squat snatch or squat clean lifts and their variations.
6. Some protection may be afforded against the "scribe effect" by applying the knee wrap over a neoprene sleeve.

PART I

THEORY & PRACTICE

GUIDELINES FOR USING KNEE WRAPS

1. Warm up the knees well prior to heavy full squat movements or other power exercises through general warm-up exercises, massage or topical rubs. Neoprene sleeves are useful to improve knee joint warmth.
2. The icing of the knees after workouts as needed will aid in recovery.
3. If knee pain appears, check the exercise techniques and consult a sports medicine expert for diagnosis and treatment.
4. Use supplementary exercises to strengthen the muscles on all sides of the knee joints.
5. Perform the squatting action correctly:

   A. Use full range of motion squatting actions.
   B. Use good technique: don't bounce at the bottom, keep back tight and arched, keep the lower leg vertical and in no case allow the knees to extend beyond the toes.
   C. Use knee wraps wisely. Do not wrap until reaching 80 percent of 1RM. Try not wrapping extremely tight most of the time. Only use competition tight wrapping for precompetition training and competition (four to six weeks).
   D. Plan for training time where knee wraps are not used at all, and, where intensity does not exceed 80% to 90% 1RM.
   E. Use many exercise variations to condition the legs and hips from many different angles: front squats, horizontal leg presses, inverted angled leg presses, hack squats, leg curls, dead lift variations, calf exercises, pulling variations, knee extensions and back squatting variations.
   F. Use the principles of periodization.

6. Develop correct technique in any squat snatching or squat cleaning exercises and their variations.

1. Harman, Everett and Frykman, Peter; The effects of knee wraps on weight lifting performance and injury; National Strength and Conditioning Association Journal, Volume 12, Number 5, 1990; pp. 30-35.

2. Totten, Leo; KneeWraps; National Strength and Conditioning Association Journal, Volume 12, Number 5, 1990; pp. 36-38.

THE USE OF WEIGHT LIFTING SHOES IN TRAINING

Weight training has become very popular over the last 30 years. Many people spend 4 to 10 hours per week in the gym. Technology has improved along with the rising popularity of weight training with the production of new equipment and development of training aids, such as super-suits, wraps, belts and lifting boots. Even with the availability of these advanced training aids, people seem to ignore the need for satisfactory footwear. Most people wear inadequate shoes when weight training. It can be observed that a variety of running shoes and general athletic shoes are worn by most people training in the gym today. Apparently, there is little consideration of footwear by the average person to their detriment.

Running shoes and general athletic shoes are designed for running and general athletic activities. These shoes cannot meet the needs for the weight lifting environment and activities. The weight lifting shoe is built to minimize deformation and to support the foot, arch and ankle. The properly designed weight lifting shoe also has a heel to enhance balance during various lifting actions. Well designed lifting shoes/boot are produced by Adidas, Nike, Pignatti and various other companies.

WEIGHT LIFTING SHOE REQUIREMENTS (GARHAMMER 1987):

1. Flat thin sole that forms a solid base.
2. Light shoe.

3. Snug fit with strap over the arch.
4. Shoe with a slightly elevated heel.
5. A shoe that minimizes the sole and shoe deformation.

In summary, the properly designed weight lifting shoe will provide for full foot support, accommodate balance shifts, short range fast movement and a rising on the toes with minimal sole and shoe deformation. The well constructed shoe supports the foot, arch and ankle.

Weight lifting shoes can also be purchased through the United States Weightlifting Federation at the address listed below:

United States Weightlifting Federation (USWF)
1750 E. Boulder Street
Colorado Springs, CO 80909

Garhammer, J.; Lower level thoughts: lifting shoes and surfaces; Strength-Power Update; Vol 2; #2; Spring 1987; pp. 2-3.

UNDERSTANDING EXERCISE EQUIPMENT

When body building and training for sport one is confronted with deciding which kind of equipment is the best. Should free weights be the choice? Are machines of any benefit? If machines are useful, which brand should be used? Should the weight trainer use constant resistance machines, variable resistance machines or accommodating resistance (isokinetic) machines? The body builder and athlete is in a quandary.

The solution is to use all equipment with all the variations in a pre-planned program using the principles of periodization (cycling) and scientific principles of weight training and body building. It is important to remember that free weights and machines are just tools. The correct application of tools permits the successful completion of the job. Once this concept is understood, then the equipment dilemma is resolved. However, it is generally accepted by most weight training and body building experts and empirically observed that free weights (including dumbbells) are the most effective equipment for training and produce the best results when programmed correctly.

The local gym equipment selection, personal preference, training objectives and level of development will dictate for most people which equipment will be used. Machines are very effective in the beginning stages of training and for general conditioning. As improvement in strength and muscular development accumulates there is a natural migration toward free weights and dumbbells. However, there is never complete independence from the use of machines. Machines provide many great exercises that are difficult to duplicate with free weights, and, therefore, various machines are an integral part of an intelligent body building and weight training program.

There is no equipment company that ranks superior to others. If machines are properly employed in a scientific body building or weight training program, the user will be successful and satisfied. The ultimate tests for the body builder and weight trainer are; **"does the exercise feel good"** and **"does using it produce results"**. **No gimmick, training plan or machine has been universally accepted unless it feels good and produces results. That is the bottom line.**

This part of the Encyclopedia of Weight Training will discuss the kinds of resistance available, research comparing constant resistance and variable resistance, the free weight versus machines controversy and unilateral, reciprocal and bilateral exercise.

THEORY & PRACTICE | PART I

KINDS OF RESISTANCE

Methods of applying resistance are classified into four categories: (1) isometric resistance; (2) constant resistance; (3) variable resistance; and, (4) accommodating resistance. All free weight equipment and machines fall into one of these four categories. "Specificity rules." This means that strength gains developed are specific for each machine, method and exercise practiced. There is little or no transfer to other unlike devices or movements. Morphological changes may occur using any type of resistance device, however, to be functional, strength training must be as specific as possible, biomechanically and neuromuscularly.

1. ISOMETRIC OR STATIC RESISTANCE

Machines or devices that allow for the application of force by muscle groups and do not permit movement are known to be isometric or static exercise machines or devices. They allow for application of force on a bar or lever at various points throughout the range of motion for a specific movement. Research has shown that isometric resistance can produce changes in strength but only at the exact positions trained. It would take exercise at a great number of positions in all movements to produce usable strength throughout the complete range of motion. This would require a long training session which would make it impractical except in the training of highly skilled elite athletes or in specific injury rehabilitation programs.

While isometric exercises have been shown to produce gains in strength, large increases in muscle mass does not result from the application of isometric exercise. Experts believe that application of other kinds of resistances are more beneficial than isometric resistance.

Furthermore, there are no general commercial resistance exercise machines that have been designed specifically for isometric training. One would have to develop various and unique techniques to use common resistance exercise machines for isometric training. This would involve extending training time, which is impractical. Generally, application of isometric training is not worth the time and energy expended unless one has the desire and a specific need for this type of training.

2. CONSTANT RESISTANCE

When the resistance (load) on a bar or machine is constant throughout the range of motion it is called constant resistance. Even though the resistance remains constant throughout the range of motion, the lifting effort changes as the system of muscles and levers (bones) change positions. Assuming the velocity of movement remains constant, the weight feels lighter or heavier as the joint angle changes throughout the range of motion, even though the weight on the machine or bar remains constant. The feeling (relative effort) of heavy or light is dependent upon the changing leverages and the speed of movement.

The amount of weight lifted is dependent upon the muscle strength at the weakest position in the range of motion. Many people try to overcome this problem by doing unusual movements (usually by cheating movements) or by trying to accelerate the weight or machine so that when the sticking point is reached there is enough momentum to carry the weight beyond this sticking point. The sticking point for any exercise is the weakest position in the range of motion. It varies with the exercise and the individual muscle-skeletal leverages.

Basically, these abnormal techniques are not recommended as they inhibit the strengthening of the muscles at the sticking points (weak points) in the range of motion of the exercise being performed. It is better to perform the exercise without cheating movements and at a speed that is commensurate with training theory (usually at a relatively slow rate of movement).

Simple fixed lever machines and pulley machines are examples of constant resistance. A simple pulldown station and the older Universal Gym Gladiator bench press and shoulder press stations are illustrations of constant resistance machines. Machines that use neutral cams (a cam that has the shape of a wheel - perfectly round) are also categorized as constant resistance exercise machines. In machines that use pulleys, the standard pulley insures that the resistance remains the same throughout the range of motion. In machines using lever arms the weight attachment is fixed so that there is no change in leverage throughout the range of motion.

Constant resistance machines and devices are very effective in producing morphological changes and strength changes, especially if the correct programs and techniques are adhered to and the speed of movement is reasonable. When these conditions are satisfied, very good results can accrue for all fitness levels. This type of resistance may be the best type for improving sport performance. Furthermore, the jury is still out regarding which type of resistance is best for producing hypertrophy.

3. VARIABLE RESISTANCE

The body is constructed in a series of levers (bones) and fulcrums (joints) with muscles pulling on the levers (bones) to produce motion. Man's skeletal system is comprised mostly of third class levers which favor speed and range of motion. In this type of lever the force (muscle pulling force) is between the fulcrum and the resistance.

Within the range of motion of any movement there is a point where the body's leverage is unfavorable (known as the sticking point or the weakest position in the range of motion). Also, there are other positions in the range of motion where the body's leverage is very good and, conversely, there are positions that are relatively weaker. The force expression of a muscle or muscle group changes throughout the range of motion. This is known as the strength curve and the strength curve for every joint is different in shape (form) and magnitude.

In movements of flexion the weakest point in the range of motion is usually at the very end of the flexion movement because the angle of pull by the muscles on the bones is most unfavorable. The angle of pull is so acute (pulling along the length of the bone) that any muscular force in this position is almost pulling the major bone out of its joint. Also, at the end of a flexion movement the muscle is almost completely contracted; and, therefore, the force development potential is small. The second weakest position for flexion exercises is near the very beginning of the flexion movement. The point of greatest strength is when the joint is at a ninety degree angle and the major muscles causing the action are pulling on the principal bone in a perpendicular direction.

In most extension lifts, the sticking point generally is slightly past the mid-range of the movement. The amount of weight that one can lift, therefore, is limited by how much can be moved through the sticking point; consequently, only a small part of the muscle being exercised receives maximum resistance. Another problem attendant to this is that of inertia (momentum). As the weight begins to move it gathers momentum, which actually makes it easier to continue to move. Again, only a small portion of the muscle receives maximum work. The point of greatest strength for extension movements is near the end of the movement.

Since the ability of the muscle or muscle group to apply force changes as one works through the range of motion and the speed of movement produces unwanted momentum, machines have been developed to match the muscle leverage changes or to minimize the effects of momentum. The leverage of the machines are manipulated to fit the changes in the muscle leverage (strength curves) over the full range of motion. This is accomplished by using either a cam or a rolling lever arm. Figure 1-4 presents two different methods of varying resistance commonly used in the construction of weight machines.

A cam changes the resistance as it rotates. The change in resistance is caused by the change in the radius of the cam as it turns. The resistance increases as the length of the cam radius increases. In Figure 1-4, Diagram 1, the radius is 6 inches at position "A" and increases to 12 inches at position "B". Thus the resistance increases as the cam moves from position "A" to position "B".

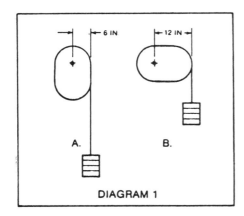
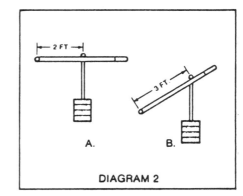

Figure 1-4.   Examples of two methods of varying resistance in the construction of weight machines.

In the rolling lever technique of varying resistance, the resistance changes as the length of the lever arm changes. In Figure 1-4, Diagram 2, the lever arm is 2 feet at position "A" and increases to 3 feet at position "B". Thus the resistance increases as the lever length increases. This change in resistance is produced when moving the rolling lever arm from position "A" to position "B".

The rolling lever arm technique of varying resistance seems to be effective for extension movements but has limited application for flexion movements in the resistance machine formats that exist today. On the other hand, cams can be configured to generally accommodate the strength curves of most movements, including flexion and extension movements. However, it must be said, it is very difficult to design a cam that will precisely match the strength curve of the joints involved in the movements of various exercise machines, so equipment companies use an approximate cam in the construction of assorted machines. Some cam machines feel good while others are very uncomfortable because the cam is mismatched for the strength curve.

Unfortunately, very little research has been published concerning strength curves of all the possible exercise movements and the related shape of the cams or the configuration of the rolling lever arms for exercise machines. Also, it has yet to be established that variable resistance is superior to all other kinds of resistance. In most real life applications of force, the resistance usually becomes less as the speed of movement accelerates and the joint approaches the end of its motion. For performance enhancement, constant resistance may be superior. On the other hand, if one is interested in maximizing muscle size and shape, variable resistance may be better. Nevertheless, there is no conclusive evidence that either constant resistance or variable resistance is superior.

The best test of the effectiveness of a cam or rolling lever arm machine is it's feel. If the movement feels good, then the chances are that it will be used abundantly by people. Variable resistance can produce good results for all fitness levels. It is not superior or inferior to other kinds of resistance for improving strength and athletic performances. It may have good potential for increasing muscle size, theoretically.

4. ACCOMMODATING RESISTANCE

When a machine allows for the automatic change of force application throughout the range of motion it is called accommodating resistance. Such machines are usually **air (pneumatic) devices**, **hydraulic devices** or **electromagnetic devices.** They permit the application of maximum force against the resistance at all points in the range of motion. Usually these devices do not allow for variable speed once the motion is started and in such case might be thought of as isokinetic in nature (ability to vary force but at a constant speed throughout the range of motion). However, there is a potential to pre-select for different speeds and assorted resistance levels prior to executing the exercise with these devices.

Some companies have introduced computer controlled machines that truly vary resistance throughout the range of motion. Examples of these computerized exercise machines using accommodating resistance are the Ariel 5000 manufactured by Ariel Life Systems (using computer controlled hydraulic push/pull resistance) and the Life Circuit Machines (using computer controlled electromagnetic positive and negative resistance) produced by Life Fitness.

Other companies use non-computerized hydraulic devices to produce accommodating resistance machines which operate in an opposing muscle group push/pull method. This type of equipment uses hydraulic cylinders to provide the resistance. When using these machines it is impossible to train the eccentric (negative) component of muscle contraction. In contrast, as mentioned above, other machines which are computerized and use electromagnetic devices to provide resistance, allow for both concentric (positive) and eccentric (negative) muscle contraction during the exercise, such as the Life Fitness computer controlled exercise machines.

It is important to remember that when using accommodating resistance machines which operate in an opposing muscle group push/pull method, the eccentric (negative) component of muscle contraction is not trained. In contrast, there are computerized electromagnetic machines which permit training both concentric (positive) and eccentric (negative) muscle contraction during the exercise. The Life Fitness computer controlled exercise machines are examples of this type of machine. It is not possible to say at this time which type of machine is superior. Both types can be effectively used in all types of training programs. Machines that allow positive and negative contractions train the muscles in the way in which they are used in real life and this may be an advantage.

Keiser Sports Health Equipment has developed some novel pneumatic exercise machines. A unique feature of the Keiser air resistance machines is the ability for the user to instantaneously change (increase or decrease) the resistance at any point in the range of motion. Also, this equipment by nature can be considered as an accommodating resistance exercise device because the air pressure increases in the system as you work through the range of motion, thus increasing the resistance. In addition, by simply pressing a foot control or a finger control, the air pressure (the resistance) can be instantly changed during the performance of the exercise. This allows the user to modulate the positive and negative machine resistance throughout the range of motion according to their specific strength curve.

A skillful and knowledgeable user can use these machines to add more effective positive and negative contractions. Nonetheless, there are few, if any, major athletes or body builders that use the Keiser equipment exclusively. These machines usually are combined with all other resistance machines or free weights which are in the training environment.

Few if any training studies have been executed demonstrating the superiority of accommodating resistance. Theoretically, these machines have value for producing good hypertrophy and strength. If they are not computer controlled and only permit push/pull training, they have limited application for performance improvement because they do not train the eccentric component of movement. However, they may be valuable for increasing strength and hypertrophy.

Computer controlled devices that allow for positive and negative components of muscle contraction at varying velocities have great potential for increasing size, strength and maximizing strength transfer to sport skills.

Clear cut superiority of accommodating exercise machines is yet to be established by scientific research. However, these devices can produce good results for strength and hypertrophy.

PART I

THEORY & PRACTICE

RELATED REFERENCES:

1. Coker, C. and Ward, P. Factors in exercise machine use and the variable resistance concept. Information Bulletin, Holiday Spa Health Clubs of California; October, 1981; p.10-11.

2. Garhammer, J. Sports Illustrated: Strength Training, Harper & Row Publishers, New York, 1986, p. 49-53.

3. Stone, M. & O'Bryant, H., Weight Training: A Scientific Approach, Burgess Publishing Company, Minneapolis, 1984, p. 151-153.

RESEARCH COMPARING CONSTANT RESISTANCE AND VARIABLE RESISTANCE

Very few research studies comparing the effectiveness of constant and variable resistance training modes on full range of motion strength development have been reported in the literature. There are many claims supporting both sides of the issue but very little scientific evidence.

In 1990, a study was reported that was conducted at the College of Health and Human Performance at the University of Florida. Manning (1990) and others, investigated the effects of constant resistance and variable resistance training on strength.

In this study a Nautilus leg extension machine was used for training. The variable resistance group trained on the Nautilus machine with it standard cam providing the variable resistance. After the variable resistance group completed training, the cam was removed from the machine and replaced with a round sprocket to create a constant resistance throughout the range of motion for the constant resistance group training.

Twenty two men and twenty seven women were randomly assigned to either the constant resistance or variable resistance group. The subjects trained either two or three times per week over a ten week period. During each training session the subjects performed one set of 8 - 12 repetitions to failure. The weight load was adjusted that allowed 8 to 12 repetitions during each training session.

Each repetition was performed in a slow controlled motion, with 2 seconds permitted for the positive portion of the lift (leg extension) and 4 seconds allowed for the negative part of the lift (lowering the weight to the starting position). When each subject was able to correctly perform 12 repetitions, the weight was increased by 2.27 kilograms (5 pounds). Prior to training and post training, isometric strength was determined at eight different points in the range of motion for each subject.

The analysis of the data showed that both the constant resistance and variable resistance groups showed significant improvements in isometric knee extension at each angle of measurement following the training period. There were no significant strength differences between the two experimental groups at any of the measured angles throughout the range of motion. The researchers concluded that the training stimulus from both constant and variable resistance knee extension exercise is sufficient to elicit full range of motion training responses when the exercise is performed slowly and with an eccentric component.

At this point in time it is impossible to state with any degree of confidence whether constant resistance, variable resistance or accommodating resistance is superior. The choice of which technique to chose as a training method is dependent upon the understanding of training theory and the personal training philosophy of those who are designing the training programs and the kinds of exercise equipment that is in the training environment. It is possible that a combination of all types of resistances will produce the best results. However, most training environments do not have enough varied equipment to allow for training with all the possible types of resistance devices. The general fitness participant, athletes and body builders have to adapt their programs to the kinds of resistance devices available in their training environment.

The tool (resistance machines) is not the critical issue. It is how the tool is applied that makes the difference in the human's response to training. In any event, good results can be achieved through the scientific application of the resistance machines available in any given environment. The ideal would be probably free weights, but even then these devices have their limitations.

Manning, R., Graves, J., Carpenter, D., Leggett, S. and M. Pollock. **Constant vs variable resistance knee extension training; Medicine and Science in Sports and Exercise, Volume 22, Number 3; June, 1990; pp 397-401.**

FREE WEIGHTS VERSUS MACHINES

DISCUSSION

Today there are many equipment manufacturers that compete for the attention of weight training enthusiasts. Much time and a lot of money are spent by these companies trying to convince the American populace that one machine is better than another for developing strength and increasing size. Some of the most well known equipment companies are: Maximus, Medx, Hoggan, Panatta, Universal Gym, Paramount, Icarian, Flex, Muscle Dynamics, Life Fitness Products, Body Masters, Nautilus, Kieser, Cybex, Mavrik, York and Elieko, et cetera.

Many of these companies focus on machines while others on free weights. Some have a combined focus, marketing machines and free weights, as well. In addition there is a movement toward computer assisted resistance machines. Six companies have led in the development of computer assisted machines: (1) Life Fitness Products; (2) Ariel Life Systems; (3) Gravitron (Stairmaster); (4) Fitnet (Universal); (5) Computerized Fitness System (Paramount); and, (6) Myotech (now defunct). The interfacing of computers with resistance machines has great potential for application in general fitness programs, body building programs and training for sport. However, there is a great need for these computer controlled exercise machines to be refined along with the conceptualization of a valid training theory and effective training programs supporting the use of these devices.

All categories of weight trainers are perplexed as to what type of equipment should be used. When determining what equipment to use, the primary factors to consider are the objectives of the training program and the level of experience of the weight trainer. Once these factors have been defined then one can select what array of equipment is to be used; free weights or a specific type of weight machines or a combination. In any case, one must always keep in mind that machines and free weights are tools. Tools do not have any inherent intelligence; therefore, it is how the human mind programs and applies these tools that determine the effectiveness of a machine or free weights.

There is great controversy about what type equipment is best for any specific training routine. This controversy exists because people don't evaluate correctly what is scientifically and empirically known regarding resistance methods and the application of machines and free weights. Furthermore, most people refuse to properly define their training objectives. The tremendous advertising pressure from the equipment companies adds to the confounding of the problem.

Both free weights and machines have distinct functional advantages and disadvantages. Both can be utilized to produce good results depending upon fitness state (level), training objectives and available training equipment.

The advantages of free weights are:

(1) Free weights work requires balancing of the weight and one's body, resulting in greater involvement of the muscle (prime movers, synergists and stabilizers) and better neuromuscular coordination during

lifting. Machines do not require the high degree of balancing and neuromuscular coordination and, therefore, the improvement of strength does not transfer to skill performance as readily as that developed with free weights.

(2)   Free weights do not limit ranges of motion. There is freedom to move in all planes (directions). This freedom allows for the strength training to be very closely allied with real life movement especially in skill performances. Machines (and this does not include pulleys) by their nature limit movement to one plane of motion. They demand specific movement patterns not necessarily related to free motion, thus forcing the human to adapt to its movement geometry instead of the opposite. Machines should adapt as much as possible to the unique movement patterns of the individual using them. This of course is not possible and, therein, lies one of the great disadvantages of machines.

(3)   Free weights allow one to execute a wide variety of movements and exercises while machines (not including pulley weights) are limited usually to one specific movement.

The advantages of machines are:

(1)   Machines are convenient. They have selectorized weight stacks and are designed to perform one primary function. They allow many people to consecutively exercise because of the simplicity of the weight changes.

(2)   Machines provide a margin of safety since they control movement in a fixed plane of motion. Also, it is almost impossible to get pinned under a heavy weight eliminating a need for spotters. Some free weight exercises require the use of spotters especially when using heavy poundage. Fixed free weights and dumbbells often come loose and present a hazard if they fall off the bar.

(3)   Machines eliminate the clutter of weight plates scattered about the gym.

(4)   Machines provide a very efficient modality for training large masses of people safely and effectively. The proper use of machines can be easily taught and learned. Furthermore, once the simple techniques have been learned about the machines, only minimum or no supervision is required.

(5)   Machines are extremely effective in circuit weight training and super circuit weight training programs. In fact the use of machines is recommended exclusively for this type of training, although, it is possible to execute circuit weight training programs with free weights.

(6)   Machines allow for the isolated training of many specific small muscle groups more effectively than free weights.

Training studies and empirical observations have shown that the use of free weights produces superior results when compared to machines. This superiority is due to better mechanical specificity, potential for using many exercise variations, and the involvement of multiple joint actions which transfer more effectively to real life movements and performances.

RELATED REFERENCES

THEORETICAL REFERENCES

1.   Garhammer, J. Equipment for the development of athletic strength and power. National Strength and Conditioning Association Journal, 3(6):24-26, 1981.

2.   Harmen, E. Resistive torque analysis of 5 nautilus exercise machines. Medicine and Science in Sports and Exercise. 15(2):113, 1983.

3. Stone, M. & O'Bryant, H. Weight Training: A Scientific Approach, Burgess Publishing Company, 1984.

4. Stone, M. Considerations in gaining a strength-power training effect. <u>National Strength and Conditioning Association Journal</u>,4(1):22-24, 1982.

RESEARCH REFERENCES

1. Coleman, A.E., Nautilus vs Universal Gym strength training in adult males. American CorrectiveTherapy Journal 31:103-107, 1977.

2. Everson, J.M. Variable resistance vs. Isotonic weight training in monozygotic male twins: a case study compiled for Dr. F. Nagle; Independent Study; University of Wisconsin.

3. Sylvester, L.J. Et Al;The effect of variable resistance and free weight training programs on strength and vertical jump. National Strength and Conditioning Association Journal; 3(6):30-33, 1981.

4. Wathen, D., A comparison of the effects of selected isotonic and isokinetic exercises, modalities, and programs on the vertical jump in college football players. National Strength and Conditioning Association Journal, 2:47-48, 1980.

5. Wathen, D. and Shutes, M., A comparison of the effects of selected isotonic and isokinetic exercises, modalities and programs on the acquisition of strength and power in collegiate football players, National Strength and Conditioning Association Journal, 4(1):40-42, 1982.

UNILATERAL, RECIPROCAL AND BILATERAL EXERCISE

INTRODUCTION

Recently, equipment manufacturers have produced exercise equipment that can be used in a bilateral way (both arms or legs together) or in a unilateral way (one arm or leg at a time). Weight training experts cannot say with confidence which method is the best for training. There is lack of research regarding this issue. Future research may show that a combination of unilateral and bilateral exercises is the most effective approach to training. Certainly the knowledgeable weight trainer uses some form of unilateral, reciprocal and bilateral exercises at some time in their training program.

Before discussing the merits of unilateral, reciprocal and bilateral exercises, three definitions are presented:

UNILATERAL is defined as moving one limb at a time in a desired direction (single action).

RECIPROCAL MOVEMENT is moving one limb in one direction while simultaneously moving the opposite limb in an opposite direction.

BILATERAL is defined as moving two comparable limbs in the same manner and at the same time; eg, a barbell or dumbbell bench press.

Bilateral exercise with free weights or machines has existed for a long time, probably because of the ease at which such exercise is executed. Unilateral exercise, while the concept has been around for a long time, has not been popular, because of the complexity of performing a unilateral task with free weights. Unilateral exercise with machines is relatively new because it is only recently that unilateral machines have been developed. However, unilateral exercise with dumbbells has been employed for a long time. Reciprocal training with dumbbells is possible but outside a very few exercises this procedure is not commonly used. Reciprocal movement with machines is possible when specially designed machines are handy but only recently (since about 1980) have such machines become available.

There is some scientific research (studied mostly in a rehabilitation environment) that has shown there is significant cross transfer from one limb to the one on the other side in unilateral training. This research supports the concept of unilateral training, but at this point in time it is difficult to say that unilateral training is superior to bilateral training. Presently, there are no studies available that have contrasted the relative merits of unilateral, reciprocal and bilateral training with respect to strength, local muscle endurance and hypertrophy or neuromuscular superiority.

Research has not been able to positively state that unilateral, reciprocal or bilateral exercise is best. The human body utilizes all three concepts in all their variations in exercise and sports actions. The most intelligent approach is to make provisions for using these methods and include unilateral, reciprocal and bilateral exercises, where possible, in one's training program.

The following is a presentation of the possible reasons for utilizing these methods in a training program.

RATIONALE FOR USING UNILATERAL AND/OR RECIPROCATING EXERCISE

1. **BALANCE OF STRENGTH:** It is generally observed by most people that the expressions of strength and/or coordination and skill of the hands and arms or feet and legs are quite different. People are generally not able to write or throw equally well with both hands and are unable to kick a soccer ball or football with the same degree of skill and force with either leg. In addition, people are not able to long jump as efficiently off the non-dominant leg. These inequalities exist for two reasons: (1) Lack of comparable strength in dominant and non-dominant limbs, and (2) Lack of comparable skill development in dominant and non-dominant limbs. The use of unilateral and reciprocating strength exercises contribute to the balancing of the strength, coordination and symmetry of comparable but opposite limbs.

2. **HUMAN MOVEMENT PATTERNS:** Many human movement patterns require unilateral movement (single action like many simple movements or reciprocating action like running). As mentioned above, many natural and athletic movements are unilateral or reciprocating in nature. The performance of unilateral or reciprocal exercises reinforce neuromuscular coordination. There is obvious improvement of skill by training the non-dominant limb with skill producing exercises.

RATIONALE FOR USING BILATERAL EXERCISE

1. **HUMAN MOVEMENT PATTERNS:** While many human movement patterns are inherently unilateral or reciprocating, there are many that involve a bilateral movement, as in some forms of jumping, skiing, gymnastics and other sports. When the requirement of movement is bilateral, it is best trained by utilizing bilateral training exercises.

2. **BILATERAL EXERCISE PROVIDES GREATER LOADING POTENTIAL:** Bilateral exercise provides for greater loading potential of the limbs involved. For example, it is difficult to conceive of a person who executes a standard bench press of 400 pounds, doing 200 pound dumbbell bench presses. **This is not impossible, just improbable.** Therefore, when maximum strength and size are the training objectives, bilateral exercise will allow the individual to train at a higher level when compared to unilateral exercises.

CONCLUSION

There are many varieties of equipment available for body building and weight training. All equipment can be implemented effectively if applied using the principles of periodization (cycling) of training and employing scientific principles of body building and weight training. Machines are most beneficial in the initial stages of training for the beginner and the re-entry program for the advanced body builder. Also, using a variety of machines is very productive in the cutting stages while preparing for an body building contest and for special exercises in general training. It makes little difference if the machines are constant resistance, variable resistance or accommodating resistance. **The bottom line is "do they feel good" and "do they produce results".** Therefore, use everything within the training environment that produces results without muscular/skeletal pain when exercising. All equipment can be used to produce outstanding results if it is used as a tool and integrated into a training program using valid principles of weight training and body building.

PRINCIPLES AND GUIDELINES FOR WEIGHT TRAINING

GENERAL PRINCIPLES OF PROGRESSIVE RESISTANCE EXERCISE

INTRODUCTION

In the past, many people have constructed their training programs on intuition, misinformation and ignorance. Furthermore, most people do not have a logical plan for training which is firmly grounded in the science of training. They try a different program every week; usually whatever appears in the latest fitness or muscle magazine. This discontinuity leads to frustration and eventually to an even more vigorous pursuit of "the golden fleece"... a magic exercise, program or dietary plan that will supposedly and instantly solve their problem. **THERE ARE NO MAGIC EXERCISES OR DIET PROGRAMS.** In this day of enlightenment, there is no need to use unsound training principles for any training program. There is ample clearly defined quality research and empirically derived principles regarding of all types of physical training that will allow one to develop very effective training programs.

The task is to identify the valid principles and then apply them in a sensible weight training program. Some selected general principles of Progressive Resistance Exercise are presented in the following paragraphs. These principles will serve as guidelines to construct valid and effective Progressive Resistance Exercise Programs.

THE KEY: YEAR ROUND TRAINING

In the past, the athlete would train just prior to the season and during the season. Post season they would not perform any regulated training regimen. With the greater desire for higher levels of performance and the demands that each sport places on the individual plus the extreme competition for sports positions, athletes are desirous and coaches are demanding year round training. The athlete can no longer afford the luxury of getting out of shape during the off season and count on a last minute conditioning program just prior to the season. Many sports have frequent mini-camps throughout the year where the athlete has to demonstrate fitness or be in jeopardy of losing their job or position on the team.

In addition to the competitive need discussed above, it has been demonstrated that improvements in performance are more long lasting and stable when training throughout the year with a periodization (cycling) of volume and intensity. It is also hypothesized that year round training not only improves performance but will profoundly reduce the potential for injury while adding significantly to the athletes sport participation longevity.

The training year for athletes can be divided into three major periods:

1. Post Competitive.
2. Pre-Season.
3. Season.

Each one of these periods play a unique role in the yearly cycle.

The average man and woman should be engaged in a physical training program daily in a year round format. The problem with most average people is that they do not periodize (cycle) their exercise programs which leads to staleness, boredom, lack of progress and results in a high drop-out rate from exercise programs. Average people need to cycle their training programs just like competitive athletes for the same reasons: efficiency, sustaining motivation and to achieve superior and longer lasting results.

A rational approach to muscular fitness assumes that there be a year-round weight training program. The three general areas of concern are: **(1) general fitness training; (2) training for sport; and, (3) body building.** This year-round training principle applies to all three categories but varies in intensity and volume throughout the training year.

When starting a progressive resistance program the intensity should be low and the volume should be moderately high until a base is developed. Subsequently, the intensity and volume are increased and manipulated in accordance with training objectives to speed up the conditioning process. This concept is known as periodization or cycling and it is thoroughly discussed under the title of Periodization (Cycling) of Physical Training Programs which appears later in this section.

Russian and American researchers in strength training have recently reported that variation of volume and intensity in weight training programs (periodization or cycling) produces better results than programs that maintain constant volume and intensity throughout the year. This cycling concept fits very nicely into the year-round training philosophy. The exact cycling pattern would be determined by the objective of the training program.

THE DAILY WORKOUT PATTERN

Table 1-10 contains a workout pattern that outlines the essential parts of a workout that are necessary to include in the daily training session for top caliber performance. This daily workout pattern is of equal importance to those training for general fitness, body building or sports. It is crucial that one follow this pattern so all important workout factors are completed and undue soreness and/or injury will not occur. This pattern considers the inter-relationships that exist between warm-up, flexibility, the specific body of the workout and the cooldown.

1. **THE WARM-UP:** Increases body temperature, circulation, facilitates metabolic processes and improves tissue elasticity to reduce the possibility of injury, as well as preparing one psychologically for the routine ahead. The activities given below have been selected as possible exercises to help accomplish an adequate warm-up.

    A. Stationary Biking - Five to fifteen minutes at low intensity.
    B. Stair Stepping Device - Five to fifteen minutes at low intensity.
    C. Jog 1/2 Mile to Mile - Easy; Make it as enjoyable as possible.
    D. Other - Any other activity where the intensity can be easily controlled. Execute from five to fifteen minutes of such exercise.

2. **FLEXIBILITY EXERCISES:** Flexibility exercises should not be performed before a general warm-up routine. The exercises performed should include every body joint. Resist all temptations of rushing through the program. There aren't any shortcuts to increasing range of motion. It is important not to rush the flexibility exercises and to approach this phase with an attitude of relaxation. The best time to do flexibility work is either after the general warm-up or after the workout, or any combination of the two.

3. **THE BODY OF THE WORKOUT:** The body of the work out relates to the specific objectives and selected activities. In general, all skill improvement should follow the warm-up and flexibility work before fatigue accumulates. Strength work should be the last element before the cool-down procedure. In specific weight training programs or body building routines, the sequence of training the body parts vary with the philosophy of training.

The body of the workout should be based on the consideration of the following elements:

A. Frequency
B. Intensity
C. Duration
D. Mode of Activity
E. Initial level of fitness
F. Length of training phases

G. Selection of exercises
H. Sequencing of exercises
I. Number of sets and repetitions
J. Rest intervals
K. Exercise speed

The precise definition of the above factors will guarantee that the training program will produce the benefits that are desired.

4. **THE COOL DOWN:** The cool down will assist in the recovery from a hard work-out. The cool down is performed to bring the body back to the resting state in a gradual manner. The cool down is the last physical activity engaged in prior to the shower. The severity of the work-out will dictate the form and extent of the cool down. This may be the most propitious time to execute flexibility training because the muscles are warm, circulation is profuse and the inherent muscle and tendon tension is reduced because the muscle spindles and the golgi tendon organs are desensitized. The cool down should extend from five to fifteen minutes and can include flexibility work, easy jogging, stationary cycling or stair stepping.

Table 1-10. Factors Making Up The Daily Training Pattern

WARM UP	BODY OF WORKOUT	COOL DOWN
5-15 MINUTES OF STATIONARY CYCLING, JOGGING OR LIGHT EXERCISE, ETC. FLEXIBILITY PROGRAM CAN BE USED HERE AFTER A GENERAL WARM UP.	20-120 MINUTES DURATION, TYPE, INTENSITY AND FREQUENCY DEPENDS ON PROGRAM OBJECTIVES.	5-15 MINUTES EASY CYCLING, JOGGING OR WALKING, ETC. FLEXIBILITY PROGRAM CAN BE USED HERE.

"OVERLOAD" - THE KEY TO IMPROVEMENT IS PROGRESSIVE RESISTANCE EXERCISE (PRE)

INTRODUCTION

Progressive resistance exercise (PRE) embodies three very important and valid principles of training:

(1) There must be application of stress (resistance, weight, speed, duration or distance) beyond what the system is accustomed. Strength of a muscle or muscle group is most effectively developed when there is an application of overload (i.e., exercising against maximal or near maximal resistance). This is commonly know as the **"principle of overload."** The degree of improvement is directly proportional to the degree of overload.

(2) The application of stress must be in a progressively greater amount to match the adaptation of the body to previously imposed stress levels. This is characteristically called the **"principle of progression."** The resistance (load) against which a muscle or muscle group must work should be periodically and systematically increased as long as strength or LME increases are desired.

(3) There must be an unloading period to manifest the delayed training effect. This is called the **"principle of unloading."** This period may last from 1 to 3 weeks when volume is reduced drastically while

THEORY & PRACTICE   PART I

intensity can vary as desired. It has been observed that large increases in strength occur after a cycle of hard training. Therefore, the delayed training effect should be planned for when formulating a training program.

FIVE GENERAL PRINCIPLES OF TRAINING

The application of progressive overload is controlled by five principles of training:

(1) **OVERLOAD:** There must be overload to produce a training effect. If the overload is insufficient (below 40% 1RM) then the exercise is of little value for improving strength and local muscle endurance. On the other hand, if there is too much overload, then the exercise becomes too much for body adaptation. Too much overload frequently leads to muscle, tendon and soft tissue injuries. In weight training, overload is produced by increasing the duration (increases in number of sets and/or repetitions), frequency (number of training sessions per day or per week) and intensity (increases in percent of 1RM). The cycling objectives will dictate the exact manner in which progression is accomplished. There must be a period of unloading to allow for the delayed training effect to become manifested.

(2) **PROGRESSION:** The overload must be progressive to induce further changes after adapting to a certain level. As one is continually exposed to an overload there is an adaptation by the body and the work is performed easily. To ensure that there be continuous improvement, one must progressively adjust their sets, repetitions or intensity. Generally, it is necessary to provide more difficult work (training sessions) as one gets bigger and stronger. **It is important to note that overload and progression must be fitted into the concept of periodization or cycling for optimum improvements.** The objectives of the cycling plan will dictate when the sets, repetitions or intensity should be changed.

(3) **USE/DISUSE PRINCIPLE OR THE PRINCIPLE OF REVERSIBILITY:** If you use the muscle or physiological support system it will improve. If you do not use the muscle or physiological support system it will deteriorate. Use promotes improved function while disuse promotes deterioration. This applies to the body as a whole and to its component systems. Exercise programs must be planned to include all components of physical fitness (strength, local muscle endurance and aerobic endurance) as well as all body parts (muscle groups). There is an optimal range of intensity, an optimal frequency and duration that relates to the exercise program objectives. As mentioned above the program objectives will dictate how much and when each component of physical fitness will emphasized.

(4) **SPECIFICITY:** One must train the muscle, muscle groups or physiological support system with a specific method in order to obtain a specific goal. There is no transfer of unlike elements between exercise programs. There are specific adaptations to imposed demands **(know as the "SAID" principle).** The body responds according to the specific demands placed upon it; i.e., sets, repetitions and percent 1RM. Improvements in strength and size, local muscular endurance and aerobic endurance require specific programs for training. Again the requirements of the exercise program and the specific performance requirements will dictate **"THE SPECIFIC PROGRAM."**

(5) **INDIVIDUAL DIFFERENCES AND UNIQUE BIOLOGY:** Everyone responds to an exercise stimulus in their own unique way in terms of magnitude and speed of improvement, as well the amount of effort needed to elicit a specified level. This factor is basically determined by the genetic organization of an individual. Heredity is the primary determinant and controlling factor for human response to exercise and nutrition programs. However, regardless of how one responds to the exercise stimulus, all people must obey the laws of biology. Other factors that may modify the genetic potential of a person involved in a weight training program are: hormone output, age, body type, obesity, rest patterns and sleep habits, nutrition, injury, disease and motivation.

THREE INVIOLATE LAWS OF PROGRESSIVE RESISTANCE EXERCISE (WEIGHT TRAINING)

In 1946 and 1948, De Lorme published the results of his research on strength training. For the first time general principles of strength training were identified and defined. De Lorme's principles are inviolate and are just as valid today as in 1946. These general training principles are simple stated as follows:

(1)   **Increase in muscle strength and size** can be accomplished by executing a few repetitions against a heavy resistance. Subsequent research coupled with empirical observations have established that the number of sets range from 3-5 and the number of repetitions should range from 1-8, at a percentage of maximum strength ranging from 70-100 percent depending upon what specific aspect of strength one wants to train (develop).

(2)   **Increase in local muscle endurance and muscle definition** can be accomplished by executing many repetitions with moderate resistance. Scientific studies combined with empirical observations have established that the number of sets be from 3-5 and the number of repetitions range from 10-15, while the intensity (load) ranges from 40-60 percent of maximum strength. Muscle definition is derived from reduction of body fat which is produced by the increased total amount of work of moderate intensity (40%-60% of 1RM) and 10-15 repetitions executed in 3-5 sets.

(3)   **The above two methods (#1 and #2) are not interchangeable; i.e., one cannot replace the other.** Each method of training produces a specific training effect; either strength/ size or local muscle endurance/definition. The training responses the human makes consequent to the application of either principle, number one or two above, does not produce training effects of the opposite principle, to a large extent. In other words, in general, **heavy weight and few repetitions** does not contribute greatly to improvement in local muscular endurance and definition; while on the other hand, **many repetitions and light weight** does not contribute, in a large way, to strength improvement. It must be noted, each method of training may enhance to a small degree the attributes produce by the opposite method but any changes will be small.

---

1.   De Lorme, T.L.; Heavy resistance exercise; Archives of Physical Medicine, 27:607-31; October, 1946.

2.   De Lorme, T.L. and Watkins, A.L.; Techniques of Progressive Resistance Exercise; Archives of Physical Medicine; 29:263-273; May, 1948.

FACTORS IN PROGRAMMING PROGRESSIVE RESISTANCE EXERCISE

The scientific and sensible approach to progressive resistance exercise programs is accomplished when all the factors of program design are considered. The factors that are important are: frequency, intensity, duration, mode of activity, fitness level, length of training, selection of exercises and sequencing of exercises. Table 1-13 contains a summary of all these factors for progressive resistance exercise prescription. **See Table 1-13, Recommendations for Prescription of PRE Programs under the topic of Periodization (Cycling) of Physical Training Programs which appears later in this section.**

FREQUENCY

Three training sessions per week is the usual number for beginners. If the intensity is low, (40%-60% 1RM) and after a minimum of four weeks of basic training, one may proceed to four or five times per week. This will hasten the development of the physiological benefits of the basic training program. One must be careful not to train too frequently too soon.

As a beginner special efforts should be made not to exceed 60% of 1RM in all exercises and training should be restricted to three times per week. After a month of steady training the beginner can expand their frequency up to six times per week if properly motivated and no training problems are existent.

For intermediate and advanced trainees a 3 day per week or a 4 or 6 day split routine can be employed. Split routines involve training upper body one day and lower body the next or some more complex muscle group pattern. The main principle to follow is: **"DO NOT TRAIN WITH THE SAME MUSCLES OR MUSCLE GROUPS ON CONSECUTIVE DAYS."** The intensity may vary from 50% to 100% 1RM depending upon the artistic formatting of the exercise program. The are many patterns one could employ in the design of resistance training programs for intermediate and advanced trainees, most of which are effective.

Advanced training for sport sometimes includes training six days a week with one day of complete rest. But it is also necessary to carefully plan the training exercises so that different muscle groups or different application of muscle groups and different intensities occur on consecutive days.

INTENSITY

Research observations show that for neophytes the exercise program drop-out rate is high if the beginning intensity of training is too high. To minimize the soreness and discomfort and to reduce this drop-out rate, it is suggested that beginners utilize a weight somewhere between 40% and 60% 1RM. However, it is unwise and difficult to test maximum lifts with beginners until a basic training foundation is established and the exercises can be performed correctly. One could use a percentage of the body weight.

AN EXAMPLE OF PERCENTAGES OF BODY WEIGHT TO USE AS STARTING WEIGHTS FOR A BEGINNING WEIGHT TRAINING PROGRAM.

1. Shoulder press	40%	5. Triceps pushdown	20%
2. Lat pulldown	40%	6. Leg press	50%
3. Bench press	40%	7. Leg curl	20%
4. Curls	20%	8. Squatting	20% - 30%

These percentages are very conservative so that the beginner could train at the beginning stages with very little stress. After two to four weeks of a starter program, the 1RM's should be determined to effectively adjust the weight loads into the 40 % to 60 % of 1RM and, thus, into the training sensitive zone.

Intermediate and advanced lifters should adjust their load somewhere between 50% and 100% 1RM in accordance with their program objectives. To determine 1RM requires a person to do a maximum lift for each exercise in their program. The weight loads are adjusted to a specific percentage of their 1RM in concert with their program objectives. The 1RM testing procedure is safe for intermediate and advanced lifters since they know how to perform the exercises correctly and have built a muscular fitness base. **It is important to remember the specificity principle and to use the appropriate training percentage that matches the objectives of the program.**

The beginner should keep their intensity between 40% and 60% 1RM and perform 10 to 15 repetitions for 2 to 3 sets not including warmup and cooldown sets. The intermediate and advanced trainer can use from 50% to 100% 1RM performing 1 to 10 repetitions for 3 to 7 sets not including warmup and cooldown sets in accordance with their training goals.

The rest between exercises in CWT is 15 seconds and for SCWT there is an aerobic rest period of 30 seconds between weight exercises. For sets and repetition training the rest period can range from 30 seconds to 5 minutes depending upon the intensity used and the condition of the exerciser. Generally, one should be fully recovered in two minutes or less except when lifting 90% to 100% 1RM. In this case it may take up to 5 minutes or more to be able to execute another set. This time seems to be relative to each individual so no firm guideline can be established.

DURATION

For beginners the duration of the training session should range between 20 and 45 minutes of continuous or broken training. Continuous training is a program where the trainee goes nonstop from one exercise to another, such as in circuit weight training or super circuit weight training. Broken training refers to a period of work followed by a period of rest/recovery, such as in the set and repetition format. The rest periods may be two minutes or longer. Intermediate and advanced trainees will adapt the rest/recovery time to meet the objectives of their training program, while the total duration of the daily training period will vary between 45 minutes and 150 minutes.

MODE OF ACTIVITY

Beginners have two objectives which influence the type of activity for their program:

(a)   Beginners generally need to learn how to perform the exercises.

(b)   Muscle, ligaments and connective tissue need to be conditioned before increasing the intensity or volume of the program. This object is valid for all people regardless of experience and should be achieved before moving to higher intensities and greater volumes.

It is recommended that beginners perform circuit weight training or sets and repetitions using 3 X 10 X 40% - 60% 1RM. (3 X 10 X 40% - 60% 1RM = 3 sets of 10 repetitions at 40% to 60% of one maximum lift [1RM]) There are many variations of sets and repetitions, but the beginner should keep it simple and not chase after rainbows. They must not lose sight of the objectives of the beginning phase for safety reasons. The body must be prepared before advancing to higher levels of stress (lifting volume and intensity). To ignore this principle is to invite unnecessary muscle soreness, injury and the possibility of non-compliance to the exercise program.

Intermediate and advanced trainees can apply any one of the many variations of circuit weight training or sets and repetitions. Their program is determined by their objectives for training. However, after long layoffs, they too need to re-establish the base before returning to high volume or high intensity training. Sometimes high repetitions (10-15) and low weight (40% - 60% 1RM) can be effective for a break in the intensity pattern. Executing an even higher number of repetitions (up to 100 per exercise) for 6 to 8 exercises per training session with very low intensity is another variation that may have some value. This type of training is endurance oriented and probably should only extend over a 3 to 6 week period. This is an extreme variation.

The variation of volume, intensity, frequency and to some degree, changing of the exercises, leads to better and longer lasting results because of using the periodization concept.

LEVEL OF FITNESS

Generally speaking, everyone who embarks on a progressive resistance exercise program (indeed any program) needs to go through a base developing training program. To circumvent this phase invites unnecessary soreness, pain, possible injury and a high potential for program participation non-compliance. It is therefore recommended that when returning to an exercise program after a layoff and when starting an exercise program, all people should participate in the General Conditioning (phase I) stage of training for at least four weeks before advancing to greater training volumes or higher intensities regardless of level of expertise.

LENGTH OF TRAINING PHASES

The length of training phases depends upon the long-range training plan and the time available for each phase. Generally, the beginning phase is four to twelve weeks and the intermediate phase is four to twelve weeks. The advanced phases should extend from two to eight weeks.

A cycling of all phases during the training year produces better results, minimizes mental fatigue, reduces boredom, reduces injuries and helps in ensuring compliance to participation in the exercise program. The exact pattern of the cycle would be determined by one's training objective and one's philosophy of training and creative talents. An example of a training pattern for a Track & Field athlete appears in Figure 1-5.

Similar weight training patterns can be constructed for general conditioning, body building or any sport based upon clearly defined objectives. A progressive resistance program must have a master plan in order to have direction. Figure 1-6 displays an example of cycling in an effective weight training program for general fitness or body building. The following paragraphs define all the training information needed to implement the weight training program presented in Figure 1-6, with the exception of specific exercises.

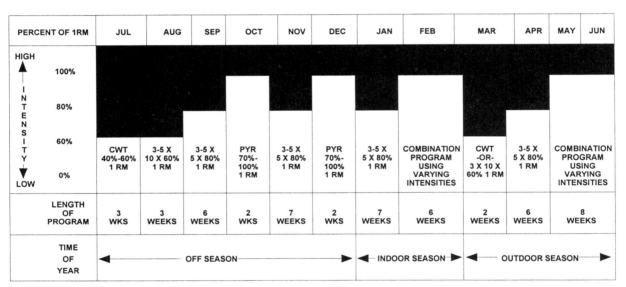

*   RECENT RUSSIAN REPORTS SHOW THAT VARYING (CYCLING) INTENSITY PROGRAMS PRODUCE BETTER RESULTS IN STRENGTH TRAINING THAN CONSTANT INTENSITY PROGRAMS.

**   PYRAMID TRAINING CORRESPONDS WITH CHAMPIONSHIP EVENTS. CIRCUIT WEIGHT TRAINING IS USED WHEN COMPETITION IS NOT A PRIORITY.

Figure 1-5.   An Example Of Cycling In A Training Program For Track And Field Athletes.

Immediately below is presented an example of cycling in an effective weight training program for general fitness or body building and is related to the information contained in Figure 1-6.

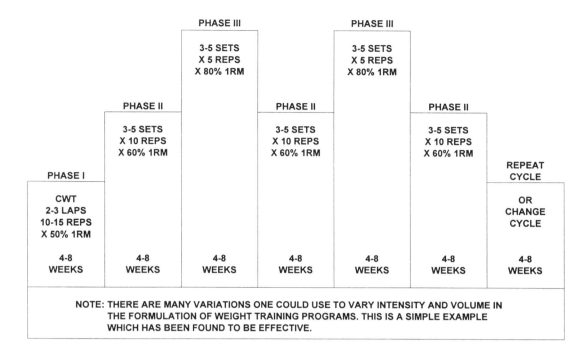

Figure 1-6.   An Example Of Cycling In An Effective Weight Training Program For General Fitness or Body Building.

Phase I is circuit weight training with the following criteria defined:

Purpose:	Preparation.
Program:	CWT or SCWT.
Intensity:	Pre-set Green, Blue or Red levels or 40% to 60% of 1RM.
Sets & Reps	3 laps of 10-15 repetitions per station.
Frequency:	3 - 6 times per week depending upon initial state of fitness.
Duration:	7.5', 15.0' or 22.5 ' for 10, 20 or 30 stations respectively.
Fitness Level:	Beginners - Start easy (green): Intermediate - Start moderate (blue): Advanced - Start higher (red). In lieu of the color scheme for training loads, 40% to 60% 1RM can be used.
Length of Cycle:	4 - 8 Weeks.
Body Parts:	All major muscle groups.

Phase II is conditioning weight training. It includes the following criteria:

Purpose:	Advanced Preparation.
Program:	Sets X Repetitions.
Intensity:	60 % of 1RM.
Sets & Reps:	3-5 sets of 10 repetitions.
Frequency:	3 times per week, unless a split routine, then 6 times per week.
Duration:	60 to 90 minutes. Can speed up by super setting 2 exercises.

THEORY & PRACTICE   PART I

Fitness Level: Stay with circuit training until fitness state is good and body fat is acceptable (men - 15% and women - 20%), **then move to sets and repetitions.**

Length of Cycle: 4 - 8 Weeks.

Body Parts: **(Chose One** **Exercise For** **Each Number)**	1. Quadriceps, buttocks, adductors: 2. Hamstrings: 3. Low Back: 4. Abdominal: 5. Shoulders: 6. Upper Back: 7. Chest: 8. Biceps: 9. Triceps:	Squat, Leg Press, Knee Extension Leg curls (Lying, Standing, Seated) Roman Chair, Low Back Machine Crunch Machine, Bent Knee Sit Up, Crunch Bench Shoulder Press, Upright Rowing Pulldown, Long Pull, Lever Bar Row Bench Press, Vertical Fly, Pullover, Incline B.P. Curls (Machine, Barbell or Dumbbells) Pushdown, French Press

Phase III is the training period. It includes the following criteria:

Purpose: Advanced Training.

Program: Sets X Repetitions.

Intensity: 80 % of 1RM, 3 - 4 sets of 5 repetitions.

Sets & Reps: 3-5 sets of 5 repetitions.

Frequency: 3 times per week unless using a split routine, then 6 times per week.

Duration: 60 - 90 minutes. Speed up by super setting 2 exercises.

**Initial State
of Fitness:**   Should go through Phase I and II before using Phase III or Higher.

Length of Cycle: 4 - 8 Weeks.

Body Parts: Same as used in Phase II or new exercises could be used with the same body parts as used in Phase II. Can utilize 2 to three exercises per body part.

EXERCISE SELECTION

Selection of exercises for any progressive resistance exercise program is very important. Generally, at least one exercise for every major muscle group should be included in all progressive resistance exercise programs regardless of the objectives of the program. Many people merely focus on selected muscle groups and overtrain those groups, ignoring the antagonistic muscle groups. Developing this muscular imbalance can interfere with athletic performance and result in asymmetrical muscle development.

Exercise selection is dependent upon the objectives of the weight training program. For general training, exercises using multiple joint action should be used with supplementation of single joint exercises where appropriate. In body building and general fitness programs one may employ more single joint action exercises. There are literally hundreds of possible exercises that could be used in the weight training program, although, it is not necessary to use unusual and unique exercises. The basic program should be composed of common basic exercises using the principles of periodization for optimal benefits. It is acceptable for advanced body builders to employ many different exercise variations at various times in their training program. One to three exercises can be selected per body part for a single training session.

EXERCISE SEQUENCE

Exercise sequences can be one of many, the most common being the following:

A. **Large muscle groups to smaller sequence.** Generally, the exercise sequence should be from larger muscle groups to the smaller muscle groups. The reason is that if the smaller muscle groups are exhausted first, it will limit the amount of weight that can be handled by the larger muscle groups. Almost all programs for basic strength should employ this principle. General fitness programs can mix muscle groups since the exercise intensity is low, between 40% and 60% of 1RM.

B. **Antagonistic muscle group exercise sequence.** This technique exercises opposing muscle groups on consecutive exercises. The antagonistic pattern can be used in CWT, SCWT, training for sport and body building.

C. **Peripheral heart action sequence.** This sequence involves exercising muscle groups in the lower body followed by an exercise in the upper body. This sequence can be applied in CWT, SCWT, general fitness training, body building or in general training programs where more than one exercise is employed for each muscle group. By alternating upper and lower body movements on consecutive exercises, the muscle fatigue level can be minimized. This permits the maximal loading of muscle groups when 2 or more exercises are included for that muscle group in the training program. This is the preferred sequence for exercises in CWT and SCWT programs or for general training where strength and size are the goals.

D. **Same muscle groups on consecutive exercises sequence.** This pattern uses exercises that condition the same muscle groups in consecutive exercises. This sequence is effectively used during the cutting phase of body building programs and also may be effective in certain low intensity phases in general training. This sequence is not recommended when increasing strength is the goal because performing consecutive exercises that work the same muscle group results in cumulative fatigue in that muscle group. This means the intensity (% 1RM) of each succeeding exercise by necessity is reduced because of fatigue. When intensity decreases the stimulus to muscle growth is reduced.

E. **Lower body then upper body sequence.** In this sequence, all the lower body exercises are performed before moving to the upper body. In addition, one can use the antagonistic muscle sequence or the same muscle group sequence in this pattern. The antagonistic pattern is recommended if this exercise sequence is used. This exercise sequence allows the larger and stronger muscles of the lower body to be maximally trained since the smaller less-strong upper body muscles have not been fatigued. Many advanced lower body exercises require the concurrent use of the upper body muscle groups.

F. **Upper body then lower body sequence.** In this sequence of exercises, all the upper body exercises are performed before moving to lower body exercises. In this pattern of exercises one can use either the antagonistic sequence or the same muscle group sequence of exercises. The antagonistic pattern is recommended if this exercise sequence is used. Training the upper body and then the lower body on the same day may not be the best pattern of training because the smaller upper body muscles are fatigued before the larger lower body muscles are employed. This may limit the amount of weight that can be used in some lower body exercises which involve the upper body muscle groups in their performance. Moreover, there may exist psychological perceptions that may interfere with the performance of exercises in this sequence which will reduce the overall intensity of the training session. This exercise sequence is probably best used by advanced weight trainers as a diversion from the regular training sequence.

For general fitness training and training for strength, the sequence of exercises is important. Generally speaking, the exercise pattern should alternate between antagonistic muscle groups and between muscle groups in various parts of the body. For example, a typical circuit weight training routine would employ an antagonistic pattern like the following: squat, shoulder press, leg curl, lat pulldown, leg adductor, bench press, back hyperextension, upright row/curl, abdominal machine, and vertical fly. Another pattern may be to perform the following sequence: bench press, pulldown, incline press and rowing. An example of an exercise sequence for overall body strength might be: power clean, incline press, squat, bench press, pulldown, pushdown and curls.

Another popular exercise sequence employs the same muscle groups on consecutive exercises. For example: power clean, squat, incline press, bench press, pulldown, rowing, curl and pushdown. This exercise sequence can be effective but empirical evidence suggests that alternating muscle groups may be more effective for increasing strength and size. Nevertheless, many weight trainers use the older less-effective method of using the same muscle groups on consecutive exercises.

Body builders traditionally use exercises that work the same muscle group in a little different way in a successive exercising sequence, for example: (for the legs - squat, knee extension and leg press; for the chest - incline press, bench press and dumbbell fly). This is an acceptable technique in the cutting/defining stages of training but it is not as good in the strength/size phase. **Basically, the key to developing strength and size is related directly to muscle tension (75% to 100% 1RM), total work performed and to one's heredity.** Muscle tension is highest only when working at maximal or near maximal strength levels (70 to 100% IRM).

Pre-exhaustion of a muscle will not allow for development of near maximal tension (75% to 100% 1RM) in consecutive exercises, and, therefore, should not be used for increasing size and strength. Examples of pre-exhaustion are: (for the legs - knee extension, leg press and then squat; for the chest - dumbbell fly, bench press and then incline press). The pre-exhaustion technique is better applied in the shaping and cutting phases of body building.

When trying to achieve size in a muscle, the successive exercises should not involve similar exercise or muscle group. Use another muscle or muscle groups and let the previously exercised muscle or muscle groups rest, and then return for another exercise and so on. Generally speaking, the larger muscle groups should be exercised before the smaller groups.

Figure 1-7 shows the components of a scientifically developed weight training program for general conditioning. Phase I displays the tools of training for beginners while Phase II shows the advanced tools for body building and sports preparation. It is important to note that at various times in the training program advanced trainers return to tools utilized in Phase I for variation, base building and/or cutting.

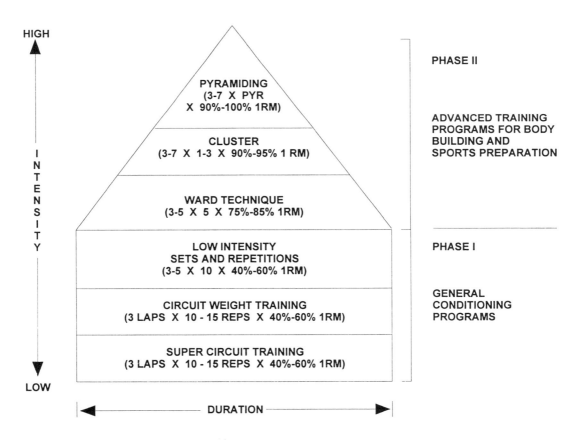

Figure 1-7.   The components of a scientifically developed weight training program for general conditioning.

GUIDELINES FOR PLANNING EXERCISE PROGRAMS

When planning exercise programs one must take into consideration the objectives of the program and the need to periodize (cycle) volumes, intensity, exercises and program emphasis. This means that time should be planned for aerobic emphasis, fat reduction emphasis as well as emphasis on strength and size. The degree of emphasis is regulated by the overall program objective of the weight trainer, be they a general fitness enthusiast, body builder or athlete.

Table 1-11 displays general guidelines for planning exercise programs for aerobic exercise, super circuit weight training, circuit weight training and progressive resistance exercise programs.

The programming factors of exercise that should be planned and prescribed are: mode or type of activity, frequency, intensity, duration, initial (starting) level of fitness and the length of each training phase. The formatting of these factors will vary with the philosophy of the coach and athlete, however, it is wise to use each one of these tools (aerobic exercise, super circuit weight training, circuit weight training, and progressive resistance exercise programs (sets and repetitions)) at some time in the yearly training plan.

If one is involved in a skill sport or activity, in addition to the physical training program, it is important to plan for and participate in a skill improvement program concurrently with the physical training program.

Table 1-11. Guidelines For Planning Exercise Programs

FACTORS OF EXERCISE	AEROBIC EXERCISE	SUPER CIRCUIT WEIGHT TRAINING (SCWT)	CIRCUIT WEIGHT TRAINING (CWT)	PROGRESSIVE RESISTANCE EXERCISE (PRE)		
				BEGINNERS	INTERMEDIATE	ADVANCED
1. MODE (TYPE) OF ACTIVITY	RUNNING, BIKING, SWIMMING, STAIR-CLIMBING, AEROBIC DANCE, RHYTHMIC CALISTHENICS, SCWT, CWT, ETC.	COMBINATION OF RUNNING OR BIKING AND CWT (WEIGHT EXERCISE FOLLOWED IMMEDIATELY BY AEROBIC ACTIVITY ETC.)	CONTINUOUS CIRCUIT WEIGHT TRAINING (ONE EXERCISE IMMEDIATELY FOLLOWING ANOTHER)	CWT OR SETS AND REPETITIONS	CWT OR SETS AND REPETITIONS	SETS AND REPETITIONS CLUSTER OR PYRAMIDING
2. FREQUENCY	3-6 DAYS/WEEK	3-6 DAYS/WEEK	3-6 DAYS/WEEK	3 DAYS/WEEK	3-6 DAYS/WEEK	3-6 DAYS/WEEK
3. INTENSITY	*60%-90% MAX. H.R. RESERVE *50%-85% VO MAX. *RULE OF THUMB: HEART RATE 130-160 BPM	*40%-60% 1RM PLUS HEART RATE OF 130-160 BPM *15 REPS/STATION *10-40 STATIONS	*40%-60% 1RM PLUS HEART RATE OF 130-160 BPM *15 REPS/STATION *20-40 STATIONS	*40%-60% 1RM *10-15 REPS/SET *2-3 SETS *6-10 EXERCISES	*60%-80% 1RM *4-6 REPS/SET *3-5 SETS *6-10 EXERCISES	*70%-100% 1RM *1-6 REPS/SET *3-7 SETS *6-10 EXERCISES
4. DURATION	15-60 MINUTES OF CONTINUOUS ACTIVITY (45 MIN. OPTIMAL)	15-60 MINUTES OF CONTINUOUS ACTIVITY	15-60 MINUTES OF CONTINUOUS ACTIVITY	20-45 MINUTES (CONTINUOUS OR BROKEN)	45-90 MINUTES (BROKEN)	45-150 MINUTES (BROKEN)
5. INITIAL (STARTING) LEVEL OF FITNESS	HIGH: CAN USE HIGHER INTENSITIES & LONGER DURATIONS. RECOMMEND: START EASY & SHORT & PROGRESS TO HARDER & LONGER WORK. LOW: SHOULD START EASY & SHORT & PROGRESS TO HARDER AND LONGER WORK.	HIGH: CAN USE HIGHER INTENSITIES & LONGER DURATIONS. RECOMMEND: START EASY & SHORT & PROGRESS TO HARDER & LONGER WORK. LOW: SHOULD START EASY & SHORT & PROGRESS TO HARDER AND LONGER WORK.	HIGH: CAN USE HIGHER INTENSITIES & LONGER DURATIONS. RECOMMEND: START EASY & SHORT & PROGRESS TO HARDER & LONGER WORK. LOW: SHOULD START EASY & SHORT & PROGRESS TO HARDER AND LONGER WORK. NOTE: START WITH REGULAR CWT THEN PROGRESS TO SCWT.	EVERYONE SHOULD START AT THE BEGINNING LEVEL BEFORE PROGRESSING TO HIGHER PHASES. NOTE: CYCLING OF INTENSITIES, SETS, REPETITIONS, AND DURATION SHOULD BE EXECUTED FOR MAXIMUM TRAINING RESULTS.		
6. LENGTH OF TRAINING PHASES	MINIMUM: 4 WEEKS MAXIMUM: LIFETIME	MINIMUM: 4 WEEKS MAXIMUM: LIFETIME OPTIMAL: 12 WEEKS	MINIMUM: 4 WEEKS MAXIMUM: LIFETIME OPTIMAL: 12 WEEKS	MIN: 4 WEEKS MAX: 12 WEEKS	MIN: 4 WEEKS MAX: 12 WEEKS	MIN: 4 WEEKS MAX: 12 WEEKS

NOTE:
THE AVERAGE PERSON SHOULD ENGAGE IN AN EXERCISE PROGRAM THAT COMBINES ENDURANCE, PROGRESSIVE RESISTANCE EXERCISE AND SKILL ACTIVITIES TO ENSURE A BALANCED FITNESS DEVELOPMENT.

PROGRAM EXAMPLES:
1. M-W-F = SCWT: T-TH-SAT = AEROBIC EXERCISE AND/OR SPORT.
2. M-W-F = PRE: T-TH-SAT = AEROBIC EXERCISE AND/OR SPORT.
3. M-W-F = CWT: T-TH-SAT = AEROBIC EXERCISE AND/OR SPORT.

PART I

THEORY & PRACTICE

PERIODIZATION (CYCLING) OF WEIGHT TRAINING PROGRAMS

INTRODUCTION

More often than not people use the "shotgun" approach to weight training. They are constantly and frequently changing their weight training program in terms of exercises, sets, repetitions and intensity without plan or design. This usually leads to complete frustration and discouragement.

A second kind of exerciser is one who never varies their program in terms of exercises, intensity or volume. They execute the same program using the same weights for weeks, months and sometimes for years without variation. This process also yields frustrating negative results.

There is yet another type of exerciser; the compulsive over worker. This person has firmly entrenched in their mind that they must work harder or they must punish themselves beyond reason in order for their body to respond. Don't misunderstand, good weight training programs require a generous degree of effort but not the masochistic effort which is counterproductive, destroys the body, increases injuries and inhibits improvements. A person should train **"SMARTER, NOT HARDER."** The overall guiding principle should be: **"TRAIN, DON'T STRAIN"** or **"STIMULATE, DON'T ANNIHILATE"**. The understanding and application of scientific principles of weight training, especially the concepts of periodization (cycling), will ensure successful training programs as well as making the training a pleasurable experience.

From a biological viewpoint, it is not prudent to follow only one type of training program over long periods. When this is done, the psychological, hormonal, nervous and muscle systems adapt to the current load (intensity), number of repetitions (volume) and to the range of motion of the exercises used in the program. Further improvement becomes impossible without increasing or decreasing the volume or intensity, or both.

It is also important to vary the exercises in the program. This in itself may introduce a new stimulus to the overall training program plus re-motivate an individual. Care must be taken, however, not to change the exercises too frequently or to use unusual or exotic exercises. **The most important determinants for exercise program success are consistency in training and the proper consideration of all the essential elements of a workout. They are:**

1. Frequency.
2. Intensity.
3. Duration.
4. Mode of activity.
5. Initial level of fitness.
6. Length of training phases.
7. Selection of exercises.
8. Sequencing of exercises.
9. Number of sets and repetitions.
10. Rest intervals.
11. Exercise speed.

Research and empirical observation have shown that the greatest improvements in athletic performance (that includes body building and general conditioning programs as well) occur when there is a variation of volume (repetitions) and intensity (percentage of 1RM) over a given period of time. The interaction between volume and intensity is determined primarily by: (1) The current level of conditioning; and, (2) The specific exercise program objectives. Beginners do not need frequent variation of volume and intensity or exercises until a conditioning base has been established. After at least a 4 to 10 week base building program one may then consider some advanced variations.

The main argument for variation of volume and intensity in the training program is that the muscle will not increase its size, strength or endurance unless it is constantly stimulated and then allowed to restore itself. Therefore, a non-varying stimulus will not continue to be as effective throughout a training program as it was in the beginning. In order to ensure continued response of the muscle or body support system to a specific exercise program, the muscle or system must be subjected to a new stimulus. This may mean an increase or decrease in the volume or intensity, possibly a rest period or maybe a change in exercises used in the program or a combination of all of these factors.

Working harder is sometimes counterproductive when extra work leads to retrogression, frustration, injuries or a plateau. Many athletes, general exercisers and body builders place themselves into these kinds of situations because they have accepted the erroneous concept of "more hard work is what it takes."

Sometimes the psychological, hormonal, nervous and muscular systems need restoration (rest) periods more than extra work. **"WORK SMARTER NOT HARDER"** should be the motto of the exerciser. However, humans are bedeviled by the erroneous cry of **"NO PAIN - NO GAIN."** This is the ultimate in folly... humans should, **"TRAIN - DON'T STRAIN"** or **"STIMULATE - DON'T ANNIHILATE"**.

The purpose of this section is to discuss a variety of periodization (cycling) principles that will assist beginning and advanced weight trainers in the formulation of a successful training program. Before discussing these principles, it is necessary to examine the fitness continuum. **The three basic components of fitness, strength, local muscle endurance (LME) and cardiovascular respiratory endurance (CVRE) can be thought of as lying on a continuum (Figure 1-8):**

STRENGTH--------------------------------LME-------------------------------CVRE

Figure 1-8. The Fitness Continuum

Each of these basic components of fitness is generally achieved by using specific exercise programs, except when using circuit weight training (CWT) or super circuit weight training (SCWT). CWT and SCWT enhances all the elements of physical fitness at the same time. It is interesting to note that when using CWT or SCWT, one will not achieve maximum training of any of these factors; however, a good balance of all three can be achieved. For the average person CWT or SCWT may be all that is needed to fulfill their exercise needs. A discussion of how one can cycle within the CWT or SCWT programs appears later in this section.

It is also important to consider the two factors that control strength development: (1) the size of the muscle (hypertrophy); and, (2) the control of the muscle fiber recruitment by the nervous system. The development of each strength factor is stimulated by a uniquely specific exercise program in terms of sets, repetitions and intensities.

The continuum concept is important to understand so that one does not use a training program that falsely attempts to generate large volumes of strength/size while expecting to achieve maximum LME/definition at the same time. This, of course, is impossible. Also, the continuum concept gives insight into why it is impossible to maximize strength gains while using aerobic programs integrated with strength building programs. A more detailed explanation of this issue is covered in the section entitled, **"TRAINING FOR STRENGTH AND ENDURANCE SIMULTANEOUSLY."**

PERIODIZATION - THE CONCEPT OF CYCLING

Periodization or cycling is the planned variation of intensity (load) and volume (repetitions or total poundage) throughout the total training year. Figure 1-9 displays Matveyev's model of periodization. This figure shows the interaction of volume and intensity as well as indicating the integration of each phase.

In reality, the training year would be composed of many undulations of the volume and intensity. Figure 1-10 illustrates Ward's theoretical model of yearly training which more accurately demonstrates the variations of volume and intensity throughout a training year. The Matveyev model usually includes the following periods or cycles:

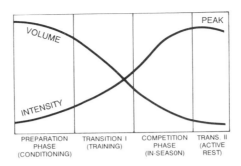

Figure 1-9.   Matveyev's Model of Periodization.

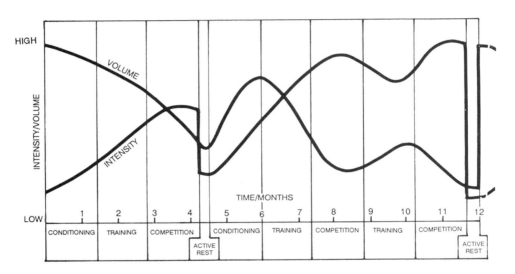

Figure 1-10.   Ward's Theoretical Model of Yearly Training.

1. **PREPARATION (CONDITIONING PERIOD):** A conditioning period is utilized when re-entering an exercise program after a period of inactivity. At this time the load (weight) is kept light and the volume (repetitions) medium. This might call for an exercise prescription of three to five sets of ten repetitions (3-5 sets X 10 reps X 40%-60% of 1RM). CWT or SCWT can also be used very effectively at this time. This type of training will condition the contractile proteins, connective tissue and the metabolic components of the muscles.

2. **TRANSITION I (TRAINING PERIOD):** During the training cycle an effort is made to increase strength and size. In this cycle the main emphasis is to focus on the structural aspect of strength, i.e., increasing the contractile proteins. This calls for an exercise prescription of three to five sets of five to eight repetitions with 75%-85% of 1RM. (3-5 sets X 5-8 reps X 75%-85% 1RM)

3. **COMPETITION (IN-SEASON PERIOD):** During the competition cycle an effort is made to focus upon the neural-muscular aspect of strength (the recruitment of motor units or developing the utilization of as much muscle fiber as possible through greater nervous control). This calls for the implementation of 3-7 sets of 1, 2, or 3 repetitions (cluster training) using 90% - 100% 1RM (3-7 SETS X 1-2-3 REPS X 90%- 100% 1RM) or pyramiding (progressively increasing the weight and reducing the repetitions performed until a near maximum lift is performed [3-7 sets X 1 rep X 90%-100% 1RM]).   The use of

cluster training (sets of 1, 2, or 3 repetitions) or pyramiding will not increase the size of the muscle, only the expression of strength as controlled by the recruitment of motor units; i.e., the central nervous system involvement.

4. **TRANSITION PERIOD II (ACTIVE REST):** During the Transition II period, one would engage in low intensity activity that might include very light weight loads and a variety of new and different exercises or various light sports activities.

Various independent researchers label the phases of periodization differently. Table 1-12 displays the classification systems for the four basic phases of periodization; three training phases and one phase of active rest and recovery. All the classifications described by these experts with the exception of Stone's characterization of Phase I as one of hypertrophy are reasonable explanations of the respective four phases of periodization.

Stone's hypertrophy description of Phase I does not seem to appropriately describe what occurs in this phase of training. It is doubtful whether much hypertrophy is generated in Phase I since the load is light (40-60% 1RM) and the repetitions performed are many (10-15 repetitions). Furthermore, empirical observations have shown that very little hypertrophy occurs during Phase I (preparation and conditioning) of periodization.

Many experts will further subdivide these four basic phases. For example, Phase I (conditioning) is sometimes divided into two sub-phases, general preparation and advanced preparation. Likewise, Phase III (competition) could be sub-divided into two sub-phases called competition training and strength maintenance. There are no absolutes with regard to classification of phases and sub-phases in periodization. This is where the "art" of coaching plays its role.

Table 1-12 also contains general ranges for intensities, volumes and the number of sets and repetitions performed in each phase of periodization.

Table 1-12. The Classification of Periodization Phases by Different Experts

EXPERT	PHASE I	PHASE II	PHASE III	PHASE IV
GENERALIZED*	BASE	LOAD	PEAK	RECOVERY
WARD	CONDITIONING	TRAINING	COMPETITION	ACTIVE REST
STONE	HYPERTROPHY	BASIC STRENGTH	STRENGTH/POWER	RECOVERY
MATVEYEV	PREPARATION	TRANSITION I	COMPETITION	TRANSITION II
PARAMETERS OF EXERCISE				
SETS	3 - 10	3 - 5	3 - 7	1 - 3
REPETITIONS	9 - 15	5 - 8	1 - 4	10 - 15+
INTENSITY	40%-60% 1RM	75%-85% 1RM	85%-100% 1RM	< 60% 1RM
PURPOSE	PREPARATION & CONDITIONING	STRENGTH AND HYPERTROPHY	STRENGTH AND POWER	REST AND RECOVERY

* PERIODIZATION FOR WEIGHT TRAINING AS UNDERSTOOD BY COACHES AND ATHLETES IN MANY SPORTS.

1. Matveyev, L.P.; Fundamentals of Sports Training; Progress Publishers; Moscow; 1981.

2. Matveyev, L.P.; Periodization of Sports Training; Fiskultura i Sport; Moscow; 1966.

3. Stone, M.H. and O'Bryant, H.; Weight Training: A Scientific Approach; Burgess Publishing Company; Minneapolis; 1984; pp. 168-187.

4. Ward, P.E.; Periodization (Cycling) Of Physical Training Programs; Information Bulletin of the Health and Tennis Corporation of America - Holiday Spa Health Clubs of California; Los Angeles; October 1982.

As mentioned above, each phase of periodization training has a specific purpose, so volume and intensity has to be very different in each of the training phases. Because the volume and intensity differs in each phase, the expected outcomes or benefits of each stage are completely different. **Phase I** basically is for conditioning and preparation (conditioning of the muscles, tendons, ligaments and connective tissue and the metabolic apparatus of the muscles). **Phase II** develops basic strength and produces maximum hypertrophy (increases in the contractile elements of the muscle). **Phase III** focuses on strength and power development (increases in the ability to recruit motor units). **Phase IV** is reserved for active rest and recovery.

The variation of intensity and volume of strength training has been studied extensively by the Russians but also by German, English and American researchers. (Dick 1980, Garhammer 1979, Matveyev 1966-1972-1981, Stone 1982, Tschiene 1979 and Ward 1982) The periodization principle also pertains to all training programs in general. This concept involves the intermittent variation of training intensities and volume throughout the years, months and weeks of a training pattern. Continuous training at high intensity or high volume levels (or both) produces plateaus or steep reductions of performance and leads to overtraining or staleness. In contrast, training with low intensities and/or low volumes leads to little improvement with frustration and despair.

Through planned variation of volume, intensity and exercises, the athlete, body builders or general fitness enthusiast can optimally achieve their goals. Lack of variation in the weight training program is one of the most common training mistakes.

Cycling of intensity and volume can be used in tapering for high level competition or just to change the program for diversity. While the former does not apply to the non-athletically involved, the latter is relevant. Changes (diversity) in the training program are a must for any level of exerciser. This involves reducing or increasing the training intensity, volume and sometimes - but not always - changing the exercises. This process creates the most favorable conditions for realizing existing potentials by storing up neuro-muscular energy and restoring freshness in the muscles and support systems of the body. Furthermore, regular and planned changes in volume and intensities greatly enhances motivation of the people participating in the training program.

RATIONALE FOR USING THE PERIODIZATION (CYCLING) CONCEPT

Dr. Hans Selye (1974 - a famous medical doctor who has studied the effects of all kinds of stresses on the human) has described a theory call the General Adaptation Syndrome (GAS). This theory has general application in the design of all exercise programs and supports the use of training cycles (periodization).

Basically, Dr. Selye's clinical observations with humans and experiments with mice and rats led him to purpose a three stage process employed by any living organism when adapting to a stimulus which tends to disrupt its normal state (known as homeostasis). In short, the theory involves three stages: (1) **Alarm**, which is the immediate response to a stressor; (2) **Resistance or Adaptation to the stressor**; and finally, (3) **Exhaustion or Fatigue**. Fatigue results when the organism can no longer adapt to the stresses. (See Figure 1-11 Selye's General Adaptation Syndrome [GAS].)

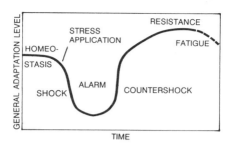

Figure 1-11. Selye's General Adaptation Syndrome (GAS).

The application of Selye's General Adaptation Syndrome (GAS) to a weight training program is shown in Figure 1-12.

The organism experiences an **alarm reaction (during the Preparation or Conditioning period)** after starting a strength training program which is followed by the **resistance reaction (during the Transition I or Training Period).** Then if the stressor (the training program) has been successfully applied there follows the **competition phase reaction (during the in-season period)** which results in higher adaptation levels. **If the exercise program stresses the body too much, then exhaustion or chronic fatigue occurs. When this occurs a cycle of active rest should be used.**

The curve in Figure 1-12 shows a double adaptation to higher levels of performance at the plateaus number 3 and number 6.

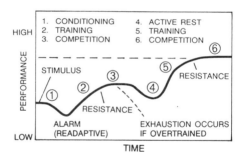

Figure 1-12. Application of the general adaptation syndrome to weight training programs.

Some format of this cycle (including most of the phases) should be repeated throughout the training history as many times as is necessary. **It is important to remember that periodization of weight training is applicable and needed for general fitness training participants and body builder's, as well as athletes.** Transition periods (active rest) are inserted after heavy training cycles to allow for the delayed training response and complete adaptation. **Note: If the sum of all stressors is too great then exhaustion (overtraining) is experienced.** This theoretical construct of Periodization (cycling) leads to **four practical reasons for the planned variation of volume, intensity and sometimes exercises in strength training programs:**

1. There must be gradual progressive preparation of the muscles and soft tissue (tendons, ligaments and connective tissue) for future exposure to greater volumes and higher intensities.

2. **There are two physiological aspects of muscular strength.** Each aspect requires the application of different volumes and intensities. The two different and unique physiological components of strength which require distinctly specific programs are:

(A) **THE HYPERTROPHY ASPECT:** Hypertrophy is the increasing of the contractile protein cross-section. In other words this means increasing the size of the muscle itself. This involves the execution of 3-5 sets of 5-8 repetitions executed with 75% to 85% of 1RM.

(B) **THE CENTRAL AND PERIPHERAL NERVOUS SYSTEM COORDINATION ASPECT:** This aspect involves teaching the total nervous system how to recruit the maximal number of motor units. This is the ability to use more of the muscle fibers. It involves the execution of 3-7 sets of 1-4 repetitions executed with 85% to 100% 1RM.

3. Continued high intensity or high volume training without recovery time leads to constant stimulation of the nervous and endocrine (hormonal) systems. The repeated energizing of these systems without rest periods can lead to overtraining and can be responsible for decreases in performance and/or training progress.

4. Increases in strength are larger and more stable when cycling programs are utilized (Dick 1980, Garhammer 1979, Matveyev 1966-1972-1981, Stone 1982, Tschiene 1979, and P. Ward 1982).

The training plan can be visualized as a pyramid. Figure 1-13 displays the components of a scientifically developed weight training program for general conditioning. The program includes the progression from general conditioning phases through advance training phases.

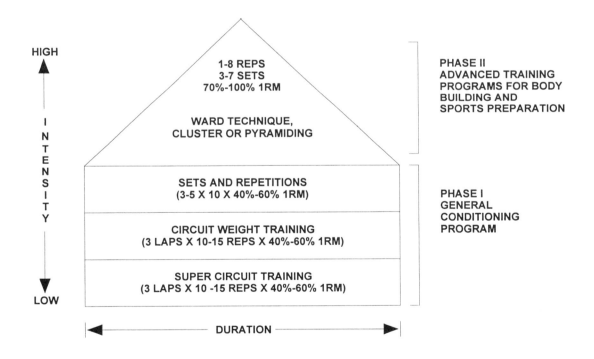

Figure 1-13. The components of a scientifically developed weight training program for general conditioning.

The **conditioning** phase forms the base with the duration long and intensity light to moderate. **More advanced training programs** are super-imposed on this base using higher intensities and varying volumes. Frequently between more advanced cycles it is advisable to return to one of the base phases or active rest cycles to allow for full restoration of the body. When weight training for general fitness, training for sport or training for body building, one should vary the volume (sets and repetitions) and intensity (% 1RM) to conform to the training goals and the training plan.

In Table 1-13 the recommendations for prescription of progressive resistance exercise programs appear. **The factors of frequency, intensity, duration, mode of activity, initial level of fitness and length of the training cycles** are displayed. These factors are quantified for beginning, intermediate and advanced training levels. Understanding the information contained in this table will assist one in the development of any training program. The term **"continuous"** refers to a pattern of exercise that does not allow for rest between exercises, such as in circuit weight training or super-circuit weight training. The term **"broken"** means that adequate periods of rest are inserted between exercises. These periods are usually not longer than two minutes; however, some high intensity programs may require longer rest periods.

The term "1RM" relates to the one repetition maximum or the maximum weight that can be lifted one time.

Table 1-13.   Recommendations For Prescriptions Of Progressive Resistance Exercise Programs.

FACTORS	PHASES		
	I. MODERATE INTENSITY - BEGINNER	II. MEDIUM/HIGH INTENSITY-INTERMEDIATE	III. HIGH INTENSITY - ADVANCED
FREQUENCY	3 DAYS/WEEK	3-5 DAYS/WEEK	3-6 DAYS/WEEK
INTENSITY	40%-60% 1RM 10-15 REPS PER SET 3-5 SETS	50%-85% 1RM 5-10 REPS PER SET 3-5 SETS	70%-100% 1RM 1-8 REPS PER SET 3-7 SETS
DURATION	20-40 MINUTES (CONTINUOUS OR BROKEN)	45-90 MINUTES (BROKEN)	45-150 MINUTES (BROKEN)
MODE OF ACTIVITY	CIRCUIT TRAINING - OR - SETS & REPETITIONS	CIRCUIT TRAINING - OR - SETS & REPETITIONS	SETS & REPETITIONS, CLUSTERS -OR- PYRAMIDING
INITIAL LEVEL OF FITNESS	HIGH = HIGH WORK LOADS LOW = LOW WORK LOADS	EVERYONE SHOULD START AT THE BEGINNING LEVEL BEFORE PROGRESSING TO HIGHER PHASES.	
LENGTH OF TRAINING PHASES	MINIMUM: 4 WEEKS MAXIMUM: 12 WEEKS	MINIMUM: 4 WEEKS MAXIMUM: 12 WEEKS	MINIMUM: 2 WEEKS MAXIMUM: 8 WEEKS

There are specific parameters of training that must be closely monitored in the application of cycling programs. Each parameter is systematically varied depending upon the program objectives. Table 1-14 contains information about cycling parameters for functional weight training programs. The information in the table describes the cycling phases and relates each phase to purpose; number of sets, repetitions, days per week, times per day, intensity and volume. By using this information one can design their progressive resistance exercise program in concert with scientific principles of weight training.

Notice that each phase varies the intensity, sets and repetitions in accordance with the purpose or objectives of each phase. Phase I, II, III, IV and V should be integrated so as to reach the overall training goal in the most efficient manner. **Developing an effective weight training cycle is part "art" and part "science".**

APPLICATIONS OF THE PERIODIZATION CONCEPT

Figure 1-14 shows an application of the periodization concept in a circuit weight training program. All phases with the exception of the in-season phase of scientific periodization are included in this format; i.e., (A) preparation, (B) conditioning, (C) training, and, (D) active rest. The competition phase is not utilized in general conditioning programs. Note that after Cycle A, B and C, an active rest cycle (D) is introduced.

Table 1-14. Cycling Parameters For Functional Strength Training Programs.

PHASE	I	II	III	IV	V
	CONDITIONING OR CWT-SCWT	TRAINING: WARD TECHNIQUE	TRANSITION: CLUSTER IN SEASON-A	PEAKING: PYRAMIDING IN SEASON-B	ACTIVE REST
PURPOSE	PREPARATION OR READAPTATION	INCREASE BASIC STRENGTH AND SIZE (HYPERTROPHY)	STRENGTH/ POWER	WORK CNS (MOTOR UNITS)	RECOVERY
SETS	3-5*	3-5*	3-7*	1-7*	1-3*
REPS	9-15	5-8	2-4	1-3	10-15
DAYS/WEEK	3-4	3-5	4-6	1-5	3-5
TIMES/DAY	1-3	1-3	1-2	1	1
INTENSITY	LOW (40%-60% 1RM)	MODERATE (75%-85% 1RM)	HIGH (90%-95% 1RM)	HIGH (90%-100% 1RM)	LOW (40%-60% 1RM)
VOLUME	HIGH 30,000 - 50,000 LBS. PER TRAINING SESSION	HIGH 40,000 - 60,000 LBS. PER TRAINING SESSION	MODERATE 20,000 - 40,000 LBS. PER TRAINING SESSION	LOW 10,000 - 20,000 LBS. PER TRAINING SESSION	LOW 10,000 - 30,000 LBS. PER TRAINING SESSION

* DOES NOT INCLUDE WARM-UP SETS.

This active rest cycle does not mean "no exercise". It merely means that the intensity and duration are low and the exercise focus changed for mental and physical rest and restoration. Activities could include stationary cycling, easy jogging, aerobic exercise or swimming, et cetera. After the active rest cycle you would merely repeat the circuit weight training cycle as many times as desired.

After the active rest cycle is fulfilled, cycles E, F and G are performed which is followed by another active rest cycle (H). This total macrocycle (A through H) could be repeated as many times as desired or a more advance cycle could be applied.

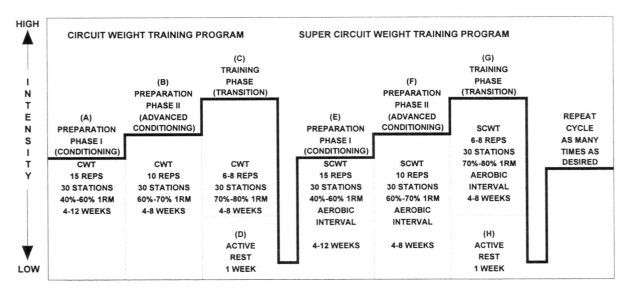

Figure 1-14. Application of the periodization concept in a circuit weight training program.

An advanced training cycle that could be applied is shown in Figure 1-15, application of the periodization concept in a beginner's general body building program. This program includes all the phases discussed; (A, B & C) preparation, (D) training, (E) competition, and, (F) active rest. This program can be very effectively used in a body builder's program. The program starts out, as it should, with a **conditioning period followed by more intense training cycles.** All the requirements for the training program are listed in the figure except the specific exercises. This is where the exerciser uses his intelligence and creativity. It is recommended that one use standard exercises with dumbbells, barbells or machines. Additionally, periods of active rest could be inserted at anytime between phases A, B, C, D and E as needed or desired.

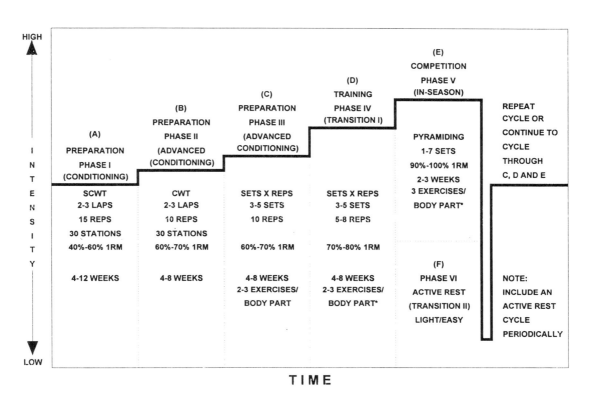

*   ONLY THE LARGE MUSCLE GROUPS SHOULD USE LOW REPS: CALVES, FOREARMS AND ABDOMINAL
     MUSCLE GROUPS SHOULD NOT USE THE PYRAMIDING PROCEDURE

Figure 1-15. Application of the periodization concept in a beginner's general body building program.

Figure 1-16 shows an example of cycling in a yearly weight training program for track and field. The cycle starts with circuit weight training; moves to sets and reps of 60% 1RM; followed by sets and reps of 80% 1RM; and them goes to pyramiding. The cycle is repeated but with shorter durations for each mini-cycle. The program would have to be specially tailored for each specific level of performance, high school, community college, university and open. Also, athletes who compete in an indoor season would have to modify this format to meet their competitive objectives. An active rest cycle could be inserted in this macrocycle at any position desired. However, it is possible to work through this macrocycle without any active rest phase. The planned and constant variation of volume and intensity produces enough change to allow physiological adaptations to occur. More examples of periodization of weight training programs for various sports appear in the section dealing with sports training.

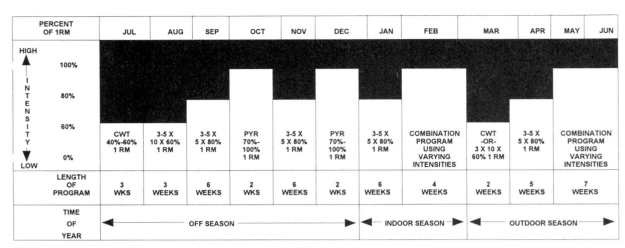

PERCENT OF 1RM	JUL	AUG	SEP	OCT	NOV	DEC	JAN	FEB	MAR	APR	MAY	JUN
	CWT 40%-60% 1 RM	3-5 X 10 X 60% 1 RM	3-5 X 5 X 80% 1 RM	PYR 70%-100% 1 RM	3-5 X 5 X 80% 1 RM	PYR 70%-100% 1 RM	3-5 X 5 X 80% 1 RM	COMBINATION PROGRAM USING VARYING INTENSITIES	CWT -OR- 3 X 10 X 60% 1 RM	3-5 X 5 X 80% 1 RM	COMBINATION PROGRAM USING VARYING INTENSITIES	
LENGTH OF PROGRAM	3 WKS	3 WEEKS	6 WEEKS	2 WKS	6 WEEKS	2 WKS	6 WEEKS	4 WEEKS	2 WEEKS	5 WEEKS	7 WEEKS	
TIME OF YEAR	◄─────── OFF SEASON ───────►						◄─ INDOOR SEASON ─►		◄─── OUTDOOR SEASON ───►			

* RECENT RUSSIAN REPORTS SHOW THAT VARYING (CYCLING) INTENSITY PROGRAMS PRODUCE BETTER RESULTS
IN STRENGTH TRAINING THAN CONSTANT INTENSITY PROGRAMS.

Figure 1-16.   An example of cycling in a training program for track and field athletes.

RELATED REFERENCES

1. Dick, F.W.; Sports Training Principles; Lepus Books; London, 1980.

2. Garhammer, J.; Periodization of strength training for athletes; Track Technique; Vol. 75; Spring 1978; pp. 2398-2399.

3. Matveyev, L.P.; Fundamentals of Sports Training; Progress Publishers; Moscow; 1981.

4. Matveyev, L.P.; Periodization of Sports Training; Fiskultura i Sport; Moscow; 1966.

5. Matveyev, L.P.; Periodisienang dos sportichen training (Translated into German by P. Tschienne with a chapter by A. Kruger) Berlin; Beles and Wernitz, 1972.

6. Selye, H.; Stress Without Stress; J.R. Lippincott; New York, 1974.

7. Stone, M., et al; A Theoretical Model of Strength Training; National Strength & Conditioning Association Journal; August/September, 1982; pp. 36-39.

8. Stone, M.H. and O'Bryant, H.; Weight Training: A Scientific Approach; Burgess Publishing Company; Minneapolis; 1984; pp. 168-187.

9. Tschiene, P.; The Distinction of Training Structure in Different Stages of Athletes's Preparation; Paper presented at the International Congress of Sports Sciences; Edmonton, Alberta, Canada; July 25-29, 1979.

10. Ward, Paul; From a speech delivered at AAHPERD Convention; Houston, Texas; April 24, 1982.

11. Ward, Paul; Periodization (Cycling) of Physical Training Programs; Information Bulletin of The Health And Tennis Corporation of America - Holiday Health Spa Health Clubs; October, 1982.

12. Yessis, M.; From Macro-To-Meso-To-Micro Cycles; National Strength and Conditioning Association Journal; August/September, 1982; pp. 45-47.

PART I

THEORY & PRACTICE

METHODS OF DETERMINING TRAINING LOADS
(LOAD PRESCRIPTION AND STARTING WEIGHTS)

THREE BASIC METHODS OF DETERMINING TRAINING LOADS

Load prescriptions or starting weights can be selected in three ways: (1) **Trial and error search**; (2) **Use of percentage of body weight**; and, (3) **Percentages of 1RM**. Each method is discussed below but before presenting the methods of determining training loads or starting weights, a few words of introduction are in order.

It is difficult to prescribe training loads without having some idea of the current functional strength capacity of the individual. However, prior to the beginning of a weight training program for the beginner and deconditioned weight trainers, one should be exposed to a conditioning/orientation training phase. During this time one would become familiarized with exercise techniques plus achieve some physical conditioning. This period can range from one to four weeks in duration. During this break-in period, the weight for the exercises should not be emphasized.

For purposes of easing into the training program, the first few weeks one can use a percent of the body weight or the trial and error method of determining training loads for the selected exercises as long as the weight loads do not produce straining. The weight loads in this conditioning period should be rather easy. This is especially acceptable for the beginner because there is a need to learn how to perform the exercises as well as undergo some conditioning before moving to higher intensities.

Ultimately, when one is prepared for serious training they must adjust their training loads in order to adequately elicit the desired and planned physiological response. Somewhere in the first 4 to 6 weeks the beginner will have to determine a more precise loading to enable maximal strength gains. This can be accomplished by implementing any one of the methods discussed below.

The intermediate and advanced weight trainer does not need to participate in a conditioning/orientation phase except when learning new exercise movements or on re-entry into a weight training program after a long lay-off. For conditioned intermediate and advanced weight trainers, one should use the 1RM procedure to determine weight loads for most of the exercises.

For those intermediate and advanced lifters who are deconditioned, it best to undergo a short training period (2 to 4 weeks) with moderate intensities until the muscle soreness has subsided and then test for 1RM. The trial and error search method or the percentage of body weight technique are acceptable methods to determine weight loads for the break-in period. But after a short period of time (2 to 4 weeks) a 1RM test should be utilized to effectively adjust the training loads for the intermediate and advanced lifter.

The three basic techniques for determining starting weights and training loads will now be discussed.

1. **THE TRIAL AND ERROR SEARCH METHOD:** The trial and error search method for selecting a training load requires a few attempts at using progressively heavier weight loads until the prescribed number of sets and repetitions can be performed.

   For example, assume the exercise prescription is three to five sets of ten repetitions (3-5 Sets X 10 Repetitions). After a warmup, one would select a weight and attempt to perform 3-5 sets of 10 repetitions. In the initial weight selection one should be conservative and select a light weight. If the selected weight can be lifted rather easily for 10 repetitions, then on the next set the weight should be increased by 10 pounds.

   A second set of 10 repetitions would then be attempted with the added weight and evaluated. If 10 repetitions can be performed easily, a third set should be attempted with an additional 10 pounds. This process should be repeated until the satisfactory performance of 10 repetitions with a moderate effort.

If the final weight is too easy, then repeat the process in the next training session until the one can perform the correct number of repetitions without straining on all ten repetitions for the prescribed number of sets. Because of cumulative fatigue and a poor conditioning state, it may be necessary to reduce the weight to enable the performance of 10 repetitions for 3-5 sets.

An alternative method would be to bracket the prospective training load. The first set would be performed and evaluated with a light weight. A second set would be performed with the addition of 20 pounds. If the second set of 10 repetitions is too easy, then a third set is performed with an additional 20 pounds. This process should be repeated until the satisfactory performance of 10 repetitions with a moderate effort. Of course, if at any weight load the prescribed 10 repetitions cannot be performed, then one should make the appropriate adjustment by reducing the weight.

This method is not the best method for determining weight loads for exercises because it is subject to psychological prejudices and usually results in a lot of wasted time. Physical training re-entry, time constraints, equipment availability and motivation will determine if this method should be applied. This trial and error search for training loads is the least desirable of all the techniques for determining training loads.

2. **THE PERCENTAGE OF BODY WEIGHT METHOD:** A percentage of the body weight can be used to select the training load for exercises used in weight training. The exact percentage will be determined by the type of equipment the exerciser is using, machines or free weights. The amount of weight that can be used for free weights and dumbbells may be quite different from the weight that can be used on machines. Also, there may be large differences in the weight that can be used for the same exercise but using different exercise machines. This is due to biomechanical differences and the method that equipment manufacturers use to define their weight stacks.

Even when using this means of training load selection, trial and error search may be necessary to precisely tune the training loads; however, the use of this technique may simplify and shorten the selection of the training loads. Table 1-15 presents some guidelines for using percentages of body weight for starting weights in selected weight training exercises with machines and free weights.

Table 1-15. An Example Of Selection Of Starting Weights Using Percentages Of Body Weight For Machines And Free Weight Exercises.

MACHINES	% BODY WEIGHT	FREE WEIGHT EXERCISE	% BODY WEIGHT
1. SQUAT	30% - 50%	1. SQUAT	30% - 50%
2. SHOULDER PRESS	20% - 30%	2. SHOULDER PRESS	20% - 30%
3. LEG CURL	15% - 20%	3. STIFF LEG DEAD LIFT	20% - 40%
4. PULLDOWN	30% - 50%	4. BENT OVER ROWING	20% - 40%
5. KNEE EXTENSION	30% - 40%	5. FRONT SQUAT	20% - 30%
6. BENCH PRESS	30% - 40%	6. BENCH PRESS	30% - 40%
7. BACK EXTENSION	20% - 30%	7. GOOD MORNING	10% - 20%
8. CURLS	15% - 30%	8. CURLS	15% - 30%
9. ABDOMINAL MACHINE	5% - 20%	9. ABDOMINAL CRUNCH	0% - 10%
10. VERTICAL FLY	10% - 20%	10. DUMBBELL FLY	5% - 15%

NOTE:
  THESE PERCENTAGES ARE ONLY GUIDELINES. THE EXACT LOADING MAY HAVE TO BE ADJUSTED UPWARD OR DOWNWARD FROM THE PERCENTAGES OF BODY WEIGHT. IT IS BEST TO USE LIGHTER WEIGHT UNTIL THE EXERCISE TECHNIQUE IS LEARNED AND SOME CONDITIONING OCCURS BEFORE USING HEAVIER WEIGHTS.

3. **THE 1RM METHOD:** The one repetition maximum (1RM) testing is the best method for determining training loads for weight training exercises. This ensures that the prescribed training loads are precisely suitable for each person and each exercise. For the beginner and the deconditioned intermediate and advanced weight trainer it is very important that an individual go through a two to four week orientation and conditioning period before attempting 1RM testing so that undue soreness will not have to be endured. The conditioned intermediate and advanced weight trainer can immediately employ the 1RM test, if desired.

There are two basic methods for determining the 1RM. The methods utilized will depend on each individual's preference. However, the basic principles of muscle physiology should still apply. No matter what individual techniques are utilized, the **ART** is to arrive at the **maximum weight levels** with the **greatest** amount of strength potential available.

A. The <u>Pyramid</u> approach insures a proper muscle temperature, good technique, and proper psychological set. A set of 1- 3 repetitions is performed followed by another set with additional weight. After one or two sets of three repetitions, the repetitions are reduced to one and the weight is increased until it is not possible to execute a correct repetition. The heaviest weight that can be correctly completed is the 1RM. This is similar to pyramid sets, except the emphasis is on <u>warm-up</u>, <u>conservation of energy</u> and <u>maximal weight</u> rather than a workout.

B. The <u>Square</u> method includes a warm-up period, but bypasses too many intermediate lifts prior to the 1RM level. After a warmup, one proceeds to perform successive sets with more weight until the 1RM is reached. In these sets only 1 repetition is performed and very few sets are executed.

Using the 1RM, intensity levels are broadly arranged into one of the following classifications:

HIGH	90% +
HEAVY	80 - 90%
MEDIUM	70 - 80%
LIGHT	60 - 70%
MINIMAL	60% or less

THE RATIONALE FOR USING 1RM TESTING

The application of 1RM testing will provide information that is used in assigning valid exercise prescriptions and impacts the adherence to the exercise program by enhancing motivation. The main reasons for performing the 1RM test are as follows:

1. To access the current strength levels and functional capacity.
2. To identify possible weaknesses by using a strength profile.
3. To evaluate the training program and individual progress.
4. To provide motivation and facilitate exercise adherence.

Reasonably accurate training loads will produce more predictable training results which will provide motivation for continuing the exercise program.

THE PHILOSOPHY FOR USING 1RM TESTING

In prescribing any kind of exercise program, one should establish the functional capacity for each component of fitness. Of course, one could assume a low level of conditioning but it would be very difficult to establish the proper intensity (training load). One could also estimate a proposed maximal but it is very difficult to make a good appraisal without some valid information. The best method for establishing the functional capacity is to test for it.

The most accurate method for establishing the functional capacity in the strength dimension is to perform a one repetition maximum test (1RM). This is defined as the largest amount of weight that can be correctly moved through the range of motion. Many people have doubts as to the safety of such a procedure arguing that the risk of injury is too great. It is the belief of the authors that this assumption is unfounded. The authors conclusion is based upon a large amount of empirical observations over 100 combined years of experience with young and old, males and females of sound and unsound bodies. People just don't injure themselves by performing 1RM tests unless pre-existing conditions are present or stupid procedures are being employed. Experience has shown that in most cases, 1RM tests are safe and can be used to effectively determine functional capacity of various muscle groups.

Insisting upon proper warmup and correct technique performance can eliminate any small chance that injury might occur plus insure that a valid estimation of strength can be made. If these principles are applied it is very easy to harmlessly determine the 1RM. Another procedure that will guarantee a safe experience when executing 1RM tests is to have a two to three week training and conditioning period prior to administering a 1RM test. Application of a short training and conditioning period before administering 1RM testing will allow for mastering the technique of performance in addition to allowing for conditioning of the muscles, tendons ligaments and connective tissue. This is the ideal situation but we live in a practical world where most of the time it is not possible to adhere to the ideal model. **Even when a short conditioning period is not practical the 1RM test can be safely administered as long as a warmup is properly executed and there is adherence to strict technique performance. The only negative result may be the soreness that may occur post testing.**

Some people use 2RM, 3RM or some other multiple repetition procedure to estimate functional strength. Multiple repetition tests are not good methods for estimating maximum strength to be used in the prescription of weight training loads.

Firstly, such procedures are based on the spurious assumption that injury while performing 1RM tests are inevitable. This false assumption, of course, has not been supported by valid research nor can one find adequate supporting empirical evidence to discredit the use of 1RM tests.

Secondly, the ability to perform repeated repetitions at assorted percentages of one's maximum strength (2RM, 3RM, etc.) varies greatly between individuals; therefore, when using multiple repetition tests there are no accurate or valid methods to predict 1RM (maximum functional strength). Using this technique is invalid because everyone has a very different capacity for performing multiple repetitions with various weight loads. For example, one person may be able to perform 2 repetitions at 97 1/2 % of 1RM while the next person can perform only one repetition with only 92 1/2 % of 1RM. Therefore, this is an invalid procedure for determine maximum strength since there is no way to know what one's maximum strength is unless it is measured.

The use of multiple repetitions tests causes an underestimating of the training loads and thus produces less than desirable effects from application of the training program. When using multiple repetitions to assign training loads, one frequently finds the training loads too low to elicit the expected physiological response to strength training; i.e., increased strength.

The proper application of the 2RM, 3RM, 5RM, 10RM or any RMs (repetitions maximum) more than 1RM, is to determine the functional capacity for local muscular endurance. Multiple repetition tests should not be used to estimate 1RM which would then be employed to determine the training loads. The 1RM should be tested to determine maximum strength for the adequate prescription of training loads while the multiple repetitions maximum (RM) tests should be used for determination of local muscular endurance.

Table 1-16 displays an example of determination of training loads using 60% of 1RM for selected exercises in a weight training program for free weight exercises and machines. The arrangement of exercises is a peripheral heart action (PHA) pattern.

Table 1-16.   An Example Of Determination Of Training Loads Using 60% Of 1RM For Selected Exercises In A Weight Training Program For Free Weight Exercises And Machines.

MUSCLE GROUPS	FREE WEIGHT EXERCISE	1RM	60% 1RM	MACHINES	1RM	60% 1RM
1. HIP/LEG/BACK	SQUAT	100 LBS	60 LBS	SQUAT	100 LBS	60 LBS
2. SHOULDERS	STANDING PRESS	50 LBS	30 LBS	SHOULDER PRESS	50 LBS	30 LBS
3. POSTERIOR THIGH	LEG CURL (MACHINE) -OR- STIFF LEG DEAD LIFT	40 LBS 100 LBS	24 LBS 60 LBS	LEG CURL	40 LBS	24 LBS
4. UPPER BACK	PULLDOWN (MACHINE) -OR- CHINS (BODY WEIGHT-PLUS)	60 LBS # REPS	36 LBS 60%/REPS	PULLDOWN	60 LBS	36 LBS
5. ANTERIOR THIGH	LEG EXTENSIONS (MACHINE) -OR- FRONT SQUAT	60 LBS 80 LBS	36 LBS 48 LBS	LEG EXTENSIONS	60 LBS	36 LBS
6. CHEST	BENCH PRESS	70 LBS	42 LBS	BENCH PRESS	70 LBS	42 LBS
7. ABDOMINAL	ABDOMINAL MACHINE -OR- BENT KNEE CRUNCH	70 LBS 40 LBS	42 LBS 24 LBS	ABDOMINAL MACHINE	70 LBS	42 LBS
8. ANTERIOR ARM	ARM CURLS	40 LBS	24 LBS	ARM CURLS	40 LBS	24 LBS
9. LOW BACK	BACK EXTENSION (MACHINE) GOOD MORNING	90 LBS 50 LBS	54 LBS 30 LBS	BACK EXTENSION	90 LBS	54 LBS
10. POSTERIOR ARM	STANDING FRENCH PRESS	30 LBS	18 LBS	PUSHDOWN	40 LBS	24 LBS

TRAINING PROGRESSION OF WEIGHT LOADS

INTRODUCTION

Progression in exercise is a natural instinct of mankind. Adults intuitively have a sense of progression when exercising, but usually lack the will or knowledge of how to sensibly progress in exercise. They need to be programmed or follow a system. Furthermore, without being specifically educated or directed, children during random playing will try to progressively lift heavier objects, jump farther or higher. Another concept of progression is the concept of two to three warmup or practice attempts before a complex or new skill is attempted. At issue is how to make progression effective and safe in weight training. The answer lies in the knowledge and application of the principles of periodization.

In good weight training programs the weight must be increased progressively to insure continued success. Also, there are times when the weight loads should be decreased instead of increased. The variation of weight loads may be formatted in hundreds of successful ways. It is important to note that while increases in weight loads are important there must be a system that allows for intelligent application of progressive resistance mixed with times of unloading and active rest.

It is not always necessary or desirable to increase the weight loads arbitrarily. There must be planned increases and decreases in weight loads throughout the training cycle. The variation of the weight load by increases and decreases is called periodization. The concept of periodization of training is thoroughly discussed under the title of **Periodization of Physical Training Programs** in this section of this book. It is sufficient at this point to state that weight progressions must occur regularly but they must be planned, be reasonable and be combined with decreases in weight loads and active rest periods.

Selectorized weight training machines with weight stacks have become popular because of the intuitive practice of increasing weight progressively and the ease of which weight can be changed. This permits a number of people with widely varying strength levels to use the same machine in an alternating manner. Presently, very sophisticated but easy to employ methods are used to change the weight load, such as selectorized weight stacks. However, free weights and dumbbells still are the most popular method of weight training but it takes more time to adjust the barbell weights. Machines and free weights allow for easy adjustment of training loads and facilitate weight progression.

It is vitally important that weight training programs allow for progressive resistance for two reasons:

1. To allow for proper physiological and psychological warmup for each exercise and training session.

2. To systematically change the training loads over time in accordance with the training plan to effectively improve strength and size.

Whatever weight training program or objectives are defined, there must be progressive overload to continue to improve strength and increase size. However, continued application of weight loads without times of reduced weight loads and active rest is counterproductive to strength and size improvements. It is important to adhere to the principles of periodization in order to maximize strength and hypertrophy gains. To randomly apply unending progressive resistance is to limit success and predispose to muscular-skeletal injuries.

Before progression can be addressed, it is important to understand how to effectively prescribe the initial starting weight loads for each exercise. It is common sense to base training on the functional capacity of each muscle group at the time of entry into the weight training program. The practical problem is; "How do you determine the functional capacity of the muscles when performing new and unusual movements while being in a deconditioned state?"

The answer is to engage in an orientation and conditioning program performing the desired new exercises at reasonably light weight loads. During this conditioning period the specific exercise movements are mastered and the muscles, tendons, ligaments and connective tissue undergo some initial conditioning. The beginning weight loads are generally accepted as the amount of weight that can be easily handled for ten repetitions of the desired movement for three sets. After two to four weeks of training a series of 1RM tests should be performed to approximate the functional capacities of various muscle groups of the weight trainer. From these 1RMs a percentage can be assigned that will effectively conditioning the muscles in agreement with the training objectives of the weight training program.

For beginners the starting weights for a strength training program is usually determined by trial and error. A common practice is to select a weight that can be correctly performed for 3 sets of 10 repetitions. Another method would be to select a percentage of the body weight for each specific exercise. A discussion of these techniques appears in a foregoing part of this section under the title of **"Factors In Programming Progressive Resistance Exercise" and the subtopic of Intensity.**

Whatever method is used, trial and error or percentage of body weight for determining starting weights, after a two to four week training session, one should perform a 1RM test to determine the functional capacity of the muscle groups for each exercise. When the functional capacity is known, a precise weight load for each exercise can be prescribed as a percentage of the 1RM in accordance with the training objectives.

Intermediate and advance weight trainers can execute 1RM tests without undergoing a conditioning phase to determine effective weight exercise loads, providing they are not coming from a detrained state. Furthermore, for all weight trainers (beginning, intermediate and advanced) **it is important to remember that the absolute maximum is not needed when testing for 1RMs.** An approximate 1RM is adequate. Moreover, the exercises that are being tested must be performed with strict technique. The 1RM approximations are acceptable for determining effective starting weight loads and subsequent progressive weight loadings. The techniques for progressive weight loadings are discussed below.

METHODS OF PROGRESSION

Once effective starting weight loads are determined and training commences, it is necessary to systematically increase the weight loads as strength and size improve. There are three basic methods of progressing in weight training: (1) **arbitrary weight progressions**; (2) **combination technique (testing 1RM and arbitrary increases)**; and, (3) **progression by repetitions.** Each of these techniques is described below.

1. ARBITRARY WEIGHT PROGRESSIONS:

Once effective and specific training loads are assigned, it is important to make sure there is progression in the weight loads in order to continue to improve strength levels. In general terms, one may arbitrarily increase the load every 3 to 6 training sessions; 5 - 10 pounds for the upper body and 10 - 20 pounds for the lower body. These are reasonable amounts of weight to add, however, smaller increments can be used if desired and if the selected weight resistance device allows for smaller weight increments. Not all exercises in the routine may or will require frequent progressions, eg., leg curls, calf and forearm exercises. Basically, most of the major exercise weight loads need to be incremented, usually on Monday of each week or every other week.

When weight increases are made it is important to make sure that the set and repetition prescription be followed. While it may be acceptable to drop one repetition per set during training, any further deviation from the set and repetition prescription means that the new weight load is too heavy and the trainer is not ready to increase. In this case, return to the previous load for 3 to 6 more workouts and then progress to higher weight loads when increases in the strength levels allow the performance of the prescribed number of sets and repetitions at the new weight loadings.

It is probable that not all weight loads for the various exercises can be increased every 3 to 6 workout periods. In this case it is recommended that increases be made in only those exercises where the increased weight load allows for the performance of the set and repetition prescription. Another way to increase weight loads is to select one half of the exercises to increase the weight loads one week and the second half to be increased the following week whenever progressive weight increases are desired.

It is not possible to continue to add weight progressively, forever. Consequently, it is important to regularly unload the muscles by reducing the volume and intensity before returning to intense training. An understanding of the principles of Periodization will allow for the proper programming of the exerciser and insure the continued success of the training program. Also, one will ultimately resort to using the 1RM technique to effectively continue to train at productive intensities without underloading or overloading. The 1RM technique is described below and, also under the heading of 1RM procedure discussed in **"METHODS OF DETERMINING TRAINING LOADS"** which appears in the previous part of this section.

2. COMBINATION TECHNIQUE (1RM TESTING AND ARBITRARY INCREASES):

The best method to insure that effective training loads are incorporated in the weight training regimen is to plan for periodic 1RM tests for the exercises in the program. Testing for 1RM can occur weekly but this frequency of testing becomes time consuming and tedious. Besides, it is not necessary to test weekly because detectable strength changes do not occur in seven days. It is better to test 1RMs every two, four or six weeks. Of course, one could test 1RMs every three, six and nine weeks, or whatever format that is desired. The authors recommend retesting between every four to six week cycle.

After the initial weight loadings are determined, the weight loads are arbitrarily increased every three to six training sessions by 5 to 10 pounds for the upper body and 10 to 20 pounds for the lower body providing that the exercise prescription of sets and repetitions is achieved. If the additional weight loadings do not allow for the performance of the exercise prescription then one should return to the

THEORY & PRACTICE

previous loadings for 3 to 6 more training sessions and progress to heavier weight loads when strength has increased.

There is no method known to man, other than testing or trial and error, that will allow one to predict when to advance in weight loads. Therefore, one must be flexible and understanding when arbitrarily increasing weight loads. **The governing principle for progression is to increase weight only if the prescribed number of sets and repetitions can be performed.**

From the 1RM test one can determine the precise training loads by determining the percentages of 1RM that are in harmony with the training objectives for the next cycle. The authors have successfully used for many years the 1RM technique to establish and reestablish precise training loads along with arbitrary increases of 5 to 10 pounds for the upper body and 10 to 20 pounds for the lower body.

The combination technique is very effective and assures that productive training loads will be used. This method, also, guards against the possibilities of over-training and helps reduce the possibility of soft tissue injuries. Using this technique, there is little chance of the exerciser constantly straining to get the desired number of repetitions with a weight load that is beyond their capacity. The philosophy that needs to applied is to **"Train, Don't Strain"** or **"Stimulate, Don't Annihilate."**

3. PROGRESSION BY REPETITIONS:

A commonly applied method of progression is the increasing repetitions method. This entails selecting weight loadings that can be performed for the prescribed number of sets and repetitions, and, over time increasing the repetitions by two or three. When the exerciser can perform all the desired number of sets with the additional repetitions the weight is increased by 5 to 10 pounds. This technique is acceptable for beginners, but really is not in accordance with the more advanced and more effective methods to determine weight progressions. Furthermore, progression by using increased repetitions may lead to underloading or overloading. Underloading does not produce acceptable results while overloading leads to overtraining or frustration.

While this technique is acceptable, it lacks the precision of testing for functional capacity (1RM) followed by the adjusting of weight loads based on true strength gains.

SUMMARY STATEMENT ON TRAINING PROGRESSION OF WEIGHT LOADS

The need for progression is a natural instinct. The difficult task is to implement progression in weight training effectively and safely. Sensible progression is needed during each training session for each exercise and, also, over the course of the training program to insure effective training loads which produce continue improvements in strength and size.

Initial starting weight loads must be effectively determined. These starting training weights can be determined by trial and error, percentages of body weight or by testing of the 1RM for each exercise with subsequent prescription of the desired percentages based on the 1RM. The 1RM method is the preferred method for people who are conditioned. For deconditioned people, it is wise to implement a two to four week orientation and conditioning period before 1RM testing.

After the proper starting weight loads are determined it is necessary to develop a system of progression. Weight progressions can be performed in three ways: (1) Arbitrary weight progressions; (2) Combination technique (1RM testing and arbitrary increases); and, (3) Progression indicated by adding repetitions to the set and repetition prescriptions.

Using the combination program (1RM testing and arbitrary weight increases) with periodic retesting of 1RMs is the best technique to effectively progress in a weight training programs. Testing 1RM have been demonstrated to be effective and safe in numerous studies and in innumerable practical applications.

SYSTEMS OF TRAINING

INTRODUCTION

There are many variations of training systems using weight machines or free weights. The "training system" relates to the technique or procedure involved in the actual application of the weight training exercises. When planning a weight training program there are many factors that have to be considered. The program that is adopted must meet the objectives for training. The integration of all the training factors are discussed in the section entitled **"Factors In Programming Progressive Resistance Exercise"** presented in **Part I of the Encyclopedia of Weight Training.** These factors are: frequency, intensity, duration, mode, level of fitness, length of training phases, exercise selection and exercise sequence. These factors are thoroughly discussed in the section mentioned above.

It is impossible, ineffective and unnecessary to present all the possible systems of training for body building. Therefore, only the most commonly used and popular systems of training are presented in this section.

The routines involving multiple-sets performed non-stop should not be used extensively, however, they can be effectively used during selected cycles of training. The concept of cycling using various routine formats should be carefully planned to take into consideration all the factors of periodization, training and competition.

SETS AND REPETITIONS

By far the most common and most popular system of training is the sets and repetitions format. In this system a specified number of repetitions are performed for a designated number of sets. The exercises to be performed are placed into an intelligent order and 2 to 7 sets of 1 to 15 repetitions are executed at an intensity that is consistent with training goals. The training procedure includes a number of sets for the warmup and cooldown for each specific exercise in the routine. These sets are not usually counted as part of the exercise prescription. The specific warm-up for an exercise usually includes the performance of a series of sets of 5 to 10 repetitions starting with a very light weight which is progressively increased up to the training weight. The number of warm-up sets ranges between 3 to 5 sets.

The rest interval between sets is dictated by the objectives of the weight training program, the physical condition of the trainee and the intensity level of the exercise. Rest periods typically are from 1 to 5 minutes. The main purpose of the rest period is to allow enough recovery so that subsequent sets can be correctly performed for the prescribed number of repetitions. Typical examples of sets and repetitions are the following:

1. Three to five sets of ten repetitions at 40%-60% 1RM. (3-5 SETS X 10 REPS X 40% - 60% 1RM)
2. Three to five sets of five repetitions at 75%-85% 1RM. (3-5 SETS X 5 REPS X 75% - 85% 1RM)
3. Four sets of eight repetitions at 60%-75% 1RM. (4 SETS X 8 REPS X 60% - 75% 1RM)
4. Other Formats: There are many other set and repetition formats. A body builder is only limited by their creativity and the program objectives.

Any number of sets and repetitions can be utilized in this format. Remember the specific number of repetitions and the intensity (% 1RM) will be dictated by the goals of the training program.

The sets and repetitions format is the system that should be used for most of the time when training. Other techniques discussed below are usually integrated into this system for training of one or two of the muscle groups within a training routine. Also, at different phases in the periodization of training many other variants or techniques of training can be effectively employed, but the majority of time, one should employ the standard sets and repetitions method.

CHEATING REPETITIONS

Cheating repetitions involve the use of unusual body movements or executing the movement faster to add momentum to the weight so that the exercise action can be easily completed. When this occurs the primary muscle or muscle groups being trained do not receive maximum stimulus and, therefore, cheating repetitions are not of great value.

Cheating repetitions are usually reserved for the last sets and last repetitions of an exercise. Examples of cheating are arching in the bench press action or swinging the barbell or dumbbell when performing a curl. The cheating repetitions method is generally employed in one of two ways:

(1)   When the trainee has performed all the possible strict repetitions, then various abnormal body configurations or the use an inordinate amount of momentum are employed to move the bar or weight machine through the weak point in the range of motion (the sticking point).

(2)   The trainee purposely selects a weight that will force them to adopt unnatural postures and movements to increase the momentum of the weight or machine which will enable them to drive the resistance through the weak point in the range of motion (the sticking point). The person consciously uses cheating movements in all the prescribed repetitions of the set. The fundamental purpose of using cheating movements is to handle as much weight as possible without regard for technique.

The use of cheating movements is not recommended. The performance of cheating repetitions is not prudent and is a bad training method because it is based on the false belief that this procedure will enhance strength and size because more of the muscle is used. It is a mistaken conclusion to assume that more muscle fiber of the same muscle will be recruited when cheating repetitions are performed. What actually happens when muscles become fatigued and the trainee resorts to performing cheating movements, is that other previously unused muscles become involved in the action. There is a change in the biomechanical patterns of exercise, some which are potentially injurious and result in over-stressing all the body systems. Furthermore, if a heavy weight is purposely selected and cheating repetitions are performed as described in # 2 above, then other muscle groups become involved in the action. Consequently, there is minimal specific conditioning of the primary muscles involved in the action.

The use of cheating repetitions when the trainee becomes fatigued or when the weight is intentionally increased so that cheating is required to perform the exercise does not improve strength and size of specific muscles. However, it is possible to increase the strength of the cheating exercises which may or may not increase the size of the many muscles involved in the movement. The potential for injury, muscle strains and overtraining is high when using these cheating practices so the risks are greater than the benefits. Certainly, there is no isolation of a muscle or muscle group when using this system.

The employment of cheating repetitions is probably not a good idea and the tendency to use this technique should be resisted. Muscle size and strength are improved by performing the correct exercise movements and appropriately applying the principles of periodization.

FORCED REPETITIONS

Forced repetitions is really another form of cheating. The application of forced repetitions is when the trainee has reached a point of muscle exhaustion, then a training partner assists in the performance of 3 to 4 additional repetitions. **The person who is performing most of the work is the training partner, not the one executing the exercise.** Forced repetitions are usually executed at the end of the last 2 sets of an exercise.

The employment of this technique is the result of misunderstanding the physiology of muscle operation and growth. When a muscle becomes fatigued, less of the muscle fibers are recruited resulting in a decrease in the force expression of muscle contraction. Less of the muscle is utilized in the action causing failure to complete the last repetition which requires the training partner to assist. Applying the forced repetition method does not result in the primary exerciser performing more work since the training partner performs much of the lifting and the accumulated fatigue reduces the potential to continue to perform exercise. The primary exerciser cannot produce the necessary force because of the accumulation of fatigue, and, consequently, the training partner has to perform most of the work.

The reasons that people employ such an ineffective method of training are:

(1)   The belief that they are pushing the muscle to the limit by using forced repetitions.
(2)   An effort to increase motivation.
(3)   The belief that they are stimulating reluctant muscles to grow by using forced repetitions.

None of these reasons are valid arguments for the use of forced repetitions as a training system. Forced repetitions do not require the muscle to increase it contraction force; therefore, there is no stimulus for the muscle fibers to grow (this requires more intensity - a percent of 1RM); and, the training partner does most of the work in allowing the forced repetition to be completed. To be very frank, forced repetitions are ineffective for developing strength and size and the concept is based on a poor understanding of exercise physiology and training theory.

The employment of forced repetitions is probably not a good idea and the tendency to use this technique should be resisted. Muscle size and strength are improved by performing the correct exercise movements and appropriately applying the principles of periodization.

PARTIAL REPETITIONS

Performing partial repetitions is another method of cheating. Partial repetitions are performed after the last repetition of the last set, when one is incapable of performing another full repetition. At this point, the trainee performs 1/2 or 1/4 repetitions until they can do no more. As with cheating repetitions and forced repetitions this technique is based on a poor understanding of exercise physiology and training theory. The person who uses this technique is not in touch with the realities of exercise physiology.

This technique is usually performed while executing joint extension movements; such as pressing movements, elbow and knee extension actions and in squatting or leg pressing exercises. However, occasionally this technique is also employed on pulling exercises like curls, rowing, pulldowns or chins.

The weaknesses of this method are:

(1)   Partial repetitions only train that part of the muscle that is active and there is no transfer of strength to other muscle parts or points in the range of motion.

(2)   When the muscle fatigues, muscle fibers start to drop out of use. The exerciser is only able to execute 1/2 or 1/4 repetitions because the leverages of the muscles and joints are favorable at the point in the range of motion where such actions are used. This is at the end of the pressing action, elbow extension, leg extension, squatting or leg pressing movements; and at the start of any of the pulling motions. More of the muscle is not recruited when the muscle becomes fatigued and forced by some artificial method to continue working.

THEORY & PRACTICE   PART I

(3)   The employment of partial repetitions is based on the erroneous concept of forcing the muscle to work harder. As the muscle fatigues, muscle fibers drop out of use so in fact the muscle is doing less work.

The employment of partial repetitions is probably not a good idea and the tendency to use this technique should be resisted. Muscle size and strength are improved by performing the correct exercise movements and appropriately applying the principles of periodization.

NEGATIVE REPETITIONS (ECCENTRIC CONTRACTIONS)

Negative repetitions (known scientifically as eccentric or lengthening contractions) are thought to produce increases in strength and size. The definition of a negative (eccentric) repetition is a muscle contraction in which a muscle exerts force while it lengthens and is overcome by resistance. An example of a negative (eccentric) contraction would be the lowering of a weight in the bench press which is heavier than one's 1RM.

Negative repetitions are performed by lowering the weight working against the pull of gravity. This kind of repetition involves the assistance of one or more partners. Extremely heavy weights (heavier than can be lifted) are used with the training partner(s) assisting in the positive direction of the repetition while the person doing the exercise controls the weight on its downward (negative) movement.

Negative repetitions can also be performed using machines by executing the positive portion of the repetition as normally done with a selected weight and then having one's training partner to push down on the weight stack to provide the heavy negative overload while the exerciser resists the return of the machine to the starting position. This same procedure can be used with free weights, also.

There is a big problem when using training-partner-assisted negative repetitions with a machine or free weight. It is impossible to quantify the amount of weight (resistance) which the training partner is applying to the bar or machine. This makes it difficult to determine the amount of extra force that should be applied to effectively train the muscles. In addition, there may be a high potential for injury using negative repetitions because there is little research that is available to identify the negative strength potential for each joint movement and, therefore, no valid manner to determine how much negative force should be applied. Also, it is very difficult for the training partner to know how much resistance should be applied.

Negative repetitions do not produce strength that can be transferred to a positive movement repetition, however, they do assist in stimulating growth. Moreover, when using free weights and exercise machines, the efficiency of the negative repetition is so low that it may not be worth the effort for the majority of the people who train with weights. Negative repetitions should be used infrequently, if at all. More research has to be conducted before a real strong statement can be made supporting the effectiveness of negative repetitions.

The use of negative repetitions is not recommended as a method to be employed to enhance strength or size. The employment of negative repetitions is probably not a good idea and the tendency to use this technique should be resisted. Muscle size and strength are improved by performing the correct exercise movements and appropriately applying the principles of periodization.

SUPER-SETS

A super-set involves performing two exercises in succession without rest. Super-sets can be performed without rest between super-sets or with a rest period between super-sets. The amount of rest will be dictated by the intensity (weight load) of the exercises involved in the super-set and the conditioning level of the participant.

Super-sets can be performed by:

(1) Using opposing muscle groups: for example; biceps (front of arm)/triceps (back of arm) combination.
(2) Using synergistic (working together) muscle groups like the pectorals (chest), anterior deltoids (shoulders) and triceps (back of arms). The synergistic format can be employed in two ways:

    (A) Using the same muscle group and employing the same muscle areas and angles of exercise.
    (B) Using the same muscle group but employing different muscle areas and different angles of exercise.

The reasons for using the super-set technique are:

(1) To shock the muscle in order to stimulate growth. This is accomplished by increasing the total amount of work at an appropriate exercise intensity. The total amount of work performed and the exercise intensity (% 1RM) will dictate the amount of stimulus to muscle growth not the specific exercise sequence.
(2) To minimize the amount of time needed to train. The super-set technique is nicely suited for training the small muscle groups and the abdominal/low back muscles groups. This technique allows for performing more work in a given time period.
(3) The super-set technique is an excellent method for introducing variation in the weight training program.
(4) The super-set technique can be effectively used in the cutting phase of body building.

The application of the super set technique creates more work for the muscle groups in a given time period. An example of the super set principle applied to opposing muscle groups (antagonistic format) would be to perform a set of curls (for the biceps) before doing a set of pushdowns (for the triceps).

In the case where there is a combination of synergistic muscles, pre-exhaustion of one muscle occurs with the first exercise, while during the second exercise the remaining muscle groups are forced to work harder. An example of the application of super sets to synergistic muscles would be to execute flying motions to stress the area of the pectorals (chest) before performing bench presses which involve the pectorals in combination with the anterior deltoids (front shoulders) and triceps (back of arms).

The first exercise in the super-set routine is performed for 6-12 repetitions (can be to failure) with 40%-75% of 1RM followed by the same number of reps and intensity for the second exercise. This procedure can be repeated for 3 - 5 laps (a lap is performance of one super-set).

Table 1-17 contains examples of the antagonistic super-set format for arms, legs, chest/back and abdominal/low back muscle groups. In Table 1-18 is displayed examples of synergistic super-sets formats using the same muscle groups working the same angles of exercise for elbow flexors, chest and shoulder muscle groups. Table 1-19 contains examples of synergistic super-set formats using the same muscle groups working different angles of exercise for elbow extensors, quadriceps and upper back muscle groups.

Table 1-17. Examples Of The Antagonistic Super-Set Formats For Arms, Legs, Chest/Back And Abdominal/Low Back Muscle Groups.

BODY AREA EXAMPLE	EXERCISE #1	EXERCISE #2	REPETITIONS	INTENSITY	CIRCUITS
1. ARM (BICEPS & TRICEPS)	ARM CURL	PUSHDOWN	6-12 REPS	40%-75% 1RM	3-5 LAPS
2. LEGS (QUADS & HAMS)	SQUAT	LEGS CURLS	6-12 REPS	40%-75% 1RM	3-5 LAPS
3. CHEST/UPPER BACK	BENCH PRESS	PULLDOWN	6-12 REPS	40%-75% 1RM	3-5 LAPS
4. ABDOMINAL/LOW BACK	CRUNCH	BACK EXTENSION	6-12 REPS	40%-75% 1RM	3-5 LAPS
1 LAP IS EQUIVALENT TO PERFORMING EXERCISE #1 FOLLOWED BY EXERCISE #2 AND IS CALLED ONE SUPER-SET.					

Table 1-18.   Examples of synergistic super-set formats using the same muscle groups working the same angles of exercise for elbow flexors, chest and shoulder muscle groups.

BODY AREA EXAMPLE	EXERCISE #1	EXERCISE #2	REPETITIONS	INTENSITY	CIRCUITS
1. ELBOW FLEXORS	EZ CURL	SEATED DB CURL	6-12 REPS	40%-75% 1RM	3-5 LAPS
2. CHEST	DB FLY (FLAT)	BENCH PRESS	6-12 REPS	40%-75% 1RM	3-5 LAPS
3. SHOULDERS	PRESS B.B.	DB PRESS	6-12 REPS	40%-75% 1RM	3-5 LAPS
1 LAP IS EQUIVALENT TO PERFORMING EXERCISE #1 FOLLOWED BY EXERCISE #2 AND IS CALLED ONE SUPER-SET.					

Table 1-19.   Examples of synergistic super-set formats using the same muscle groups working different angles of exercise for elbow extensors, quadriceps and upper back muscle groups.

BODY AREA EXAMPLE	EXERCISE #1	EXERCISE #2	REPETITIONS	INTENSITY	CIRCUITS
1. ELBOW EXTENSORS	FRENCH PRESS	PUSHDOWN	6-12 REPS	40%-75% 1RM	3-5 LAPS
2. QUADRICEPS	FRONT SQUAT	BACK SQUAT	6-12 REPS	40%-75% 1RM	3-5 LAPS
3. UPPER BACK	SEATED ROW	PULLDOWN	6-12 REPS	40%-75% 1RM	3-5 LAPS
1 LAP IS EQUIVALENT TO PERFORMING EXERCISE #1 FOLLOWED BY EXERCISE #2 AND IS CALLED ONE SUPER-SET.					

TRI-SETS (INCLUDING 3 MUSCLES OR MUSCLE GROUPS)

Tri-sets involve using 3 different exercises, one after the other, without rest between exercises. Tri-sets can be performed without rest between each tri-set or with a rest period between each tri-set. The amount of rest will be dictated by the intensity (weight load) of the exercises involved in the tri-set and the conditioning level of the participant.

The application of the tri-set technique creates more work for the muscle groups in a short time period. Using exercises that condition three different muscle groups allows for more emphasis on general endurance as well as the local muscle endurance of the specific muscles involved. It may be possible to enhance size and strength using this technique to a moderate degree. The tri-set technique is best applied in the low intensity and high repetition phases of the periodization of training or as a short term training variation.

In the case where the same muscle group and same angle of exercise is performed there is a definite impact on the local muscle endurance. Using the same muscle group and same angle of exercise may be useful in muscle defining and body fat reduction programs, but certainly not for increasing muscle mass.

Tri-sets can be performed by:

(1)   Using three different muscle groups. This is the best application of the tri-set technique.

(2)   Using synergistic (working together) muscle groups like the pectorals (chest), anterior deltoids (shoulders) and triceps (back of arms). The synergistic format can be employed in two ways:

(A)   Using the same muscle group and employing the same muscle areas and angles of exercise. This method is less efficient because all the muscles involved become progressively fatigued and, therefore, the weight that is used must be reduced.

(B)   Using the same muscle group but employing different muscle areas and different angles of exercise.

The reasons for using the tri-set technique are:

(1)   To shock the muscle in order to stimulate growth. This is accomplished by increasing the total amount of work at an appropriate exercise intensity in a given time period. The total amount of work performed and the exercise intensity (% 1RM) will dictate the amount of stimulus to muscle growth not the specific exercise sequence.

(2)   To minimize the amount of time needed to train. The tri-set technique is nicely suited for training most of the muscle groups. This allows performing more work in a given time period.

(3)   The tri-set technique is excellent for use to reduce body fat, to produce muscle definition and to increase local muscle endurance.

(4)   The tri-set technique is an excellent method for introducing variation in the weight training program.

In tri-setting, one set of each exercise for three different muscles or synergistic muscle groups is performed in a successive non-stop fashion. A total of 3, 6 or 9 sets can be performed. In this case, 3 different exercises are performed for one set each so that each lap is equal to 3, 6 or 9 sets in a successive manner using the three separate exercises. Usually, 3 tri-sets are performed for each distinct muscle or muscle groups, although up to 5 tri-sets may be acceptable.

For example: One tri-set involves the execution of one set of the press exercise (1 set); followed by one set of pulldowns (1 set); followed by one set of the bench press (1 set) for a total of 3 sets. A second tri-set is equal the execution of another set of presses (1 set); followed by another set of pulldowns (1 set); followed by another set of bench presses (1 set) for a total of 6 sets. A third tri-set is equivalent to the execution of another set of presses (1 set); followed by another set of pulldowns (1 set); followed by another set of bench presses (1 set) for a total of nine sets. One set of each exercise is performed for 6 to 12 repetitions (could be to muscle failure) with 40% to 75% of 1RM. Depending upon one's level of conditioning and the objectives of the body building program, 1 to 3 laps of the tri-set could be performed. One lap is the performance of one tri-set. The above example is shown in Table 1-20.

Table 1-20 also contains an example of a tri-set program using different muscle groups. Table 1-21 includes an example of a tri-set program for the shoulders using the same muscle groups but various angles of exercise. Table 1-22 contains an example of a tri-set program for the chest using the same muscle groups and the same angles of exercise. In Table 1-23 is shown an example of a tri-set program for the hips and legs using three different angles of exercise.

Table 1-20. An Example Of A Tri-Set Program Using Different Muscle Groups.

EXERCISE	REPETITIONS	INTENSITY	CIRCUITS
1. PRESS	6-12 REPS	40%-75% 1RM	
2. PULLDOWN	6-12 REPS	40%-75% 1RM	1-3 LAPS
3. BENCH PRESS	6-12 REPS	40%-75% 1RM	
* 1 LAP IS EQUIVALENT TO THE PERFORMANCE OF 1 SET OF THE 3 EXERCISES LISTED IN TABLE IN A NON-STOP FASHION AND IS CALLED ONE TRI-SET.			

Table 1-21.   An Example Of A Tri-Set Program For The Shoulders Using The Same Muscle Groups But Various Angles of Exercise. *

EXERCISE	REPETITIONS	INTENSITY	CIRCUITS
1. LATERAL DELTOID	6-12 REPS	40%-75% 1RM	
2. PRESS BEHIND NECK	6-12 REPS	40%-75% 1RM	1-3 LAPS
3. UPRIGHT ROWING	6-12 REPS	40%-75% 1RM	
* 1 LAP IS EQUIVALENT TO THE PERFORMANCE OF 1 SET OF THE 3 EXERCISES LISTED IN TABLE IN A NON-STOP FASHION AND IS CALLED ONE TRI-SET.			

Table 1-22.   An Example Of A Tri-Set Program For The Chest Using The Same Muscle Groups And The Same Angles of Exercise. *

EXERCISE	REPETITIONS	INTENSITY	CIRCUITS
1. BENCH PRESS	6-12 REPS	40%-75% 1RM	
2. FLY	6-12 REPS	40%-75% 1RM	1-3 LAPS
3. DUMBBELL BENCH PRESS	6-12 REPS	40%-75% 1RM	
* 1 LAP IS EQUIVALENT TO THE PERFORMANCE OF 1 SET OF THE 3 EXERCISES LISTED IN TABLE IN A NON-STOP FASHION AND IS CALLED ONE TRI-SET.			

Table 1-23.   An Example Of A Tri-Set Program For The Hips And Legs Using Three Different Angles of Exercise. *

EXERCISE	REPETITIONS	INTENSITY	CIRCUITS
1. SQUAT	6-12 REPS	40%-75% 1RM	
2. FRONT SQUAT	6-12 REPS	40%-75% 1RM	1-3 LAPS
3. LEG PRESS	6-12 REPS	40%-75% 1RM	
* 1 LAP IS EQUIVALENT TO THE PERFORMANCE OF 1 SET OF THE 3 EXERCISES LISTED IN TABLE IN A NON-STOP FASHION AND IS CALLED ONE TRI-SET.			

QUAD-SETS (INCLUDING 4 SYNERGISTIC MUSCLES OR MUSCLE GROUPS)

Quad-sets involve using 4 different exercises in sequence without rest between exercises. Quad-sets can be performed without rest between each quad-set or with a rest period between each quad-set. The amount of rest will be dictated by the intensity (weight load) of the exercises involved in the quad-set and the conditioning level of the participant.

Quad-setting involves performing exercises that utilize four muscles or muscle groups in a non-stop procedure. In quad-setting one set of each exercise for four different muscles or the same muscle groups is performed in a successive non-stop fashion. A total of 4, 8 or 12 sets can be performed. In this case, 4 different exercises are performed for 4, 8 or 12 sets in a successive manner. Usually 3 quad-sets are performed for each distinct muscle or muscle groups, although up to 5 quad-sets may be acceptable.

For example: One quad-set is equal to the consecutive execution of a fly (1 set); incline press (1 set); bench press (1 set); decline bench press (1 set) for a total of four sets. A second quad-set is equal to execution of another fly (1 set); incline press (1 set); bench press (1 set); decline bench press (1 set) for a total of 8 sets. A third quad-set is equivalent to the execution of another fly (1 set); incline press (1 set); bench press (1 set); decline bench press (1 set) for a total of 12 sets. One set of each exercise is performed for 6 to 12 repetitions (could be to muscle failure) using 40% to 75% of 1RM. Depending upon one's level of conditioning and the objectives of the body building program, 1 to 3 laps of the quad-set could be performed. The above example is shown in Table 1-24.

Quad-sets can be performed by:

(1)   Using four different muscle groups. This is the best application of the quad-set technique.
(2)   Using synergistic (working together) muscle groups like the pectorals (chest), anterior deltoids (shoulders) and triceps (back of arms). The synergistic format can be employed in two ways:

    (A)   Using the same muscle group and employing the same muscle areas and angles of exercise. This application is best used in a low intensity phase of training, if at all.
    (B)   Using the same muscle group but employing different muscle areas and different angles of exercise. This is more realistic application of the quad-set technique when synergistic muscles are utilized.

The reasons for using the quad-set technique are:

(1)   To shock the muscle in order to stimulate growth. This is accomplished by increasing the total amount of work at an appropriate exercise intensity in a given time period. The total amount of work performed and the exercise intensity (% 1RM) will dictate the amount of stimulus to muscle growth not the specific exercise sequence.
(2)   To minimize the amount of time needed to train. The quad-set technique is nicely suited for training a combination muscle groups. This allows performing more work in a given time period.
(3)   The quad-set technique is excellent for use to reduce body fat, produce muscle definition and increase local muscle endurance.
(4)   The quad-set technique is an excellent method for introducing variation in the weight training program.

Table 1-24 also contains an example of a quad-set program for the chest using the same muscle groups and different exercise angles. Table 1-25 displays an example of a quad-set program using four different muscle groups.

Table 1-24.   An Example Of A Quad-Set Program For The Chest Using The Same Muscle Groups And Different Exercise Angles.*

EXERCISE	REPETITIONS	INTENSITY	CIRCUITS
1. FLY	6-12 REPS	40%-75% 1RM	
2. INCLINE PRESS	6-12 REPS	40%-75% 1RM	1-3 LAPS
3. BENCH PRESS	6-12 REPS	40%-75% 1RM	
4. DECLINE BENCH PRESS	6-12 REPS	40%-75% 1RM	

* 1 LAP IS EQUIVALENT TO THE PERFORMANCE OF 1 SET OF THE 4 EXERCISES LISTED IN TABLE IN A NON-STOP FASHION AND IS CALLED ONE QUAD-SET.

PART I

THEORY & PRACTICE

Table 1-25. An Example Of A Quad-Set Program Using The Four Different Muscle Groups.*

EXERCISE	REPETITIONS	INTENSITY	CIRCUITS
1. PRESS	6-12 REPS	40%-75% 1RM	
2. PULLDOWN	6-12 REPS	40%-75% 1RM	1-3 LAPS
3. BENCH PRESS	6-12 REPS	40%-75% 1RM	
4. CURLS	6-12 REPS	40%-75% 1RM	

* 1 LAP IS EQUIVALENT TO THE PERFORMANCE OF 1 SET OF THE 4 EXERCISES LISTED IN TABLE IN A NON-STOP FASHION AND IS CALLED ONE QUAD-SET.

GIANT-SETS (INCLUDING 5 OR MORE SYNERGISTIC MUSCLES OR DIFFERENT MUSCLE GROUPS)

Giant-sets involve using 5 or more different exercises in sequence without rest between exercises. This procedure is like a mini-circuit. Giant-sets can be performed without rest between each giant-set or with a rest period between giant-sets. The amount of rest will be dictated by the intensity (weight load) of the exercises involved in the giant-set and the conditioning level of the participant.

Giant-sets are for the very advanced weight trainer or body builder. It involves performing exercises that utilize five synergistic muscles or independent muscle groups or more in a non-stop procedure. One set of 6-12 repetitions (could be to muscle failure) are performed for each successive exercise with 40% -75% of 1RM.

An example of one giant-set for the quadriceps would be to perform one set of knee extensions (1 set), squats (1 set), leg presses (1 set), front squats (1 set) and inverted leg presses (1 set) for a total of 5 sets. The second giant-set using the same exercises would produce a total of 10 sets. A third giant-set using the same exercises would yield a total of 15 sets. Depending upon one's level of conditioning and the objectives of the weight training or body building program, 1 to 3 giant-sets could be performed with or without rest between them. The above example is shown in Table 1-26.

A giant-set example is presented in Table 1-26 which emphasizes conditioning the quadriceps. Displayed in Table 1-27 is an example of a giant-set program for the shoulders employing exercises that use different angles of pull. Table 1-28 contains an example of a giant-set program for the abdominal muscle group employing exercises that use different angles of pull.

Giant-sets can be performed by:

(1) Using five or more different muscle groups. This is the best application of the giant-set (mini-circuit) technique.
(2) Using synergistic (working together) muscle groups like the pectorals (chest), anterior deltoids (shoulders) and triceps (back of arms). The synergistic format should be employed in one way, using the same muscle group but employing different muscle areas and different angles of exercise. This pattern is probably not the best application of the giant-set technique.

The reasons for using the giant-set technique are:

(1) To shock the muscle in order to stimulate growth. This is accomplished by increasing the total amount of work at an appropriate exercise intensity. The total amount of work performed and the exercise intensity (% 1RM) will dictate the amount of stimulus to muscle growth not the specific exercise sequence.
(2) To minimize the amount of time needed to train. The giant-set technique is nicely suited for training the most muscle groups. This results performing more work in a given time period.

(3) The giant-set technique is excellent for use to reduce body fat, produce muscle definition and increase local muscle endurance.

(4) The giant-set technique is an excellent method for introducing variation in the weight training program.

Table 1-26. An Example Of A Giant Set Program For The Legs Focusing On The Quadriceps. *

EXERCISE	REPETITIONS	INTENSITY	CIRCUITS
1. KNEE EXTENSION	6-12 REPS	40%-75% 1RM	
2. SQUATS	6-12 REPS	40%-75% 1RM	
3. LEG PRESS	6-12 REPS	40%-75% 1RM	1-3 LAPS
4. FRONT SQUAT	6-12 REPS	40%-75% 1RM	
5. INVERTED LEG PRESS	6-12 REPS	40%-75% 1RM	
* 1 LAP IS EQUIVALENT TO THE PERFORMANCE OF 1 SET OF THE 5 EXERCISES LISTED IN TABLE IN A NON-STOP FASHION AND IS CALLED ONE GIANT-SET.			

Table 1-27. An Example Of A Giant Set Program For The Shoulders Employing Exercises That Use Different Angles Of Pull.*

EXERCISE	REPETITIONS	INTENSITY	CIRCUITS
1. PRESS	6-12 REPS	40%-75% 1RM	
2. REVERSE FLY	6-12 REPS	40%-75% 1RM	
3. LATERAL RAISES	6-12 REPS	40%-75% 1RM	1-3 LAPS
4. FORWARD RAISES	6-12 REPS	40%-75% 1RM	
5. UPRIGHT ROW	6-12 REPS	40%-75% 1RM	
* 1 LAP IS EQUIVALENT TO THE PERFORMANCE OF 1 SET OF THE 5 EXERCISES LISTED IN TABLE IN A NON-STOP FASHION AND IS CALLED ONE GIANT-SET.			

Table 1-28. An Example Of A Giant Set Program For The Abdominal Muscle Group Employing Exercises That Use Different Angles Of Pull. *

EXERCISE	REPETITIONS	INTENSITY	CIRCUITS
1. CRUNCH	6-12 REPS	40%-75% 1RM	
2. TWISTS	6-12 REPS	40%-75% 1RM	
3. LEG LIFTS (HIGH CHAIR)	6-12 REPS	40%-75% 1RM	1-3 LAPS
4. SIDE BENDS	6-12 REPS	40%-75% 1RM	
5. REVERSE CRUNCH	6-12 REPS	40%-75% 1RM	
* 1 LAP IS EQUIVALENT TO THE PERFORMANCE OF 1 SET OF THE 5 EXERCISES LISTED IN TABLE IN A NON-STOP FASHION AND IS CALLED ONE GIANT-SET.			

PART I

THEORY & PRACTICE

PYRAMID TRAINING

Pyramid training offers a unique and interesting way to train. The main application for pyramid training is to train the CNS to recruit as many muscle fibers as possible and is used in peaking or as a variation for the training program. Do to the fact that it is not considered to be a conditioning program or a muscle mass enhancer and requires the use of very high intensities, pyramiding should only be used for short time periods of 1 to 4 weeks. It is very easy to over-stress the total body systems and, therefore, slide into an over-trained state using the pyramiding system.

The pyramid technique involves performing 3-7 sets of 90% to 100% of 1RM not including warm up sets. This technique could be used for all the major exercises in the weight training routine but is not suited for the training of smaller muscle groups, such as the calf or forearm muscles. Also, it is not recommended that the abdominal or low back muscles be conditioned using this technique. It is not necessary to specifically stress the abdominal and low back muscle groups at very high intensities. They are more adequately stressed at high intensities in multiple joint complex exercises like squatting, dead lifting, high pulls, power cleans and power snatches. It is important that adequate specific warm-up be performed before using this procedure. It may also be of benefit to perform a set or two of eight to ten repetitions after using the pyramiding technique to maintain some muscle mass.

Pyramiding can be employed for the following reasons:

 (1)   To train the central nervous system to recruit more motor units (more muscle).
 (2)   To increase strength without increasing muscle mass.
 (3)   As a peaking routine during the competitive period for an athlete.
 (4)   As a training diversion.

The pyramiding technique can be one of the following forms:

 (1)   Ascending pyramid. The weight is increased and the repetitions are reduced.
 (2)   Descending pyramid. The weight is decreased and the repetitions are increased.
 (3)   Ascending/descending pyramid. The weight is increased and the repetitions are reduced until the maximum weight is lifted followed by the weight decreasing and the repetitions increasing in the succeeding sets until exhaustion occurs.

The ascending pyramid technique is employed for the training of the central nervous system (recruitment of motor units [more muscle]) by applying a progressive sequence of increasing the weight and reducing the repetitions during one specific exercise. This technique is used during the competition/peaking phase or to unload the person during the periodization of training.

Using the ascending pyramid technique will increase strength without increasing muscle mass. The length of time this technique should be used is between 1 to 4 weeks and sometimes longer. Longer application of this technique leads to staleness and plateaus because it takes extremely large amounts of mental energy to use this technique. A thorough warmup is recommended before engaging in the ascending pyramiding technique.

The descending pyramid and the ascending/descending pyramid techniques are popular variations for the general weight trainer and body builders. Unfortunately, this technique is used too much by most people who weight train. It should be applied infrequently and, in general, for no longer than four weeks. A thorough warmup is recommended before engaging in the ascending/descending pyramiding technique.

Table 1-29 contains examples of ascending, descending and ascending/descending pyramid techniques for the bench press exercise. It is important that a proper warm-up be performed before using any of the pyramiding formats. It is especially important when using the descending pyramid format because this technique starts at a very high intensity and progressively decreases.

Table 1-29. Examples of ascending, descending and ascending/descending pyramids for the bench press exercise.

ASCENDING			DESCENDING			ASCENDING - DESCENDING		
SET #	REPS	WEIGHT	SET #	REPS	WEIGHT	SET #	REPS	WEIGHT
1	12	135	1	1	235	1	10	155
2	10	155	2	2	225	2	8	175
3	8	175	3	4	210	3	6	195
4	6	195	4	6	195	4	4	210
5	4	210	5	8	175	5	2	225
6	2	225	6	10	155	6	1	235
7	1	235	7	12	135	7	4	210
						8	6	195
						9	8	175
						10	10	155

Body builders frequently employ a variation of the descending pyramid technique in conjunction with the regular training program. They call it the multi-poundage system. After the completion of the usual exercise prescription and without rest, some weight is removed from the bar and the last few sets are performed until failure. This procedure is repeated for 1 to 5 sets.

Some body builders never go below a specified number of repetition when using the multi-poundage system in a descending pyramid. They usually perform between 3 to 6 repetitions in all sets. In this case, fewer and fewer muscle fibers are recruited because of the muscle fatigue produced by previous repetitions of the same exercise. No research exists to define just what physiological effects occur in the muscle when using this variation of pyramiding.

The use of this variation of descending pyramiding is thought to increase strength but any gains in the strength attribute would be very small. Regardless, there may be some hypertrophy because more total work has been performed. The probable net gain as a result of using this body building variation of descending pyramiding is an increase in local muscle endurance, some slight increase in muscle size and improvement of the metabolic apparatus (energy production enhanced).

The pyramiding technique and, all its variations, can be effective tools in the periodization of training. However, these techniques are not good methods of training to use over long periods of time and will result in overtraining and possibly injuries, if overused. The major benefits of using the pyramiding technique are to train the central nervous system to recruit more motor units and to provide variation in the training program. This technique requires great mental effort and it is doubtful if a high mental effort can be sustained over long time periods. Pyramiding is most useful for very short time periods during a peaking phase or as a short term training variation.

CIRCUIT WEIGHT TRAINING (CWT)

Circuit weight training is employed at the start of a training program or could be used in the cutting phase of a body builders program. It can also be used as a short term program for training variety. Some high level body builders have also used a very low intensity CWT program as a warm up for their regular training program. It can also be used as a flushing technique after the regular training program has been completed.

The concept of CWT includes completing a series of ten exercises with weight resistance machines that systematically conditions all the major muscle groups. This provides for well balanced body conditioning and contouring. In the process of CWT a person would normally execute two to three laps around a ten station circuit in each training session. This translates into 20 exercise stations completed in 15 minutes or 30 exercise stations completed in 22.5 minutes. CWT can be biased for any physical fitness component; used with equipment or free exercise; and can be group or individually directed.

The load at each station can vary from 40% to 60% of one repetition maximum (1RM), but usually 50% of 1RM is used. The number of repetitions executed at each station should not be more than fifteen and generally no less than ten for general conditioning when using free weights or weight machines. Figure 1-14 presents a body building variation of CWT. This figure is found earlier in this section under the title of **"PERIODIZATION (CYCLING) OF WEIGHT TRAINING PROGRAMS."** The length of time at each exercise station is 30 seconds (10 to 15 repetitions) and the rest/rotate to next station time period is 15 seconds. In CWT where free exercises (calisthenics) are used instead of equipment, the repetitions performed can be as many as 25, depending upon the physical condition and training objectives.

A more complete understanding of CWT is presented in this book in Part II, General Fitness Training.

SUPER CIRCUIT WEIGHT TRAINING (SCWT)

Super circuit weight training can be employed for the same reason that regular CWT is employed. It can be used as a stand alone exercise entry program or an exercise reentry program; as a training variation; as a warmup for regular training; as a flushing program for after regular training, or as a training system during the cutting phase for body builders.

A series of 10 exercise stations working every major muscle group is performed. A person would normally execute 2 to 3 laps around this circuit in each training session. This means that there are 20-30 exercises performed on the weight machines or with free weights with an aerobic exercise used between weight stations. For each weight exercise station the work period is 30 seconds (10-15 repetitions) and the aerobic work period is 30 seconds. The aerobic exercises could be running, cycling, stepping or free exercises. The time needed to perform 20 stations is 20 minutes and the time needed to perform 30 stations is 30 minutes. Figure 1-14 presents a body building variation of SCWT. This figure is found earlier in this section under the title of **"PERIODIZATION OF WEIGHT TRAINING PROGRAMS."**

The load at each station can vary from 40% to 60% of one repetition maximum (1RM), but usually 50% of 1RM is used. The number of repetitions executed at each station should not be more than fifteen and generally no less than ten for general conditioning when using free weights or weight machines. In SCWT where free exercise is used instead of equipment, the repetitions performed can be as many as 25, depending upon the physical condition and training objectives.

A more complete understanding of SCWT is presented in this book in Part II, General Fitness Training.

PART II

THE ENCYCLOPEDIA OF WEIGHT TRAINING

Weight Training For General Fitness

GENERAL FITNESS   PART II

PART II

GENERAL FITNESS

THE ENCYCLOPEDIA OF WEIGHT TRAINING: WEIGHT TRAINING FOR GENERAL CONDITIONING, SPORT AND BODY BUILDING

PART II: WEIGHT TRAINING FOR GENERAL FITNESS

TABLE OF CONTENTS — PART II

PART II

GENERAL FITNESS

TABLE OF CONTENTS — PART II (CONTINUED)

PART II

GENERAL FITNESS

THE ENCYCLOPEDIA OF WEIGHT TRAINING: PART II

LIST OF FIGURES

GENERAL FITNESS   PART II

THE ENCYCLOPEDIA OF WEIGHT TRAINING: PART II

LIST OF TABLES

PART II

GENERAL FITNESS

LIST OF TABLES — PART II (CONTINUED)

PART II

GENERAL FITNESS

PART II

GENERAL FITNESS

PART II

PART II — WEIGHT TRAINING FOR GENERAL FITNESS

INTRODUCTION

As mentioned in the previous section, physical fitness has four components: strength, local muscle endurance, cardiovascular-respiratory endurance and optimal body composition. Traditionally, there has been the application of specific programs for the training of each of these separate physiological elements that comprise physical fitness; e.g., running for cardiovascular-respiratory fitness; and a variety of specific weight training programs for strength, local muscle endurance and body building. All exercise programs contribute to the reduction of body fat, depending upon duration, intensity and frequency. Some programs are more efficient than others.

The safest and least stressful method of beginning a fitness training program is the application of progressive resistance exercise (weight training). The use of running programs for beginners produces orthopedic stress on the skeletal system, while the skeletal stress in weight training programs can be easily and safely controlled by adjusting the weight used during each exercise. Moreover, weight training creates immediate increases in lean body mass.

In any fitness program it is essential to develop a conditioning base in order to prepare the muscles, tendons, ligaments and connective tissues for more intense physical training. The length of a conditioning phase ranges between 4 to 12 weeks, although, most programs range between 4 to 6 weeks of preparation training. When a conditioning base is developed, one can extend the fitness program progressively into other dimensions of general fitness training (for example, running, cycling and even body building).

It is very important that all dimensions of fitness be developed as humans progress in age, especially the cardiovascular-respiratory dimension. However, the exclusion of strength and local muscular endurance exercise severely limits one's appearance, performance and overall fitness capacities. Many people focus only on the cardiovascular-respiratory to the detriment of their physical appearance and their abilities to enjoy leisure time sports. **There must be balance in all physical conditioning programs.**

Because there exists a great number of possible conditioning programs using a wide variety of exercise equipment, the discussion in this part of the book will focus on training principles, theory and tools (weight training programs) for obtaining general balanced physical fitness; i.e., a program that includes provisions for strength, local muscular and cardio-vascular-respiratory endurance while reducing body fat and increasing lean body mass. As each physical exercise tool (weight training program) is presented an example will follow to help the understanding.

APPLICATIONS OF WEIGHT TRAINING PROGRAMS FOR GENERAL FITNESS

Prudent planning of a conditioning program requires the preparation of the body in a basic starter program before advancing to higher intensities or volumes of training. Periodization of basic exercise programs needs to be considered for optimal physiological changes to occur and for good psychological health. Motivation to stay in a fitness program usually decreases as the individual continues to train. Periodization helps to ease the trainer through these tough periods by an effective planned variance of volume, intensity, frequency, exercises and program formats. There are three basic weight training programs that can be utilized for beginning general fitness training:

PART II

GENERAL FITNESS

(1)   Circuit Weight Training (CWT).
(2)   Super Circuit Weight Training(SCWT).
(3)   Sets and Repetitions Program (3-5 Sets X 10 Reps X 40% - 60% of 1RM).

Each one of these programs will be generally outlined in the following pages. Moreover, periodization of these programs will be discussed at the end of this chapter. Examples will be given of how to periodize weight training programs for general fitness.

Figure 2-1 presents in a graphical form the basic concept of a scientifically designed weight training program for general conditioning. SCWT is at the bottom of the pyramid. As one ascends the pyramid they find the next program to be CWT which is then followed by a program of low intensity sets and repetitions. The length of time for each phase may be as low as four weeks and as high as 12 weeks. The training objectives and motivation will dictate the length of time at each stage. The upper portion of the pyramid (Phase II) contains programs for body building and sport preparation.

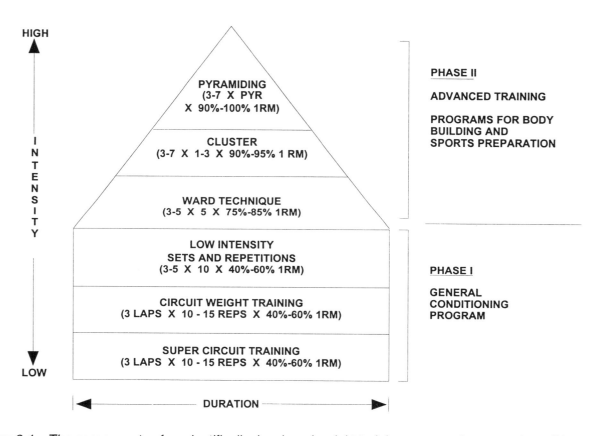

Figure 2-1.   The components of a scientifically developed weight training program for general conditioning.

CIRCUIT WEIGHT TRAINING AND SUPER CIRCUIT WEIGHT TRAINING

INTRODUCTION

The pace of living in these days requires that a person develop an efficient pattern of living. Physicians and experts in exercise physiology all agree that some form of exercise be performed daily. The search for effective methods of exercising has produced what might be called the ultimate in exercise programs, especially when considered in the context of the time constraints of today's society. The system of exercising is called Circuit Weight Training (CWT) and involves regular circuit weight training (CWT) or super circuit weight training (SCWT) which will be discussed in the following pages.

CWT and SCWT are scientifically founded systems of exercising with weights that provides a balanced approach to physical fitness training. Through CWT and SCWT a male or female of all ages can increase strength, local muscle endurance (LME), cardiovascular respiratory endurance and flexibility while very effectively decreasing body fat and increasing lean body mass. With slight procedural modifications the CWT program can focus more directly upon any component of the physical fitness component continuum. All these objectives can be obtained concurrently in a relatively short time period when engaging in CWT or SCWT.

THE HISTORY OF CIRCUIT WEIGHT TRAINING (CWT)

Circuit Weight Training is a scientifically documented program for general fitness training. CWT has probably been in existence longer than history records, however, under no such precise name. The origin of CWT is not precisely known, however, it appears as a organized and systematized program for improving muscular development and aerobic fitness at the University of Leeds in 1953. R. E. Morgan and G. T. Adamson, implemented this system of exercising at the University of Leeds.

1. **Morgan, R.E. and Adamson, G.T., Circuit Training, London, G. Bell and Sons, Ltd., 1961.**

2. **R. Sorani; Circuit Training; Wm. C. Brown Co; Dubuque, Iowa; 1966, p. 1.**

Since 1953, many applications of CWT have been utilized in various training situations, including the military, school fitness classes at all educational levels and in the training of athletes at all age levels and including males and females.

In 1960, CWT was added to the curriculum at the University of British Columbia on an experimental basis. It became so popular that the number of students training voluntarily with CWT exceeded the number enrolled in the required classes.

R. Sorani; Circuit Training; Wm. C. Brown Co; Dubuque, Iowa; 1966, p. 1.

At the University of Wisconsin-Parkside in 1969, P. Ward introduced CWT in the curriculum at that University as part of a class entitled the American Training Pattern. Cantello in 1969, the cross country coach at the Naval Academy, developed and introduced a CWT program for shipboard use by the cadet cross country runners.

P. Ward, T. Rosandich and B. Lawson; American Training Pattern, Circuit Training Patterns, Olympia Sport Publications; Upson, Wisconsin, 1969.

In (1974), CWT was introduced as a means of mass physical training in the commercial health club setting by Dr. Paul Ward (Director of Education, Research and Development for the Health and Tennis Corporation of America) in the Chicago Health Clubs.

Dr. Paul Ward organized, systematized and researched the many facets of CWT and SCWT and has implemented it across the United States in over 325 commercial health clubs that are part of the Health and Tennis Corporation of America. This was the first commercial health club setting in the history of the fitness industry where a truly effective program for general fitness was implemented impacting muscular development as well as conditioning the cardio-vascular-respiratory system. Scientific documentation of the efficacy of CWT and SCWT would lag

PART II

GENERAL FITNESS

behind the "in the trenches" view that these programs were effective programs that change all the major components of physical fitness (strength, local muscular endurance, aerobic endurance and optimization of body composition) in a very positive way.

Subsequently, most first class health and fitness clubs have adopted this method of training the general public which was first introduced by Dr. Paul Ward in 1974, in the commercial health club setting.

In 1976, Allen, et al, studied the hemodynamic consequences of circuit weight training in men only. He analyzed the effects of a 12 week program conducted three days a week and found no significant changes in aerobic capacity, maximum cardiac output, stroke volume or arteriovenous oxygen-content difference measured on a cycle ergometer that provided arm and leg work. The work/rest intervals involved work periods of 30 seconds followed by rest periods of 60 seconds for a total training session of 30 minutes. Training sessions were conducted three time a week. In retrospect, the lack of aerobic improvement was due to the long one-minute rest intervals which permitted too much recovery (primarily the lowering of heart rate) between weight stations to improve aerobic fitness.

These researchers used the average training weight for strength appraisal and described a 71% increase for the leg press strength and a 44% improvement in the bench press strength after participating in their CWT program. This method of reporting strength does not accurately reflect the strength improvement. The reported percentage increases seem to be greatly inflated. One would not expect to observe strength changes of over 25% to 30% in well designed strength studies. The obvious conclusion is that the training loads may have been extremely low at the start of the program. The low training loads coupled with the long rest periods between exercise stations account for the inability of these researchers to demonstrate any aerobic improvements. Analysis of later studies substantiate this conclusion.

Allen, T.E., Byrd, R. J., Smith, D. P.: Hemodynamic consequences of circuit weight training. Res Q 47:299-306, October, 1976.

Dr. Paul Ward instituted a series of CWT studies starting in 1976. Prior to that time, studies had been performed but they demonstrated that CWT did not significantly change aerobic capacity. The first study that demonstrated good aerobic improvement using CWT was commissioned by HTCA and Universal Gym jointly. Dr. Ward and Chuck Coker (Universal Gym) commissioned Dr. Jack Wilmore to conduct the study at the National Athletic Health Institute in Inglewood, California.

Wilmore, Jack; et al; Physiological alterations consequent to circuit weight training; Medicine and Science in Sports; VOL. 10, NO. 2. PP 79-84, 1978.

As mentioned above, this study was the first to demonstrate significant improvements in aerobic capacity as well as substantial improvements in strength, flexibility and body composition. The basic design of the study was outlined by P. Ward and Coker, who applied "in the trenches knowledge" to direct scientific research. The results of this study demonstrates the fact that most good ideas in fitness training emanate from the trenches.

In this study, Wilmore, et al, studied the efficacy of a 10 week circuit weight training program to produce physiological changes in a group of men (N = 16) and a group of women (N = 12). An additional group of men (N = 10) and a group of women (N = 11) were used as control groups. The circuit included 10 weight exercises performed on multi-station standard resistance Universal Gym, 3 circuits per day (22.5 minutes/day), 3 days a week. Each subject used 40-55% of 1RM, executing as many repetitions as possible in 30 seconds at each station, followed by a 15 second rest interval as the subjects moved to the next station.

After the completion of the training program the experimental groups demonstrated significant increases in lean body weight, flexed biceps girth, treadmill endurance time, aerobic capacity (women only), flexibility and strength.

An improvement in aerobic capacity of 10.7% was observed for the women as a result of the application of CWT over ten weeks. On the other hand, the men did not show any improvement. The researchers explained that this finding may be due to the fact that the women were training at a higher percentage of their maximum heart rate compared to the men.

Pre and post training determinations were made for men and women for the following strength exercises:

1.	Shoulder Press	5.	Lat Pulldown
2.	Bench Press	6.	Leg Press
3.	Arm Curl (men only)	7.	Leg Flexion
4.	Upright Row	8.	Leg Extension (men only)

The percentage increases in strength for men ranged from 6.0% in the shoulder press and leg flexion up to 15% in the leg extension. For women the percentage increases ranged from 12.0% for the upright row to 53% for the leg flexion exercise. These changes in strength were found to be similar to the relative strength changes reported by others for women who participated in general programs of weight training.

Table 2-1 contains information about the strength changes of males and females consequent to participation in this 10 week program of circuit weight training (CWT).

Table 2-1.   Strength Changes In Males And Females After Ten Weeks Of Circuit Weight Training.

EXERCISES	PERCENTAGE INCREASE	
	MEN	WOMEN
1. SHOULDER PRESS	6.0%	14.0%
2. BENCH PRESS	8.0%	20.0%
3. ARM CURL (MEN ONLY)	10.0%	--------
4. UPRIGHT ROW	6.0%	12.0%
5. LAT PULLDOWN	7.0%	35.0%
6. LEG PRESS	7.0%	27.0%
7. KNEE FLEXION	6.0%	53.0%
8. KNEE EXTENSION (MEN ONLY)	15.0%	--------

Wilmore, et al; Physiological Alterations Consequent To CWT; Med & Science in Sport, Vol 10, # 2, pp. 79-84, 1978.

Also, significant decreases were found in selected skinfold measurements. There were no changes in body weight but there were reductions in body fat of 8.6% for men and 6.4% for women in terms of absolute percentages. The changes in body fat was statistically significant only for the females. Both males and females also demonstrated statistically significant increases in lean body weight. Males displayed an absolute increase of lean mass of 2.7% while the females showed a 2.1% absolute increase in lean mass.

Author's note: For scientific work statistical significance is extremely important. However, for in-the-trenches empirical observations, any reduction in body fat is important and motivating to people.

PART II

GENERAL FITNESS

The women in this study, in general, displayed equal or greater changes when compared to the men for all variables studied. This could be a result of the women starting at a lower level or the women training at higher intensities. The women in this study were reported as training at a greater percentage of their heart rate Maximum (87.6%) compared to the men (78.2%). Besides, the women were training at 46.8% of their aerobic capacity while the men were training at 41.1% of their aerobic capacity.

The overall conclusion was that circuit weight training is a good general conditioning activity which improves all the major dimensions of physical fitness.

Gettman and others, conducted a 20 week study on CWT with the idea that greater training effects would accrue from participation in a longer training program. The results were reported in 1978.

They studied 11 men performing 30 minutes of CWT, three days per week, using 50% of 1RM. The rest interval started at 30 seconds during the first part of the study and was reduced to 20 seconds for the last part of the project. The men demonstrated a 3.5% improvement in aerobic capacity after the 20 week training program. This aerobic improvement was statistically significant which indicates that CWT had an aerobic component. Again, a retrospective view leads one to believe that the rest intervals were too long to induce any large aerobic changes.

Strength increases were reported in isotonic bench pressing of 32% while the isokinetic leg press strength improved 43 percent.

Gettman, L.R., Ayres, J.J., Pollock, M.L., et al: The effect of circuit weight training on strength, cardio-respiratory function, and body composition of adult men, Med Sci Sports 10:171-176, Fall 1978.

In 1978, Gettman and Ayers examined CWT in men using isokinetic devices as training tools. This 10 week study involved one group using a slow (60 degrees/second) and another group using a fast (120 degrees/second) movement pattern. Both groups progressed from 10 repetitions to 12 to 15 repetitions with 30 seconds recovery between exercises. The slow speed group averaged more total time and more total work per workout than the fast speed group. This fact impacted the results, as would normally be expected, with the slow speed group improving 10% in aerobic fitness while the fast speed group only improved 3%. It is intuitively obvious that the extent of fitness improvement is dependent upon the total training time and the total work accomplished.

These authors reported a 11% increase in isotonic bench pressing strength for the group that used slow speed isokinetic training. In contrast, the groups that used fast speed isokinetic training demonstrated a 9% improvement in isotonic bench pressing strength.

Gettman, L.R., Ayres, J.J.: Aerobic changes through 10 weeks of slow and fast speed isokinetic training (abstract). Med Sci Sports 10:47, Fall 1978.

Gettman, Ayres and Polluck studied the physiological training effects of participation in CWT and jogging reported in 1979. They examined the interplay of CWT and running programs by having the subjects circuit weight train for eight weeks followed by eight weeks of jogging and finally participation in either CWT or jogging for another eight weeks. The study had two purposes: (1) To compare CWT to jogging; and, (2) to evaluate CWT after training by jogging.

The first eight weeks of CWT produced only a 3% improvement in aerobic fitness. Sixteen men performed 10-15 repetitions per set and trained three days per week. The subsequent jogging program produced an added 8% increase in aerobic fitness which was significantly superior to the CWT program. The intensity of the jogging program was 85% of maximum heart rate. At the end of the jogging program, half of the group continued to jog while the other half returned to the CWT program format.

In the final eight weeks of training, both the jogging and CWT groups maintained equivalent aerobic fitness. CWT was shown to effectively maintain aerobic fitness but only to have very little effect in attaining aerobic fitness as demonstrated in the first eight weeks. The subjects in this study exhibited an 18% increase in strength for isotonic leg pressing and 38% increase for isokinetic strength testing. For the bench press, there was an improvement of 11% for the isotonic test and 22% for the isokinetic test.

Gettman, L.R., Ayres, J.J., Pollock, M.L, et al: Physiological effects on adult men of circuit strength training and jogging, Arch Phys Med Rehabil 60:115-120, March 1979.

To validate the result of the 1978 NAHI study and to demonstrate that good changes in all the major physical fitness dimensions could occur regardless of the type of equipment utilized, Dr. Paul Ward (HTCA) and Lloyd Lambert Jr. (Dynamics Health Equipment Company, South Houston, Texas) collaborated to commission another CWT study using Dynamics Health equipment at Syracuse University in 1978. This was the second in a series of circuit weight training studies designed by Ward.

Garfield, Ward, et al, reported this study in 1979. This study analyzed the effectiveness of a 12 week circuit weight training program to produce changes in aerobic capacity, strength and body composition. This study involved men and women participating in CWT for 12 weeks, training three times a week, using 30 second work intervals with weight equipment followed by 15 seconds of rest while moving to the next weight station. Twelve to fifteen repetitions were performed in each 30 second work interval at 40% 1RM.

In the first six weeks, the exercise protocol called for execution of two full circuits; 15 stations per circuit for a total of 30 stations in a 22.5 minute training session. The second 6 weeks called for executing 3 full circuits (45 stations) for a total workout time of 33.75 seconds. Both men and women increase the absolute aerobic capacity by 9%, whereas the relative aerobic capacity increased 6.4% for men and 5.6% for women.

Both men and women increased their ability to run on the treadmill for time. The increase in treadmill running time of 6.1% for men and 2.6% for women, also indicates the improvement in aerobic fitness. The improvement in aerobic capacity was 6.36 % for the men and 5.56 % for women who participated in this study.

Body composition changes were observed in both men and women. Body fat decreased an average of 4.0 lbs. for men and an average of 2.2 lbs. for women. This represented a reduction of 16.9% for men and 6.8% for women. The men increased their lean body mass by 2.6 lbs. for a 1.8% change while the women demonstrated a negative change. Women unexpectedly lost 1.6 lbs. for a negative change of 1.7% in lean body mass. There is no explanation for this observation except possibly the women severely restricted their diet. However, no attempt was made to control caloric intake. One would expect to see a positive change in lean body mass in women as was demonstrated in the males, but to a lesser magnitude. Total body weight loss for men was 1.4 lbs. for a negative change of .8%. The women showed a loss of total body weight of 3.8 lbs. for a negative change of 3.0%.

Change in body weight alone cannot be used to correctly evaluate the efficacy of a training program. Through relatively small changes in total body weight were recorded, the net fat losses reflect substantial changes in body composition in both men and women.

Six skinfold sites were measured pre and post training. These included the chest, mid-axial, iliac, abdominal, thigh and triceps sites. All skinfold measures for the men exhibited a decrease except the chest which showed an increase. The skinfold decreases ranged from 11.2% for the triceps to 37.2% for the iliac crest. The total amount of skinfolds (sum of six sites) showed a 16.2 mm decrement or a 20.6% decrease. The women subjects showed a decrease in all six skinfold measurements. The decreases ranged 3.8% for the triceps skinfold to 28.2% for the mid-axillary (underarm) skinfold. The total amount of skinfolds showed a 14.2 mm decrease which is loss of 15.0%.

The underwater weighing and skinfold measurement results indicate that circuit weight training is very effective in decreasing body fat.

All strength measures for males and females increased. The 1RM was determined pre and post training for each of the following exercises: shoulder press, bench press, arm curl, knee extension and leg curl. The men demonstrated strength increases of from 3.80% in the arm curl exercise to 27.51% in the leg curl exercises. The women manifested strength increases of from 4.19% in the arm curl exercise to 25.88% in the leg curl exercise.

Table 2-2 contains the percentage increases for males and females in five strength exercises after 12 weeks of participation in circuit weight training (CWT).

The post-training strength scores reflected what could be considered to be the expected strength gains for circuit weight training programs despite the fact that the loads used during the training program were only 40% of the 1RM. It is also important to note that the women in this study made good strength gains while showing no significant increases in body measurements. The myth that women "bulk up" while weight training dies hard.

Table 2-2.   Strength Changes in Males and Females After Twelve Weeks of Circuit Weight Training.

	PERCENTAGE INCREASE	
EXERCISES	MEN	WOMEN
1. SHOULDER PRESS	6.28%	10.30%
2. BENCH PRESS	8.86%	10.18%
3. ARM CURL	3.80%	4.19%
4. KNEE EXTENSION	15.15%	9.52%
5. KNEE FLEXION	27.51%	25.88%

Garfield, D., Ward, P. and Disch, J.; Dynamics Health Equipment; Houston, TX, 1979.

This study outlined some advantages for using circuit weight training. They are:

1. Circuit weight training can produce substantial increases in aerobic fitness as well as all other areas of total physical conditioning.

2. The time investment of three 30-minute workouts a week is realistic, even for the busiest executive.

3. The systematic management of time for each workout facilitates daily exercise planning.

4. The reduction of orthopedic wear and tear helps to prevent exercise-induced injuries.

5. The ability to control environmental conditions solves the problems inherent in the following exercise hazards:
    a. extreme temperature (hot or cold)
    b. unfavorable humidity
    c. air pollution and car exhaust
    d. irregularities of running surfaces
    e. aggressive and unsympathetic motorists

6. The physiological benefits are generalizable to sports and recreation in the broadest sense, rather than highly specific to a particular activity.

7. Circuit weight training facilitates close supervision of the workout by an exercise leader.

8. The exercise prescription can be accurately determined and is easily upgraded using the same protocol, which is also a built-in measure of progress.

9. Circuit weight training is conducive to an enjoyable, non-competitive social atmosphere that can contribute to an individual's persistence in exercise.

The results of this study corroborated the study done at NAHI by again demonstrating a significant improvement in aerobic fitness, strength and body composition.

Garfield, D., Ward, P. and Disch, J; Circuit Weight Training (CWT); An Unpublished Report, Dynamics Health Equipment Manufacturing Co., Inc, South Houston, Texas, 1979.

In 1979, Ward, P. conceived a third CWT study and arranged for Health and the Tennis Corporation of America to collaborate with Universal Gym to commission the prestigious Institute of Aerobics Research in Dallas, Texas to complete the study. This time Dr. P. Ward wanted to study the physiological effects of his conceptualized, systematized and implemented super circuit weight training as well as to validate the results of his previous circuit weight training studies. Dr. Larry Gettman was appointed the director of the research project.

The super circuit weight training (SCWT) concept was first implemented in the commercial health club environment in 1976 at the Mt. Prospect Chicago Health Club by Dr. Paul Ward. The impact of this "in-the-trenches" application of SCWT was the motivating force that stimulated the research effort. It had been noted that a large number of health club members were experiencing exceptional body fat losses and outstanding improvements in strength and aerobic endurance.

Gettman, et al, reported the results of this research in 1982. The purpose of the study was to compare the physiologic effects of a program of combined running and weight training (RUN-CWT) with a program of circuit weight training (CWT). Thirty-six females (average age = 35.7 years) and 41 males (average age = 36.1 years) were randomly assigned to RUN-CWT, CWT and control groups.

The training groups trained three days per week, executing three circuits of 10 weight stations using 12-15 repetitions performed in 30 seconds at 40% 1RM. The RUN-CWT group involved a 30 second run around an indoor track following each weight station for a total training session lasting 30 minutes. The regular CWT group exercised for a total time of 22.5 minutes each training session and had only a 15 second time period between weight stations.

Both groups increased their aerobic capacity. The RUN-CWT group improved 17% in aerobic capacity for both males and females. In contrast the CWT group improve 12% in aerobic capacity for both males and females. However, there was not a statistically significant difference between the RUN-CWT and CWT groups.

The RUN-CWT and the CWT groups increased aerobic capacity considerably beyond what had been reported in the literature with the exceptions of the Wilmore, et al (1978), and the Gettman and Ayers (1978) studies. Wilmore, et al (1978), described a 10.7% increase in aerobic capacity for females in his study. Gettman and Ayers (1978) demonstrated a 10% improvement in aerobic capacity for slow isokinetic training.

Body fat was significantly reduced for both experimental groups for males and females. For females there was an absolute change of 11.2% which was a real reduction of body fat of -3.2% for the RUN-CWT group. The female CWT group showed a change of 10% which is a real reduction of body fat of -2.8%. For males there was an absolute change of 17% which was a real reduction of body fat equivalent to -4.1% for the RUN-CWT group. The male CWT group showed a change of 14% which is a real reduction of body fat of -3.1%.

Lean body mass showed significant increases for both experimental groups for men but only the CWT group for females showed significant lean mass increases. The absolute lean body mass change for females in the RUN-CWT group showed a gain of 1.0 kilograms which was not significant while the females in the CWT group had an improvement of 1.9 kilograms which was significant. The absolute lean body mass change for males in the RUN-CWT and CWT groups were precisely the same, showing a gain of 1.8 kilograms which was statistically significant.

Both males and females in the RUN-CWT and CWT groups demonstrated significant strength increases in the bench press and leg press. The increases in the strength scores averaged 22% (bench press and leg press summed and divided by two) for the females in the RUN-CWT group and 19% for the females in the CWT group. For males, the increases in the strength scores averaged 21% for the RUN-CWT group and 15% for the CWT group. These strength scores are analogous to those reported in the literature for other CWT studies.

The results of this study, again, dramatically confirmed what coaches had known for years and what had been found in the NAHI and Syracuse studies. Furthermore, this study demonstrated that super circuit weight training (SCWT) and circuit weight training were effective beyond wildest expectations in producing changes in aerobic fitness, strength and body composition.

Gettman, L., Ward, P. and Hagan, D.; A comparison of combined running and weight training with circuit weight training; Medicine and Science in Sports and Exercise, Vol. 14, No 3, pp. 229-234, 1982.

The utilization of CWT and SCWT has been shown to be very effective in stimulating the desired physiological responses in all the major components of physical fitness. The beauty of the program is that a high degree of improvement can be experienced in a very short period of time in all these physical fitness components concurrently, through the employment of CWT and SCWT programs and principles at relatively moderate training intensities.

The main reason why early research in CWT did not demonstrate a good aerobic training effect was that the time between each station was between 30 and 45 seconds. This allowed the heart rate to drop well below the training sensitive zone (60% to 90% of maximum heart rate reserve). It wasn't until the recent studies designed and commissioned by Dr. Paul Ward that the time between stations was set at 15 seconds and the work period set at 30 seconds. As mentioned above, the research began to demonstrate good aerobic training effects as a result of participating in CWT and SCWT programs using the correct time and intensity format.

It is important to point out that training theory is first demonstrated to be effective on the athletic training field (**"in the trenches"**) and then finally documented in the exercise physiology laboratories. Little or no usable training theory has ever originated in the exercise physiology laboratories. This is the case with CWT and SCWT for they were applied in the trenches years before any significant research had been conducted.

Strong confidence can be put in the concept that CWT and SCWT are the most productive methods for general physical training for all levels of fitness and for males and females of all ages because of the large empirical evidence and now the accumulation of carefully controlled scientific research.

THE DEFINITION OF CIRCUIT WEIGHT TRAINING

"Circuit Weight Training is interval training striving to obtain strength, local muscle endurance, cardiovascular respiratory endurance and reducing body fat by timed control of submaximal exercise."

Ward, Paul; Health and Tennis Corporation Certification Manual, 1975.

Interval training involves the concept of alternating short periods of intensive work with short periods of rest. The interval training technique has been shown to be effective in swimming, running and cycling programs and is well documented by research.

Fox, E. and Mathews, D.; Interval Training: Conditioning For Sports and General Fitness; W.B. Saunders Company, Philadelphia, 1974.

THE CONCEPT OF CIRCUIT WEIGHT TRAINING

The concept of CWT includes, completing a series of ten or more exercise stations with weight resistance machines that systematically conditions all major muscle groups. This provides for well balanced body conditioning and contouring. In the process of CWT a person would normally execute two to three laps around a ten station circuit in each training session. This translates into 20 to 30 exercise stations. CWT can be biased for any physical fitness component; used with equipment, with free weights or free exercise; and can be group or individually directed. Table 2-3 contains an example of CWT or SCWT exercises using free exercises, machines and free weights.

The load at each station can vary from 40% to 60% of one repetition maximum (1RM), but usually 50% of 1RM is used. The number of repetitions executed at each station should be not more than fifteen (15) and, generally, no less than ten (10) for general conditioning when using free weights or weight machines. In CWT where free exercise is used instead of equipment or free weights, the repetitions performed can be as many as 25, depending upon the physical fitness level and training objectives.

Using weights that allows the execution of more than fifteen (15) repetitions requires that the weight used drop below the training threshold level of 40 % 1RM. On the other hand, weight loads that are too heavy to allow at least ten (10) repetitions, are more than 60 % 1RM and the training routine becomes too intense for maintaining the effort long enough to derive aerobic benefit.

The work period should be not longer than thirty (30) seconds while the rest period including the time needed to move to and adjust the next station should be no longer than 15 seconds. **Extending rest periods to longer than 15 seconds is the reason why the very earliest research demonstrated little aerobic training effect.** Approximately fifteen repetitions can be completed in a thirty second work period when the work load is between forty to sixty percent of one's maximum strength.

It is important to realize that the body will normalize it's measurements in response to a specific exercise program and specific person in it's own way. **The spot reduction of fat, from the male and female body is impossible.** The human organism in response to increased energy demands will mobilize the fat generally from all over the body. The increase in the size of the muscle groups in response to weight training is related to one's genetic design, sex, hormonal levels, load levels (intensity) and repetitions.

Table 2-3.   An Example Of CWT Or SCWT Exercises Using Free Exercises, Machines And Free Weights.

MUSCLE GROUP	FREE EXERCISES	MACHINES	FREE WEIGHTS
1. HIP-LEG-BACK	SQUAT	HORIZONTAL LEG PRESS	SQUAT
2. SHOULDERS	DECLINE PUSHUP -OR- HANDSTAND PUSHUP	SHOULDER PRESS	SHOULDER PRESS
3. POSTERIOR THIGH	STEP UP	LEG CURL	STIFF LEG DEAD LIFT
4. UPPER BACK	OVERHAND GRIP PULLUP	PULLDOWN	BENT OVER ROWING
5. MISCELLANEOUS LEG	SQUAT THRUST	ADDUCTOR MACHINE	FRONT SQUAT
6. CHEST	PUSHUP	BENCH PRESS	BENCH PRESS
7. ABDOMINAL	ABDOMINAL CRUNCH	ABDOMINAL MACHINE	ABDOMINAL CRUNCH
8. ANTERIOR ARM	REVERSE GRIP CHINS	ARM CURL	ARM CURL
9. LOW BACK	HORIZONTAL BACK ARCH	BACK EXTENSION	GOOD MORNING
10. POSTERIOR ARM	DIPS	PUSHDOWN	FRENCH PRESS

NOTE:
1.   THERE ARE MANY EXERCISES THAT COULD BE USED IN A CWT/SCWT PROGRAM. ONE IS ONLY LIMITED BY THEIR IMAGINATION AND CREATIVITY.
2.   FOR EXECUTING SCWT ONE WOULD MERELY INTERJECT AN INTERVAL OF RUNNING, STEPPING, BIKING OR OTHER AEROBIC ACTIVITIES BETWEEN WEIGHT EXERCISES.
3.   THE INTENSITY FOR FREE EXERCISE CAN BE A SELECTED NUMBER OF REPETITIONS, WHILE FOR MACHINES & FREE WEIGHT INTENSITY CAN BE CONTROLLED BY REPETITIONS, WEIGHT, LAPS AND REST INTERVAL TIME.

Women need not worry about excessive muscle build-up (hypertrophy), because the normal low level of androgens (testosterone) prevents this from occurring in the average women. This is not to say that women cannot create muscle. Women who train with weights just do not develop the massiveness seen in men who train with weights. However, in CWT and SCWT lower repetition and higher intensity prescriptions can be used during the thirty second work period for focusing on strength and size for both men and women. **One must remember that women do not hypertrophy like men.**

THE DEFINITION OF SUPER CIRCUIT WEIGHT TRAINING (SCWT)

SCWT is interval training striving to obtain strength, CVRE and LME by timed control of sub-maximal exercise. It is differentiated from conventional CWT by alternating periods (30 seconds) of work with resistance machines with periods (30 seconds) of aerobic activity (running, jogging in place, stepping devices or stationary cycling).

THE CONCEPT OF SUPER CIRCUIT WEIGHT TRAINING (SCWT)

A series of 10 exercise stations working every major muscle group is laid out. This format requires the execution of a weight exercise followed by the performance of an aerobic activity which is repeated until the exercise prescription is completed. A person would normally execute 2 to 3 laps around this circuit in each training session. This means that there are 20-30 exercises performed on the weight machines with an aerobic device or exercise used between weight stations. These aerobic devices or exercises are running, jogging in place, stepping devices or stationary cycling.

It is important to plan the sequence of exercise so that different muscle groups are exercised at succeeding stations. A PHA (peripheral heart action) arrangement of equipment is preferred, i.e., an arrangement of exercises that works lower body then upper body on successive exercises. A person should execute 12 to 15 repetitions in the 30 second work interval with 40 - 60% 1RM at each station followed by 30 seconds of aerobic work.   Fifty percent of the 1RM is typically used for the training intensity in SCWT, but, of course, any intensity could be selected to emphasize a specific component of fitness.

SCWT can be biased for any physical fitness component; used with equipment or free exercise; group or individually directed; and can be used effectively with running, cycling, rowing or stairclimbing. Table 2-3 contains an example of CWT or SCWT with free exercises, machines or free weights. Other examples of free weight and machine exercises for CWT or SCWT are found in Tables 2-5, 2-6 and 2-7.

THE RATIONALE FOR USING CIRCUIT WEIGHT TRAINING (CWT) AND SUPER CIRCUIT WEIGHT TRAINING (SCWT)

People need to have effective, safe and time efficient exercise in our society. CWT and SCWT provide an efficient and safe means of obtaining physical fitness and reducing body fat. Below are some reasons for using these kinds of programs:

1. **Complete Adaptability.** Members of both sexes and of all ages can be accommodated in a circuit weight training setting. Because of this, coeducation exercise becomes a reality with very few problems. The specific training patterns of any conditioning program can be accommodated merely by changing the load, repetitions or laps.

2. **CWT and SCWT can be group or individually directed.** When few people are in the gym they can execute the CWT program without the help of an instructor. Also, when large volumes or people are present, the circuit is best conducted using a regimented group technique under the direction of an instructor or a voice recorded on tape. The concept is so simple and easy to use that it is appropriate for all age groups when machines are utilized.

3. **Each individual works at their own capacity and work rate.** Progression is implemented by increasing the load, repetitions, and/or the number of laps around the circuit. Selectorized weight machines allows for quick and easy changes of weight so that people with different levels of fitness can train at the same time. Also, when using an individual circuit, time to complete two or three laps can be reduced as a means of progression.

4. **CWT and SCWT provide a vigorous and effective period of activity in a relatively short time period.** No longer is it necessary for the individual to stay in the gym for hours to get a good workout. The intensity of CWT or SCWT provides safe and excellent results in a short time span.

5. **CWT or SCWT has built-in motivation.** Achievement of a certain heart rate, performance of a selected number of repetitions, lifting a specific weight or executing a predetermined number of laps are various ways in which motivation can be expressed.

6. **CWT and SCWT are low impact.** CWT and SCWT do not require high impact activities executed over long time periods in order to produce aerobic benefits.

THE COMPONENTS OF PHYSICAL FITNESS AND THE FITNESS CONTINUUM

CWT and SCWT produces improvements in all the components of physical fitness by using one program. This has been demonstrated in various current research studies. It is important to remember that the strength and CVRE adaptations will not be maximal when using CWT or SCWT but can still be very substantial while the LME adaptation will be near maximal. The components of physical fitness and how they are related in the fitness component continuum are discussed below.

1. **STRENGTH:** The ability to execute one maximum contraction.
2. **LME:** The ability to perform sub-maximal repetitions.
3. **CVRE:** Long duration low intensity work (aerobic activities).
4. **BODY COMPOSITION:** The minimizing of body fat and increasing of the muscle mass. (This dimension of fitness is by its nature not part of the fitness continuum, but is still one of the components of physical fitness.)

PART II

GENERAL FITNESS

THE FITNESS CONTINUUM

CVRE----------------------------------LME----------------------------STRENGTH

CVRE and strength are at opposite ends of the continuum and usually require separate and unique training programs for development. LME resides on a sliding scale between them and can be biased toward either end of the continuum. When CWT and SCWT programs are used all components of physical fitness can be dramatically improved plus effectively reducing body fat and increasing lean body mass.

THE OBJECTIVES OF CIRCUIT WEIGHT TRAINING (CWT) AND SUPER CIRCUIT WEIGHT TRAINING (SCWT)

CWT and SCWT are the best systems of exercising to improve all the major components of physical fitness when using one exercise program. CWT and SCWT are scientifically documented methods of exercise that improve all the components of physical fitness. There are five training objectives in CWT and SCWT:

1. **To develop physical work capacity (cardiovascular respiratory endurance or aerobic capacity).** This is the ability to execute long duration work of low to moderate intensity.

2. **To increase local muscle endurance.** This is the ability of muscle or a muscle group to make repeated contractions of moderate intensity without a significant stress on the cardiovascular respiratory system.

3. **To increase strength.** Strength is the ability of a muscle or a muscle group to make one maximum contraction. In CWT and SCWT there is limited strength improvement because the intensity of effort is between forty and sixty percent of 1RM for each station. Never-the-less, strength improvements for the participant can be substantial.

4. **To improve flexibility.** Flexibility is related to the extent of the range of motion of selected joints. In scientifically designed CWT and SCWT programs, where opposing muscle groups are trained through the full range of motion, flexibility will be improved.

5. **To decrease body fat and normalize body measurements.** CWT and SCWT reduces body fat while increasing lean body mass which contributes to the body's natural contouring tendencies.

THE PHYSIOLOGICAL TRAINING EFFECTS CONSEQUENT TO PARTICIPATION IN CIRCUIT WEIGHT TRAINING (CWT) AND SUPER CIRCUIT WEIGHT TRAINING (SCWT)

With the minimal levels of intensity, frequency and duration satisfied there are certain physiological adaptations and training effects that occur with CWT and SCWT. These physiological adaptations are as follows:

1. Increase in maximum oxygen consumption (aerobic capacity).
2. Decrease in body fat and increase in lean body weight.
3. Increase in flexibility.
4. Increase in strength.
5. Increase in local muscle endurance.

THESE PHYSIOLOGICAL CHANGES CONSEQUENT TO PARTICIPATION IN CWT OR SCWT PROGRAMS HAVE BEEN THOROUGHLY DOCUMENTED IN RECENT RESEARCH STUDIES.

PART II

GENERAL FITNESS

THE INTENSITY OF CIRCUIT WEIGHT TRAINING (CWT) AND SUPER CIRCUIT WEIGHT TRAINING (SCWT)

To force the body to adapt to higher levels of fitness requires the application of stress in the form of specific exercise performed at intensities and durations beyond what has been required of it. This is called the "overload" principle. To produce the desired training effect (adaptations) there is a threshold intensity that must be surpassed. For CWT and SCWT the specific (local) load for each distinctive exercise must be between forty and sixty percent of the one repetition maximum (1RM).

A rule of thumb that can be used is: if ten (10) to fifteen (15) repetitions can be performed in thirty seconds without straining, the load is approximately forty to sixty percent of 1RM. If more than fifteen repetitions can be performed in thirty seconds the load is too light. Similarly, if less than ten repetitions are performed in thirty seconds the load is too heavy. Using 40% - 60% of 1RM is the most precise method of adjusting the training intensity.

The general intensity of the exercise program is reflected by the exercise heart rate. The exercise heart rate for CWT and SCWT should range between 130 and 160 beats per minute (60 to 90 percent of the maximum heart rate reserve). **(American College of Sports Medicine Standards - See Part I)** In Table 2-4 is shown the method for determining the training heart rate range (THRR).

Higher heart rates can be tolerated but this is dependent upon one's state of condition and level of motivation. The higher the exercise heart rate the less aerobic and more anaerobic the exercise becomes. Heart rate can be accurately determined by taking the pulse within five seconds post-exercise or at any time during the exercise program. It can be felt at the radial artery by placing the tips of the fingers of the free hand on the thumb side of the wrist, or by placing the tips of the fingers of either hand at the carotid artery on the side of the neck. Figure 2-2 displays how to take the exercise heart rate.

As mentioned above, the exercise heart rate can be determined by using the radial or carotid pulse. As soon as the pulse is found, count for six seconds and add a zero. This will give an estimate of the exercise heart rate without referring to a table or using complicated math. It is very important to take the heart rate immediately after stopping the exercise because heart rate will start to rapidly decrease once the exercise stimulus is absent. It is acceptable to use longer time periods for determining exercise heart rates (10 to 15 seconds), however, it requires the use of mental mathematical manipulations that are not easily performed by most people and requires more effort when the heart is vigorously beating. The six second count is easy to perform and yields valid estimates of exercise heart rates.

For resting heart rate determinations, the wrist pulse is best. Count for fifteen seconds and multiply by four. For more precision, count for thirty seconds and multiply by two. The resting heart rate should be taken in a seated position. Resting heart rate is used as a baseline to ascertain the speed of post exercise heart rate recovery. It can be used as an indicator for how effectively the exercise program is working. Over time the resting heart rate will be reduced as heart and the circulatory system adapts to the stimulus of the exercise program.

THE DURATION OF CIRCUIT WEIGHT TRAINING (CWT) AND SUPER CIRCUIT WEIGHT TRAINING (SCWT)

The duration of CWT and SCWT programs depends upon one's fitness state, objectives, and motivation level. The overall length of a training session can vary considerably. For CWT the duration ranges from 7 1/2 minutes for beginners to 22 1/2 minutes or more for advanced trainers. In SCWT, beginners start at 10 minutes and advance to as much as 60 minutes. Initially, the duration would be short while advancing progressively in time as physiological adaptation occurs and motivation improves.

Table 2-4.   How To Find Your Training Heart Rate Range (THRR).

FOR EXERCISE TO BE AEROBIC IT MUST BE PERFORMED IN A SPECIFIC TRAINING HEART RATE RANGE (THRR). THE AMERICAN COLLEGE OF SPORTS MEDICINE RECOMMENDS THE USE OF A HEART RATE RANGE CORRESPONDING TO 60-90 PERCENT OF MAXIMUM HEART RATE RESERVE. THE HEART RATE RANGE IS USED TO DETERMINE THE INTENSITY OF THE AEROBIC WORKOUT. TO TRAIN OUTSIDE THIS RANGE IS INEFFECTIVE IF BELOW THE LOW END OF THE RANGE AND TOO INTENSE TO SUSTAIN THE EXERCISE LONG ENOUGH TO ACHIEVE BENEFITS IF BEYOND THE HIGH END OF THE RANGE. THE AEROBIC TRAINING HEART RATE RANGE "RULE OF THUMB" OF 130-160 BEATS PER MINUTE IS ADEQUATE IM MOST CASES. PEOPLE OVER 50 YEARS OF AGE HAVE A LOWER "RULE OF THUMB" AEROBIC RANGE OF 110-140 BEATS PER MINUTE. HOWEVER, TO BE VERY SPECIFIC FOR EACH INDIVIDUAL, THE FORMULA PRESENTED BELOW CAN BE USED TO DETERMINE THE PERSONAL AEROBIC TRAINING HEART RATE RANGE.

TRAINING HEART RATE RANGE (THRR)

TO DETERMINE LOW END:

	220	CONSTANT NUMBER
-		MINUS AGE
=		ESTIMATED MAXIMUM H.R.
-		MINUS RESTING H.R.
=		HEART RATE RESERVE
X		MULTIPLY BY .6 (USED TO DETERMINE 60% OF MAXIMUM H.R. RESERVE)
=		% OF H.R. RESERVE
+		PLUS RESTING H.R.
=		TRAINING HEART RATE RANGE (THRR)

TO DETERMINE HIGH END:

	220	CONSTANT NUMBER
-		MINUS AGE
=		ESTIMATED MAXIMUM H.R.
-		MINUS RESTING H.R.
=		HEART RATE RESERVE
X		MULTIPLY BY .9 (USED TO DETERMINE 90% OF MAXIMUM H.R. RESERVE)
=		% OF H.R. RESERVE
+		PLUS RESTING H.R.
=		TRAINING HEART RATE RANGE (THRR)

SAMPLE TRAINING HEART RATE RANGE CALCULATION

PROFILE: A 30 YEAR OLD WOMAN WHOSE RESTING HEART RATE IS 70 BEATS PER MINUTE.

TO DETERMINE LOW END:

-	220	CONSTANT NUMBER
	30	MINUS AGE
=	190	ESTIMATED MAXIMUM H.R.
-	70	MINUS RESTING H.R.
=	120	HEART RATE RESERVE
X	0.60	MULTIPLY BY .6
=	72	% OF H.R. RESERVE
+	70	PLUS RESTING H.R.
=	142	TRAINING HEART RATE RANGE (THRR)

TO DETERMINE HIGH END:

-	220	CONSTANT NUMBER
	30	MINUS AGE
=	190	ESTIMATED MAXIMUM H.R.
-	70	MINUS RESTING H.R.
=	120	HEART RATE RESERVE
X	0.90	MULTIPLY BY .9
=	108	% OF H.R. RESERVE
+	70	PLUS RESTING H.R.
=	178	TRAINING HEART RATE RANGE (THRR)

WARD, PAUL; FUTURE FITNESS FORMULA; SHAPE MAGAZINE; FEBRUARY, 1986.

Ward, Paul; Future Fitness Formula; Shape Magazine; February, 1986.

FIND YOUR CAROTID ARTERY   FIND YOUR RADIAL ARTERY

1. LOCATE THE CAROTID ARTERY WITH THE TIPS OF THE FINGERS - IT IS IN THE FRONT STRIP OF MUSCLE RUNNING VERTICALLY DOWN THE NECK - OR FIND THE RADIAL ARTERY BY PRESSING THE FINGERS LIGHTLY ON THE INSIDE OF THE WRIST JUST BELOW THE THUMB. REFER TO THE ILLUSTRATIONS FOR FINGER PLACEMENT.

2. TAKE THE EXERCISE HEART RATE IMMEDIATELY AFTER EXERCISING BY COUNTING THE NUMBER OF TIMES THE HEART BEATS IN SIX SECONDS. (THE FIRST BEAT IS ZERO.)

3. MULTIPLY THE HEART RATE BY 10 BY JUST ADDING A ZERO TO THE NUMBER THAT HAS BEEN COUNTED. FOR EXAMPLE, IF YOUR HEART BEATS 18 TIME IN 6 SECONDS, MULTIPLY 18 BY 10 AND THE EXERCISE HEART RATE WOULD BE 180. BY JUST ADDING A ZERO TO THE NUMBER THAT HAS BEEN COUNTED IS MULTIPLYING BY 10. ONE COULD COUNT FOR 10, 15 OR 30 SECONDS BUT USING THESE TIME PERIODS MAKE IT DIFFICULT TO ASCERTAIN THE EXERCISE HEART RATE QUICKLY. THE SIX SECOND TIME PERIOD IS BEST. THE PULSE SHOULD BE TAKEN EVERY FIVE TO TEN MINUTES DURING AEROBIC EXERCISE TO MAKE SURE THE HEART RATE IS NOT TOO LOW OR TOO HIGH. IF IT IS HIGH, REDUCE EXERCISE INTENSITY. IF IT IS TOO LOW, INCREASE THE INTENSITY OF THE EXERCISE TO MOVE INTO THE TRAINING SENSITIVE ZONE.

4. TAKE A ONE MINUTE RECOVERY HEART RATE. THE PULSE AFTER ONE MINUTE OF RECOVERY (REST) SHOULD DROP BETWEEN 30 AND 50 BEATS PER MINUTE IF ONE IS IN GOOD PHYSICAL CONDITION. A SLOW RECOVERY HEART RATE INDICATES LACK OF AEROBIC FITNESS.

Figure 2-2.   How to take the exercise heart rate.

THE FREQUENCY OF PARTICIPATION IN CIRCUIT WEIGHT TRAINING (CWT) AND SUPER CIRCUIT WEIGHT TRAINING (SCWT)

The number of times that a person participates in CWT or SCWT during a week is dependent upon the fitness state, training objectives and motivation level. Initially, the frequency might be two to three times per week and as one adapts that may increase to a seven day a week pattern. The reason that a daily pattern can be followed after an initial adaptation training period of just three days per week, is because the specific and general intensity of exercise is low enough for the body to adapt (recover) from day to day. As the frequency of CWT and SCWT increases so do the benefits.

It is important to use reason when deciding to increase the frequency of CWT or SCWT. While a five day pattern is acceptable an alternate day pattern may be optimal, especially when CWT and SCWT are alternated with other aerobic exercise programs like aerobic dance, swimming, running, cycling or stair climbing and even higher intensity weight training programs. An alternate day approach in CWT or SCWT will enhance exercise adherence for the serious fitness enthusiast. The alternate day, three days a week format is recommended for the beginner and deconditioned people.

GENERAL FITNESS   PART II

THE SELECTION OF EXERCISES AND EXERCISE SEQUENCE FOR CIRCUIT WEIGHT TRAINING (CWT) AND SUPER CIRCUIT WEIGHT TRAINING (SCWT)

The exercises included in CWT or SCWT as well as the sequence of exercises determine to a large degree the success of motivating people to continue their efforts. In addition, the exercises and sequences also determine the effectiveness of the CWT or SCWT program along with other factors such as intensity, duration and frequency of training. The majority of both males and females start to exercise because they want to lose body fat. Most other fitness objectives are secondary.

To accomplish the objective of burning calories requires a moderate intensity exercise performed over an extended period of time. CWT and SCWT are natural methods for doing this if conducted according to scientific principles. These forms of exercise spread the work load over a variety of muscle groups in a sequential manner so that no one muscle group gets overly fatigued. This allows for more work to be performed. Below is a list of five criteria for the selection and sequencing of exercises included in CWT and SCWT.

1. **The exercises included in the circuit should condition every major muscle group in the body.** The universally bad practice of over emphasizing selected muscle groups results in failure to improve, frustration, poor performance, unbalanced contouring and bad posture.

2. **Attention should be given to the sequence (order of exercise) so that consecutive exercises work antagonistic (opposite) muscle groups or muscle groups in opposite ends of the body (Peripheral Heart Action -PHA).** When PHA is not used there is too much local fatigue which produces a work slowdown or stoppage. It is important to remember that CWT is based on the principle of moderate sustained effort carried out over a specified period of time. To fatigue a body segment to the point of fatigue is counterproductive.

3. **Exercises in the circuit should be strenuous.** Donkey kicking or other low intensity exercise is not sufficiently vigorous to produce a training effect on the muscles or the cardiovascular respiratory system.

4. **Exercise in CWT and SCWT should be simple and not require a complicated adjustment of the seats, machinery or require instructor assistance.** The circuit trainer should merely adjust the resistance (load) and prepare for execution of the repetitions upon command.

5. **The performance of the exercises should be standardized as well as the traffic pattern.** All exercises should be performed so that the machine is moved through the full range of motion while executing the prescribed number of repetitions. Ideally, the sequence of going through the circuit should be the same in every training session, however, in practice this concept may have to be violated because of the large number of people using the circuit.

   When a large number of people are executing circuit weight training, like in a large health club, it is impossible to start at the same station in the circuit every training session without causing some problem. In this case a compromise would be to start at any station that was open and perform the prescribed number of stations (10, 20 or 30).

The sequence of exercises performed in CWT and SCWT needs special attention. If the exercises are randomly performed it is difficult to continue to execute the circuit because one or two muscle groups get overly fatigued because of poor selection of exercise sequence. The are two basic patterns for arranging exercises in CWT and SCWT. They are as follows:

1. **Antagonistic Muscle Group Arrangement: (See Table 2-5)**

   This method of arranging pairs of exercises in CWT and SCWT involves arranging successive exercises so that they work the antagonistic muscle group of the previous exercise. Another different pair of antagonistic muscle groups follows the first pair and this selection is followed until all the major muscle groups have been conditioned.

This pattern usually involves using the larger muscle groups first and then as fatigue accrues, the exerciser trains the smaller muscle groups.

This is not the best way to design the exercise pattern for CWT or SCWT because it allows for the over-fatigue of certain muscle groups in the upper and lower extremities. When this occurs, the perception that the circuit trainer gets is that only the arms or legs are being used. This can frustrate beginners who are not programmed or motivated to push themselves. The antagonistic muscle group pattern can be used most effectively with intermediate and advanced trainers. However, the PHA pattern is probably the best method for arranging exercise sequence in CWT and SCWT.

2.   Peripheral Heart Action (PHA): (See Table 2-6 and Table 2-7)

This method involves the working of the lower body then the upper body on each succeeding exercise until all the muscle groups have been conditioned. This is the best method of arranging exercises in CWT and SCWT because it spreads the workload all over the body and eliminates a fatiguing of upper or lower limbs. When using the PHA method of sequencing exercises more work can be accomplished in a short time period compared to the antagonistic exercise pattern because no one part of the body fatigues prematurely.

Table 2-8 presents examples of PHA circuit weight training programs using a variety of equipment commonly found in a typical commercial health club. This table defines many of the basic factors needed to conduct a circuit weight training program. The companies whose equipment is represented are: Cybex, Paramount, Universal Gym, Polaris and Body Masters. In addition, the table exhibits the muscle groups, exercises, companies, laps around the circuit, repetitions and intensity.

Table 2-5.   An Example Of An Antagonistic Exercise Pattern For CWT Or SCWT. *

MUSCLE GROUPS	MACHINES	FREE WEIGHTS
1. ANTERIOR THIGH	SQUAT/LEG PRESS	SQUAT
2. POSTERIOR THIGH	LEG CURL	STIFF LEG DEAD LIFT
3. ABDOMINAL	CRUNCH MACHINE	CRUNCH
4. LOW BACK	BACK HYPEREXTENSION	GOOD MORNING
5. SHOULDERS	SHOULDER PRESS	STANDING PRESS
6. UPPER BACK	PULLDOWN	BENT OVER ROWING
7. CHEST	BENCH PRESS	BENCH PRESS
8. POSTERIOR CHEST	REVERSE FLY	REVERSE D.B. FLY
9. ANTERIOR ARM	ARM CURL	ARM CURL
10. POSTERIOR ARM	PUSHDOWN	FRENCH PRESS
* SCWT INTERPOSES AN AEROBIC ACTIVITY BETWEEN EACH EXERCISE (RUN, STATIONARY RUN, STATIONARY CYCLING, ROWING OR STAIRCLIMBING).		

PART II

GENERAL FITNESS

Table 2-6. An Example Of A Peripheral Heart Action (PHA) Pattern For CWT And SCWT.*

MUSCLE GROUPS	MACHINES	FREE WEIGHTS
1. ANTERIOR THIGH	SQUAT/LEG PRESS	SQUAT
2. SHOULDERS	SHOULDER PRESS	STANDING PRESS
3. POSTERIOR THIGH	LEG CURL	STIFF LEG DEAD LIFT
4. UPPER BACK	PULLDOWN	BENT OVER ROWING
5. MISCELLANEOUS (LEG)	KNEE EXTENSION	FRONT SQUAT
6. CHEST	BENCH PRESS	BENCH PRESS
7. LOW BACK	BACK HYPEREXTENSION	GOOD MORNING
8. ANTERIOR ARM	ARM CURLS	ARM CURLS
9. ABDOMINAL	CRUNCH MACHINE	CRUNCH
10. MISCELLANEOUS (CHEST)	VERTICAL FLY	D.B. FLY

* THE PHA PATTERN OF EXERCISE SEQUENCE IS THE PREFERRED METHOD
  FOR GENERAL FITNESS TRAINING.
* SCWT INTERPOSES AN AEROBIC ACTIVITY BETWEEN EACH EXERCISE (RUN,
  STATIONARY RUN, STATIONARY CYCLING, ROWING OR STAIRCLIMBING).

Table 2-7. An Example Of A Peripheral Heart Action (PHA) Exercise Pattern For Super Circuit
Weight Training (SCWT).

MUSCLE GROUPS	MACHINES	FREE WEIGHTS
1. ANTERIOR THIGH	1. SQUAT/LEG PRESS	1. SQUAT
2. AEROBIC ACTIVITY	2. BIKE-STEP-JOG	2. BIKE-STEP-JOG
3. SHOULDERS	3. SHOULDER PRESS	3. STANDING PRESS
4. AEROBIC ACTIVITY	4. BIKE-STEP-JOG	4. BIKE-STEP-JOG
5. POSTERIOR THIGH	5. LEG CURL	5. STIFF LEG DEAD LIFT
6. AEROBIC ACTIVITY	6. BIKE-STEP-JOG	6. BIKE-STEP-JOG
7. UPPER BACK	7. PULLDOWN	7. BENT OVER ROWING
8. AEROBIC ACTIVITY	8. BIKE-STEP-JOG	8. BIKE-STEP-JOG
9. MISCELLANEOUS (LEG)	9. KNEE EXTENSION	9. FRONT SQUAT
10. AEROBIC ACTIVITY	10. BIKE-STEP-JOG	10. BIKE-STEP-JOG
11. CHEST	11. BENCH PRESS	11. BENCH PRESS
12. AEROBIC ACTIVITY	12. BIKE-STEP-JOG	12. BIKE-STEP-JOG
13. LOW BACK	13. BACK HYPEREXTENSION	13. GOOD MORNING
14. AEROBIC ACTIVITY	14. BIKE-STEP-JOG	14. BIKE-STEP-JOG
15. ANTERIOR ARM	15. ARM CURLS	15. ARM CURLS
16. AEROBIC ACTIVITY	16. BIKE-STEP-JOG	16. BIKE-STEP-JOG
17. ABDOMINAL	17. CRUNCH MACHINE	17. CRUNCH
18. AEROBIC ACTIVITY	18. BIKE-STEP-JOG	18. BIKE-STEP-JOG
19. MISCELLANEOUS (CHEST)	19. VERTICAL FLY	19. D.B. FLY
20. AEROBIC ACTIVITY	20. BIKE-STEP-JOG	20. BIKE-STEP-JOG

NOTE:
1. THE PHA PATTERN OF EXERCISE SEQUENCE IS THE PREFERRED METHOD
   FOR GENERAL FITNESS TRAINING.
2. ONE CAN CHOOSE TO BIKE, STEP, ROW OR RUN FOR THE AEROBIC INTERVAL. IT IS
   ALSO ACCEPTABLE TO FORMAT ALL FOUR AEROBIC MODALITIES AT RANDOM IN ANY
   DESIRED PATTERN OF USE.

PART II

GENERAL FITNESS

Table 2-8.   Examples Of PHA Circuit Weight Training Programs With Selected Equipment.

| MUSCLE GROUP | COMPANIES AND EQUIPMENT | | | | | EXERCISE PARAMETERS | | |
	CYBEX	PARAMOUNT	UNIVERSAL	POLARIS	BODY MASTER	LAPS	REPS	INTENSITY
1. ANTERIOR THIGH	HORIZONTAL LEG PRESS	SQUAT	SQUAT	LEG EXTENSION	HORIZONTAL LEG PRESS	1-3	12-15	40%-60% 1RM
2. SHOULDERS	SHOULDER PRESS	SHOULDER PRESS	SHOULDER PRESS	SHOULDER PRESS	SHOULDER PRESS	1-3	12-15	40%-60% 1RM
3. POSTERIOR THIGH	LEG CURL	LEG CURL	LEG CURL	LEG CURL	LEG CURL	1-3	12-15	40%-60% 1RM
4. UPPER BACK	PULLDOWN	PULLDOWN	PULLDOWN	SEATING ROWING	SEATED ROWING	1-3	12-15	40%-60% 1RM
5. MISCELLANEOUS LEG	LEG EXTENSION	LEG ADDUCTION	LEG EXTENSION	LEG ADDUCTION	LEG EXTENSION	1-3	12-15	40%-60% 1RM
6. CHEST	VERTICAL CHEST PRESS	CHEST PRESS	VERTICAL CHEST PRESS	VERTICAL CHEST PRESS	CHEST PRESS	1-3	12-15	40%-60% 1RM
7. LOW BACK	BACK EXTENSION	BACK EXTENSION	BACK EXTENSION	BACK EXTENSION	LOWER BACK MACHINE	1-3	12-15	40%-60% 1RM
8. ANTERIOR ARM	ARM CURL	ARM CURL	ARM CURL	ARM CURL	ARM CURL	1-3	12-15	40%-60% 1RM
9. ABDOMINALS	CRUNCH MACHINE	CRUNCH MACHINE	CRUNCH MACHINE	CRUNCH MACHINE	CRUNCH MACHINE	1-3	12-15	40%-60% 1RM
10. POSTERIOR ARM	TRICEPS MACHINE	PUSHDOWN	TRICEPS MACHINE	PUSHDOWN	TRICEPS MACHINE	1-3	12-15	40%-60% 1RM

SELECTING STARTING WEIGHTS IN CIRCUIT WEIGHT TRAINING (CWT) AND SUPER CIRCUIT WEIGHT TRAINING (SCWT)

Determining starting weights for the various circuit weight training exercises for participants can be done a number of ways: (1) Percentage of body weight; (2) Pre-set color levels (green, blue, red); (3) Percentage of 1RM.

In Table 2-9 is presented an example of selection of starting weights in circuit weight training and super circuit weight training using percentages of body weight for machines and free weight exercises. This is not the preferred method, but can be used in some instances when size of class or time constraints may be of primary consideration.

The best method is to use the preset levels for a one to four week conditioning program and then execute a 1RM and use 50% 1RM for the training loads. Of course, time, facilities and motivation will probably dictate which method will be employed for a given environment. In Table 2-9 is shown some guidelines for adjusting training loads for circuit weight training using percentages of body weight for respective exercises. Tables 2-10, 2-11 and 2-12 show pre-set green, blue and red levels for beginning, intermediate and advanced exercisers, respectively. This method of determining weight loads for circuit weight training is very simple and is exceptionally adequate for large group formats and where time and personnel are limited.

As mentioned above, the most accurate and best method for accurately determining starting weights for CWT and SCWT is to test 1RM and then use 50% 1RM for the training load. This method will ensure that the proper physiological stress will be used to obtain optimal training objectives. This should occur only after a short orientation period (one to four weeks). This orientation period permits the exerciser to learn the exercises and circuit training format while achieving some physical conditioning.

When using 1RM technique for determining starting weights for circuit weight training, one should execute the tests in the same order that the circuit program will be performed. This will keep the loads consistent with the training pattern and enhance improvement.

It is important to keep in mind that some people, regardless of physical condition, may become nauseated when starting any exercise program. If one becomes too aggressive in their participation in circuit weight training or super circuit weight training, this condition may be aggravated. It is always best to start easy and progress to more intense levels as physical conditioning improves.

PART II

GENERAL FITNESS

Table 2-9. An Example Of Selection Of Starting Weights In CWT And SCWT Using Percentages Of Body Weight For Machines And Free Weight Exercises.

MACHINES	PERCENT BODY WEIGHT	FREE WEIGHT EXERCISES	PERCENT BODY WEIGHT
1. SQUAT	30% - 50%	1. SQUAT	30% - 50%
2. SHOULDER PRESS	20% - 30%	2. SHOULDER PRESS	20% - 30%
3. LEG CURL	15% - 20%	3. STIFF LEG DEAD LIFT	20% - 40%
4. PULLDOWN	30% - 50%	4. BENT OVER ROWING	20% - 40%
5. KNEE EXTENSION	30% - 40%	5. FRONT SQUAT	20% - 30%
6. BENCH PRESS	20% - 40%	6. BENCH PRESS	20% - 40%
7. BACK EXTENSION	20% - 30%	7. GOOD MORNING	10% - 20%
8. CURLS	15% - 30%	8. CURLS	15% - 30%
9. ABDOMINAL MACHINE	5% - 20%	9. ABDOMINAL CRUNCH	0% - 10%
10. VERTICAL FLY	10% - 20%	10. DUMBBELL FLY	5% - 15%

NOTE:
THESE PERCENTAGES ARE ONLY GUIDELINES. THE EXACT LOADING MAY HAVE TO BE ADJUSTED UPWARD OR DOWNWARD FROM THE PERCENTAGES OF BODY WEIGHT. IT IS BEST TO USE LIGHTER WEIGHTS UNTIL EXERCISE TECHNIQUES ARE LEARNED AND SOME CONDITIONING OCCURS BEFORE USING HEAVIER WEIGHTS.

Table 2-10. An Example Of CWT Levels Using Selected Chrome Universal Gym And Paramount Weight Machines.

CIRCUIT WEIGHT TRAINING LEVELS
PRESIDENT'S HEALTH CLUB - DALLAS TEXAS

MUSCLE GROUP	EXERCISE	COMPANY	GREEN	BLUE	RED
1. ANTERIOR THIGH	LEG PRESS (DVR)	UNIVERSAL GYM	74/126	109/177	160/211
2. SHOULDERS	SHOULDER PRESS	PARAMOUNT	28/39	33/61	39/83
3. POSTERIOR THIGH	LEG CURL (DVR)	UNIVERSAL GYM	13/20	28/36	43/51
4. UPPER BACK	PULLDOWN	UNIVERSAL GYM	30/70	40/100	60/130
5. MISCELLANEOUS LEG	ADDUCTOR (INNER)	PARAMOUNT	30/60	50/80	70/100
6. CHEST	SEATED BENCH PRESS	UNIVERSAL GYM	29/71	35/89	41/110
7. LOW BACK	BACK HYPEREXTENSION	PARAMOUNT	55/70	70/100	85/130
8. ANTERIOR ARM	UPRIGHT ROW/CURL	UNIVERSAL GYM	20/20	30/30	40/50
9. ABDOMINAL	ABDOMINAL MACHINE	POLARIS	20/40	40/80	70/115
10. MISCELLANEOUS CHEST	PULLOVER	UNIVERSAL GYM	15/31	23/38	31/46
11. ANTERIOR THIGH	SQUAT (DVR)	UNIVERSAL GYM	66/89	89/146	112/192
12. SHOULDERS	SHOULDER PRESS (DVR)	UNIVERSAL GYM	28/30	33/61	39/83
13. POSTERIOR THIGH	LEG CURL (DVR)	UNIVERSAL GYM	13/20	28/36	43/51
14. UPPER BACK	PULLDOWN	UNIVERSAL GYM	30/70	40/100	60/130
15. ANTERIOR THIGH	KNEE EXTENSION	PARAMOUNT	40/60	60/80	80/110
16. CHEST	CHEST PRESS (DVR)	UNIVERSAL GYM	29/71	35/89	41/110
17. LOW BACK	BACK HYPEREXTENSION	PARAMOUNT	55/70	70/100	85/130
18. ANTERIOR ARM	UPRIGHT ROW/CURL	UNIVERSAL GYM	20/20	30/30	40/50
19. ABDOMINAL MACHINE	ABDOMINAL MACHINE	PARAMOUNT	15/30	25/55	45/85
20. MISCELLANEOUS CHEST	VERTICAL FLY	UNIVERSAL GYM	14/21	21/33	29/44

NOTE:
1. THE NUMBER ON THE LEFT SIDE OF THE SLASH IS THE LOAD FOR WOMEN WHILE THE NUMBER ON THE RIGHT OF THE SLASH IS THE LOAD FOR MEN. EXPRESSED IN POUNDS.
2. THESE LOADS WERE APPLICABLE FOR THE TRAINING PROGRAM PRIOR TO 1988.

PART II

GENERAL FITNESS

Table 2-11.   An Example Of CWT Levels Using Selected Cybex, Polaris and Paramount Machines.

CIRCUIT WEIGHT TRAINING LEVELS
PRESIDENT'S HEALTH CLUB - DALLAS TEXAS

MUSCLE GROUP	EXERCISE	COMPANY	GREEN	BLUE	RED
1. LEGS AND HIPS	LEG PRESS	CYBEX	4/7	6/9	8/12
2. SHOULDERS	SHOULDER PRESS	CYBEX	1/4	2/6	3/8
3. POSTERIOR THIGH	LEG CURL	CYBEX	3/5	4/7	5/9
4. UPPER BACK	PULLDOWN	CYBEX	4/7	5/9	6/11
5. ANTERIOR THIGH	LEG EXTENSION	CYBEX	3/5	5/7	7/10
6. CHEST	CHEST PRESS	CYBEX	4/6	6/8	8/10
7. ABDOMINAL	ABDOMINAL MACHINE	POLARIS	20/40	40/80	70/115
8. UPPER BACK	ROWING	CYBEX	2/4	3/6	4/8
9. MISCELLANEOUS CHEST	VERTICAL FLY	POLARIS	15/50	25/70	35/90
10. LEG AND HIP	LEG PRESS	CYBEX	4/7	6/9	8/12
11. SHOULDER	SHOULDER PRESS	POLARIS	15/45	30/60	45/90
12. POSTERIOR THIGH	STANDING LEG CURL	POLARIS	20/40	30/60	40/80
13. REAR SHOULDERS	REAR DELTOID MACHINE	POLARIS	20/50	30/70	40/90
14. ANTERIOR THIGH	LEG EXTENSION	POLARIS	30/60	50/60	70/100
15. CHEST	CHEST PRESS	CYBEX	2/6	3/8	4/10
16. UPPER ARM	ARM CURL	POLARIS	10/30	15/45	20/60
17. MIDDLE SHOULDER	LATERAL RAISE	CYBEX	1/2	1/3	2/4
18. ABDOMINAL MACHINE	ABDOMINAL MACHINE	POLARIS	20/40	30/80	50/110
19. MISCELLANEOUS CHEST	VERTICAL FLY	PARAMOUNT	15/30	25/70	35/90
20. LOW BACK	BACK EXTENSION	CYBEX	2/4	3/5	4/6

NOTE:
1.   THE NUMBER ON THE LEFT SIDE OF THE SLASH IS THE LOAD FOR WOMEN WHILE THE NUMBER
     ON THE RIGHT OF THE SLASH IS THE LOAD FOR MEN.   EXPRESSED IN POUNDS.
2.   SINGLE AND DOUBLE DIGIT NUMBERS RELATE TO THE NUMBER OF PLATES FOR CYBEX MACHINES
     AND DOES NOT INDICATE DIRECTLY THE NUMBER OF POUNDS.
3.   THESE LOADS WERE APPLICABLE FOR THE TRAINING PROGRAM PRIOR TO 1988.

PART II

GENERAL FITNESS

Table 2-12. An Example Of CWT Levels Using Selected Machines.

CIRCUIT WEIGHT TRAINING LEVELS
PRESIDENT'S HEALTH CLUB - DALLAS TEXAS
GUEST NEW MEMBER CIRCUIT

MUSCLE GROUP	EXERCISE	COMPANY	GREEN	BLUE	RED
1. ANTERIOR THIGH	SQUAT (DVR)	UNIVERSAL GYM	66/89	89/146	112/192
2. SHOULDERS	SHOULDER PRESS	UNIVERSAL GYM	28/30	33/61	39/83
3. POSTERIOR THIGH	LEG CURL (DVR)	UNIVERSAL GYM	13/20	28/36	43/51
4. UPPER BACK	PULLDOWN	UNIVERSAL GYM	30/70	40/100	60/130
5. MISCELLANEOUS LEG	ADDUCTOR (INNER)	PARAMOUNT	30/60	50/80	70/100
6. CHEST	CHEST PRESS (DVR)	UNIVERSAL GYM	29/71	35/89	41/110
7. LOW BACK	BACK HYPEREXTENSION	PARAMOUNT	55/70	70/100	85/130
8. ANTERIOR ARM	UPRIGHT ROW/CURL	UNIVERSAL GYM	20/20	30/30	40/50
9. ABDOMINAL	ABDOMINAL MACHINE	POLARIS	20/40	40/80	70/115
10. MISCELLANEOUS CHEST	VERTICAL FLY	UNIVERSAL GYM	14/21	21/33	29/44

NOTE:
1. THE NUMBER ON THE LEFT SIDE OF THE SLASH IS THE LOAD FOR WOMEN WHILE THE NUMBER
    ON THE RIGHT OF THE SLASH IS THE LOAD FOR MEN.   EXPRESSED IN POUNDS.
2. THESE LOADS WERE APPLICABLE FOR THE TRAINING PROGRAM PRIOR TO 1988.

THE METHODS OF PROGRESSION IN CIRCUIT WEIGHT TRAINING (CWT) AND SUPER CIRCUIT WEIGHT TRAINING (SCWT)

Progression in CWT and SCWT can be effected very simply. Depending upon the format of the CWT or SCWT program, progression is accomplished by varying one or more of the following factors:

A. Load
B. Repetitions
C. Laps
D. Time

All these factors interact to produce the correct stress needed or desired by the participant.

For beginners the load is very low or can be prescribed by computing 50% of 1RM and executing 10 - 15 repetitions for 10 to 20 stations. As soreness subsides and there is some initial physiological adaptation another ten stations (for a total of 30 stations) can be added to the prescription. Intermediate and advanced trainers can proceed to test 1RM and determine 50% of 1RM for training loads. They can also execute 30 stations of the circuit. This assumes that intermediate and advanced participants have been training at least two weeks before testing 1RM.

Beginners usually start out using ten repetitions and building up to fifteen repetitions before adding weight and/ or stations. Intermediate and advanced trainers can execute fifteen repetitions immediately with 50% of 1RM.

Usually beginners start with one lap (10 stations) around the circuit. Intermediate and advanced trainers can start with 2 to 3 laps (20 to 30 stations). As conditioning is achieved and if the proper number of repetitions (15 repetitions) can be performed at each station, additional laps (10 stations) can be added to the training program. The usual number of stations for CWT is 30 stations or 3 laps. This is equivalent to 22 1/2 minutes of CWT (7 1/2 minutes for each 10 station circuit). More laps can be performed but rarely do people complete more than four. In SCWT, twenty stations seems to be the most common number performed. It is recommended that a SCWT program consist of 20 to 30 stations. This is equivalent to 20 to 30 minutes of SCWT (10 minutes for each ten station super circuit). Most people are not motivated to complete more than 30 stations or thirty minutes of SCWT.

EQUIPMENT PURCHASE AND ARRANGEMENT FOR CIRCUIT WEIGHT TRAINING (CWT) AND SUPER CIRCUIT WEIGHT TRAINING (SCWT)

To properly implement CWT, SCWT and/or any other system of training for the masses of people requires some careful planning of equipment purchase and layout. There are eight basic criteria used in the selection of exercise equipment for use in CWT and SCWT programs in sophisticated exercise environments. They are:

1. Durability and appearance
2. Safety and ease of operation
3. Selectorized weight stacks
4. Small space requirement
5. Scientific validation
6. Single function machine used
7. Biomechanically correct pattern for movement
8. Reasonable cost

There are an infinite number of ways to arrange the equipment for CWT and SCWT. Space and room configuration will dictate to a large degree the equipment layout. CWT and SCWT are best executed where single station units are placed in a cafeteria style traffic pattern. This may take the form of a row of equipment along a wall or down the middle of a room. On the other hand, the equipment can be placed around the perimeter of the room in a circular fashion. All patterns mentioned above have been used successfully with the circular pattern being the most common and effective when more than ten machines are used. Also, when more than ten machines are used a broad diversity of equipment is recommended. This produces the necessary variety to avoid mental staleness.

Care must be taken to insure that all major muscle groups are included in the circuit and that in successive circuits (groups of ten stations), corresponding numbers condition the same muscle groups; for example, # 3, #13 and # 23 should all condition the same muscle group. When only ten single station units are used in the circuit weight training plan the row arrangement is best.

The traffic flow is very important to efficient application and operation of CWT and SCWT. Figure 2-3 and Figure 2-4 illustrate the recommended layout for circuit weight training and super-circuit weight training in a peripheral heart action format, respectively.

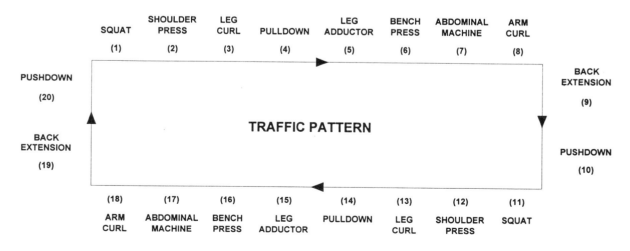

TWENTY PEOPLE MOVE IN A COUNTER CLOCKWISE OR IN A CLOCKWISE DIRECTION AFTER PERFORMING THE PRESCRIBED NUMBER OF REPETITIONS AT EACH STATION.

Figure 2-3. An example of a recommended equipment layout for circuit weight training in a peripheral heart action format.

PART II

GENERAL FITNESS

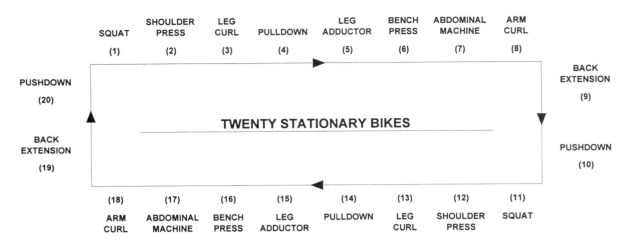

NOTE:
1. AN ALTERNATIVE EQUIPMENT LAYOUT OF SUPER CIRCUIT WEIGHT TRAINING WOULD BE TO PLACE A BIKE BETWEEN EACH PIECE OF EQUIPMENT. HOWEVER, THIS IS NOT ADVISED UNLESS THERE IS PLENTY OF SPACE AVAILABLE. THE ABOVE EQUIPMENT LAYOUT IS PREFERABLE.
2. AS MANY AS 40 PEOPLE AT ONE TIME CAN BE INVOLVED IN SUPER CIRCUIT WEIGHT TRAINING USING THE ABOVE EQUIPMENT LAYOUT. TWENTY ON THE 20 MACHINES AND 20 ON THE 20 BIKES. AT THE END OF THE 30 SECOND WORK PERIOD THEY SWITCH PLACES, ALWAYS MOVING IN EITHER A CLOCKWISE OR COUNTER CLOCKWISE DIRECTION.

Figure 2-4.   An example of a recommended equipment layout for super circuit weight training in a peripheral heart action format.

FIVE PHASES OF CIRCUIT WEIGHT TRAINING (CWT) AND SUPER CIRCUIT WEIGHT TRAINING (SCWT)

In pure CWT and SCWT there are five phases:

1. **TEACH:** This involves teaching the concept, exercises, breathing, traffic flow, heart rate monitoring and recording.

2. **TEST:** One needs to ascertain the 1RM for each lift included in the circuit in order of their execution. The training load is computed by multiplying the 1RM by 50%. Additionally, one must determine how many repetitions can be executed in one minute with 50 % of the 1RM. When this is determined one can compute the training repetitions by multiplying by 50 %. The preceding two steps will usually take two separate days.

3. **TIMING:** Once the prescription of load and repetitions have been ascertained it is time to determine a target time. This is accomplished by using the prescribed load and repetitions in the correct sequence for three laps around the circuit. The time is noted and a target time computed by multiplying by two thirds (66%) of that time. Example: Time to complete three laps of the circuit is thirty minutes. Two thirds (66%) of thirty minutes is twenty minutes. **Twenty minutes is the target time.** Normally this step is omitted.

4. **TRAINING:** Once the prescribed load, repetitions and target time have been established the trainer should follow the training pattern. Upon reaching the target time it would be necessary to change the circuit or repeat the evaluation process.

5. **RE-TEST:** When the target time is reached, steps 1-4 are repeated or a new pattern of training is developed.

One can readily see that this procedure is too time consuming for the general public. To shorten this process, arbitrary levels of intensity or percentages of body weight can be used to determine training loads. Additionally, the repetitions can be set arbitrarily ranging from 10 to 15 repetitions per station. Furthermore, two rules of thumb can utilized to insure that adequate training levels are employed. They are:

1. **For adequate general stress the heart rate should range between 130 and 160 beats per minute.** When the heart rate goes beyond this range the beginner should stop and cool down on the bike or walk on the track or treadmill. Advanced people can continue in accordance with their fitness state and level of motivation. It is important to remember that it is better to **"train not strain"** so even for advanced trainers it would be indicated to reduce the training loads so that the heart rate will be between 130 and 160 beats per minute.

2. **No more than fifteen repetitions or less than ten repetitions should be executed in the thirty second work period.** This will insure that the load will be at an optimal strength level at each station. If more precise load levels are desired then one should determine their 1RM at each station and then use 50% of 1RM for their training load.

Earlier in this section, Tables 2-10, 2-11 and 2-12 have shown examples of arbitrary training levels (loads) for males and females using circuit weight training as performed in selected Health and Tennis Corporation of America Health Clubs across the United States prior to 1988.

In addition, the previously presented Table 2.8 contains examples of a circuit weight training programs with selected equipment from various companies.

THE ADVANTAGES OF CIRCUIT WEIGHT TRAINING (CWT) AND SUPER CIRCUIT WEIGHT TRAINING (SCWT)

1. It combines into one program three major factors of physical fitness which are most often accomplished through separate programs.
2. It is goal oriented. (target time, heart rate, weight, repetitions or laps)
3. Adaptability: men/women; boys/girls; one/100; any time requirements can be met; elaborate or expensive equipment is not necessary.
4. Progression assured: load, time, reps or laps.
5. Time factor and goals build in motivation.
6. Flexibility: one can bias the focus or fit it into tight time schedules.
7. Gives a vigorous period of activity in a short time.
8. Can be group or individually directed.

VARIATIONS OF CIRCUIT WEIGHT TRAINING (CWT)

CWT, being quite flexible enables one to alter it in ways to match most training objectives and desires of the participants. This means that it can be altered to match specific objectives and special goals of the participants and can focus on more aerobic benefit or can be biased to enhance muscular size and shape while increasing local muscular endurance. One is only limited by their imagination in the implementation of CWT. In the following paragraphs, some unique variations are presented to illustrate this point. Before presenting these variations it must be emphasized that for most people, simplicity must override all other factors and that these variations may not be appropriate for all circumstances.

MUSICAL CIRCUIT WEIGHT TRAINING

Music is best used with standard CWT only. Musical CWT has been successfully used in health club operations like the Chicago Health Clubs and Holiday Spa Health Clubs in California. When the music is playing the participants perform the exercise. When the music stops, it is signal to rotate to the next station. The music selected should be ergogenic (up-beat) in nature and varied. Using music to control the work and rest rotation cycle of the circuit does two things:

1. Eliminates the need for an instructor to call the time and rotation. This frees them to provide basic instruction and to generally supervise the circuit.

2. The motivation levels of the individual using the circuit increases, especially if there is variety in the music used in successive exercise sessions. It is vitally important that the work and rest intervals be precisely thirty seconds and fifteen seconds, respectively. During the fifteen second rest and rotation intervals, "pearls of wisdom" concerning exercise, nutrition and weight control can be interjected.

REVERSING THE TRAFFIC PATTERN

It may be productive to reverse the direction of traffic periodically in CWT. This will break the monotony and may improve one's motivation.

CHANGING THE ORDER OR SEQUENCE OF EXERCISES

Occasionally it is good to change the order of the exercises. When changing the order or sequence of the exercises it is important to make sure all major muscle groups are conditioned and that the sequence is in a peripheral heart action mode. Otherwise the balance of the circuit is broken. Also, it is important that the numbers (exercises) in each ten stations circuit work the same muscle group, i.e., # 3, # 13 and # 23 work the same muscle group, et cetera.

CHANGING THE EXERCISES IN THE CIRCUIT

Changing the specific exercises included in the regular circuit weight training or super circuit weight training programs is difficult if one is training in a preset institutional or commercial health club program. However, if one is training on an individual basis at an institution or commercial health club it would be very simple to change the specific exercises in the circuit or super circuit program.

When changing the exercises, care must be taken to maintain the PHA sequencing as well as including exercises for all the major muscle groups. Of course, if program objectives dictate violation of these principles and it makes scientific sense, then any sequence or exercise can be justified.

Commercial health clubs should change the exercises and equipment in their circuit every two or three years as equipment improvements are introduced into the market place. Of course, this would be dependent upon the philosophy of the club owner or operator and the financial success of the respective health club.

This may not be possible in the institutional or school setting because of the restriction in funds available for program restructuring. This is an unfortunate happenstance, since it does not allow schools and institutions to stay current with the ever changing equipment and fitness technology. This fact, to some degree is responsible for the failure of many weight training and fitness programs offered by schools, community colleges and universities.

LOW INTENSITY SETS AND REPETITIONS

In accordance with the concept of periodization, the next logical level of intensity and volume is a sets and repetitions program where the intensity is comparable to CWT and SCWT but the volume is increased significantly. Furthermore, there is a shift of the emphasis away from the aerobic toward the muscularity components of fitness; i.e., strength, local muscular endurance and reduction of body fat. This is accomplished by increasing the intensity a little (up to 60% 1RM) and allowing longer rest periods (1-2 minutes) between sets and exercises.

THE DEFINITION OF LOW INTENSITY SETS AND REPETITIONS

Sets and Repetitions is a system of progressive resistance exercises that requires 3 to 5 sets of 10 repetitions with approximately 40-60 % of one repetition maximum. Usually 60 % of 1RM is used, however the intensity can vary between 40 % and 60 % of 1RM.

THE CONCEPT OF LOW INTENSITY SETS AND REPETITIONS

A series of exercises are selected working every major muscle group in the body for 3-5 sets of 10 repetitions for each exercise not including the warm-up exercises. All three to five sets are executed before going to the next exercise. No more than two minutes of rest is used between sets.

THE RATIONALE FOR USING LOW INTENSITY SETS AND REPETITIONS

For general fitness training, low intensity Sets and Repetitions provides a little different format that reduces the aerobic component and focuses on the muscularity components of the fitness continuum. At the same time body fat is very effectively reduced while body curves and muscle shaping are optimized. Besides, continued training effort needs variation in load, intensity and volume for sustained motivation and continued physiological improvement. Low intensity Sets and Repetitions permit one to provide physiological, psychological and training variation in the exercise program. An additional benefit is that various exercises can be employed to enhance and improve weak areas in the muscle structure and in the strength profile.

THE PURPOSES OF LOW INTENSITY SETS AND REPETITIONS

It is unwise to move too quickly to higher intensities even though one's body and mind may ostensibly adapt to it. With poor preparation the body will break down over time. If the body and mind are not effectively prepared, training progress is retarded and the over-trained state is experienced. The purposes of the conditioning weight training cycle are:

1. To condition the muscles, tendons, ligaments and connective tissue in preparation for heavier lifting.
2. To develop to a high degree of local muscle endurance, to increase lean body mass (LBM) and increase strength.
3. To assist in reducing body fat.
4. To break out of a plateau.
5. To develop a limited amount of strength.

OBJECTIVES OF LOW INTENSITY SETS AND REPETITIONS PROGRAMS

Low intensity sets and repetitions programs condition strength, local muscular endurance, increase flexibility and are extremely effective for reducing body fat and increasing lean body mass. These programs are scientifically documented as methods of exercise that improve the strength, local muscle endurance and body composition components of physical fitness. There are five training objectives for low intensity sets and repetitions:

1. **To increase local muscle endurance.** This is the ability of muscle or a muscle group to make repeated contractions of moderate intensity without a significant stress on the cardiovascular respiratory system.

2. **To increase strength.** Strength is the ability of a muscle or a muscle group to make one maximum contraction. In Sets and Reps there is limited strength improvement because the intensity of effort is between forty and sixty percent of 1RM for each exercise. Nevertheless, strength improvements for the participant can be substantial.

GENERAL FITNESS   PART II

3. **To improve flexibility.** The extent of the range of motion performed in the exercises selected for the training program will impact flexibility. Flexibility will be improved by employing scientifically designed Sets and Reps programs where exercises are performed through the full range of motion and where all opposing muscle groups are trained.

4. **To decrease body fat and normalize body measurements.** Sets and Reps programs reduce body fat while increasing lean body mass which contributes to the body's natural contouring tendencies. The reduction of fat occurs because there is a high amount of work performed in a Sets and Reps program resulting in many calories being expended.

5. **To build a physical structure that will respond to higher levels of intensity and greater volumes, should the exerciser desire to direct their program into more advanced dimensions of fitness.**

PHYSIOLOGICAL TRAINING EFFECTS CONSEQUENT TO PARTICIPATION IN LOW INTENSITY SETS AND REPETITIONS PROGRAMS.

With the minimal levels of intensity, frequency and duration satisfied there are certain physiological adaptations and training effects that occur with participation in low intensity sets and repetitions programs.

These physiological adaptations are as follows:

1. Decrease in body fat and increase in lean body weight.
2. Increase in flexibility.
3. Increase in strength.
4. Increase in local muscle endurance.

Low intensity sets and repetitions cut the body fat more effectively than any other system of training. When one executes 3-5 sets of 10-15 repetitions at 40-60 % intensity, there is a larger amount of work produced. For example, if one were to compute the amount of work produced in two sample training programs but with differing sets, repetitions and intensities, the amount of work completed would be more when lighter weights and more repetitions are executed.

Consider the information contained in Table 2-13. From a comparison of the total work shown it can be seen that for the same exercises and the same individual, the total amount of work is about 1/3 more with the 5 X 10 X 60% 1RM exercise prescription. The difference in this example is 6,000 pounds. This accounts for the greater fat reduction observed in programs using lower intensities and higher repetitions.

One must keep in mind that the figure for the total work is not precisely the amount of work that would be calculated. The definition of work is weight (load) multiplied by the distance moved. For simplicity and ease of understanding, in the above example, the total poundage was accumulated without multiplying by the distance the weight was moved. This results in a relative total work value that is adequate to demonstrate the point of increased overall work output in programs using lower intensities and higher repetitions (5 X 10 X 60% 1RM).

It is crucial to maintain the optimal intensity that matches the training goals. Higher training intensities (70 to 100% 1RM) generate more muscle mass and strength; while lower intensities (40 to 60% 1RM) develop local muscle endurance and reduction of body fat. Intensities below 40% 1RM are of questionable values for impacting muscle hypertrophy or for reducing body fat. However, there may be some presently undefined reasons for using higher repetitions performed at very low intensities. This method certainly does not induce muscle hypertrophy. This concept needs to be researched to precisely define its physiological impact, if any.

A further benefit is the stimulus of some muscular growth that occurs when the intensity is kept between 40 and 60% 1RM. It is important to note that the more effective hypertrophy programs use higher intensities and lower repetitions. Even so, a little hypertrophy does occur when using a Sets and Reps program with intensities ranging between 40% and 60% 1RM. The maximum effective intensity for this intensity range (40% to 60% 1RM) would be at the higher end of this range.

It has been empirically observed and scientifically shown, that when one drops below the 40 to 60% 1RM range, the effectiveness of stimulating muscle growth by performing high repetitions (beyond 15 repetitions) is not good. The physiological impact of this very low intensity training on the muscles is strictly metabolic with very little bearing on the contractile protein in the muscle. The muscles just are not stimulated enough to produce hypertrophy. Regardless, there may be other reasons to use high repetitions and extremely low intensity exercise. However, at this time there is no research, body of knowledge or believable theory to base valid conclusions concerning the effectiveness of using very high repetition training patterns performed with extremely low intensities.

All other things being equal, when total work is increased there is a higher caloric output producing a larger reduction in body fat. This is how body builders "cut-up" in preparation for a contest.

THESE PHYSIOLOGICAL CHANGES CONSEQUENT TO PARTICIPATION IN LOW INTENSITY SETS AND REPETITIONS PROGRAMS HAVE BEEN THOROUGHLY DOCUMENTED IN RESEARCH STUDIES.

Table 2-13. An Example Of The Effect Of 5 x 10 x 60% 1RM And 5 x 5 x 80% 1RM On Total Work Load (Total Pounds Lifted).

MUSCLE GROUP	1RM	LOWER INTENSITY AND HIGHER VOLUME		HIGHER INTENSITY AND AND LOWER VOLUME		
		5 X 10 X 60% 1RM	TOTAL WORK	5 X 5 X 80% 1RM	TOTAL WORK	DIFFERENCE
1. SQUAT	100 LBS	50 REPS X 60 LBS =	3,000	25 REPS X 80 LBS =	2,000	1,000
2. SHOULDER PRESS	50 LBS	50 REPS X 30 LBS =	1,500	25 REPS X 40 LBS =	1,000	500
3. LEG CURL	40 LBS	50 REPS X 24 LBS =	1,200	25 REPS X 32 LBS =	800	400
4 PULLDOWN	60 LBS	50 REPS X 36 LBS =	1,800	25 REPS X 48 LBS =	1,200	600
5. LEG EXTENSION	60 LBS	50 REPS X 36 LBS =	1,800	25 REPS X 48 LBS =	1,200	600
6. BENCH PRESS	70 LBS	50 REPS X 42 LBS =	2,100	25 REPS X 56 LBS =	1,400	700
7. ABDOMINALS	60 LBS	50 REPS X 36 LBS =	1,800	25 REPS X 48 LBS =	1,200	600
8. ARM CURL	40 LBS	50 REPS X 24 LBS =	1,200	25 REPS X 32 LBS =	800	400
9. LOW BACK	90 LBS	50 REPS X 54 LBS =	2,700	25 REPS X 24 LBS =	1,800	900
10. POSTERIOR ARM	30 LBS	50 REPS X 18 LBS =	900	25 REPS X 24 LBS =	600	300
		TOTAL VOLUME =	18,000 LBS	TOTAL VOLUME =	12,000 LBS	6,000 LBS*

* = TOTAL DIFFERENCE

INTENSITY UTILIZED IN A LOW INTENSITY SET AND REPETITIONS PROGRAM

The intensity of the exercises during this cycle need not be high. It is recommended that the intensity range between 40% and 60% of 1RM, with 60 % 1RM usually being the most commonly used intensity for this cycle. With complex exercises such as squats or power cleans, the intensity may be less until the execution of the movement is perfected and strength and skill are improved. It is a good idea to keep the repetitions to no more than six when performing complex exercises like the power clean or power snatch.

In Table 2-14 is found an example of exercise selection, intensity, sets and repetitions for a low intensity program using machines and free weights in a PHA arrangement.

Table 2-14.   An Example Of Exercise Selection, Intensity, Sets And Repetitions For A Low Intensity
             Conditioning Program Using Machines And Free Weights In A Peripheral Heart Action (PHA) Format.

MUSCLE GROUP	FREE WEIGHT EXERCISES	MACHINE EXERCISES	SETS	REPS	INTENSITY
1. HIP/LEG/BACK	SQUAT	LEG PRESS	3-5	10	60% 1RM
2. SHOULDERS	STANDING PRESS	SHOULDER PRESS	3-5	10	60% 1RM
3. POSTERIOR THIGH	LEG CURL (MACHINE) -OR- STIFF LEG DEAD LIFT	LEG CURL	3-5	10	60% 1RM
4. UPPER BACK	PULLDOWN (MACHINE) -OR- CHINS (BODY WEIGHT-PLUS)	PULLDOWN	3-5	10	60% 1RM
5. ANTERIOR THIGH	LEG EXTENSIONS (MACHINE) -OR- FRONT SQUAT	LEG EXTENSIONS	3-5	10	60% 1RM
6. CHEST	BENCH PRESS	BENCH PRESS	3-5	10	60% 1RM
7. ABDOMINALS	ABDOMINAL MACHINE -OR- BENT KNEE CRUNCH	ABDOMINAL MACHINE	3-5	10	60% 1RM
8. ANTERIOR ARM	ARM CURLS	ARM CURLS	3-5	10	60% 1RM
9. LOW BACK	BACK EXTENSION (MACHINE) -OR- GOOD MORNING	BACK EXTENSION	3-5	10	60% 1RM
10. POSTERIOR ARM	STANDING FRENCH PRESS	PUSHDOWN	3-5	10	60% 1RM

DURATION OF LOW INTENSITY SETS AND REPETITIONS

The duration of each exercise session during this low intensity sets and repetitions cycle ranges from one hour to one and one half hours, depending upon the state of conditioning and the number of sets performed at each exercise. It is not advisable to extend the training period much beyond the 1 1/2 hour limit. The pace of the training session should be regulated so that training sessions do not extend beyond this time goal.

FREQUENCY OF LOW INTENSITY SETS AND REPETITIONS

The number of training sessions per week in low intensity sets and repetitions is three times per week with a day of rest between each training session. It is not necessary nor desirable to engage in this system of exercise more than three times per week. Moreover, to train more than every other day (daily or some other pattern with no days of rest between training sessions) may be too physiologically intense to allow adequate recovery of the musculoskeletal apparatus. This may lead to overtraining and all sorts of soft tissue injuries and possible skeletal problems.

SELECTION OF EXERCISES AND EXERCISE SEQUENCE FOR LOW INTENSITY SETS AND REPETITIONS

Like CWT and SCWT the selection of exercises and the sequence of their performance will have a major impact on the success of the Sets and Reps training cycle. There are three criteria that should govern the selection of exercises for this cycle. They are:

1. Every major muscle group should be trained.

2. The sequence of exercises can be one of the following:

    A. Antagonistic arrangement where first the muscles on one side of the joint are exercised followed by an exercise that conditions the muscles on the opposite side of the joint (antagonists). Table 2-15 contains an example of an antagonistic exercise format in a low intensity sets and repetitions program for general conditioning.

B. Peripheral Heart Action Arrangement (PHA). An upper body exercise followed by a lower body exercise should be executed (PHA). This method is preferred for the large muscle groups, however, the antagonistic arrangement is effective also. Using the PHA method of arranging exercises does not result in fatiguing the muscle groups that move the body segments and therefore allows for optimal loading throughout the workout because fatigue is minimized. See Tables 2-16, 2-17 and 2-18.

3. It is very important to use basic standard exercises. Unusual and different exercises are not very effective at this stage of the general conditioning process. Tables 2-15, 2-16, 2-17 and 2-18 contain examples of standard exercises which could be used in this program. There are many other simple exercises that could be employed also, if desired.

4. It is best to work from the larger/stronger muscle groups to the smaller/weaker muscle groups in the training program. This is true for both the antagonistic format or the PHA format. If smaller/weaker muscles become fatigued first, it will limit the training load that could be handled by the larger/stronger muscle groups.

Table 2-15. An Example Of A Low Intensity Sets and Repetitions Conditioning Program With Universal Gym and Paramount Exercise Machines In An Antagonistic Format.

MUSCLE GROUP	EXERCISE	COMPANY	SETS	REPETITIONS	INTENSITY
1. ANTERIOR THIGH	SQUAT	UG*	3-5	10 - 15	40% - 60% 1RM
2. POSTERIOR THIGH	LEG CURL	UG*	3-5	10 - 15	40% - 60% 1RM
3. MISC. LEG	LEG ADDUCTION	UG*	3-5	10 - 15	40% - 60% 1RM
4. ABDOMINAL	ABDOMINAL MACHINE	UG*	3-5	10 - 15	40% - 60% 1RM
5. LOW BACK	BACK EXTENSION	PARA*	3-5	10 - 15	40% - 60% 1RM
6. SHOULDERS	SHOULDER PRESS	UG*	3-5	10 - 15	40% - 60% 1RM
7. UPPER BACK	PULLDOWN	UG*	3-5	10 - 15	40% - 60% 1RM
8. CHEST	BENCH PRESS	UG*	3-5	10 - 15	40% - 60% 1RM
9. ANTERIOR ARM	ARM CURL	UG*	3-5	10 - 15	40% - 60% 1RM
10. POSTERIOR ARM	TRICEPS MACHINE	UG*	3-5	10 - 15	40% - 60% 1RM

EXERCISE MACHINES FROM ANY COMPANY CAN BE USED, E.G., BODY MASTER, POLARIS, CYBEX, PARAMOUNT, ICARIAN, KIESER OR HOGGAN.

Table 2-16. An Example Of A Low Intensity Sets and Repetitions Conditioning Program With Cybex and Paramount Exercise Machines In A Peripheral Heart Action (PHA) Format.

MUSCLE GROUP	EXERCISE	MACHINE	SETS	REPETITIONS	INTENSITY
1. ANTERIOR THIGH	HORIZ. LEG PRESS	CYBEX*	3-5	10 - 15	40% - 60% 1RM
2. SHOULDERS	SHOULDER PRESS	CYBEX*	3-5	10 - 15	40% - 60% 1RM
3. POSTERIOR THIGH	LEG CURL	CYBEX*	3-5	10 - 15	40% - 60% 1RM
4. UPPER BACK	PULLDOWN	CYBEX*	3-5	10 - 15	40% - 60% 1RM
5. MISC. LEG	LEG ADDUCTION	PARA*	3-5	10 - 15	40% - 60% 1RM
6. CHEST	BENCH PRESS	CYBEX*	3-5	10 - 15	40% - 60% 1RM
7. LOW BACK	HYPEREXTENSION	CYBEX*	3-5	10 - 15	40% - 60% 1RM
8. ANTERIOR ARM	ARM CURL	CYBEX*	3-5	10 - 15	40% - 60% 1RM
9. ABDOMINAL	ABDOMINAL MACHINE	CYBEX*	3-5	10 - 15	40% - 60% 1RM
10. POSTERIOR ARM	TRICEPS MACHINE	CYBEX*	3-5	10 - 15	40% - 60% 1RM

EXERCISE MACHINES FROM ANY COMPANY CAN BE USED, E.G., BODY MASTER, POLARIS, CYBEX, PARAMOUNT, ICARIAN, KIESER OR HOGGAN.

PART II

GENERAL FITNESS

Table 2-17. An Example Of A Low Intensity Sets and Repetitions Conditioning Program With Free Weights In A Peripheral Heart Action (PHA) Format.

	MUSCLE GROUP	EXERCISE	SETS	REPETITIONS	INTENSITY
1.	HIP/LEG/BACK	POWER CLEAN/SNATCH	3-5	5 - 6	40% - 60% 1RM
2.	SHOULDERS	SHOULDER PRESS	3-5	10 - 15	40% - 60% 1RM
3.	POSTERIOR THIGH	STIFF LEG DEAD LIFT	3-5	10 - 15	40% - 60% 1RM
4.	UPPER BACK	BENT OVER ROW	3-5	10 - 15	40% - 60% 1RM
5.	MISC. LEG	SQUAT/FRONT SQUAT	3-5	10 - 15	40% - 60% 1RM
6.	CHEST	BENCH PRESS	3-5	10 - 15	40% - 60% 1RM
7.	LOW BACK	GOOD MORNING	3-5	10 - 15	40% - 60% 1RM
8.	ANTERIOR ARM	ARM CURL	3-5	10 - 15	40% - 60% 1RM
9.	ABDOMINAL	BENT KNEE CRUNCH	3-5	10 - 15	40% - 60% 1RM
10.	POSTERIOR ARM	FRENCH PRESS	3-5	10 - 15	40% - 60% 1RM

* THERE ARE MANY EXERCISES THAT COULD BE USED IN THIS PROGRAM EMPLOYING BARBELLS OR DUMBBELLS.

Table 2-18. An Example Of Selection Of Starting Weights For Low Intensity Sets And Repetitions Programs Using Percentages Of Body Weight For Machines And Free Weight Exercises.

MACHINES	PERCENT BODY WEIGHT	FREE WEIGHT EXERCISES	PERCENT BODY WEIGHT
1. SQUAT	30% - 50%	1. SQUAT	30% - 50%
2. SHOULDER PRESS	20% - 30%	2. SHOULDER PRESS	20% - 30%
3. LEG CURL	15% - 20%	3. STIFF LEG DEAD LIFT	20% - 40%
4. PULLDOWN	30% - 50%	4. BENT OVER ROWING	20% - 40%
5. KNEE EXTENSION	30% - 40%	5. FRONT SQUAT	20% - 30%
6. BENCH PRESS	30% - 40%	6. BENCH PRESS	30% - 40%
7. BACK EXTENSION	20% - 30%	7. GOOD MORNING	10% - 20%
8. CURLS	15% - 30%	8. CURLS	15% - 30%
9. ABDOMINAL MACHINE	5% - 20%	9. ABDOMINAL CRUNCH	0% - 10%
10. VERTICAL FLY	10% - 20%	10. DUMBBELL FLY	5% - 15%

NOTE:
THESE PERCENTAGES ARE ONLY GUIDELINES. THE EXACT LOADING MANY HAVE TO BE ADJUSTED UPWARD OR DOWNWARD FROM THE PERCENTAGES OF BODY WEIGHT. IT IS BEST TO USE LIGHTER WEIGHTS UNTIL EXERCISE TECHNIQUES ARE LEARNED AND SOME CONDITIONING OCCURS BEFORE USING HEAVIER WEIGHTS.

STARTING WEIGHTS IN THE LOW INTENSITY SETS AND REPETITIONS

Starting weights can be selected in three ways: (1) Trial and error search; (2) Percentage of body weight; and, (3) Percentages of 1RM. Each method is discussed below.

Prior to the beginning of weight training program, one should be exposed to a conditioning/orientation phase. During this time one would become familiarized with exercise technique plus achieve some physical conditioning. This period can range from one to four weeks in duration. During this break-in period, the weight for the exercises need not be emphasized. When one is prepared for serious training they must adjust their training loads in order to adequately elicit the physiological response.

TRIAL AND ERROR SEARCH METHOD: The trial and error search method for selecting a training load requires a few attempts at using progressively heavier weight loads until the prescribed number of sets and repetitions can be performed. In this case, 3-5 sets of 10 repetitions is the training objective. Two to three training sessions will be needed to find the proper training loads that will allow for the execution of the exercise prescription of sets and repetitions. This method is not the best method for determining weight loads for exercises. However, time constraints, equipment availability and motivation will determine if this method should be applied. This trial and error search for a training load is the least desirable of all the techniques for determining training loads.

PERCENTAGE OF BODY WEIGHT METHOD: A percentage of the body weight can be used to select the training load for exercises used in weight training. The exact percentage will be determined by the type of equipment the trainer is using, machines or free weights. One cannot use the same weight loads for all similar machine exercises because of the great differences in the feel between the machines and the accuracy of the weights indicated on the machines.

Likewise, training loads for free weights will be different than those for machines. The percentages of body weight will the same but the absolute loads will be different. There has been no research to correlate the weight loads of various machines with similar free weight loads for the same exercises. Furthermore, machine biomechanics greatly influences the feel of the weight in exercise throughout the range of motion. It is entirely possible that the strength curve of machines are not even remotely related to what is experienced in the real world of free weight exercises.

Using percentages of body weight to determine training loads will require some trial and error search to precisely tune the training loads; however, the use of this technique may simplify and shorten the process of determining the training loads if 1RM testing is not used.

Table 2-18 presents examples of selection of starting weights for low intensity sets and repetitions programs using percentages of body weight for machines and free weight exercises.

1RM METHOD: The one repetition maximum (1RM) testing is the best method for determining training loads. This ensures that the training loads are precisely suitable for each person. It is very important that an individual go through a two to four week orientation and conditioning period before attempting 1RM testing so that undue soreness will not have to be endured. For the low intensity sets and repetition cycle, 60 % of 1RM is utilized. A higher percentage could be used but it is not necessary since the purpose of this phase is to prepare the muscles, tendons, ligaments and connective tissue for more intense work.

Table 2-19 displays an example of selection of training loads using 60 % of 1RM for selected free weight exercises and machine exercises in a low intensity sets and repetitions training program. The arrangement of exercises is a peripheral heart action (PHA) pattern.

PART II

GENERAL FITNESS

Table 2-19. An Example Of Selection Of Training Weights Using 60% Of 1RM For Selected Exercises In Low Intensity Sets And Repetitions Programs For Free Weight Exercises And Machines (PHA).

MUSCLE GROUP	FREE WEIGHT EXERCISES	1RM	60% 1RM	MACHINES	1RM	60% 1RM
1. HIP/LEG/BACK	1. SQUAT	100 LBS	60 LBS	1. SQUAT	100 LBS	60 LBS
2. SHOULDERS	2. STANDING PRESS	50 LBS	30 LBS	2. SHOULDER PRESS	50 LBS	30 LBS
3. POSTERIOR THIGH	3. LEG CURL (MACHINE) -OR- STIFF LEG DEAD LIFT	40 LBS 100 LBS	24 LBS 60 LBS	3. LEG CURL	40 LBS	24 LBS
4. UPPER BACK	4. PULLDOWN (MACHINE) -OR- CHINS (BODY WEIGHT-PLUS)	60 LBS # REPS	36 LBS 60%/REPS	4. PULLDOWN	60 LBS	36 LBS
5. ANTERIOR THIGH	5. LEG EXTENSIONS (MACHINE) -OR- FRONT SQUAT	60 LBS 80 LBS	36 LBS 48 LBS	5. LEG EXTENSIONS	60 LBS	36 LBS
6. CHEST	6. BENCH PRESS	70 LBS	42 LBS	6. BENCH PRESS	70 LBS	42 LBS
7. ABDOMINAL	7. ABDOMINAL MACHINE -OR- BENT KNEE CRUNCH	70 LBS 40 LBS	42 LBS 24 LBS	7. ABDOMINAL MACHINE	70 LBS	42 LBS
8. ANTERIOR ARM	8. ARM CURLS	40 LBS	24 LBS	8. ARM CURLS -	40 LBS	24 LBS
9. LOW BACK	9. BACK EXTENSION (MACHINE) GOOD MORNING	90 LBS 50 LBS	54 LBS 35 LBS	9. BACK EXTENSION	90 LBS	54 LBS
10. POSTERIOR ARM	10. STANDING FRENCH PRESS	30 LBS	18 LBS	10. PUSHDOWN	40 LBS	24 LBS

METHODS OF PROGRESSION FOR LOW INTENSITY SETS AND REPETITIONS

Program progression is performed by varying one of the following:

1. Load
2. Repetitions
3. Sets

LOAD PROGRESSION

The easiest method of progression is to arbitrarily add weight after six training sessions but only if all prescribed sets and repetitions can be performed. There is arbitrary incrementing of the training loads for each exercise. A good "rule of thumb" is to add:

1.   5 lbs to 10 lbs for upper body exercises
2.   10 lbs to 20 lbs for lower body exercises

If more precise monitoring is desired, one can execute a 1RM test and readjust the training loads by using 60% of the newly tested 1RM. This can be done every six training sessions, however, this becomes a tedious process when testing so frequently. A possible compromise would be to use the "rule of thumb" for 3 to 4 weeks then test 1RM and readjust loads. The length of this cycle would dictate the number of times necessary for testing 1RM.

REPETITIONS PROGRESSION

Repetition progression is effectuated by incrementally increasing the number of repetitions used in the exercise by an arbitrary number until the preset number has been reached. For example, if the exercise prescription is 5 sets of 10 repetitions (prescription could be any number), the exerciser would add a repetition for each set in every workout until 5 sets of 12-15 repetitions can be performed.

In the subsequent training session, 5 to 10 pounds would be added to the exercise training load and the process repeated. One would start again at 5 sets of 10 repetitions working up to 5 sets of 12-15 repetitions. The weight would be incremented and the process repeated. This method is the least effective method of progression.

SETS PROGRESSION

Increasing the number of sets for each exercise over a few training session is another method of progressing. It is usually employed for a few weeks at the beginning stages of a training cycle. For example, when starting a cycle one could start with two sets of ten repetitions for the first week and progress to three sets of ten repetitions for the second week; four sets of ten repetitions for the third week; and five sets of ten repetitions for the fourth week up to the end of the cycle.

The set progression method is very effective for easing into a Sets and Reps type of program. After the prescribed number of sets and repetitions can be performed, the weight for each exercise should be incremented every 6 training sessions or when appropriate, until the end of the training cycle.

SUMMARY

The best method of progression, after selecting the appropriate starting weight, is to arbitrarily increase the weight loads over the training cycle. At the end of the cycle a 1RM test would be performed to adjust the training loads for the next cycle if the same exercises were going to be used in the next training cycle. If new exercises are going to be used, 1RM tests must be performed to assign effective training loads. Thereafter, progression should occur as needed.

The progression by sets is another method that is effective in the early part of a training cycle. Once the prescribed number of sets can be performed, one progresses by using the arbitrary load incrementing method until the end of the training cycle. Progression by repetitions seems to be the least popular method of progression.

PERIODIZATION OF GENERAL FITNESS PROGRAMS
FOR GENERAL FITNESS TRAINING

The most important part of any program, plan or theory is its application or implementation. There are two basic periodization applications for general fitness training presented in this discussion. They are: (1) The application of the periodization concept to a general conditioning program using circuit weight training; and (2) The application of the periodization concept for a beginner's general body building program. It is important to understand that there are many other possible applications. It is sufficient to illustrate the periodization concept at this point by presenting just two of many applications.

To ensure that weight training programs are applied intelligently over a long period of time, it is important to know how to get the most out of these programs, or any other training routine. The application of the principles of periodization provides the method for maximizing the benefits of participation in a general fitness program or body building program.

Periodization is the art of variation -changing the volume and intensity of exercises to keep the muscles "guessing" and growing! One might very well perform CWT or SCWT for the rest of one's life, and even enjoy excellent overall fitness as a result. However, it is a lot better to maximize one's potential and be efficient with one's training time by learning how to "cycle" all weight training programs. This way one can get the maximum physiological benefit for the time and effort invested, as well as minimizing tedium.

THE APPLICATION OF THE PERIODIZATION CONCEPT IN A CIRCUIT WEIGHT TRAINING (CWT) PROGRAM

Figure 2-5 shows an application of the periodization concept for a Circuit Weight Training Program. This training program starts with CWT and progresses to SCWT. It would be acceptable to start with SCWT and progress to CWT, also. There is no magic to the order of the circuit weight training programs. The total

GENERAL FITNESS   PART II

program is called a macrocycle and is made up of eight mesocycles (short cycles) that can extend from 1 to 12 weeks.

In this figure there are eight mesocycles represented as A, B, C, D, E, F, G and H. The optimal length of the basic work phases (mesocycle) is from 4 to 6 weeks, while in this example, the active rest cycles are 1 week in duration. This program includes all the basic cycles of periodization except the competition cycle; i.e., the conditioning cycle, the training cycle and the transition (active rest) cycle. A thorough discussion of Periodization is presented in Part I of this book under the title of Periodization. A competition cycle would not be appropriate in a general conditioning program and is not included in this application.

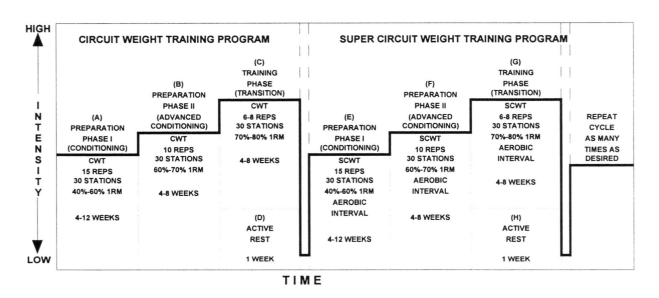

Figure 2-5.   Application of the periodization concept in a circuit weight training program.

In most health clubs, schools and universities that have structured and unstructured weight training programs, this Circuit Weight Training concept can be easily applied. All repetitions performed at the prescribed weight loads should be executed in the standard 30 second work interval. The standard 15 second rest/rotation interval is sufficient, especially when the circuit stations are arranged in a peripheral heart action format (stations are arranged lower body, upper body, lower body, upper body; et cetera).

This CWT and SCWT program can extend from 26 weeks to 58 weeks, as desired. For most people a four to six week cycle for each phase is most effective making the total training program (macrocycle) from 26 to 38 weeks.

Phase I (A) involves CWT where 15 repetitions are performed at 30 stations using 40% to 60% 1RM in the standard 30 second work period with a following 15 second rest and rotate period. Phase II (B) uses the same CWT format and the same exercises where 10 repetitions are executed for 30 stations using 60%-70% 1RM in the same work and rest/rotate time sequence. The same CWT format is used in Phase III (C) with the same exercises performed for 6-8 repetitions for 30 stations using 70%-80% 1RM in the same work and rest rotate time sequence. Phase IV is a one week active rest cycle. A 1RM test for each exercise should be applied at the end of each phase to appropriately prescribe the training loads for the next cycle and to evaluate progress.

The second half of the program starts with another Phase I (E) where SCWT is performed using 15 repetitions for 30 stations with 40% to 60% 1RM performed in the 30 second work period followed by a 30 second aerobic interval between each exercise. The aerobic interval can involve running, biking, rowing or stairclimbing as desired. Phase II (F) involves the same SCWT program and the same exercises performed for 10 repetitions for

30 stations using 60% to 70% 1RM with aerobic intervals using the same work and aerobic interval time sequence. The same SCWT format is used in Phase III (G) with the same exercises performed for 6-8 repetitions for 30 stations using 70% to 80% 1RM performed with aerobic intervals using the same work and aerobic interval time sequence. A 1RM test for each exercise should be applied at the end of each phase to appropriately prescribe the training loads for the next cycle and to evaluate progress. Phase IV (H) is a one week active rest cycle which could be followed by the same macrocycle or a new advanced body building macrocycle.

THE APPLICATION OF THE PERIODIZATION CONCEPT IN A BEGINNER'S GENERAL BODY BUILDING PROGRAM

Figure 2-6 displays an application of the periodization concept in a beginner's general body building program. This training program starts with SCWT and progresses to CWT, Sets and Reps, Pyramiding and ends with an Active Rest cycle. In this figure there are six mesocycles represented as A, B, C, D, E and F in the figure. As mentioned above, the optimal length of the basic work phases (mesocycle) is from 4 to 6 weeks, while the active rest cycles can be from 1-2 weeks in duration. The total length of this general body building program ranges from 19 to 41 weeks.

This program includes all the basic cycles of periodization; i.e., the conditioning cycle (Phase I, II and III), the training cycle (Transition I), the competition cycle (In-Season) and the active rest (Transition II) cycle. A thorough discussion of Periodization is presented in Part I of this book under the title of Periodization.

This beginner's body building cycle starts with Phase I (A) which is a SCWT program where 15 repetitions are performed at 30 exercise stations using 40% to 60% 1RM performed in the 30 second work periods followed by a 30 second aerobic interval between each exercise. The aerobic interval can employ running, biking, rowing or stairclimbing as preferred. Phase I is employed from 4 - 12 weeks and is followed by Phase II (B) which is a CWT program where 10 repetitions are performed at 30 exercise stations using 60%-70% 1RM in the standard 30 second work period with a following 15 second rest and rotate period. Phase II is applied for 4 to 8 weeks.

Phase II is followed by Phase III (C) where a Sets and Reps program is applied using 10 repetitions at 60% to 70% 1RM for 3 to 5 sets and 2 or 3 exercises per body part. Phases I, II and III are directed at preparation of the body by conditioning the muscles, tendons, ligaments and connective tissues for the higher intensities and volumes that will be applied in the advanced body building phases.

Phase IV (D) is a Sets and Reps program where 3 to 5 sets of 5 to 8 repetitions are performed with 70% to 80% 1RM over a 4 to 8 week cycle. There may be 2 or 3 exercises per body part selected for training in this cycle. During this phase an effort is made to dramatically increase muscle mass and strength. After a 4 to 8 week exposure to Phase IV the body builder using this program moves to the last heavy training phase.

Phase V (E) involves a pyramiding program which progressively increases the weight and reduces the repetitions on successive sets. The primary purpose of this phase is to train the central nervous system to enhance the body builders ability to call upon all the motor units (muscle mass) which results in ability to demonstrate more strength. Two to three exercises per body part can be designated for training in this phase. Frequently, during this cycle the body builder experiences a tremendous increase in strength and size, which is a delayed training response by the previous training cycle (Phase IV [D]).

The last phase of this training plan is Phase VI (F) which is called Active Rest. This active rest cycle does not mean "no exercise". It merely means that the intensity, duration and volume is low and the exercise focus changed for mental and physical rest and restoration. Activities could include stationary cycling, easy jogging, aerobic exercise, swimming and some easy weight training. The training sessions during this phase should be non-vigorous and short. Weight training programs can be used but should extend no longer than 30 minutes to 45 minutes in length and be of very easy intensity and low volume.

After the active rest cycle one would repeat the total body building cycle or consider designing another body building cycle.

The general length of each cycle should be 4 to 8 weeks, with training occurring 3 to 6 times a week. Each muscle group should be trained no more than three days per week and if this frequency proves to be too exhausting, then the training days should be reduced to two days per body part with one or more days of rest between exercise exposures.

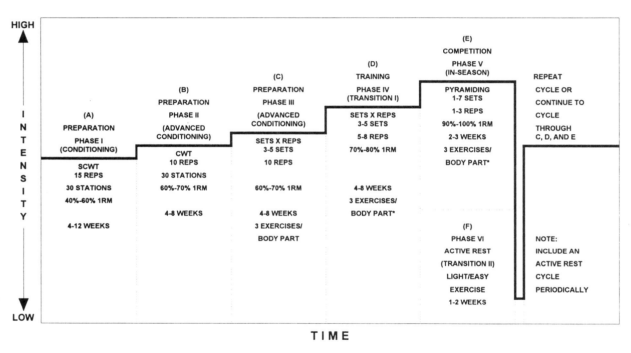

* ONLY THE LARGE MUSCLE GROUPS SHOULD USE LOW REPS: CALVES, FOREARMS AND
  ABDOMINAL MUSCLE GROUPS SHOULD NOT USE THE PYRAMIDING PROCEDURE.

Figure 2-6. Application of the periodization concept in a beginner's general body building program.

The training can include the following exercise formats:

1. Training all body parts on each training day, three days per week.

2. A split routine with upper body one day and lower body the next day.

3. A more sophisticated pattern involving 3 days of training followed by one day of rest. An example would be chest, shoulders and abdominals on day one. Day 2 would train the legs, hips, calves and abdominals. Day 3 would train the arms, back and abdominals. Day 4 would be a rest day. This format would them be repeated until the end of the cycle.

Incidentally, one should execute a 1RM test at the beginning of each cycle to determine the effective training loads. Another important guideline is to use standard exercises with dumbbells, barbells or machines.

SUMMARY OF GENERAL FITNESS PROGRAMS

For general fitness training it is best to use SCWT or CWT first, and then follow it with the Sets and Repetitions (3-5 X 10 X 40% to 60% 1RM), if desired. Some people find that SCWT and CWT, alone, meets their time constraints very favorable. CWT or SCWT can be applied in any sequence desired or each variation can be used as a primary method of training. Some method of changing the volume and intensity should be integrated into whatever format is used in training. The main advantages of SCWT and CWT are:

1. SCWT and CWT give a vigorous exercise program in a short time period.

2. SCWT and CWT work on all the major components of fitness at one time.

3. SCWT and CWT can be performed in a group, or individually in a gym or at home with machines or free weights.

The low intensity Sets and Repetitions system of training allows a needed and effective method to change from a generalized conditioning program (CWT and SCWT), to a program more focused on the muscularity and fat reducing components of physical fitness. This is done by again changing the load, intensity and volume which enhances the continued acquisition of physiological training effects as well as intensifying psychological motivation. It also prepares the body for more intense work, if movement into more intense training programs is desired.

Generally, as people continue to train with weights one experiences physiological and psychological metamorphosis. All of a sudden, they want to become body builders, involving greater efforts executed at higher intensities and greater volumes. If this phenomenon occurs after cycling from SCWT to CWT to low intensity Sets and Repetitions, then it is easier to take the more advanced step in weight training toward serious body building. Nevertheless, if the motivation and desire remains focused on the general fitness realm, then cycling of SCWT, CWT and low intensity Sets and Repetitions will provide a lifetime of success, including good aerobic capacity, good strength and local muscular endurance levels while minimizing the body fat and increasing the lean body mass and normalizing the body curves. This general fitness cycling program can be followed throughout life with good results and a healthy mental attitude toward weight training and physical fitness.

For the more serious and devoted body builder (male and female), the sets and repetitions programs have a great number of variations. Hundreds of exercises exist and there are many effective combinations of sets and repetitions and sequencing of exercises. This topic will be explored in the section on Body Building.

There is no need to over-complicate one's training programs. The basic exercises using free weights or machines should be used. Remember, the most important physical training principle is the periodic variation of the training volume and intensity. Correct use of this variation based on the principles presented in this book will produce good results stimulating even greater training effects and resulting in a rewarding exercise experience. This, in turn, will generate the large amount of enthusiasm and motivation needed to maintain the life-long exercise habit.

PART II

GENERAL FITNESS

PART II

GENERAL FITNESS

PART III

THE ENCYCLOPEDIA OF WEIGHT TRAINING

Weight Training For Sport

PART III

SPORT

THE ENCYCLOPEDIA OF WEIGHT TRAINING: WEIGHT TRAINING FOR GENERAL CONDITIONING, SPORT AND BODY BUILDING

PART III: WEIGHT TRAINING FOR SPORT

TABLE OF CONTENTS — PART III

PART III

SPORT

TABLE OF CONTENTS — PART III (CONTINUED)

PART III

SPORT

THE ENCYCLOPEDIA OF WEIGHT TRAINING: PART III

LIST OF FIGURES

SPORT PART III

ENCYCLOPEDIA OF WEIGHT TRAINING: PART III

LIST OF TABLES

PART III

WEIGHT TRAINING FOR SPORT

INTRODUCTION

There are many similarities between training for sport and general conditioning programs in the beginning stages of the training program. The foundation must be built strongly before advancing to higher training levels. Part II of this book explains in detail all the factors that need to be considered when engaging in the conditioning weight training cycle. The concept of periodization must be applied for maximizing the weight training program for sport. In fact, the total integrated program of physical training and skill training must be placed in a periodization pattern to insure maximal performance.

Figure 3-1 displays the components of a scientifically developed weight training program used in training for sport. It includes general conditioning programs and advanced training programs for body building and sports preparation. At the top of the training pyramid is presented a progressive approach to in-season training. This format aids in maintaining and possibly enhancing strength levels during in-season cycles.

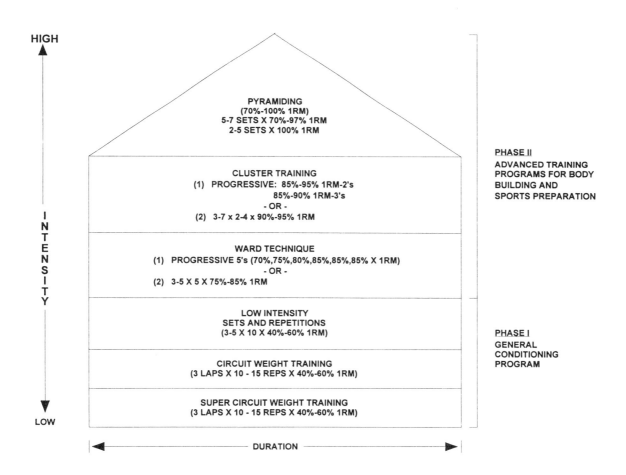

Figure 3-1. *The components of a scientifically developed weight training program for sports training.*

In Figure 3-2 is shown a training scheme that integrates the conditioning period, training period and in-season training period. The in-season cycle is less aggressive and is focused on strength maintenance programs.

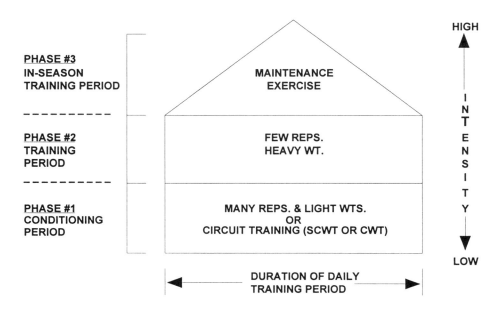

Figure 3-2.   A sports weight training scheme integrating the conditioning period, training period and in-season training period.

Once the conditioning period is completed, there are other factors that must be considered. Among them are:

1. An analysis of the specific movement patterns of the sport determines the muscle groups that need the most emphasis.

2. Analysis of the specific energy system(s) used in the sport determines how to design the program.

3. The testing of various motor performance factors are used to evaluate the current status of the athlete and the efficiency of the training program:

    A. Strength (various lifts)
    B. Sprinting speed over short distances
    C. Explosive power (various jumps and throws)
    D. Body Composition (underwater weighing)

More factors and sub-factors can be considered, but these factors are the most important. It is critical not to include too many tests and administer them too often. This becomes a unnecessarily burdensome record keeping task and also takes significant time away from the training process. However, of all the items mentioned above, strength should be tested frequently, every four to six weeks. This allows for a more precise exercise loading during training. Furthermore, it provides great motivation for the athlete involved in the strength training program. The other tests can be performed every twelve weeks.

The most accurate method of estimating body fat is by hydrostatic weighing. Skinfolds equations for estimating body fat, while convenient, are highly population specific and are usually very inaccurate.

DEVELOPING THE PROGRAM

Training for sport involves analysis of the time constraints of the specific performance to make sure the proper conditioning program is developed. Basically, there are long duration sports (distance running, swimming, cycling or a combination of the three [triathlon]) and short duration sports (sprinting, jumping and throwing like in basketball, baseball, football and track). Although there are components of cardiovascular-respiratory endurance and strength in all sporting activities, one needs to ensure that the one component or components that contribute the greatest to athletic performance are emphasized and enhanced.

All other components are trained in accordance with their percent contribution to a specific sports performance. It has been empirically observed that some type of strength training is very beneficial for all sports performances. The increase in power output that accrues with weight training programs is the basis for improvement in many sports performances. Moreover, in a weight training program the total muscular-skeletal system experiences strengthening that helps to eliminate or minimize the occurrence of serious injuries.

Most sports activity is short-term in nature and reliant upon the application of skillful actions which are applied over a very short time period. Generally speaking, training for strength and/or local muscle endurance will condition the same energy systems utilized in most skill performances. Therefore, there is a large amount of physiological transfer. It must be remembered that although the muscle physiology of sport performance can be enhanced by progressive resistance exercise programs, one must spend a large amount of time practicing the specific skills involved in the sports performance.

Weight training programs only prepare the body for sports performance. **SPECIFIC SPORTS SKILL DEVELOPMENT PROGRAMS MUST BE USED TO DEVELOP SPECIFIC SKILLS.** Moreover, it is important to remember that strength enhancement provided by weight training, is a very important stimulus for skill improvement. Whenever power is part of performance, and power is important to most sports skill performances, then the benefits of strength enhancement programs should be eagerly pursued.

It can be concluded from a kinesiological and biomechanical analysis that many sporting activities utilize the same muscle groups in creating the predominate amount of forces for performances. Most activities require the coordination of a series of muscles and muscle groups. This idea supports the wisdom of the utilization of multiple-joint exercise for sports training.

The most important muscle groups for any sports performance are those that flex and extend the ankle, knee, hip and trunk. Since the force generated by the lower extremities is transmitted through the trunk and upper extremities to some object, it is intuitively prudent to include the training of the muscle groups that move the upper body segments in all sports training programs. Moreover, a balanced muscular development of all major antagonistic muscle groups in the upper and lower body contribute to body aesthetics and, more importantly, facilitates optimal sport performance. Therefore, the principle of conditioning all major muscle groups is an inviolate principle of training for all sport training programs.

A YEAR-ROUND TRAINING PATTERN: THE RATIONAL APPROACH

The principle of developing a base before introducing high intensity workloads has applications in most training patterns; it has definite merit relative to strength development programs for sports. A rational approach to strength development assumes that there be a year-round weight training program. The year-round concept is naturally separated into three divisions: (1) the conditioning period; (2) the training period, and (3) the in-season period. The total scheme may be illustrated by a pyramid. (Figures 3-1 & 3-2)

The first phase is called the **conditioning period**. It consists of large volumes of exercise done at low intensity. This phase forms the base upon which all future strength training phases can be supported. High intensity and large volumes of exercise characterize the **training period** which makes up the second phase. During this

SPORT **PART III**

phase, an all out effort is made to increase size and strength. The top of the pyramid is the **in-season period**. It consists of high intensity exercises of small volumes for strength improvement and maintenance during the competitive season or at selected times during a training cycle.

Each division in the pyramid is differentiated in terms of load, sets and repetitions mainly, and to a small degree, by exercises. The principle followed is that there is a design or pattern for strength training as there must be design in all training programs. Figure 3-2 displays the basic concept of sports training programs. At the beginning of a training cycle, it is useful to test motor performance variables to use as a comparison at later dates. With regard to training, at first the base is laid down using general conditioning programs. Strength testing is beneficial for prescribing training loads and for comparison of retesting data at future dates. After 4-12 weeks of general conditioning, the athlete is re-tested to determine the changes in motor performance variables and strength.

Motor performance testing may include one or more of the following depending upon the specific requirements of the specific sport for which one is training:

TESTING OF MOTOR PERFORMANCE VARIABLES

1. 50 yard sprint.
2. Vertical Jump
3. Standing Long Jump
4. 25 yard hopping on one leg (both right and left)
5. Flying 50 yard sprint
6. Agility Run
7. Throwing various implements for distance

STRENGTH TESTING

It is important to test the strength for all body segments, especially those involved in the sport action in which one is participating. The testing of all or selected weight training exercises (preferably all exercises utilized in the training program with the exception of those exercises for the forearm, calves and neck) enables the development of the a total body strength profile. This involves determining the 1RM for all the exercises used in the training program. The coach and athlete can then do the following:

1. Effectively and precisely set the training loads.
2. Determine the strengths and weaknesses in the strength profile of the athlete.
3. Develop a strength training program that will address the deficiencies in the strength profile as well as enhance the total body strength.
4. Provide a method of setting short term and long term strength goals which greatly enhances the motivation of the athlete.

BODY COMPOSITION TESTING

Body composition is very important for maximizing sports performance. It is important to get baseline body fat figures to help in planning the weight training program and to provide motivation for the athlete. There are many ways to assess body fat. The most accurate method and, therefore, the most meaningful is hydrostatic weighing. Circumferential and skinfold measurements provide very useful measurements to determine the changes that are occurring in the body as a result of weight training programs as well as providing motivation for the athlete. **Skinfolds and circumferential measurements should not be used to determine percent fat because they result in spurious results.** They can be effectively used as a raw score to demonstrate changes.

The following physical measurements should be made:

1. Circumferential measurements (to ascertain where muscle imbalances are).
2. Skinfolds (to demonstrate where the subcutaneous fat resides).
3. Hydrostatic weighing (to determine percent body fat).

RATIONALE FOR TESTING STRENGTH AND MOTOR PERFORMANCE VARIABLES

Testing for testing sake is without value; however, when testing is specific and correctly performed it can give a lot of information regarding the effectiveness of the exercise program and the athlete.

The purpose of testing is fourfold:

(1) Evaluation of the present status of the athlete.
(2) Evaluation of the effectiveness of the training program.
(3) To serve as a basis for exercise prescription (determination of weight loads).
(4) To produce motivation in the athlete.

Such testing should occur intermittently throughout the year. Strength and motor performance testing should occur approximately every 6-8 weeks and body composition twice per season or about every 12 weeks.

THE CONDITIONING PERIOD

The general purpose of the conditioning period is preparation of the body for higher levels of intensity and volumes. It is not important during this period of training to lift heavy weights. The intent of this program is to **"stimulate"** the muscular system to grow, **not annihilate it**. This phase of training provides the foundation for more advanced weight training programs.

Super circuit weight training and circuit weight training are good tools to use, especially at the beginning of a yearly training cycle. SCWT and CWT have been thoroughly discussed in Part II of this book. If more information is desired regarding SCWT and CWT please refer to Part II of this book. It is sufficient here to restate a few facts about SCWT and CWT to assist in program development:

CWT AND SCWT FACTORS

1. **GENERAL OBJECTIVE:**   Preparation

2. **INTENSITY:**   40 % to 60 % 1RM

3. **DURATION:**   15 to 60 minutes

4. **FREQUENCY:**   3 to 6 times per week

5. **PROGRESSION:**   At 50 % 1RM start at 10 reps & increase to 15 reps. Add 5 to 10 pounds weekly and return reps to 10 working back to 15 reps. Another progression is to start with 20 stations and progress to 30 or 40 stations as desired in the CWT or SCWT program.

6. **LENGTH OF CYCLE:**   4 to 12 weeks.

SPORT PART III

It is not necessary to go through a SCWT and CWT cycle before moving on to low intensity sets and repetitions cycles. On the other hand, it may be exciting and motivating to include both in the preparation program. This is where the art of coaching and the art of psychology interact to enhance the implementation of the program. Figure 3-3 displays the application of the periodization concept in a circuit weight training program.

The next step in the training program during the conditioning cycle is the application of a low intensity sets and repetitions program. During this period the intensity is low (40% - 60% 1RM) with high repetitions (10-15 repetitions) and large volumes of work (three to five sets per exercise may be used). The total volume of work may be between 25,000 pounds and 50,000 pounds for women and 45,000 pounds to 70,000 pounds for men each training session. Because of the high work load (volume) the weight training sessions may extend from one and one-half to two hours.

The primary purpose of this period is to learn proper lifting techniques and to condition the muscles, tendons, ligaments and connective tissues for the high intensity work that will follow. Experience has shown that advancement to higher levels of strength and performance is faster and more stable when the foundation is laid with the conditioning period. A solid muscular conditioning base will help prevent injuries while at the same time minimizing any future injuries. Furthermore, recovery from injuries will be much faster when a good muscular and soft tissue conditioning base are achieved.

As in all good weight training programs, every muscle group should be exercised. If any gross strength deficiencies exist, they can be very effectively upgraded during the conditioning period. Again, basic exercises should be employed. There is no need to utilize unusual or novel exercises. Either an antagonistic or peripheral heart action format can be employed very effectively in this cycle for the CWT/SCWT programs.

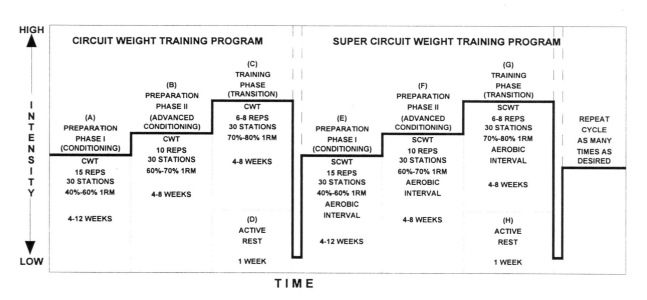

Figure 3-3. Application of the periodization concept in a circuit weight training program.

During the conditioning period the amount of weight used is low to moderate and the repetitions are many. Rest periods between sets should be no longer than 2 minutes. The duration of the daily workout may be of considerable length. As an alternative, circuit weight training or super circuit weight training may be employed at this time if desired. The conditioning regimen is usually followed for a four week period but can be extended if desired to a maximum of 12 weeks. As soon as the base of good local muscle endurance is developed and the soft tissue have been conditioned, the program shifts gears for work at higher intensity.

Below is a summary of the factors that need to be considered in the conditioning cycle using low intensity sets and repetitions in the weight training program. A more detailed description of the conditioning cycle can be found in Part II of this book.

LOW INTENSITY SETS AND REPETITIONS FACTORS

1. **GENERAL OBJECTIVE:**   Preparation

2. **INTENSITY:**   40%-60% 1RM

3. **DURATION:**   1 1/2 to 2 hours

4. **FREQUENCY:**   3 times per week

5. **PROGRESSION:**
1st week -	3 Sets X 10 Reps X 60% 1RM
2nd week -	4 Sets X 10 Reps X 60% 1RM
3rd - 5th week -	5 Sets X 10 Reps X 60% 1RM

NOTE: After the completion of the third week, 5 to 10 pounds of weight may be added to each exercise but only if the prescribed number of sets and repetitions can be performed correctly. If desired a 1RM test can be performed and the training loads readjusted accordingly.

6. **LENGTH OF CYCLE:**   4 to 12 weeks

In Table 3-1 and Table 3-2 are found two distinct examples of training exercises, load and volume for two separate low intensity sets and repetitions cycles for elite female and male athletes using sets of approximately 50 % 1RM (Power Snatch and Power Cleans 60 % 1RM). Note that the volume (total weight lifted) ranges from 41,846 to 44,836 pounds for women and from 60,030 to 70,268 pounds for men.

Table 3-1.   An example of training exercises, load and volume for a low intensity sets and repetitions weight training cycle for elite male and female athletes during a conditioning cycle at 50% to 60% 1RM. (Example # 1)

EXERCISES	WOMEN'S PRESCRIPTION		TOTAL POUNDS	MEN'S PRESCRIPTION		TOTAL POUNDS
1. POWER CLEANS	4 X 6 X 154	=	3,696	4 X 6 X 220	=	5,280
2. INCLINE PRESS	5 X 10 X 135	=	6,750	5 X 10 X 185	=	9,250
3. SQUAT	5 X 10 X 198	=	9,900	5 X 10 X 250	=	12,500
4. BENCH PRESS	5 X 10 X 150	=	7,500	5 X 10 X 200	=	10,000
5. PULLDOWN	5 X 10 X 150	=	7,500	5 X 10 X 200	=	10,000
6. CURL	5 X 10 X 50	=	2,500	5 X 10 X 100	=	5,000
7. FRENCH PRESS	5 X 10 X 40	=	2,000	5 X 10 X 80	=	4,000
8. ABDOMINAL CRUNCH	5 X 10 X 40	=	2,000	5 X 10 X 80	=	4,000
	TOTAL VOLUME	=	41,846 LBS	TOTAL VOLUME	=	60,030 LBS

* ALL EXERCISES COULD BE PERFORMED ON THE SAME THREE DAYS OF THE WEEK OR THEY CAN BE APPROPRIATELY SPREAD OUT OVER 6 DAYS OF THE WEEK. IN THE CONDITIONING PHASE, ALL EXERCISES SHOULD BE PERFORMED AT LEAST 3 TIMES PER WEEK.

SPORT   PART III

Table 3-2. An example of training exercises, load and volume for a low intensity sets and repetitions weight training cycle for elite male and female athletes during a conditioning cycle at 50% to 60% 1RM. (Example # 2)

EXERCISES	WOMEN'S PRESCRIPTION		TOTAL POUNDS	MEN'S PRESCRIPTION		TOTAL POUNDS
1. POWER SNATCH	4 X 6 X 110	=	2,640	4 X 6 X 187	=	4,480
2. POWER CLEANS	4 X 6 X 154	=	3,696	5 X 10 X 220	=	5,280
3. PRESS	5 X 10 X 132	=	6,600	5 X 10 X 200	=	10,000
4. SQUAT	5 X 10 X 198	=	9,900	5 X 10 X 300	=	15,000
5. BENCH PRESS	5 X 10 X 150	=	7,500	5 X 10 X 250	=	12,500
6. PULLDOWN	5 X 10 X 150	=	7,500	5 X 10 X 200	=	10,000
7. CURL	5 X 10 X 50	=	2,500	5 X 10 X 100	=	5,000
8. PUSHDOWN	5 X 10 X 50	=	2,500	5 X 10 X 80	=	4,000
9. ABDOMINAL CRUNCH	5 X 10 X 40		2,000	5 X 10 X 80		4,000
	TOTAL VOLUME	=	44,836 LBS	TOTAL VOLUME	=	70,268 LBS

* ALL EXERCISES COULD BE PERFORMED ON THE SAME THREE DAYS OF THE WEEK OR THEY CAN BE APPROPRIATELY SPREAD OUT OVER 6 DAYS OF THE WEEK. IN THE CONDITIONING PHASE, ALL EXERCISES SHOULD BE PERFORMED AT LEAST 3 TIMES PER WEEK.

THE TRAINING PERIOD

Once the base program and subsequent testing is completed the athlete can begin the application of advanced training routines and programs. The purpose of this advanced phase of training is to work on the structural aspect of strength development, i.e., increasing the overall muscle mass. The foundation has been developed in the conditioning period. Now is the time to concentrate all energies upon strength and lean mass development.

The training period emphasizes exercising the large muscle groups with heavy loads and performing few repetitions. This is best done with repetitions between 5 and 8 and performing 3 to 5 sets between 75% and 85% of 1RM. There are other effective formats of sets, repetitions and intensities, but the above format has been shown to be the most effective with male and female athletes ranging from beginners to elite in all age categories.

It is not necessary to perform sophisticated and unusual exercises in this cycle. The basic power lifts, olympic lifts and related exercises, and other assistance and basic exercises should be given preference. The duration of the weight training session is long (total program = 2 hours; split program 1 hour) with higher intensity and in moderate volumes. Depending upon the local conditions and the sport, this period may extend well into the competitive season with microcycles of various intensities and varying volumes. During out of season programs the off days should be devoted to work on fundamentals of basic movement skills of all types and limited and wisely applied cardiovascular conditioning.

Below is presented the basic concepts of the training cycle with general characteristics of the program application.

THE WARD TECHNIQUE (3-5 X 5 X 75% - 85% 1RM)

The concept of three to five sets of five repetitions with 75% to 85% 1RM for the major training emphasis has been used in training athletes over many years by one of the authors with outstanding success. This format has been successful with males and females of all ages and level of skill.

DEFINITION:

The Ward Technique involves determining one's maximum strength (1RM) on a variety of lifts. During the training program, eighty percent of the maximum (80% 1RM) is performed for each exercise for 3 to 5 sets of 5 repetitions, after a one, two or three set warmup for each exercise. The exercise intensity can range between 75% and 85% 1RM to meet the goals of the training phase which are increasing the size and the strength of the athlete.

CONCEPT:

A series of exercises are selected using all the major muscle groups. Many compound exercises like cleans, snatches and squats are used. After a 2 to 3 set warmup is completed at the beginning of each exercise; 3 to 5 sets of 5 repetitions of between 75% and 85% of 1RM is executed. Rest periods of two to three minutes between sets are adequate.

PURPOSE OF THE WARD TECHNIQUE:

The purpose of the Ward Technique is to develop muscle size, increase functional body weight (lean body mass) and to improve strength. This particular exercise prescription seems to be more effective that any other prescription. Maximum lean mass (muscle) is developed when using this method or one similar to it. During this particular exercise prescription (cycle) the athlete should make every effort to complete the scheduled training sessions, receive adequate rest and nutrition. This cycle is the core of the functional strength training program for any sport.

SELECTION OF EXERCISES AND EXERCISE SEQUENCE:

Like CWT, SCWT and Low Intensity Sets and Repetitions the selection of exercises and the sequence of their performance will have a major impact on the success of the Sets and Reps training cycle. There are four criteria that should govern the selection of exercises for this cycle. They are:

1. Every major muscle group should be trained.

2. The sequence of exercises can be one of the following:

    A. **Antagonistic arrangement** where first the muscles on one side of the joint are exercised followed by an exercise that conditions the muscles on the opposite side of the joint (antagonists).

    B. **Peripheral Heart Action Arrangement (PHA).** An upper body exercise followed by a lower body exercise should be executed (PHA). This method is preferred for the large muscle groups, however, the antagonistic arrangement is effective, also. Using the PHA method of arranging exercises does not result in fatiguing the muscle groups that move the body segments and, therefore, allows for optimal loading throughout the workout because fatigue is minimized.

3. It is very important to use the basic standard exercises. Unusual and different exercises are usually not very effective. Experience has shown that successful athletes use some variation of the basic weight training exercises for 95% of their training program. Using the basic exercises for training is especially important in the early stages of the athlete's career, as well as, during all phases of the yearly training cycle for advanced training.

4. It is best to work from the larger/stronger muscle groups to the smaller/weaker muscle groups in the training program. This is true for both the antagonistic format or the PHA format. If smaller/weaker muscles become fatigued first, it will limit the training load that could be handled by the larger/stronger muscle groups.

INTENSITY:

Intensities between 75% and 85% of 1RM have been scientifically and empirically demonstrated to be very effective for producing increases in size and strength if used in a 3 - 5 sets times 5 repetitions format. The specific intensity of eighty percent 1RM has been proven to be very effective for males and females of all ages and skill levels.

The intensity level for the Ward technique is 5 sets of 5 repetitions which should be performed between 75% - 85% of 1RM. For beginners it is acceptable to train three times per week with a day of rest between training sessions or use a split routine (upper body one day and lower body the next day) with intensity remaining at 80% for all three days. As the athlete becomes stronger, it becomes necessary to have an easy day interposed between the two heavier days. Usually this involves reducing the intensity to between 60% and 70% 1RM on the middle day and performing 3 sets of 8-10 repetitions. An example of this concept is shown in the next section which discusses frequency of the training program.

Table 3-3 displays an example of the intensity utilized in the Ward Technique for the bench press exercise using 5 sets of 5 repetitions performed at 80% of 1RM. This table includes the warmup, training and cool down loadings.

A variation of the Ward Technique is the progressive 5's method. Progressive fives can be used to provide diversity to the periodization concept and at the same time combine, to some degree, the hypertrophy and motor unit recruitment objectives into one program. This variation is biased toward the improvement in size but involves the motor unit recruitment to a small degree. All the training parameters and exercises remain the same as with the standard Ward Technique method with the exception of intensity, which obviously varies.

After a 1 to 3 set warmup, the athlete performs sets of 5 reps with progressively increasing intensities. The intensity percentage of 1RM should vary between 70% and 85% of 1RM. In Table 3-4 is shown an example of the Progressive 5's variation of the Ward Technique using the bench press exercise. The 1RM in this example is 310 pounds. The training percentages successively used are 70% (1 set), 75% (1 set), 80% (1 set) and 85% (3 or more sets), followed by a cool down set of 10 repetitions with 60% of 1RM.

Table 3-3.   An example of the Ward Technique (5 X 5 X 80% 1RM) using the bench press exercise.
              (1RM is 310 pounds)

SET #	PURPOSE	WEIGHT	% 1RM	# OF REPS
1	WARMUP	135 LBS	45%	10
2	WARMUP	185 LBS	60%	5
3	WARMUP	205 LBS	65%	5
4	TRAINING	250 LBS	80%	5
5	TRAINING	250 LBS	80%	5
6	TRAINING	250 LBS	80%	5
7	TRAINING	250 LBS	80%	5
8	TRAINING	250 LBS	80%	5
9	COOLDOWN	185 LBS	60%	10

PART III SPORT

Table 3-4.   An example of the Progressive 5's variation of the Ward Technique using the bench press exercise. (1RM is 310 pounds)

SET #	PURPOSE	WEIGHT	% 1RM	# OF REPS
1	WARMUP	135 LBS	45%	10
2	WARMUP	185 LBS	60%	5
3	WARMUP	205 LBS	65%	5
4	TRAINING	215 LBS	70%	5
5	TRAINING	230 LBS	75%	5
6	TRAINING	250 LBS	80%	5
7	TRAINING	260 LBS	85%	5
8	TRAINING	260 LBS	85%	5
9	TRAINING	260 LBS	85%	5
10	COOL DOWN	185 LBS	60%	10

DURATION:

The duration of the daily training session when using the Ward Technique may extend from 1.5 hours to 2.5 hours depending upon the state of conditioning of the athlete. If lack of time becomes a problem, the number sets can be cut to 4 and the warmup sets limited. If this procedure doesn't reduce the duration of the daily training sessions to a manageable time period, then the number of exercises should be reduced to include only the exercises that provide the most contribution to improvement of the specific skill involved.

Another way to reduce the daily training time is to use a split routine where the upper body is trained on one day and the lower body is trained on the next day. This method requires the athlete to be in the gym 6 days a week. Another limitation of this 6 days per week weight training program is finding time to include skill practice concurrent with weight training. Some compromises may need to be implemented in the weight training program.

FREQUENCY:

The number of training sessions per week in the Ward Technique is three times per week with a day of rest between training sessions for beginners. (Monday - Wednesday - Friday or Tuesday - Thursday - Saturday) This format is effective for novices since for them there seems to be easy recovery with a day of rest between training sessions. This may be due to the relatively lower training weights they use and the lower training volume that results from their training.

If a split (upper body one day and lower body the next day) format is utilized then, of course, a daily training session using only one part of the body is executed followed the next day by the opposite body area. For example: Monday, Wednesday and Friday upper body and Tuesday, Thursday and Saturday lower body. This concept can be used by the novice as well as the advanced athlete. The athlete's time schedule will dictate what procedure should be employed. For advanced athletes (those who have achieved a high level of strength development) it is advisable to have an easy day (3 X 8 X 60% - 70%) between the two heavy days (5 X 5 X 80% 1RM). A typical example of varying intensity is shown in the following:

LEVEL	WEEKLY TRAINING FREQUENCY	INTENSITY
1. BEGINNERS	MONDAY-WEDNESDAY-FRIDAY	5 X 5 X 80% 1RM
2. INTERMEDIATE AND ADVANCED	MONDAY-FRIDAY WEDNESDAY	5 X 5 X 80% 1RM 3 X 8 X 60 - 70% 1RM

SPORT   PART III

When using a split routine one should interpose an medium intensity day between the hard days for both the upper body and lower body training day sequences. An example is shown below:

DAYS	BODY AREA	PRESCRIPTION	RELATIVE NTENSITY
1. Monday	Lower Body	5 X 5 X 80% 1RM	HARD
2. Tuesday	Upper Body	5 X 5 X 80% 1RM	HARD
3. Wednesday	Lower Body	3 X 8 X 60% 1RM	MEDIUM
4. Thursday	Upper Body	3 X 8 X 60% 1RM	MEDIUM
5. Friday	Lower Body	5 X 5 X 80% 1RM	HARD
6. Saturday	Upper Body	5 X 5 X 80% 1RM	HARD
7. Sunday	Rest	Rest	REST

The training load percentages do not have to be exactly the same as prescribed above. There is an envelope of training percentages from which to select an effective training intensity. For the hard days, Monday, Tuesday, Friday and Saturday the effective training percentage envelope ranges between 75% and 85% 1RM. For the easy days, Wednesday and Thursday the effective training percentage ranges between 60% and 70% 1RM.

SELECTING STARTING WEIGHTS IN THE TRAINING CYCLE

Selecting starting weights for the various exercises for participants is done by testing for 1RM and then adjusting the training loads to 80% (75% - 85%) 1RM. This program should only be followed after a 4 to 8 week conditioning cycle (mesocycle). The purpose of the conditioning cycle is for preparation of the muscles, tendons, ligaments and connective tissue for exposure to greater intensities and larger volumes. There is always the temptation to by-pass this program. This practice is unwise and may lead to injury or retarded progression of training.

LENGTH OF TRAINING CYCLE

The length of the training cycle for the Ward Technique can range from 4 to 12 weeks. Longer cycles can be used but they don't seem to fit into the American competitive schedules and are not as effective as the shorter ones. The advantage of the shorter cycle may be purely psychological. Research and empirical observations suggest that cycles between 6 and 8 weeks may be optimal.

PROGRESSION

The training weight for each exercise should be increased every 3 to 6 training sessions, usually on the first training session in the week (Monday). The increments should be 5 to 10 pounds for the upper body and 10-20 pounds for the lower body. Testing for 1RM can occur every four weeks if more precise load adjustments are desired. A set-progression technique is useful in the first three weeks of a training cycle. An example is presented below:

PROGRESSION:	1st week -	3 Sets X 5 Reps X 80% 1RM
	2nd week -	4 Sets X 5 Reps X 80% 1RM
	3rd - 8th week	5 Sets X 5 Reps X 80% 1RM

After the third week the athlete can increase the weight as long as the sets and repetitions prescription can be performed. It is not necessary to make the training loads so heavy that the athlete has to generate large volumes of psychological energy to complete the exercise prescription. **"TRAIN, DON'T STRAIN."**

SUMMARY

The Ward Technique (muscle structure emphasis) can be employed for a period ranging from four to twelve weeks. The optimal length of time for using this technique may vary from sport to sport and, also, during the competitive season. Some sports may effectively use this training phase (3-5 X 5 X 80% 1RM) during the early part of the season. Sports like track and field allow for the utilization of this technique throughout the good part of the competitive season while football, basketball and baseball, do not. However, in the off season training programs of all sports, this tool can be utilized very effectively.

After completion of the prescribed time in the Ward Technique cycle it is time to increase the intensity to specifically train the nervous system aspect (ability to call upon the motor units) of strength development.

THE IN-SEASON CYCLE

The in-season training program is really an extension of the training period. The main objective is to maintain the strength and muscle mass, if possible, that has been developed during earlier training. The in-season cycle utilizes cluster training, pyramid training or a combination strength intensity program. The specific programming is dependent upon the judgement of the coach and athlete and the sport for which one is training. Another objective is to employ the central nervous system in the recruitment of motor units. The exact application of this very high intensity training may vary from sport to sport and between athletes.

During cluster and pyramid training or when using a combination strength intensity program, the routine is altered to implement only those exercises that are absolutely necessary to maintain performance levels and an injury free competitive existence. In other words, there must be absolute specificity of training, while some attention should be given to injury prevention. The time devoted to weight training during the competitive season is necessarily short; however, the intensity of the work can be high. It is obvious that priorities of specific skills and the sport be observed.

It is interesting to note that many coaches and athletes do not employ in-season weight training, even in this enlightened day. Consequently, many hours of diligent and arduous training go down the drain and are paralleled by poor performances, increased injuries and risk of injuries. There must be an effort to maintain strength at the desired level without consuming vast quantities of time and energy. Weight training programs can be used effectively during the season of all sports and the prudent progressive coaches utilize in-season weight training programs.

Obviously, the duration and intensity cannot be, and indeed, need not be the same as used in the off-season period. There is no reason to believe, and no evidence to indicate that there is any negative effect upon performance as a result of participating in weight training during the season. In fact, performance is enhanced by reduction of injuries and maintaining the strength at high levels, insuring maximum performance of skills.

The in-season weight training cycle may include a combination of sets and repetitions consonant with the specificity of training for the selected sport. The sets and repetitions can vary as needed and the intensity can vary between 70% and 100% 1RM.

CLUSTER TRAINING

Cluster training is the next step in the periodization of training. It represents the transition between the program that maximally enhances the muscle hypertrophy and a program that maximally calls upon motor unit recruitment (employment of the central nervous system). Cluster training teaches the athlete how to more effectively recruit the motor units in the muscle groups involved in movements related to sports performance. Cluster training can be effectively employed in the off-season and in-season weight training programs. It is merely the extension of the periodization of training which can be employed during the competitive season, if desired.

SPORT PART III

DEFINITION

Cluster training involves executing sets (3-7 sets or more) with fewer repetitions (2 to 3 reps) at higher intensities (90% to 95% 1RM).

CONCEPT

A list of exercises is selected using all the major muscle groups. In the standard cluster program, three to seven sets of 2-3 repetitions are performed at between 90% and 95% 1RM after a two to four set warm-up for each exercise. In the standard cluster program after the warm-up sets, the basic intensity does not change for all the prescribed sets. In contrast when using the progressive cluster method, after a two to four set warm-up for each exercise, approximately three to seven sets of 2 to 3 repetitions are performed at increasingly higher percentages of 1RM (85% - 95% 1RM). A rest period of up to 5 minutes between sets may be required in either variation of this program.

PURPOSE OF CLUSTER TRAINING

The purpose of cluster training is to train the neuromuscular system to activate a greater number of motor units during a specific exercise. This technique will not develop a large amount of hypertrophy since the focus is on the motor unit recruitment and the energy system that supports the execution of such a program. This aspect of strength (facilitation of motor unit recruitment) must be specifically trained. Once all the muscle mass has been developed, it has to be trained to specifically contract at or near maximal intensities. The application of cluster training is one of the methods one can utilize in training the motor unit recruitment. The use of the progressive cluster technique intensifies the motor unit recruitment.

SELECTION OF EXERCISES AND EXERCISE SEQUENCE

Like CWT, SCWT, Low Intensity Sets and Repetitions and the Ward Technique, the selection of exercises and the sequence of their performance will have a major impact on the success of the Cluster Training cycle. There are four criteria that should govern the selection of exercises for this cycle. They are:

1. **Every major muscle group should be trained.**

2. **The sequence of exercises can be one of the following:**

   A. **Antagonistic arrangement** where first the muscles on one side of the joint are exercised followed by an exercise that conditions the muscles on the opposite side of the joint (antagonists).

   B. **Peripheral Heart Action Arrangement (PHA).** An upper body exercise followed by a lower body exercise should be executed (PHA). This method is preferred for the large muscle groups, however, the antagonistic arrangement is effective, also. Using the PHA method of arranging exercises does not result in fatiguing the muscle groups that move the body segments and, therefore, allows for optimal loading throughout the workout because fatigue is minimized.

3. **It is very important to use the basic standard exercises.** Unusual and different exercises are usually not very effective. Experience has shown that successful athletes use some variation of the basic weight training exercises for 95% of their cluster training program. Using the basic exercises for cluster training is especially important in the early stages of the athlete's career, as well as, during all phases of the yearly training cycle for advanced training.

4. **It is best to work from the larger/stronger muscle groups to the smaller/weaker muscle groups in the training program.** This is true for both the antagonistic format or the PHA format. If smaller/weaker muscles become fatigued first, it will limit the training load that could be handled by the larger/stronger muscle groups. Cluster training for small muscle groups probably is not needed; for example, calves, forearms and neck.

INTENSITY

The intensity of the training weight in standard cluster training ranges from 90% to 95% of 1RM. Each specific percentage will determine the number of repetitions that can be performed. The progressive cluster technique employs the application of increasing intensities ranging from 85% to 95% of 1RM. Not every one will be able to execute the same number of repetitions with various percentages of 1RM, therefore individual percentages will have to be determined in some cases. There is no rule of thumb that can determine these percentages, so the trial and error method should be employed. Straining is not the purpose in this phase. One must attempt to perform each repetition without straining and complete each set without failing to execute the desired number of repetitions.

Examples are displayed in Tables 3-5 and 3-6 for standard cluster training using 3 repetitions and 2 repetitions, respectively. Tables 3-7 and 3-8 contain examples of progressive cluster training for 3 repetitions and 2 repetitions, respectively.

Table 3-5. An example of the standard cluster program employing 3 repetitions per set and using the bench press exercise. (1RM is 310 pounds)

SET #	PURPOSE	WEIGHT	% 1RM	# OF REPS
1	WARMUP	135 LBS	45%	10
2	WARMUP	220 LBS	70%	3
3	WARMUP	250 LBS	80%	3
4	CNS TRAINING	280 LBS	90%	3
5	CNS TRAINING	280 LBS	90%	3
6	CNS TRAINING	280 LBS	90%	3
7	CNS TRAINING	280 LBS	90%	3
8	CNS TRAINING	280 LBS	90%	3
9	COOL DOWN	185 LBS	60%	10

Table 3-6. An example of the standard cluster program employing 2 repetitions per set and using the bench press exercise. (1RM is 310 pounds)

SET #	PURPOSE	WEIGHT	% 1RM	# OF REPS
1	WARMUP	135 LBS	45%	10
2	WARMUP	220 LBS	70%	2
3	WARMUP	250 LBS	80%	2
4	WARMUP	280 LBS	90%	2
5	CNS TRAINING	295 LBS	95%	2
6	CNS TRAINING	295 LBS	95%	2
7	CNS TRAINING	295 LBS	95%	2
8	CNS TRAINING	295 LBS	95%	2
9	CNS TRAINING	295 LBS	95%	2
10	COOL DOWN	185 LBS	60%	10

Table 3-7. An example of a progressive cluster program employing 3 repetitions per set and using the bench press exercise. (1RM is 310 pounds)

SET #	PURPOSE	WEIGHT	% 1RM	# OF REPS
1	WARMUP	135 LBS	45%	10
2	WARMUP	205 LBS	65%	3
3	WARMUP	235 LBS	75%	3
4	CNS TRAINING	260 LBS	85%	3
5	CNS TRAINING	260 LBS	85%	3
6	CNS TRAINING	270 LBS	87%	3
7	CNS TRAINING	270 LBS	87%	3
8	CNS TRAINING	280 LBS	90%	3
9	CNS TRAINING	280 LBS	90%	3
10	CNS TRAINING	280 LBS	90%	3
11	COOL DOWN	185 LBS	60%	10

Table 3-8. An example of a progressive cluster program employing 2 repetitions per set and using the bench press exercise. (1RM is 310 pounds)

SET #	PURPOSE	WEIGHT	% 1RM	# OF REPS
1	WARMUP	135 LBS	45%	10
2	WARMUP	185 LBS	60%	3
3	WARMUP	220 LBS	70%	3
4	CNS TRAINING	260 LBS	85%	2
5	CNS TRAINING	270 LBS	87%	2
6	CNS TRAINING	280 LBS	90%	2
7	CNS TRAINING	285 LBS	92%	2
8	CNS TRAINING	295 LBS	95%	2
9	CNS TRAINING	295 LBS	95%	2
10	CNS TRAINING	295 LBS	95%	2
11	COOL DOWN	185 LBS	60%	10

PART III   SPORT

DURATION

The duration of the daily training session in cluster training varies from 1.5 hours to 2.5 hours depending upon the state of conditioning of the athlete. The rest periods tend to be longer, up to five minutes in this cycle, extending the total length of the training session. While one may be ready to perform another set physiologically within two minutes, there is a need to extend the rest periods to mobilize the mental energy. The length of the training session can be reduced by training different exercises (body parts) on consecutive days.

FREQUENCY

Three times per week with a day of rest between training sessions is the most commonly used pattern. Lifting extremely heavy weights (high percentages of maximum) may require two to five days of rest between training sessions. It may be wise to use this tool on a Monday and Friday and use a medium load (60% to 70%) on Wednesday. This pattern must be tailored to fit the requirements for each sport for the in-season training program.

The number of training sessions per week in the Cluster Training is three times per week with a day of rest between training sessions for beginners. (Monday - Wednesday - Friday or Tuesday - Thursday - Saturday)

This format is effective for novices since for them there seems to be easy recovery with a day of rest between training sessions in this group. This may be due to the relatively lower training weights they use and the lower training volume that results from their training.

If a split (upper body one day and lower body the next day) format is utilized then, of course, a daily training session using only one part of the body is executed followed the next day by the opposite body area. For example: Monday, Wednesday and Friday upper body and Tuesday, Thursday and Saturday lower body. This concept can be used by the novice as well as the advanced athlete.

For advanced athletes (those who have achieved a high level of strength development) it is advisable to have an easy day (3 X 8 X 60% to 70% 1RM) between the two heavy days (cluster training). A typical example of varying intensity is shown below:

LEVEL	WEEKLY TRAINING FREQUENCY	INTENSITY
1. BEGINNERS	MONDAY-WEDNESDAY-FRIDAY	3-7 X 2-3 X 90% - 95% 1RM
2. INTERMEDIATE AND ADVANCED	MONDAY-FRIDAY WEDNESDAY	3-7 X 2-3 X 90% - 95% 1RM 3 X 8 X 60% - 70% 1RM

When using a split routine then interpose an easy day between the hard days for both the upper body and lower body training day sequences. For in-season weight training it is necessary to modify and adapt cluster training to the specific sport.

SELECTING STARTING WEIGHTS IN THE CLUSTER CYCLE

Selecting starting weights for the various exercises for participants is done by testing for 1RM and then adjusting the training loads to appropriate intensity (85-95% 1RM). This program should only be followed after a 4 to 8 week training cycle (mesocycle). The purpose of the training cycle is for increase in size and strength. The purpose of cluster training is to learn to recruit the motor units and for tapering.

LENGTH OF CYCLES

This technique can be used for extended periods of time especially when time is limited and a good base has already been developed. Also, 2-3 repetitions may be the best number of repetitions for power development in sophisticated lifting movements. Certainly cluster training can be integrated into a program where hypertrophy is the focus but just on the sophisticated lifting movements like variations of the snatch and clean and jerk.

This period may extend from 2 to 4 weeks. The length of application of this technique can be extended as part of a combined program in special competitive circumstances (such as extension of the competitive season like in making the Olympic Team or going to the Football Superbowl).

PROGRESSION

The training weight for each exercise should be increased every 3 to 6 training sessions, usually on the first training session in the week (Monday). The increments should be 5 to 10 pounds for the upper body and 10-20 pounds for the lower body. Testing for 1RM can occur every four weeks if a more precise load adjustment is desired.

THE PYRAMIDING TECHNIQUE

Pyramiding forces the central nervous system to become maximally involved in the performance of exercises in the strength training program. Pyramiding involves the progressive increase in weight in consecutive sets and the decreasing of the repetitions until maximum or near maximum weight is lifted. In the performance of this procedure the brain calls upon as much muscle as possible (near maximal recruitment of the motor units without extreme circumstances prevailing - motor units are a nerve and its branches and the muscle fibers they activate).

Many people neglect this very important aspect of strength training (application of the mind). There are times in all sport performances, individual and team, when near maximal strength applications produce superior performance. However, it is almost impossible to produce maximal contractions without specific training, except in very unusual emergency situations when maximal contractions become an automatic response to danger.

The prospect of injury when executing maximal contractions exists only when the athlete is improperly conditioned or when they make foolish errors in judgement in the execution of maximal contractions. Even when there are foolish actions and unwise procedures undertaken, it is commonly observed that it is very difficult to sustain injuries when performing maximal contractions.

Highly active children and young adults engage in maximal contractions in their daily living patterns with impunity. Consider the youngster jumping out of high trees, lifting heavy awkward objects, throwing rocks for maximal distances, fighting with others, playing tackle football without pads, wrestling, and performing the many very difficult dares of peers. Athletes at all ages and levels of competition routinely subject themselves to maximal contractions and performances. The younger humans do these things as a matter of daily routine and there are very few injuries resulting from maximal contractions.

Can you imagine the gymnastics coach telling a gymnast to perform a half-speed double back somersault on a floor exercise routine? What about going half speed in a competitive wrestling match, football game, basketball game, soccer match or sprinting event? This is absurd! This is said to dispel the undeserved fear and concern with regard to performing maximal contractions. Maximal or near maximal contractions are frequently performed in various sporting movements and general activities of life at all ages.

In the training environment, the progressive coach and athlete control the situations where maximum contractions are employed. Therefore, the small risk of injury during maximum contractions is reduced to almost nothing.

Training for maximal contractions is a part of athletic training. How can one learn to more effectively apply muscular force without training that function of the neuromuscular apparatus. To not train the central nervous system aspect of strength is to improperly and incompletely train the athlete for maximal performance. Near maximal and maximal muscular contractions do not cause or predispose one to injury as long as reasonable training procedures are not compromised.

Pyramiding is the highest level of periodization of weight training. It can be effectively employed in the off-season and in-season weight training programs. It is merely the extension of the periodization of training which can be employed during the competitive season, if desired.

DEFINITION

The pyramiding technique involves executing a decreasing number of repetitions with a corresponding increase in load (weight) for each selected exercise. It corresponds somewhat to determining one's 1RM. This technique is usually applied for short lengths of time and sometimes in combination with other prescription formats, depending upon the competitive circumstances.

CONCEPT

A series of exercises is selected that use all the major muscle groups. Two, three or more warmup sets are performed and then the pyramiding program is implemented. In this cycle 5 to 10 sets of 1 to 5 repetitions are performed after a specific warmup of 1 to 3 sets. One would start with approximately 70% 1RM and increase the weight in 10 to 15 pound increments until the 90% of 1RM is reached. Thereafter, the increments should be smaller (2.5 to 5 pounds) until the 1RM is reached.

At the 1RM one would attempt to perform 2 to 5 sets. After completion of the 1RM sets, perform 10 repetitions at 60% 1RM to complete the exercise. The rest periods between efforts are usually longer because of the need to focus the mental and physical energy into the lift. Therefore the length of the rest period between sets may range between 5 to 10 minutes and sometimes longer, depending upon the individual and the exercise.

PURPOSE OF PYRAMIDING

The objective of this cycle is to train the brain to involve the greatest number of motor units in a strength movement. Also, this method can be used effectively to maintain and improve strength when accumulation of muscle mass is a limiting factor (like in gymnastics, boxing or wrestling).

SELECTION OF EXERCISES AND EXERCISE SEQUENCE:

Like CWT, SCWT, Low Intensity Sets and Repetitions, the Ward Technique and cluster training, the selection of exercises and the sequence of their performance will have a major impact on the success of the Pyramiding Training cycle. There are four criteria that should govern the selection of exercises for this cycle. They are:

1. **Every major muscle group should be trained.**

2. **The sequence of exercises can be one of the following:**

    A. **Antagonistic arrangement** where first the muscles on one side of the joint are exercised followed by an exercise that conditions the muscles on the opposite side of the joint (antagonists).

    B. **Peripheral Heart Action Arrangement (PHA).** An upper body exercise followed by a lower body exercise should be executed (PHA). This method is preferred for the large muscle groups, however, the antagonistic arrangement is effective, also. Using the PHA method of arranging exercises does not result in fatiguing the muscle groups that move the body segments and, therefore, allows for optimal loading throughout the workout because fatigue is minimized.

3. **It is very important to use the basic standard exercises.** Unusual and different exercises are usually not very effective. Experience has shown that successful athletes use some variation of the basic weight training exercises for 95% of their pyramid training program. Using the basic exercises for pyramid training is especially important in the early stages of the athlete's career, as well as, during all phases of the yearly training cycle for advanced training.

4. **It is best to work from the larger/stronger muscle groups to the smaller/weaker muscle groups in the training program.** This is true for both the antagonistic format or the PHA format. If smaller/weaker muscles become fatigued first, it will limit the training load that could be handled by the larger/stronger muscle groups. **Pyramid training for small muscle groups probably is not needed, for example; calves, forearms and neck.**

All major muscle group exercises can be used in this phase. Pyramiding on minor exercises may not be of great value. Certainly the major exercises where pyramiding can be used are:

Pyramiding For Major Lifts

Squats
Back Squats
Hack Squats
Leg Presses
Power Cleans
Power Snatches
High Pulls
Dead Lifts
Presses
Incline Presses
Bench Presses
Pullovers
Pulldowns
Rowing
Various Relevant Exercise Machines

Optional Pyramiding For Assistance Lifts

Curls
Pushdown
French presses
Leg Extensions
Leg Curls
Various Relevant Exercise Machines

INTENSITY

Intensity varies up to 100% maximum. While it is to difficult to determine if your limit has been reached until you have failed to complete a lift, the emphasis in this cycle should be on completing every attempt at progressively heavier weights. In fact, it may be more beneficial to perform more complete lifts at 97% to 99% 1RM than attempt to execute one 100% 1RM and fail. The pyramid program should never be used without some preparation of the muscles, ligaments, tendons and connective tissues regardless of age, sex or skill level.

Table 3-9 contains an example of pyramiding using the bench press exercise with a 1RM of 310 pounds. The set number, weight used, percentage of 1RM and number of repetitions for each set are shown.

Table 3-9. An example of a pyramiding program using the bench press exercise. (1RM is 310 pounds)

SET #	PURPOSE	WEIGHT	% 1RM	# OF REPS
1	WARMUP	135 LBS	45%	10
2	WARMUP	185 LBS	60%	5
3	WARMUP	205 LBS	65%	5
4	CNS TRAINING	220 LBS	70%	5
5	CNS TRAINING	250 LBS	80%	3
6	CNS TRAINING	275 LBS	90%	2
7	CNS TRAINING	295 LBS	95%	1
8	CNS TRAINING	310 LBS	100%	1
9	CNS TRAINING	310 LBS	100%	1
10	CNS TRAINING	310 LBS	100%	1
11	CNS TRAINING	310 LBS	100%	1
12	COOL DOWN	185 LBS	60%	10

DURATION

The duration of the training session is long when using this cycle. Therefore, it is important to cut the number of exercises to the bare minimum to save time if it becomes a factor. If time is not a large factor then a reasonable number of exercises can be performed using this concept. The length of the daily training session can vary from 2 to 3 hours depending upon the state of conditioning of the athlete and their motivation.

The duration of the daily training session can be shortened if a split routine is used. A warning is necessary on this point. It is likely that the body will not tolerate the application of the pyramid concept in a split routine for too long of a time. The reason is that it (the body) perceives that every day is a maximal training day even though different exercises are performed and the muscles are training in a slightly different manner from day to day. The overtrained syndrome appears very rapidly.

Another concept for a daily training pattern in this cycle is a variation of the Bulgarian approach. This involves selecting just one lift and executing a series of maximum pyramiding efforts and then a long resting period followed by another similar training session using completely different lift. There may be two or three training sessions performed each training a different lifting exercise for each selected weight training day. It is doubtful that this variation can be broadly applied in the American system of competition and social structure. However, it could conceivably be applied in a limited way.

FREQUENCY:

The number of training sessions per week for the Pyramiding Technique is three times per week with a day of rest between training sessions for beginners. (Monday - Wednesday - Friday or Tuesday - Thursday - Saturday) This format is effective for novices since for them there seems to be easy recovery with a day of rest between training sessions. This may be due to the relatively lower training weights they use and the training volume that results from their training.

If a split (upper body one day and lower body the next day) format is utilized then, of course, a daily training session using only one part of the body is executed followed the next day by the opposite body area. For example: Monday, Wednesday and Friday upper body and Tuesday, Thursday and Saturday lower body. This concept can be used by the novice as well as the advanced athlete.

For advanced athletes (those who have achieved a high level of strength development) it is advisable to have an easy day (3 X 8 X 60% - 70%) between the two heavy days (pyramiding). The exercises may be completely different than those performed on the heavy training days. A typical example of varying intensity is shown below:

LEVEL	WEEKLY TRAINING FREQUENCY	INTENSITY
1. BEGINNERS	MONDAY-WEDNESDAY-FRIDAY	PYRAMIDING 100%
2. INTERMEDIATE AND ADVANCED	MONDAY-FRIDAY WEDNESDAY	PYRAMIDING 100% 3 X 8 X 60% - 70% 1RM

When using a split routine one should interpose an easy day between the hard days for both the upper body and lower body training day sequences.

SELECTING STARTING WEIGHTS IN THE PYRAMIDING TECHNIQUE

Selecting starting weights for the various exercises for participants is done by testing for 1RM and then adjusting the training loads to appropriate intensity (70-100% 1RM). It may be appropriate to use the most recent 1RM test to compute the most suitable training load for each set. In the process of applying the pyramiding technique, one will quickly establish the new 1RM and the appropriate percentages can be applied to training plan.

LENGTH OF CYCLE

Generally speaking, the pyramid cycle should not exceed three to four weeks. Many coaches and athletes stay in this mode of training for long periods of time. When this occurs, there is a flattening of the strength increase curve while there is minimal increase in muscle mass or even a slight loss of muscle mass in some cases. The training stimulus (work) is not enough to induce muscle hypertrophy.

The optimal length of time for implementing this program is 2 to 4 weeks. Longer periods can be used but the athlete runs the risks of leveling in strength acquisition and cessation of muscle mass development.

PROGRESSION

Progression is evident as strength improves, i.e., the ending weight level of each exercise in the pyramid program becomes heavier. The rate of strength gain is specific to the individual and related to methods of training, motivation, restoration, rest and nutrition.

COMBINATION STRENGTH INTENSITY PROGRAM

In-season strength training is very important. A good in-season weight training program maintains the conditioning of the muscles and connective tissues at a high level throughout the season. There is a gradual deterioration of strength of athletes as the season progresses, especially if no strength program is used. This results in a weak athlete at the time when the championships approach. This, of course is undesirable because it will reduce the performance level and increase the chances of injury.

In many sports, such as football, basketball and volleyball, it is very difficult to maintain high intensity strength programs during the season. A combination program involving varying intensities in the weekly cycle may prove beneficial. The combination strength program includes two to three strength training sessions per week. Each strength training session would vary in intensity based upon the sport, the competitive schedule and the training philosophy.

There are many variations and formats for a combination strength intensity program. For instance, one series of exercises, intensities and repetitions would be executed on one day and a different series of exercises, intensities and repetitions would be performed on the second weight training day. Tables 3-10 and 3-11 contain a proposed weekly weight training pattern for basketball and football, respectively. In sport training the strength training usually occurs after practice. It may be more beneficial to weight train in the morning and practice the sport the late afternoon. However, the practice facilities and time schedules will dictate the timing of the training format. Figures 3-4, 3-5 and 3-6 display examples of cycling training for basketball, football and track and field, respectively.

Table 3-12 contains an example of a year-round football weight training program. All the cycles of periodization are presented in this example; conditioning cycle, training cycle and the in-season cycle.

Table 3-10. A Proposed Weekly Weight Training Pattern For The Competitive Basketball Season.

MONDAY	TUESDAY	WEDNESDAY	THURSDAY	FRIDAY	SATURDAY	SUNDAY
STRENGTH TRAINING 70%-100% 1RM	-----	GAME	STRENGTH TRAINING 40%-70% 1RM	-----	GAME	-----
AND						
PRACTICE	PRACTICE	-----	PRACTICE	PRACTICE	-----	REST

Table 3-11.   A Proposed Weekly Weight Training Pattern For The Competitive Football Season.

MONDAY	TUESDAY	WEDNESDAY	THURSDAY	FRIDAY	SATURDAY	SUNDAY
STRENGTH TRAINING CWT 40%-60% 1RM AND PRACTICE	----- PRACTICE	----- PRACTICE	STRENGTH TRAINING 70%-100% 1RM PRACTICE	----- PRACTICE	GAME -----	----- REST

PERCENT OF 1RM	MAR	APR	MA	JUN	JUL	AUG	SEP	OC	NOV	DEC	JAN	FEB
HIGH 100% INTENSITY 80% 60% LOW 0%	CWT 40%-60% 1RM	3-5 X 10 X 60% 1RM	3-5 X 5 X 80% 1RM	PYR 70%-100% 1RM	3-5 X 5 X 80% 1RM	PYR 70%-100% 1RM	3-5 X 5 X 80% 1RM	PYR 70%-100% 1RM	3-5 X 5 X 80% 1RM	COMBINATION PROGRAM USING VARYING INTENSITIES		COMBINATION PROGRAM USING VARYING INTENSITIES
LENGTH OF PROGRAM	3 WEEKS	3 WEEKS	4 WEEKS	2 WKS	5 WEEKS	2 WKS	5 WEEKS	2 WKS	4 WEEKS	10 WEEKS		12 WEEKS +
TIME OF YEAR	←————————————————— OFF SEASON PROGRAM —————————————————→								PRE-SEASON PROGRAM		IN-SEASON PROGRAM

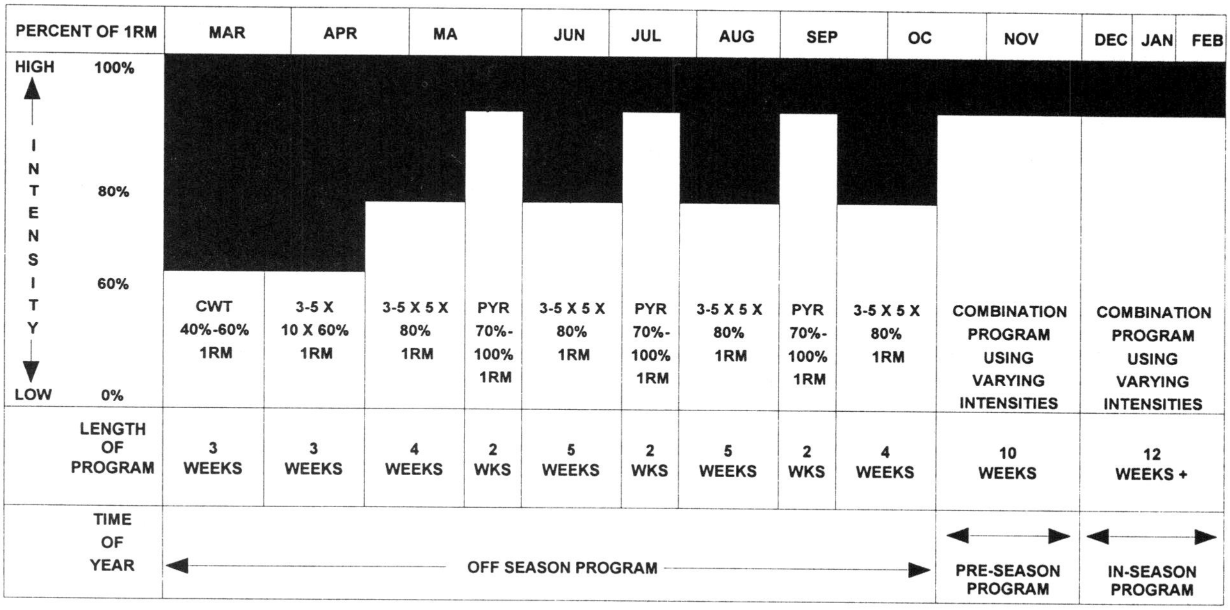

* RECENT RUSSIAN REPORTS SHOW THAT VARYING (CYCLING) INTENSITY PROGRAMS PRODUCE BETTER RESULTS
IN STRENGTH TRAINING THAN CONSTANT INTENSITY PROGRAMS.

Figure 3-4.   An Example Of Cycling In A Yearly Weight Training Program For Basketball.

SPORT PART III

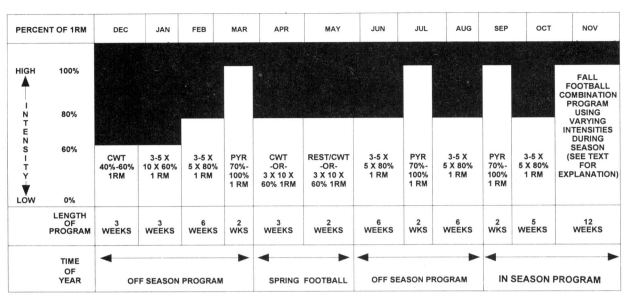

* RECENT RUSSIAN REPORTS SHOW THAT VARYING (CYCLING) INTENSITY PROGRAMS PRODUCE BETTER RESULTS
  IN STRENGTH TRAINING THAN CONSTANT INTENSITY PROGRAMS.

Figure 3-5.   An Example Of Cycling In A Yearly Weight Training Program For Football.

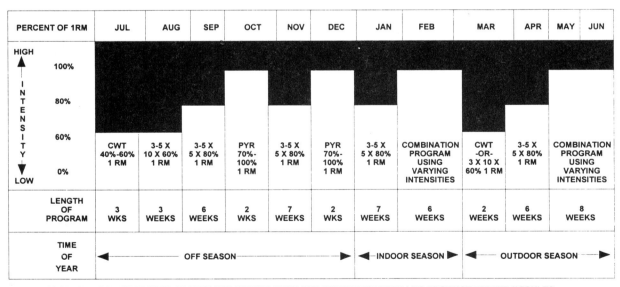

* RECENT RUSSIAN REPORTS SHOW THAT VARYING (CYCLING) INTENSITY PROGRAMS PRODUCE BETTER RESULTS
  IN STRENGTH TRAINING THAN CONSTANT INTENSITY PROGRAMS.

Figure 3-6.   An Example Of Cycling In A Yearly Weight Training Program For Track And Field.

Table 3-12.   An Example Of A Year-Round Football Weight Training Program.

I. CONDITIONING PERIOD (SCWT & CWT)

EXERCISE	SETS	REPS	INTENSITY
1. LEG PRESS	2-3	10-15	40%-60%
2. SHOULDER PRESS	2-3	10-15	40%-60%
3. LEG CURL	2-3	10-15	40%-60%
4. PULLDOWN	2-3	10-15	40%-60%
5. ABDOMINAL	2-3	10-15	40%-60%
6. BENCH PRESS	2-3	10-15	40%-60%
7. SQUAT	2-3	10-15	40%-60%
8. CURLS	2-3	10-15	40%-60%
9. BACK EXTENSION	2-3	10-15	40%-60%
10. PUSHDOWN	2-3	10-15	40%-60%
11. NECK	---	------	----------

II. CONDITIONING PERIOD (SETS X REPS)

EXERCISE	SETS	REPS	INTENSITY
1. POWER CLEANS	3-5	6	40%-60%
2. INCLINE PRESS	3-5	10	40%-60%
3. SQUATS	3-5	10	40%-60%
4. PULLDOWN	3-5	10	40%-60%
5. BACK EXTENSION	3-5	10	40%-60%
6. BENCH PRESS	3-5	10	40%-60%
7. ABDOMINAL	3-5	10	40%-60%
8. CURLS	3-5	10	40%-60%
9. LEG CURLS	3-5	10	40%-60%
10. FRENCH PRESS	3-5	10	40%-60%
11. NECK	---	---	----------

III. TRAINING PERIOD

EXERCISE	SETS	REPS	INTENSITY
1. POWER CLEANS	3-5	5	80%
2. INCLINE PRESS	3-5	5	80%
3. SQUATS	3-5	5	80%
4. PULLDOWN	3-5	5	80%
5. ABDOMINAL	3-5	15	W/WT
6. BENCH PRESS	3-5	5	80%
7. BACK EXTENSIONS	3-5	5	80%
8. CURLS	3-5	5	80%
9. KNEE EXTENSIONS	3-5	5	80%
10. FRENCH PRESS	3-5	5	80%

IV. IN-SEASON PERIOD

A.   CIRCUIT PROGRAM -- DURING TWO A DAY
AND SPRING PRACTICE OR OPTION #2 BELOW.
B.   DURING SEASON -- OPTION #1 OR #2 BELOW.

OPTION #1

MON	WEDNESDAY	SETS	REPS	INTENSITY
CWT	1. POWER CLEAN	3-4	3	70%-80%
	2. INCLINE PRESS	3-4	3-5	70%-80%
	3. SQUAT	3-4	3-5	70%-80%
	4. PULLDOWN	3-4	3-5	70%-80%
	5. ABDOMINAL	3	15	W/WT
	6. CURLS	2-3	6	70%-80%
	7. PUSHDOWN	2-3	6	70%-80%
	8. LEG CURLS	2-3	6	70%-80%
	9. NECK	---	---	----------

OPTION #2

MONDAY	SETS	REPS	INTENSITY
1. FRONT SQUATS	3-4	3-5	70%-80%
2. INCLINE PRESS	3	3-5	70%-80%
3. LEG CURLS	3	6	70%-80%
4. UPRIGHT ROW	3	6	70%-80%
5. ABDOMINAL	3	15	W/WT
6. CURLS	3	6	70%-80%
7. NECK	---	---	----------

WEDNESDAY	SETS	REPS	INTENSITY
1. POWER CLEAN	3-4	3	70%-80%
2. INC. PRESS	3-4	3-5	70%-80%
3. SQUAT	3-4	3-5	70%-80%
4. BENCH PRESS	3-4	3-5	70%-80%
5. ABDOMINAL	3	15	W/WT
6. PULLDOWN	3	6	70%-80%
7. NECK	---	---	----------

SPORT PART III

SUMMARY

The foregoing is an overview of the scientific approach to year-round weight training. The key to success of any weight training program is its design and implementation. This section of the Encyclopedia of Weight Training has focused on how to develop the weight training program, a year-round approach to training, testing of strength and motor performance variables and has discussed the basic cycling tools (conditioning cycle, training cycle [Ward Technique], in-season cycle [cluster, pyramiding and combination training]). Moreover, examples of weight training programs for basketball, football and track and field have been presented.

The remaining section of this part of the Encyclopedia of Weight Training (Part III) is devoted to selected physiological principles related to strength training and to empirical derived weight training principles.

SELECTED PHYSIOLOGICAL PRINCIPLES
RELATED TO STRENGTH

Quite often coaches and athletes become mesmerized by new concepts and, consequently, stray from valid principles of training. When this happens, sometimes success is experienced and when this happens there is something added to the body of knowledge. Unfortunately, in many of these experimentations, success does not occur, and the coach and athlete are forced to return to the established methods of training. In the meantime much time and energy has been wasted chasing the "golden fleece".

Any approach to training is doomed to failure if not based on sound and appropriate physiological principles. Many athletes have had their progress impeded, if not stymied, by following an unsound training program projected by some misinformed coach or ivory tower exercise physiologist that derived some interesting but unsound training theory.

The following physiological principles have been gleaned from research relative to progressive resistance training. They are presented to assist the coach and athlete in planning strength (power) training programs. Every program will be reflective of local conditions, facilities, equipment, objectives and motivations. Nevertheless, the adherence to sound principles is imperative for maximizing the benefits of training.

1. Weight training has proven to be the quickest way to develop functional strength in athletes. People who train regularly with free weights and machines produces significant increases in muscle mass, strength, local muscle endurance (LME), flexibility and power.

2. To increase muscle strength, there has to be progressive overloading of the muscle or muscle groups beyond that which is normal for them. As the muscle adapts to this overloading, to get further increases in strength, size and LME, additional stress must be applied. This process continues as long as the athlete continues to train. This is known as the "progressive overload principle."

   A second concept that goes hand in hand with the "progressive overload principle" is the "said" principle. This principle states that there is **"specific adaptation to imposed demands"**. This means that the training program demands must be specific to derive the desired effects. In other words, strength programs must be employed to gain strength while local muscle endurance (LME) is developed by a specific muscle endurance program. Furthermore, aerobic endurance is developed as a result of participating in some aerobic program. These specific programs do not develop attributes outside of their specificity.

   The overload must be of sufficient intensity to produce strength improvement. The intensity should generally range between 70% and 100% one repetition maximum; however, some studies have reported that small amounts of strength can be gained by using 40% to 60% of 1RM. One can say that strength can be obtained by using loads that range from 40% to 100% 1RM, but the optimal range for strength and hypertrophy is between 70% and 100% 1RM.

3. Periodization (cycling) of strength training produces better and longer lasting results. Periodization has four phases: (1) The conditioning phase; (2) The training phase; (3) The competition phase; and, (4) The active rest phase.

4. Muscle fibers grow larger with increased strength, but there is no increase in the number of fibers. Hyperplasia (increasing of the number of muscle fibers) has not been demonstrated in humans. There is coincidental growth of connective tissue also. There may be an increase in strength without an increase in size of muscle. The increase in strength, in this case, appears to be due to a change in the central nervous system. This means that there are two aspects of strength development: a physiological (structural) component and a nervous system component. These components need separate programs for development.

5. Strength is dependent upon the size of the muscles and the ability to recruit motor units (the nerve, it's branches and the muscle fibers it activates). Hypertrophy and motor unit recruitment each require a distinct weight training programs to enhance them.

   Hypertrophy is produced by performing 3-5 sets of 5-8 repetitions with 75% to 85% 1RM in cycles of 4 to 8 weeks. Motor unit recruitment is produced by performing 3-7 sets of 1-3 repetitions with 90% to 100% 1RM for short cycles of 2-4 weeks.

6. Capillarization occurs with increased strength, even more with local muscular endurance training. This is in concert with the increased demand for oxygen, nutrients and the removal of waste products from the working muscle.

7. Weight training produces increases in muscle protein (contractile tissue).

8. Strength of males increases rapidly from 12 to 19 years of age. This indicates that the ideal physiological time to start weight training is around the seventh grade (12 years of age). Research and empirical evidence indicates that weight training is effective at even younger ages. Sensible weight training programs can be and should be employed at any age.

9. It is not wise to distort the muscle balance by concentrating only on a single muscle or muscle group. This increases the chance of muscle strain, tear, faulty body mechanics and impaired sport performances. A general program which conditions antagonistic muscle groups with emphasis on deficient areas is prudent practice.

10. General weight training principles:

   A. Increase in muscle strength can be accomplished by a few repetitions against heavy resistance. One to eight repetitions; three to five sets; and a resistance ranging from 70% to 100% 1RM.

   B. Increase in local muscular endurance can be accomplished by many repetitions with light resistance. Ten to fifteen repetitions; three to five sets; and a resistance ranging from 40% to 60% 1RM.

   C. These two methods are not interchangeable; one cannot replace the other.

11. The training stimulus for increasing strength is muscle tension and not the prolongation of the exercise. Intensity relates to a high percentage of the 1RM and not to fatigue displayed after performing ten to fifteen repetitions or more. This statement gives further insight into the general weight training principles addressed above.

12. The amount of work done per unit of time is the critical variable upon which improvement in performance depends. This is associated with high muscle tension which is the stimulus to muscle growth. The work rate may be intensified by increasing the speed of movement (this is inefficient and ineffective in weight training programs) or by increasing the load.

   Rapidly contracting muscles exhibit a reduction in the ability to produce force as speed of contraction increases and involve an uneconomical expenditure of energy, making increases in speed of exercise unacceptable. An increase in work load (intensity) is more advantageous.

   With the increase in work load, the speed of movement is slow, but the muscle tension remains high. Consequently, a greater improvement in strength and hypertrophy. A.V. Hill states that "...the mechanical efficiency (work/total energy) of muscle is greatest at about 1/5 of maximum speed." The implications for strength training is that a moderate rhythm should be used when executing exercises.

PART III

SPORT

13. The trainability of muscles is high during summer and autumn months and low in the winter (December, January and February).

14. Reasonable amounts of ultra-violet radiation, natural and artificial enhances strength development.

15. A training stimulus of as low as one-third has demonstrated increases in strength: however, empirical evidence indicates that the training stimulus should be between 70 to 100 percent of maximum.

16. There appears to be changes in the central nervous system as a result of training. Strength may depend not only on the increase in contractile strength and size of muscle fibers, but also on neuromuscular changes. The ability to develop maximal tension appears to be dependent on the proprioceptive facilitation with which overloading is associated, as well as disinhibition of sensory nervous structures.

17. Strength of muscle contraction depends upon: (1) the number and frequency of stimuli, and (2) the number of motor units called upon. From empirical observations it seems more advantageous to encourage heavy weight exercises executed at a moderate rhythm, rather than light weight done very rapidly. It is interesting to note that increases in the rate of muscle contraction decreases the ability to produce high tensions. Heavy weight produces the ability to activate a maximum number of motor units.

18. There is a strong relationship between gain in speed and gain in strength. Speed of movement has been significantly increased by isometric, isotonic and isokinetic programs. Isotonic programs are preferred as indicated by research. It should be emphasized that simply training the muscle groups alone, apart from a specific speed movement, increases speed of that movement.

19. For increasing strength and size, four to five sets of five repetitions at 75% to 85% 1RM seems to be most effective. An alternative program design might include a pyramiding (progressive increasing) of weight and decreasing of the repetitions.

    Pyramiding is not as effective as the former, however, it is good variation for three to six workout sessions. After pyramiding, an athlete should return to four to five sets of five repetitions at 80% 1RM. A periodization (cycling) concept of training at varying intensities and volumes over time, is well documented by research, especially, Russian research.

20. Strength gains are specific to the angle in the range of motion at which the resistance is met in training.

21. The rate of strength gain is most rapid when a muscle has achieved only a small proportion of its possible maximal end strength. The rate of gain slows down as muscle strength approaches its maximal end strength. For most people, strength develops rather slowly and requires constant work for continued improvement.

22. The rate of strength loss after training ends is a very much slower process than strength gain. Retention of strength can probably be brought about by as little as one maximal contraction per week.

TRAINING PRINCIPLES

One must have more than a knowledge of the physiological principles of strength (power) training to effectively implement weight training programs. They must be able to implement and adapt those principles to a program and local environment. The following training principles have been formulated through many years of experience. They are presented as guidelines based upon experience in an effort to assist the coach and athlete in deriving optimum benefits from strength training.

1. All heavy lifting programs should be preceded by a three to four week conditioning period. This conditioning period is necessary to strengthen the muscles, tendons, connective tissue and ligaments to withstand the stress of heavy training. Another reason is to learn the correct technique for each specific exercise. Many neophytes and veterans as well fail to understand the wisdom of this practice. Consequently, they find themselves suffering with various joint and muscle injuries. This greatly retards their progress.

   During the conditioning period, the weight should be moderate and the repetitions many. If the athletes adhere to the training dose of repetitions, they cannot use too much weight. There is a built-in discipline in a high repetition program in terms of training load. Emphasis should be placed on the proper execution of lifting technique and breathing. During this conditioning period, the athletes should perform three to five sets of ten repetitions with approximately 40% to 60% of 1RM (3-5 X 10 X 40% - 60% 1RM).

   A shorter conditioning period might be considered if: (1) the athletes are in good physical condition; (2) if one desires to rapidly increase in strength and size, however, this involves a risk of extra soreness and possible joint and soft tissue problems.

2. The training program includes the power lifts (bench press, squat, and dead lift), Olympic lifts and their variations (snatch and clean and jerk) and associated lifts (press, incline press and front squat). Other exercises associated with these lifts and specific muscle group development are incorporated.

   After the initial conditioning period, the weight is increased and the repetitions are reduced. The recommended dosages of sets and repetitions is 3-5 sets of 5 repetitions at 80% 1RM, although other set and repetition formats may be effective, also. It should be noted that exercises are designed for development of large muscle groups while attention is also given to antagonistic muscle groups.

3. Consistency in workouts is paramount and ensures improvements. The loss of a workout period per se is not the problem; what does cause trouble is the fact that once one misses a training session, it becomes progressively easier to miss others. Soon you are training irregularly, if at all. You cannot expect to make satisfactory gains unless there is training regularity and training discipline.

4. Training sessions should occur every other day unless scheduled and planned for in the overall training scheme. A Monday-Wednesday-Friday or Tuesday-Thursday-Saturday format is acceptable. The length of the training sessions should extend from one and one half hours to two and one half hours. Shorter periods, although beneficial, are not long enough for maximum results. Off days can be used for skill development and recreation.

5. If time is short, a split routine format can be used. In this technique, one works the upper body one day, and the lower body the next. This means the workout week is extended to six days. However, the workout sessions are shorter. The same exercises can be used as with the regular format.

6. One will retrogress before they improve. This will discourage some, especially those who insist on using heavy weights without a conditioning period and/or reject the principles of the periodization of weight training. Persist with a scientific training plan and results will be forthcoming.

7. Perform a general warm up before training. The Europeans, especially the Russians, spend up to 1/2 hour in warming-up before touching the weights. This makes good sense in terms of preventing injury and increasing performance during the workout. The warm-up can be achieved using a variety of methods such as running, biking, stairclimbing, or free exercises and calisthenics. The duration of the warm-up ranges from 5 minutes to 30 minutes. It is important to keep the warm up procedures very low in intensity. Specific warm-up should be performed for each exercise.

SPORT PART III

8. The achievement of high level of strength takes a long period to develop, for the average person. Once it is obtained, it needs maintenance exercise. This calls for in-season strength training programs. Two days a week devoted to weight training is sufficient for strength maintenance during in-season training. A medium day and a heavy day lifting sequence is a good training pattern that can be followed. A routine emphasizing local muscle endurance could also be effectively used on one of these days. CWT or SCWT can be employed also as alternatives.

9. There is specificity of training, i.e., if training for endurance, the result will be endurance. If training for strength, the results will be strength. This is known as the "said" principle which means there is **"specific adaptation to imposed demands"**.

10. Think of strength as an integral part of the whole performance capacity. Strength isn't an end in itself. Strength forms the basis for improvement in speed of movement, application of force, and enhancement of athletic performance.

11. When planning training routines, think of muscle groups. Muscles rarely operate independently of each other in any athletic movement. Multiple joint actions are always the case in athletic performance. Single joint exercise has minimal value.

12. Sequence of exercise needs careful consideration. This is necessary to insure maximum work of muscle groups with the least amount of fatigue. It is prudent to work a specific muscle group with one exercise then work the antagonistic muscle group or another muscle group in some other part of the body. For example, after performing presses, one might do pulldowns, or after squats one might do leg curls for antagonistic training. To train different body locations on successive exercises, one would do presses followed by squats followed by pulldowns followed by leg curls, et cetera. This latter procedure is known as peripheral heart action (PHA) training.

13. Proper rest and sleeping habits must be firmly entrenched. There is a wide variation between individuals in terms of number of hours of sleep that is needed. Eight to ten hours is a reasonable amount for a growing athlete in vigorous training. Burning the candle at both ends will severely hamper the efforts in strength training.

14. Diet is of great importance in rigorous training. Adequate amounts of protein, carbohydrates, fats, water, vitamins, and minerals must be included in the diet. If weight gaining is the objective non-fat milk provides an inexpensive way to supplement the diet with protein (as much as a gallon a day). Additional benefits can be obtained if Dry Milk is mixed with the non-fat milk. Other protein supplements, powdered or amino acid tablets, can be used effectively if money is not a problem. Recent research in the United States and Russia has demonstrated the need for as much as 2 to 5 grams of protein per kilogram of body weight per day for athletes in heavy weight training for optimal growth.

15. If one is training for strength and increase in muscle mass, do not run athletes great distances or compel them to participate in long sessions of calisthenics. Calisthenics are for warm-up not for strength training. Aerobic training detracts from the increase in strength and mass, however, there should be some time devoted to aerobic training at various times of the year for health reasons.

16. Constantly strive to lift as much weight as possible but without straining. A good coaching phrase is, **"TRAIN, DON'T STRAIN"** or **"STIMULATE, DON'T ANNIHILATE'**.

17. Starting weights in the conditioning phase should be a percentage of the 1RM, in general. If the athletes are not in good enough shape to perform a 1RM then there must be an arbitrary selection of starting weights. A good rule to follow is: select a weight and perform as many repetitions as possible in one set. If the repetitions are as high as twenty or more, the training load should be 10 to 20 pounds

heavier. The athletes should train two to three weeks at these training loads and then execute a 1RM. From the 1RM tests, it is possible to prescribe effective training loads.

18. Sets and Repetitions: During the conditioning period many repetitions and moderate weights are the order of the day (3-5 X 10 X 40% - 60% 1RM). During the training period few repetitions and heavy weight should be executed (3-5 X 5 X 75% - 85% 1RM).

19. Weight increases: After the first week, the weight should be increased five to ten pounds for the upper body exercises, and ten to twenty pounds for the lower body exercises. With the increase in training weight, the repetitions may drop. Work with the increased weight until the prescribed number of repetitions can be performed. When this occurs, go six more work-out periods, then increase the weight again if the prescribed number of repetitions can be executed. Improvement will not be manifested unless there is progressive overloading.

20. Insist on proper form and technique in performing the exercises. Cheating, in general, is not a good practice.

21. It is not judicial practice to make up exercises for specific sport skills. Determine the muscles involved in the desired movement, then use the standard exercises for their development. Attention might be focused on the angle of force application when choosing the exercises. Always work through full range of motion. In general, full range movements are preferred.

22. Motivation of the athletes is important in strength training. First you must convince the athlete that he will benefit from weight training; secondly, provide experiences whereby they can see their progress. By nature weight training is self-motivational. The athlete can see changes in their muscle mass and body proportions and experience the increase in strength and power. These experiences are highly motivating.

23. Breathing is extremely important, especially while handling heavy weights. In general lifting, the rule is: exhale during the working phase of the movement and inhale on the non-working phase. The rule needs slight modification in heavy lifting. One should inhale on the non-working phase of the movement and hold the breath until the weight has passed the sticking point and then forcefully exhale.

24. One gets out of training what they put into it. If only a little time and energy is devoted to training, the results will not be the same as the results of a person who trains hard and regularly. If maximum development is desired, one must be dedicated to the weight training program.

25. Coaches cannot expect their athletes to discipline themselves in their strength training program. They must supervise and encourage their athletes to seek higher strength levels.

26. Frequently athletes get stuck at a certain weight load. Improvement seems impossible. An effective technique used to break this plateau is to reduce the weight and increase the repetitions (for example, 3 sets of 10 repetitions). Carry out this procedure for three to six training sessions, then return to heavy lifting. This should shock the system and stimulate improvement. If results are not forthcoming, look for other causes for the plateau; e.g., poor nutrition, lack of sleep or an absence of periodization of volume and intensity in the weight training program.

27. It is advisable to test strength at the beginning of the training period and periodically thereafter, about every 6 to 8 weeks. The athlete should also keep a record of their training weights and repetitions. Both provide a basis for accurate evaluation.

SPORT PART III

28. Don't be duped by equipment manufacturers. Force them to show you research substantiating their claims. Machines are only a tool and must be scientifically employed to get maximum results. Some factors to consider are:

   A. Scientifically designed and engineered with documented claims by reputable research institutions.
   B. Constructed with the highest quality components.
   C. Excellent workmanship and durability.
   D. Ease of operation.
   E. Availability of machines for the conditioning of all major joint actions.
   F. Minimal maintenance.
   G. Safety.
   H. Small space requirement.
   I. Best possible value per dollar invested.

29. Do all of the above and pick up your medals.

PART IV

THE ENCYCLOPEDIA OF WEIGHT TRAINING

Weight Training For
Body Building

BODY BUILDING PART IV

PART IV

BODY BUILDING

THE ENCYCLOPEDIA OF WEIGHT TRAINING: WEIGHT TRAINING FOR GENERAL CONDITIONING, SPORT AND BODY BUILDING

PART IV: WEIGHT TRAINING FOR BODY BUILDING

TABLE OF CONTENTS — PART IV

BODY BUILDING PART IV

TABLE OF CONTENTS — PART IV (CONTINUED)

THE ENCYCLOPEDIA OF WEIGHT TRAINING: PART IV

LIST OF TABLES

BODY BUILDING PART IV

LIST OF TABLES — PART IV (CONTINUED

PART IV

WEIGHT TRAINING FOR BODY BUILDING

INTRODUCTION

Body building has become one of the most popular physical activities in the last two decades of the twentieth century. Potentially this physical activity, in all its variations, can make the most significant contribution to the pursuit of physical excellence. Coupled with the excellent opportunities available in modern society for intellectual and spiritual refinement, mankind could be on the threshold of levels of development never before known by humans. The Roman poet, Decimus Junius Juvenalis (Juvenal), expressed this concept in a simple phrase; **"Mens sana in corpre sano."** Translated into contemporary English this phrase is interpreted as **"a sound mind in a sound body."**

DEFINITION OF BODY BUILDING

Body building is considered both a sport and an art form. It is a sport because it diverts one's attention from the critical problems of life in activities that provide amusement. The word sport is derived from the Latin "des", meaning away, and "porto", meaning carry. In other words, to carry away from one's work or business. It is an art form because the final product is an expression of what is aesthetic, appealing or of more than ordinary significance.

Although scientific principles are sometimes utilized in the sport of body building, many of the concepts and patterns used by body builders represent an artful and clever synthesis of mostly empirical observations. However, it must be pointed out that in recent years, the sport of body building is being powerfully drawn to more scientifically defensible training programs and practices.

GUIDE TO BODY BUILDING

Body building as a sport has certain characteristics that must be displayed by the competitors. The guidelines used in judging body building competition include: symmetry, proportion, development, definition, structure, posing and general appearance. To become a champion the body builder must possess the highest degree of all these physical characteristics.

The person who has no motivation or intention to compete at a high level should also use these guidelines to construct their program of body building. This assures that a balanced development occurs.

SYMMETRY: This means that there is balance between the limbs on opposite sides of the body as well as balance between the upper body and lower body. The development of the upper body should be proportionate to the lower body while the right and left side should be equally developed. No one body part should be more prominent than any other body part.

PROPORTION: Proportion is a matter of skeletal structure. This means the upper body should be in proportion to the lower body in terms of body build and weight category. Size should be in proportion to body and limb skeletal girths, hands to feet, and head in proportion to body length.

SHAPE AND DEVELOPMENT: All major muscle groups should be equally prominent and appropriate to body build and weight category. The shape of a muscle can be as important as size. Muscles can be

PART IV

BODY BUILDING

sculptured in slightly different ways by various combinations of exercises, sets, repetitions and intensities. The body builder's and the contest judges' aesthetic perception play important roles in this area.

DEFINITION: One of the most important qualities in body building is the removal of subcutaneous fat resulting in the display of striated muscularity through the skin. This is accomplished by sensible cutting routines and intelligent, but highly disciplined eating patterns.

SKELETAL STRUCTURE: The body should have no distorting curvature of the spine, knock knees or bow legs. Muscle development should not further add to the structural distortion. The over-development of massive arms on narrow shoulders would exaggerate the narrowness of the shoulders.

POSING: The contestant's posing routine is the expression of their muscular development and the artistic presentation of their body on stage. It is important that the poses match the muscular development and be presented in a graceful unstrained manner. The contestant must execute a full posing routine making no attempt to hide a weak area or body part.

GENERAL APPEARANCE: The performer should project an image of neatness. Their posture must be impressive, the hair well-styled and the posing garment commensurate with the standard of competition.

THE FITNESS CONTINUUM

The three basic physical fitness components (cardio-vascular-respiratory endurance, local muscle endurance and strength) can be arranged on a continuous line. Cardio-vascular-respiratory endurance (CVRE) is at one end of the line while strength resides at the opposite end of the line. Local muscle endurance (LME) is in between CVRE and strength. By changing the training parameters, LME can favor either CVRE or strength.

The body composition components such as muscle mass, proportionality, symmetry, shape and development and definition (lack of sub-cutaneous fat) are goals that must be achieved in the body building program. These are outcomes of the proper application of periodization of exercises, sets, repetitions and intensities as well as sensible and rigid nutritional practices and are influenced by genetics as well as training. Concomitant improvements of physiological components of physical fitness (strength, local muscle endurance, cardiovascular endurance and changes in body compositions components) are, also, impacted by intelligent manipulation of all training and nutritional factors.

It is important to remember that training for strength produces large increases in muscle mass while the focus of training for local muscle endurance generates cuts and defines the muscle while at the same time reducing body fat levels. CVRE training helps in the elimination of body fat and, of course, fosters cardio-vascular-respiratory health by increasing the functional capacity of the heart, lungs and circulatory system. CVRE training by its nature (especially high impact aerobic activities) has a negative impact on the development and maintenance of strength levels as well as a tendency to decrease muscle size. **HOW MANY MARATHON RUNNERS WOULD WIN A BODY BUILDING CONTEST? Research and empirical observations have demonstrated that this negative effect on muscle mass can be minimized if non-impact CVRE training (stationary cycling, stepping or rowing) is employed as opposed to long runs or other high-impact aerobic activities.**

The body builder must carefully select the type of aerobic training; when in the training cycle it should be used; and, how much and the intensity of aerobic (cardio vascular respiratory endurance [CVRE]) training. During the cycle where the goal is to increase mass, aerobic activity should not be used or greatly minimized. When the goal is to cut and define, aerobic activity can help to reduce subcutaneous fat levels by using a lot of calories. However, low impact aerobic activity is recommended over jogging and other high impact aerobic activities to minimize the loss of muscle mass.

There are certain physiological relationships that must be understood before one can plan and implement a body building program. Unfortunately, many body builders have little understanding of the physiological principles that form the foundation for the body building program and how they relate to each other.

Table 4-1 displays the relationship between physical fitness components that form the "Fitness Continuum"; size of muscles and definition of muscles (muscularity components); and, defines the exercise parameters that control the magnitude and quality of muscular development.

Table 4-1. The Relationship Between Physical Fitness Components And Muscularity Components.

PHYSICAL FITNESS COMPONENTS	CVRE*------------------------------- LME**----------------------------- STRENGTH (NOTE: CAN BIAS LME PROGRAM TOWARD STRENGTH OR CARDIOVASCULAR ENDURANCE) ◄——————————— SLIDING SCALE ———————————►		
MUSCULARITY COMPONENTS	DIMINUTION IN MUSCLE SIZE AND FURTHER LOSS OF SUBCUTANEOUS FAT	DEFINITION (MUSCULARITY)	SIZE (BULK)
REPETITIONS	CWT/SCWT (10-15 REPS)	9-15 REPS	1-8 REPS
SETS	3-4 LAPS OF CIRCUIT	3-5 SETS	3-5 SETS
TIME OR REST BETWEEN SETS	CONTINUOUS ACTIVITY	CONTINUOUS ACTIVITY OR MINIMAL REST (UP TO 2 MINUTES)	2-5 MINUTES REST BETWEEN EXERCISES
INTENSITY	40%-60% OF 1RM	40%-70% OF 1RM	70%-100% 1RM
TRAINING DAYS PER WEEK	DAILY IF DESIRED OR 3 DAYS PER WEEK	DAILY IF DESIRED OR 2-3 DAYS PER WEEK FOR EACH BODY PART	2-3 DAYS PER WEEK FOR EACH BODY PART
* CVRE = CARDIOVASCULAR ENDURANCE ** LME = LOCAL MUSCLE ENDURANCE			

The **first phase** of a body building program is devoted to a **general conditioning period**. The purpose of this cycle is to prepare the body physiologically (**getting in shape to do more work**) and structurally - **gradually preparing the muscles, tendons, connective tissue and mind to engage in more strenuous training.** The **second phase** in a body building program should focus on the **development of muscular size and symmetry with the minimization of body fa**t. When size, symmetry and proportion have been achieved, a **third phase** is introduced in which **specific defining of the muscle groups is the primary goal of training.** The **continued reduction of body fat** is another very important goal in this third phase. A **fourth phase** of a body building program is to **continue to enhance and improve muscular size and shape while concurrently improving any weak areas in muscle development.**

All phases of the body building program exist and revolve around the fifth stage. The **fifth phase** of a general body building program is the **competition phase.** Every effort is made to reduce body fat to a minimum while maintaining muscle size and shape. Also, there must be development of the presentation of the body on the stage. The ultimate goal is competition in a body building contest. A **sixth stage** involves a **rest and restoration cycle of training (active rest)** in which volume, intensity and duration of training are minimal. The main purpose of this last cycle is to permit rest for the total organism before moving into advanced body building programs. This should be the general plan for all body building programs.

BODY BUILDING **PART IV**

The attempt to train simultaneously for maximum size and maximum definition and low body fat is just not very successful. Training for size and definition at the same time does not produce the desired results. One cannot have their cake and eat it also. The body builder must identify their objective and then plan the program that will specifically meet the objective. **INTENSITY** is the key to increased muscle size. Intensity is not to be construed as fatigue, the "metabolic burn" or the pumped feeling. Intensity is the degree of force needed to move a load. Intensity is a percentage of the one repetition maximum (1RM) and the level of intensity dictates when and the magnitude of muscle hypertrophy and when local muscle endurance (LME) and definition are developed.

Total work is another factor in building muscle. The body builder must combine both intensity and a high volume of work to produce good muscularity. The body builder should work for size first and then work on definition, cutting and shaping the muscles. Size is controlled by performing exercises with fewer repetitions (5-8 repetitions) executed at higher intensities (75% to 85% 1RM) resulting in large volumes of work being accomplished. Weight training under these conditions, maximally increases the contractile elements of the muscle resulting in muscle enlargement or hypertrophy.

Defining, cutting and shaping of the muscle can be achieved using lower intensities (40% - 75% 1RM) which are performed for a high number of repetitions (9-15 repetitions) resulting in very large volumes of work. Cutting and shaping are associated with the **"metabolic burn"** or the **"pumped feeling"**. This physiological phenomenon is the result of performing an exercise for many repetitions with low to moderate intensity to momentary muscle failure (fatigue). Higher intensities can be used but it requires the sacrifice of proper exercise technique and is usually not effective because the body builder has to stop the exercises before an intense **"metabolic burn"** can be produced.

The **"pumped feeling"** or **"metabolic burn"** is produced by a combination of factors, including:

1. An engorgement of the muscle with blood.
2. A shift of other fluids into and between the muscle cells.
3. Increase in lactic acid.
4. Increasing the number of hydrogen ions which decreases the cellular pH which in turn interferes with energy production and the contraction process within the muscle.
5. Decrease in creatine phosphate (CP).
6. Decrease in adenosine triphosphate (ATP).
7. Decrease in muscle glycogen.
8. The sensitization of pain receptors caused by low pH.

The **"muscle pumping procedure"** results in a short term increase in the muscle size brought about by increased blood engorgement in the muscle and fluid shifts within and in between the muscle cells. However, this procedure decreases the number of muscles fibers involved in the specific pumping movement progressively as the muscle becomes fatigued. Consequently, this procedure does not stimulate the muscle fibers optimally for growth. Furthermore, often times the **"muscle pumping procedure"** necessitates a gross alteration of exercise technique which may predispose to injury or lead to the **"overtrained syndrome."**

The employment of the "muscle pumping procedure" is a best a pseudo-psychological experience that contributes very little to increased muscle mass. However, it does facilitate the cutting and shaping procedure, helps in the reduction of body fat while enhancing the anaerobic metabolic processes (the creation of energy without the immediate use of oxygen). Moreover, this technique is employed before going on stage at body building competitions to enhance the presentation of the musculature to the judges and audience. "The muscle pumping procedure" thus has its proper place in the body building program but it should not be used as a primary builder of muscle mass.

It is important to understand that training for size/strength and training for cuts, definition and low body fat involves two very different training programs. These two programs involve training at very different intensities which can only be performed for a specific number of repetitions; low (5-8 reps) repetitions for size and strength, and high (9-15 reps) repetitions for cutting, definition, shaping and local muscle endurance. For size and strength improvement, absolute intensity (percent of 1RM [between 70% and 100% 1RM]) is very important. When training for definition, cutting and shaping, absolute intensity is of lesser importance. Total work is the most important factor in the cutting, defining and shaping phase. The body builder can easily and effectively adjust their total training load (work) to match their cutting objectives. A very high volume of work sculptures the musculature while, at the same time reduces body fat. In this case intensity should be between 40% and 70% 1RM. One must be careful to apply the appropriate intensities and repetitions in order to achieve a pre-defined training goal.

Fatigue does not produce increases in size and strength. Fatigue yields enhancement of the energy making process (the muscle physiology); defines, shapes and cuts the muscles while improving local muscle endurance (the ability to perform many repetitions). Pre-exhaustion of a particular muscle or muscle group does not involve any more muscle fiber, it just fatigues the fibers involved in the pre-exhaustion movement at the specific intensity resulting in a lowered work output in subsequent efforts.

For the bulking phase of the body building program, pre-exhaustion exercises are probably not of value. On the other hand, for the cutting and defining stage, the pre-exhaustion technique may be very valuable because the absolute volume of work is of greater value than absolute intensity for these purposes.

GENETIC POTENTIAL

All people are born with certain limits of growth, muscular development, rates of gain and loss and intelligence, etc. All these traits and others can be optimized or refined but never beyond the genetic potential. The difficulty in dealing with this reality is, how do we measure one's genetic potential for muscle growth? The potential for muscle growth has to be determined by evaluation of practical experience. One must expose themselves to a scientific weight training program over time and then evaluate their potential for body building by the observing the ease at which strength and hypertrophy of muscles are acquired. The potential for body building will be indicated after weight training for six months to a year.

If response to the weight training program is very good to excellent, there is hope for being a high level body builder. Only by exposure to extended periods of scientific body building will the capacity to become a body builder be fully revealed. However, it must be said that if a person has the motivation, the energy and the knowledge, they can refine their body in accordance with their genetic capacity. There is always room for improvement whatever the genetic structure may dictate.

Present indications are that somatotype (body type) changes during growth and, also, that physical training changes the somatotype of both young and old people. This means that one's muscularity components can be modified both by the growth process and physical training. The degree and rate of changing the muscularity components are genetically controlled, all other things being equal. Indeed scientific training and nutrition must interact to allow for optimal muscular development.

> **STRUCTURE:** The basic skeletal stature (height) and structure (width and bone density) is basically determined by the genetic pattern.

> **GROWTH RATES:** Growth rates (hypertrophy: the synthesizing of protein) are basically determined by the genetic profile. Adequate work (exercise), rest and nutrition are needed to insure attainment of the genetic potential.

> **GENERAL SCULPTURING:** The basic lines and sculpturing of one's body is determined genetically. One has to train to maximize the genetic strong points and at the same time develop those areas in muscle sculpture that appear to be less than perfect.

BODY BUILDING FOR MALES AND FEMALES

The body building program for males and females should follow the same basic pattern. However, the increasing of muscle mass in women is generally not a great a men because of the lack of the muscle building hormone (testosterone). In contrast, males have a large volume of the anabolic (muscle building) testosterone produced in the testicles. Females and males have been shown to develop outstanding muscle mass but males, obviously, develop greater muscle mass. Also, it must be remembered that definition is brought about by the reduction of subcutaneous fat so that the muscular striations are visible; however, it is a process that requires scientific training, nutrition and rest. It has been shown that both male and female body builders can achieve very impressive muscular striations that are vividly displayed by low subcutaneous fat levels.

The shaping and sculpturing of the muscles are accomplished by applying the correct exercises and proper dosages of load (intensity), repetitions (volume) and sets (volume). Strength in females appears to be due to increases in the neuromuscular facilitation (activation of the motor units) and not necessarily by muscle hypertrophy. Although, empirical observations show that females who have large muscles are generally stronger those with little muscle mass. Strength in females can be produced both by neuromuscular facilitation and hypertrophy of the muscles. The strength in males is produced by both neuromuscular facilitation and muscle hypertrophy.

Recent general observations of female body builders have demonstrated that many women do indeed have the capacity to produce a great amount of hypertrophy (size) while achieving a very low body fat percentage. It is thought that these women have been genetically selected to produce higher testosterone levels which accounts for their unusual muscular development.

The female body builders of today are awesome examples of hard work, scientific training and nutrition, uncommon discipline and genetic selection. More females from the general population are becoming involved in body building programs and, therefore, many heretofore undetected talents are being identified.

PRINCIPLES OF BODY BUILDING

As indicated at the start of this section, body building is an art. Programming for body building is more art than science. There are many body building techniques and practices, some valid and some bogus, that one can utilize in training. Only the most common body building techniques and practices are discussed in this section of The Encyclopedia of Weight Training. When a body building technique or practice is unscientific or unreasonable, the authors have made strong statements about the ineffectiveness of these training procedures. Furthermore, many general principles and practices are discussed to assist in the pursuit of body building.

It is difficult to find valid and reliable information regarding body building. Scientific studies conducted to elucidate the various aspects of body building are hard to find. Most body building information comes from the **"gyms"**, which are in actuality, large laboratories where hundreds of training concepts are tested by **"trial and error"**. Ultimately, reasonable body building programs and practices emerge from these **"GYM LABORATORIES"** and are accepted as valid and effective methods of muscle training because they have produced results **"IN THE REAL WORLD"**.

The research and principles that support any weight training program can also be used to build a framework for a body building program. The principles of training don't change, just the application of them in accordance with the body building objectives. A great amount of research regarding weight training has been conducted over the years. This research has provided many useable principles of weight training and body building that can be and should be applied to body building programs. As mentioned above, there is a lot of valid empirical knowledge regarding body building. However, this practical information takes a long time to accumulate and must be applied over a long time in a large group of body builders to validate the effectiveness of its implementation.

PART IV

BODY BUILDING

This empirical body of knowledge is a very significant source of information; however, care must be given to how much of the empirical information regarding body building should be adopted and implemented. The beginning and advanced body builder must evaluate the source of information to make sure that these self-proclaimed experts are, in fact, knowledgeable authorities. In addition the information disseminated from these **"body building gurus"** needs to be measured with regard to its validity. The proof of any projected idea is the track record of success.

The general training program for body builders should include the following phases:

1. Conditioning (preparation).
2. Increasing size, muscle development and reducing body fat.
3. Cutting, defining, shaping and reducing body fat.
4. Enhancement of size and shape; improvement of weak areas and reduction of body fat.
5. Training for competition.
6. Rest and rehabilitation (active rest).

A training pattern including all of these phases should be followed throughout one's body building career. It is important to remember that each phase requires the use of different volumes and intensities. Also, the periodization of training can be directly applied to body building to ensure success in training. The principles of periodization are thoroughly discussed in Section I of this book.

THE STIMULUS TO MUSCLE GROWTH

In order to produce muscle growth (hypertrophy) it is necessary to apply some kind of overload. Overload can be in many forms, i.e., isotonic, isokinetic or isometric exercise or a combination of these forms. Isotonic exercise is defined as any dynamic resistive exercise involving free weights, machines or calisthenics. Isokinetic exercises use special machines where the speed of exercise is constant while the application of force can vary throughout the range of motion. Isokinetic machines may be in the form of hydraulic machines, air machines or electro-magnetic devices. Isometric exercises are any static (non-moving) exercise where muscles are contracted against an immovable object.

The most effective method of resistance exercise at this point in time is isotonic exercise, that is dynamic positive and negative contractions. This may be because isotonic exercises are the most refined and commonly used mode rather than any innate superiority. As other methods are refined they may be very effective in producing good muscularity changes, especially the isokinetic approach if such training includes positive and negative training.

Overload is needed to produce some kind of muscle adaptation. It is important that the overload be progressive. This is accomplished by applying the principles of progressive resistance in any of its forms. When the muscles are subjected to stress as in weight training, they soon make a specific adaptation and cease to grow bigger and stronger. If further improvement is desired the body builder must again increase the stress (the weight or the amount of work [volume]) beyond what the muscle has adapted to. This is done by progressively increasing the amount of resistance (weight) a muscle must work against in a particular exercise or expanding the total amount of work (volume) completed. All components of physical fitness can be modified by scientifically and skillfully varying the sets, repetitions, number of exercises and time.

INTENSITY

Intensity is defined as the percentage of one repetition maximum (1RM) that is used when performing an exercise. Intensity is not to be confused with fatigue ("the metabolic burn") or local muscle endurance. Since individuals vary in their response to exercise programs it is difficult to exactly prescribe a specific intensity. Generally, for increasing the strength-only (neural) component, only 1 to 4 repetitions are performed at an

PART IV

BODY BUILDING

intensity of 85% to 100% of 1RM. To increase the structural component (muscle mass and protein synthesis), 5 to 8 repetitions are performed at an intensity of 75% to 85% 1RM. For extreme cutting and sculpturing 10 to 15 repetitions should be used at an intensity of 40% to 60% of 1RM.

There are two basic variables that interact to create greater intensity, however, the training effects have different consequences. If more weight is used to increase intensity, the results will be reflected in greater tissue (muscle) growth. If time between sets is reduced the metabolic intensity is greater; however, the results are reflected in the metabolic machinery (facilitation of the muscle to create energy and better handle the increased lactic acid and hydrogen ion build up) with some increase in lean mass. The methods for increasing intensity are:

OPTION ONE: <u>**Absolute intensity (increase in absolute weight used, usually represented as a percent of 1RM)**</u> You can add more weight to the exercise in the program producing greater muscle mass. **It is important to remember that muscle mass and protein synthesis is achieved by performing 3-5 sets using 5-8 repetitions with 75% to 85% 1RM. This method is the preferred method of increasing intensity for the majority of training.**

OPTION TWO: <u>Metabolic intensity:</u> Time can be varied to regulate intensity in different ways. You can train for longer time periods or train for shorter time periods more often. Another way to increase intensity by using time, is to do more exercises in the same time frame or the same exercises in a shorter time frame. Also, one can vary time between sets and exercises. However, when time between sets is reduced the body builder is forced to reduce the training weight (absolute intensity), because of the fatigue accumulation, in order to correctly perform the exercises. **This option for increasing intensity should not be used when attempting to increase size and strength. This method specifically increases the metabolic intensity (local muscle endurance [LME] and the ability to produce energy) and does not produce a large amount of hypertrophy in the contractile proteins of the muscles. It is best applied during the preparation and conditioning phases or during the cutting, defining and shaping program.**

Manipulation of time reduces the amount of weight lifted and is probably counter-productive if strength and size is the training objective. **Muscle tension, not fatigue is the stimulus for increasing size and strength and muscle tension is only increased as weight increases.** A weight load of between 75% and 85% of 1RM performed for 3-5 sets of 5-8 repetitions is considered to be the optimal intensity and repetition prescription to increase mass and strength. Beginners can benefit greatly from option one above, while more advanced body builders will use both options stated above to make additional progress, but only in the appropriate phases of training.

SHAPING AND SCULPTURING THE BODY

It is vitally important that every major muscle group in the body be optimally shaped. This involves many hours of work, scientific understanding of the anatomy and creative intelligence in the application of exercises, intensities, sets, repetitions, volumes, frequencies and durations of the various cycles within the training program. At the same time, there is a certain genetic shape potential for each muscle for each individual. The body builder should be realistic in their shaping goals and not go chasing after unobtainable goals.

While the general shape of a muscle is predetermined genetically, it can be greatly enhanced by intelligent application of resistance exercises. It is, therefore, important to perform as many different exercises as possible to potentiate shape after basic size has been achieved. Exercises that work the muscle from all different angles helps to achieve this goal. The intensity, sets, repetitions and volume will dictate the magnitude of the training effects produced by the application of the selected exercises.

The most important guiding principle in shaping the muscles is, after a basic general conditioning and preparation program, to first work for size (hypertrophy) and then train for the shaping and definition of the muscles. Also, it is important to vary the training volumes and intensities periodically to optimize the increase in size, strength and shaping of the muscles. This periodization, also, helps to fix the gains in size and strength that have been experienced.

WEEKLY TRAINING PATTERNS OR FORMATS (SPLITS)

There are countless ways to organize the weekly training pattern. Beginners generally train all body parts on one training day, initially. Training usually occurs three days per week with a day of rest between training sessions. Intermediate and advanced body builders use more sophisticated weekly training patterns with varying work and rest day combinations. They usually switch to a weekly training pattern which trains each muscle group at least twice per week. This is called a split routine requiring more than three training sessions per week which may extend from 6 to 18 training sessions per week, depending upon the training objectives.

In addition to the beginners training pattern where all body parts are trained on one day spread over a seven day week, there are split training patterns. A **single split** involves training once a day with various body part training spread out over the seven day week. A **double split** is a pattern where the body builder trains twice a day with various body part training spread out over the seven day week while the **triple split** involves training three times a day where body part training is spread out over the seven day week. There are many variations of the single, double and triple split training patterns.

The single, double and tipple split training formats usually apply one of the following patterns: (1) The muscles that are related to each other in function (synergistic muscles) are trained on the same day; (2) An antagonistic muscle group format is used on the same day; or, (3) A mixed upper body/lower body muscle group format is used on the same day. All these formats permit good recovery before the next training session where the same muscle groups will be trained again. The muscle groups that are not trained on a specific training day from other body areas are exercised in similar patterns on a different day for the same reason.

Whatever the split design or format, the split should be designed to permit maximal intense individual workouts for the selected muscle groups with one or more days of recovery before the next training session of using these same muscle groups. This allows a higher quality overload which produces the greatest gains possible. It is absolutely essential to design the training pattern so that no muscle or muscle group is overtrained. For successive training days, this is accomplished by using an antagonistic muscle format, or an upper body/lower body/upper body (or vice versa) daily training format or any other logical muscle group arrangement.

The upper body/lower body/upper body/rest or similar split design provide the most intelligent training format for the mass building phase of training. The principle is to give maximum rest to muscle groups between workouts when training for muscle mass with high intensity and volume levels. Moreover, the body builder must remember that to some degree many muscles are used is some way in upper body pushing and pulling movements so that training upper body movements on consecutive days may be counter productive in the mass building stage.

In this weekly training format, a muscle or muscle group is trained vigorously and then allowed to rest before engaging again in training. On the next training day, it is best to train muscles at the opposite end of the body. An example would be to train chest, shoulders and triceps on day one. On day two the quadriceps, hamstrings, gluteals and low back are trained. The third day involves the upper back and biceps. The fourth day is a day of rest and then the cycle is repeated. Of course, there are many other similar weekly training formats that are equally effective.

The four basic weekly training patterns are briefly discussed below:

ALL BODY PARTS ON ONE DAY - BEGINNERS TRAINING PATTERN: The main purpose of a beginning body builder's program is to introduce people to the sport of body building and to acquire some basic muscle development and physical fitness. This training pattern can also be used as a re-entry training pattern for a body builder after a lay-off or to start a new cycle of training. In both cases, this pattern prepares the body builder for more advance body building training patterns and routines.

As mentioned above, in the beginner's training pattern, all body parts are trained on one day, usually three days per week with a day of rest between training sessions. In Table 4-2 is displayed an example of a weekly training pattern for beginning body builders. When all body parts are trained on the same day, usually only one exercise per body part is performed. The exercises could be arranged in an antagonistic pattern (opposing muscle groups used in consecutive exercises) or a upper body/lower body pattern (peripheral heart action - PHA). Table 4-3 contains an example of weekly antagonistic and PHA training patterns for beginning body builders.

Since many muscles work as assistive (synergistic) or stabilizers in the training of upper body prime movers, it is wise to let them rest by placing a lower body exercise between upper body exercises. This exercise arrangement results in less acute muscle fatigue in the muscle areas being trained and results in greater over all work. This is the PHA pattern.

Table 4-2.   An Example Of A Weekly Training Pattern Training All Body Parts Each Training Session For Beginning Body Builders.

WEEKLY TRAINING PATTERN						
DAY 1	DAY 2	DAY 3	DAY 4	DAY 5	DAY 6	DAY 7
TOTAL BODY	REST	TOTAL BODY	REST	TOTAL BODY	REST	REST

Table 4-3.   An Example Of Weekly Antagonistic and PHA Training Patterns For Beginning Body Builders.

ANTAGONISTIC PATTERN		PHA PATTERN	
MUSCLE GROUPS	EXERCISES	MUSCLE GROUPS	EXERCISES
1. Shoulders	Press	1. Shoulders	Press
2. Upper Back	Pulldown	2. Hips/Legs	Squat
3. Chest	Bench Press	3. Upper Back	Pulldown
4. Biceps	Curls	4. Miscellaneous Leg	Leg Curls
5. Triceps	Pushdown	5. Chest	Bench Press
6. Abdominals	Crunch	6. Abdominals	Crunch
7. Low Back	Hyperextension	7. Biceps	Curl
8. Quadriceps	Squats	8. Low Back	Hyperextension
9. Hamstrings	Leg Curls	9. Triceps	Pushdown
10. Adductors	Hip Adduction	10. Miscellaneous Leg	Hip Adduction

SINGLE SPLIT (BEGINNING, INTERMEDIATE & ADVANCED BODY BUILDERS): The single split is a training pattern where the body builder trains one time each day. One to four body parts are trained each training session. Most body builders commonly train one to two body parts in their daily training pattern. Three to four body parts per training session is less frequently employed, but can be effective.

The number of training days per week range from 3 to 6 days and depends upon the training philosophy, number of body parts trained per day, the fitness state of the body builder and the specific phase of training. Table 4-4 displays some very simple training patterns employing 4, 5 and 6 days of training per week.

Table 4-4.   Simple Single Split Training Patterns For 4, 5 And 6 Days Per Week.

DAYS	4 DAYS	5 DAYS	5 DAYS	6 DAYS
MONDAY	Upper Body	Upper Body	Chest	Upper Body
TUESDAY	Lower Body	Lower Body	Shoulders	Lower Body
WEDNESDAY	Rest	Upper Body	Back	Upper Body
THURSDAY	Upper Body	Lower Body	Rest	Lower Body
FRIDAY	Lower Body	Upper Body	Triceps/Biceps	Upper Body
SATURDAY	Rest	Rest	Legs	Lower Body
SUNDAY	Rest	Rest	Rest	Rest
COMMENT	None	Reverse Cycle Following Week	Abs/Calves Each Day or 3 X Week	None

The most common single split is the push/pull format. The upper body pushing muscle groups (triceps, chest, and shoulders) are trained on one day and the upper body pulling muscle groups (biceps, upper and lower back) are trained on the next day. The legs, midsection, forearms and calves can be included on either day or can be split between the days. Example # 1 for the upper body push/pull training pattern with legs and midsection training included is shown in Table 4-5.

Table 4-5.   An Example Of A Push/Pull Training Pattern - Example # 1.

DAYS	MUSCLE GROUPS
1	Triceps, Chest, Shoulders, Midsection
2	Biceps, Back, Legs
3	Triceps, Chest, Shoulders, Midsection
4	Biceps, Back, Legs
5	Triceps, Chest, Shoulders, Midsection
6	Biceps, Back, Legs
7	Rest
8-14	Repeat Cycle

PART IV

BODY BUILDING

A second method for designing the push/pull training split is to include training the quadriceps (pushing) and hamstrings (pulling) on the respective training day while including the midsection on either the pushing day or the pulling day. The calves are usually trained on the pulling day.   Table 4-6 contains a training pattern where the quadriceps, chest, shoulders and triceps are trained on the pushing day. Meanwhile, the hamstrings, calves and midsection are included with the biceps and back on the pulling day.

Table 4-6.   An Example Of A Push/Pull Training Pattern - Example # 2.

DAYS	MUSCLE GROUPS
1	Chest, Shoulders, Triceps, Quadriceps
2	Biceps, Back, Hamstrings, Calves, Midsection
3	Chest, Shoulders, Triceps, Quadriceps
4	Biceps, Back, Hamstrings, Calves, Midsection
5	Chest, Shoulders, Triceps, Quadriceps
6	Biceps, Back, Hamstrings, Calves, Midsection
7	Rest
8-14	Repeat Cycle

Another popular single split is a more generalized approach where the body builder performs a mixture of push/pull exercises for the chest, shoulders and arms on Monday, Wednesday and Friday. Meanwhile, on the alternate days of Tuesday, Thursday and Saturday, the body builder uses a mixture of push/pull exercises for the legs, back and midsection. Table 4-7 displays an example of a generalized single split training pattern.

Table 4-7.   An example of a generalized single split training pattern.

DAYS	MUSCLE GROUPS
1	Chest, Shoulders, Arms
2	Legs, Back, Midsection
3	Chest, Shoulders, Arms
4	Legs, Back, Midsection
5	Chest, Shoulders, Arms
6	Legs, Back, Midsection
7	Rest
8-14	Repeat Cycle

Tables 4-8, 4-9, 4-10, 4-11, 4-12, 4-13, 4-14 and 4-15 display various **single split training patterns** for champion body builders as reported in selected issues of the Muscle & Fitness magazine which is published by Weider Publications of Woodland Hills, California. The following tables are introduced by the source for each single training split that is presented.

Table 4-8. Shelley Beattie - 1990 NPC USA Champion
How The Champs Peak - Part II: Sooner Is Better And Less Is More For
This Ms. O Challenger
Muscle & Fitness: May, 1992 - Page 72

DAY	1	2	3	4	5	6
BODY PARTS	Chest Biceps	Back Triceps	Thighs Calves	Shoulders Trapezius	Rest	Repeat Cycle

Table 4-9. Laura Creavalle - 1990 Ms International
A Body-Sculpting Back Program
Muscle & Fitness: December, 1993 - Page 106

DAY	1	2	3	4	5	6	7-12
BODY PARTS	Back Calves	Shoulders Biceps Abdominals	Rest	Legs Calves	Chest Triceps Abdominals	Rest	Repeat Cycle

Table 4-10. Lee Labrada - Second Place - 1993 Ironman & Arnold Classic
Granite Thighs
Muscle & Fitness: September, 1993 - Page 154

DAY	1	2	3	4	5	6	7-12
BODY PARTS	Chest Shoulders Triceps	Back Biceps	Rest	Legs	Chest Shoulders Triceps	Rest	Repeat Cycle

Table 4-11 Cory Everson - 6 Time Ms. Olympia
The Breast - An Uplifting Guide To: Anatomy, Self-examination, Training For Shape,
Sport Bras and Implant Safety
Muscle & Fitness: April, 1992 - Page 122

DAY	1	2	3	4	5-8
BODY PARTS	Chest Shoulders Triceps	Legs Low Back Calves	Back Biceps	Rest	Repeat Cycle

PART IV

BODY BUILDING

Table 4-12. Kevin Levrone - 1992 Second - Mr. Olympia
Burnin' Arms In Glen Burnie
Muscle & Fitness: December, 1993 - Page 162

DAY	1	2	3	4	5-8
BODY PARTS	Chest Shoulders Triceps	Back Biceps Hamstrings	Quadriceps	Rest	Repeat Cycle

Table 4-13. Mike Matarazzo - IFBB USA Champion
Dreadnought Delts
Muscle & Fitness: November, 1993 - Page 74

DAY	1	2	3	4	5	6	7-12
BODY PARTS	Chest Forearms Aerobics	Back Aerobics	Shoulders Trapezius Aerobics	Quadriceps Hamstrings Calves	Arms Aerobics	Rest	Repeat Cycle

Table 4-14. Lenda Murray - 1991, 1992, 1993 Ms. Olympia
Beating Thunder Thighs: Here's A Common Sense Guide For Altering Leg Shape
And Size With Diet and Training
Muscle & Fitness: January, 1994 - Page 82

DAY	1	2	3	4	5-8
BODY PARTS	Chest Triceps Shoulders Abdominals	Back Biceps Forearms Calves	Quadriceps Hamstrings Glutes Abdominals	Rest	Repeat Cycle

Table 4-15. Dorian Yates - 1992, 1993, 1993, 1994 Mr. Olympia
Lat Me Go!
Muscle & Fitness: January, 1993 - Page 175

DAY	1	2	3	4	5	6	7-12
BODY PARTS	Chest Biceps	Quadriceps Hamstrings	Rest	Shoulders Triceps	Back	Rest	Repeat Cycle

DOUBLE SPLIT (INTERMEDIATE & ADVANCED BODY BUILDERS): The **double split training pattern** is one that requires the body builder to train twice per day. A selected number of body parts, usually one to three body parts, are trained in the morning while different body parts (one to three) are trained in the afternoon or evening. These patterns involve training each body part two to three times per week. The double split routine can be designed using different muscles or muscle groups in various combination of work days and rest days. There are many combinations possible.

Tables 4-16, 4-17, 4-18, 4-19, 4-20, 4-21 display various double split training patterns for selected champion body builders as reported in various issues of the Muscle & Fitness magazine which is published by Weider Publications of Woodland Hills, California. The following tables are introduced by the source for each double split training program that is presented.

Table 4-16. Achim Albrecht - IFBB World Amateur Champion
Wideload
Muscle & Fitness: June, 1993 - Page 158

DAY	1	2	3	4	5	6-10
BODY PARTS						
AM	Chest	Back	Biceps Forearms	Quadriceps	Rest	Repeat Cycle
PM	Shoulders	Hamstrings Low Back	Triceps Abdominals	Calves	Rest	Repeat Cycle

Table 4-17. Cory Everson - 6 Times Ms. Olympia - Post Competitive Training
Cory Goes Ballistic!
Muscle & Fitness: November, 1993 - Page 110

DAY	1	2	3	4	5	6	7	8-14
BODY PARTS								
AM	Chest	Legs	Back	Chest	Legs	Back	Rest	Repeat Cycle
PM	Shoulders	Nothing	Biceps Triceps	Shoulders	Nothing	Biceps Triceps	Rest	Repeat Cycle

BODY BUILDING **PART IV**

Table 4-18. Lenda Murray - 1991, 1992, 1993, 1994 Ms. Olympia
         How The Champs Peak: Part 9 - Conquering Her Only Weak Point Brought Her
         A Second Ms. Olympia Title!
         Muscle & Fitness: March, 1992 - Page 80

DAY	1	2	3	4-6	7	8-14
BODY PARTS						
AM	Chest Calves	Quadriceps Hamstrings	Back Shoulders	Repeat Cycle	Rest	Repeat Total Cycle
PM	Biceps Triceps Abdominals	Stationary Bike	Stairclimber	Repeat Cycle	Rest	Repeat Total Cycle

Table 4-19. Sonny Schmidt - IFBB Pro
         Pecs Won't Grow? Force'em!
         Muscle & Fitness: October, 1993 - Page 168

DAY	1	2	3	4	5	6	7	8-14
BODY PARTS								
AM	Chest	Shoulders	Biceps	Chest	Shoulders	Biceps	Aerobics	Repeat Cycle
PM	Back	Triceps	Legs	Back	Triceps	Legs	None	Repeat Cycle

Table 4-20. Vince Taylor - 1992 Arnold Classic Champion
         Massive Chest
         Muscle & Fitness: July, 1993 - Page 170

DAY	1	2	3	4	5	6	7	8-14
BODY PARTS								
AM	Chest	Back	Quadriceps	Chest	Back	Quadriceps	Rest	Repeat Cycle
PM	Shoulders Triceps	Trapezius Biceps Hamstrings	None	Shoulder Triceps	Trapezius Biceps Hamstrings	None	Rest	Repeat Cycle

Table 4-21. Flex Wheeler - 1993 IFBB Arnold Classic Champion
How I Won The Arnold Classic - Mega Mass Workout Program
Muscle & Fitness: July, 1993 - Page 128

DAY	1	2	3	4	5	6
BODY PARTS						
AM	Chest	Hamstrings	Shoulders	Back	Rest	Repeat Cycle
PM	Triceps	Quadriceps	Biceps	None	Rest	Repeat Cycle

TRIPLE SPLIT (ADVANCED BODY BUILDER): The **tipple split training pattern** is a very radical approach to training. The application of this training pattern must be very carefully used because it could easily lead to overtraining. The tipple split should be applied for only short periods possibly only three to eight weeks.

This training pattern requires being able to train three times per day. One body part is trained in each training session. The pattern involves three days of work followed by a day of rest and then the repetition of the cycle. Their many other variations in the sequencing of the body parts that can be used. One is only limited by their imagination. Example # 1 is shown in Table 4-22 which demonstrates an example of a **tipple split training format** for advanced body builders. Table 4-23 displays example # 2 of **triple split training format** for advanced body builders.

Table 4-22. An Example Of A Tipple Split Training Format For Advanced Body Builders-Example # 1.

TIME OF DAY	DAY 1	DAY 2	DAY 3	DAY 4	DAY 5-7
MORNING	Shoulders	Low Back	Upper Back	Rest	REPEAT CYCLE
AFTERNOON	Calves	Triceps	Quadriceps	Rest	
EVENING	Chest	Hamstrings	Biceps	Rest	

PART IV

BODY BUILDING

Table 4-23. An Example Of A Triple Split Training Format For Advanced Body Builders-
            Example # 2.

KIM CHIZEVSKY - 1992 IFBB NORTH AMERICAN CHAMPION
HOW WE WON THE IFBB NORTH AMERICAN CHAMPIONSHIPS:
PAUL DILLETT & KIM CHIZEVSKY ARMED FOR BATTLE

MUSCLE & FITNESS: FEBRUARY, 1993 - P. 154

TRAINING FORMAT

TRAINING SPLIT			
DAY	A.M.	NOON	P.M.
1	AEROBICS (1 HOUR)	LARGE MUSCLE GROUP	SMALLER MUSCLE GROUPS (TRICEPS, CALVES, ABDOMINALS) & AEROBICS
2	AEROBICS (1 HOUR)	SHOULDERS	BICEPS & AEROBICS
3	AEROBICS	BACK	HAMSTRINGS & AEROBICS
4	QUADRICEPS & AEROBICS	NONE	NONE
5	AEROBICS	NONE	NONE
6	REST	REST	REST
7	REPEAT CYCLE	REPEAT CYCLE	REPEAT CYCLE

BODY BUILDING ROUTINES

A prudent plan for body building initially includes the attainment of basic size and minimization of body fat by using the standard weight training exercises and proven methods of training. After basic size has been achieved, a training plan can be devised to enhance and potentiate the shape of the muscles using a great many varied exercises. During all phases of body building, attention should be paid to low fat, high carbohydrate diets with reasonable protein intake. It is best to fight the fat battle throughout the year.

There are ten (10) major anatomical areas of concern for the body builder:

1. Chest
2. Arms (biceps & triceps)
3. Upper Back
4. Shoulders (anterior, middle, posterior,)
5. Thighs (quadriceps, hamstrings, adductors & abductors)
6. Calves
7. Forearms
8. Abdominal
9. Lower Back
10. Neck

Within these areas are many muscles and muscle groups, all that must be conditioned and shaped by specific exercises. There are literally hundreds of training exercises that can be employed and one is only limited by their imagination and availability of equipment.

There are no "magic" exercises or "secret routines" that makes any approach to body building superior. The efficacy of any exercise or routine is determined by the results that its produces and not the hype that its advocates project.

There are many ways to put together a series of exercises (a routine) for each body part. Also, as demonstrated in the previous sections, there are many ways of combining these various routines into daily and weekly training patterns. In most cases, the training pattern is an individual preference. Moreover, the training goals and training phases will dictate to a large degree what format will be followed. The methods, techniques and training patterns will change depending on which phase of the body building plan is implemented: (1) conditioning; (2) increasing size and muscle development; (3) cutting, defining and shaping; (4) enhancing size, shape and reducing body fat; (5) training for competition, or, (5) rest and restoration.

Beginners and advance body builders have very different training patterns, which is an obvious necessity. Beginners need to develop a conditioning base; learn how to perform the many exercises that will be used in the advanced body building routines; and, acquire the discipline that is needed to be successful in body building. Advanced body builders have developed a good conditioning base; have learned the proper technique for performing a large number of weight training and body building exercises; and, have developed the discipline needed to become a competent body builder. Therefore, the advanced body builder uses many different machine and free weight exercises in a variety of exercise formats. The complexity of their body building programs reflects the degree of training maturity and knowledge of anatomy and muscle physiology of the body builder.

The following concepts need to be considered when designing body building routines:

NOVICE ROUTINES (PATTERNS)

The novice routine is used to introduce the beginner to weight training and body building and to develop a good training base. These programs are aimed at conditioning the muscles, tendons, ligaments and connective tissue in preparation for more arduous training and to reduce the body fat as much as is possible. All body parts are trained in each training session and training sessions occur three times a week lasting from one to two hours. There is usually a day of rest between training sessions.

ADVANCED ROUTINES (PATTERNS)

There are many variations of advanced routines. These routines are not for the beginner. Once the beginner has a good base they can advance to more sophisticated routines. Basically, these programs adjust the frequency, intensity, duration and length of program in a personalized and artful format. The major objectives are to increase the size of all the muscles, to maximize the shape of the muscles, improve muscle definition and continue to reduce body fat to optimal levels. Advanced training patterns include the single split, double split and triple split systems. Moreover, there are times when the simple daily total body training pattern can be performed three times per week as a re-entry program after a long lay-off or for training diversity.

REPETITIONS

A "rep" or repetition is defined as one complete movement cycle of an exercise. The repetition cycle extends from the starting position through the range of motion and then back to the starting position. The number of repetitions is dependent upon the program objectives and usually ranges from 1 to 15 repetitions. Table 4-1, which was presented earlier in Part IV, displays information regarding the specific number of repetitions to perform for the achievement of training objectives.

SETS

A set is the number of prescribed repetitions performed in a consecutive manner. The number of repetitions performed in a set varies according to the training objective and individual preference. Most body builders execute from six to twelve repetitions per set. The amount of weight (% of 1RM) used in each set will dictate the number of repetitions that can be performed. The rest time between sets will also greatly affect the training weight. Longer times between sets allows training at higher intensities (% 1RM) which increases muscle mass and strength. Shorter time between sets increases the metabolic intensity and impacts local muscle endurance and assists in reducing body fat. See Table 4-1 presented earlier in Part IV.

NUMBER OF SETS AND REPETITIONS

The number of sets and repetitions that a body builder would employ depends entirely upon the objectives of the body building program. The number of repetitions (and to a lessor degree the number of sets) will dictate the intensity (% 1RM) that can be utilized in training. For increases in strength and size, 3 to 5 sets of 1 to 8 repetitions are used at intensity levels of 70% to 100% 1RM. Most body builders use from 5 to 8 repetitions for 3 to 5 sets for increasing size. For cutting (defining the muscle and reduction of subcutaneous fat) most body builders use from 10 to 15 repetitions and sometimes up to 20 repetitions at intensity level of 40% to 70% 1RM. It is important to remember that just the selection of sets and repetitions without any consideration of the intensity (% 1RM) will result in less than desirable results. **INTENSITY (% of 1RM)** must receive attention when designing the body building program.

See Table 4-1 presented earlier in Part IV.

NUMBER OF EXERCISES PER BODY PART

The number of exercises that should be used per body part is dependent upon the objectives of the body building program and the level of development of the body builder. Other factors involved in determining the number of exercises to use for each body part are: (1) The kind of weekly training pattern (split) utilized; (2) How many body parts are trained in each training session; (3) What cycle is being applied (conditioning, mass development, cutting and defining, enhancement of size and shape, competition or restoration); and, (4) The number of sets, repetitions and intensity level (% 1RM).

For general body building and conditioning, 1 to 2 exercises per body part is acceptable and this training pattern can be performed two to three times per week with a day of rest between training sessions.

Advanced training patterns for size and strength usually involve 3 to 4 exercises per body part and training sessions usually occur two to three times per week depending upon the training pattern. The advanced body builder needs to be very careful in using more than four exercises per body part in order to keep from becoming over-trained. Another consideration in determining the number of exercise per body part is the intensity and the number of sets and repetitions that are being performed. It is reasonable to use more exercises in a selected body part (5-8 exercises) while using only 3 to 4 exercises in the other body parts. This procedure is usually applied to body parts that need emphasis and is applied for short training cycles.

The body builder must remember that it is easy to develop a state of overtraining when they overwork. The training philosophy should be to **"STIMULATE NOT ANNIHILATE". The overtrained state is characterized by persistent soreness of muscles and joints, elevated resting heart rate and resting blood pressure, difficulty in warming up and general lack of motivation to train.** If these symptoms are present, it is time to re-evaluate the training program and make the appropriate changes. It is probable that some restorative program needs to be implemented before moving on to more sophisticated training programs.

During the cutting and/or other low intensity and high repetition programs the bodybuilder may use from 2 to 8 exercises per body part. This may help in producing motivation because of the exercise diversity. Furthermore, working the muscle and muscle groups from many different angles help to shape them. This requires the application of a variety of exercises. When performing a high number of exercises per body part one needs to make sure the intensity is rather low (40% to 60% 1RM). If any tendonitis is present, it would be best not to over-stress the affected area.

The authors of this Encyclopedia of Weight Training have surveyed the training routines of the top international male and female body builders as reported in Muscle & Fitness in the years 1992, 1993, 1994 and 1995. The Muscle & Fitness Magazine is published by Weider Publications of Woodland Hills, California. It is the premier magazine for body building and nutrition for body building in the world.

This information related to the number of exercises per body part is taken directly from the Muscle & Fitness issues for the four years listed above. The authors assume that the information presented in the Muscle & Fitness issues reviewed, accurately represents what the top male and female body builders actually execute in their training programs. Caution should be used when deciding to apply what the champion body builder's report as their training program. There is a tendency to exaggerate and embellish such reports. Moreover, the genetic qualities of champion body builders allow them to use more sophisticated and intensive training programs. The application of training routines of champion body builders should be done thoughtfully. **THE KEY TO VALID EVALUATION OF ANY INFORMATION IS THE RESULTS OF THE APPLICATION OF THE KNOWLEDGE.**

Table 4-24 presents the results of this survey of the number of exercises per body part used in training as reported by international male and female body builders as published in the Muscle & Fitness Magazine from 1992-95. This survey involve 245 male and 65 female body builders. In this survey, it was found that the champion body builders used from 2 to 8 exercises per body part depending upon what part of the training cycle was being used. The desires and practices regarding the number of sets per body part used by male and female body builders is approximately the same. The information in Table 4-24 demonstrates that most champion male and female body builders use an average 3 to 4 exercises per body part in training. Eighty-one body builders used 3 exercises per body part in training while 79 body builders used four exercises per body part. There was a small tendency to use fewer exercises for the arms and abdominals. This difference is probably not of any significance.

The following recommendations are given for beginning, intermediate and advanced body builders:

      1. Beginners . . . . 1-3 exercises per body part.
      2. Intermediates . . . . 3-4 exercises per body part.
      3. Advanced . . . . 3-6 exercises per body part.

PART IV

BODY BUILDING

Table 4-24. Number Of Exercises Per Body Part Used In Training As Reported By International Male and Female Body Builders In The Muscle & Fitness Magazine In Years 1992-95.

| BODY PARTS | SEX | NUMBER OF EXERCISES PER BODY PART | | | | | | | AVG EX/ B.P.* |
		2	3	4	5	6	7	8	
SHOULDERS	M	4	9	11	4	5	1	0	4.00
	F	0	0	6	1	2	0	0	4.56
CHEST	M	3	10	10	4	1	1	0	3.76
	F	0	3	2	3	0	0	0	4.00
BACK	M	5	3	12	8	9	3	0	4.55
	F	1	4	1	2	2	0	0	4.00
ARMS	M	15	31	11	12	7	1	1	3.64
	F	1	6	9	1	1	0	0	3.72
ABDOMINALS	M	8	4	3	2	0	0	0	2.94
	F	2	0	0	1	0	0	0	3.00
LEGS	M	5	7	10	8	10	6	1	4.70
	F	0	4	4	4	2	2	1	4.82
NUMBER OF OBSERVATIONS	M	40	64	57	38	32	12	2	245
	F	4	17	22	12	7	2	1	65
	TOTAL	44	81	79	50	39	14	3	310

* AVG EX/BP . . . . . The average number of exercises for each separate body part.

** The numbers recorded in the boxes adjacent to the respective body part and in the respective column for number of exercises per body part, represent the number of surveyed body builders reporting the use of the respective number of exercises for each specific body part.

NUMBER OF REST DAYS BETWEEN TRAINING THE SAME MUSCLE GROUPS:

At least one day and sometimes two days should separate training of the same muscle groups depending upon the intensity and volume of exercise performed. The muscles need time to recover, and while constant and frequent stimulus can be tolerated for a short period, eventually the overtrained state occurs if the muscles are not allowed to recover and rest. In split training formats, adequate rest for various muscle groups can be planned by carefully formulating the weekly training cycle.

The number of rest days will be dictated by the intensity (% 1RM), the number of sets and repetitions being performed and the number of exercises per muscle group being executed in each training session. There is a lot of room for creativity in varying the time between training sessions working the same muscle groups. Working

PART IV

BODY BUILDING

the muscles at different angles and intensities can allow for more frequent exposure for the same muscle groups, however, one has to be very careful not to overtrain.

Also, using more frequent training of the same muscle groups may be acceptable in the cutting, shaping, enhancing and competition phases of body building because the exercise intensity (% 1RM) is usually low. If the intensity drops below 50% 1RM it is possible to use exercises that involve the same muscle groups on consecutive days for longer periods of time. This practice could be used in the cutting, shaping, enhancing and competition phases of training or maybe as a diverse training pattern to stimulate motivation. In general, it is probably not advisable to engage the same muscle groups on consecutive days for long periods of time. This is especially true if the training intensity is above 70% 1RM or if the training volume (total work) is very large.

In Table 4-25 is found a summary of four general programs for body building. These four programs include a novice plan and three different approaches for the advanced body builder. The table contains information regarding the number of training days per week, body parts for each training session, workout length and program (cycle) length. It is very important to apply the principles of periodization for optimal training efficiency and maximal muscle growth and body fat reduction and to maintain motivation to sustain the training efforts. The principles of periodization are thoroughly discussed in Section I of this book.

There are many variations of the weekly training pattern that are successful. The adoption of any training plan requires the **careful** consideration of periodization principles and many other principles of exercise physiology, training and competition.

Table 4-25. Four Generalized Body Building Programs.

PROGRAM LEVEL	DAYS/WEEK	BODY PARTS	WORKOUT LENGTH	PROGRAM LENGTH
NOVICE	3 DAYS PER WEEK (M,W,F) OR (T,TH,SAT)	ALL BODY PARTS	1-2 HOURS	3-6 MONTHS (PERIODIZED)
ADVANCED OPTION #1 SPLIT ROUTINE	6 DAYS PER WEEK (M,W,F) AND (T,TH,SAT)	UPPER BODY - M,W,F	1-1 1/2 HOURS	INDEFINITE (PERIODIZED)
		LOWER BODY - T,TH,SAT	1 - 1 1/2 HOURS	
ADVANCED OPTION #2 DOUBLE SPLIT ROUTINE	A. 3 DAYS PER WEEK (M,W,F) OR (T,TH,SAT) OR B. (M,T) - REST - (TH,F) REST - (SUN,M) - REST ETC.	A.M. 2 BODY PARTS	1 HOUR	INDEFINITE (PERIODIZED)
		REST	6 - 8 HOURS	
		P.M. 2 BODY PARTS	1 HOUR	
ADVANCED OPTION #3 3 DAYS ON & 1 DAY REST	6 DAYS PER WEEK M,T,W - REST - F, SAT, SUN - REST, ETC.*	MON/FRI - CHEST & SHOULDERS & ABS	1 - 1 1/2 HOURS	INDEFINITE (PERIODIZED)
		TUES/SAT - LEGS & CALVES & ABS	1 - 1 1/2 HOURS	
		WED/SUN - ARMS & BACK & ABS	1 - 1 1/2 HOURS	
		THUR - REST		

* OPTION # 2B AND # 3 REQUIRES THE ABILITY TO TRAIN ON DIFFERENT DAYS EVERY WEEK. THIS PLAN IS GOOD BUT DIFFICULT TO APPLY UNLESS HIGHLY MOTIVATED AND SOMEWHAT FINANCIALLY INDEPENDENT.

PART IV

BODY BUILDING

SYSTEMS OF TRAINING

INTRODUCTION

There are many variations of training systems using weight machines or free weights. The "training system" relates to the technique or procedure involved in the actual application of the weight training exercises. When planning a body building program there are many factors that have to be considered. The program that is adopted must meet the objectives for training. The integration of all the training factors are discussed in the section entitled "Factors In Programming Progressive Resistance Exercise" presented in Part I of the Encyclopedia of Weight Training. **These factors are: frequency, intensity, duration, mode, level of fitness, length of training phases, exercise selection and exercise sequence. All these factors are thoroughly discussed in the section mentioned above.**

It is impossible, ineffective and unnecessary to present all the possible systems of training for body building in this book. Therefore, only the most commonly used and popular systems of training are presented in this section.

The routines involving multiple-sets performed non-stop should not be used extensively, however, they can be effectively used during selected cycles of training. The concept of cycling using various routine formats should be carefully planned to take into consideration all the factors of periodization, training, competition and restoration.

SETS AND REPETITIONS

By far the most common and most popular system of training is the sets and repetitions format. In this system a specified number of repetitions are performed for a designated number of sets. The exercises to be performed are placed into an intelligent order and 2 to 7 sets of 1 to 15 repetitions are executed at an intensity that is consistent with training goals.

The training procedure includes an number of sets for the warmup and cooldown for each specific exercise in the routine. These warmup and cooldown sets are not usually counted in the exercise prescription. The specific warm-up for an exercise usually includes the performance of a series of sets of 5 to 10 repetitions starting with a very light weight which is progressively increased up to the training weight.

The number of warm-up sets ranges between 3 to 5 sets depending upon the exercises. There may be some exercises where warm-up sets are not needed. This situation usually occurs where exercises working the same muscle group are performed in a consecutive sequence. Also, some small muscle groups which are placed at the end of the workout often do not need a warm-up set because the body is already warm and the specific area has been used in previous exercises. If there is any doubt, always use at least one warmup set with light weight performing 10 repetitions.

The rest interval between sets is dictated by the objectives of the weight training program, the physical condition of the trainee and the intensity level of the exercise. Rest periods typically are from 1 to 5 minutes and are related to the objectives of the training program. The main purpose of the longer rest period is to allow enough recovery so that subsequent sets can be correctly performed for the prescribed intensity and number of repetitions. Typical examples of sets and repetitions are the following:

1. Three to five sets of ten repetitions. (3-5 SETS X 10 REPS X 60% 1RM)
2. Three to five sets of five repetitions. (3-5 SETS X   5 REPS X 80% 1RM)
3. Four sets of eight repetitions. (4 SETS X   8 REPS X 70% 1RM)
4. OTHERS FORMATS (Note: There are many other set and repetition formats. One is only limited by their creativity and the program objectives.)

Any number of sets and repetitions can be utilized in this format. Remember the specific number of repetitions and the intensity (% 1RM) will be dictated by the goals of the training program.

The sets and repetitions format is the system that should be used for most of the time when training. Other techniques discussed below are usually integrated into this system for training of one or two of the muscle groups within a training routine. Also, at different phases in the periodization of training many other variants or techniques of training can be effectively employed, but the majority of time, one should employ the standard sets and repetitions method.

CHEATING REPETITIONS

Cheating repetitions involve the use of unusual body movements or executing the movement faster to add momentum to the weight so that the exercise action can be completed. When this occurs the primary muscle or muscle groups being trained do not receive maximum stimulus and, therefore, cheating repetitions are not of great value.

Cheating repetitions are usually reserved for the last sets and last repetitions of an exercise. Examples of cheating are arching in the bench press action or swinging the barbell or dumbbell when performing a curl. The cheating repetitions method is generally employed in one of two ways:

(1) When the trainee has performed all the possible strict repetitions, then various abnormal body configurations or the use an inordinate amount of momentum are employed to move the bar or weight machine through the weak point in the range of motion (the sticking point).

(2) The trainee purposely selects a weight that will force them to adopt unnatural postures and movements to increase the momentum of the weight or machine which will enable them to drive the resistance through the weak point in the range of motion (the sticking point). The person consciously uses cheating movements in all the prescribed repetitions of the set. The fundamental purpose of using cheating movements is to handle as much weight as possible without regard for technique.

The use of cheating movements is not recommended. The performance of cheating repetitions is not prudent and is a bad training method because it is based on the false belief that this procedure will enhance strength and size because more of the muscle is used. It is a mistaken conclusion to assume that more muscle fiber of the same muscle will be recruited when cheating repetitions are performed. What actually happens when muscles become fatigued and the trainee resorts to performing cheating movements, is that other previously unused muscles become involved. Moreover, there is a change in the biomechanical patterns of exercise, some which are potentially injurious and result in over-stressing all the body systems. Furthermore, if a heavy weight is purposely selected and cheating repetitions are performed as described in # 2 above, then other muscle groups become involved in the action. Consequently, there is minimal specific condition of the primary muscles involved in the action.

The use of cheating repetitions when the trainee becomes fatigued or when the weight is intentionally increased so that cheating is required to perform the exercise does not improve strength and size of specific muscles. However, it is possible to increase the strength expressed in the cheating exercises which may or may not increase the size of the many muscles involved in the movement. Cheating movements do not involve more muscle fibers of the primary muscle or muscle groups being trained. What occurs is that many other muscle groups come into play and the training benefit is spread across a greater part of the body. The potential for injury, muscle strains and overtraining is high when using these cheating practices so the risks are greater than the benefits. Certainly, there is no isolation of a muscle or muscle group when using this system.

The employment of cheating repetitions is probably not a good idea and the tendency to use this technique should be resisted. Muscle size and strength are improved by performing the correct exercise movements and appropriately applying the principles of periodization. However, application of cheating exercises may be

PART IV

BODY BUILDING

beneficial if done **infrequently**, and with a reasonable amount of overload. The body builder must understand that more muscles than the primary muscle will be conditioned and the primary muscle is not fully activated. This system can be used to introduce variety into the body building programs. Cheating exercises should not become a major part of the body building program.

FORCED REPETITIONS

Forced repetitions is really another form of cheating. The application of forced repetitions is when the trainee has reached a point of muscle exhaustion, then a training partner assists in the continued performance of 3 to 4 additional repetitions. **The person who is performing most of the work is the training partner, not the one executing the exercise.** Force repetitions are usually executed at the end of the last 2 sets of an exercise.

The employment of this technique is also the result of misunderstanding the physiology of muscle operation and growth. When a muscle becomes fatigued, less of the muscle fibers are recruited resulting in a decrease in the force expression of muscle contraction. Less of the muscle is utilized in the action causing failure to complete the last repetition which requires the training partner to assist. Forcing the muscle to work more does not happen because it cannot produce the necessary force and consequently the training partner has to perform most of the work. The use of forced repetitions produces the **"metabolic burn"** but does not result in enhancing muscle size and strength.

The reasons that people employ such a useless method of training are:

(1) The belief that they are pushing the muscle to the limit by using forced repetitions.
(2) An effort to increase motivation.
(3) The belief that they are stimulating reluctant muscles to grow by using force repetitions.

None of these reasons are valid if forced repetitions are used as a training system. Forced repetitions do not require the muscle to increase its contraction force; there is no stimulus for the muscle fibers to grow (this requires more intensity - a percent of 1RM); and, the training partner does most of the work in allowing the forced repetition to be completed. **To be very frank, forced repetitions are ineffective for developing strength and size and the concept is based on a poor understanding of exercise physiology and training theory.**

The employment of forced repetitions is probably not a good idea and the tendency to use this technique should be resisted. Muscle size and strength are improved by performing the correct exercise movements and appropriately applying the principles of periodization.

PARTIAL REPETITIONS

Performing partial repetitions is another method of cheating. Partial repetitions are performed after the last repetition of the last set, when one is incapable of performing another full repetition. At this point, the trainee performs 1/2 or 1/4 repetitions until they can do no more. As with cheating repetitions and forced repetitions this technique is based on a poor understanding of exercise physiology and training theory. The person who uses this technique is not in touch with the realities of exercise physiology.

This technique is usually performed while executing joint extension movements; such as pressing movements, elbow and knee extension actions and in squatting or leg pressing exercises. However, occasionally this technique is also employed on pulling exercises like curls, rowing, pulldowns or chins.

The weaknesses of this method are:

(1) Partial repetitions only train that part of the muscle that is active and there is no transfer of strength to other muscle parts or points in the range of motion.

(2) When the muscle fatigues, muscle fibers start to drop out of use. The exerciser is only able to execute 1/2 or 1/4 repetitions because the leverages of the muscles and joints are favorable at the point in the range of motion where such actions are used. This is at the end of the pressing action, elbow extension, leg extension, squatting or leg pressing movements; and at the start of any of the pulling motions. More of the muscle is not recruited when the muscle becomes fatigued and forced by some artificial method to continue working.

(3) The employment of partial repetitions is based on the erroneous concept of forcing the muscle to work harder. As the muscle fatigues, muscle fibers drop out of use, so, in fact, the muscle is doing less work.

The employment of partial repetitions is probably not a good idea and the tendency to use this technique should be resisted. Muscle size and strength are improved by performing the correct exercise movements and appropriately applying the principles of periodization.

NEGATIVE REPETITIONS (ECCENTRIC CONTRACTIONS)

Negative repetitions (known scientifically as eccentric or lengthening contractions) are thought to produce increases in strength and size. The definition of a negative (eccentric) repetition is a muscle contraction in which a muscle exerts force while it lengthens and is overcome by resistance. An example of a negative (eccentric) contraction would be the lowering of a weight in the bench press which is heavier than one's 1RM.

In the gym, negative repetitions are performed by lowering the weight working against the pull of gravity. This kind of repetition involves the assistance of one or more partners. Extremely heavy weights (heavier than can be lifted) are used with the training partner(s) assisting in the positive direction of the repetition while the person doing the exercise, controls the weight on its downward (negative) movement.

Negative repetitions can also be performed using machines or a free weight bar by executing the positive portion of the repetition as normally done with a selected weight and then having one's training partner push down on the weight stack or on the free weight bar to provide the heavy negative overload while the exerciser resists the return of the machine or free weight bar to the starting position.

Research has shown that the strength gain by performing negative repetitions does not transfer to positive repetitions. However, there is some research indicating that there may be some benefit to enhancing the size of the muscle by performing negative repetitions.

The negative (eccentric) strength curves of muscles have not been completely studied. It appears that the ability of the muscle to produce negative (eccentric) force varies from 0% to 300% or more when compared to the positive (concentric) strength. Unpublished research using the Life Circuit computerized exercise machines has demonstrated that the shapes and magnitudes of negative strength curves is very different from positive strength curves. **(Ward, P.; Garhammer, J.; Rozenek, R.; Unpublished Research for Life Fitness; 1987-88)** More research has to be conducted before a real strong statement can be made supporting the effectiveness of negative repetitions.

There is a big problem when using training-partner-assisted negative repetitions with a machine or free weight. It is impossible to quantify the amount of weight (resistance) which the training partner is applying to the bar or machine. This makes it difficult to determine the amount of extra force that should be applied to effectively train the muscles. In addition, there may be a high potential for injury using negative repetitions because there is little research that is available to identify the negative strength potential for each joint movement and, therefore, no valid manner to determine how much negative force should be applied and when. Also, it is very difficult for the training partner to know how much resistance should be applied.

As mentioned above, negative repetitions do not produce strength that can be transferred to a positive movement repetition, however, they do assist in stimulating growth. Moreover, when using free weights and exercise

PART IV

BODY BUILDING

machines, the efficiency of the negative repetition to produce increases in muscle mass is so low that it may not be worth the effort for the majority of the people who train with weights. **Negative repetitions should be used infrequently, if at all**. Only future research on negative contractions can fully explain how and when to correctly apply negative training and what should be the magnitude of negative loading. More research has to be conducted before a real strong statement can be made supporting the effectiveness of negative repetitions.

The use of negative repetitions is not recommended as a method to be employed to enhance strength or size. The employment of negative repetitions is probably not a good idea for people not familiar the science of muscle training and the tendency to use this technique should be resisted. Muscle size and strength are improved by performing the correct exercise movements and appropriately applying the principles of periodization. However, limited use of negative training may have some benefits for the very advanced body builder but should be used with caution.

SUPER-SETS

A super-set involves performing two exercises in succession without rest. Super-sets can be performed without rest between super-set sequences or with a rest period between super-set sequences. The amount of rest will be dictated by the intensity (weight load) of the exercises involved in the super-set and the conditioning level of the participant.

Super-sets can be performed by:

(1) Using opposing muscle groups: for example; biceps (front of arm)/triceps (back of arm) combination.

(2) Using synergistic (working together) muscle groups like the pectorals (chest) or the anterior deltoids (shoulders) or the triceps (back of arms). The synergistic format can be employed in two ways:

    (A) Using the same muscle group and employing the same muscle areas and angles of exercise.
    (B) Using the same muscle group but employing different muscle areas and different angles of exercise.

(3) Using different muscle groups: for example; squats and bench press or incline press and seated rowing, et cetera.

The reasons for using the super-set technique are:

(1) To shock the muscle in order to stimulate growth. This is accomplished by increasing the total amount of work at an appropriate exercise intensity. The total amount of work performed and the exercise intensity (% 1RM) will dictate the amount of stimulus to muscle growth not the specific exercise sequence.

(2) To minimize the amount of time needed to train. The super-set technique is nicely suited for training opposing muscle groups and the abdominal/low back muscles groups. This technique allows for performing more work in a given time period.

(3) The opposing muscle super-set technique is excellent in the mass building, cutting, shaping and the definition cycles. Some strength and size occurs as well as increasing local muscle endurance (LME) and producing a small amount of aerobic endurance.

(4) The super-set technique is an excellent method for introducing variation in the weight training program.

(5) The super-set technique can be effectively used in the cutting phase of body building.

The application of the super set technique creates more work for the muscle groups in a given time period. An example of the super set principle applied to opposing muscle groups (antagonistic format) would be to perform a set of curls (for the biceps) before doing a set of pushdowns (for the triceps).

In the case where there is a combination of synergistic muscles, pre-exhaustion of one muscle occurs with the first exercise, while during the second exercise the remaining muscle groups are forced to work harder. An example of the application of super sets for synergistic muscles would be to execute flying motions to stress the area of the pectorals (chest) before performing bench presses which involve the pectorals in combination with the anterior deltoids (front shoulders) and triceps (back of arms).

The first exercise in the super-set routine is performed for 6-12 repetitions (can be to failure) with 40% -75% of 1RM followed by the same number of reps and intensity for the second exercise. This procedure can be repeated for 3 - 5 laps (a lap is the performance of one super-set).

Table 4-26 contains examples of the antagonistic super-set format for arms, legs, chest/upperback and abdominal/low back muscle groups. In Table 4-27 is displayed examples of synergistic super-sets formats using the same muscle groups working the same angles of exercise for elbow flexors, chest and shoulder muscle groups. Table 4-28 contains examples of synergistic super-set formats using the same muscle groups working different angles of exercise for elbow extensors, quadriceps and upper back muscle groups.

Table 4-26. Examples Of The Antagonistic Super-Set Formats For Arms, Legs, Chest/Back And Abdominal/Low Back Muscle Groups.

BODY AREA EXAMPLE	EXERCISE #1	EXERCISE #2	REPETITIONS	INTENSITY	CIRCUITS
1. ARM (BICEPS & TRICEPS)	ARM CURL	PUSHDOWN	6 -12 REPS	40% - 75% 1RM	3 - 5 LAPS
2. LEGS	SQUAT	LEG CURL	6 -12 REPS	40% - 75% 1RM	3 - 5 LAPS
3. CHEST/UPPER BACK	BENCH PRESS	PULLDOWN	6 -12 REPS	40% - 75% 1RM	3 - 5 LAPS
4. ABDOMINAL/LOW BACK	CRUNCH	BACK EXTENSION	6 -12 REPS	40% - 75% 1RM	3 - 5 LAPS

* 1 LAP IS EQUIVALENT TO PERFORMING EXERCISE #1 FOLLOWED BY EXERCISE #2 AND IS CALLED ONE SUPER-SET.

Table 4-27. Examples Of Synergistic Super-set Formats Using The Same Muscle Groups Working The Same Angles Of Exercise For Elbow Flexors, Chest And Shoulder Muscle Groups.

BODY AREA EXAMPLE	EXERCISE #1	EXERCISE #2	REPETITIONS	INTENSITY	CIRCUITS
1. ELBOW FLEXORS	EZ CURL	SEATED DB CURL	6 -12 REPS	40% - 75% 1RM	3 - 5 LAPS
2. CHEST	DB FLY (FLAT)	BENCH PRESS	6 -12 REPS	40% - 75% 1RM	3 - 5 LAPS
3. SHOULDERS	PRESS B.B.	DB PRESS	6 -12 REPS	40% - 75% 1RM	3 - 5 LAPS

* 1 LAP IS EQUIVALENT TO PERFORMING EXERCISE #1 FOLLOWED BY EXERCISE #2 AND IS CALLED ONE SUPER-SET.

Table 4-28. Examples Of Synergistic Super-set Formats Using The Same Muscle Groups Working Different Angles Of Exercise For Elbow Extensors, Quadriceps And Upper Back Muscle Groups.

BODY AREA EXAMPLE	EXERCISE #1	EXERCISE #2	REPETITIONS	INTENSITY	CIRCUITS
1. ELBOW EXTENSORS	FRENCH PRESS	PUSHDOWN	6 -12 REPS	40% - 75% 1RM	3 - 5 LAPS
2. QUADRICEPS	FRONT SQUAT	BACK SQUAT	6 -12 REPS	40% - 75% 1RM	3 - 5 LAPS
3. UPPER BACK	SEATED ROW	PULLDOWN	6 -12 REPS	40% - 75% 1RM	3 - 5 LAPS

* 1 LAP IS EQUIVALENT TO PERFORMING EXERCISE # 1 FOLLOWED BY EXERCISE # 2 AND IS CALLED ONE SUPER-SET.

PART IV

BODY BUILDING

TRI-SETS (INCLUDING 3 MUSCLES OR MUSCLE GROUPS)

Tri-sets involve using 3 different movements in subsequent exercises without rest between exercises. Tri-sets can be performed without rest between each tri-set or with a rest period between each tri-set sequence. The amount of rest will be dictated by the intensity (weight load) of the exercises involved in the tri-set, the conditioning level of the participant and design of the tri-sets.

The application of the tri-set technique creates more work for the muscle groups in a short time period. Using exercises that condition three different muscle groups allows for more emphasis on general endurance as well as the local muscle endurance of the specific muscles involved. It may be possible to enhance size and strength using this technique to a moderate degree. The tri-set technique is best applied in the low intensity and high repetition phases of the periodization of training or as a short term training variation.

In the case where the same muscle groups and same angle of exercise is performed in successive exercises there is a definite impact on the local muscle endurance and some small impact on general endurance. Using the same muscle group and same angle of exercise may be useful in muscle defining, shaping and body fat reduction programs, but certainly not for increasing strength and muscle mass.

When using the same muscle group but different muscle areas and different angles of exercise, one may possibly enhance the size and strength to a moderate degree. However, there will be an specific emphasis on the local muscular endurance with some small impact on general endurance when using this variation of the tri-set method.

Tri-sets can be performed by:

(1)   Using three different muscle groups. This is the best application of the tri-set technique.

(2)   Using synergistic (working together) muscle groups like the pectorals (chest) or the deltoids (shoulders) or the triceps (back of arms). The synergistic format can be employed in two ways:

    (A)   Using the same muscle group and employing the same muscle areas and angles of exercise. This method is less efficient because all the muscles involved become progressively fatigued and, therefore, the weight that is used must be reduced.
    (B)   Using the same muscle group but employing different muscle areas and different angles of exercise.

The reasons for using the tri-set technique are:

(1)   To shock the muscle in order to stimulate growth. This is accomplished by increasing the total amount of work at an appropriate exercise intensity in a given time period. The total amount of work performed and the exercise intensity (% 1RM) will dictate the amount of stimulus to muscle growth not the specific exercise sequence.

(2)   To minimize the amount of time needed to train. The tri-set technique is nicely suited for training a combination of all the muscle groups especially when 3 different muscle groups are utilized. This allows performing more work in a given time period.

(3)   The tri-set technique is excellent for use to reduce body fat, to produce muscle definition and shaping, to increase local muscle endurance and produce some impact on general endurance.

(4)   The tri-set technique is an excellent method for introducing variation in the weight training program.

In tri-setting, one set of each exercise for three different muscles or synergistic muscle groups is performed in a successive non-stop fashion. A total of 3, 6 or 9 sets can be performed. In this case, 3 different exercises are performed for one set each so that each lap is equal to 3, 6 or 9 sets in a successive manner using the three separate exercises. Usually, 3 tri-sets are performed for each distinct muscle or muscle groups, although up to 5 tri-sets may be acceptable.

An example of a tri-set using different muscle groups is: One tri-set involves the execution of one set of the press exercise (1 set); followed by one set of pulldowns (1 set); followed by one set of the bench press (1 set) for a total of 3 sets. A second tri-set is equal the execution of another set of presses (1 set); followed by another set of pulldowns (1 set); followed by another set of bench presses (1 set) for a total of 6 sets. A third tri-set is equivalent to the execution of another set of presses (1 set); followed by another set of pulldowns (1 set); followed by another set of bench presses (1 set) for a total of nine sets. One set of each exercise is performed for 6 to 12 repetitions (could be to muscle failure) with 40% to 75% of 1RM. Depending upon one's level of conditioning and the objectives of the body building program, 1 to 3 laps of the tri-set could be performed. The very advanced body builder can perform 3-5 tri-sets. One lap (performing all three exercises in succession) is considered one tri-set. This example is shown in Table 4-29.

Table 4-29 contains an example of a tri-set program using different muscle groups. Table 4-30 includes an example of a tri-set program for the shoulders using the same muscle groups but various angles of exercise. Table 4-31 contains an example of a tri-set program for the chest using the same muscle groups and the same angles of exercise. In Table 4-32 is shown an example of a tri-set program for the hips and legs using three different angles of exercise.

Table 4-29.   An Example Of A Tri-Set Program Using Different Muscle Groups.

EXERCISE	REPETITIONS	INTENSITY	CIRCUITS
1. PRESS	6 -12 REPS	40% - 75% 1RM	
2. PULLDOWN	6 -12 REPS	40% - 75% 1RM	1 - 3 LAPS
3. BENCH PRESS	6 -12 REPS	40% - 75% 1RM	

*   1 LAP IS EQUIVALENT TO THE PERFORMANCE OF 1 SET OF THE 3 EXERCISES LISTED IN THE TABLE IN A NON-STOP FASHION AND IS CALLED ONE TRI-SET.

Table 4-30.   An Example Of A Tri-Set Program For The Shoulders Using The Same Muscle Groups But Various Angles of Exercise. *

EXERCISE	REPETITIONS	INTENSITY	CIRCUITS
1. LATERAL DELTOID	6 -12 REPS	40% - 75% 1RM	
2. PRESS BEHIND NECK	6 -12 REPS	40% - 75% 1RM	1 - 3 LAPS
3. UPRIGHT ROWING	6 -12 REPS	40% - 75% 1RM	

*   1 LAP IS EQUIVALENT TO THE PERFORMANCE OF 1 SET OF THE 3 EXERCISES LISTED IN THE TABLE IN A NON-STOP FASHION AND IS CALLED ONE TRI-SET.

PART IV

BODY BUILDING

Table 4-31. An Example Of A Tri-Set Program For The Chest Using The Same Muscle Groups And
          The Same Angles of Exercise. *

EXERCISE	REPETITIONS	INTENSITY	CIRCUITS
1. BENCH PRESS	6 -12 REPS	40% - 75% 1RM	
2. FLY	6 -12 REPS	40% - 75% 1RM	1 - 3 LAPS
3. DUMBBELL BENCH PRESS	6 -12 REPS	40% - 75% 1RM	

* 1 LAP IS EQUIVALENT TO THE PERFORMANCE OF 1 SET OF THE 3 EXERCISES LISTED
IN THE TABLE IN A NON-STOP FASHION AND IS CALLED ONE TRI-SET.

Table 4-32. An Example Of A Tri-Set Program For The Hips And Legs Using Three Different
          Angles of Exercise.*

EXERCISE	REPETITIONS	INTENSITY	CIRCUITS
1. SQUAT	6 -12 REPS	40% - 75% 1RM	
2. FRONT SQUAT	6 -12 REPS	40% - 75% 1RM	1 - 3 LAPS
3. LEG PRESS	6 -12 REPS	40% - 75% 1RM	

* 1 LAP IS EQUIVALENT TO THE PERFORMANCE OF 1 SET OF THE 3 EXERCISES LISTED
IN THE TABLE IN A NON-STOP FASHION AND IS CALLED ONE TRI-SET.

PART IV

BODY BUILDING

QUAD-SETS (INCLUDING 4 SYNERGISTIC MUSCLES OR MUSCLE GROUPS)

Quad-sets involve using 4 different exercises in sequence without rest between exercises. Quad-sets can be performed without rest between each quad-set or with a rest period between each quad-set sequence. The amount of rest will be dictated by the intensity (weight load) of the exercises involved in the quad-set and the conditioning level of the participant.

Quad-setting involves performing exercises that utilize four muscles or muscle groups in a non-stop procedure. In quad-setting one set of each exercise for four different muscles or the same muscle groups is performed in a successive non-stop fashion. A total of 4, 8 or 12 sets can be performed. In this case, 4 different exercises are performed for 4, 8 or 12 sets in a successive manner. Usually three quad-sets are performed for each distinct muscle or muscle groups, although up to five quad-sets may be acceptable.

An example of a quad-set program for the chest using the same muscle groups and different exercise angles is: One quad-set is equal to execution of a fly (1 set); an incline press (1 set); a bench press (1 set); a decline bench press (1 set) for a total of four different sets. A second quad-set is equal to execution of an another set of flys (1 set); an incline press (1 set); a bench press (1 set); a decline bench press (1 set) for a total of 8 sets. A third quad-set is equivalent to the execution of an another set of flys (1 set); an incline press (1 set); a bench press (1 set); a decline bench press (1 set) for a total of 12 sets.

One set of each exercise is performed for 6 to 12 repetitions (could be to muscle failure) using 40% to 75% of 1RM. Depending upon one's level of conditioning and the objectives of the body building program, 1 to 3 laps of the quad-set could be performed. The above example is shown in Table 4-33, which displays an example of a quad-set program for the chest using the same muscle groups and different exercise angles.

Quad-sets can be performed by:

(1) Using four different muscle groups. This is the best application of the quad-set technique.

(2) Using synergistic (working together) muscle groups like the pectorals (chest) or the deltoids (shoulders) or the triceps (back of arms). The synergistic format can be employed in two ways:

(A) Using the same muscle group and employing the same muscle areas and angles of exercise. **This application is best used in a low intensity phase of training, if at all.**
(B) Using the same muscle group but employing different muscle areas and different angles of exercise. **This is more realistic application of the quad-set technique when synergistic muscles are utilized and is best applied in the cutting, defining, shaping and body fat reduction training cycles.**

The reasons for using the quad-set technique are:

(1) To shock the muscle in order to stimulate growth. This is accomplished by increasing the total amount of work at an appropriate exercise intensity in a given time period. The total amount of work performed and the exercise intensity (% 1RM) will dictate the amount of stimulus to muscle growth not the specific exercise sequence.

(2) To minimize the amount of time needed to train. The quad-set technique is nicely suited for training a combination of muscle groups. This allows performing more work in a given time period.

(3) The quad-set technique is excellent for use to reduce body fat, produce muscle definition and increase local muscle endurance and has good impact on general endurance.

(4) The quad-set technique is an excellent method for introducing variation in the weight training program.

Table 4-33 contains and example of a quad-set program for the chest using the same muscle groups and different exercise angles. Table 4-34 displays an example of a quad-set program using four different muscle groups.

Table 4-33. An Example Of A Quad-Set Program For The Chest Using The Same Muscle Groups And Different Exercise Angles.*

EXERCISE	REPETITIONS	INTENSITY	CIRCUITS
1. FLY	6 -12 REPS	40% - 75% 1RM	
2. INCLINE PRESS	6 -12 REPS	40% - 75% 1RM	1 - 3 LAPS
3. BENCH PRESS	6 -12 REPS	40% - 75% 1RM	
4. DECLINE BENCH PRESS	6 -12 REPS	40% - 75% 1RM	

*   1 LAP IS EQUIVALENT TO THE PERFORMANCE OF 1 SET OF THE 4 EXERCISES LISTED IN THE TABLE IN A NON-STOP FASHION AND IS CALLED ONE QUAD-SET.

PART IV

BODY BUILDING

Table 4-34.   An Example Of A Quad-Set Program Using Four Different Muscle Groups.*

EXERCISE	REPETITIONS	INTENSITY	CIRCUITS
1. PRESS	6 -12 REPS	40% - 75% 1RM	
2. PULLDOWN	6 -12 REPS	40% - 75% 1RM	1 - 3 LAPS
3. BENCH PRESS	6 -12 REPS	40% - 75% 1RM	
4. CURLS	6 -12 REPS	40% - 75% 1RM	

*   1 LAP IS EQUIVALENT TO THE PERFORMANCE OF 1 SET OF THE 4 EXERCISES LISTED
    IN THE TABLE IN A NON-STOP FASHION AND IS CALLED ONE QUAD-SET.

GIANT-SETS (INCLUDING 5 OR MORE SYNERGISTIC MUSCLES OR DIFFERENT MUSCLE GROUPS)

Giant-sets involve using 5 or more different exercises in sequence without rest between exercises. This procedure is like a mini-circuit. Giant-sets can be performed without rest between each giant-set or with a rest period between giant-set sequences. The amount of rest will be dictated by the intensity (weight load) of the exercises involved in the giant-set and the conditioning level of the participant.

Giant-sets are for the very advanced weight trainer or body builder. It involves performing exercises that utilize five synergistic muscles or independent muscle groups or more in a non-stop procedure. One set of 6-12 repetitions (could be to muscle failure) are performed for each successive exercise with 40% -75% of 1RM.

An example of one giant-set for the quadriceps would be to perform one set of knee extensions (1 set), squats (1 set), leg presses (1 set), front squats (1 set) and inverted leg presses (1 set) for a total of 5 sets with five separate exercises which are performed in a consecutive fashion. The second giant-set using the same exercises would produce a total of 10 sets. A third giant-set using the same exercises would yield a total of 15 sets. Depending upon one's level of conditioning and the objectives of the weight training or body building program, 1 to 3 giant-sets could be performed with or without rest between each giant-set. The very advanced and highly motivated body builder could perform 4 to 5 giants sets.

A giant-set example is presented in Table 4-35 which emphasizes conditioning the quadriceps. Displayed in Table 4-36 is an example of a giant-set program for the shoulders employing exercises that use different angles of pull. Table 4-37 contains an example of a giant-set program for the abdominal muscle group employing exercise that use different angles of pull.

Giant-sets can be performed by:

(1) Using five or more different muscle groups. **This is the best application of the giant-set (mini-circuit) technique.**

(2) Using synergistic (working together) muscle groups like the pectorals (chest) or the deltoids (shoulders) or the triceps (back of arms). The synergistic format should be employed in one way, using the same muscle group but employing different muscle areas and different angles of exercise. **This pattern is probably not the best application of the giant-set technique.**

The reasons for using the giant-set technique are:

(1) To shock the muscle in order to stimulate growth. This is accomplished by increasing the total amount of work at an appropriate exercise intensity. The total amount of work performed and the exercise intensity (% 1RM) will dictate the amount of stimulus to muscle growth not the specific exercise sequence.

(2) To minimize the amount of time needed to train. The quad-set technique is nicely suited for training the most muscle groups. This results performing more work in a given time period.

(3) The quad-set technique is excellent for use to reduce body fat, produce muscle definition and increase local muscle endurance and has good impact on general endurance.

(4) The quad-set technique is an excellent method for introducing variation in the weight training program.

Table 4-35. An Example Of A Giant Set Program For The Legs Focusing On The Quadriceps. *

EXERCISE	REPETITIONS	INTENSITY	CIRCUITS
1. KNEE EXTENSION	6 -12 REPS	40% - 75% 1RM	
2. SQUATS	6 -12 REPS	40% - 75% 1RM	
3. LEG PRESS	6 -12 REPS	40% - 75% 1RM	1 - 3 LAPS
4. FRONT SQUAT	6 -12 REPS	40% - 75% 1RM	
5. INVERTED LEG PRESS	6 -12 REPS	40% - 75% 1RM	

*   1 LAP IS EQUIVALENT TO THE PERFORMANCE OF 1 SET OF THE 5 EXERCISES LISTED IN THE TABLE IN A NON-STOP FASHION AND IS CALLED ON GIANT-SET.

Table 4-36. An Example Of A Giant Set Program For The Shoulders Employing Exercises That Use Different Angles Of Pull.*

EXERCISE	REPETITIONS	INTENSITY	CIRCUITS
1. PRESS	6 -12 REPS	40% - 75% 1RM	
2. REVERSE FLY	6 -12 REPS	40% - 75% 1RM	
3. LATERAL RAISES	6 -12 REPS	40% - 75% 1RM	1 - 3 LAPS
4. FORWARD RAISES	6 -12 REPS	40% - 75% 1RM	
5. UPRIGHT ROW	6 -12 REPS	40% - 75% 1RM	

*   1 LAP IS EQUIVALENT TO THE PERFORMANCE OF 1 SET OF THE 5 EXERCISES LISTED IN THE TABLE IN A NON-STOP FASHION AND IS CALLED ONE GIANT-SET.

Table 4-37. An Example Of A Giant Set Program For The Abdominal Muscle Group Employing Exercises That Use Different Angles Of Pull. *

EXERCISE	REPETITIONS	INTENSITY	CIRCUITS
1. CRUNCH	6 -12 REPS	40% - 75% 1RM	
2. TWISTS	6 -12 REPS	40% - 75% 1RM	
3. LEG LIFTS (HIGH CHAIR)	6 -12 REPS	40% - 75% 1RM	1 - 3 LAPS
4. SIDE BENDS	6 -12 REPS	40% - 75% 1RM	
5. REVERSE CRUNCH	6 -12 REPS	40% - 75% 1RM	

*   1 LAP IS EQUIVALENT TO THE PERFORMANCE OF 1 SET OF THE 5 EXERCISES LISTED IN TABLE IN A NON-STOP FASHION AND IS CALLED ONE GIANT-SET.

BODY BUILDING   PART IV

PYRAMID TRAINING

Pyramid training offers a unique and interesting way to train. The main application for pyramid training is for peaking of strength or as a variation for the training program. A series of major exercises are defined in the body building routine for application for pyramid training. Each exercise is completed before moving to the next exercise. This technique is primarily used to train the central nervous system to recruit as many muscle fibers as possible in the performance of an exercise. **Due to the fact that it is not considered to be a conditioning program or a muscle mass enhancer and requires the use of very high intensities, pyramiding should only be used for short time periods of 1 to 4 weeks.** It is very easy to over-stress the total body systems and, therefore, slide into an over-trained state using the pyramiding system.

This technique could be used for all the major exercises in the body building routine but is not suited for the training of smaller muscle groups, such as the calf or forearm muscles. Also, it is not recommended that the abdominal or low back muscles be conditioned using this technique. It is not necessary to specifically stress the abdominal and low back muscle groups at very high intensities. They are more adequately stressed at high intensities in multiple joint complex exercises like squatting, dead lifting, high pulls, power cleans and power snatches. It is important that adequate specific warm-up be performed before using the procedure. It may also be of benefit to perform a set or two of eight to ten repetitions after using the pyramiding technique to maintain some muscle mass.

Pyramiding can be employed for the following reasons:

    (1) To train the central nervous system to recruit more motor units (more muscle fibers).
    (2) To increase strength without increasing muscle mass.
    (3) As a peaking routine during the competitive period for an athlete.
    (4) As a training diversion.

The pyramiding technique can be one of the following forms:

    (1) Ascending pyramid. The weight is increased and the repetitions are reduced.
    (2) Descending pyramid. The weight is decreased and the repetitions are increased.
    (3) Ascending/descending pyramid. The weight is increased and the repetitions are reduced until the maximum weight is lifted followed by the weight decreasing and the repetitions increasing in the succeeding sets until reaching the starting weight, or some arbitrarily selected weight or until exhaustion occurs.

As mentioned above, the ascending pyramid technique is employed for the training of the central nervous system (recruitment of motor units [more muscle]) by applying a progressive sequence of increasing the weight and reducing the repetitions during one specific exercise. This technique is used during the competition/peaking phase or to unload the person during the periodization of training.

Using the ascending pyramid technique will increase strength without increasing muscle mass. The length of time this technique should be used is between 2 to 4 weeks. Longer application of this technique leads to staleness and plateaus because it takes extremely large amounts of mental energy to use this technique. A thorough warmup is recommended before engaging in the ascending pyramiding technique.

The descending pyramid and the ascending/descending pyramid techniques are popular variations for the general weight trainer and body builders. Unfortunately, these techniques are used too much by most people who weight train. These should be applied infrequently and, in general, for no longer than four weeks. A thorough warmup is recommended before engaging in the descending or ascending/descending pyramiding technique.

Table 4-38 contains examples of ascending, descending and ascending/descending pyramid techniques for the bench press exercise. It is important that a proper warm-up be performed before using any of the pyramiding formats. It is especially important when using the descending pyramid format because this technique starts at a very high intensity and progressively decreases.

Table 4-38. Examples Of Ascending, Descending And Ascending/Descending Pyramids For The Bench Press Exercise.

ASCENDING			DESCENDING			ASCENDING - DESCENDING		
SET #	REPS	WEIGHT	SET #	REPS	WEIGHT	SET #	REPS	WEIGHT
1	12	135	1	1	235	1	10	155
2	10	155	2	2	225	2	8	175
3	8	175	3	4	210	3	6	195
4	6	195	4	6	195	4	4	210
5	4	210	5	8	175	5	2	225
6	2	225	6	10	155	6	1	235
7	1	235	7	12	135	7	4	210
						8	6	195
						9	8	175
						10	10	155

Body builders frequently employ a variation of the descending pyramid technique in conjunction with the regular training program. They call it **the multi-poundage system**. After the completion of the usual exercise prescription and without rest, some weight is removed from the bar and another set is performed until failure. This procedure is repeated for 1 to 5 sets.

Some body builders never go below a specified number of repetitions, between 3 to 6 repetitions. In this case, fewer and fewer muscle fibers are recruited because of the muscle fatigue produced by previous repetitions of the same exercise. No research exists to define just what physiological effects occur in the muscle when using this variation of pyramiding.

The use of this variation of descending pyramiding is thought to increase strength but any gains in the strength attribute would be very small. Regardless, there may be some hypertrophy because more total work has been performed. The probable net gain as a result of using this body building variation of descending pyramiding is an increase in local muscle endurance, some slight increase in muscle size and improvement of the metabolic apparatus (energy production enhanced).

The pyramiding technique and, all its variations, can be effective tools in the periodization of training. However, these techniques are not good methods of training to use over long periods of time and will result in overtraining and possibly injuries, if overused. The major benefits of using the pyramiding technique are to train the central nervous system to recruit more motor units and to provide variation in the training program. This technique requires great mental effort and it is doubtful if a high mental effort can be sustained over long time periods. Pyramiding is most useful for very short time periods during a peaking phase or as a short term training variation.

CIRCUIT WEIGHT TRAINING (CWT)

Circuit weight training is employed at the beginning of a training program or could be used in the cutting phase of a body builders program. It can also be used as a short term program for training variety. Some high level body builders have also used a very low intensity CWT program as a warm up for their regular training program. It can also be used as a flushing technique after the regular training has been completed.

PART IV

BODY BUILDING

The concept of CWT includes completing a series of ten exercises with weight resistance machines that systematically conditions all the major muscle groups. This provides for well balanced body conditioning and contouring. In the process of CWT a person would normally execute two to three laps around a ten station circuit in each training session. This translates into 20 exercise stations completed in 15 minutes and 30 exercise stations completed in 22.5 minutes. CWT can be biased for any physical fitness component; used with equipment or free exercise; and can be group or individually directed.

The load at each station can vary from 40% to 60% of one repetition maximum (1RM), but usually 50% of 1RM is used. The number of repetitions executed at each station should not be more than fifteen and generally no less than ten for general conditioning when using free weights or weight machines. The length of each exercise station is 30 seconds (10 to 15 repetitions) and the rest/rotate to next station time period is 15 seconds. In CWT where free exercises (calisthenics) are used instead of equipment, the repetitions performed can be as many as 25, depending upon the physical condition and training objectives.

A more complete understanding of CWT is presented in this book in Part II, General Fitness Training.

SUPER CIRCUIT WEIGHT TRAINING (SCWT)

Super circuit weight training can be employed for the same reason that regular CWT is employed. It can be used as a stand alone exercise entry or reentry program, as a training variation, as a warmup for regular training, as a flushing program for after regular training or as a training system during the cutting phase for body builders.

A series of 10 exercise stations working every major muscle group is performed. A person would normally execute 2 to 3 laps around this circuit in each training session. This means that there are 20-30 exercises performed on the weight machines or with free weights with an aerobic exercise used between weight stations. For each weight exercise station the work period is 30 seconds (10-15 repetitions) and the aerobic work period is 30 seconds.

The aerobic exercises could be running, cycling, stepping or free exercises. The time needed to perform 20 stations is 20 minutes and the time needed to perform 30 stations is 30 minutes. The load at each station can vary from 40% to 60% of one repetition maximum (1RM), but usually 50% of 1RM is used. The number of repetitions executed at each station should not be more that fifteen and, generally, no less than ten for general conditioning when using free weights or weight machines. In SCWT where free exercise is used instead of equipment, the repetitions performed can be as many as 25, depending upon the physical condition and training objectives.

A more complete understanding of SCWT is presented in this book in Part II, General Fitness Training.

PART IV

BODY BUILDING

PART V

THE ENCYCLOPEDIA OF WEIGHT TRAINING

Nutritional Support of Weight Training Programs for General Fitness, Sport and Body Building

NUTRITION PART V

PART V NUTRITION

THE ENCYCLOPEDIA OF WEIGHT TRAINING: WEIGHT TRAINING FOR GENERAL CONDITIONING, SPORT AND BODY BUILDING

PART V: NUTRITIONAL SUPPORT OF WEIGHT TRAINING PROGRAMS FOR GENERAL FITNESS, SPORT AND BODY BUILDING

TABLE OF CONTENTS — PART V

NUTRITION PART V

TABLE OF CONTENTS - PART V (CONTINUED)

TABLE OF CONTENTS - PART V (CONTINUED)

NUTRITION PART V

THE ENCYCLOPEDIA OF WEIGHT TRAINING: PART V

LIST OF TABLES

PART V

NUTRITION

LIST OF TABLES — PART V (CONTINUED)

NUTRITION PART V

PART V NUTRITION

PART V

NUTRITIONAL SUPPORT OF WEIGHT TRAINING PROGRAMS FOR GENERAL FITNESS, SPORT AND BODY BUILDING

INTRODUCTION AND HISTORICAL OVERVIEW

This part of the Encyclopedia will discuss concepts of nutrition, weight control and supplementation of nutritional substances that will enhance body building, sports training and performance and general fitness training.

In this age of "enlightenment", people cannot reject the basic nutritional principles. There is a vast amount of research as well as empirical evidence that can be used to form valid conclusions regarding nutrition. Nutrition is applied biochemistry. Hickson and Wolinsky (1989) have identified basic nutritional principles that apply to all people:

1. Each essential nutrient has a specific chemical structure and molecular configuration tailored to fit a precise metabolic pattern.

2. Each essential nutrient participates either as an enzyme, coenzyme, co-factor or substrate in the metabolic process.

3. All essential nutrients have the common characteristics of a vital role in health; a fundamental function in metabolism; a need met by comparatively small amounts; an inability to be formed or synthesized in the body in needed quantities; a relative lack of toxicity or capacity to do harm in physiologic amounts; and, in most instances, a deficiency-induced distinctive disease syndrome.

4. Nutritional imbalance may be provoked not only by a lack of proper food intake, but also by conditioning factors that interfere with digestion, absorption, and assimilation of food in persons consuming apparently adequate diets.

5. Excessive intake of some essential food factors will not compensate for others that may be in short supply.

6. Limited storage facilities in the body make nutritional replenishment of the tissues a daily task, tissue hunger a constant threat, and tissue breakdown an inevitable consequence of unfulfilled needs. When faced with nutritional impoverishment, cellular action is slowed or suspended, growth ceases, size is diminished, and shape altered. Built-in-stress-breakers and safety devices in the form of alternate metabolic pathways, reduced functional levels, and tissue redistribution of essential nutrients temporarily forestall nutritive failure.

7. Time is the prime factor in the development of malnutrition. Weeks, months, or even years may be required to deplete the tissues of particular nutrients or to manifest overt evidence of dietary excess.

Hickson, James and Wolinsky, Ira; Nutrition in Exercise and Sport; CRC Press; Boca Raton, Florida; 1989; P.P. 12.

People fall into two basic categories regarding nutrition and exercise: general fitness enthusiasts and athletes.

PART V

NUTRITION

First, there are the individuals who are concerned with general fitness, involving reduction of body fat, improvement of physical appearance and comprehensive health. Within this group there are many levels ranging from those people with casual interest and those individuals with a high interest who would do just about anything to improve their appearance and, to a lesser degree, their ability to perform. Then, there are those who try to control body weight (fat) by ineffective and sometimes dangerous dietary manipulation; and, finally, those who are obsessively addicted to exercise. The best strategy to reduce body fat in a general fitness program is a balanced approach including a sensible eating pattern with intelligent dietary supplementation, where needed, combined with the application of a scientific exercise program. The goals of such a strategy would be to reduce body fat, normalization of body curves and improved physical performance.

Athletes are the second category of people who are interested in nutrition and exercise. Because of the immense intrinsic motivation and the great pressure to win, athletes become very susceptible to nutrition faddism and addiction, in addition to invalid exotic physical training methods and erroneous technical strategies. Moreover, the athletic nutrition world suffers from hugh amounts of misinformation, numerous misconceptions and great amounts of misguided enthusiasm. Athletes are exposed to body building myths, quick energy myths, technical and nutritional performance enhancing myths, food myths and many dangerous misapplication of drugs.

Because of gullibility, ignorance or hope and the heightened desire to perform at high levels, athletes waste large amounts of money on worthless nutritional supplements. This is not to say that all nutritional supplements are inconsequential, but it is essential to make intelligent decisions about the use of nutritional supplements and to make sure that any supplements that are used have a scientific basis. Athletes must be able to evaluate the validity of the claims of unique nutritional practices and special supplementation products. To make sound judgements, athletes must acquire legitimate nutritional biochemical knowledge.

It is tempting to associate dietary modification or special supplementation with improved physical performance. However, increased physical performance may not have any correlation with special dietary practices or unique kinds of food supplementation. On the other hand, intelligent augmentation of the diet with valid nutritional products will enhance training levels leading to improved physical performance.

It is impossible to overestimate the importance of good nutrition to achieve and maintain excellent results from participation in exercise programs. It is a simple fact that the nutritional practices of individuals participating in exercises programs directly impacts the expected results of such programs. Many people do not experience good results from their exercise program primarily because of poor nutritional practices. Similarly, many people do not experience satisfying results of a high level nutritional program simply because they do not integrate a scientific exercise program. Furthermore, body builders and people training for general conditioning can retard the expected results of their exercise program because of poor nutritional practices.

Body fat reduction research and empirical observations have shown that diet alone does not produce long lasting weight (fat) loss. Crash Diets and Fad Diets are unbalanced. They can produce malnutrition and they may place stresses on the body that are destructive to health. Crash diets are not recommended. The combination of proper nutrition and exercise are the building blocks to produce lean, healthy, functional, vibrant and vigorous people.

Reliable statistics show that 50 million American men and 60 million American women are too fat and need to remove excess fat. Scientific weight reduction depends on maintaining a negative energy balance (a caloric intake which is less than energy expenditure) preferably based on the combination of both decreasing food intake while increasing energy expenditure through exercise and physical work. This means eat less calories than expended but maintain a balanced nutritional intake, eating proteins, carbohydrates and fats from the four basic food groups.

Every calorie that is consumed, over and above the body's need, either must be stored as fat or burned by additional exercise. This is an undeniable law of nature. People get fat from refusing to exercise enough and eating too much of any food: carbohydrate, fat or protein. If one is on a weight reduction program, every calorie eaten over those needed to attain the desired weight loss simply slows the progress and means that additional calories must be burned to achieve the desired results.

On the other hand, one may want to generate large amounts of muscle while training to improve sport performance or maximize muscle development by body building. How does one design a proper eating program with supplementation of various nutrients and substances that will enhance athletic training and performance or maximize lean body mass and reduction of body fat while body building or training for general fitness? This is accomplished by proper application of valid principles of nutrition combined with verified physical training principles that are found in this book.

There are no magic substances or sophisticated training programs that will instantly create a Mr. or Miss America or an Olympic athlete. Genetics for the most part, determines to a large degree what level of fitness, body building or athletics a person can attain. However, it is possible to achieve good results in performance, body building and/or general fitness by hard intelligent work and application of scientifically valid principles of training (work), rest and nutrition.

NUTRITIONAL QUACKERY

Despite the abundant support in the scientific literature for taking a variety of supplements, there are still many worthless nutritional products available in the marketplace. These worthless products fall into two basic categories: either the formulas are outdated and/or there is no real scientific basis for using some of the supplements. These products are marketed by deceitful entrepreneurs that hook the public with slick misleading advertisement based on false claims. This is a big problem and many people waste a lot of money purchasing these worthless products. Unfortunately, it seems that people who trust and hope in these useless nutritional products are usually the ones that are most sincerely interested in physical fitness, sport and body building. Their gullibility is driven by the genuine desire to maintain or acquire improved performance, aesthetic bodies and good health.

To optimize physical fitness, increase lean body mass with good fat reduction and improve physical performance capacity, it is important to learn as much as possible regarding nutritional products and their impact on growth, development and physical performance. An informed human has a better chance of avoiding being deceived, and, therefore an improved chance of making correct decisions when purchasing and using nutritional supplements.

Williams (1988) provides a series of questions that will help to distinguish nutritional quackery from valid scientific nutritional advice. Some of these questions are presented below with comment.

1. Does the nutritional product promise quick increases in physical performances? Nutritionally induced metabolic responses take time to produce noticeable effects. In no instances are metabolic responses immediately dramatic unless some drug is used.

2. Does the nutritional product contain some secret ingredient or formula? There are no secret or magical formulas.

3. Is the nutritional product advertised primarily by use of case histories or testimonials? Case histories and testimonials are not objective and frequently lead to many misinterpretations and misapplication of the facts. Scientific research is more reliable. Also, case histories and testimonial information are sometimes influenced by moneymaking interests.

4. Are currently popular star athletes used in the nutritional product's advertising? Famous spokespeople from various sports and the entertainment industry are not creditable and reliable sources of valid

PART V

NUTRITION

information. Many of these people have a large financial stake in the success of such products so there is a conflict of interest.

5. Does the advertising of such nutritional products take a simple truth about a nutrient and exaggerate its claims relative to physical performance? Most worthless nutritional products exaggerate the effects of using the product.

6. Does the nutritional product use the results of a single study or dated and poorly controlled research to support its claims? Single studies and poorly executed research are not reliable sources of information. They usually do not contain enough information to make valid judgments. Furthermore, many of these studies may be significantly flawed in the scientific design.

ADAPTED FROM: Williams, M.H.; Nutrition For Fitness and Sport; Wm. C. Brown Publishers; Dubuque, Iowa; 1988; p. 14.

It is always best to consult recognized authorities to evaluate the claims of nutritional products. A professionally trained nutritionist (R.D.), Registered Dietician or a Clinical Nutritionist with degrees from accredited Universities that have focused on physical performance and sport nutrition are good resources. **However, it is important to remember that those nutrition professionals who have not been specifically trained in sport and performance nutrition may not provide the correct information to the athlete, body builder and general fitness participant.** Therefore, one has to be very judicious and selective when seeking nutritional advice, even from those who are supposed to be experts.

In lieu of qualified sports nutritionists, a general nutritionist may substitute, but sometimes they are not up to date with current products, research, theory and especially application of nutritional principles and products to improve training and performance. It is important for the fitness enthusiast, athlete and body builder to educate themselves as much as possible with regard to performance nutrition and general nutrition. This is a difficult process which is never ending but will help one make the correct decisions regarding the use of nutrition supplements and practices.

It is important to realize that most registered dieticians and professionally trained nutritionists take a general position that is strongly anti-supplements. These professionals ignore preventive medicine research findings and are usually too conservative in their nutritional approach.

Books dealing with sports nutrition are good sources of valid sport nutrition information and guidance. However, it is important to check the credentials of the authors and the publishers as well as the accuracy of the related references used to support the concepts presented in the book.

There are many professional journals that provide factual and authoritative nutritional information. Some examples are:

1. Medicine and Science In Sport And Exercise; The American College Of Sports Medicine.
2. Sport Medicine; An International Journal of Applied Medicine and Science in Sport and Exercise; ADIS Press Limited, New Zealand.
3. The American Journal Of Clinical Nutrition.
4. The Physician and Sports Medicine.
5. The International Journal of Sports Medicine.

It is important for those interested in performance nutrition and general nutrition to search for valid and authoritative sources of information. The sources listed above are only a few of the many books, journals and publications that contain valid information concerning performance nutrition.

THE BASIC FOUR FOOD GROUPS

In 1958, the U.S. Department of Agriculture (USDA) devised the Four-Food-Group Plan. This plan was based on consuming a variety of foods. Foods are categorized into groups that provide similar nutrient contributions. The basic four food groups are: (1) dairy products; (2) meat, poultry, fish and high proteins; (3) vegetables and fruits; and, (4) grains and cereals. The basic guidelines for the Four-Food-Group Plan are presented in Table 5.1. The plan recommends the appropriate number of daily servings from each category to meet the requirement for adequate nutrition. Adequate nutrition is assured when the number of recommended servings are supplied from the variety in each group and when cooking and handling are proper.

Table 5.1 The Four-Food-Group Plan.

FOOD GROUPS	EXAMPLE	RECOMMENDED DAILY SERVING (c)
MILK & MILK PRODUCTS (a)	milk, cheese, ice cream, sour cream, yogurt, cottage cheese	2(e)
MEAT, POULTRY, FISH & HIGH PROTEINS (b)	beef, fish, poultry, eggs- with dried beans, peas, nuts, or peanut butter as alternatives	2
VEGETABLES & FRUITS (d)	dark green or yellow vegetables; citrus fruits or tomatoes	4
GRAINS & CEREALS	enriched breads, cereals, flour, baked goods, or whole-grain products	4

(a) If large quantities of milk are normally consumed, fortified skim (non-fat) milk should be substituted, to reduce the quantity of saturated fats.
(b) Fish, chicken and high protein vegetables contain significantly less saturated fats than other protein sources.
(c) A basic serving of meat or fish is usually 100 g or 3.5 oz of edible food; 1 cup (8 oz) milk; 1 oz cheese; ½ cup of fruit, vegetables, juice; 1 slice bread; ½ cup cooked cereal or 1 cup ready-to-eat cereal.
(d) One should be rich in vitamin C; at least one every other day rich in vitamin A.
(e) Children, teenagers, and pregnant and nursing women-4 servings.

NUTRITION PART V

THE EATING RIGHT PYRAMID

While the Four-Food-Group plan is a practical guideline for a daily eating pattern, it has been observed that this plan included to much fat from meats and milk products. Thirty-five years of research in cancer, heart disease and nutrition has demonstrated that high fat diets are a significant risk to one's health. To reflect this thinking the "Eating-Right Pyramid" concept has been developed by the USDA. The "Eating-Right Pyramid" maintains the concept of variety recommended in the Basic Four-Food-Group Plan, but places a greater emphasis on grains, vegetables and fruits. This plan places food into six categories: (1) fats, oils and sweets; (2) milk, yogurt and cheeses; (3) meat, poultry, fish, dry beans, eggs and nuts; (4) vegetables; (5) fruits; and, (6) bread, cereal, rice and pasta. The Eating-Right-Pyramid accentuates the eating of grains, vegetables and fruits. In addition, this plan reduces the amount of fats, dairy products and foods that are high in animal protein. Table 5.2 illustrates this new model for good nutrition as conceptualized by the USDA.

Table 5.2   The Eating-Right Pyramid: A Guide To Daily Food Choices.

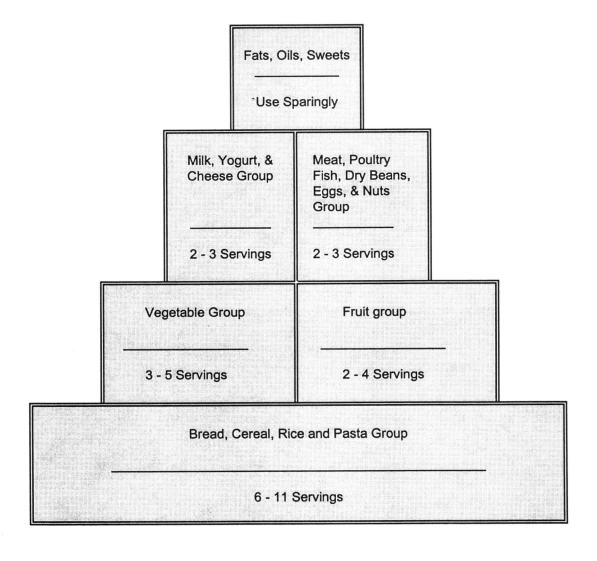

Whether you use the Basic Four Food Group Plan or the Eating Right Pyramid Plan, the nutrition program should consist of a **variety** of healthy foods which one normally eats. In addition, if weight reduction is desired, one should lower the caloric intake 500 calories per day and include 300 to 500 calories of exercise daily.

It is the number of calories and the caloric balance, not the type of food or the order in which it is eaten, that affects the accumulation of body weight (fat). There is no magic metabolic mixture that can be eaten to accelerate weight loss. Any diet claiming so is based on false premises.

Similarly, there is no magic metabolic mixture that can be eaten to produce functional weight gain (increase in muscle mass). Increased muscle mass is produced by appropriate weight training or body building programs, proper nutritional supplementation and adequate rest. If adequate protein is included in the diet then it is the amount of calories (presumably from carbohydrate) and the amount (volume) and intensity of the weight training program that determines the amount of lean mass gained.

There is no need for specialized foods. A reasonable combination of the foods normally eaten, including some from the basic four food groups or from the six categories included in the USDA Food Guide Pyramid in the recommended proportions, is prudent practice. Supplementation of vitamins, minerals, protein and other nutrients is a value and will discussed later in this section.

THE BASIC NUTRIENTS

The body requires six basic nutrients for operation: carbohydrates, protein, fats, vitamins, minerals and water. These nutrients have three major impacts on the human body: (1) They provide energy for metabolism; (2) They are responsible for growth, development, repair and building; and, (3) They regulate metabolism. Metabolism is the sum total of the chemical changes or reactions occurring in the body. Too much or too little of any of the basic nutrients will tend to produce health risks and will indeed inhibit physical performance or curtail the improvements desired from participation in physical training programs.

In addition to the six basic nutrients, fiber is also needed to facilitate movement of solids through the digestive tract. Fiber is fibrous substance that is contained in vegetables, grains and fruits which are resistant to human digestion. Diets that are high in fiber have been shown to reduce the incidence of colon cancer, diverticulosis and other intestinal disorders.

High fiber foods are vegetables, fruits and whole grains. Diets high in soluble fiber (oats, beans, dried peas and fruit) have demonstrated reductions in cholesterol levels in the blood which may protect against atherosclerosis and coronary artery disease. Table 5-3 displays the recommended percentages of calories from proteins, fats and carbohydrates in a well balanced diet.

Table 5-3. Recommended Percentages Of Calories From Proteins, Fats And Carbohydrates In A Well-Balanced Diet.

FOOD SOURCE	PERCENTAGE OF DAILY CALORIC INTAKE
PROTEIN	15% - 20% OF DAILY CALORIC INTAKE
FAT	20% - 30% OF DAILY CALORIC INTAKE
CARBOHYDRATES	50% - 60% OR MORE OF DAILY CALORIC INTAKE

PART V

NUTRITION

CARBOHYDRATES. Carbohydrates are the main source of fuel for the body when exercising. Also, the central nervous system operates almost exclusively on carbohydrates and people who deprive themselves of carbohydrates are actually starving the brain and nervous system. Furthermore, adequate intake of carbohydrates assists in maintaining tissue protein. A lack of adequate carbohydrates severely limits moderate to high intensity exercise as well as the functioning of the nervous system.

When carbohydrates reserves are reduced to low levels the body converts protein to carbohydrate. The daily diet should include at least 100 - 150 grams of carbohydrate to prevent the breakdown of protein. Carbohydrates have four (4) calories per gram.

Also, carbohydrates are needed to burn fat more efficiently. There must be enough carbohydrate present in the cell to provide substances for the breakdown for free fatty acids. When carbohydrate is depleted by exercise or limited because of low carbohydrate intake, there is limited utilization of free fatty acids. Fats will not be efficiently metabolized without an adequate supply of carbohydrate at the cell level.

Nutritionists often subdivide carbohydrates into two groups: (1) Natural or "complex" carbohydrates (the good guys); and (2) Processed or "refined" carbohydrates (the bad guys). The complex carbohydrates (foods as grown and unprocessed) consisting of fruits, vegetables and whole grain products are more desirable because they convert into blood sugar slowly providing energy over a longer time. Furthermore, complex carbohydrates promote glycogen storage better than refined carbohydrates. They are also a good source of vitamins, minerals and roughage needed for sound nutrition.

The refined carbohydrates are essentially empty calories, low in nutritional value and high in calories. They include sugar, sweets, soft drinks, white bread, sugary cereals, et cetera. Refined carbohydrates are converted into glucose rapidly causing blood sugar imbalances. These refined sugars enter the bloodstream very quickly but this energy supply is rapidly depleted. An excess consumption has been associated with many medical disorders ranging from tooth decay to diabetes and heart disease.

An excess of carbohydrates is converted to fat and stored in the fat cells. It is recommended that fifty (50%) to sixty (60%) percent or more of the daily caloric intake should come from carbohydrates; ideally unrefined complex carbohydrates.

There are some authorities that recommend a carbohydrate intake of more than 60% of the total caloric intake. For example, the Pritikin program suggests that as much as 80% of the caloric intake should consist of complex and unrefined carbohydrates, with 10% of the total calories provided by protein and 10% of the total calories coming from fat.

The Pritikin program is an extreme approach, never-the-less, it has produced some good results in lowering cholesterol levels, reducing body fat and reversing atherosclerosis - demonstrated with angiograms. For the average person with no manifestation of coronary heart disease or aggravated risk factors the Pritikin approach may be too spartan with the fat and protein content of this diet program too low. Data reported at the 1983 meeting of the American Heart Association (Dr. McGee) suggested that people with a diet containing less that 25% from fat had a higher risk for developing heart disease and cancer.

Pritikin, N.; The Pritikin Program For Diet And Exercise. New York,; Grosset and Dunlap; 1979.

PROTEIN. Protein contains many amino acids which are the basic building blocks for tissue maintenance, growth and repair. It makes up the cell membranes and nucleus as well as the hair, skin, nails, tendons, ligaments and muscles. Proteins are used in numerous metabolic reactions; the blood contains protein; and, amino acids are the basic building blocks for hormones and enzymes. Recent studies have shown that protein contributes to energy needed during exercise of long duration (10% to 15% of the total energy expenditure).

PART V   NUTRITION

Proteins are obtained from animal meats, vegetables, eggs and dairy products. A specific amino acid from any of these sources is equal in terms of quality. Twenty distinct amino acids are required by the body for operation and maintenance. A list of these amino acids appears in Table 5-4.

There are nine amino acids which cannot not be synthesized in the body which must be provided in the food eaten. These are called essential amino acids. A list of essential amino acids appear in Table 5-4. The classification and listing of amino acids in this table represent a simple scheme for better understanding of amino acid classification. Later in this section, under the topic of protein supplementation for athletes, body builders and active people, Table 5-24 presents a more precise biochemical classification of the amino acids in which biochemical interactions are taken into account.

Besides building muscle, some important roles that proteins play in the human body are:

1. They act as enzymes to speed up chemical reactions.
2. Help maintain water balance.
3. Help maintain acid base balance.
4. Confer resistance to disease.
5. Are hormones.
6. Carry nutrients into and out of cells.
7. Carry nutrients in the circulatory system.
8. Carry oxygen.
9. Are involved in blood clotting.
10. Help make scar tissue, bones and teeth.
11. Are part of vision.
12. Are used in growth and maintenance.

It is well known that muscle and liver protein is unstable and can be altered quickly and used for energy when unusual conditions exists; such as: severe trauma requiring immobility; inactivity; low carbohydrate or protein intake in the daily eating pattern (especially in body weight reduction diets) or when people remain sedentary while dieting to lose weight. The proteins in nervous and connective tissues appear not to be broken down for energy when carbohydrate is not available for fuel.

Non-essential amino acids number eleven and can be synthesized by the body from the essential amino acids when needed for body growth and maintenance. A list of nonessential amino acids is found in Table 5-4.

Table 5-4. Twenty Amino Acids That Are Necessary For Protein Synthesis In The Body.

ESSENTIAL AMINO ACIDS	NON-ESSENTIAL AMINO ACIDS
1. HISTIDINE (CHILDREN)	1. ALANINE
2. ISOLEUCINE	2. ARGININE
3. LEUCINE	3. ASPARAGINE
4. LYSINE	4. ASPARTIC ACID
5. METHIONINE	5. CYSTEINE
6. PHENYLALANINE	6. GLUTAMIC ACID
7. THREONINE	7. GLUTAMINE
8. TRYPTOPHAN	8. GLYCINE
9. VALINE	9. PROLINE
	10. SERINE
	11. TYROSINE

PART V

NUTRITION

Proteins that contain all the "essential" amino acids are known as **complete proteins** and are considered to be of high quality. Those proteins that lack one or more of the essential amino acids are known as **incomplete proteins** and are considered to be of lower quality. It is important to make sure that one's diet contain the essential amino acids to insure optimal nutrition, growth and development. If a single amino acid is not present in the correct amount, protein synthesis will be blocked. Furthermore, there is an infinite number of amino acid combinations allowing for an infinite number of protein designs for use in the body.

Protein from animals (meat and milk products), fish and poultry (meat and eggs) provide all the essential amino acids in the correct proportions for use in the body. Protein from eggs is considered to be the best protein source. Proteins from plant foods generally lack some essential amino acids in the quantities needed. However, proteins from various plants (grains and beans) can be can be combined in a way so that the proteins complement each other. In this way, amino acids may combine to form balanced proteins. It is possible to be a strict vegetarian, but only with great effort. Including milk products or eggs with a vegetarian diet is an easier approach to ensuring that all essential amino acids are available in the diet.

Any excess of protein is converted to fat and stored in the fat cells. For average people, fifteen (15%) to twenty (20%) percent of the daily caloric intake should come from protein. One gram of protein has the equivalent of 4 calories. **Research has shown that athletes, weight trainers, body builders and very physically active people may require from 1-3 grams of protein per kilogram (1 kg = 2.2 pounds) of body weight. This can also be expressed as .45 to 1.36 grams per pound of body weight. (Laritcheva [1978]; Lemon, et al [1984]; Lemon [1991]; Paul [1989]; & Tarnopolsky [1992]).**

---

1. **Laritcheva, K.A.; Yalovaaya, N.I.; Shubin, V.I. and P.V. Smirnov: Study of Energy Expenditure and Protein Needs of Top Weight Lifters: Parizkova, J. and Rogozkin, V.A.; Nutrition, Physical Fitness and Health; University Park Press, Baltimore, 1978; pp.155-163.**

2. **Lemon, P.; Yarasheski, K.E.; and Dolny, D.G.; The Importance of Protein For Athletes; Sports Medicine; November/December 1984; Vol 1, No. 6; pp.474-484.**

3. **Lemon, P.W.R., Effect of exercise on protein requirements. J. Sports Sci., 49: Special Issue, 53-70, 1991.**

4. **Paul, G., Dietary Protein Requirements of Physically Active Individuals, Sports Med., 8(3):154-176, 1989.**

5. **Tarnopolsky, M.A., Atkinson, S.A., MacDougall, J.D., et al., Evaluation of protein requirements for strength trained athletes. J. Appl. Physiol., 73(5):1986-1995, 1992.**

PART V

NUTRITION

FATS. Fat is the body's major source of energy and the main storage form of energy. The basic functions of fat are: (1) energy source for prolonged low to moderate intensity physical activities; (2) serves as cushion against mechanical shock and for protection of vital organs; (3) provides insulation from heat and cold; (4) acts as carriers of vitamins A, D, E and K; (5) provides structural material for many tissues.

The average American eats too much fat; between 30% and 40% of the total caloric intake. The recommended intake of fat is twenty (20%) percent to thirty (30%) percent of the total caloric intake, preferably most of it from unsaturated fat sources. Excessive fat intake has been associated with obesity, coronary artery disease and stroke. It is important to minimize the intake of fat in the diet at all age levels.

Fats are found in both plants and animals. All fat has 3500 calories per pound and one gram of fat has the equivalent of 9 calories. Fats can be classified into three main groups: simple fats, compound fats and derived fats. Each category is discussed below.

   A. **SIMPLE FATS:** Simple fats consist mainly of triglycerides. Triglycerides are the most abundant fat in the body and are the main storage form of fat in the body. Some authorities state that triglycerides make up 95% of the body fat. Simple fats are sub-categorized into saturated fatty acids and unsaturated fatty acids.

Saturated fats are solid at room temperature and are essentially found in animal meats, egg yolks, dairy products and shellfish. Coconut and palm oil, vegetable shortening and margarine are derived from plant sources and are considered saturated fats. The real difference between fats from animal and plant sources is that animal fats are more saturated and plant fats (oils) less saturated. Large amounts of ingested saturated fats have been linked to the development of vascular disease.

Unsaturated fats are from plant sources and are liquid at room temperature. Some examples of plant sources of unsaturated fats are: corn oil, safflower oil, olive oil, and peanut oil.

B. **COMPOUND FATS:** Compound fats are the combination of simple fats with other chemicals. There are two important compound fats: phospholipids and lipoproteins.

Phospholipids. Most of the phospholipids are formed in the liver, however, all cells formulate them. Phospholipids assist in the process of blood clotting and are a part of the insulating sheath surrounding the nerves and are an important part of the structure of the cell membrane.

Lipoproteins. The lipoproteins are formed in the liver where protein is combined with either triglycerides, phospholipids or cholesterol. The lipoproteins are the main form of transport for fat in the blood. There are high density lipoproteins (HDL), low density lipoproteins (LDL) and very low density lipoproteins (VLDL).

The **HDL** is considered good and is thought to be protective against heart disease in two ways: (1) It carries the cholesterol away from the wall of the arteries and takes it to the liver where it is degraded to bile and excreted through the intestines. (2) It competes with the LDL for entrance into the cells of the arterial walls and thus prevents fatty deposits from being formed.

The **LDL's** are the bad guys and elevated levels are thought to increase the risk of heart disease. The LDL's transport fat throughout the body where they deposit fat in the fat depots, including the walls of the arteries. Fat deposited in the arteries becomes involved in the process of atherosclerosis (narrowing of the arteries). Low saturated fat intake and low caloric intake may reduce the levels of the LDL's.

Exercise and moderate amounts of wine may increase the HDL level. According to the American Heart Association and the American College of Sports Medicine position papers, one should exercise for 20 minutes at least three times per week at 60% to 90% of maximal heart rate reserve to promote cardiovascular fitness and reduce LDL levels and increase HDL levels. Furthermore, data from exploratory research indicate that the vitamins C (1000 mg per day) (Herman, W., 1991) and E (600 mg per day) (Livesley, B., 1991) were able to increase HDL levels.

The minimal physical activity is 1,000 calories of energy expenditure per week for the development of a preventative level of HDL. According to a Harvard Alumni study, increases in energy expenditure beyond 2,000 calories per week (approximately the amount of energy expended in walking or running 20 miles) did not appreciably affect the risk of coronary heart disease. Most forms of physical activities result in HDL levels greater than those of sedentary control subjects.

PART V

NUTRITION

---

1.   Vitamin E; Herman, W. Dr.; Memorial City General Hospital; Houston, Texas; Quoted in Preventive Medicine Update; Volume 4: # 12; March, 1991.

2. **Vitamin C; Livesley, Brian Dr.; Clinical Gerontology; St. Francis Hospital; London, England; Quoted in Preventive Medicine Update; Volume 4: # 12; March, 1991.**

C. **DERIVED FATS:** Derived fats are substances that combine simple and compound fats. Cholesterol is the most widely known of the derived fats and is of primary concern in this discussion. Cholesterol is required for many sophisticated body functions including the synthesis of vitamin D, adrenal hormones, estrogens, androgens and progesterone. It also plays a big role in the formation of bile secretions that emulsify fat during digestion.

Cholesterol is present in all cells. It is synthesized within the cell (this type is endogenous cholesterol) or ingested with the food that is eaten (this type is known as exogenous cholesterol). It has been shown that severe dietary restriction of exogenous cholesterol is not damaging to one's health.

The sources of dietary cholesterol are found in foods of animal origin including egg yolks, organ meats such as liver, kidney and brains, shellfish (especially shrimp) and dairy products that have not had the fat removed. Cholesterol is not present in any foods from plants. It has a waxy consistency and is odorless.

Endogenous cholesterol production ranges from 500 mg to 2000 mg per day regardless of the magnitude of dietary (exogenous) cholesterol. The liver is the main producer for cholesterol although other tissues can synthesize this substance.

The National Cholesterol Education Program has established general guidelines for total blood cholesterol for people over 20 years of age. The information presented below includes suggested standards for total cholesterol levels. It should be noted that only a physician can evaluate the overall impact of total cholesterol on one's health. **Below are the general standards for cholesterol levels in the blood:**

Desirable Blood Cholesterol.................................. Less than 200 mg/dl
Borderline-High Blood Cholesterol........................ 200-239 mg/dl
High Blood Cholesterol.. 240 mg/dl and above

The American Heart Association makes the following recommendations with regard to controlling cholesterol in the body:

1. Cholesterol intake should not exceed 300 milligrams per day.
2. To reduce dietary cholesterol, limit the intake of meat, seafood and poultry to no more than 4-6 ounces per day.
3. Use not more than two egg yolks per week.
4. Limit the ingestion of shrimp, lobster and organ meats.

The National Cholesterol Education Program recommends the following strategies for lowering blood cholesterol:

1. Decrease the intake of saturated fat.
2. Increase the intake of soluble fiber.
3. Decrease the intake of cholesterol.
4. Increase the HDL level by exercise, quitting smoking and reducing body weight.

It is generally true that the lower the total cholesterol level, the less likely it is to have a heart attack. However, the total cholesterol, regardless of whether the level is high or low, does not give the complete picture regarding the risk of heart attack.

The total cholesterol is carried in high density fatty particles (named HDL-cholesterol), low density fatty particles (named LDL-cholesterol) and a small amount in very low density fatty particles (named VLDL-cholesterol with triglycerides). The higher the HDL-cholesterol level in the blood, the less likelihood of fatty cholesterol deposits in the arteries and a heart attack. The reason is that the HDL-cholesterol transports the cholesterol away from the walls of the arteries and moves it to the liver for destruction. Furthermore, HDL-cholesterol competes with the LDL-cholesterol for entrance into the cell walls of the arteries. Large amounts of HDL-cholesterol will prevent fat deposition in the arteries.

There is no distinct level of total cholesterol above which most deaths from heart disease occur. Rather, at levels above 180 mg/dl, the risk of cardiovascular diseases increases as the level of total cholesterol rises. However, just having a low total cholesterol level does not mean you have a decreased risk of having coronary heart disease. Conversely, having a high total cholesterol level does not mean that there is a high risk of having coronary heart disease independent of the influences of other risk factors. The reason is related to the amount of HDL-cholesterol. Cholesterol is not soluble in water, and hence it is not soluble in blood. The way that the body circumvents this problem is to transport cholesterol in a "package" that is soluble in water. This takes the form of lipoprotein, made up of fat (triglycerides), cholesterol and blood protein. Combining the blood protein with cholesterol makes it soluble in blood plasma which allows the body to transport to places where it is used or eliminated.

The size of these fatty-cholesterol particles has a lot to do with whether or not they will result in fatty-cholesterol deposits in the walls of arteries. The small particles have a high density and are called high density lipoproteins (HDL). The cholesterol carried in these packages is call HDL-cholesterol. The higher the level of HDL-cholesterol, the less likely one is to develop coronary heart disease.

Individuals who have HDL-cholesterol levels below 40 mg/dl have a increased risk of developing coronary heart disease even if the total cholesterol level is below 200 mg/dl. That helps explain the many cases in which the total cholesterol level is really quite low, yet coronary artery disease develops. Apparently, at HDL-cholesterol levels below 40 mg/dl there is significant deposition of fat in the arteries.

In contrast, those individuals with a high total cholesterol level of 260 mg/dl or more, but who also have HDL-cholesterol levels of 60 mg/dl or more, have a low risk of developing coronary heart disease. In other words, a total cholesterol level alone is not adequate to assess the real risk of heart attack or stroke.

A critical review of the cholesterol by Smith (1991) contends that much of the cholesterol data are either incorrect or blown out of proportion. Smith's statements seem to be at odds with the conventional wisdom of the prevailing medical authorities.

Table 5-5, 5-6, 5-7, 5-8 and 5-9 contains guidelines for blood levels of triglycerides, HDL, LDL, total cholesterol and various total cholesterol/HDL ratios with appropriate coronary risks. These components make up the lipid profile which can be determined by the analysis of a blood sample. The lipid profile analysis is performed by a physician who obtains a blood sample with subsequent analysis by a qualified testing laboratory. The interpretation of test results and control of any excessive amounts of blood lipids should be under the direct management of a qualified physician. However, sufficient exercise and healthy nutritional habits have been shown to effectively lower all of the blood lipids.

1. The Health Letter, Volume 29, No. 5, March, 1987.

2. McArdle, W.D.; Katch, F.I.; Katch, V.L.: Exercise Physiology: Energy, Nutrition and Human Performance; Lea And Febiger; Philadelphia; Third Edition; 1991; pp. 19-27.

3. Smith, Russell L.; The Cholesterol Conspiracy; Warren H. Green Publisher; St. Louis, Missouri; 1991.

NUTRITION   PART V

Table 5-5.   Coronary Risk Values For Total Cholesterol In Males And Females.

CHOLESTEROL	CLASSIFICATION FOR AGE 20+ YEARS
< 200 MG/DL	DESIRABLE BLOOD CHOLESTEROL
200 - 239 MG/DL	BORDERLINE HIGH BLOOD CHOLESTEROL
> 240 MG/DL	HIGH BLOOD CHOLESTEROL
DATA BASED ON N.I.H. CONSENSUS DEVELOPMENT CONFERENCE J.A.M.A. (1985) 253, 2080 AND NATIONAL CHOLESTEROL EDUCATION PROGRAM.	

Table 5-6.   Coronary Risk Values For Fasting Triglyceride Levels In Males And Females.

INCREASED RISK	AGE
> 126 MG/DL	15 - 19
> 140 MG/DL	19 - 29
> 150 MG/DL	30 -39
> 160 MG/DL	40 -49
> 190 MG/DL	> 49
DATA BASED ON N.I.H. CONSENSUS DEVELOPMENT CONFERENCE J.A.M.A. (1985) 253, 2080 AND NATIONAL CHOLESTEROL EDUCATION PROGRAM.	

Table 5-7.   Coronary Risk Values For HDL Cholesterol Levels In Males And Females.

CORONARY RISK	MALES	FEMALES
DECREASED RISK	> 45 MG/DL	> 55 MG/DL
AVERAGE RISK	45 MG/DL	55 MG/DL
INCREASED RISK	< 45 MG/DL	< 55 MG/DL
SMITHKLINE BIO-SCIENCE LABORATORIES, VAN NUYS, CALIFORNIA, 12/11/90.		

PART V

NUTRITION

Table 5-8.   Coronary Risk Values For LDL Cholesterol Levels In Males And Females.

CORONARY RISK	CLASSIFICATION FOR AGE 20+ YEARS
130 MG/DL & LOWER	DESIRABLE LDL LEVEL
130 - 159 MG/DL	BORDERLINE HIGH RISK
160 MG/DL & ABOVE	HIGH RISK LDL CHOLESTEROL
SMITHKLINE BIO-SCIENCE LABORATORIES, VAN NUYS, CALIFORNIA 12/11/90	

Table 5-9.   Coronary Risk Values For Total Cholesterol/HDL Ratios In Males And Females.

CORONARY RISK	CHOLESTEROL/HDL MALE RATIOS	CHOLESTEROL/HDL FEMALE RATIOS
1/2 AVERAGE RISK	3.4	3.3
AVERAGE RISK	5.0	4.4
2 X AVERAGE RISK	9.6	7.1
3 X AVERAGE RISK	23.0	11.0
1. A LOWER RATIO IS DESIRABLE.		
2. DATA BASED ON FRAMINGHAM STUDY, SMITHKLINE BIO-SCIENCE LABORATORIES, VAN NUYS, CALIFORNIA 12/11/90.		

VITAMINS: Vitamins regulate metabolism, facilitate energy release and play an important role in bone and tissue building. Vitamins do not supply energy, but are involved in energy metabolism. Vitamins can be obtained from food or from a daily vitamin pill. Vitamins are classified as: fat soluble which include A, D, E and K; and water soluble which include C and the B-complex. It is thought that a balanced diet alone contains sufficient vitamins, although there are some experts that claim that even the so-called balanced diet does not contain adequate vitamins. (See references 1 and 2 below) It is recommended that one contact a physician or qualified nutritionist for guidance regarding vitamin supplementation. A general discussion of vitamins appears later in this section under the title of vitamin and mineral supplementation.

MINERALS: Minerals are found in meats and vegetables that are eaten. The primary role of minerals is in cellular metabolism where they act as enzymes to regulate chemical reactions in the cells. Minerals are also important in muscle contraction and the development of hormones. It is thought that a balanced diet includes an adequate mineral supply, however there are some experts that claim that even a balanced diet does not contain adequate amounts of minerals. (Kugler, 1991) It is recommended that one contact a physician or qualified nutritionist for guidance regarding mineral supplementation. A general discussion of minerals appears later in this section under the title of vitamin and mineral supplementation.

1. **Cheraskin, E.; Ringsdorf, W. and Medford, F.; The Ideal Daily Vitamin E Intake; International Journal For Vitamin and Nutrition Research; 1:58-60; 1976.**

2. **Reference for ODR: Kugler, Hans; Editor; Preventive Medicine Update; Vol 4; # 2; March, 1991.**

WATER: Humans cannot live without water. One should drink 8 - 10 glasses or intake a little more than 2 quarts of water per day including all that is contained in the food eaten and the fluid drunk. About 60% of the body weight is water. Water is needed for all processes in the body and very important for temperature regulation,

PART V

NUTRITION

especially while exercising. In vigorous exercise, especially in high temperatures and humidity, water replacement is the most important action to be taken by the exerciser.

FIBER: Fiber is not a nutrient and is included here for purposes of convenience. Fiber supplies bulk for digestion and elimination. The dietary fiber is provided by the fruits, vegetables and whole grain products that are eaten. Fiber is that part of the fruits, vegetables and whole grains that are resistant to digestive enzymes and serves as bulk to move waste products quickly through the digestive tract. Fiber is water soluble and water insoluble. Whole wheat products include more of the water insoluble fiber which increases the bulk in the digestive track. This maximizes the dilutant effect and increases the speed of movement through the intestinal track. Water soluble fiber include beans and oat bran and have a more binding effect and are thought to lower serum cholesterol. The average American has a fiber intake of 18-20 grams per day. The National Cancer Institute recommends 25-40 grams of fiber per day.

ENERGY SOURCES

The body uses food in two ways: (1) as a source of fuel for body heat, metabolism, muscular activity and work; and, (2) as a source of nutrients for continual repair and maintenance of all tissues. All foods can be used as a fuel for energy but no one food provides all the nutrients needed by the body. Therefore, one needs a balanced diet of different foods.

Carbohydrates, fats, and sometimes, proteins that are eaten are converted to ATP (fuel for metabolic processes and muscle contraction) to provide energy needed for metabolism, activity and repair. The kinds of foods that one eats not only will affect the results that can be attained in a physical training program, but, also, over-all health and vitality. Furthermore, it is important to limit the total number of calories eaten and eliminate the junk food, if one's goal is to lose body fat. During the process of losing body fat the body more than ever needs a balanced diet with a full range of nutrients, while at the same time intelligently restricting caloric intake and increasing energy expenditure with exercise.

If the goal is body building or a superior sports performance, good nutritional eating patterns are very important. Moreover, it may be important to consider vitamin and mineral supplementation along with ingestion of various metabolic optimizers (supplements that aid in energy metabolism and facilitate recovery from training), amino acids and naturally occurring anabolic substances that support high level training.

The body uses three food substances for fuel: carbohydrates, fats and proteins. The intensity of the activity will dictate to a large degree which of these fuels are utilized for a specific activity. Furthermore, the body prefers to utilized just carbohydrates and fats for fuels in exercise. However, when the need arises, muscle protein can converted to carbohydrate by a process called gluconeogenesis. The greatest protein breakdown results when carbohydrate (glycogen) stores are low. When people engage in vigorous physical activity at any level it is important to maintain a high carbohydrate intake to preserve muscle protein.

THE THREE BASIC ENERGY SYSTEMS

There are three basic energy systems that supply fuel (ATP) for exercise: (1) **The ATP-PC system** - the stored quick energy; (2) **Anaerobic Glycolysis**; and, (3) **The oxygen (aerobic) system** which includes **aerobic glycolysis** and **fatty acid oxidation.** As mentioned above, the intensity of the activity controls which energy system will produce the predominate amount of energy (ATP) for exercise. However, at any instant, all energy systems are working concurrently in an integrated manner to supply energy required for activity and life itself.

THE PHOSPHAGEN SYSTEM (ATP-PC): ATP (adenosine triphosphate) and PC (phosphocreatine) are stored in the muscle cells to supply the immediate energy for muscle contractions. The amount of ATP-PC stored in the muscle cells can only sustain the energy requirements in maximal muscle contractions for a few seconds (approximately 6 - 10 seconds). **This energy source supplies the energy for very high intensity and short term speed and explosion activities.**

Examples of movements of short duration and very high intensity are jumping, sprinting, swinging, kicking, individual skills of various positions in team sports, weight lifting (1-3 reps) and like actions. All of these activities are energy dependent upon the stored ATP-PC in the muscle cells. ATP-PC stores are rapidly depleted but are also very quickly restored. Training the ATP-PC system requires repeated efforts of very high intensity with rest periods of 30 seconds to 120 seconds (.5 minutes to 2 minutes). The repetition of maximum performances requires longer periods of rest. The ATP-PC stores can be significantly increased by specific very high intensity training programs and creatine supplementation.

ANAEROBIC GLYCOLYSIS: Anaerobic glycolysis is the breakdown of carbohydrates (glycogen) in the absence of oxygen. Glycogen in the active muscle fibers is broken down to provide ATP for muscle contraction in the absence of oxygen producing the metabolic by-product lactic acid. **This energy source supplies the energy for high intensity and short duration activities.** The utilization of anaerobic glycolysis ranges from 30 seconds to 180 seconds (.5 minutes to 3 minutes).

Examples of physical activities requiring the use of this energy system are running 300 meters through 800 meters, the sprint at the end of a mile of 1500 meter race, gymnastic routines, wrestling (2 minute periods), boxing (3 minute rounds), 100 meter through 200 meter swims and team sports. All these activities are essentially reliant upon the energy supplied by anaerobic glycolysis.

The limiting factor in high intensity short duration performance is the accumulation of lactic acid. A large accumulation of lactic acid is responsible for muscle fatigue and the amount of energy that can be supplied is rather limited. In exhaustive performance lactic acid removal is best accomplished by performing low intensity exercise for about 10 to 20 minutes.

Anaerobic glycolysis can best be trained by performing some type of interval training specific to the time requirements of the activity for which one is training. This energy system can be effectively trained by repeated repetitions of 30 seconds to 180 seconds (.5 minutes to 3 minutes) followed by an active rest period of ranging from 1 to 5 minutes. Usually the more intense the repetition the longer the rest period should be.

Training the anaerobic glycolysis system produces:

1. Increases in the resting levels of ATP, PC and glycogen.
2. Increases in the quality and activity of key enzymes that control anaerobic glycolysis.
3. Increases in the ability to tolerate higher levels of lactic acid during high intensity and short duration activities.
4. Maximal increases in the strength of heart contractions which result in pumping more blood with every heart beat.

THE OXYGEN (AEROBIC) SYSTEM: This system uses glycogen and fats (free fatty acids) to produce large amounts of ATP without producing fatiguing by-products (lactic acid). In a normal state of nutrition and adequate physical fitness the human can perform large quantities of aerobic work. **The aerobic system supplies the energy for low intensity and long duration physical activities.**

Examples of physical activities that require the use of this energy system are extended climbing, walking, running, swimming, cross country skiing, biking and other like low intensity and long duration exercises.

Aerobic glycolysis is the breakdown of carbohydrate (glycogen) in the mitochondria (the aerobic energy producing mechanism for the cells) in the presence of adequate supplies of oxygen. This process is limited by the amount of oxygen that is delivered to the active muscle cells. Aerobic glycolysis occurs

PART V

NUTRITION

only at low exercise intensities. If the exercise intensity increases to a level where the oxygen supply cannot match the need there is an unrelenting accumulation of lactic acid which leads to fatigue. Too much lactic acid will produce drastic lowering of exercise intensity. Aerobic glycolysis is used in activities that are at the upper levels of low intensity and long duration work that extends past 3 minutes.

Fatty acid oxidation is the metabolism of free fatty acids to produce large quantities of ATP in active muscle cells. This process also transpires in the mitochondria of the active muscle cells. This process requires a endless supply of oxygen just like aerobic metabolism of glycogen (aerobic glycolysis). Free fatty acid utilization as a fuel occurs only at very low intensity levels of physical activity performed for 20 minutes or more.

Both glucose and fatty acids are used for energy when the body is at rest with the ATP being produced aerobically. The supply of oxygen easily meets the demand because of the very low level of energy metabolism. As one begins to exercise the requirement for oxygen becomes difficult to meet. Since glycogen utilization requires less oxygen than fatty acid metabolism the working muscles will employ more glycogen for energy production and lower amounts of fat as the intensity of exercise increases. To maximize the utilization of fat in the energy production process in exercise, low intensity exercise of long duration is required. As aerobic exercise intensity increases the chief fuel source for aerobic energy metabolism is glycogen.

The aerobic energy system can be conditioned by using interval training, continuous training (long slow distance) or Fartlek training (speedplay). Any type of physical activity can utilize these forms of training to condition the aerobic energy system. Training produces many physiological changes. A few of them appear in a generalized list below:

1. Improvement in the function of the heart.
2. Positive blood vessel and blood chemistry changes. This is manifested by reduced blood pressure, increased blood supply to muscles and heart, improved blood lipid (fat) profile, more efficient exchange of oxygen and carbon dioxide and increased blood volume.
3. Improved respiratory function.
4. Increased neural, endocrine (hormone) and metabolic functioning.

Table 5-10 displays the anaerobic and aerobic systems of ATP (energy) production. This table includes the activity category, the performance time and the respective major energy system utilized.

Table 5-10. Anaerobic And Aerobic Systems Of ATP (Energy) Production.

PHASE	MAJOR ENERGY SYSTEM USED	PERFORMANCE TIME	ACTIVITY CATEGORY
I	PHOSPHAGEN SYSTEM (ATP-PC)	1 SECOND - 10 SECONDS	VERY HIGH INTENSITY SHORT TERM SPEED AND EXPLOSION ACTIVITIES
II	ANAEROBIC GLYCOLYSIS (LACTIC ACID)	.5 MINUTE - 3 MINUTES	HIGH INTENSITY SHORT DURATION ACTIVITIES
III	AEROBIC GLYCOLYSIS	3 MINUTES PLUS	LOWER INTENSITY LONGER DURATION ENDURANCE
IV	FATTY ACID OXIDATION (AEROBIC)	20 MINUTES PLUS	LOWER INTENSITY LONGER DURATION ENDURANCE ACTIVITIES

PART V

NUTRITION

THE ENERGY CONTINUUM SCHEME

The three basic energy systems can be visualized as existing on a horizontal line with the phosphagen system at one end and the oxygen (aerobic) system on the opposite end. Anaerobic glycolysis is in the middle. This concept is illustrated vividly by relating the energy usage to running events in Track. On one end of the continuum is found the 100 meter sprint which is categorized as a short term very high intensity activity in which the total energy requirement is produced by the phosphagen system. On the opposite end is marathon running which is classified as long term and low intensity activity that is almost exclusively supplied with energy by the oxygen (aerobic) system. In the middle are the 400 and 800 meter dashes which are ranked as high intensity activities and the energy is supplied predominately by anaerobic glycolysis.

While the body derives energy from three separate energy making processes none of them operates alone. Each energy system supplies a percentage of the total energy needed to perform a specific activity. As intensity and duration varies the relative percentage of each system contribution changes. High intensity and short term activities receive most of their energy from the phosphagen system while only minuscule amounts are supplied by the oxygen system. On the other hand, low intensity long duration activities receive 99 percent of their energy from the aerobic system and 1 percent from the anaerobic system. Activities of intermediate intensities and durations have receive varying percentages from the anaerobic and aerobic energy systems.

For very short work durations (up to 10 seconds) and extremely high work outputs, the body uses stored levels of high energy phosphates and adenosine triphosphate (ATP). There is a relatively small amount of this energy source available for use in the muscle, and fortunately, it is re-synthesized rather quickly (usually within one to two minutes) when the body is in recovery and rest.

Carbohydrates (glycogen) are utilized for short term very intense activity. For low intensity activity and long duration work (over 20 minutes of sustained activity), **free fatty acids** are the main source of fuel. A **combination of carbohydrates and free fatty acids** provide energy for intermediate intensities and intermediate time periods.

Table 5-11 exhibits the four phases of the energy continuum. This table contains the different phases of energy use, the corresponding performance times, the major energy system used and specific exercise examples. **Careful examination of the this table demonstrates the overlapping of the energy systems.**

Table 5-11.   The Four Phases Of The Energy Continuum.

PHASE	PERFORMANCE TIMES	MAJOR ENERGY SYSTEM USED	EXAMPLES
I	0 - 30 SEC	PHOSPHAGEN (ATP-PC)	SHOTPUT, WEIGHT LIFTING, 100M,
II	30 - 90 SEC	ATP-PC AND LACTIC ACID	300M - 400M SPRINT, 100M SWIM
III	90 - 180 SEC	LACTIC ACID AND AEROBIC SYSTEM	800M RUN, WRESTLING (2'), GYMNASTICS, BOXING (3'), TEAM SPORTS
IV	BEYOND 180 SEC	AEROBIC SYSTEM	EXTENDED RUN, SWIM, BIKE, WALK

PART V

NUTRITION

Adapted and modified from Fox, Edward: Sports Physiology; Saunders College Publishing; N.Y.: 1984, p. 35.

Phase 1 involves the ATP-PC energy system. The letters ATP-PC represent adenosine triphosphate - phosphocreatine which is a high energy compound stored in the muscles cells. It is the major form of energy available for immediate use in the muscles for short-term and very high-intensity exercise. It is the predominant energy source for activities ranging from 0 to 30 seconds (.5 minute).

Phase 2 involves both the ATP-PC and the lactic acid energy systems. The lactic acid system is an anaerobic (without oxygen) energy system in which ATP is manufactured when carbohydrate is broken down to lactic acid. Lactic acid is a fatiguing metabolite of the lactic acid system resulting from the incomplete breakdown of carbohydrate. High intensity efforts requiring 1 to 3 minutes to perform, extract energy (ATP) primarily from this system. If the circulatory system cannot remove lactic acid faster than it is formed it begins to accumulate. This produces temporary muscular fatigue which is manifested as "the burn" that is felt in the muscles involved in an effort. This phase involves physical activities performed at high intensities that range from 30 - 90 seconds (.5 to 1.5 minutes).

Phase 3 is a combination of using the lactic acid (anaerobic glycolysis) and oxygen (aerobic glycolysis and fatty acid oxidation) energy systems. This phase includes physical activities that extend from 90 to 180 seconds (1.5 to 3 minutes).

Phase 4 includes those physical activities that require performance times that are longer than 180 seconds (3 minutes). The oxygen system supplies most of the energy utilized in these long duration and low intensity physical activities.

HOW MUCH OR HOW LITTLE SHOULD ONE EAT?

To optimize one's nutritional state it is necessary to first determine how much or how little one should eat. In order to remain at one's present body weight requires approximately 15 calories per pound per day. This is not an absolute number, but merely an estimate to establish a starting point for daily caloric need. To determine how many calories that are necessary to consume to maintain one's present body weight, multiply body weight by the factor 15. The resulting number represents the number of calories needed to consume in order to maintain one's present body weight.

Various numbers can be used when computing the estimate of how many calories should be eaten per day depending upon the activity level or the goal for reduction of body weight. These estimates are not absolutes and are just guidelines. The numbers derived from this computation may underestimate or overestimate the actual daily caloric need. Because of individual biological differences, one may need to use a higher or lower factor (number) to get a more precise estimate of daily caloric need. This may take some experimentation to accurately estimate the daily caloric intake necessary to correspond with the body weight goal.

Table 5-12 contains activity levels and the corresponding calorie factor for multiplication.

PART V

NUTRITION

Table 5-12. Levels Of Activity And Calorie Factors That Can Be Used To Estimate The Needed
             Daily Caloric Intake.

LEVEL OF ACTIVITY	CALORIE FACTOR*
SEDENTARY	12 - 14
MODERATELY ACTIVE	15 - 17
HIGHLY ACTIVE	18 & ABOVE

*** MULTIPLY THIS NUMBER BY BODY WEIGHT
TO ESTIMATE THE DAILY CALORIC NEED.**

Ward, Paul; Nutritional Guidance Program; Health And Tennis Corporation Of America; 1987; p. 5.

To reduce body weight one must reduce the caloric intake below what is estimated for the present body weight.
Also, adjustments should be made for age; one calorie less per pound per day should be used for each 10 year
period over 30 years of age. Some example calculations are presented below:

1. **Female Under 30 years of age:**   116 Lbs. X 15 = 1,740 calories per day.
2. **Female 31 to 40 years of age:**   116 Lbs. X 14 = 1,624 calories per day.
3. **Female 41 to 50 years of age:**   116 Lbs. X 13 = 1,508 calories per day.

Table 5-13 contains methods for determining daily caloric need for ideal body weight and daily caloric need for
present body weight.

Table 5-13.   Daily Caloric Need For Ideal Body Weight And For Present Body Weight For The Moderately
              Active Person.

> **A. Daily Caloric Need For Ideal Body Weight* Can Be Computed By:**
> **Daily Caloric Need** = Ideal Body Weight X 15 = _____ X 15 = _____
> **Daily Caloric Need** = _____ Calories Per Day.
>
> *** Ideal Body Weight** should be determined by a body composition analysis or
> it could be a reasonable arbitrarily selected body weight.
>
> **B. Daily Caloric Need For Present Body Weight Can Be Computed By:**
> **Daily Caloric Need** = Present Body Weight X 15 = _____ X 15 = _____
> **Daily Caloric Need** = _____ Calories Per Day.

Sometimes it is helpful to compare estimates of energy needs from other authoritative sources like that listed
below to make sure the estimate is reasonable. Table 5-14 contains the 1980 standards published by the Food
and Nutrition Board of the National Academy of Sciences - National Research Council.

PART V

NUTRITION

Table 5-14.   1980 Standards For Range of Recommended Energy Intake For Males And Females Of
              Selected Ages, Heights and Weights.

CATEGORY	AGE	WEIGHT (LBS)	HEIGHT (IN)	ENERGY NEEDS (CALORIE RANGE)
MALES	15 - 18	145	69	2100 - 3900
	19 - 22	154	70	2500 - 3300
	23 - 50	154	70	2300 - 3100
	51 - 75	154	70	2000 - 2800
FEMALES	15 - 18	101	62	1200 - 3000
	19 - 22	120	64	1700 - 2500
	23 - 50	120	64	1600 - 2400
	51 - 75	120	64	1400 - 2200

Adapted from: Recommended Dietary Allowances, Revised 1980. Food and Nutrition Board National Academy of Sciences - National Research Council, Washington, D.C.

PHYSIOLOGY OF WEIGHT (FAT) LOSS

Humans who have a consistent high level of physical activity do not accumulate body fat. This outcome is rarely accomplished in the world today. Modern people just are not active enough in contemporary society and therefore accumulate body fat. Once the body fat has accumulated, it takes a lot of effort, dedication, motivation and perspiration to remove.

The best way to stay lean is to maintain an high activity level and learn as much as possible about the physiology of fat accumulation and exercise metabolism. Below is listed some general information regarding the physiology of weight (fat) loss.

1. One calorie is the energy needed to raise the temperature of one Kilogram (2.2 pounds) (slightly more that a quart) of water one degree centigrade.
2. Fat provides energy that is needed between meals and during low intensity prolonged exercise.
3. Fat is more concentrated than protein or carbohydrate. It contains 2 1/4 times more energy per unit of weight.
4. Fat contains 9 calories per gram; protein contains 4 calories per gram; carbohydrate contains 4 calories per gram; alcohol contains 7 calories per gram.
5. One pound of fat contains 3500 calories.
6. There are three basic food sources needed by the human body: carbohydrate, fat and protein. The body prefers to use carbohydrates and fats for fuel in exercise. Protein is primarily used for tissue building, maintenance and repair except when no carbohydrates are available. In this case body protein is converted to carbohydrate for use by the brain and nervous system. When no carbohydrates are available, amino acids are broken down into carbohydrates (by a process known as gluconeogenesis) and fats are broken into glycerol and free fatty acids (FFA) to be used as a fuel for exercise. When protein is used as a source for carbohydrates, muscle protein is one of the first proteins to be utilized in this process.

7. Any food (carbohydrate, protein or fat) eaten in excess of the body's immediate needs are stored as fat for when extra energy is needed. Therefore, it is important to balance energy intake with energy output. In other words, one should not eat more than the sum of the energy needs for basal metabolism, digestion, exercise and routine daily activities for any given 24 hours.

8. The approach to correct weight (fat) reduction is to lower the caloric intake by 500 calories per day while eating a variety of foods and increase the physical activity by 300 to 500 calories per day. This will result in an 800 to 1000 calorie deficit per day. Over a seven day period one would expect a caloric deficit of 5600-7000 calories. This translates into a fat loss of between 1.6 to 2 pounds.

FAT CELLS

There are many health risks associated with obesity. It is important to identify these risks so that intelligent actions can be taken to reduce the risks. Some or the known risks of obesity are: (1) Reduced efficiency of the heart; (2) High blood pressure; (3) Diabetes; (4) Kidney diseases; (5) Gallbladder disease; (6) Lung diseases; (7) Skeletal problems and gout; (8) Blood lipid imbalances and disturbance of lipoprotein concentrations. The more that is known about fat the more effective can be the "battle against fat." **Fat accumulation in the human body occurs in three ways:**

1. By storage of larger quantities of fat in existing adipose (fat) cells. This is called fat cell hypertrophy or increase in existing fat cell size. When adults get fat they increase the size of the existing fat cells. This is just one of the methods by which children and adolescents get fat.

2. By formation of new fat cells. This is called hyperplasia and occurs during childhood and adolescence. It is thought that adults do not add new fat cells when they accumulate fat.

3. By a combination of hypertrophy of existing fat cells and hyperplasia (increasing the number of fat cells). Children and adolescents get fat in both of these ways. Once fat cells have been developed they do not disappear in weight reduction programs, they just get smaller.

Fat cell number increases in three critical periods in humans:

1. The fetus in the third trimester of pregnancy.
2. The first year of life.
3. In childhood and adolescence.

In adults, the number of fat cells apparently cannot be altered significantly. However, in adults the size of the fat cells increases or decreases according to the caloric balance. Table 5-15 contains the estimated number of fat cells in various types of people.

Table 5-15. Fat Cell Numbers In Humans.

PEOPLE TYPES	FAT CELL NUMBERS
AVERAGE PEOPLE	27 BILLION
OBESE PEOPLE	75 BILLION
EXTREMELY OBESE PEOPLE	235 BILLION

Adapted and tabled from: McArdle, W.D.; Katch, F.I.; Katch, V.L.: Exercise Physiology: Energy, Nutrition and Human Performance; Lea And Febiger; Philadelphia; Third Edition; 1991; pp. 662 - 664.

NUTRITION   PART V

BODY COMPOSITION

Body weight as shown on the scale is not a good indicator of body composition. The absolute weight does not indicate what portion of the body weight is fat and/or muscle. Therefore, it is necessary to determine what percent fat an individual has and then strive to reduce it by proper nutrition and exercise programs.

There are many ways to estimate body fat. The most valid method is by hydrostatic weighing (underwater weighing). There are other methods of estimating percent body fat. Among them are: skinfold measurements, circumferential measurements, ultra-sound measurement and bio-electrical impedance. All of these methods are validated by using hydrostatic weighing and are population specific (only applicable to population similar to that in the study). Contrary to popular belief, it is very difficult to get good estimates of body fat using these alternative techniques.

It is best to take circumferential measurements and skinfold measurements and not convert them to percent fat. Record them in the raw state and use changes in them as an indicator for fat reduction. If one wants a percent determination, it should be through the hydrostatic weighing process.

Another practical and more simplified way to determine if you are too fat is to look in the mirror or pinch the fat at the side of the naval. If one can "pinch an inch", it indicates too much fat.

In Table 5-16 is found the average percent fat values for selected age groups of males and females. It is important to remember that these values may vary greatly when humans are very active or are quite inactive.

Table 5-16. Average Percent Fat Values For Selected Ages In Humans

AGE	MALE %	FEMALE %
15 YEARS OLD	12	20
20 YEARS OLD	15	25
30 YEARS OLD	19	28
40 YEARS OLD	22	30
50 YEARS OLD	26	35
ATHLETES	6 - 20	6 - 20

GUIDELINES FOR FAT CONTROL

It is best to prevent the accumulation of body fat. This means that it is important to start at a young age to develop sensible daily exercise habits as well as intelligent and disciplined eating habits. It is unfortunate but most humans end up reacting to a body fat accumulation rather than preventing body fat accumulation.

Faced with fat accumulation how can a person effectively remove accumulated body fat? Below is a list of facts that will help one to understand the method of body fat reduction and control.

GENERAL INFORMATION:

1. There are three ways to reduce fat:

    A. Reduce the amount of food eaten. Food reduction alone is not recommended, as the weight loss is not all fat under this circumstance. A good amount of muscle is lost, also. Drastic reductions in food intake are associated with large losses of muscle mass. Loss of muscle mass results in a lowering of the basal metabolic rate (the resting energy usage rate) and results in less calories utilized throughout a 24 hour period. Also, when muscle mass is lost, physical performance capacity and appearance are reduced and one becomes more prone to muscular and skeletal injuries.

B. Increase the amount of energy expended by expanding the level of physical activity.

C. Intelligently reduce food intake **AND** increase activity level. **THIS IS THE PREFERRED METHOD FOR FAT REDUCTION**.

Methods B and C are recommended because of their superior effectiveness in reducing fat while producing positive physical fitness and appearance changes.

2. Fat loss is long, hard work and good results may take several months to become evident. Short-term fat reduction programs are usually ineffective. **THE FAT FIGHT IS A LIFE-LONG BATTLE.**

3. One must become active and begin a vigorous regular exercise program to lose fat. Some fat can be lost by dieting but vigorous exercise and caloric restriction produce the best results.

4. Fad diets do not work. It is estimated that there are over 17,000 fad diets, all of which are usually ineffective for long lasting results.

5. Expend more energy than is eaten. When more energy is put into the body than used, it is stored as fat. However, research shows that the basic cause of excess fat storage is inactivity, and not necessarily overeating.

6. Recommended weight (fat) loss is 1 to 2 pounds per week. A loss of more than two pounds is usually produced by losing muscle protein, water and minimal body fat. It is mathematically impossible to lose more than 2 pounds of fat in seven days. One would have to reduce the caloric intake by 7000 calories per week (1000 per day) or run seventy miles per week (10 miles per day) or combine caloric reduction and running just to lose two pounds of fat in one week. It is highly unlikely that one who is over-fat and deconditioned could run 70 miles per week or exercise a comparable amount without exposing themselves to many health risks or muscular-skeletal injuries.

7. Any effective fat-loss plan must be adaptable to life-long use.

8. Successful eating (diet) programs must be nutritious and balanced. A good nutrition program should include adequate amounts of the basic nutrients: protein, carbohydrates, fat, vitamins, minerals, water and fiber. Proper nutrition cannot be maintained in diets of fewer than 1200 calories per day. This is especially true for people involved in a strenuous exercise program. One should never consume less than 1200 calories per day when involved in a strenuous training program, in general. Fasting should be restricted to no more than a twenty four hour duration, if at all. Fasting is not appropriate for weight loss programs.

9. Successful weight loss programs result in only small regular losses of weight (fat) each week. Large weekly losses are often accompanied by sickness and other health problems and usually reflect large losses of muscle tissue and dehydration (water loss) with little fat loss.

10. Record calorie intake and calories used by exercise daily. Make a concentrated effort to use more calories than are eaten.

11. Body weight may not decrease dramatically with exercise programs, however, measurements of various segments will decrease. One should not be alarmed at the small increases in scale weight, especially in

PART V

NUTRITION

the beginning stages of training. Basically, it is a common occurrence to lose fat and gain muscle mass with a slight gain in body weight. However, as consistent physical training occurs over time there will be a reduction in body measurements as well as reduction in body weight especially when exercise and caloric restriction programs are combined.

Muscle is more dense than fat and occupies less space per pound than fat, therefore, at the outset of an exercise program blended with a diet, one usually gains a small amount of body weight while maintaining or losing inches in body measurements. After the first week or two, the gain in muscle mass will slow down while body fat reduction speeds up which results in greater reductions in various body circumferential measurements.

12. Remember that one usually eats until they are "full". By reducing fats and refined carbohydrates, and replacing them with bulky foods like vegetables, salads and whole grain products, one can avoid that "empty stomach" feeling that makes one overeat.

HOW TO INCREASE THE AMOUNT OF ENERGY OUTPUT

The solution to a body fat problem and the explanation of how body fat accumulates is directly related to the amount of physical activity included in the daily patterns of movement. To control the amount of body fat accumulated one has to increase the amount of energy used. This increased energy output should be a combination of increased general daily activity patterns and expanded planned regular exercise sessions. Below is a list of general rules that will assist one in increasing energy output.

GENERAL RULES:

1. Moderate and high intensity exercise decreases the appetite.

2. Exercise increases muscle mass which produces an increase in the calories used during daily activities and at rest. When more calories are expended in exercise and at rest there is general reduction of body fat. It is highly recommended that resistive exercise (weight training) as well as aerobic exercise be combined into a daily exercise pattern. This will increase the muscle mass, normalize body curves as well as reducing body fat.

3. **Long duration** exercise increases the body's ability to burn fat by increasing fat-burning enzymes. However, endurance exercises have little impact on the contractile proteins of the muscle. It is, therefore necessary to include weight training programs along with endurance training.

4. Activities that work the larger muscle groups produce the best results for fat loss; Circuit Weight Training, Super Circuit Weight Training, running, biking, stairclimbing and walking are all good calorie burners.

5. Exercise frequency, intensity, duration, type and periodization:

   A. **Frequency:** At least three times per week, however, daily exercise is recommended.

   B. **Intensity:** In circuit weight training and super circuit weight training, 40% to 60% or one repetition maximum strength and approximately 10 - 15 repetitions per station at a heart rate of 130-160 beats per minute. For other endurance exercises the intensity should be between 60% and 90% maximum heart rate reserve or the "rule of thumb" of 130 to 160 beats per minute.

   Intensities for standard weight training programs may vary from 40% to 100% 1RM depending on the program goals.

C. **Duration:** Exercise no less than 15 minutes daily and for best results, 45 minutes daily. Remember to start easy (short) and progress to harder (longer) durations. Morris, J. (1973), et al, suggests that at levels of 30 minutes or more (when exercise is performed a least three times per week AND pulse rate in the right range) heart disease protection jumps to more than 1,000%.

D. **Type of Exercise:** Large muscle activity which uses all the major muscle groups.

E. **Periodize (cycle)** your training by changing the type of exercise, duration of exercise and intensity to provide psychological and physiological variation.

6. The goal for calories burned per daily workout is from 300 to 500 calories. This is approximately equivalent to running 3 to 5 miles per workout, or about 1 to 2 hours of vigorous weight training, or 45 to 60 minutes of circuit weight training.

---

1. **American College of Sports Medicine Position Statement: The Recommended Quantity and Quality of Exercise for Developing and Maintaining Fitness in Health Adults; Indianapolis, Indiana; 1991.**

2. **Morris, J., et. al.; Vigorous exercise in leisure time and the incidence of coronary heart disease; Lancet; # 1; 1973; pp. 333-38.**

BEHAVIORAL CHANGES THAT ASSIST IN CONTROLLING BODY FAT

To be absolutely successful in any endeavor, one must use every dimension of human existence possible. Discipline is the key to success. To be successful it is important to restrict calories, eat well balanced meals, exercise intelligently and regularly and follow simple, yet effective general rules of behavior. The following general rules of behavior will assist in the **"battle against fat."**

GENERAL RULES:

1. Eat in only one room and at only one spot. Sit down and do nothing except eat. No TV.

2. Buy non-fattening, low calorie food. Avoid junk foods which contain empty calories (for example: Potato chips which are high in calories but low in vitamins and minerals.)

3. Keep problem foods out of sight.

4. Plan meals and develop a shopping list.

5. Shop from a list and eat before going shopping.

6. Make small food portions appear large; use small plates.

7. Measure each portion of food.

8. Avoid second helpings; make them hard to get.

9. Eat quality foods. Eat breakfast like a king; lunch like prince; and, dinner like a pauper.

10. Keep a variety of safe snack foods on hand; such as, carrot strips; cauliflower and celery strips.

11. Keep a running total of daily caloric intake and daily caloric expenditure through exercise.

NUTRITION   **PART V**

12. Eat slowly - put the fork down between bites.

13. Do not consume alcohol. If one must drink, do it moderately and remember that alcohol has many empty calories.

THE PHYSIOLOGY OF WEIGHT GAIN

There are some people, who for various reasons want to increase their body weight. Increasing body weight for most people is very easy. However, in these cases most of the weight gain is fat. Gains in fat are undesirable while gains in muscle normalize body contours and increases the ability of the person to perform various physical activities. The important thing to remember is that the increased body weight should be muscle, not fat. Muscle is functional and contributes to one's physical appearance while fat destroys normal body curves and is harmful to health. One can insure that the increase in body weight is, in fact muscle, by employing a weight training program based on scientific principles of periodization.

Before deciding to increase body weight one should investigate the medical and health risk factors involved if body weight is increased. A qualified exercise physiologist, coach, physician or nutritionist are the best people from which to obtain advice and guidance. Make sure that guidance is from a qualified person and not just some self-appointed expert or guru. Factors such as age, height, frame size, health status, blood pressure, blood fat profile, family history of diabetes, heart and vascular disease are among some of the important considerations.

PHYSIOLOGICAL RULES OF GAINING WEIGHT

There are no special food substances that will increase functional tissue (muscle) without effective weight training. Nor will eating more protein, by itself, produce functional muscle. **The stimulus to muscle growth (protein synthesis) is muscular work** in the presence of adequate nutrition and rest. The greater the intensity and volume of work the more the need for the muscle to adapt by increasing its size and under these circumstances additional protein, carbohydrate, vitamins and minerals and other body building nutrients may be indicated. Without muscular work of sufficient intensity, no food, vitamin, hormone or drug will increase functional tissue (muscular mass).

Many people participating in activities such as weight lifting, weight training, and body building have used a variety of nutritional supplements in an effort to gain body weight, increase muscle mass and improve strength. However there is relatively little scientific information regarding the effects of supplementation on the above mentioned parameters when combined with resistance training. On the other hand, there seems to be a lot of "in the trenches" or empirical evidence that demonstrates the efficacy of nutritional supplements combined with weight training programs.

Short term non-supplemented weight training studies lasting from 7-10 weeks have been shown to produce increases in strength in selected exercises from 9-29% in males and females (Kraemer, Deschenes, Fleck 1988) (Garhammer, Long, Rozenek, Ward 1994). Likewise, increases in fat-free weight, segmental circumferences and decreases in percentage body fat have also be demonstrated in non-supplemented weight training as reported by Fleck (1987) and Garhammer, Long, Rozenek, Ward (1994). What impact does nutritional supplementation and increase caloric intake have on gaining strength, lean muscle mass and increasing segmental circumferences?

The importance of nutritional supplementation including extra carbohydrate, protein, and selected body building nutrients compared to just a carbohydrate supplementation or just weight training for gaining strength, lean muscle mass and increasing segmental circumferences was demonstrated in a unpublished study completed in 1994 (Garhammer, Long, Rozenek, Ward 1994). The study involved males subjects between the ages of 18 to 35 years and included two experimental groups and one control group. This double blind study involved using the same weight training program plus the addition of 2000 kilocalories per day above the normal diet for both experimental groups, but one experimental group received additional protein and other selected body building nutrients in their nutritional supplementation. The control group was non-supplemented and followed the same weight training program. The subjects in all the groups followed a four day weight training split, working various body parts twice per week. The weight training routine included training on Monday and Tuesday, followed by a rest day on Wednesday, and training again on Thursday and Friday. Saturday and Sunday were considered rest days. Each training session lasted between 60 to 90 minutes.

The results of this study suggest that the addition of nutritional supplements of 2000 kilocalories per day above the normal diet produces significant gains in body weight and fat-free weight when combined with a well-designed weight training program emphasizing high volume and moderate intensity. Furthermore, the use of the nutritional supplements in combination with a well-designed weight training program did not significantly affect fat weight or the percentage of body fat. In addition, the use of the nutritional supplements in combination with a well designed weight training program did significantly increase the strength in the criterion strength measures. The group which used the weight training program with the nutritional supplement which contained the carbohydrate calories, increased protein and other body building nutrients did not prove to be superior to the group using just the carbohydrate supplementation in combination with the weight training program. Finally, the control group which did not use any nutritional supplementation produced smaller gains in body weight and fat free weight while also slightly reducing the percentage of body fat.

Increased calories along with adequate protein intake in the diet combined with an effective weight training program are important factors in developing lean body mass. Although, controversy does exist regarding the effects of additional protein, carbohydrate, calories, vitamins, minerals and other substances in the diet on facilitating improvements in muscular strength, muscle size, and body composition. What should a person do who is engaged in weight training and is desirous of gaining weight?

Below is a list of rules that govern the gaining of functional body weight:

1. Caloric intake must exceed caloric expenditure in order to increase muscle mass.

2. The rate of gaining muscle mass is different for each person. Fleck (1987) reports up to .75 of a pound of lean mass can be gained per week during an effective weight training program for average **non-supplemented** college aged males. He also reported that average non-supplemented college age females gained approximately .19 pounds per week from weight training. In contrast, Garhammer, Long, Rozenek and Ward (1994) found that an eight week supplemented weight training program for average college males increased muscle mass which averaged 0.789 and 0.923 pounds per week, respectively for the two experimental groups. Meanwhile the non-supplemented weight training control group demonstrated an average increase in muscle mass of 0.389 pounds per week. Moreover, it was observed that there were eleven males (some from both experimental groups) that gained between 1.41 and 2.88 pounds of lean muscle mass per week over the eight week nutritionally supplemented weight training program. This finding demonstrates that the gain in muscle mass is highly individualistic.

   Empirical observations suggest that there may be even greater increases in lean mass possible when using nutritional supplementation (vitamins, minerals, protein and other metabolic optimizers) and added caloric intake (carbohydrate) combined with more sophisticated weight training programs of moderate to high intensities and moderate to high volumes.

3. The number of calories or the form of these calories needed to gain one pound of muscle has not been precisely defined by exercise and nutrition scientists. It is thought that to gain one pound of muscle requires 2500 - 3000 calories in excess of what is needed to maintain one's weight.

   NOTE: An excess of 2500 - 3000 calories should not be eaten in one day. It should be spread out over 2 to 3 days. If a consistent and vigorous weight training program is followed, adding 720 to 860 calories a day to the usual diet will supply adequate energy to build two pounds of muscle per week. An addition of only 360 to 430 calories a day to the usual diet will supply adequate energy to create one pound of muscle per week providing a weight training regimen is being followed.

4. Not more than 1 to 2 pounds per week is recommended for weight (muscle) gain. Research has not precisely identified the maximum amount of muscle that can be gained over any time period.

5. To increase lean body mass (muscle mass) it is necessary to have adequate amounts of protein in the diet. The amount of protein should be 15% to 20% of the total caloric intake. High energy diets that are low in protein cause lean body mass to fall as weight is gained (Kleiner 1991; Miller and Mumford 1967). **When the protein content of the diet is adequate it is the amount of calories consumed (preferably carbohydrate), the total work (volume) and the intensity (% of 1RM) of the weight training program that determines the amount of lean mass gained.**

6. **Individuals involved in heavy weight training may require increased amounts of protein ranging from 1.2 - 3.9 grams of protein per kilogram of body weight. Expressed in pounds of body weight this would translate into .55 grams to 1.77 grams per pound of body weight.** The sensible increase of protein and calorie intake combined with weight training of sufficient volume (total work) and adequate intensity (% 1RM) is necessary for lean mass weight gain. It is vitally important to engage in a weight training or body building program when increasing protein and/or caloric (preferably unrefined carbohydrate) intake to ensure that the weight gain is, in fact, lean body mass (muscle).

7. A consistent and vigorous strength training program should be followed to insure the weight gain will be primarily muscle. The stimulus to muscle growth is exercise at high intensity, i.e., high muscle tension which should be expressed as a percent of one repetition maximum (1RM). The best level of muscle tension for increases in lean muscle mass is between 75% and 85% 1RM. This intensity should be performed for 3-5 sets of 5-8 repetitions. Moreover, all major muscle groups should be included in the training pattern.

   In addition, total work (volume) is another important factor for the gaining of functional body weight (lean muscle mass). It is difficult to place an exact number on the amount of total work needed. Also, it is important to monitor closely the total amount of work and intensity and the body's response to them, over time, to ensure that symptoms of overtraining are prevented.

8. If a person's body fat percentage is more than 15 percent for males and 20 percent for females, the exercise and nutrition program should focus on reducing body fat and increasing muscle mass.

9. For gaining functional weight (muscle mass) it is crucial to employ a scientific weight training program along with the augmentation of the diet with a proportionate formula of free form amino acids combined with a balanced vitamin and mineral supplement. There are 454 grams (16 ounces) in a pound of muscle, but only 22 percent of that is protein. Twenty two percent of 454 grams is approximately 100 grams. If 100 grams is divided by 7 days, it would take approximately 14 grams of additional protein per day over and above the requirement for one's body weight to synthesize one pound of muscle. This assumes that there is sufficient exercise stimulus and enough other energy available to facilitate protein synthesis.

1. Fleck, S. and Kraemer, W.J., Designing ResistanceTraining Programs, Human Kinetics Books, Champaign, Il, 1987.

2. Garhammer, J., Long, S., Rozenek, R., and Ward, P., Effects of the Mega Mass 4000 nutritional supplement on body composition, anthropometric measures, and muscular strength following an eight week training program. Unpublished research for the Weider Corporation, September, 1994.

3. Kraemer, W.J., Deschenes, M., and Fleck, S., Physiological adaptations to resistance exercise: implications for athletic conditioning. Sports Med., 6:246-256, 1988.

4. Kleiner, S.M., Performance-enhancing aids in sport: health consequences and nutritional alternatives. J. Amer. Coll. Nutr., 10(2):163-176, 1991.

5. Miller, D.S. and Mumford, P., An experimental study of overeating low- or high-protein diets. Am. J. Clin. Nutr., 20:1212-1229, 1967.

VITAMINS AND MINERALS

This section includes discussions regarding vitamins - natural or synthetic, fat soluble vitamins, water soluble vitamins, should one use natural or synthetic vitamins and minerals. General information is provided about these topics for the reader.

VITAMINS - NATURAL OR SYNTHETIC?

Many people believe that there are significant differences between vitamins derived from natural sources and those created synthetically. Nutrition scientists and biochemists state unequivocally that vitamins as they occur naturally in foods are not different from those created synthetically in the laboratory and put into foods.

A simple definition of vitamins is that they are organic substances in foods which are essential in small amounts for body processes. This definition includes the following requirements:

1. Vitamins are organic which distinguishes them from minerals.
2. Vitamins are needed in very small amounts which distinguishes them from other organic nutrients such as fats, proteins and carbohydrates.
3. Vitamins are created outside human cells meaning they must be secured from food.
4. Body processes are impaired when vitamin supplies are inadequate.

Both "natural" vitamins extracted from and contained in foods and "synthetic" vitamins synthesized in the laboratory meet all the requirements of the above stated definition. When synthetic vitamins are utilized instead of natural vitamins, no vitamin deficiency is demonstrated. Furthermore, if a vitamin deficiency exists, it can be corrected by the administration of synthetic vitamins.

Any marketing scheme that claims vitamins are natural, implies that the natural vitamin includes some other special substance which potentiates or improves it's use. This, of course, is not true. A vitamin is a vitamin, equivalent whether occurring naturally or synthesized in the laboratory. The only difference between natural and synthetic vitamins is that vitamin supplements produced from natural sources are very costly. Biologically, natural and synthetic vitamins are equivalent.

FAT SOLUBLE VITAMINS

The fat soluble vitamins are A, D, E and K, and are soluble in fat but not in water. These substances are dissolved and accumulated in the body fat making daily consumption unnecessary.

The excessive supplementation of these fat soluble vitamins can be deleterious to one's health. Deficiencies of the fat soluble vitamins are uncommon. It is thought that overdoses or A and D are toxic, while overdoses of E and K seldom occur. Table 5-17 contains a list of the fat soluble vitamins and their major functions in the body.

WATER SOLUBLE VITAMINS

Water soluble vitamins are dissolvable in water and need to be replaced on a regular basis because they are not stored in the body. Deficiency states develop rather quickly, within 2-4 weeks, and can produce reductions in

PART V

NUTRITION

physical performances. Excessive intakes of the water soluble vitamins are not thought to be damaging and are normally discharged in the urine. Water soluble vitamins include nine vitamins: vitamin C (ascorbic acid) and eight in the B-complex. The B complex include the following:

1. Thiamine (B-1)
2. Riboflavin (B-2)
3. Niacin
4. Pyridoxine (B-6)

5. Cyanocobalamin (B-12)
6. Folic Acid (Folacin)
7. Pantothenic Acid
8. Biotin

In Table 5-17 is found the water soluble vitamins and their major functions in the body.

Table 5-17.   The Thirteen Vitamins And Their Major Functions In The Body.

FAT SOLUBLE VITAMINS:	MAJOR FUNCTIONS IN THE BODY
1. VITAMIN A	MAINTENANCE OF EPITHELIAL TISSUES; PRODUCTION OF RHODOPSIN; PROMOTES BONE GROWTH. TOXIC IN LARGE AMOUNTS.
2. VITAMIN D	FACILITATES ABSORPTION OF CALCIUM AND PHOSPHOROUS; PROMOTES TEETH AND BONE GROWTH. TOXIC IN LARGE AMOUNTS.
3. VITAMIN E	FUNCTIONS AS AN ANTIOXIDANT TO PROTECT CELL MEMBRANES. HELPS IN THE FORMATION OF RED BLOOD CELLS.
4. VITAMIN K	NECESSARY FOR BLOOD CLOTTING AND BONE METABOLISM. TOXIC IN LARGE AMOUNTS.
WATER SOLUBLE VITAMINS:	MAJOR FUNCTIONS IN THE BODY
B COMPLEX	
5. THIAMIN (VITAMIN B-1)	COENZYME IN CARBOHYDRATE METABOLISM. INVOLVED IN FUNCTIONING OF CENTRAL NERVOUS SYSTEM.
6. RIBOFLAVIN (VITAMIN B-2)	HELPS IN FREE FATTY ACID METABOLISM; PROTEIN AND CARBOHYDRATE METABOLISM.
7. NIACIN	HELPS IN FREE FATTY ACID AND GLYCOGEN METABOLISM (ENERGY PRODUCTION ANAEROBICALLY AND AEROBICALLY); FAT SYNTHESIS.
8. PYRIDOXINE (B-6)	COENZYME FOR GLYCOGEN AND AMINO ACID METABOLISM; PARTICIPATES IN HEMOGLOBIN FORMATION. ASSISTS IN METABOLISM OF FATS.
9. COBALAMIN (B-12)	COENZYME IN PROTEIN SYNTHESIS; DNA AND RED BLOOD CELL FORMATION; ACTIVE IN FORMATION OF NERVE FIBERS.
10. FOLIC ACID	COENZYME IN AMINO ACID METABOLISM; DNA FORMATION AND RED BLOOD CELL DEVELOPMENT.
11. BIOTIN	COENZYME FOR PROTEIN, FATS AND CARBOHYDRATE METABOLISM.
12. PANTOTHENIC ACID	COMPONENT OF COENZYME A IN ENERGY (FAT, CARBOHYDRATE AND PROTEIN) METABOLISM.
13. VITAMIN C (ASCORBIC ACID)	IMPORTANT IN CONNECTIVE TISSUE FORMATION (CARTILAGE, TENDON AND BONE). SERVES AS AN ANTIOXIDANT; ASSISTS IN IRON ABSORPTION; AIDS IN FORMATION OF HORMONES; HELPS REGULATE CHOLESTEROL AND AMINO ACID METABOLISM. FACILITATES HEALING.

PART V

NUTRITION

MINERALS

Minerals are inorganic elements widely distributed in nature which have vital roles in the structure of the body and its functioning and regulation. A nutritional definition declares that minerals are elements that are essential to life. Minerals regulate metabolism but are not, in themselves, a source of energy.

There are **six major (macrominerals) minerals:** calcium, phosphorous, magnesium, potassium, sodium and chloride. They are considered major because the daily requirement is greater than 100 mg per day and they have a known biologic function. Deficiencies or excesses of these macrominerals may impair health or degrade physical performances.

Trace or microminerals are those needed in quantities less than 100 mg per day and are present in small quantities in the body.

National nutritional surveys have shown that there is either deficient mineral intake or excessive mineral intake in the general population. It is thought that the deficiencies or excesses are a contributing factor in the development of assorted health afflictions. These deficiencies or excesses are, also, prevalent in athletes, body builders and people who are in vigorous physical training. Furthermore, it is known that mineral deficiencies are detrimental to physical performance. In contrast, mineral inadequacies and damaged mineral metabolism may be a direct result of vigorous physical activity.

Plants absorb minerals from the soil in which they are grown and incorporate them into their structures. Plant and animal foods are major sources of minerals for humans. An additional source of some of the minerals can be the drinking water which varies in quality in different geographical areas. It is an established fact that a balanced dietary intake of minerals is necessary for optimal health and optimal physical performances. Absorption of minerals is in the small intestine.

Table 5-18 contains the RDA, ESADDI (estimated safe and adequate daily dietary intake) and the physiologic function of the 20 essential minerals found in the body.

Williams (1988 - page 160) states a basic principle of mineral nutrition.

> "A basic principle of mineral nutrition is to eat natural foods that are rich in calcium and iron. If you select a diet to provide your RDA for these two minerals, you will receive adequate amounts of the other major and trace minerals at the same time. Dairy products and animal meats are excellent sources of these minerals, but other foods also may provide significant amounts if selected wisely, such as legumes and dark green leafy vegetables."

There is some research and a vast amount of empirical observations in athletes, body builders and general fitness participants that may indicate the need for mineral supplementation because of mineral loss due to training in combination with nutritionally inadequate diets. **It is prudent to consult a qualified sports nutritionist or a nutritionally oriented physician for guidance in mineral supplementation.**

Despite strongly stating the ineffectiveness of vitamin and mineral supplementation for all people except those who have identified nutritional deficiencies, many nutritionists and physicians make qualifying disclaimers like that embodied in a statement made by Williams (page 161).

> **"Nevertheless, it may be prudent behavior to recommend a one-a-day vitamin-mineral supplement to those athletes whose poor nutritional habits are documented. The tablet should contain no more than 100 percent of the RDA for any mineral. In the meantime, efforts should be undertaken to educate the athlete concerning sound nutritional practices."**

Williams, Melvin; Nutrition for Fitness and Sport; Wm. C. Brown Publishers; Dubuque, Iowa; 1988. Page 160.

NUTRITION **PART V**

Table 5-18. The RDA, ESADDI And The Physiologic Function Of The 20 Essential Minerals Found In The Body.

MINERAL	RDA (MG)		ESADDI (MG)	PHYSIOLOGIC FUNCTION
MAJOR MINERALS	M	F	RANGE	
1. CALCIUM (Ca)	800	800	N/A	TOOTH AND BONE FORMATION. BLOOD CLOTTING. MUSCLE CONTRACTION AND RELAXATION. HEART ACTION. NERVE TRANSMISSION.
2. CHLORIDE (Cl)	N/A	N/A	1,700 - 5,100	WATER BALANCE. FORMATION OF HYDROCHLORIC ACID DIGESTION. ELECTRICAL IMPULSE TRANSMISSION.
3. MAGNESIUM (Mg)	350	350	N/A	CONSTITUENT OF TEETH AND BONES. ACTIVATOR AND COENZYME IN CARBOHYDRATE METABOLISM AND PROTEIN SYNTHESIS. ACTIVE IN ATP USE.
4. PHOSPHORUS (P)	800	800	N/A	TOOTH AND BONE FORMATION. ENERGY METABOLISM. ACID-BASE BALANCE.
5. POTASSIUM (K)	N/A	N/A	1,875 - 5,625	MAINTENANCE OF BODY FLUIDS. GENERATION OF ELECTRICAL IMPULSE IN NERVES, SKELETAL AND HEART MUSCLE. ENERGY METABOLISM OF GLUCOSE, GLYCOGEN AND HIGH-ENERGY COMPOUNDS.
6. SODIUM (Na)	N/A	N/A	1,100 - 3,300	WATER BALANCE AND OSMOTIC PRESSURE. IMPACTS BLOOD PRESSURE. CRITICAL OF NERVE NERVE-IMPULSE TRANSMISSION AND MUSCLE CONTRACTION. ACID-BASE BALANCE.
TRACE MINERALS	M	F	RANGE	**PHYSIOLOGIC FUNCTION**
1. CHROMIUM (Cr)	N/A	N/A	0.052 - 0.2	USED IN GLUCOSE AND ENERGY METABOLISM. RELATED TO INSULIN ACTION.
2. COBALT (Co)	NOT ESTABLISHED			FORMATION OF RED BLOOD CELLS. COMPONENT COMPONENT OF VITAMIN B-12.
3. COPPER (Cu)	N/A	N/A	2 - 3	BONE FORMATION. IRON ABSORPTION AND TRANSPORT. OXYGEN METABOLISM. HELPS IN FORMATION OF HEMOGLOBIN.
4. FLUORINE (Fl)	N/A	N/A	1.5 - 4.0	TOOTH AND BONE FORMATION.
5. IODINE (I)	0.15	0.15	N/A	FORMATION OF THYROID HORMONES.
6. IRON (Fe)	10	18	N/A	HEMOGLOBIN AND MYOGLOBIN FORMATION. TRANSPORT OF OXYGEN. ENERGY METABOLISM.
7. MANGANESE (Mn)	N/A	N/A	2.5 - 5.0	ENZYMES IN ENERGY METABOLISM AND PROTEIN SYNTHESIS. BONE FORMATION. SYNTHESIS OF FATTY ACIDS.
8. MOLYBDENUM (Mo)	N/A	N/A	0.15 - 0.20	WORKS WITH ENZYMES IN CARBOHYDRATE AND AND FAT METABOLISM.
9. NICKEL (Ni)	NOT ESTABLISHED			NOT KNOWN BUT UNDER STUDY.
10. SELENIUM (Se)	N/A	N/A	0.05 - 0.2	FORMATION OF CONNECTIVE TISSUE. ASSOCIATED WITH METABOLISM. FUNCTION WITH VITAMIN E AS AN ANTIOXIDANT. PROTECTS RED BLOOD CELL MEMBRANES.
11. SILICON (Si)	NOT ESTABLISHED			FORMATION OF CONNECTIVE TISSUE.
12. TIN (Sn)	NOT ESTABLISHED			NOT KNOWN BUT UNDER STUDY.
13. VANADIUM (V)	NOT ESTABLISHED			NOT KNOWN BUT UNDER STUDY.
14. ZINC (Zn)	15	15	N/A	PART OF ENZYMES INVOLVED IN DIGESTION. INVOLVED IN PROTEIN SYNTHESIS, GROWTH PROCESS AND HEALING.

ESADDI = ESTIMATED SAFE AND ADEQUATE DAILY DIETARY INTAKES.
N/A = NOT APPLICABLE.
M = MALE.
F = FEMALE.

VITAMIN AND MINERAL SUPPLEMENTATION

Nutrition scientists continue to claim that athletes, body builders and people training for general fitness can adequately meet their nutrition requirements on a balanced and varied diet. They contend that the consumption of a selection of foods from fruits; vegetables; dairy products; meats, fish and poultry; and, grains in sufficient quantity to supply the energy requirements, will contain enough of all the essential nutrients. They refer to this as a normal balanced diet.

While a balanced diet is thought to provide the recommended dietary allowance (RDA) amounts of vitamins and minerals, the individual nutritional requirements may not be satisfied. This may exist because the RDA amounts are not correct, vitamin and mineral content of foods may vary, individual exposure to very high levels of physiological and psychological stresses, environmental pollution and a plethora of negative influences on the human and their foods. Furthermore, the suggested governmental RDA standards should not be used to estimate the nutritional requirement for individuals because everyone has a unique requirement based on activity levels, food intake, environmental stress, psychological stress and individual biological programming. Finally, the practical observation is that people just do not eat a "balanced diet".

Research that has extended over the past forty years or more has failed to define a demonstrated need for vitamin and mineral supplementation when people eat a normal balanced diet; however, coaches, athletes, body builders, general fitness participants and average people have a different perspective. There is a world wide popular belief that vitamin, mineral, protein and miscellaneous supplementation is required for average people and especially people who are participating in vigorous physical training.

This view is largely supported by volumes of empirical observations where improvement in health, well being and performance are noted. Along with this belief there is corresponding widespread use of food and nutrient supplementation. While there is a strong practice of vitamin, mineral, protein and miscellaneous supplementation in western society, it is difficult to objectively interpret the impact of using nutritional substances because a lack of scientific controls. These observations do not rule out the influence of the "placebo" effects of using these nutritional supplements.

The masses are in a dilemma. What is the truth? To supplement or not to supplement? That is the question! The truth probably lies somewhere between the opinions of hard core professional nutritionists and the basic understanding of the masses.

A RATIONALE SUPPORTING VITAMIN AND MINERAL SUPPLEMENTATION

There are three major areas of research that support taking vitamin/mineral supplements:

1. Computerized diet evaluations of thousands of people have shown that the statement "if you eat a cross-section of foods from the four basic food groups, you will get all the vitamins and minerals you need" is NOT correct (referring to meeting the RDA). (Cheraskin and Ringsdorf, 1972; Kugler, Hans, 1977.)

2. Literally hundreds of medical publications (best summarized and quoted in "Diet and Disease", by E. Cheraskin, et. al., 1977) show that the "average diet" (faulty diet, and not getting the RDA of vitamins and minerals) are major contributing factors to many (literally all) diseases. Werbach (1991), a professor at UCLA, states that a faulty diet and not getting enough vitamins/minerals are factors that greatly contribute to the onset of about 150 diseases, and that special nutritional regimens and supplementation programs are very effective in treating many of these diseases. Werbach's book could be called "the nutritional PDR (physicians desk reference)."

3. Longevity studies on animals, using vitamins/minerals in higher than RDA amounts have given excellent life span increases. Dietary evaluation of several thousand people by Cheraskin (1976), using the Cornell Medical Index Questionnaire, concurrently, suggests that vitamin intake should be 4 to 8 times greater than the RDA for optimal health. (Walford, R. [1980]; Cheraskin, E. [1976]) Harman (1980 and 1990) studied the impact of vitamins and minerals (A, C, E, selenium, etc) on intervention of causes of aging (the free radical theory). The use of these vitamin and mineral supplements appear to slow down the aging process.

---

1. **Cheraskin, E. and Ringsdorf, W.; Clinical Findings Before and After Dietary Counsel; Geriatrics; Number 27; 1972; pp. 121-26.**

2. **Cheraskin, E., et. al.; Diet and Disease; Keats Publishing; 1977.**

PART V

NUTRITION

3. Cheraskin, E.; The Ideal Daily Vitamin A Intake; International Journal of Vitamin and Nutrition Research; Volume 1; 1976; pp. 58-60.

4. Harman, Denham; The Free Radical Theory of Aging; Age; Vol 3:100; 1980.

5. Harman, Denham; Free Radicals and Aging; Lecture at the November, 1990 ACAM meeting; Disneyland Hotel; Anaheim, California.

6. Kugler, H.; Diet and Health Practices as Related to the Onset of Disease; Journal of the International Academy of Preventive Medicine; Winter 1977; pp. 68-76.

7. Walford, Roy; Maximum Life Span; Avon Books, New York; 1984.

8. Werbach, Melvin; Nutritional Influences on Illness; Third Line Press; Tarzana, California; 1990.

Practicing doctors and researchers associated with prevention-oriented medical organizations (ICAN, AHMA, IAHHM - see below for organization identification) strongly feel that the RDA for vitamins and minerals is not sufficient for achieving optimum health. Many of these nutrition experts suggest establishing an ODR (optimal daily requirement) which they feel is a vitamin and mineral intake level recommended to achieve optimum health.

These doctors and scientists believe that the average person eating a cross section of healthy foods does not get enough of the RDA of vitamins and minerals from these food sources only. They recommend that the optimal health daily requirement (ODR) for vitamins is 4 to 8 times the RDA (Kugler, 1991 and Ceraskin, E., et al, 1976). Furthermore, they state that the RDA for minerals is on the low side, but is considered to be an adequate amount if in fact the RDA is obtained from the daily food intake.

1. ACAM: American College for the Advancement in Medicine; 23121 Verdugo Dr., Suite 204, Laguna Hills, California 92653.

2. IAHHM: International Academy of Holistic Health and Medicine; 218 Ave B, Redondo Beach, California, 90277.

3. AHMA: American Holistic Medical Association; 2002 Eastlake Ave East, Seattle, Washington 98102.

4. Cheraskin, E. and Ringsdorf, W.; Psychodietetics; Stein and Day Publishers; New York; 1974.

5. Cheraskin, E.; Ringsdorf, W. and Medford, F.; The Ideal Daily Vitamin E Intake; International Journal For Vitamin and Nutrition Research; 1:58-60; 1976.

6. Kugler, Hans; The Anti-aging Weight-Loss Program; Stein and Day Publishers; New York; 1985.

7. Reference for ODR: Kugler, Hans; Editor; Preventive Medicine Update; Vol 4; # 2; March, 1991.

8. Williams, Roger; Nutrition Against Disease; Bantam; New York; 1973.

It is also important to remember that excessive amounts of vitamins and minerals can be toxic and may produce a variety of reactions including allergic reactions such as rashes, itching, hives, headaches, nausea, diarrhea and in some cases disease. A variety of factors controls the toxicity levels that may be experienced with unreasonable usage or vitamins and minerals. These factors include the amount of the overdose of vitamins and minerals, the body weight, activity levels, diet and the quality of the supplement as well as the unique individual biological response to radical use of supplements.

Vitamin and mineral analysis may be beneficial to determine the specific need for supplementation. This analysis should be performed by a qualified sports nutritionist.

PART V

NUTRITION

Further action that will help the individual to objectively control their supplementation program is to read all supplement labels and keep track of intake. In addition, one should record the impact of supplementation on health and physical performance over a four to six month time period.

Supplementation is very beneficial when a need has been discovered and supplementation is intelligently used.

Another good reason to consider vitamin and mineral supplementation is the impact of nutrition upon the function and health of important body tissues. It is thought that muscles, tendons, ligaments and bones experience permanent injuries because of sub-optimal supply of nutrients. If this is true, then reasonable vitamin, mineral and protein supplementation would be considered appropriate health and physical performance insurance.

There was a time when a balanced and varied diet provided sufficient nutrition. During those times the food was grown in healthy soil, picked fresh and used locally, grains were used unrefined, beef was fed on pastureland and most of the food moved directly from the farm to the table. This is not the case today.

Presently, crops are grown in depleted and polluted soil, irrigated with polluted water, grains are highly refined, insecticides and other chemicals are used in the growing stages, food coloring and other chemicals are used to delay spoilage and enhance appearance, beef and poultry are fed in feedlots and given hormones to accelerate the growth process, most food is highly processed and/or frozen, fish come from highly polluted waters and all food arrives at the marketplace after long waiting periods in warehouses and travel over long distances to the marketplace. All these circumstances attenuate the nutrition of the food that comprises the diet of modern man. Today it is impossible to identify the quality of the nutrients that is found in the contemporary diet.

Considering all the negative aspects of food growth, harvesting, processing and shipment to the point of sale, it seems certain that some vitamin and mineral supplementation is indicated.

There are many distinct factors that determine the vitamin and mineral need of each individual. Among them are the following:

1. Intensity of physical training	6. Physiological stress level.
2. Duration of physical training.	7. Psychological stress level.
3. Age.	8. Environmental stress level.
4. Sex.	9. Genetics.
5. Medical history.	

The need for vitamin, mineral, protein and miscellaneous supplementation should be determined by a careful analysis of each specific individual and their biological individuality as it has, and is, presently interacting with their dietary practices along with the impact of the environment and physical activity patterns. There are 24 arguments that should be considered in the decision to supplement the diet with vitamins and minerals (Deters 1989). These justifications are listed below. Not all the reasons are applicable in all cases.

1. Poor Digestion.	13. Accidents and Illness
2. Hot Coffee, Tea and Spices	14. Physical and Psychological Stress
3. Alcohol	15. Pre Menstrual Syndrome
4. Smoking	16. Teenage Years of the Life Cycle
5. Laxatives	17. Pregnancy
6. Usage of Fad Diets	18. Usage of Oral Contraceptives
7. Overcooking of Foods	19. Light Eaters
8. Food Processing	20. Old Age
9. Eating of Convenience Foods	21. Lack of Sunlight
10. Usage of Antibiotics	22. Bio-Individuality
11. Food Allergies	23. Low Body Reserves
12. Crop Nutrient Losses	24. Participation in Vigorous Physical Activity

PART V

NUTRITION

SUMMARY STATEMENT ON VITAMIN, MINERAL AND NUTRIENT SUPPLEMENTATION

It is very difficult to get the scientist and professional sports nutritionist to agree with the masses regarding the need for vitamin, mineral, protein and miscellaneous supplementation. The best approach is to consider intelligent supplementation as health and physical performance insurance. To prevent the use of worthless substances and to avert using supplements that represent health risks, one should become educated and rely on valid sources of information before making a commitment to supplement the diet.

Also, one needs to objectively evaluate the impact of any supplementation program and product. This evaluation usually will take an extended length of time since any supplementation would not impact training and physical performance levels over brief time periods. Furthermore, it is necessary to objectify any observations of training or performance improvement to make a valid assessment of the cause of the improvement.

Certainly the use of a daily multiple vitamin and mineral supplement would be the very least a highly active person should do. This is usually recommended by sports nutritionists as insurance. Furthermore, dependent upon the activity level, there may be a need for protein supplementation in highly active fitness participants, body builders, and strength and endurance athletes. Other metabolic optimizers may be of benefit and assist in improving training levels, speed of recovery from training and performance as well as improving performance levels.

THE ANTIOXIDANT WARRIORS

Body builders, athletes, and fitness enthusiasts are keenly aware of what is required for good health. Moreover, people that are physically active are interested in optimal and sometimes high level physical performance. Billions of dollars are spent each year for nutritional supplements with the expectation of enhancing or optimizing health, physical training and physical performance. These people are bombarded with great volumes of information, some of it valid and some of it invalid, concerning vitamins, minerals, protein supplements, carbohydrate drinks, electrolyte replacements, metabolic optimizers, antioxidants and phytochemicals.

Considerable attention has been given to the use of antioxidant supplementation for improved health, prevention and management of degenerative (chronic) diseases, control of infectious diseases (bacterial and viral), to prevent exercise induced tissue damage and to ensure rapid recovery between exercise training sessions. This approach is supported by numerous research studies that demonstrate the efficacy of using nutritional antioxidant supplementation to achieve good health, prevent diseases, facilitate exercise and to recover quickly from exercise sessions. It is estimated that there are approximately 6,000 articles in research and scientific journals cited in the references listed at the end of this section alone, concerning the body's natural antioxidants and supplementation of nutritional antioxidants in exercise, general health maintenance and disease states. There seems to be voluminous scientific research the supports the efficacy of using antioxidant supplementation as aids in physical training and in the amelioration and prevention of non-germ based diseases.

An antioxidant is a compound that protects others from oxidation by being oxidized itself and without producing free radicals. The body constructs various antioxidant enzymes at the cell level as the first line of defense against free radicals. The second line of defense consists of the nutritional antioxidants. The major protective antioxidant nutrients include vitamins A (or beta Carotene), C and E, and the trace mineral selenium. New evidence is mounting that other nutritional antioxidants may be important also, such as coenzyme Q10, proanthocyanidins, melatonin and others.

Antioxidants are used in the body to neutralize or prevent the formation of free radicals which are implicated in virtually every major disease and pathological process. Free radicals are renegade oxygen molecules that must be controlled so that they will not cause damage to the cell membranes, cell contents, DNA, proteins or lipids (fats). Free radicals are controlled by the body's natural (endogenous- internal police force) antioxidant enzyme system and by nutritional antioxidants (the nutritional green berets) which are absorbed from the consumption of certain foods and by using various nutritional supplements.

Nutritional antioxidant supplementation is needed to defend against the free radical assault on the body. It is important to remember that free radicals are the natural consequence of living in an oxidative environment. Although some free radicals are beneficial, we are at risk for all kinds of health problems when the body's defenses are overwhelmed by excessive free radical production.

Research has shown that nutritional antioxidants function to prevent or minimize free radical damage to biological systems. Adequate antioxidant defense provided by sensible nutritional supplementation can protect the body from the high free radical concentrations that are a consequence of daily living experiences and may enhance success in physical training. There are many primary sources of free radicals: air, water and soil pollution; stress (emotional); basic metabolism, exercise, diseases and infections, inflammation and the aging process itself. Everyone is exposed to all of these major sources of free radicals. The person who minimizes the damages caused by free radicals is the one who knows and applies the truth about free radical pathology and implements a strategic defense initiative including avoidance techniques, engaging in sensible exercise programs, eating a rational diet and uses the daily supplementation of nutritional antioxidants.

The scientific community is finally recognizing that vitamin and mineral supplementation has health effects beyond just the prevention of deficiency diseases. Vitamin and mineral supplementation are now considered to have new biochemical functions such as enhancing the immune system and providing antioxidants to fight against free radical formation and propagation. Consequently, in the minds of progressive scientists, the RDA standard is being replaced by what is called the **optimal daily requirement (ODR)** which recommends significantly higher dosages of vitamins and minerals.

Prevention-oriented medical organizations strongly feel that the older and passe' RDA standards for vitamins and minerals are not sufficient for achieving optimal health and improving physical performance. They state that the ODR for vitamins is 4 to 8 times the RDA and in some cases, a lot more. **(ACAM - American College for the Advancement of Medicine, Laguna Hills, California: IAHHM - International Academy of Holistic Health and Medicine, Redondo Beach, California: AHMA - American Holistic Medical Association, Seattle, Washington)**

There is accumulating scientific evidence suggesting that dietary changes and **nutritional antioxidant supplementation** can prevent, slowdown and stop degenerative diseases; help prevent the overtraining syndrome in exercise; protect against environmental pollution and radiation exposure; help to offset the effects of high stress; prevent or minimize infections and diseases; prevent some activity related injuries and facilitate recovery from injuries; and slow down the aging process.

A number of environmental, behavioral and health habits—including intense exercise and poor dietary habits—can be detrimental to your health by triggering the formation in the body of highly reactive and unstable oxygen molecules called "free radicals." Before discussing the antioxidants and the necessary strategic battle plan for controlling free radicals and optimizing health and fitness, it is necessary to discuss "the enemy."

THE ENEMY WITHIN — FREE RADICALS

Free radicals are not seen nor do you feel them; but they leave behind cumulative traces of their presence. It is estimated that the number of oxidative hits **(a free radical attack)** to the DNA alone, per cell per day is about 10,000 in the human. **(Ames, Bruce et al, Proc Natl. Acad. Sci USA, Vol 90, pp 7915-7922, September 1993)** Your body is sustaining a constant bombardment every single day from these biological renegades and the results can be devastating if not controlled. When the body cannot control the generation of these free radicals, it results in a threat to your health and physical performance.

NUTRITION   PART V

The latest research has linked these miscreants to the following health problems: heart and blood vessel disease; cancer; cataracts; premature aging, reduced physical performance and exercise induced muscle damage. In addition, **Ken Cooper, MD (1994)**, states that many other diseases have been linked by medical research to the treacherous operation of free radicals in your body. Among them are: stroke, asthma, pancreatitis, inflammatory bowel diseases such as diverticulitis, ulcerative colitis, peptic ulcers, chronic congestive heart failure, Parkinson's disease, sickle cell disease, leukemia, rheumatoid arthritis, bleeding within a cavity of the brain, and high blood pressure.

WHAT ARE FREE RADICALS?

The basic building blocks of nature are molecules such as oxygen, fatty acids, amino acids, glucose and DNA. These normal molecules are held together by paired electrons which make them stable compounds. Free radicals (unstable molecules resulting from oxygen reactions) are formed by essential metabolic reactions involving oxygen and, also, other oxygen reactions with toxic substances. These free radicals are formed as a result of metabolic circumstances where one electron is either lost or gained.

A free radical is molecule with one or more unpaired electrons which make them highly reactive and dangerous. The gain or loss of one electron converts a normal stable compound into a free radical form. When free radicals are created in the body they start chain reactions that results in a destructive biological fireworks. These unstable oxygen molecules start a chain reaction by literally stealing an electron from any available molecule in a random manner. Thousands of free radical reactions occur within seconds. Once a stable molecule loses an electron, it becomes another free radical. Each time a molecule loses an electron it is damaged and will damage another molecule. If not controlled these free radicals become biological renegades or terrorists that will create severe damage to the tissues and cells of the body. **This is called oxidative stress.**

Free radicals (the hydroxyl radical and the superoxide radical) and other reactive oxygen species (ROS) (oxygen singlet, hydrogen peroxide and others) are by-products of normal oxygen metabolism. They are produced in the body's tissues and cells. Free radicals and reactive oxygen species (ROS) are different compounds and have different structures, but they behave the same way. These compounds are the main enemies to the health and proper function of the human body and they are a consequence of oxidative metabolism. For the purposes of this discussion free radicals and reactive oxygen species are placed under the general term of free radicals.

Free radicals can damage practically every component of a cell including its proteins, nucleic acids and particularly the fatty acid bilayer membrane. A damaged cell cannot reproduce itself, does not function properly, and dies from starvation or from the pollution of waste products. Also, damage to the cell membrane by free radicals can cause them to rupture, spilling cellular contents, including damaging enzymes into the surrounding tissue. Moreover, when the DNA is attacked by free radicals it alters the genetic code which increases the likelihood of abnormal cell duplication and growth.

This kind of damage accelerates the aging process as the tissues lose their function due to the steadily decreasing number of cells. In addition, a damaged cell cannot function properly. It is known that aging is accelerated when tissues lose their function due to a steady decrease in the number of cells. As tissues lose their function there is a steady decrease in the number of functional cells which accelerates the aging process.

The damage caused by free radicals is suspected to contribute to premature aging, cancer, impaired immune function, atherosclerosis and many other disorders. The damage to the cell by free radicals can be so severe that they are not capable of replenishing their components and, therefore, die. Moreover, aging tissues show an accumulation of debris from the damage cells. Also, free radicals are implicated in cancer development by their damage to chromosomes and nucleic acids which initiate irregular cell growth. It is thought that the promotion stage of cancer might also involve free radicals.

Also, free radicals play a significant part in the development of atherosclerosis and cardiovascular disease. Free radicals are thought to damage cell membranes of the blood vessels which encourage the accumulation of cholesterol in the injured cell membranes. Moreover, free radicals have be been implicated in the oxidation of LDL-cholesterol which is linked to heart disease.

For the most part these biological renegades are controlled by cellular enzymes (the internal police force) and antioxidant nutrients (biological green berets) which will be discussed below.

THE MAKING OF A RENEGADE! (WHERE DO FREE RADICALS COME FROM?)

Free radicals come from three sources. (1) The body makes free radicals every moment as a by-product of producing energy (basal metabolism). This energy is derived from reactions involving various substances and oxygen. Free radicals are a by-product of this metabolism. (2) Other sources of free radicals are exercise, diseases, inflammations, infections, environmental pollution (air, water, chemicals), tobacco smoke, excessive radiation, ultraviolet light, stress, and the aging process itself. All these sources increase oxygen-related reactions in our bodies, and consequently a large number of free radicals are created. (3) Free radicals have some positive actions. Our immune systems intentionally produces free radicals to fight and kill bacteria and viruses. They also contribute to the control of blood flow by influencing the tone of tissue lining the blood vessels.

If the production of free radicals, by whatever means, exceeds the body's ability to neutralize them they begin to proliferate uncontrollably and more free radicals are produced as the cells are damaged. It is important for the body to control the creation of free radicals to prevent damage to the healthy tissue in the body.

EXERCISE AND FREE RADICAL FORMATION

With regard to exercise, free radicals are produced by all types of exercise, but there is a greater creation of free radicals in long duration and high intensity training. While most of the oxygen consumed by the body in exercise combines with hydrogen to form water, up to 5% will form free radicals. **(McArdle et al, 1994 P 168) Ken Cooper, MD (1994)** states that it is well known that exercise results in free radical activity and that this free radical action is associated with damage in the muscles, liver, blood and other tissues.

Most of the research regarding free radical damage, antioxidants, and exercise have focused on high intensity endurance exercise. However, **Cooper MD (1994) and Kanter, Ph.D. (1995 in ESSR p. 379)** have pointed out that a number of suggestive findings and observations have emerged to implicate strength training and body building, as well, in the creation of free radicals.

Some of the more important observations are:

Strenuous physical exercise is associated with a remarkable increase in oxygen consumption, and hence, a challenge to the antioxidant systems. Exercise may promote free radical production in a number of ways. During exercise there is a 10-20 fold increase in oxygen consumption that can promote free radical generation. Also, the increase in catecholamine levels and lactic acid production and an elevated rate of hemoglobin autoxidation during and after exercise may increase free radical production.

The increase of body temperature caused by exercise may provoke free radical proliferation. Also, free radical damage may result simply from the act of putting extra pressure on joints and muscles during exercise. Mechanical processes such as the forces involved in joint compression have been shown to produce free radicals. Activity-related joint trauma may result from free radicals induced by a combination of joint compression, inflammation and reperfusion injury.

An "ischemia-reperfusion" phenomenon occurs during weight training exercise. During the performance of weight training exercises, there is a short term or transient restriction of blood flow (ischemia) caused by contracting muscles which is followed by the blood rushing back into the deprived tissues (reperfusion) when the muscle is resting. More aggressive body building examples of this process are "working to failure" or working for "the pumped effect." This "ischemia-reperfusion" process is known to trigger the generation of free radicals which increases the potential for damage to the body's cells. These techniques of body building also generate large volumes of lactic acid which may in part account for the "metabolic burn" and result in the production of free radicals. **(Kanter, Mitchell 1995 in ESSR P. 379)**

Finally, Dr. Paul Ward, one of the authors of this book was the Elite Athlete Coordinator from 1972 through 1984 for male and female throwers for the federation controlling track and field in the United States. In Olympic level discus throwers and shotputters, it has been observed that very high levels of CPK (creatine phospho kinase) were present in the blood on the days following heavy weight training. CPK is indicative of damage to muscle. In fact, in one case while reviewing the results of a routine blood test the athlete was asked by his physician to report to the emergency room because it was feared that he had experienced a heart attack. Subsequent analysis determined that the high CPK level was in fact due to a long and very heavy weight training session and that the athlete's heart and cardiovascular system were in perfect condition. Muscle damage is known to produce a release of free radicals. The endogenous antioxidant enzymes and dietary nutritional antioxidants help control free radical damage that may occur in exercise.

Regular physical exercise is recommended for maintenance of optimal health and prevention or management of some of the chronic diseases, as well as in training programs for general fitness, and amateur and professional athletes. It is generally recommended that both aerobic and body building exercises be included in the balanced fitness exercise program. There is strong evidence that implicates strenuous exercise with an increased free radical generation which is essentially due to a dramatic increase in oxygen uptake at the whole body and tissue levels, mechanical forces within the muscles, connective tissues and joints, production of lactic acid, increased body temperature and ischemic/reperfusion activities. **(Ji (1995)in ESSR P 135)**

Although the benefits of exercise are well known, evidence is accumulating to suggest that strenuous physical exercise can be damaging. It has been shown that strenuous exercise is associated with elevation of free radical production and increased lipid peroxidation, and results in increased requirements for nutritional antioxidants. Also, acute exposures to intense exercise has been shown to increase the production of free radicals and evidence of muscle damage. This is strong motivation for maintaining an exercise program of moderate intensity combined with nutritional antioxidant supplementation throughout life.

Demonstration of oxidative damage associated with exercise appears to depend on the training level of the subjects and the intensity level of the exercise (Witt et al [1992] in Frei [1994] p. 568) (McArdle [1994] et al p. 168). People who randomly submit their muscles to high levels of work and those advanced body builders and athletes that "push the envelop" are at risk for greater oxidative damage. **This is reason enough to increase the dietary intake of vitamins A (or beta-carotene), C, E and selenium and other nutritional antioxidants as insurance against tissue damage produced by free radicals generated in the exercise process.** These antioxidant scavengers neutralize free radicals and blunt their potential to cause damage. In addition, periodization of training factors is another protective measure which should be employed to prevent excessive free radical stress.

Muscle damage occurs during exercise and is greater with exhaustive exercise or when unusual amounts of negative (eccentric) muscle contractions are experienced, even in highly trained athletes. The damage is demonstrated by leakage of enzymes from muscle to plasma (Dillard et al. [1978] in Frei [1994] p 569). Duration and intensity of exercise are the primary factors affecting the degree of enzyme leakage. Substantial increases in serum creatine kinase activity have been observed 24 to 48 hrs after a 42.2 km marathon race. Following a marathon race, men incur significant skeletal muscle injury. Damaged or injured muscles produce free radicals. It is conceivable to believe that extended body building and exercise sessions of high intensity produce free radicals which will damage cells if not controlled by the "the internal police" and the "nutritional green berets."

The enzymic antioxidant defense systems (the internal police force) appear to increase in regularly exercised muscle tissue but they are not enough if free radicals start to proliferate out of control. When this happens, the second line of defense the nutritional green berets are available to engage in the battle to control free radicals. It appears that living in our society and engaging in strenuous physical exercise and body building programs that there is increased need for vitamins A (or beta carotene preferred), C, E and selenium and other antioxidants to help fight in the battle against free radicals. Apparently the dietary antioxidant supplements have the ability to decrease the oxidative damage that develops during exercise (Goldfarb [1993] in Frei p. 52). Recent research has demonstrated that antioxidants, especially vitamin E, can protect the body from free radical damage associated with strenuous exercise. (Lester Packer, Abraham Reznick & Sharon Landvik in Frei p. 567)

THE WARRIORS

The body has a complex defense system against the attack of these biological renegades. This complex network of antioxidants attacks free radicals and protects membranes, nucleic acids, and other cellular constituents from destruction. The "strategic defense system" includes the **endogenous antioxidant enzymes (superoxide dismutase, glutathione peroxidase, glutathione reductase, catalase, amino acids and other compounds)** and the **nutrient antioxidants which are vitamins, minerals and other herbal substances.** Antioxidants are compounds that combine readily with oxygen and neutralize oxygen radicals; the free radical chains are thus broken and other compounds and body components are enhanced or constructed.

This complex network of antioxidants (the biological strategic defense force) attack and neutralize the free radicals which protects cell membranes, nucleic acids, proteins and other cellular constituents from damage and destruction. This strategic defense force defends the tissues by scavenging free radicals before they interact with cells to cause free radical chain reactions which produces cell damage. The free radicals are rendered harmless because the antioxidants defense forces bind to and neutralize them.

This defense force involves the **endogenous cellular antioxidant enzymes (the internal police force)** and **the nutritional antioxidant defense system (the nutritional green berets).**

1. ## THE ENDOGENOUS CELLULAR ANTIOXIDANT ENZYMES (THE INTERNAL POLICE FORCE)

    Superoxide dismutase (SOD), catalase (CAT), glutathione peroxidase (GSH) and glutathione reductase (GR) are the internally produced antioxidant police force. However, these main enzymes are supported by a number of other enzymes. This cellular enzyme system is the body's first line of defense. These enzymes are naturally developed in the body and not much can be done to enhance their production other than to optimize nutrition and perform reasonable physical exercise. In addition, it is important to ensure adequate intake of the trace minerals copper, zinc, manganese, selenium and iron because they are needed for antioxidant enzyme production. Superoxide dismutase is marketed as a supplement to the natural formation of this substance in the body and may be effective in the control of free radicals.

    The efficiency of the cellular antioxidant defense system is of vital importance in determining the extent of oxidative stress and subsequent cell or tissue damage. **(Ji [1995] in ESSR p.136)** Moreover, it appears that this internal police force is augmented and becomes more efficient with reasonable physical training. In the body the skeletal muscle demonstrates the most responsive adaptations with regard to cellular antioxidant enzymes. However, in extended training at high intensity the "internal police force" may be overwhelmed. In this case the **nutritional antioxidant green berets** spring into action.

2. ## THE NUTRITIONAL ANTIOXIDANT DEFENSE SYSTEM: (THE NUTRITIONAL GREEN BERETS)

    Nutrition and nutritional supplementation permits us to greatly enhance our antioxidant defense system. The principal nutritional green berets are vitamins A (or beta-carotene), C and E, and the trace mineral

NUTRITION   PART V

selenium. The fat soluble vitamin E, A and beta-carotene, the water soluble C and the trace mineral selenium have the most support in scientific research. However, there are many other nutritional antioxidants that join the free radical battle and support the antioxidant defense system, such as: coenzyme Q10, proanthocyanidins, melatonin, phytochemicals and others.

It has been demonstrated that these nutritional antioxidants play preventative roles in many diseases like: cancer, cataracts, cardiovascular disease and premature aging. Moreover, they can minimize exercise induced free radical generation and prevent the subsequent damage they can cause. They have now taken the center stage and have become the **nutrient warriors of the 21st century.**

It is important to remember that antioxidants work together as teams to protect the body. Combinations of nutritional antioxidants (vitamins A [or beta-carotene], C and E, and selenium) provide better protection than just supplementing one or more of them. The effect of this combination is synergistic, which means that a combination of vitamins A (or beta-carotene preferred), C, E and trace mineral selenium is better than taking large amounts of just one or two of the nutritional antioxidants alone.

An example of this teamwork is a follows. Vitamin C recycles vitamin E after it has neutralized a free radical, which permits vitamin E to immediately reengage in the battle. Water soluble vitamin C also works to neutralize free radicals in cellular fluids. Also, the antioxidant mineral selenium cooperates closely with vitamin E. Selenium aids vitamin E and scavenges free radicals missed by the vitamin.

Other examples of the antioxidant teamwork is the coenzyme Q10 and vitamin E link and the proanthocyanidins vitamin C and E connection. Coenzyme Q10 helps to regenerate vitamin E which in turn protects cell membranes from damage caused by free radical terrorists. Proanthocyanidins are known to work synergistically with vitamin C by preventing vitamin C oxidation, and vitamin C in turn recycles vitamin E. Future research is bound to further demonstrate the efficacy of the nutritional antioxidants as well as identify and define the role of new nutritional antioxidants.

Beta-carotene is split to form two molecules of Vitamin A but beta-carotene itself is a quencher of singlet oxygen (a type of free radical). The antioxidant characteristics of beta-carotene are well documented, but it is just one of more than 400 carotenoid compounds that exist in nature. Other carotenoids that possess antioxidant functions are lycopene and lutein. Vitamin A is an antioxidant that helps protect cell membranes against free radicals and also has significant antiradical activity which helps prevent many undesirable reactions. (Barilla [1995] p. 53)

Each enzymic and nutritional antioxidant plays a unique role in protecting the tissues from exercise-induced oxidative damage. Any deficiency of an antioxidant nutrient can severely hamper the corresponding antioxidant system during exercise **(Ji [1995] in ESSR p. 159).**

The nutritional antioxidants have another significant function in the maintenance of one's health. All of them are strong stimulants to the immune system. Antioxidant supplements appear to strengthen the immune system by lowering the production of those chemical substances in the blood that suppress the immune functions. (Cooper [1994] p. 30) Also, they protect the immune cells and tissues from harmful free radical reactions that could impair their function. Poor nutrition is one of the most common causes of impaired immunity. Optimal intake of protein, vitamins and minerals and consumption of a low fat diet enhance the immune system and reduce the risk for infection and disease. Table 5-19 contains the recommended dietary allowances (RDA) for some antioxidant vitamins.

PART V

NUTRITION

Table 5-19. The recommended dietary allowances (RDA) for vitamins A, C, and E.

Vitamin	Men	Women
Vitamin A (RE[b]/day)	1000	800
Vitamin C (mg/day)[c]	60	60
Vitamin E (mg α-tocopherol/day)	10	8

[a]From NRC (1989)
[b]1 RE + 1 mcg all-trans-retinol = 6 mcg all-trans-β-carotene.
[c]The recommended dietary allowance of vitamin C for smokers is 100 mg/day.

Table 5-20 shows two recommended supplementation approaches from two different authorities which are very aggressive compared to the RDA. **ALWAYS CHECK WITH A HEALTH PROFESSIONAL WHO HAS NUTRITIONAL COMPETENCY RELATED TO PHYSICAL TRAINING AND BODY BUILDING BEFORE USING ADDITIONAL NUTRITIONAL SUPPLEMENTATION.**

NUTRITION PART V

Table 5-20. Best food sources and recommended amounts of nutritional antioxidants.

ANTIOXIDANT	BEST FOOD SOURCES	U.S. RDA	BARILLA[1]	COOPER[2]	
				General Fitness	Athletic Fitness
BETA-CAROTENE	Carrots & juice sweet potatoes, pumpkin, cantaloupe, leafy greens, winter squash, apricots, mangoes, persimmon, broccoli	No RDA* Established	15 mg ≈25,000 IU	15-30 mg ≈25,000-50,000 IU	30 mg ≈50,000 IU
OR VITAMIN A	Milk, eggs, liver, cheese, fish oil, butter	4,000 IU ♀ 5,000 IU ♂	12,500[3]-25,000 IU[4]	None[2+5]	None[2+5]
VITAMIN C	Melons, citrus fruits, red & green peppers, leafy greens, strawberries, papaya, kiwi, mangoes, cruciferous veg., tomatoes, sweet potatoes, blackberries, raspberries	60 mg	1,000[3]-18,000 mg[4]	500-2,000 mg	2,000-3,000 mg
VITAMIN E	Seeds, nuts, peanut butter, vegetable oils, wheat germ, leafy greens, fish & shellfish, avocados, mangoes, whole grains	12 IU ♀ 15 IU ♂	300[3]-1,600 IU[4]	400-600 IU	1,200 IU
SELENIUM	Cashews, halibut, meat, oysters, salmon, scallops, tuna, eggs, garlic	50 mcg ♀ 70 mcg ♂	100-200 mcg	50 mcg	100 mcg
Proanthocyanidins	Pine bark, grape seeds	None	100-150 mg	None[2]	None[2]
COENZYME Q10	Fish, nuts, lean meats, polyunsaturated fats, (Q10 made in body)	None	30-100 mg	None[2]	None[2]

OTHER IMPORTANT NUTRITIONAL ANTIOXIDANTS

1. **COENZYME Q10:** Q10 (known as ubiquinone) is found in every cell of the body and is the key to the process that generates 95 percent of cellular energy. It is used in the mitochondria where most of the body's energy is derived. Coenzyme Q10 is considered essential for the health of all the body cells, tissues and organs. **(Lee in Barilla p 220)** Coenzyme Q10 is marketed as a nutritional supplement at affordable prices. **(Lee in Barilla [1995] p. 216-217)**

   The major sources of coenzyme Q10 in the human diet are soybean oil, meats, migratory fish (e.g., mackerel and sardine), nuts, wheat germ, and some vegetables (e.g., beans, spinach, cabbage, and garlic). It helps to recycle the antioxidant vitamin E in the body. Q10 reacts with oxygen radicals and thus prevents direct damage to molecules and inhibits the initiation of lipid peroxidation which is a major factor in the destruction of cell membranes. It, also, is an effective singlet oxygen quencher (a reactive oxygen compound). **(Briviba, Karlis and Sies, Helmut in Frei p. 113-114)**

   It appears that Q10 enhances the power of vitamin E in protecting cell membranes from oxidative damage from free radicals, much as vitamin C does. (Cooper [1994] p. 72) As an antioxidant, it may play a role in preventing heart disease and congestive heart failure, controlling hypertension and normalizing periodontal disease. **(Cooper [1994] p. 214-215) (Lee in Barilla [1995] p. 217)** Coenzyme Q10 should be included in the supplementation of antioxidants (antioxidant cocktail) and should be used over a long period of time. **(Lee in Barilla [1995] p. 241-2)**

   Q10 has been shown to be effective in widely diverse health conditions ranging cardiomyopathy to periodontal disease. It is often effective in managing diabetes and obesity, in detoxification, enhances longevity, and stimulates the immune system. **(Lee in Barilla [1995] p. 215)** Q10 has no known harmful side effects and seems to be safe to use. The supplementation of Q10 is beneficial to body builders and all exercise enthusiasts in the following ways:

   A. Q10 may be effective in controlling the accumulation of fat and reducing the body fat by facilitating energy production.
   B. Improvement in aerobic capacity and retardation of fatigue.
   C. Enhancement of the immune system.

2. **PROANTHOCYANIDINS - THE NEW SUPER ANTIOXIDANT, PLUS:** Proanthocyanidins are a special blend of a type of bioflavonoid. Proanthocyanidins were originally isolated in 1951 from the bark of the French maritime pine tree. The term "proanthocyanidins" actually describes and entire complex of plant flavonoids all with exceptional antioxidant activity.

   Proanthocyanidins have been found also in various plants including grape seed, lemon tree bark, peanuts, cranberries and citrus peels. Both grape seed and pine bark are the best sources of proanthocyanidins. Some studies indicate that the grape seed extract may be more potent and effective since it contains chemical forms of proanthocyanidins not present in pine bark extracts. It is also more economical to extract these compounds from grape seeds than from pine bark.

   Proanthocyanidins are effective antioxidants which help our bodies resist blood vessel and skin damage, mental deterioration, inflammation and other damage caused by harmful free radicals. They reduce free radical-caused tissue damage many times more effectively than vitamin E, potentiate the health-giving effects of vitamin C, and protect brain and nerve tissue with its unique ability to penetrate the blood-brain barrier. To explain it another way, it can protect vitamin C, and vitamin C can regenerate vitamin E that has already been "spent" by sacrificing itself to free radicals.

   They also reduce inflammation and improve circulation, both relieving the distresses of arthritis, diabetes and stroke and promoting prevention of cardiovascular disease and cancer. As noted earlier, free radical

NUTRITION   **PART V**

damage is a common factor in a host of non-germ diseases, including heart disease, cancer, arthritis and accelerated aging.

The versatile action of proanthocyanidins appear to result from their being a potent antioxidant and from their function as a unique vitamin C and bioflavonoid helper. Because this bioflavonoid blend is such a strong antioxidant, it directly prevents vitamin C from being oxidized to dehydroascorbate. It is believed that another important way in which proanthocyanidins help is by their action on the enzyme, ascorbic oxidase, that metabolizes (breaks down) vitamin C in the body. Another way it helps vitamin C is by providing hydrogen ions to reduce glutathione, The reduced form of glutathione converts oxidized vitamin C (dehydroascorbate) back into its active form (ascorbate) which then can reengage in the battle against free radicals.

Proanthocyanidins do more than protect. They help repair by improving and stabilizing the skin protein collagen and improving the condition of arteries and capillaries. There a four biochemical properties of these substances that are responsible for their many benefits: (1) free-radical scavenging; (2) collagen (a skin protein) binding; (3) inhibition of inflammatory enzymes; (4) inhibition of histamine formation.

Proanthocyanidins reduce inflammation and improve circulation which relieves the distresses of arthritis, diabetes and stroke. In addition they promote the prevention of cardiovascular disease and cancer. Its ability to bond to collagen has wide implications as to its benefits for those who bodybuild and exercise.

3. **MELATONIN:** Research evidence suggest that melatonin may posses potent antioxidant properties. It is effective in fighting free radicals and molecular fragments which experts identify as causing the degenerative effects associated with aging. It is believed that melatonin may help prevent alzheimer's disease, fight depression, fight cancer and prevents premature aging. One of its chief applications is the regulation and normalization of biological rhythms. **MELATONIN SHOULD ONLY BE TAKEN BEFORE THE SLEEP CYCLE.**

THE STRATEGIC DEFENSE INITIATIVE AGAINST FREE RADICALS

We exist in an oxygen environment which means that many oxidative reactions will naturally occur. There is moment by moment exposure to oxidative stress. Oxidative stress means that the balance of oxidants (free radical compounds—the biological renegades) versus antioxidants (enzymic-internal police force and nutritional green berets) has shifted in favor of the oxidants. When the oxidants rule the free radical renegades proliferate. The results are cell damage that contributes to the development of diseases, injuries and lowered physical performance. The ultimate outcome of this damage to the cells is premature aging.

Free radical have beneficial actions which produce energy, hormones and to fight infections. And, free radicals are also part of many necessary enzymatic reactions. However, the uncontrolled creation of free radicals causes cellular damage and must be stopped. That is the function of the endogenous enzymes ("the internal police force") and the nutritional antioxidant warriors (nutritional green berets).

The natural endogenous enzymes are the first line of defense. In addition, the nutritional green berets which are vitamins A (or beta-carotene preferred), C, E, and selenium, work together as a team to control these biological renegades. Each of the nutritional supplements has its own unique method of controlling these free radicals, but they all work in concert. Vitamin E works in the fat containing areas of the body, like the membranes surrounding the cells. It resides in the membranes and neutralizes the free radicals when they are produced. Without antioxidant protection, the cell membrane is damaged and cell functioning is impaired. Selenium works with vitamin E and is part of many antioxidant enzymes made in the body.

Vitamin C works in the watery environments between and inside the cells. It recycles vitamin E after it has destroyed a free radical and has become inactive. Vitamin C converts the inactive vitamin E back to its antioxidant form so that it can reengage the battle against the free radicals. Beta-carotene is active in the energy producing factories of the cell. Creation of free radicals in the mitochondria will stop energy production and can kill the cell. Vitamin A can be created from beta-carotene when needed or can exist as assimilated from dietary sources. Vitamin A is a strong antioxidant which helps protect cell membranes against undesirable oxidation.

Coenzyme Q10 is involved in the creation of 95% of the cellular energy. Proanthocyanidins reduce free radical caused tissue damage, potentiates vitamin C and protects the brain and nerve tissue. They are effective in reducing inflammation, improving circulation, relieving the distresses of arthritis, diabetes and stroke, and promoting prevention of cardiovascular disease and cancer. So you see that the strategic defense forces used to fight against the free radical onslaught is a highly coordinated interactive force that involves the natural enzymes (internal police force) and the antioxidant nutrients (the nutritional green berets).

There are five ways to fight against the onslaught of free radical damage: (1) Employ a super-nutrition eating pattern; (2) Control your environment as much as possible; (3) Reduce as much unnecessary emotional stress in your life as possible; (4) Engage in a rational regular physical training program; and, (5) Supplement your diet with nutritional antioxidants daily.

<u>First</u>, employ a super-nutrition eating pattern. Include as much raw fruits and vegetables in your daily eating pattern as possible. Only 9% of Americans eat **five servings** of fruit and vegetables per day—the intake recommended by the National Cancer Institute and the National Research Council. Make sure your diet is high in antioxidant foods which are the fruits and vegetables. Buy fresh fruits and uncut vegetables and eat them raw or prepare them with the minimum of cooking. Avoid wilted produce. Minimize excess trimming, cutting, chopping, slicing, washing or soaking. Frozen fruits and vegetables are acceptable but they do have lower nutritional values. The best cooking methods to preserve antioxidants are microwave, steam or stir-fry. Use the minimum amount of water for cooking and consume the water in some way with your meal. Avoid use of excessive heat in cooking. Store once cooked food in air tight containers. Avoid eating left-overs. **Table 5-20** presents the best food sources of nutritional antioxidants.

<u>Second</u>, control your environment as much as possible. Water pollution, soil pollution, air pollution, cigarette smoke, car exhaust, various chemicals, ultraviolet light and ozone produce free radicals in our bodies. While it is not possible to eliminate the impact of all of these environmental factors, you can minimize some of them and eliminate some of them. Cigarette smoke can be eliminated for the most part by not smoking and avoiding cigarette smoking environments. Ozone and air pollution exposure can be avoided by exercising in air conditioned environments or outside in the early mornings or after sundown when air pollution is less.

Water pollution is generally not a problem in our society. However, special drinking and cooking water can be purchased or effective filtration devices can be attached to kitchen water supplies. Soil pollution is generally not a big concern except in various instances of known pollution levels. Car exhaust can be avoided by using car air conditioners and driving in free moving traffic. Traffic is unavoidable in most cases but it is well known that freely moving traffic produces less air pollution. If possible drive in non stop-and-go situations. Seek freely moving alternative routes to your destination.

Excessive ultraviolet radiation can be prevented by staying out of the sun, wearing protective clothing or by using any one of dozens of skin protectants. Avoid exposure to various chemicals that have toxic effects and may produce free radicals. The use of protective gloves and clothing will afford some protection. Thorough washing of your hands and exposed skin is effective, also.

The objective is to identify, avoid and eliminate as many environmental triggers of free radicals as possible. One does not have to become rabid anti-pollution nut, just be aware of the problems and take reasonable evasive actions. Some decisive and silent shifts in one's behavior can reduce significant exposure to factors that produce free radicals which may reduce the immune system functioning, cause disease, accelerate aging, and inhibit body building and exercise progress.

NUTRITION PART V

Third, one must reduce as much unnecessary emotional stress in life as possible. This can be done by changing the attitude, planning times of low or no stress activities, and engaging in activities that vent some of the pent-up emotions. This may take the form of exercise, music, reading, rest or spiritual activities.

Fourth, is to engage in a rational regular training program. Effective body building programs are periodized (by varying the main factors of the program in cycles or phases). Cycles of 6 to 8 weeks should be planned. Subsequent cycles should vary the frequency, intensity (% 1RM), duration, mode (free weights, dumbbells, machines and combinations), sets and repetitions. In addition, any collateral cardiovascular program should be periodized (cycled) by varying the frequency, intensity, duration, and mode of this kind of exercise (stationary bike, stepper, treadmill, step classes, etc). Most people fail to reach their goals because they do not cycle their training. Proper variation of the basic training factors will reduce the oxidative stress on the system as well as enhancing your motivation to train. Lee Haney, often uses the phrase, **"stimulate, don't annihilate."** The authors of this book believe it is more important to **"train, don't strain."**

Fifth, you should supplement your diet with nutritional antioxidants daily. Use a variety of nutritional antioxidants in a **"antioxidant cocktail."** This **"antioxidant cocktail"** should include the combination of vitamin A (or beta-carotene preferred), C, E, the trace mineral selenium, coenzyme Q10, proanthocyanidins, and melatonin. Other nutritional supplements should be ingested as needed or desired. Nutritional antioxidant supplements (the green berets) augment and support the interior police forces (endogenous enzymatic defenses). Table 5-20 shows two recommended approaches by Barilla (1995) and Cooper (1994). Safe ranges are given to meet the needs of a wide variety of living requirements. If you are involved in heavy training, in a high stress daily living pattern or exposed to environmental pollution, you will require higher amounts of antioxidants, and, therefore, use larger amounts of the antioxidants. **CONSULT WITH A NUTRITIONALLY COMPETENT PHYSICIAN, DIETICIAN OR NUTRITIONAL BIOCHEMIST FOR PRECISE GUIDANCE BEFORE USING THE ANTIOXIDANT COCKTAIL.**

Additional vitamin and mineral supplementation is always a prudent practice in an effort to prevent oxidative damage. You need all the important antioxidant nutrients. It would be foolish to rely on vitamin A, C, E, beta-carotene and selenium alone. The combination cocktail is needed for synergism and to optimize the effects of all the nutrient antioxidants. **(Barilla [1995] p. 187)**

CONCLUSION

Premature aging and continued good health can be promoted by knowing the enemies within (the formation of excessive free radicals) and taking steps to reduce them in your lifestyle. Below is a summary of some environmental and personal behaviors that trigger the production of damaging free radicals which put one at risk for excessive oxidative stress and premature aging. They are: (1) excessive physical activity and overtraining; (2) inadequate eating patterns; (3) cigarette smoke; (4) pollution (water and air); (5) pesticides and other chemical contaminants; (6) inflammation; (7) infections; (8) radiation; (9) ultraviolet radiation; (10) certain drugs; and, (11) excessive emotional stress.

Application of a sound "strategic defense initiative" against free radicals will increase the results of training, improve physical performance, enhance health, prevent chronic diseases and may increase one's lifespan. Do not forget to ingest an " antioxidant cocktail" that is tailored to one's biological system and one's specific needs. It will add "life to your years and years to your life!"

ANTIOXIDANT AFTERTHOUGHTS

ANTIOXIDANT PROFILE: It isn't just what we eat, but how well it is absorbed, that determines our nutritional antioxidant defenses. You may eat well and take supplements, but do you know if the nutrients are actually getting into your system? There are scientific laboratories which can provide a comprehensive "antioxidant profile" based on the analysis of blood serum.

The diet is a factor in the antioxidant defenses, because the needed nutrients must be in the diet in the first place. However, nutrients won't help unless they are absorbed. We can control what is eaten, but our antioxidant defenses are influenced by other variables that are outside our control. The only solution is to measure the blood levels directly and then make adjustments as necessary based on these measurements.

Blood concentrations of more than 20 different substances can be measured in human blood serum that are related to the antioxidant defense system. Among the nutritional antioxidants that can be assessed are beta-carotene and other carotenes, vitamins A, C, E, coenzyme Q10, the trace mineral iron and other related substances. It is simple to determine what relative deficiencies actually exist so that they can be targeted for correction.

If deficiencies are found, the consumption of significantly higher levels of micronutrients in the form of nutritional supplements can elevate the serum levels. Subsequent tests will demonstrate the effectiveness of the dosages and the duration of antioxidant supplementation.

This antioxidant profile allows the potential hazards of antioxidant deficiencies to be recognized long before they become problems. With regard to physical training, this antioxidant profile will indicate deficiencies that may interfere with training success.   When unfavorable situations are recognized early, small corrections can be made that help individuals avoid serious disease or optimize nutritional antioxidant defenses that will ensure training success.

VITAMIN C IS MORE THAN AN ANTIOXIDANT! In addition to the use of vitamin C as an antioxidant and in prevention and treatment of infectious diseases and degenerative diseases, Jean Barrilla, M.S. lists other benefits of Vitamin C: **(Barilla [1995] p. 92-94)**

1. Vitamin C is effective in helping individuals suffering from all kinds of allergies. It will not cure the allergies, but is useful in suppressing symptoms. The allergy symptoms are ameliorated by the vitamin's antihistamine effect and by improving the immune system's regulatory mechanism.

2. Vitamin C helps wounds to heal more quickly. Higher intakes of vitamin C speeds the healing process. In combination vitamins C and E increases the rate of the healing of burns without formation of painful scar tissue. Also, it is used postoperative to reduce the time needed for recovery.

3. Vitamin C offers protection against air pollution. When combined with vitamins A and E, the protection against the effects of air pollution is multiplied.

4. Vitamin C inhibits carcinogens and other toxins found in food or produced in the digestive tract from foods and food additives. When present in the digestive tract, vitamin C blocks the production of nitrosamines which are manufactured in the digestion of meats containing nitrites or nitrates. Nitrosamines are known to be among the most powerful carcinogens.

5. Vitamin C offers protection against radiation. It is believed the vitamin C slows the rate of cell division.

6. Vitamin C enhances the development of prostaglandin E1 which may reduce the risk of cancer.

7. Vitamin C in combination with B vitamins may benefit schizophrenics and other psychiatrically ill people.

8. Vitamin C in combination with B6 is useful in treating arthritic symptoms.

9. Vitamin C helps us combat a variety of physical and psychological stresses.

PART V

NUTRITION

10. Vitamin C assists alcoholics and drug addicts in breaking their addiction because it competes for the same receptor sites as alcohol or drugs. If vitamin C bonds with the receptor site, the alcohol or narcotic cannot.

11. Vitamin C may be helpful in reducing the pain and discomfort of hemorrhoids in some individuals. Increased vitamin C intake can maintain soft stools and strengthen the walls of the veins in the anus.

RELATED LITERATURE

1. Barilla, Jean, M.S.; The Nutrition Superbook: Volume I: The Antioxidants; Keats Publishing, Inc., New Canaan, Connecticut, 1995.

2. Frei, Balz Ph.D.; Natural Antioxidants In Human Health And Disease; Academic Press, Inc.; San Diego, California; 1994.

3. Cooper, Kenneth, M.D.; Antioxidant Revolution; Thomas Nelson Publishers, Nashville, 1994.

4. Diplock, Anthony; Machlin, Lawrence; Packer, Lester; Pryor, William; Editors; Vitamin E: Biochemistry and Health Implications; Annals of the New York Academy of Sciences, Volume 570; The New York Academy of Sciences, New York, 1989.

5. Holloszy, John, M.D.; Editor; Exercise And Sport Sciences Review, American College Of Sports Medicine Series; Williams & Wilkins, Baltimore, 1995.

6. Ji, Li Li, Ph.D.; Exercise and Oxidative Stress: Role of the Cellular Antioxidant Systems; Exercise and Sport Sciences Reviews, John Holloszy, M.D., Editor; American College of Sports Medicine Series, Williams & Wilkins, Baltimore; 1995; pp. 135-166.

7. Kanter, Mitchell, Ph.D.; Free Radicals and Exercise: Effects of Nutritional Antioxidant Supplementation; Exercise and Sport Sciences Reviews, John Holloszy, M.D., Editor; American College of Sports Medicine Series, Williams & Wilkins, 1995; Baltimore; 1995; pp. 375-397.

8. McArdle, William (Ph.D.); Katch, Frank (Ed.D.) & Katch, Victor (Ed.D.); Essentials of Exercise Physiology, Lea & Febiger, Philadelphia, 1994; p. 168.

9. Levine, Stephen, Ph.D.; Kidd, Parris, Ph.D.; Antioxidant Adaptation: Its Role in Free Radical Pathology. Biocurrents Division, Allergy Research Group, 400 Preda Street, San Leandro, California 94577.

10. Passwater, Richard A, Ph.D.; The New Superantioxidant - Plus: The Amazing Story of Pycnogenol, Free-Radical Antagonist And Vitamin C potentiator; Keats Publishing. Inc., New Canaan, Connecticut, 1992.

11. Sauberlich, Howerde; Machlin, Lawrence; Editors; Beyond Deficiency: New Views on the Function and Health Effects of Vitamins; Annals of the New York Academy of Sciences, Volume 669; The New York Academy of Sciences, New York, 1992.

PROTEIN SUPPLEMENTATION FOR ATHLETES, BODY BUILDERS AND ACTIVE PEOPLE

The protein needs of athletes, body builders and highly active humans has been debated for many years. Some believe that a balanced diet can meet the protein needs of people who exercise vigorously. On the other hand, many experts believe that exercise at high intensities or of long durations will increase the demand for dietary protein, and, thus, there must be increased protein intake and/or utilization of a protein supplementation to maintain a positive nitrogen balance. A positive nitrogen balance means that there is no muscle breakdown.

The Food and Nutrition Board of the National Academy of Sciences has consistently not recognized any special protein requirement for athletes or highly active people. This position is diametrically opposed to the practices and thinking of athletes and highly active people over the years. The reality is, that regardless of scientific opinion and nutritional policies, athletes and highly active people have continued to consume a high amount of protein in their daily eating pattern. What should be the protein intake for highly active people and should protein intake be supplemented? This question will be answered in the following paragraphs.

Adequate amounts of protein are needed as basic building blocks for tissue maintenance, growth and repair. Protein is not considered an important source of fuel in exercise, although in long duration endurance exercise protein contributes from 10% to 15% to the total energy utilized. (**MCARDLE 1991**) In general, the preferred fuels for exercise are carbohydrates and fats, depending upon the intensity and duration of the exercise. Carbohydrates are used in repeated short duration movements executed at moderate to high intensity. A mixture of carbohydrates and fats are utilized for moderate intensity activities while fats are employed almost exclusively in low intensity and long duration exercise.

McArdle, W.D.; Katch, F.I.; Katch, V.L.: Exercise Physiology: Energy, Nutrition and Human Performance; Lea And Febiger; Philadelphia; Third Edition; 1991; p. 37.

Before discussing the recommended daily allowance (RDA) and the need for additional dietary protein in physically active people, body builders and athletes, a examination of amino acids; anabolism, catabolism and nitrogen balance and branched chain amino acids will be presented.

THE RECOMMENDED DIETARY ALLOWANCE FOR PROTEIN

The recommended dietary allowance (RDA) or protein for an adult is determined by the Food and Nutrition Board of the National Academy of Sciences. This value has been established with regard to age. Table 5-21 contains the number of grams of protein needed per kilogram/pound of body weight for selected ages.

Table 5-21. The RDA In Number Of Grams Of Protein Needed Per Kilogram/Pound Of Body Weight For Selected Ages.

AGE	GRAMS/KG BODY WEIGHT	GRAMS/LB BODY WEIGHT
7 - 10	1.2	.55
11 - 14	1.0	.45
15 - 18	0.9	.41
19 - 22	0.8	.36
OVER 23	0.8	.36

NOTE: Infants and growing children have an RDA of protein intake of 2 - 4 grams per kilogram of body weight (1 - 2 grams per pound). Pregnant women and nursing mothers should increase their intake of protein by an additional 10 to 20 grams over the RDA, respectively.

PART V

NUTRITION

1. National Research Council, Food and Nutrition Board; Recommended Dietary Allowances; 9th Edition; Washington, D.C.; National Academy of Sciences; 1980; PP. 39-54.

2. Table 5-21 adapted from: Williams, Melvin; Nutrition for Fitness and Sport; Wm. C. Brown Publishers; Dubuque, Iowa; 1988; p. 103.

Some authorities define protein requirements in another way. The American standard for protein is that 12% - 15% of the daily total caloric intake should be from protein. This standard permits up to approximately 1.32 grams of protein per kilogram of body weight. This is more than the RDA standard. The British state that only 10% of the daily total caloric intake should be from protein. This standard falls below the RDA standards. The World Health Organization standard for protein intake is a very low 5% of the total daily caloric intake. This is an inferior standard for protein needs. As will be shown later, all these standards are well below the recommended level for daily dietary protein intake for people engaged in vigorous weight training and other anaerobic and aerobic conditioning programs.

While these standards are good guidelines, athletes, body builders and physically active people are seeking ways to optimize their performance. Recent research studies (see references below) have demonstrated that athletes and highly active people need more daily dietary protein compared to the established standards. This is true for the endurance athlete as well as the body builder and weight lifting participants. This higher requirement for protein is discussed below.

References Indicating A Higher Protein Demand For Athletes And Highly Active People:

1. Brotherhood, J.R.; Nutrition and Sports Performance; Sports Medicine; 1:350-389; 1984.

2. Celejowa, I. and Homa, M: Food intake, nitrogen and energy balance in Polish weight lifters during training camp; Nutrition and Metabolism; 12:259-274; 1970.

3. Dragon, G; Vasiliu, H and Georgescu, E.; Effect of increased supply of protein on elite weight-lifters. IN: Milk Proteins; Galesloot, T.E. and Tinbergen, B.J. (Editors); Wageningen, The Netherlands: Pudoc, 1985; pp. 99-103.

4. Lathan, H.; The diet of weightlifters; IN: European Weightlifting Federation Official Bulletin; #3; pp 39-47; European Weightlifting Federation, Yugoslavia; 1982.

5. Laritcheva, K. A.; Yalovaya, N. I.; Shubin, V. I. and Smirnov, P. V.; Study of Energy Expenditure and Protein Needs of Top Weight Lifters; In Parizkova, Jana and Rogozkin, V. A.; Nutrition, Physical Fitness and Health; University Park Press; Baltimore; 1978; pp. 155-163.

6. Lemon, P.W.R., Effect of exercise on protein requirements. J. Sports Sci., 9: Special Issue, 53-70, 1991.

7. Lemon, Peter; Protein and Exercise: Update; Medicine and Science in Sports and Exercise; Vol. 19; # 5; 1987; pp. S179-S190.

8. Lemon, P.; Yarashki, K. E. and Dolny, D.A.; The importance of protein for athletes; Sports Medicine; 1:474-484; 1984.

9. Lemon, Peter and Nagel, F.; Effects of exercise on protein and amino acid metabolism; Medicine and Science in Sports and Exercise; 13:141-149; 1981.

10. Tarnopolsky, M.A., Atkinson, S.A., MacDougall, J.D., et al., Evaluation of protein requirements for strength trained athletes. J. Appl. Physiol., 73(5):1986-1995, 1992.

PART V

NUTRITION

11. Tarnopolsky, M.A.; MacDougall, J.D. and Atkinson, S.A.; Influence of protein intake and training status on nitrogen balance and lean body mass. Journal of Applied Physiology; 64:187-193; 1988.

12. van Erp-Baart, A.M.J., W.H.M. Saris, R.A. Binkhorst, J.A. Vos and J.W.S. Elvers. Nationwide survey on nutritional habits in elite athletes: Part 1. Energy, carbohydrate, protein and fat intake. International Journal of Sports Medicine 10:suppl 1, S3-S10, 1989.

13. Williams, Melvin; The role of protein in physical activity; IN: Nutritional Aspects of Human Physical Performance; 2nd Edition; Springfield, IL; Charles C. Thomas; 1988; pp. 120-146.

14. Wilmore, Jack and Freund, B.; Nutritional enhancement of athletic performance; Nutritional Abstracts Reviews; A 54:1-16; 1984.

Historically, athletes and coaches have intuitively thought that more dietary protein is needed during heavy weight training. While the evidence is accumulating that supports the effectiveness of a high protein intake by highly active humans, the intake of additional protein in conjunction with arduous physical training makes good sense. To build muscle tissue requires the stimulus to grow (weight training) and the raw materials for protein synthesis and the energy needed to enable the construction of new protein.

The need for a higher protein intake is especially true for those people who are weight training at high intensities in long training sessions. This kind of training requires an increased level of daily dietary protein intake to prevent a negative nitrogen balance (loss of muscle mass) and, also to enhance the development of more muscle mass. Empirically it has been observed over at least 40 years, that athletes and body builders have used higher protein intakes in their diets. Meanwhile, no epidemiological (the study of diseases) evidence has been presented that demonstrates adverse side effects or health risks from high protein intake.

There are three minor concerns with high protein intake that have been addressed by Lemon. They are:

1. Water balance disturbances (water deficiency).
2. Undesirable increased total energy intake.
3. Calcium balance disturbances (deficiency).

To overcome these problems the following guidelines are suggested:

1. Increase water intake to minimize the dehydration affects with increased protein intake.
2. Keep track of the daily total number of calories ingested to minimize the accumulation of body fat.
3. Increase calcium intake to offset any tendency toward developing osteoporosis. Also, the increase weight training to produce structural adaptation of the bones in the presence of balanced and adequate nutrition.
4. Seek the help of a qualified sports nutritionist if any nutritional problems become manifest.

Lemon (1984) makes the following recommendations for individuals (male and female, young or old) with regard to increased daily protein intake associated with highly vigorous weight training and long duration endurance programs.

"Athletes should consume 1.8 to 2.0 grams of protein per kilogram of body weight per day. This is approximately twice the recommended requirement for sedentary individuals. For some athletes this may require supplementation; however, these quantities of protein can be easily obtained in a diet when 12% to 15% of the total energy is from protein!"

Lemon, Peter; Yarasheski, Kevin; Dolny, Dennis; The Importance of Protein For Athletes: Sports Medicine; ADIS Press Limited; Langhorne, PA; Vol 1:474-484; 1984.

PART V

NUTRITION

In a study of elite Romanian weight lifters, Dragon, et al (1985), found that maintaining a more positive nitrogen balance produced a greater protein synthesis resulting in enlarged muscle mass and enhanced strength performances. These weight lifters made impressive gains in muscle mass (approximately 6%) and increases in strength (approximately 5%) when the dietary protein was increased from 225% to 438% of Recommended Dietary Allowance (RDA). This is translated into absolute values of 2.0 - 3.9 grams per kilogram of body weight or 1 - 2 grams per pound of body weight.

The Russians have done some advanced nutritional research. Laritcheva, et al (1978) reported the following results of high protein diets combined with vigorous Russian weight lifters.

1. **"At protein intake levels of less the 2 grams per kilogram of body weight in some athletes during intensive training, a negative nitrogen balance was observed despite high nitrogen assimilation (95%)."**

2. **"During periods when athletes are not exposed to increased physical and psychic stress, a protein intake of 2 grams per kilogram of body weight was enough to sustain nitrogen balance."**

3. **"The protein requirement of athletes during a period of intensive training corresponds to 2.2 - 2.6 grams per kilogram of body weight."**

Laritcheva, K. A.; Yalovaya, N. I.; Shubin, V. I. and Smirnov, P. V.; Study of Energy Expenditure and Protein Needs of Top Weight Lifters; In Parizkova, Jana and Rogozkin, V. A.; Nutrition, Physical Fitness and Health; University Park Press; Baltimore; 1978; pp. 155-163.

CONCLUSION:

People who are vigorously involved in weight training and endurance training have a higher protein need. Sports nutrition authorities recommend 1.0 - 3.0 grams of protein per kilogram of body weight or .45 - 1.36 grams per pound of body weight. This is considerably above the minimum RDA value of .8 grams per kilogram of body weight or .36 grams per pound of body weight and represents 1.25 to 3.78 times the minimum standard.

AMINO ACIDS

Amino acids are the basic structural units of plant and animal protein. The protein eaten by humans are broken down by the digestive tract into various amino acids which are subsequently utilized by the body for tissue growth, repair and maintenance.

WHY AMINO ACIDS?

Magendie (1783-1855), a French physiologist, carried out early feeding experiments on laboratory animals using different kinds of food. All of these kinds of food had one feature in common: none of them contained nitrogenous substances. Magendie was the first contemporary scientist who had experimentally shown that nitrogenous foods are essential for humans. Then the Dutch biochemist, Mulder, recognized the similarity of different nitrogen containing albuminous substances in animal and plant tissues and coined the term "protein" to describe these substances. Magendie after getting acquainted with Mulder's work assessed his discovery as the nutritional essentiality of proteins for humans.

Today, it is known that living cells contain thousands of different proteins, the most abundant class of large biological molecules. Proteins, as many other biological molecules, exhibit functional versatility. Table 5-22 presents some biological functions of proteins.

Biochemistry has established that all proteins are composed of building blocks call amino acids. The number of amino acids in a protein, the chemical nature of these amino acids, and the sequential order of amino acids in a protein chain determine the characteristic chemical behavior of this protein. These 3 factors determine the ability of a protein to perform its biological functions. Absence of certain amino acids in a diet makes it impossible for a body to build a protein where these amino acids are part of the structure. The lack of a specific protein means the lack of a specific function in the body, and this could be catastrophic. Now it is possible to see why amino acids are so important in the diet. An eminent nutritional biochemist, Dr. Konrad Lang, states: "Actually, the body needs amino acids and not proteins."

Table 5-22.   Some Biological Functions of Proteins (Animo Acids).

FUNCTION	EXAMPLES
ENZYMES	GLYCOLATE OXIDASE OF GLYCOSOMES. ALCOHOL DEHYDROGENASE IN ALCOHOL FERMENTATION.
TRANSPORT	HEMOGLOBIN - OXYGEN TRANSPORT IN BLOOD VERTEBRATES. CERULOPLASMIN - COPPER TRANSPORT IN BLOOD.
STORAGE	FERRITIN - IRON STORAGE (SPLEEN). CASEIN - AMINO ACID STORAGE (MILK).
CONTRACTION	MYOSIN - THICK FILAMENT IN SKELETAL MUSCLE. ACTIN - THIN FILAMENT IN SKELETAL MUSCLE.
PROTECTION	ANTIBODIES - INTERACT WITH FOREIGN PROTEIN. FIBRINOGEN - PROTEIN REQUIRED FOR BLOOD CLOTTING.
HORMONES	INSULIN - REGULATOR OF GLUCOSE METABOLISM. GROWTH HORMONE - REQUIRED FOR BONE GROWTH.
TOXINS	SNAKE VENOM - HYDROLYTIC (DEGRADATIVE) ENZYMES. CLOSTRIDIUM BOTULINUM TOXIN - LETHAL FOOD TOXINS.

Armstrong, F.B. and Bennett, T.P.; "Biochemistry", Oxford University Press; N.Y.; 1979; p. 61.

TYPES OF AMINO ACIDS

All the amino acids existing in living forms can be divided into two groups. The first group encompasses all the amino acids which could be incorporated in protein chains. Their main role is to be building blocks of proteins. Their main biological function is to participate as a team with the other amino acids in a specific function of a protein entity. There are twenty such amino acids. All of them, under special circumstances, exist in a body as free amino acids and consequentially they may perform special individual functions. For instance, they could be used as regulators or precursors of regulators of the nervous system. They could, also, be used for the construction of many other important chemicals in the body. Table 5-23 contains examples of some multiple functions of products constructed of individual amino acids in humans.

NUTRITION   PART V

Table 5-23.   Examples of some multiple functions of products constructed of individual amino
            acids in humans.

AMINO ACID	PRECURSOR OF:
GLYCINE	CREATINE, BILE ACIDS, PORPHYRINS, GLUTATHIONE, HIPPURATE.
SERINE	ETHANOLAMINE AND CHOLINE, I.E., OF PHOSPHOLIPIDS; ACETYLCHOLINE (NEUROTRANSMITTER).
CYSTEINE	TAURINE (NEUROTRANSMITTER), GLUTATHIONE.
ARGININE	CREATINE.
ASPARTATE	NUCLEIC ACID, NUCLEOTIDES, B-ALANINE, ANSERINE, CARNOSINE.
TYROSINE	EPINEPHRIN, NOREPINEPHRINE (NEUROTRANSMITTERS), THYROXINE HORMONE, MELANINS.
TRYPTOPHAN	SEROTONIN (NEUROTRANSMITTER).
METHIONINE	METHYL GROUP FOR CREATINE AND CHOLINE, AND POST-TRANSLATIONAL METHYLATIONS.

The second group are amino acids which exist individually as members of the free amino acid pool performing their biological role and never as building blocks of a protein chain, or a peptide chain (a shorter protein-like chain).

Nutritionists suggest a second way of classifying amino acids in the human body: "essential" amino acids (indispensable) and "non-essential" amino acids (dispensable). "Essential" describes a compound that the body is unable to synthesize: the compound must be supplied as food. "Non-essential" characterizes a compound which could be made in the body from other chemicals.

Of the twenty amino acids which could be, and, mostly are, incorporated into proteins, ten are essential for growing humans. This includes histidine and arginine which are pseudo-essential and which are required for growth related to early life and growth related to repair and replacement throughout life. Adults usually need only eight amino acids.

All other amino acids in the first ("biochemical") classification of these compounds can be made in the body. In this sense they are "non essential" or "dispensable" or "provisionally dispensable." It should be remembered that "dispensable" amino acids are also very important in the metabolism and any difficulty in their production in the body means a disturbance of metabolism.

The specific metabolic functions of individual essential and metabolically related amino acids are:

Arginine participates in the biosynthesis of creatine and participates in the formation of urea and thus accelerating the removal of potential toxic ammonia.

Histidine deficiency causes anemia and the decrease of carnosine in muscle. Larger doses of histidine may act as an antiketogenic substance and cause the accumulation of glycogen in the liver.

Leucine, Isoleucine and Valine are called branch-chain amino acids (BCAA). They are expended normally, in their free form by the heart, kidney, diaphragm, brain, leukocytes, skin fibroblasts, adipose tissue and the liver. Lack of leucine impairs the functions of the liver, thymus, adrenals and gonads. Lack of isoleucine disturbs the nitrogen balance severely. Lack of valine causes hyperaesthesia and lack of muscle coordination.

Methionine protects the liver, stimulates blood formation and growth. Lack of methionine causes cirrhosis of the liver, anemia, kidney damage, muscle atrophy and decrease of general resistance.

Lysine strongly affects bone formation, length growth and genital function.

Phenylalanine and Tyrosine affect the function of thyroid gland, adrenals and blood formation.

PART V   NUTRITION

Tryptophan contributes to the formation of nicotinic acid (niacin), eye pigments and genital function.

Cystine (or Cysteine) maintains liver function and contributes to the formation of albumin, glutathione and insulin. Lack of this amino acid causes similar effects to those in methionine deficiency.

Threonine deficiency affects the utilization of other amino acids.

Table 5-24 contains a nutritional biochemical classification of the amino acids. This table is different from Table 5-4 presented in the foregoing section dealing with protein. Table 5-4 is a more generalized listing of amino acids which is targeted for the average person. The information in Table 5-24 is a more precise biochemical classification of the amino acids in which biochemical interactions are taken into account.

Table 5-24.   A Nutritional Biochemical Classification Of The Amino Acids.

INDISPENSABLE (ESSENTIAL)	PROVISIONALLY DISPENSABLE (PROVISIONALLY NON-ESSENTIAL)	DISPENSABLE (NON-ESSENTIAL)
LYSINE	CYSTINE (OR CYSTEINE) (C)	GLYCINE
TRYPTOPHAN	TYROSINE (D)	SERINE
METHIONINE		ALANINE
PHENYLALANINE		ASPARTIC ACID
HISTIDINE (A)		GLUTAMIC ACID
THREONINE		PROLINE
LEUCINE		HYDROXYPROLINE
ISOLEUCINE		
VALINE		
ARGININE (B)		

(A) DISPENSABLE FOR MAINTENANCE IN HUMAN ADULT.
(B) RATE OF SYNTHESIS ADEQUATE FOR MAINTENANCE IN THE ADULT AND FOR MODERATE GROWTH.
(C) SYNTHESIS REQUIRES SULFUR FROM METHIONINE.
(D) SYNTHESIZABLE FROM PHENYLALANINE.

ANABOLISM, CATABOLISM AND NITROGEN BALANCE

One of the best general indicators of the correctness of amino acid metabolism in the body is the nitrogen balance. Anabolism and catabolism will be defined before the discussion of nitrogen balance.

Most of the metabolic reactions in the body (often called metabolic pathways as they occur in an organized sequence) can be classified into two main groups: anabolic pathways or anabolism, and, catabolic pathways or catabolism.

Catabolic pathways degrade food that is eaten to produce precursors for biosynthesis. The second function of catabolism is to generate chemical energy for energy requiring reactions in the body. The third function of catabolism is to convert waste material to chemical compounds suitable for excretion from the cells and finally from the organism.

Anabolic pathways synthesize complex molecules in the body needed to build, maintain and reproduce cells and tissues. Anabolism uses precursors formed by catabolism and uses energy (the anabolic reactions usually require good amounts of energy) also provided by catabolism. In the absence of adequate carbohydrate, muscle protein is broken down by the process called gluconeogenesis to provide carbohydrate for the operation of the brain and nervous system. This is also protein catabolism.

For amino acids, it is noticed that catabolism isolates amino acids from foods and transforms them into nitrogen containing compounds or supplies them without transformation for anabolic purposes: building proteins or other complex biomolecules. Some nitrogen containing compounds the body considers as waste (e.g., urea or creatinine) and excretes them. This leads to a consideration of nitrogen balance.

The human body takes in as food: proteins, peptides, amino acids and other nitrogen containing compounds in addition to many non-nitrogen containing foodstuffs (carbohydrates and fats). As a result of catabolic and anabolic processes certain amounts of nitrogen wastes are generated. If nitrogen input equals nitrogen output there is nitrogen balance.

Positive nitrogen balance occurs when more nitrogen containing compounds are retained by the body than are excreted. One can observe positive nitrogen balance in growth, during pregnancy, during lactation, in times of convalescence after injury or disease or during stress.

Negative nitrogen balance takes place when the body loses more nitrogen containing compounds than it obtains from the diet. Negative nitrogen balance takes place when the body loses more nitrogen containing compounds that it obtains from the diet. Negative nitrogen balance occurs most frequently when the supply of amino acids is inadequate. Either the essential amino acids have not been supplied or the "non-essential" are supplied in smaller than necessary quantities and the nitrogen of these amino acids does not cover the nitrogen requirements of the body. In these situations the anabolic processes of nitrogen metabolism is impaired and malnutrition develops.

Loss of non-nitrogen containing compounds while nitrogen balance is maintained is observed during optimum weight-loss programs. The supply of amino acids is critical at this time. The negative nitrogen balance during a weight-loss diet would mean that the diet program is not suitable for the person who uses it. Moreover, lack of essential amino acids in the diet leads to a very serious restriction of protein biosynthesis in the body and all the protein functions previously mentioned are in such cases impaired. The consequences of a negative balance involve the impairment of biosynthesis of proteins and the appearance of specific deficiency symptoms related to biological functions of individual amino acids.

RELATED LITERATURE

1. Armstrong, F.B. and Bennett, T.P.; "Biochemistry"; Oxford University Press; N.Y.; 1979.

2. Krebs, H.A.; "Evolutionary Concepts in Biological Thought"; IN: "Metabolism and Clinical Implications of Branched Chain Amino Acids and Keto Acids"; Editors: M. Walser and J.R. Williamson; Elsevier; Amsterdam; 1981.

3. Meduski, J.W.; "Lecture Notes on Nutritional Biochemistry"; Fifth Edition; University of Southern California; Los Angeles; 1983.

4. Meduski, J.W.; Introduction to Amino Acids; Unpublished monograph; Nutritional Consultants Group, Inc.; 1985.

BRANCHED CHAIN AMINO ACIDS (ANABOLIC)

Leucine, isoleucine and valine are known as the branched chain amino acids (BCAA). BCAA are essential amino acids and together comprise 40% of the minimum daily requirement in humans. Unlike most other amino acids, after absorption from the small intestine, the BCAA are channeled directly to the muscles for growth and repair. The BCAA are a source of energy and can induce an anabolic effect in the active muscle.

BCAA must be present in the muscle for growth and development to occur. A deficiency in any one of the BCAA will result in muscle catabolism.

Madsen (1982) proposes three principal metabolic roles of the BCAA:

1 . Peripheral calorie source - BCAA in the skeletal muscle are substances used for generating calories.

2. Anabolic - the presence of BCAA promotes protein synthesis. BCAA not only decrease the breakdown (catabolism) of protein but also increase its formation (anabolism).

3. BCAA also act as regulators to normalize the metabolism of brain neurotransmitters.

Stone (in Comereski 1986) makes a strong statement suggesting the need for supplementation with BCAA in those people involved in heavy training:

> **"There's evidence to show that in heavy work, especially aerobic work, they (BCAA) are very easily converted into alanine. In other words, they're the primary amino acids involved in gluconeogenesis. (A process which converts protein to glycogen for use as energy when carbohydrate stores are low.) Because of that, there might be an increased need for the branched-chain amino acids. If you're talking about someone doing sets of squats for multiple sets of 10, lots of large muscle mass exercise, I think the branch-chain amino acids might help."**

Hickson states, ".... **supplementation of BCAA would be desirable for athletes especially as an energy source and potential anabolic agent."** There have been no reported scientific studies on the use of BCAA to induce muscle growth in conjunction with weight training programs.

Dr. Peter Lemon in the 1980s demonstrated that exercise depletes some amino acids much faster than others. Through research it has been established that large quantities of alanine and glutamine (nonessential amino acids) are released from the muscle during exercise. (Felig 1971 & Roth 1990) Since there is not enough quantities of alanine and glutamine stored in the muscles that account for this loss it is surmised that much of these amino acids that are released are made in the muscles from other amino acids during exercise.

Approximately one-third of the muscle is made up of the three branched chain amino acids (BCAA), leucine, isoleucine and valine. It is believed that the BCAA supply the material for the construction of alanine in exercise. Lemon (1982) states that exercise depletes more leucine than any other amino acid. In addition, it has been demonstrated that this rapid loss of leucine occurs in both endurance exercise (Henderson, et al 1985) and anaerobic exercise (Babji, et al 1983).

The depletion of leucine has been shown by research to be substantial during exercise even at moderate intensities. Evans, et al (1983), found that leucine oxidation increased 240% in exercise performed at moderate levels. Measurement of isoleucine and valine is more difficult, but it is believed that there are similar losses in these amino acids during exercise. Support for this hypothesis comes from recent studies that have shown that exercise directly increases the enzyme branched-chain keto-acid dehydrogenase, which controls the degradation of all three BCAAs (Kasperek 1987).

There are three possible sources of the BCAA loss during exercise:

1. Increased uptake of free BCAA from the blood.
2. Reduced use of BCAA in muscle protein synthesis.
3. Breakdown of muscle protein.

To avoid the muscle breakdown in exercise, the exerciser should ensure an adequate supply of BCAA prior to and post exercise. There are studies that suggest that eating BCAA can easily increase the blood levels (Felig

NUTRITION **PART V**

1971 & Matthews, et al 1980). BCAA taken 1-2 hours before intense training spare muscle BCAA and spare testosterone during training, and increase testosterone levels after training (Kraemer 1988 & Wagenmakers, et al, 1989).

The sensible practice should be BCAA supplementation 1-2 hours before the workout to spare the breakdown of muscle and spare testosterone during and after training (Carli 1992).

How much BCAA are needed? There are no definitive studies to suggest the BCAA requirement. Furthermore, is has been demonstrated that even sedentary men require higher amounts of leucine than the recommended RDA. The RDA level for leucine in average men is approximately 14.28 mg/kg/day. At leucine intakes of 20 mg/kg/day (a 40% larger value) average men were found to be in negative leucine balance. Therefore, it is impossible for even average men to maintain optimal muscle maintenance.

A research group from MIT make the following conclusion about current requirements for leucine.

> **"Current values for leucine requirements may underestimate significantly intake levels actually needed to maintain protein nutritional status." (Meguid et al 1986).**

Colgan (1993) estimates that people in **vigorous training** have the following requirements for BCAA:

Leucine	- 60 mg/kg/day
Valine	- 50 mg/kg/day
lsoleucine	- 20 mg/kg/day

The only form of BCAA that an athlete should use are those that specify singular, free-form L-amino acids on the label. There are three different forms of amino acids that can be obtained, L form, D form and the DL form. **The body can only use the L-amino acids to make proteins.** It is also important that the BCAA be protected from light to prevent attenuation, so buy BCAA products that are placed in dark glass bottles with expiration dates and lot numbers displayed on the labels.

---

1. Babij, P., et al. Changes in blood ammonia, lactate and amino acids in relation to workload during bicycle ergometer exercise in man. European J of Appi Physiol 1983;50:405-411.

2. Comerski, John; Amino Mania - a round-table interview of the experts; Joe Weider's Sports Fitness Magazine, September 24,1986.

3. Colgan, M.; Optimum Sports Nutrition; Advanced Research Press, New York; 1993.

4. Carli, G., et al. Changes in the exercise-induced hormone response to branched chain amino acid administration. Eur J Appi Physiol 1992;64:272-277.

5. Evans, W.J., et al. Protein metabolism during exercise. Physician and Sports Med 1983;11:63.

6. Felig, P., Wahren, J., Amino acid metabolism in exercising man. J. Clin Invst, 1971; 50:2703.

7. Felig, P, Wahren, J.; The glucose-alanine cycle. Metabolism 1973;22:179.

8. Hatfield, Frederick; Ergogenesis: Achieving peak athletic performance without drugs; Fitness Systems, Inc.; Canoga Park, CA; 1985; pp. 15-16.

9. Henderson, S.A., et al. Leucine turnover and oxidation in trained rats during exercise. Am J Physiol 1985;249:El37-El44.

10. Hickson, James and Wolinsky, Ira; Nutrition in Exercise and Sport; CRC Press, Inc.; Boca Raton, Florida; 1989; pp. 136-137.

11. Kasperek, G.J., Snider, R.D.; Effect of exercise intensity and starvation on activation of branch-chain keto acid dehydrogenase by exercise. Am J Physiol 1987;252:E33-E37.

12. Kraemer, W.J.; Endocrine response to resistance exercise. Med Sci Sport Exer 1988;(Suppl)20:Sl52-Sl57.

13. Lemon, P., et al. In vivo leucine oxidation at rest and during two intensities of exercise. J Appi Physiol 1982;53:947-954.

14. Madsen, D.C. and Johnson, Ivan D.A. (Editor), Branched-chain amino acids; metabolic roles and clinical applications; Symposium: Branched-chain amino acids; MTP Press Ltd.; 1982; pp 1-21.

15. Matthews, D.E., et al. Measurement of leucine metabolism in man from a primed, continuous infusion of L-(I-C) leucine. Am J Physiol 1980;238:E473.

16. Meguid, M.M., et al.; Leucine kinetics at graded leucine intakes in young men. Am J Clin Nutr 1986:43:770.

17. Roth, E. et al. Glutamine: An anabolic effector? J. Parent Ent Nutr 1990;14:1305-1365.

18. Wagenmakers, A.J.M., et al. Exercise-induced activation of branched-chain 2-oxo acid dehydrogenase in human muscle. Eur J Appi Physiol 1989;59:159-167.

A FEW METABOLIC OPTIMIZERS FOR HIGH ACTIVITY LEVELS

In this day of understanding and enlightenment there are still nutritionists and physicians that say a balanced diet will provide sufficient fuel and nutrients that will sustain vigorous training and high performance. They still believe that highly active people can receive all their nutrient requirements from careful selection of foods and increased caloric intake. An analysis of the typical American's eating habits and considering the questionable nutritional content of American food (raw and processed) demonstrates that this type of thinking is seriously flawed. Empirically, athletes and progressive coaches and nutritionists know differently. Moreover, studies performed on physically active people and athletes have shown them to be short of many key nutrients despite their increased food intake.

Dr. Jezy Meduski, M.D. and leading authority of nutritional biochemistry makes the following statement:

> *"It is not just a question of needing more calories for fuel to maintain a higher activity level, but of maintaining the body's systems at the upper limits of performance. Exhaustive physical work puts a tremendous burden on the immune, recovery and other systems of the body. The ratio of special nutrients (those directly related to exercise, endurance, muscle breakdown, reconstruction and immunity) to total caloric nutrients is significantly changed. There is an increased need for certain vitamins, minerals, fatty acids, phytochemicals and amino acids. Merely eating more does not supply these specific substances."*

The key to successful nutritional support is to adopt a scientific approach to eating patterns and nutritional supplementation. By using this approach the athlete, weight trainer and body builder can optimize the results of the many hours of training in the gym. People who train vigorously, use supplements for eleven general reasons besides survival and eating for pleasure. They are:

1. To get stronger.
2. To gain muscle mass.
3. To lose fat.
4. For anaerobic energy.
5. For aerobic energy.
6. To reduce pain and inflammation.
7. For more rapid tissue healing.
8. For faster post-exercise recovery.
9. For better mental focus or arousal.
10. For general health.
11. To improve training and performance.

PART V

NUTRITION

There are many substances that have been touted to improve performances, facilitate recovery from training and aid in cellular metabolism. It would take another book to present all the nutritional supplementation possibilities. To stimulate the thinking process, just a few metabolic optimizers for high activity levels are presented below. There are other substances that could have been presented, but there are other books that focus on the identification of effective metabolic optimizers plus the science and application of these substances. **The objective of this section is to make the reader aware of the need for a more sophisticated approach to nutrition and nutritional supplementation to support training and recovery from training.**

The number of nutritional supplements on the market is staggering. One is seriously challenged to find effective nutritional supplements as well as generating the money to support their use. Certainly, it is important to use a multiple vitamin and mineral supplement; to use protein supplements; to use additional antioxidant vitamins, minerals and phytochemicals; and, to use specialized nutritional and herbal substances that meet one or more of the 11 objectives presented above. Each individual needs to develop a plan for nutritional supplementation that is consistent with their training and performance goals and the amount of their budget they can devote to nutritional supplements.

BORON (ANABOLIC AGENT)

Bodies require a number of minerals for efficient metabolism. Boron is one of them. Human bodies cannot make minerals, they are found in the food that is grown in soil that has an adequate content of minerals. If minerals are not in the soil, then they cannot be in the food that is grown in the soil, and, therefore, will not be found in the person who eats food grown in the mineral deficient soil.

Without consuming all the essential minerals in adequate amounts, no weight trainer can expect good improvement is muscle mass and performance. Food that is grown in the mineral deficient soil of today makes it impossible to get optimal mineral intake. Therefore, the vigorous weight trainer can be seriously deficient in the essential minerals including boron.

Boron is essential for the manufacture of hormones that control bone and muscle growth. Furthermore, it is understood from clinical observations that an adequate boron status is necessary for normal testosterone production. Because of this there is interest in using boron as a possible anabolic supplement for people who train with weights.

It is believed that the average person who trains with weights does not consume sufficient boron to meet the demands of a vigorous strength training. The Colgan Institute (Colgan 1988) performed an analysis of the boron content of the American diet in 1987. They found that the average boron intake in a good mixed diet in America is 1.9 mg per day. This data is in correspondence with an analysis of the average diet in Finland which reported a boron intake of 1.7 mg per day. (Varo 1980) These studies just looked at the intake of average people who were not engaged in vigorous physical training.

The question is, how much boron should the active weight trainer consume per day? It has been suggested that 2.0 mg per day may be sufficient for the average person. However, when you add the hormonal demand of very active people, the requirement may be higher. The Colgan Institute supplements athletes with 3.0-6.0 mg/day of boron citrate and aspartate. They recommend that you do not use more than 50 mg/day because it may interfere with phosphorus and riboflavin metabolism. (Pinto 1978) Large doses are not a good idea.

Boron does not, by itself, increase testosterone levels, but it is an essential part of the process. The testosterone levels are strictly controlled by multiple factors. Taking mega-doses of boron will interfere with the metabolism of other nutrients.

1. Colgan, M., Optimum Sports Nutrition; Advanced Research Press; New York, 1993; p. 205, 231-232.

2. Colgan, M., Boron; Nutrition & Fitness; 1988;7:33,46.

3. Varo, P., et al. Acta Agric Scand; 1980;22:27-171 (Suppl).

4. Pinto, J., et al. J. Lab Clin Med; 1978;92:126-134.

CAFFEINE (ERGOGENIC AGENT)

Most people are aware that caffeine is a classic stimulant. It is consumed on as regular basis in coffee, some soft drinks, chocolate, in headache and pain medicine as well as cough and cold remedies. Caffeine is one of the oldest and most commonly used stimulants in the world. Everyone knows that it stimulates the central nervous system to increase alertness and fight drowsiness.

Caffeine comes close to being the safest stimulant known, although overdosing can be unpleasant and extreme abuse can be fatal (for example drinking over 200 cups of coffee or swallowing 50 Vivarin tablets in a short time).

Studies involving serious athletes have demonstrated significant improvement in performance or physiological responses or both. For those people who are not a serious trainer there seems to be no effects on physical performance or on physiology (Bucci 1989).

When caffeine is properly used, it is very effective for increasing physical performance. Williams has published some good reviews that show that caffeine stimulates the central nervous system, increases the release of adrenaline increases the use of bodyfat as fuel and spares glycogen (Van Handel in Williams 1983 & Williams 1985).

If a person is a habitual user of caffeine in the form of coffee, tea, cocoa, sodas that include caffeine, or chocolate, then extra caffeine will not benefit training or sport performance.

If you want to use caffeine as an ergogenic aid it is imperative to purge it from you diet four or more days before it's application. Even then the impact of caffeine on performance or training is smaller than those people who would in their daily lifestyle avoid caffeine. The best procedure is to use caffeine only to enhance performance or training. Save the use of caffeine for you hard training days or for competition.

How much caffeine is enough? No one knows the correct dosage. It appears that there are large individual differences in response to caffeine ingestion (Essig, D, et al. 1980). The Colgan Institute states that 1000 mg of caffeine is over the top for most athletes, especially if they do not use caffeine in their everyday life (Colgan, 1993). Body weight does influence the amount one needs to get an effect.

Caffeine ingestion (3-9 mg/kg body weight) prior to exercise enhances performance of both prolonged endurance exercise and short-term intense exercise lasting about 5 minutes in the laboratory. Practical observations have shown that caffeine should be ingested 30-60 minutes before intense weight training to be effective. The timing seems to be individualistic. Some experimentation with the timing should define the correct sequence.

It is important to remember that if frequent use of caffeine to stimulate a person to train is required, then it is time to evaluate you work, rest and nutrition pattern. The training pattern should be varied by changing the volume, intensity, exercises and training frequency so that recovery is optimized. It is a foregone conclusion that rest and nutrition must be considered, also. Overuse of caffeine without the periodization of training will invariably lead to overtraining and other health problems.

PART V

NUTRITION

1. **Bucci, L.R.; Nutritional Ergogenic Aids. In: Hickson, J.F. and Wolinsky, I.; Nutrition In Exercise and Sport. Boca Rotan, FL.; CRC Press, 1989; pp. 107-185.**

2. **Colgan, M.; Optimum Sports Nutrition; Advanced Research Press, New York; 1993; p. 301.**

3. **Essig, D., Costill, D.L., and Van Handel, P.J.; Effects of caffeine ingestion on utilization of muscle glycogen and lipid during leg ergometer cycling. J. Sports Med 1980; 1:70-74,**

4. **Van Handel, P., Caffeine. In: Williams, M.H.; Ergogenic aids in Sports. Human Kinetics Publishers, Champaign, IL; 1983:128.**

5. **Williams, M.H.. Drug foods - alcohol and caffeine. In: Nutritional Aspects of Human Physical and Athletic Performance, 2" Ed. Charles C. Thomas, Springfield, IL; 1985:272.**

CARNITINE (ENERGY BOOSTING AGENT)

Carnitine is found in all the human tissues. Carnitine is a non-essential amino acid, which can be manufactured from other amino acids in the liver. Also, the kidney, brain and possibly the testis are able to synthesize carnitine from its precursor, 4-butyrobetaine. The 4-butyrobetaine, is produced not only in the liver, kidney and brain, but, also in the testis, skeletal muscle, cardiac muscle and epididymis. In addition to being formed in the body, carnitine can be obtained from the food consumed.

Carnitine is a vitamin-like nutrient related to the vitamins of the B-complex and is naturally found in foods of animal origin. Major sources of carnitine in the diet are meat and diary products. People who eat mainly cereals, fruits and vegetables (all carnitine-poor) should either complement their diet with fermented soybean products or use a L-carnitine supplement. It is essential for energy production and fat metabolism and is primarily synthesized in the human liver, yet insufficient amounts are produced in infants, adolescents and adults under certain physiological conditions.

Humans are able to synthesize carnitine but only under specific metabolic conditions and they may produce too little of it. A carnitine deficiency may develop if not enough is made. Carnitine biosynthesis requires two essential amino acids (lysine and methionine), three vitamins (vitamin C, niacin and vitamin B-6) and reduced iron (that is a bivalent iron ion). It is known that carnitine biosynthesis is regulated not only by age and metabolic status of an organism, but specifically by diet. Generally, a poor diet and specifically the deficiency of nutrients involved in carnitine biosynthesis lead to a poor carnitine status and to carnitine deficiency. It is then necessary to supplement the diet with carnitine to restore carnitine-linked functions of the body. Dietary carnitine does affect tissue carnitine concentration.

For nutrition of athletes it is of additional importance to note that carnitine has an important role in the utilization of branched-chain amino acids. These amino acids (leucine, valine and isoleucine) are utilized in exercising muscles. Carnitine, by improving the utilization of branched-chain amino acids, contributes to the effectiveness of muscle work of an athlete. Moreover, it may be of benefit to the athlete in long duration weight training sessions.

Approximately 95% of the L-carnitine in the body is located in the musculature, and, theoretically, it may impact both aerobic and anaerobic energy production during exercise. Carnitine is very important for the aerobic endurance athlete since most of the energy for endurance training and performance comes from fatty acid oxidation. Fats, to be used as an energy source, are oxidized in the body.

Carnitine is a component of several enzymes that facilitate the transport of fatty acids across the inner mitochondrial membrane. Carnitine absolutely controls fat use because it forms the transport system that moves the fatty acid molecules into the mitochondria of the cell where they are used as fuel.

The oxidation occurs in the part of cells of all body tissues called the mitochondrial matrix. Carnitine is "absolutely required for the transport of long chain fatty acids into the mitochondrial matrix." In other words, carnitine makes it possible to deliver fatty acids to the mitochondria where the process of oxidation does occur. Carnitine may be of assistance in the reduction of body fat by athletes and body builders.

Research has shown that carnitine supplements increases the maximum use of oxygen in athletes. The use of 4 grams of L-carnitine daily as a dietary supplement, increased maximal oxygen consumption (Marconi 1985 & Angeline 1986).

The person who trains seriously has a demand for carnitine that can easily exceed the body's ability to manufacture it. Moderate exercise (at 55% of maximum oxygen uptake) causes a 20% drop in muscle carnitine. Training at higher levels of exercise intensity causes a much greater drop in muscle carnitine, which places the person into the same carnitine status as patients with carnitine deficiency diseases (Lennon 1983).

In addition to the above functions, carnitine plays a role in thermogenesis (helps in cold acclimation). Other functions of carnitine are oxidation of medium chain fatty acids, oxidation of fatty acids in peroxisomes, removing toxic concentrations of acetylcoenzyme A, producing energy from ketone bodies, pyruvate, amino acids and regulating blood ammonia concentrations.

Carnitine deficiency is easily corrected by ingesting oral L-carnitine. Research shows that L-carnitine supplements inhibit the decline of free carnitine in muscle caused by maximal exercise, and completely prevent the decline in free carnitine during endurance exercise (Arenas 1991).

The supplementation of L-carnitine has demonstrated reduced post-exercise levels of lactate and pyruvate, and significantly increased maximal work output (Siliprandi 1990). Moreover, L-carnitine supplements have shown significant improvement in endurance (aerobic) exercise (Canale 1988). It appears that L-carnitine supplementation can boost both anaerobic and aerobic performance.

A dose of 2-4 grams taken for 2 weeks, one hour before exercise appears to be effective. That is many times the recommended dietary intake which is about 100-300 mg per day (Borum 1982). No toxicity has been demonstrated at 4 grams daily of L-carnitine supplementation (Angeline 1986).

The L-carnitine form is the only form recommended for human supplementation. L-carnitine appears to be very effective as a supplement for endurance athletes. There has been sufficient empirical evidence of the use of L-carnitine by body builders to successfully reduce body fat to warrant consideration for supplementation. However, definitive research needs to be conducted to support the use of this substance in the enhancement of aerobic endurance performance and the reduction of body fat.

The D,L-carnitine form of carnitine is less expensive but is of no use in the human body. In fact, it actually has a negative effect on metabolism. The use of D, L-carnitine has demonstrated muscle weakness in hemodialysis patients. The D, L-carnitine form is thought to block the cellular uptake of L-carnitine and inhibits the enzymes which allow the transportation of fat into the cell by L-carnitine. This process suppresses the fat burning mechanism. The D, L-carnitine form is not recommended for dietary supplementation.

Japanese and European (Siliprandi, et. al., 1980) research have indicated that carnitine supplementation can help lower triglycerides in individuals with elevated blood fats. Furthermore, contemporary studies with carnitine show its usefulness in normal and abnormal metabolism. The nutritional studies indicate effectiveness of carnitine supplementation in certain cases of the infant diet, in the vegetarian diet or in cases of a diet where a main source of protein is soy protein isolate, casein or egg white protein.

PART V

NUTRITION

---

1. Angeline, C., et al. Clinical study of efficacy of L-carnitine and metabolic observations in exercise physiology. Clinical Aspects of Human Carnitine Deficiency, Pergamon Press, NY:1986:38.

2. Arenas, J., et al. Carnitine in muscle, serum, and urine of non-professional athletes: effects of physical exercise training and L-carnitine administration. Muscle & Nerve; 1991;14:598-604.

3. Borum, P.R.: Carnitine in human nutrition. Nutrition and the MD, 1982;9:1.

4. Canale, C., et al. Bicycle ergometer and echocardlographic study in healthy subjects and patients with angina pectoris after administration of L-carnitine: semiautomatic computerized analysis of M-mole tracing. Int J Clin Pharmacol Ther Toxicol, 1988;26:221.

5. Colgan, M.; Optimum Sports Nutrition; Advanced Research Press, New York; 1993; p. 301.

6. Hatfield, Frederick; Ergogenesis: Achieving peak athletic performance without drugs; Fitness Systems, Inc.; Canoga Park, California; 1985; pp. 37-38.

7. Hickson, James and Wolinsky, Ira; Nutrition in Exercise and Sport; CRC Press; Boca Raton, Florida; 1989; pp. 127-129.

8. Khan-Siddiqui, L. and Bamji, M.S.; Plasma Carnitine Levels in Adult Males in India: Effects of High Cereal Low Fat Diet, Fat Supplementation and Nutritional Status; American Journal of Clinical Nutrition; 33:1259-63; 1980.

9. Lennon, D.L.F., et al. Effects of acute moderate-intensity exercise on carnitine metabolism in men and women. J Appl Physiol; 1983;55:489.

10. Marconi, C., et al. Effects of L-carnitine loading on the aerobic and anaerobic performance of endurance athletes. Eur J Appi Physiol; 1985;54:131-135.

11. Siliprandi, N. and Ramacci, M.T.; Carnitine as a "Drug" Affecting Lipid Metabolism; in Drugs Affecting Lipid Metabolism; Eds: R. Fumagaiii, D. Kritchevsky and R. Paoletti; Elsevier Publishing Company; New York; 1980.

12. Siliprandi, N., et al. Metabolic changes induced by maximal exercise in human subjects following L-carnitine administration. Biochem Biophys Acta, 1990;1034:17-21.

13. Williams, Melvin; Nutrition for Fitness and Sport: Wm. C. Brown Publishers; Dubuque, Iowa; 1988; pp. 90 + 91 + 93.

CHROMIUM (ANABOLIC AGENT)

Biologically active chromium is necessary to utilize insulin. Chromium is responsible for the binding of insulin to the cell membrane receptor sites. Insulin is a powerful hormone that controls protein, fat and carbohydrate metabolism; performs a principal role in affecting blood sugar and cholesterol levels, enlarging muscle mass and creating energy. Insulin also constrains the breakdown of proteins, especially in muscles cells.

Chromium is part of the glucose tolerance factor (GTF) associated with the metabolism of insulin. Without the GTF chromium, insulin is ineffective and incapable of affecting the body's metabolism. If GTF mediated (chromium) insulin is not present, protein catabolism continues as usual with no replacement.

Chromium is important to insulin function and insulin assists in fat metabolism, growth and protein synthesis. Some researchers have stated that exercise-induced trace mineral losses combined with a dietary intake of lower than RDA, produces suboptimal nutritional status and suboptimal health in exercising individuals. Individuals who train vigorously are at risk due to repeated losses of chromium (Campbell and Anderson 1987).

PART V

NUTRITION

Furthermore, other stresses on the body such as infections, intense heat or cold and physical trauma can cause increased chromium losses placing the human at risk. (Borel and Anderson 1984) In addition, research has shown that Americans do not consume enough chromium. (Anderson and Kozlovsky 1985) Food processing is the cause for the low chromium intake in the American diet. A scientific report declares that 80% of the chromium in the food is removed during processing. (Borel and Anderson 1984) The problem is exacerbated by food being grown in chromium depleted agricultural soil. Also, diets high in simple sugars increase chromium losses from 1 0% to 300%. (Koziovsky 1986)

Recently, chromium has been praised by newspapers and health and nutrition magazines as a "cholesterol fighter" and a "natural anabolic steroid alternative". Many athletes and body builders have jumped on the bandwagon. There are two forms that are being marketed, one which is less effective (chromium picolinate) and the other which shows good results and promise (chromium nicotinate). The controversy centers around the effectiveness of the formulation of the chromium product. More will be said about this controversy latter.

The trace mineral chromium intake for the general population is considered to be suboptimal. Research studies have shown that 9 out of 10 Americans do not get adequate amounts of chromium from the food they eat. Moreover, it has been shown in vigorous exercise that a large amount of chromium is lost. Furthermore, consuming high amounts of sugar, also, depletes the body's chromium store. The soil in which food grows has become deficient in chromium as well as other minerals. The diets of the American people are low in chromium, but also refining and processing of food removes up to 80% of the chromium. Recent reports by the US Department of Agriculture indicates that 90% diets of Americans contain less than 50 mcg of chromium per day (Anderson 1985).

Foods that are good sources of chromium include: brewers yeast, whole breads and cereals, molasses, brown rice, cheese. and lean meats.

The safe recommended dietary allowance (RDA) has been established by the National Research Council as 130 mcg per day for adults (range: 50-200 mcg per day) (RDA 1989).

Athletes use about twice the amount of chromium as the sedentary person, even when they perform exercise at moderate intensity. This means that they have insufficient dietary intake of chromium and in exercise they lose large amounts which results in decreased muscle mass and impaired use of bodyfat as fuel. Therefore, athletes may require twice as much chromium as the average non-active person.

The Colgan Institute supplements their athletes with 200 to 800 mcg of chromium daily depending upon body weight. They contend that to effect permanent fat loss one must *maintain chromium status* (Colgan, 1993). It is impossible to get sufficient chromium from food. It is just not in the food we eat. Moreover, it would be necessary to consume up to 5,500 calories a day to obtain even the lower end of the 50-200 mcg of chromium considered adequate by the Food and Nutrition board of the National Academy of Sciences. It must come from supplementation.

Chromium picolinate and chromium polynicotinate are the most common forms found in health food stores. Chromium polinicotinate (niacin-bound chromium) is absorbed and retained up to 311% better than chromium picolinate and 672% better than chromium chloride (Olin, 1992).

The widespread practice of consuming refined sugars and refined carbohydrates results in chromium loss and depletion of chromium stores. This sustained intake of diets high in sugars and refined carbohydrates can lead to chromium deficiencies. Dietary supplementation of chromium would appear beneficial to any body type or lifestyle.

The use of a chromium supplement is important for good health, may reduce the risk of adult onset diabetes, cardiovascular disease, reduce body fat and increase muscle mass. Oral supplementation of chromium at the estimated safe and adequate daily dietary intake level appears to be safe.

PART V

NUTRITION

The use of chromium will not increase your muscle mass and reduce your fat overnight. It is the combination of sensible work, rest, nutrition and supplementation carried out over time that gives optimal results.

Products where the chromium is bound to nicotinic acid (the chemical name for niacin) which is called chromium nicotinate are considered safe and very effective. The other form of chromium is bound to picolinic acid (called chromium picolinate) and is considered biologically inert and ineffective at activating insulin - which is the primary function of biologically active chromium.

It has been mentioned that chromium picolinate is not considered to be biologically effective. Picolinic acid forms very strong chemical bonds with chromium. The strength of this bond interferes with the chromium's insulin-potentiating effect. The chromium is so tightly attached to the picolinic acid that the body is unable to convert this compound into a form usable by insulin. Cellular metabolism is hampered by this ineffective form of chromium even though picolinic acid facilitates the absorption through the intestines. Furthermore, the use of picolinic acid has not been declared safe for human consumption. The long term studies on picolinic acid demonstrate that picolinic acid literally competes with niacin and could be a health hazard.

On the other hand, chromium nicotinate has been shown to posses the greatest biological activity and safety when contrasted to other chromium supplements. The niacin in this formulation creates less rigid bonds with chromium so that it is easily transformed to a form insulin can use. This substance is thought to facilitate protein, fat and carbohydrate metabolism; to reduce cholesterol levels; to increase muscle mass and to act strongly in generating energy.

The human chromium problem, simply defined, is that vigorous exercise reduces chromium levels; there is documented low levels of chromium in the diet; food is grown in chromium depleted soils; normal stresses of living depletes chromium stores and a diet high in simple sugars increases chromium losses. These facts combined with the fact that chromium, an essential trace element, is required for metabolism of proteins, fats and carbohydrates presents a strong argument for the dietary supplementation of chromium nicotinate.

The dietary supplementation of chromium nicotinate has not been definitively studied with respect to its impact on muscle building and improvement in strength and endurance activities. However, there are numerous medical studies plus a large amount of anecdotal evidence observed concerning body builders and athletes who use chromium, to stimulate the consideration of chromium's potential use as dietary supplementation to increase muscle mass, reduce fat, lower cholesterol, and improve strength and endurance performances.

PART V

NUTRITION

1. **Anderson, R. and Koziovsky, A.; Chromium Intake, Absorption and Excretion of Subjects Consuming Self-Selected Diets; American Journal of Clinical Nutrition; Vol. 41(6); 1985; pp. 1177-1183.**

2. **Borel, J. and Anderson, R; Biochemistry of the Essential Ultra Trace Elements; Plenum Publishing Corporation; 1984; pp. 175-199.**

3. **Campbell, W.W. and Anderson, R.A.; Effects of aerobic exercise and training on trace minerals; chromium, zinc and copper; Sports Medicine, 1987; Jan/Feb; Vol 4 (1); pp. 9-18.**

4. **Clarkson, Priscilla; Nutritional ergogenic aids: chromium, exercise and muscle mass. International J Sport Nutrition; 1991; 1:289-293.**

5. **Colgan, M.; Optimum Sports Nutrition; Advanced Research Press, New York; 1993; p. 301.**

6. **Evans, G.W., The effect of chromium picolinate on insulin controlled parameters in humans. Int J Biosocial Med Research, Vol. 11(2);163-180,1989.**

7. **Koziovsky, A., et al; Effects of diets high in simple sugars on urinary chromium losses; Metabolism; Vol. 35(6); 1986; pp. 515-518.**

8. Lefavi, R.G., et al. **Efficacy of chromium supplementation in athletes: emphasis on anabolism; International J Sport Nutrition; 1992; 2:111-122.**

9. Olin, K., et al. **Annual Meeting of the American College of Nutrition, Oct. 10, 1992; University of California-Davis.**

10. **Recommended Dietary Allowances. 10th Ed. Washington DC, National Academy Press; 1989.**

11. **Rosenbaum, Michael; Properties of A New Chromium-Niacin Complex; Nutrition Update; May 1988.**

12. **Rosenbaum, Michael; GTF Chromium And Athletic Performance; Sports Science Update; March, 1988.**

13. **The Interhealth Chromium Series: # 1; Interhealth Company; Concord, California; 1990.**

14. **The InterHealth Chromium Series: # 2; Interhealth Company; Concord, California; 1991.**

15. **The Science Behind Chromium Polynicotinate; ChromeMate, Interhealth. From notes of The Nutritional Consultants Group; Playa Del Rey, CA; March, 1991.**

CREATINE MONOHYDRATE (ENERGY BOOSTING AGENT)

Creatine is one of the hottest supplements of the 1990's. The supplementation of creatine is currently one of the most popular practices in sports nutrition. It is being used to help increase lean muscle mass and muscular power for anaerobic performances. Paul Greenhaff, PhD, (1995) from the Department of Physiology and Pharmacology, at the University Medical School, Queens Medical Centre, Nottingham, England makes the following statement:

> **"Creatine should not be viewed as another gimmick supplement; its ingestion is a means of providing immediate, significant performance improvements to athletes involved in explosive sports. In the long run, creatine may allow athletes to train without fatigue at an intensity higher than that to which they are accustomed. For these reasons alone, creatine supplementation should be viewed as a significant development in sport nutrition."**

Creatine is a nitrogenous compound synthesized in the body by the liver, pancreas and kidneys from the amino acids glycine, arginine and methionine. The body makes creatine by combining the amino acids glycine and arginine and then attaching a methyl group from methionine. Over 95% of the total creatine content of the body is stored in the skeletal muscles. Creatine is also directly absorbed from the diet (primarily from meat and fish) and is eventually stored in the skeletal muscles in the form of creatine phosphate. Vegetarians have a noticeable lack of creatine in their muscles and have a great increase in muscle stores of creatine when creatine supplementation is used.

Creatine is combined with phosphate to form creatine phosphate (phosphocreatine). Creatine phosphate is a supply of high energy phosphates in muscle and nerve cells that maintains the ATP level during high intensity-short duration physical activities. Creatine phosphate which is primarily stored in the muscles, does not supply energy, but it does provide a simple, one-step reaction to restore ATP level in the active muscle.

When muscles are used in high intensity speed and explosion activity, the ATP is broken down to ADP (adenosine diphosphate) and energy is released. The muscle stores of ATP will only fuel a maximum effort for 10-15 seconds. After that, the muscle must rely on creatine phosphate to replenish its supply of ATP.

Creatine phosphate is a precursor of adenosine triphosphate (ATP) which is the energy source for all muscular contractions. It combines with ADP (adenosine diphospate) to regenerate ATP. In other words, when it combines

PART V

NUTRITION

with ADP, it recharges ADP to ATP. ATP stores are important for maximal and near maximal contractions while creatine phosphate stores are important for extended repetitions of maximal and near maximal contractions.

Creatine phosphate can be rapidly metabolized in the formation of ATP and its concentration can fall to nearly zero and, therefore, is thought to make a significant contribution to the energy supply that is needed for short duration and high intensity muscle contraction. It is believed that supplementation of creatine is beneficial for increasing creatine phosphate stores and is of help to performance in strength, speed and explosion sporting events. Theoretically, increases in cellular levels of creatine phosphate would postpone fatigue in repetitive, high intensity-short term physical activities. This would make it useful for the serious weight trainer and body builder. Increasing the creatine phosphate content of the muscle by dietary supplementation will enhance the ability to perform high intensity work and result in greater lean mass and strength gains.

As mentioned above, creatine is supplied in the diet by meat and fish. The estimated daily requirement for creatine for the average individual is about 2 grams, however, most people have a daily intake of less than 1 gram.

The liver synthesizes creatine by using arginine, glycine and methyl sources. It has been shown that oral supplementation and/or intramuscular injection has been able to increase muscle creatine stores. Oral creatine is readily absorbed and merged into the muscle and nerve tissues. Large amounts of creatine (1 gram per day for several weeks or 10 grams daily for 10 days) supplementation is required to produce significant increases in the body creatine pool sizes.

CREATINE LOADING AND MAINTENANCE

It appears that creatine concentration can be increased in two ways: **(1) Through creatine loading**. Ingesting 20 grams of creatine (5 gms in 4 doses spread throughout the day) for six days. This is followed by ingesting 2-3 grams of creatine daily after the initial loading phase. **(2) Through long term low dosage administration**. Ingesting of 3 grams of creatine for 28 days is as effective as creatine loading with higher amounts.

Creatine is best taken in a glass of warm water about 1-2 hours prior to the workout with complex carbohydrates and, if desired just after the workout with complex carbohydrates. Creatine transport into the muscle is increased with by insulin. Therefore, taking creatine on an empty stomach with water may not provide optimal results because of the lack of insulin. Creatine should be ingested with meals or a complex carbohydrate to maximize the transport of creatine into the muscle cells.

It has been found that mixing creatine with juices neutralizes the activity of creatine monohydrate. When creatine is mixed with juices it quickly creates a waste product call creatinine which, of course is useless. Do not over-supplement creatine. After the loading cycle, 2-3 grams per day is sufficient to maintain high energy stores. Using more is not helpful and is costly. An additional recommendation is to drink more water when using creatine. It seems that creatine takes water from other parts of the body for its energy work in the cells.

Research has demonstrated that creatine supplementation plays a prominent role in speed and explosion activities and even helps to increase the muscle mass. The intelligent use of creatine provides for more productive training as well as improve protein synthesis.

Creatine offers bodybuilders and athletes more energy for extended, high-intensity workouts and a faster recovery period between sets or efforts and, also, between training sessions. Creatine supplementation allows athletes and body builders to train without fatigue at an intensity higher than that to which they are accustomed. It is suggested by some scientists and trainers that creatine should be taken both before and after the workout for optimal restoration of the muscle energy stores. Others recommend that creatine should be consumed before training. Experiment and see what works best for you.

Creatine is a natural amino acid and no side effects have been noted in research when supplemented at the recommended levels. Creatine monohydrate is the most stable of all creatines in dry form. However, once it is mixed in liquid, it should be consumed immediately (within 15 minutes) to prevent the waste product creatinine from developing which makes the drink useless.

Although creatine has been used by many international class athletes from Russia and Eastern Europe the use of creatine has been basically by trail and error in the West. It is reported that athletes from Russia and Eastern European nations may have had the benefit of the results of sport science studies in the application of this substance to improve performance and training levels.

There is a need for the study of creatine supplementation and its effects on increasing human performance and elevating training levels. Athletes generally reserve the use of this substance for performance experiences or intensive physical training sessions.

1. Balsom, P.D.; Soderlund, K.;Sjodin, B. and Ekbiam, B.; Skeletal muscle metabolism during short duration high-intensity exercise: influence of creatine supplementation. Acta Physiol Scan 154:303-310,1995.

2. Birch, R.; Noble, D. and Greenhaff, P.L.;The influence of dietary creatine supplementation on performance during repeated bouts of maximal isokinetic cycling in man. Eur. J. Appi. Physio. 64:268-270.1994.

3. Greenhaff, P.L.; Creatine and its application as an ergogenic aid. International Journal of Sport Nutrition; 5:SIOO-SIIO; 1995.

4. Greenhaff, P.L.; Casey, A.; Short, A.H.; Harris, R.; Soderlund, K and Hultman, E.: Influence of oral creatine supplementation on muscle torque during repeated bouts of maximal voluntary exercise in man. Clinical Science, 84:565-571, 1993.

5. Harris, R.C.; Soderlund, K.; and Hultman, E.; Elevation of creatine in resting and exercised muscle of normal subjects by creatine supplementation. Clinical Science, 83:367-374, 1992.

6. Hickson, James and Wolinsky, Ira; Nutrition in Exercise and Sport; CRC Press; Boca Raton, Florida; 1989; pp. 127-129.

COENZYME Q-10 [UBIQUINONE] (ENERGY BOOSTING AGENT)

Coenzyme Q-10 is found in every cell in the body and is a vital part of the process that produces most of the energy for the cells. Variations of this substance are found in humans, animals and plants. The human body manufactures coenzyme Q-10 and deficiencies may occur which can be effectively handled with dietary supplementation of coenzyme Q-10. The variation found in animals is upgraded to coenzyme Q-10 in the human body and is readily used. There is some question that the plant variation of this substance can be used by the body as a supplementation without chemical modification.

Coenzyme Q-10 is the cofactor in the electron transport chain which is the biochemical pathway in cellular respiration from which ATP and the majority of the energy used by the body are secured. Because of its role in energy production, any deficiency could limit physical performance (Lee 1987). It plays an important function in maintaining immunity (Folkers 1985) and in normal heart function (Liebovitz 1991). Moreover, it is a strong antioxidant (Folkers 1984).

Coenzyme Q-10 plays a key role in ATP production for endurance activities. A daily dose of 60 milligrams of oral Coenzyme Q-10 has been shown to improve submaximal and maximal exercise capacities by 3% to 12% after four and eight weeks of supplementation and training (Vanfrachem 1981).

PART V

NUTRITION

Coenzyme Q-10 is beneficial to the athletes in the following ways:

1. May be effective in controlling the accumulation of fat and reducing the body fat by facilitating energy production.
2. Improvement in aerobic capacity and retardation of fatigue.
3. Enhancement of the immune system (Bliznakov, E.G. 1970 and Folkers 1980).

In 1985, Japanese researchers (Kamikawa, et al 1985) found a 17.7% increase in exercise time in patients with angina pectoris. Furthermore, there was also a significant correlation between CoQlO administration and increase in treadmill exercise time. This study suggest the CoQlO is a safe and promising treatment for angina patients and seems to support the hypothesis that use of CoQlO may improve muscular endurance performances. Hundreds of thousands of heart patients are being successfully treated with CoQlO in Japan. Meanwhile in the United States there are large number of studies reporting the effectiveness of CoQlO (Liebovitz 1991).

Colgan (1993) reports of a scientific study conducted at the University of Bologna in Italy where trained runners using 100 mg of CoQlO per day out-performed a placebo group of well trained runners. At the Colgan Institute, CoQlO is recommended in doses of 10-60 mg/day in some athletes (Colgan 1993, p. 186).

No studies on the effect of Coenzyme Q-10 combined with training in strength athletes and body builders have been reported. This substance appears to be safe, available, has known mechanism of action and has shown good empirical results when combined with training of endurance athletes. More research needs to be executed to document and amplify the efficacy of combining the ingestion of Coenzyme Q-10 with training with respect to improvement in aerobic endurance, body building and speed and explosion physical performances.

Given the accumulating research showing the positive effects of CoQlO, it would seem wise to supplement the diet with this substance. It has been shown to be a powerful antioxidant as well as enhancing endurance performance, and may be effective in managing diabetes, obesity, in detoxification, enhances longevity and stimulates the immune system.

1. **Bliznakov, E.G., et al; Coenzyme Q: stimulants of the phagocytic activity in rats and immune response in mice; Experientia; 266:953; 1970.**

2. **Bliznakov, E.G. and Hunt, G.L.; The Miracle Nutrient - Coenzyme Q10; Bantam Books, Inc.; New York; 1986.**

3. **Colgan, M.; Optimum Sports Nutrition; Advanced Research Press, New York; 1993; p. 186.**

4. **Folkers, K and Yamura, Y.; (Editors); Biomedical and Clinical Aspects of Coenzyme Q; Vol. 2; Amsterdam; Elsevier/North Holland Biomedical Press; 1980; pp. 333-347.**

5. **Folkers, K and Wolaniuk, A.; Drugs Under Exper Clin Res; 11:539-546;1985.**

6. **Folkers, K & Yamamura, Y., eds. Biomedical and Clinical Aspects of Coenzyme Q Vol. IV. New York: Elsevier:201-208:291-300:1984.**

7. **Kamikawa, T.; Kobayash, A.; Yamashita, T.; Hayashi, H. and Yamazaki, N.; American Journal of Cardiology, 1985; Aug 1: Vol 56 (4); pp. 247-51.**

8. **Liebovitz, B.; Coenzyme Q. Nutrition & Fitness; 10;47-48:1991.**

9. **Lee, William; Coenzyme Q-10; Keats Publishing, INC.; New Canaan, Connecticut; 1987.**

10. **Vanfrachem, J.H.P. and Folkers, K.; Coenzyme Q-10 and Clinical Aspects of Coenzyme 9; Amsterdam; Biomedical Press; 1981.**

GINSENG (ANABOLIC AGENT AND GENERAL TONIC)

Ginseng is used world wide as a general stimulant for physical activity and a health tonic. The Eastern forms of ginseng have been employed successfully in China, Tibet, Korea, Indochina and India for thousands of years for prevention of aging, as a general health tonic and as medicine in a wide variety of illnesses. All ginsengs are considered to be an adaptogenic which helps the body manage stress, normalize the body systems, balance hormonal levels and improve immunity. An adaptogen is a substance that is able to improve the ability of an organism to adapt to differing external or internal disturbances. There are many variations and strengths of ginseng plants and commercial preparations. Not all commercial preparations produce the same effects.

The active ingredients in ginseng have been identified as ginsenosides. There are 12 (some scientists say 13) of these ginsenosides called triterpenoid saponin glycosides. However, some extracts may not even contain ginsenosides and, therefore, are of little value. Currently, there are two standardized ginseng products that are in the marketplace, **Ginsana** and **Sports Ginseng** which is produced by Nature's Herbs. To properly evaluate the effect of various ginsengs it is important to use only those products that have standardized the percentage of the active ingredient, ginsenosides.

Ginseng extracts containing ginsenosides have demonstrated a glycogen sparing effect and augmented oxidation of fatty acids in animals when using high doses. The use of ginseng has been shown to reduce fatigue, decrease cholesterol, alleviate insomnia and diminish depression. It produces a general supporting of the functioning of all the systems of the body.

Basically, there are three genuine types of ginseng plants of the family Araliaceae. Panax ginseng (panax schinseng) is the original Korean and Chinese herb. A second type is Sanchie or Tienchi (panax notoginseng) which is another form of ginseng from the far East. The third type of ginseng is the American (panax quinquefolium). The three types produce the same fundamental effects in the human body and are equally useful.

Many of the early studies on ginseng did not use standardized ginseng extract, and, therefore, they contribute little to the knowledge of it's efficacy. Recently, the Swiss have formulated a standardized ginseng extract which is called GI 15 (Ginsana). Since 1971 there have been many independent studies that have shown that the use of a standardized ginseng extract does indeed have benefits for health and physical training.

Study of clinical observations on the combination of ginseng, vitamins and trace elements have shown the following benefits in humans (Vigue 1972 and Bensky, et al 1986).

1. There is a great increase in the capacity for manual work. The quality of the physical work seems to be improved as well as the quantity. The effects of ginseng on working capacity can last up to 30 days after the discontinuation of its use. The stimulating effect of ginseng is different from the noticeable stimulating effect as experienced in the use of caffeine or amphetamines which are manifested as a subjective sensation of excitement. Ginseng stimulation is not consciously perceived but, nevertheless, effective.

2. There is a great increase in the capacity for intellectual work. in studies ginseng has produced a psycho-stimulating effect which enables continued intellectual effort.

3. Ginseng has demonstrated good impact on the nervous system by shortening the latency period of nerve reflexes, speeding the transmission of the nerve impulses and strengthening conditioned reflexes.

4. Ginseng has been shown to have anti-inflammatory action and stimulates the formation of permanent fibrous tissue in the healing of wounds.

5. Ginseng has been shown to produce a general stimulating effect on the all systems of the body.

PART V

NUTRITION

6. Ginseng increases the synthesis of proteins and nucleic acids. The use of ginseng produces a carbohydrate sparing effect, enhances resynthesis of glycogen and high energy phosphates.

7. Ginseng has been shown to improve the immune system.

8. Ginseng has excellent anti-stress capabilities.

A number of research studies using humans and animals from 1975 to 1989 have demonstrated improvement in various parameters of performance with the use of standardized ginseng extract (Avakian 1980 & 1984) (Dorling 1980) (Forgo & Kurchdorfer 1981) (Forgo & Schimert 1985) (Kakru 1975) (McNaughton 1989) (Samura 1985) (Singh 1984). The use of standardized ginseng extract demonstrated the following:

1. Produced pronounced stimulating effects on brain activity.
2. Produced significant resistance to fatigue.
3. Improved psychomotor performances by maintaining alertness.
4. Delayed fatigue.
5. Spares glycogen and increases oxidation of free fatty acids.
6. Increased lung function: VC, FEV, PEF, and maximum breathing capacity.
7. Significantly reduced lactic acid levels at various workloads in athletes.
8. Produced faster recovery rates from exercises.
9. Showed impressive strength gains for the quadriceps and pectorals muscle groups post training.

The literature has not revealed any acute or chronic toxicity of using ginseng and no side affects associated with the use of ginseng have been reported. The effective dose of standardized ginseng extract appears to be 200 mg/day. The G1 15 ginseng extract sold by Ginsana is the only product that has been subjected to repeated studies (Colgan 1993). Colgan (1993) states: ***"The number of studies is still small, but the consistent results do qualify ginseng as a legitimate ergogenic aid."***

In view of the demonstrated positive effects of using ginseng and to no manifestation of side effects with prolonged use of ginseng, the addition of ginseng to the diet of physically active people, athletes and body builders may have significant constructive impact on training and physical performance. Ginseng may be beneficial in improving strength and endurance, increasing muscle mass, boosting physical performance, enhancing resistance to disease, facilitating recovery and counteracting stress. Research regarding the use of ginseng on training and physical performance is indicated and needed.

The use of ginseng will produce positive effects on performance if used over time with a consistent scientific training program. The improvements will be slow and steady, so do not expect overnight success.

---

1. **Avakian, E.V. & Sugimoto, B.R.; Effect of panax ginseng on energy substrates during exercise. Fed Proc; 39:287:1980.**

2. **Avakian, E.V. et al. Effect of Panax ginseng extract on energy metabolism during exercise in rats. Planta Medica; 50:151:1984.**

3. **Bensky, D and Gamble, A.; Chinese Herbal Medicines: Materia Medica; Eastland Press; Seattle; 1986; pp. 450-454.**

4. **Dorling, E. et al. Do ginsenosides influence performance? Results of a double blind study. Notaben Medici: 10:241-246:1980.**

5. **Forgo, 1. & Kirchdorfer, A.M.: On the question of influencing the performance of top sportsmen by means of biologically active substances. Arztiiche Praxis:33:17841786:1981.**

6. Forgo, 1. & Shimert, G.; The duration of effect of the standardized ginseng extract G115 in healthy competitive athletes. NotabeneMedica:15:636-640:1985.

7. Hatfield, Frederick; Ergogenesis: Achieving peak athletic performance without drugs; Fitness Systems, Inc.; Canoga Park, California; 1985.

8. Hickson, James and Wolinsky, Ira; Nutrition in Exercise and Sport; CRC Press; Boca Raton, Florida; 1989; pp. 146-147,158.

9. Kaku,T.; Chemicopharmacological studies on saponins of P ginseng CA Meyer. Arzniem Forsch:25:539-547:1975.

10. McNaughton, L.; Egan, G.; and Caelil, G.; A comparison of Chinese and Russian ginseng as ergogenic aids to improve various facets of physical fitness. Int Clin Nutr Rev;9:3237:1989.

11. Popov, Ivan M. and Goidwag,William J.; A review of the properties and clinical effects of ginseng; American Journal of Chinese Medicine; Vol. 1, No. 2; 1973; pp. 263-270.

12. Samura, M.M. et al. Effect of standardized ginseng extract G1 15 on the metabolism and electrical activity of the rabbit's brain. J Int Med Res;13:342-348:1985.

13. Singh, V.K. et al. Planta Medica;50:462:1984.

14. Vigue, Roger; Prof. Med. Int. Centre Hospitalier, Argenteuil, France. Rapport D'Experimentation/Clinique; Sept. 1972. Reported in Popov, I.M. and Goidwag, W.J.; A review of the properties and clinical effects of ginseng; American Journal of Chinese Medicine; Vol. 1; No. 2; 1973; pp. 263-270.

GLUTAMINE (ANABOLIC AGENT)

Glutamine may be more important than the use of creatine monohydrate in weight training and physical training programs. **Glutamine is the single most important amino acid in the body to facilitate anabolic conditions in the muscles; to protect from overtraining by its anti-catabolic action; and, to strengthen the immune system. Furthermore, glutamine enhances the health of the entire gastro-intestinal system. Its action in the gut increases the biological value and utilization of all nutrients in the diet, especially protein.**

Glutamine is a non-essential amino acid because it can be made by the body and is not required to be obtained by dietary intake. However, recent studies now classify glutamine as **"conditionally essential"** because it is not obtained in sufficient quantities in the normal diet and it is needed in large quantities under exercise conditions and times of stress. Remember, the body does not differentiate types of stress and considers all kinds of stress (physical, mental and psychological) as additive. That means the different kinds of stress are added together to represent the "total body stress factor."

The muscle tissue is the main site for the creation and storage of glutamine. It is the most abundant amino acid in the muscle tissue. It accounts for 60% of the free amino acid pool in the muscle cells. The large amount of glutamine stored in the muscles is a source for glutamine to maintain plasma levels and to provide other tissues with needed glutamine. Moreover, the level of glutamine is highly correlated with muscle protein synthesis and efficient immune system functioning.

It is known that large amounts of alanine and glutamine are released from the muscle during and post exercise. Also, trauma and stress result in the use of large amounts of alanine and glutamine. Moreover, the loss of alanine and glutamine caused by exercise is beyond the amounts stored in the muscle and is more than 50% of the total loss of muscle amino acids during exercise. This means that other amino acids have to be broken down to produce the needed alanine and glutamine under exercise and stress conditions.

Moreover, research has shown that the branched chain amino acids (BCAA) provide the building materials for alanine and glutamine during and after exercise. It is well known that the supplementation of BCAA support protein synthesis. The BCAA prevent catabolism of the muscle by supplying the substrates for the creation of large amounts of alanine and glutamine which are lost during and after exercise. (Colgan, p. 376-377)

Furthermore, the optimal functioning of the immune system requires a large source of glutamine. There is a lot of scientific evidence to support that all cell replication in the immune system requires adequate supply of glutamine. The immune system uses a large amount of it. Therefore, the muscles have to continuously supply large amounts of glutamine to the immune system.

Intense physical training which produces a highly catabolic effect on the muscles can overwhelm the body's ability to produce glutamine. The more intense and the longer the training session, the greater the use of glutamine in the muscles. **Glutamine is the main anti-catabolic amino acid in the muscle which helps preserve the muscle during and after exercise.** With this anti-catabolic requirement of the muscles coupled with the large need of the immune system for glutamine, it is easy to see the need for glutamine supplementation.

When the muscles and the immune system get inadequate supplies of glutamine, there is consequent loss of muscle mass, strength and performance along with a decline in immunity. **There is a definite need to use supplemental glutamine.** Colgan (1993) recommends the use of alpha-ketoglutarate which supplies the ammonia-free carbon skeleton of glutamine in the place of glutamine. In addition, the branched chain amino acids help to increase the supply of glutamine because they provide the substrate for the creation of glutamine by the muscles.

The range of glutamine supplementation has been reported to be between 2 grams to 30 grams per day. Each individual will have to determine what is effective for them.

The research seems to support the theory that glutamine supplementation is important to maximizing muscle growth. In addition, glutamine is also very important to maintain good health by enhancing the functioning of the immune system. Deficiencies may result in increased risk of infections, colds, and flu. **The scientific evidence shows that glutamine administered orally increases synthesis of muscle protein while reducing the catabolic effect of stress hormones related to vigorous physical exercise.**

1. Bergstrom, J., et al. Intracellular Free Amino Acid Concentration in Human MuscleTissue. J Appl Physiol, 36 (1974):693-701.

2. Colgan, Michael; Optimum Sports Nutrition; Advanced Research Press; New York; 1993.

3. Griffith, M.& Keast, D.; The effect of glutamine on murine splenic leukocyte responses to T and B-cell mitogens. Cell Biology, 1990;68:405-408.

3. Lacey, J. & Willmore, D.; Is glutamine a conditionally essential amino acid? Nutrition Reviews; 1990:48: 297-309.

4. Milward, D.J. & Rivers, P.W.; The need for indispensable amino acids: The concept of anabolic drive. Diabetes Metab Rev; 1989;5:191-21 1.

5. Roth, E., et al. Glutamine: An anabolic effector. J Parent Ent Nutr 1990;14:1305-1365.

6. Roufs, James B.; L-Glutamine, Anabolic Steroids, and Muscle Protein Synthesis. Journal of Optimal Nutrition: 2(2):110-116, 1993.

PART V

NUTRITION

7. Vaubourdolle, M., et al; Action of enterally administered ornithine alpha-ketoglutarate on protein breakdown in skeletal muscle and liver of the burned rat. J Parent Ent Nutr; 1991;5:517-520.

8. Welbourne, T.C.; Enteral Glutamine Spares Endogenous Glutamine in Chronic Acidosis; JPEN 17 (1993):23S.

9. Wernerman, J., et al; Alpha-ketoglutarate and postoperative muscle catabolism. Lancet; 990;335: 701-703.

NUTRITION PART V

PART V

NUTRITION